THE HOLY SPIRIT—
In Biblical Teaching,
through the Centuries,
and Today

THE HOLY SPIRIT—
In Biblical Teaching,
through the Centuries,
and Today

To Professor Alan Ford
with affectionate good wishes

Anthony C. Thiselton

Anthony C. Thiselton

WILLIAM B. EERDMANS PUBLISHING COMPANY
GRAND RAPIDS, MICHIGAN / CAMBRIDGE, U.K.

© 2013 Anthony C. Thiselton
All rights reserved

Published 2013 by
Wm. B. Eerdmans Publishing Co.
2140 Oak Industrial Drive N.E., Grand Rapids, Michigan 49505 /
P.O. Box 163, Cambridge CB3 9PU U.K.
www.eerdmans.com

Printed in the United States of America

19 18 17 16 15 14 13   7 6 5 4 3 2 1

Library of Congress Cataloging-in-Publication Data

Thiselton, Anthony C.
The Holy Spirit — in biblical teaching, through the centuries, and today /
Anthony C. Thiselton.
pages   cm
Includes bibliographical references and index.
ISBN 978-0-8028-6875-6 (pbk.: alk. paper)
1. Holy Spirit.   I. Title.

BT121.3.T45   2013

231′.3 — dc23

2013002916

To Rosemary
in the year of our
golden wedding anniversary

Contents

PART III
The Holy Spirit in Modern Theology and Today

Preface

This book began as a work on the Holy Spirit solely with reference to biblical teaching. I initially aimed to study the biblical material in its own right, but with the secondary aim of initiating and developing a mutual dialogue with Pentecostals and those influenced by the Renewal Movement. I hoped to write with respect for both sides, to try to reach across a dangerously widening chasm of church practice.

In the event, I discovered more and more material on the Holy Spirit through the centuries and today, and came to realize that, if my work were to be taken seriously, it would be essential to examine the substance and context of historical and contemporary thought as well as biblical teaching. In practice this meant writing a book of three or four times the original size. The work of some Pentecostal and Renewal writers added yet more to the task.

Unexpectedly a double bonus emerged. First, the historical and contemporary material conveys fascinating and sometimes little-known insights. Second, this book now becomes unique in offering a thorough biblical and historical study of the Holy Spirit in systematic form. H. B. Swete had provided a book on the New Testament groundwork, but this was first written in 1909, followed by a historical study of the Church Fathers in 1912, a hundred years ago. Howard Watkin-Jones extended this to the medieval Church in 1922, but this is more variable and now ninety years old. James Dunn does not include historical work but is taken seriously by Pentecostals. Moltmann, Pannenberg, Congar, Lossky, and Zizioulas remain invaluable, but do not attempt the same degree of either specific and systematic biblical exegesis or historical comprehensiveness. Stanley Burgess is helpful on much historical work, but is less systematic and comprehensive than ideally we need.

Pentecostals and exponents of the Renewal Movement have important things to say to the established churches, but self-criticism has emerged only relatively recently among Pentecostals, and seems hardly to have touched the Renewal Movement, with few exceptions, including perhaps Congar, Smail,

Purves, and a handful of others. We badly need self-criticism and correction on both sides, in the light of deeper biblical and historical exploration. Scripture and history teach so many needed lessons.

Contemporary writing and research show that this is an immensely fast-growing subject. New insights on prophecy, tongues, the miraculous, the range and nature of "the gifts of the Spirit," and the Holy Spirit in relation to the Holy Trinity clamor for attention. Moltmann, Pannenberg, and Rogers have opened up and explored a "narrative" approach to the Holy Trinity which not only does justice to the New Testament but also helps preachers to know where to start in explaining the doctrine of the Trinity.

I offer here twenty-three chapters of scholarly work on specific biblical, historical, and contemporary themes, often citing writers with carefully researched sources and sometimes with a direct use of their words. But I have not forgotten that Pentecostals and Renewal writers often value the testimony of the heart above intellectual discussion. We need both. I have tried to provide this. However, Chapter 24 offers entirely my own reflections, for which I alone am responsible. Admittedly these are suggested in the light of previously thorough biblical and historical study and prayer. Since this chapter also constitutes a summary and conclusion, it is offered without a single footnote. It rests on the documentation of the previous twenty-three chapters.

This last chapter sets out seven fundamental themes or principles. I have added to each a practical consequence for worship or life. I then seek to engage in mutual dialogue with Pentecostals and the Renewal Movement. I recognize, I hope, their strengths, including not least the dramatic growth and widespread appeal of these movements. But I also express some reservations. Like Congar, I could not share the hope that *everyone* would wish to follow these paths. They can, however, give fresh intimacy with God, and vigor to an overformalized and overroutinized faith. Third, for the second time in this book, I have endorsed the comments of the many who insist that the deepest divisions arise from different understandings of hermeneutics. I hope that after a lifetime's study of this subject, I can offer something in the way of disentangling some deep-seated misconceptions and mistakes. I make these suggestions entirely in the hope of facilitating mutual understanding.

I owe a great debt of thanks, first, to my secretary, Mrs. Karen Woodward, who typed most of the manuscript. Second, my wife, Rosemary, took on much of the remaining typing when the University of Nottingham made me "Emeritus Professor." She has also helped tirelessly with all the proofreading and indexing, as I have been fairly useless at this task, in view of poor eyesight. I should also like to thank my PhD graduate, Dr. Andrew Talbert, for helping to compile indices and check proofs, and Mr. Milton Essenburg of Eerdmans for his meticulous and painstaking editing. I should also thank Mr. Jon Pott and others at Eerdmans for once more risking time and expenditure on a very large book.

The compiling of the indices of subjects and names raised the problem of where to allocate pre-modern names. In the end, I have perhaps arbitrarily placed pre-modern names in the index of subjects, and placed all names from 1800 onwards under modern authors. ***Bold type and italics*** indicate major discussions of a subject or a pre-modern person, to distinguish the main references from more incidental or marginal ones.

University of Nottingham, U.K. ANTHONY C. THISELTON

Abbreviations

ANF	*Ante-Nicene Fathers*
BDAG	W. Bauer, F. W. Danker, W. F. Arndt, and F. W. Gingrich, *A Greek-English Lexicon of the New Testament and Other Early Christian Literature*. Chicago: University of Chicago Press, 3rd ed. 2003.
CCSL	Corpus Christianorum, Series Latina
C.D.	*Church Dogmatics* by Karl Barth
CSEL	Corpus Scriptorum Ecclesiasticorum Latinorum
EKKNT	Evangelisch-katholischer Kommentar zum Neuen Testament
ICC	International Critical Commentary
JBL	*Journal of Biblical Literature*
JPT	*Journal of Pentecostal Theology*
JPTSS	Journal of Pentecostal Theology Supplement Series
JSNT	*Journal for the Study of the New Testament*
JSNTSS	Journal for the Study of the New Testament Supplement Series
JTS	*Journal of Theological Studies*
LCC	Library of Christian Classics
NICNT	New International Commentary on the New Testament
NIDOTTE	*New International Dictionary of Old Testament Theology and Exegesis*
NIDPCM	*New International Dictionary of Pentecostal and Charismatic Movements*
NIGTC	New International Greek Testament Commentary
NovTSup	Supplements to Novum Testamentum
NPNF	*Nicene and Post-Nicene Fathers*
NTS	*New Testament Studies*
PG	*Patrologia Graeca*, ed. J-P. Migne
PL	*Patrologia Latina*, ed. J-P. Migne

SNTSMS   Society for New Testament Studies Monograph Series
TDNT   *Theological Dictionary of the New Testament*
TDOT   *Theological Dictionary of the Old Testament*
WUNT   Wissenschaftliche Untersuchungen zum Neuen Testament

PART I
=========

The Holy Spirit in Biblical Teaching

1

The Spirit of God in the Old Testament

1.1. Introduction: Seven Practical Themes

The details of relevant Old Testament passages and themes are often complex. Hence it will help to offer a preliminary outline of themes which we shall then amplify and develop. Thus, before looking at the Old Testament in any detail, we may anticipate several practical theological points which we shall try to establish by more technical investigations of passages and themes.

(1) First, if "spirituality" is due to the workings of the Spirit of God within the human heart, the Old Testament sees the Spirit as *transcendent* or *"other,"* in contrast to *innate human aspirations.* As we shall see, the Spirit of God can act like a warrior. The Spirit guards the Israelites from marauders in the wilderness as if they were cattle (Isa. 63:14); the Spirit can breathe life into a dead Israel which has rotted into dry bones, and set it on its feet as a living human body (Ezek. 37:12-14); the Spirit can empower Samson, so that Samson can tear a lion apart with his bare hands, as if it was a young kid (Judg. 14:6).

(2) Second, although God gives the Spirit to *chosen individuals* to perform special tasks, the Spirit of God makes these tasks possible only within the framework of God's wider purposes for the *community* of Israel. Both Testaments stress the individual and the community, even if with different emphases and purposes. Even the well-known gift of the Spirit to various judges has as its purpose the deliverance from oppression of a repentant Israel. Thus the judges in question are called "saviors" of Israel (Judg. 3:7-11, 12-30; 6:1–8:35; 13:1–16:31). Many current thinkers stress this corporate aspect, as we shall note later.

(3) Third, the Old Testament begins to represent the Spirit of God, along with Wisdom, as an Agent of God, or extension of God, who necessarily imparts *revelation and inspiration,* and who begins the long path toward *holiness and renewal of the heart.* Wisdom is given to Bezalel by the Spirit for craftsman-

3

ship in Exod. 31:3-5, and the Spirit inspires Micaiah to prophesy in 1 Kings 22:11-28. The Spirit who reveals and inspires does so because he is often understood as more than the Agent of God; *he represents God's presence.* It would be anachronistic to suggest that Old Testament writers consciously anticipated the later doctrine of the Holy Trinity, but they certainly laid the groundwork for such a doctrine by associating God's Spirit with God himself. This came about initially by closely associating angels with the functions of the Spirit. For example, "a man . . . with a drawn sword" appeared before Joshua as commander of the Lord's hosts (Josh. 5:13-14), and Joshua "fell on his face . . . and worshiped," and was commanded to remove his sandals, "for the place where you stand is holy" (5:15). God *creates* through the Spirit (Gen. 1:2; NRSV translates *rûach*, "Spirit," by "wind" here). God's Spirit is called "your Holy Spirit" three times in the Old Testament (Ps. 51:11; Isa. 63:10-11; *rûach qodhsh^ekā*, "your Holy Spirit"; *rûach qodh^eshô*, "his Holy Spirit"). "Holy" is often referred to as that which belongs to God. To seek the Spirit is to seek *God.*

(4) Fourth, the work of the Spirit of God can usually be seen by the Spirit's *effects.* Wind as such may be invisible; but when it blows over a field of corn, we know that the wind is blowing by looking at the effects on the field of corn, not on the wind. This is helpful in making the operation of the Spirit observable and concrete; but it can constitute a pitfall. Too often we make judgments about the Spirit by looking only at the *phenomena* which the Spirit produces. The Hebrews were familiar with the effects of wind. Isaiah declares, "The heart of his people shook as the trees . . . shake before the wind" (Isa. 7:2). The wind carries chaff away (Isa. 41:16). But we must not confuse the ultimate (acts of God) with the penultimate (the effects of his acts), as in different ways Paul Tillich and Karl Barth remind us. This would have the unwanted further effect of reducing the transcendence of the Spirit of God.

(5) The Spirit of God is *creative,* as Wolfhart Pannenberg, among others, stresses, and the image of the dove can mislead us. We speak of the dove of peace in everyday life. But in Gen. 1:2, "swept over the face of the waters" (NRSV) probably indicates the hovering or brooding of the creative Spirit, who is about to produce order out of chaos. It is strange that some associate the Spirit with chaos or lack of order, when from the first the Spirit is associated with order; and strange that "peace" often obscures creativity. The picture of Isa. 63:11-14 is that of a dynamic, powerful, creative Agent of God, who in the days of Moses "brought them up out of the sea . . . who divided the waters . . . led your people." The Spirit is the Guide and Protector of onward-journeying Israel. Haggai exclaims, "Take courage . . . for I am with you. . . . My Spirit abides among you; do not fear" (Hag. 2:4-5).

(6) Sixth, *the Spirit of God is life-giving.* God breathes. Ezekiel has this theme: "I will put my Spirit within you, and you shall live" (Ezek. 37:14; cf. vv. 1-14). The Spirit of God can animate the "dry bones" of a long-dead Israel (37:5;

cf. vv. 6-14) into an undivided nation (vv. 15-22), cleansed and active (vv. 23-27). The Psalmist declares, "When you take away their breath, they die and return to the dust. When you send forth your Spirit [NRSV, 'spirit'], they are created" (Ps. 104:29-30). The life in question is creative life, not merely existence. This is largely because God is seen to be the source of all life: "Where can I go from your Spirit [NRSV, 'spirit']? Or where can I flee from your presence?" (Ps. 139:7). Again, this is referred to creation: "The Spirit [NRSV, 'spirit'] of God has made me, and the breath of the Almighty gives me life" (Job 33:4).

(7) The seventh striking characteristic of the work of the Spirit of God is the *Spirit's capacity for being "shared out" from one figure to others.* The classic example is that of Moses and the seventy elders. Moses has been anointed by the Spirit for the task of serving as leader of the people, but later complains that the "burden" of leading such a large number of people has become a heavy strain. Hence "the LORD . . . took some of the Spirit [NRSV, 'spirit'] that was on him and put it on the seventy elders; and when the Spirit rested upon them, they prophesied" (Num. 11:25). Similarly, Joshua derives the Spirit through Moses and the laying on of hands (Deut. 34:9), and Elisha from the gift of the Spirit to Elijah (2 Kings 2:15; cf. 2:9, 13-14). This principle will have considerable consequences in the New Testament for the sharing of the Messianic Spirit by all Christians.

These are the most striking themes which became a practical basis for the gift of the Holy Spirit to Christians in the New Testament. We have not yet discussed every aspect comprehensively. Other themes concern the ambiguity of the precise meaning of the Hebrew term *rûach*, which at different times and in different contexts may mean not only "the Spirit of God," but also "wind," "breath," or "the human spirit." This is why from now on we propose to translate the Hebrew *rûach* by "Spirit" when it denotes the Spirit of God, even when the NRSV translates the term as "spirit" (lowercase letter). We have also not fully discussed the renewal of God's people by the Spirit, the future promises of the gift of the Spirit in the New Age, and the Messianic Spirit. We shall now explore these seven themes in greater detail, investigating, when necessary, how they interact with some scholarly opinion.

1.2. The "Otherness" or Transcendence of the Spirit from Beyond

The usual Hebrew term for Spirit is *rûach*. This word is regularly translated as "Spirit" or "spirit," but also as "breath" or "wind."[1] *Rûach* occurs about 387

---

1. Francis Brown, with S. R. Driver and C. A. Briggs (eds.), *The New Hebrew and English Lexicon* (Lafayette, IN.: Associated Publishers, 1980), pp. 924-26; G. J. Botterweck and H. Ringgren (eds.), *Theological Dictionary of the Old Testament (TDOT)* (Grand Rapids: Eerdmans, 1980), vol. 2, p. 836; W. Van Gemeren (ed.), *New International Dictionary of Old Testament Theology and Exegesis (NIDOTTE)*, 5 vols. (Carlisle: Paternoster, 1997), vol. 3, p. 1073.

times in the Old Testament. The Septuagint (Greek Old Testament) translates it uniformly as *"pneuma"* some 264 times, except when it translates it as *"anemos,"* "wind" (49 times).

One of the popular misconceptions of today is that "spiritual" or "spirituality" denotes a religious human aspiration or capacity. If the term denotes, in a biblical sense, "what is of the Spirit" (as it does usually in Paul), nothing could be further from the truth. In Paul we shall see this more clearly, where the adjective "spiritual" (Greek, *pneumatikos*) denotes precisely what issues from God, not from humankind, especially in 1 Cor. 2:6-16, and most explicitly in v. 12: "We have received not the spirit of the world, but the Spirit that is from God" (Greek, *to pneuma to ek tou theou*).

As we have already seen, the Spirit in Ezek. 37:7-14 is specifically "put" (v. 14) within Israel as it were from "outside," to give Israel life which the community does not possess. Cyril Powell comments on the Spirit: "It does not belong to him whose native sphere is that of *bāśār,"* that is, "flesh."[2] In the Old Testament context, flesh *(bāśār)* represents humankind in its earthly frailty (not "the mind of the flesh" in Paul in its more theological sense). A contrary notion could arise only by unwisely confusing "spirit of human beings" with "Spirit of God." This then makes "spirit" or "Spirit" *seem* to denote a merely *human capacity.* Even under the heading "The Spirit of God as the Principle of Life," Walter Eichrodt's normally judicious *Theology of the Old Testament* confuses passages about the Spirit of God with many about the human spirit. Thus Eichrodt cites Gen. 45:27, "When he [Jacob] saw the wagons that Joseph had sent to carry him, the spirit of their father Jacob revived."[3] In the same note he cites Judg. 15:19, "When he [Samson] drank, his spirit returned, and he revived." The refreshment of water patently has nothing to do with the return of the Spirit of God but with the disposition of Samson's spirit. His third example in the same note follows this pattern: "When he had eaten, his [the Egyptian's] spirit revived" (1 Sam. 30:12). Eichrodt is admittedly making a general comment about *rûach,* but *rûach* denoting "Spirit of God" must not be confused with *rûach* when the term denotes the human spirit. Similarly, in Josh. 5:1 "there was no longer any spirit in them" is in synonymous parallelism with "their heart melted." So also in Isa. 65:14 "anguish of spirit" is parallel with "pain of heart."[4]

The Hebrew *rûach,* "spirit," often denotes the human spirit as a disposition or even as evidence of life, although *nephesh* ("life," or more rarely "soul") and *nᵉshāmâ* ("breath") are used in a similar way. *Nᵉshāmâ* occurs as the principle of life in at least nine of twenty-four uses, but even "blood" (Hebrew, *dām*) is

---

2. Cyril H. Powell, *The Biblical Concept of Power* (London: Epworth, 1963), p. 26.

3. Walter Eichrodt, *Theology of the Old Testament,* 2 vols. (London: SCM, 1964), vol. 2, p. 47, n. 4.

4. Eichrodt, *Theology of the Old Testament,* vol. 2, p. 47, n. 3.

said to be every creature's "life" (Lev. 17:14). Of the son of the widow of Zarephath it is said, "There was no *n*^e*shāmâ* left in him" (1 Kings 17:17). Job states, "All my *n*^e*shāmâ* is still in me" (Job 27:3). Although it is claimed that *nephesh* occurs 754 times, the word sometimes perhaps means "soul"; but it may also denote "life" (like the Greek *psychē*), or do duty for a personal pronoun, for example, "me," and even once denotes a dead body.

The Old Testament can speak of "the spirits of all flesh" (Num. 16:22), or of the "breath *(rûach)* of every human being" (Job 12:10). On occasion the term "spirit" seems to approach the Greek, German, and English notion of "spirit" as the psychological, cognitive, intellectual, and nonmaterial "core" of a human being, as in Ps. 77:6: "I meditate and search my spirit," which is in poetic parallelism with "I commune with my heart" in the same verse. But contrary to its use in Greek, it does not convey a sharp dualism between body and spirit. Both terms, "flesh" and "spirit," denote different modes of being, or functions, of the same self in a unitary way. When *rûach,* "spirit," is used of a human person, the term may also denote a human "disposition," as we have begun to see. In Hosea God condemns his people, "for a spirit of whoredom has led them astray, and they have played the whore, forsaking God" (Hos. 4:12 and 5:4). Isa. 54:6 speaks of being "grieved in spirit." Hos. 4:12 speaks of "the spirit of lust."

We can easily see how far these anthropological meanings have taken us away from the properly transcendent meaning of "Spirit" in much of the Old Testament. By contrast, the translation of *rûach* as "wind" in appropriate contexts can have the opposite effect of enhancing the transcendence of *rûach,* even when it does not denote "Spirit." The scorching east wind can represent the wrath of God (Jer. 18:17: "Like the wind from the east I will scatter them"); while the west wind may bring relief from hardships: "A very strong west wind . . . lifted the locusts" (Exod. 10:19).

Ezekiel's emphasis is on the transcendent. He provides a peak of references to the Spirit of God in the postexilic period. Ezekiel has been called "the Prophet of the Spirit," not least because he mentions the Spirit some forty-two times. The throne of God is carried along with the speed of lightning by four fearsome "living creatures," who "moved straight ahead; wherever the Spirit would go, they went" (Ezek. 1:12). The creatures "were full of eyes" (1:18), which in the book of Revelation implies the Spirit's omniscience. In his vision of the awesome and transcendent throne of God, he writes, "The Spirit lifted me up and bore me away" (Ezek. 3:14), while he also recounts "the sound of loud rumbling . . . the wings of the living creatures brushing against one another" (3:13). He also says, "Wherever the Spirit would go, they went . . . for the spirit [Spirit?] of the living creatures was in the wheels" (1:20). The imagery of apocalyptic "throne-visions" represents the transcendence of God himself, not simply the stage setting of the throne. The Spirit of God now lifts the prophet Ezekiel, and bears him, as the Spirit bore Elijah (Ezek. 3:12, 14; 8:3; 11:1, 24; 37:1).

One of the most debated translations of *rûach* arises in Gen. 1:2: "The *rûach* [NRSV, 'wind'] from God swept over the face of the waters." The KJV/AV translate the same verse, "The Spirit of God moved upon the face of the waters"; and the RSV, "The Spirit of God was moving over the face of the waters." In the earlier, traditional translation, the Spirit of God brings order out of chaos, or perhaps acts in creation like a mother bird "brooding" over a creative process, like the appearance of a dove at the baptism of Jesus (Mark 1:10 parallel to Matt. 3:16; Luke 3:22). "Chaos" or "formless wasteland" translates the well-known Hebrew phrase *tōhû wābōhû*, which signifies unproductive empty space. Even if *rûach* is translated as "wind," it signifies what Vawter calls "a wind that was superhuman, almighty, and inconceivable in ordinary terms."[5] In this light, Spirit or "wind" acts as a transcendent, more-than-human Agent of God, representing the action of God, as so often in the Old Testament. C. K. Barrett adopts the rendering "the Spirit" in Gen. 1:2, which he sees as suggesting the brooding or hovering of a bird. He strongly associates this creative Spirit with the Spirit who will initiate the new creation in the conception of Jesus in the Virgin Mary.[6] This creativity is seen elsewhere. For example, Ps. 33:6 declares: "By the word of the LORD the heavens were made, and all their host by the *rûach* [NRSV, 'breath'] of his mouth." Ps. 104:30 affirms: "When you send forth your Spirit, they are created." Job exclaims in 33:4, "The Spirit of God has made me, and the breath of the Almighty gives me life."

Although the Old Testament ascribes many meanings to *rûach*, there can be little doubt that a major theme is that of the Spirit of God as *creative, dynamic, and transcendent*. Some popular uses of "Spirit of God" today seem to suggest the very opposite, even seeing the "dove" in Genesis and the Gospels as "gentle" rather than creative and awesomely "from Beyond." If "spirituality" is understood as a natural human disposition toward religious aspiration, this may seem to have more in common with the Greek Stoics than with the Old Testament. We explore this notion elsewhere in these pages. A typical sentence which underlies this idea is found in Isa. 31:3: "The Egyptians are human, and not God; their houses are flesh, not spirit *(rûach)*." The whole point of the passage in Isaiah is to indicate that "those who go down to Egypt for help and who rely on horses, who trust in chariots" (Isa. 31:1), are placing their confidence in human beings, who are weak and vulnerable, in comparison with God and his Spirit. *Rûach* is strong and transcendent, not frail and feeble, like *bāśār*, "flesh" (or humanity). "Spirituality," even if such a term has any currency with reference to the Old Testament alone, comes from Beyond, not from within human-

---

5. Bruce Vawter, *On Genesis: A New Reading* (New York: Doubleday, 1977), p. 40; cf. E. A. Speiser, *Genesis*, Anchor Bible (New York: Doubleday, 1964), pp. 10-13; and Gordon Wenham, *Genesis 1–15*, Word Biblical Commentary (Nashville: Nelson, 1987), pp. 15-17.

6. C. K. Barrett, *The Holy Spirit and the Gospel Tradition* (London: SPCK, 1958), pp. 18-24.

kind; and the "Spirit" in the Old Testament comes to humanity as God's transcendent action.

1.3. The Anointing of the Spirit of
Chosen Individuals for Particular Tasks

Many writers set the Old Testament view of the Holy Spirit in sharp contrast to that of the New Testament. It is often said that the Old Testament depicts the Spirit as a *temporary* gift for chosen *individuals* only, who are empowered for special tasks, whereas the New Testament depicts the Spirit as a *permanent* gift for the whole *community* of God's people. Yet the gift of the Spirit is given to individuals only to promote *the welfare of the community* of Israel. There can be no question that this Spirit of God is identified as the same "Holy Spirit" when Jesus identifies "the Spirit of the LORD [who] is upon me because he has anointed me to bring good news to the poor; he has sent me to proclaim release to the captives . . . the year of the Lord's favor" (Luke 4:18-19) with "the Spirit of the Lord [who] shall rest upon him . . ." (Isa. 11:2). This is confirmed by Peter's sermon at Pentecost, where "I will pour out my Spirit on all flesh . . ." (Acts 2:17) is seen as the fulfillment of Joel 2:28-29, both of which speak of "the last days" and of a communal gift of the same Holy Spirit. In Isa. 11:2 the Spirit of God rests on the Messiah, is creative and transforming, and transforms hearts of stone into hearts of flesh (Ezek. 36:26-27).[7]

Without doubt, the most characteristic gift of the Spirit of God in the Old Testament is to empower and inspire chosen individuals to perform special tasks. Many of these tasks further God's redemptive purposes within the wider frame of the history of Israel. Hence, although there are gifts for an individual at a particular moment in time, their ultimate function and purpose relate to the good of the community in a permanent way. These gifts range from wisdom, administration, craftsmanship, and military leadership to prophecy and physical strength. They are not dissimilar to "gifts of the Spirit" in the New Testament. "The divine Spirit" gives wisdom and insight to inspire Bezalel "with ability, intelligence, and knowledge in every kind of craft to devise artistic designs, to work in gold, silver and bronze, and in cutting stones for setting, and in carving wood" (Exod. 31:3-5). This is the kind of intelligence and craftsmanship which led to what today we might think of as the design of great cathedrals. Here, however, our main point is that this is not merely an individual gift, but a gift to an individual for the benefit of the whole community. Incidentally,

---

7. Friedrich Baumgärtel, *"Pneuma,"* in *Theological Dictionary of the New Testament (TDNT),* ed. Gerhard Kittel and Gerhard Friedrich, 10 vols. (Grand Rapids: Eerdmans, 1964-76), vol. 5 (1968), p. 365.

it can hardly be "charismatic" or "spontaneous," for good craftsmanship requires many years of patient training and learning.

The book of Judges shows how all the elements identified in the above paragraph blend together. Judges mainly concerns individual deliverers: Othniel (Judg. 3:7-11), Ehud (Judg. 3:12-30), Deborah and Barak (Judg. 4:1-24), Gideon (Judg. 6:1–8:35), Abimelech (Judg. 9:1-57), Jephthah (11:1–12:7), and Samson (Judg. 13:1–16:31), as well as some "minor" judges in the intervening verses. With the exception of Abimelech, who is a victim of his own ambition, at least seven of the judges receive the enabling of the Spirit of the Lord to perform salvific functions on behalf of the whole community of Israel. They are explicitly called "saviors." Each receives the enabling of the divine Spirit, but each is also marked by human weakness. In this interim period between the leadership of Moses and Joshua and the anointing of kings, namely, Saul and David, the disarray and survival of the community of Israel are traced to Israel's sin and to God's saving Spirit.

A cycle of five similar events occurs repeatedly. In the story of Othniel, for example, (1) "The Israelites did what was evil in the sight of the LORD, forgetting the LORD their God" (Judg. 3:7); (2) "Therefore the anger of the LORD was kindled . . . , and he sold them into the hand of King Cushan-rishathaim . . . eight years" (3:8); (3) But "when the Israelites cried out to the LORD, (4) the LORD raised up a deliverer [Hebrew, *wayyāqem YHWH môshîyʿa*) for the Israelites, who delivered them, Othniel . . . , Caleb's younger brother. The Spirit of the LORD came upon him . . . , he went out to war . . . , his hand prevailed" (3:9-10); (5) "So the land had rest forty years" (3:11). The same cycle of events occurs in the case of Ehud. "The Israelites again did what was evil" (3:12). (2) The Lord delivered Israel to King Eglon of Moab, with the Ammonites and Amalekites, and they served King Eglon for eighteen years (3:12-14). (3) Israel "cried out to the LORD; the LORD raised up . . . Ehud" (Hebrew, *wayyāqem YHWH lāhem môshîyʿa,* as above) (3:15). (4) Ehud delivered Israel with the sword, and "they killed about ten thousand Moabites" (3:16-29). (5) "And the land had rest eighty years" (3:30). The cycle is repeated. Israel did evil (4:1). (2) The Lord delivered them to King Jabin of Canaan (4:2). (3) Israel "cried to the LORD for help" (4:3). (4) Deborah, the judge, summoned Barak, the general, while she and Jael seduced Sisera, the general of Jabin's army (4:4-22), and "God subdued Jabin of Canaan" (4:23). (5) Deborah and Barak exult in a victory song (5:1-31).

We need not repeat the cycle for all those whom we have named. Gideon constitutes our final example. (1) The Israelites did what was evil (6:1). (2) The Lord gave them over to the hand of Midian for seven years (6:1). (3) Israel "cried to the LORD" (6:7). (4) The Lord commissioned Gideon "to deliver Israel from the hand of Midian" (6:14); "The Spirit of the LORD took possession of Gideon" (6:34), and Gideon put the enemy army to flight (7:22-25). (5) A vast store of booty was won for Israel (8:26-27), and "the land had rest forty years"

(8:28). But as soon as Gideon died, a new cycle began: "the Israelites relapsed . . . [and] did not remember the LORD their God, who had rescued them . . . from all their enemies" (8:33-34).

Three factors deserve to be noted for an understanding of the work of the Spirit of God. In Part III we will see that Michael Welker stresses these, and their diversity.

(1) *First,* every "judge" *has a human weakness or frailty.* Ehud is left-handed (Judg. 3:15), which was regarded in the ancient world as a weakness in battle. Deborah was a woman, who would hardly be expected to show military leadership. A degree of guile was needed for Deborah and Jael (4:7, 9, 18-21). Gideon was commanded by God to reduce the size of his army (7:2), first from twenty-two thousand to ten thousand (7:3); then from ten thousand to three hundred. Clearly the reason was to give credit for victory to God and the Spirit of God, not to Gideon and his army.

Abimelech was too obsessed with personal ambition to be an agent of good: "God sent an evil spirit" (9:23). In the case of Jephthah, "the Spirit of the LORD came upon [him]" (11:29), but he made a rash and foolish vow, which led to the death of his daughter (11:31, 34). "The Spirit of the LORD rushed on [Samson], and he tore the lion apart barehanded, as one might tear apart a kid" (14:6). But for much of his life he played the fool (15:4-5), pursued revenge, and lusted after foreign women. In the end Delilah was his downfall (16:4-22). Yet one last time "he called to the LORD" and brought down the house in which many Philistines gathered, in addition to three thousand on the roof (16:27-30).

(2) The *second* point is that each of these manifestations of the Spirit of God ultimately *preserved Israel* from broadly the era of Joshua to that of Saul or the kings, while "in those days there was no king in Israel" (Judg. 18:1). Even if the Spirit anointed chosen individuals, this served *the people of God as a whole.* We may study the individual gifts of military powers, or (in Samson's case) brute strength, but these served a redemptive end for Israel, which, even in relation to ancient narratives, was interwoven with Israel's moral and spiritual conduct. The Hebrew word for "savior" applies to the judges, and constitutes an early model of what "salvation" means. Hence, while there is some justification for claiming that in the Old Testament the Spirit is given to individuals on a temporary basis, this is not the whole picture, and it should be firmly qualified.

(3) *Third,* writers often speak of "empowering" leaders and judges by the Spirit of God. I use the word "enabling" because we shall note in due course that certain problems arise over the excessive use of the word "power." Later I shall argue that "power" is often misinterpreted as an analogy from the industrial age, where it is seen in quasi-mechanical terms in analogy with steam power or electrical power. Karl Barth and others rightly see this enabling in terms of *effectiveness* or *efficaciousness.* It is true that, as Norman Snaith declared, "Men are able to do those things, which of themselves and in their own

strength, they are incapable of doing."[8] But this speaks of *ability, effectiveness,* and *heightened capacity,* not of raw power. Even among biblical scholars the term "power" can rest on older, now discredited, notions of power. When he speaks of the "empowerment of humans in the Old Testament," Cyril Powell works with an old-fashioned notion of being "charged with psychic power" in blessing and cursing, which we have exposed as false.[9] Moreover, he quotes Gerhard von Rad's criticism of J. Pedersen "for providing a predominantly magical interpretation . . . of power."[10] Powell then frequently uses energy as a synonym for power. The contrast is not only, or perhaps even primarily, between strength and weakness, but rather between effective and ineffective, and possible and impossible.

Our main objective in this section, however, is to discuss the relation between the gift of the Spirit to individuals and its wider context in the welfare, even salvation, of the community. This becomes especially important when we consider the "gifts of the Spirit" in the Pauline writings. When he sums up the relation between the two Testaments with special attention to Paul, Floyd Filson declares, "It is likewise true that chosen individuals are given the Spirit for special tasks; but this does not mean that some are left without the Spirit" (i.e., in the New Testament).[11]

1.4. The Spirit as an "Extension" of God: Revelation, Inspiration, and Holiness

Like the Wisdom of God and the Word of God (and perhaps also the angel of God, the glory of God, and the Law of God), the Spirit of God is both distinct from God, and yet can convey God's presence or "face" (Hebrew, *pānîm*). To seek the Spirit is to seek *God,* as Gordon Fee insists. God's face can denote his gracious attention. While the Old Testament insists that no one can literally "see" God, in a metaphorical sense to see God means to experience God's gracious presence or face (Ps. 17:15; Job 33:25-26).[12] Indeed, "to seek the face of God" becomes a biblical phrase (Ps. 24:6; cf. 1 Chron. 21:30). Wisdom and Word

---

8. Norman Snaith and Vincent Taylor (eds.), *The Doctrine of the Holy Spirit,* Headingly Lectures (London: Epworth, 1937), p. 11.

9. Powell, *The Biblical Concept of Power,* p. 20. See Anthony C. Thiselton, "The Supposed Power of Words in the Biblical Writings," *JTS* 25 (1974): 282-99; repeated in *Thiselton on Hermeneutics: Collected Works with New Essays* (Grand Rapids: Eerdmans, and Aldershot: Ashgate, 2006), pp. 53-68.

10. Powell, *The Biblical Concept of Power,* p. 22.

11. Floyd V. Filson, *The New Testament against Its Environment* (London: SCM, 1950), p. 78.

12. Eichrodt, *Theology of the Old Testament,* vol. 2, pp. 35-39; cf. Gordon Fee, *God's Empowering Presence: The Holy Spirit in the Letters of Paul* (Carlisle: Paternoster, 1995), pp. 6-9.

can become what Eichrodt calls "a form of self-manifestation of the transcendent God."[13] This foundation becomes important when, on the basis of a *later* theology of the Holy Spirit, *some seem to seek or pray to the Spirit as if he were somehow different from God, or independent of God.* In the same vein, "statements about the Word . . . in many cases overlap with those about the Spirit."[14] Both Word and Spirit reveal the divine will and purpose, which otherwise might remain hidden.

Often the Spirit of God is found in synonymous parallelism with God, for example, in "do not take your Holy Spirit from me" (Ps. 51:11). The parallel, "Do not cast me away from your presence," makes "Holy Spirit" and "your presence" synonymous. The confession of sin (prompted traditionally by Nathan's parable) and restoration depend wholly on God, and communion with God constitutes a key theme. Ps. 104:29-30 has a similar emphasis on God's presence and his Spirit. It reads: "When you hide your face [Hebrew *pānîm,* also 'presence'], they are dismayed. . . . When you send forth your Spirit *(rûach),* they are created; and you renew the face of the ground." These verses associate creation and renewal with the work of the Spirit of God as well as with the presence of God. Similarly, "God's Spirit" is in synonymous parallelism with "your presence" in Ps. 139:7: "Where can I go from your Spirit? Or where can I flee from your presence?"

After the Exile during the period of the Restoration, God's people needed assurance and reassurance that God was still with them. Thus Haggai assures the people, "My Spirit abides among you; do not fear" (Hag. 2:5). God will remain true to his covenant promises, hence Zerubbabel and Joshua must take courage (Hag. 2:4). Again, "My Spirit abides with you" (v. 5) is parallel with "I am with you" (v. 4). The Spirit of God is clearly a mode of God's activity, whose nature and identity are inseparable from God. Indeed, many begin to define or to explicate the Spirit as "God in action." A famous verse appears in another writer of the same era, Zechariah: "This is the word of the LORD to Zerubbabel: 'Not by might, nor by power, but by my Spirit,' says the LORD of hosts" (Zech. 4:6). By the Spirit of God mountains become plains (v. 7). Zerubbabel, therefore, may lay the foundation of the temple (v. 9). The Spirit represents the omniscient God, symbolized by the seven eyes (or complete knowledge) of God (v. 10). Perhaps even the "oil" from the olive trees conveys the notion in symbol of Zerubbabel's anointing by the Spirit, together with Joshua's ("the two anointed ones, who stand by the Lord," v. 14; cf. vv. 11-13).

The Spirit's identification and conceptualization as an angelic being is less clear. Joshua saw a "man" with a drawn sword (Josh. 5:13) who shared in his commissioning and anointing. "The angel of the LORD" appeared to Manoah (Judg. 13:13). The NRSV often translates entities or agents denoted by the He-

---

13. Eichrodt, *Theology of the Old Testament,* vol. 2, p. 38.
14. Eichrodt, *Theology of the Old Testament,* vol. 2, p. 79.

brew *śārāph* ("burning ones," "seraphim") as "fiery serpents" (Isa. 14:29; 30:6). More directly associated with the presence of the Lord are the angelic cherubim (Exod. 25:18-22), where cherubim are associated with the Ark of the Covenant and God's presence. In 2 Sam. 22:2-20 David sings of "the LORD my rock, my fortress, and my deliverer," who is of awesome majesty: "Thick darkness was under his feet. He rode on a cherub, and flew; he was seen upon the wings of the wind." The *k^erûbîm* are winged beings who may transport the Lord and guard the divine throne (Ezek. 1; Rev. 4:8-10). Their functions are like those of the Spirit, especially in Ezekiel.

The notion of the Spirit as an Agent of revelation persists in rabbinic thought, and into the New Testament and Church Fathers. Theodore Vriezen writes, "The Spirit of God may occur in the Old Testament as a means to grant revelations, but this happens far less frequently than we might think on a super-ficial view."[15] Isa. 40:13 asserts what is later quoted by Paul: "Who has directed the Spirit of the LORD, or as his counselor has instructed him?" (cf. also 1 Cor. 2:16). The close association of the Spirit with God can be seen in the synony-mous parallelism of Ps. 139:7: "Where can I go from your Spirit? Or where can I flee from your presence?" In later writings communion with God came to re-ceive more attention than the miraculous.[16] Hence an emphasis on renewal finds expression in Ezek. 36:23-33: "I will sanctify my great name" (v. 23). This leads to: "A new heart will I give you. . . . I will remove from your body the heart of stone. . . . I will put my Spirit within you, and make you follow my statutes" (vv. 26-27). Eichrodt observes, "Man's relationship with God is no longer left to his own efforts, but is given him by the spirit."[17] Hence, he adds, the Spirit now becomes a permanent influence.

This enables us to grasp and to clarify a fundamental difference between revelation and inspiration. The revealing of God can be an event which God en-acts through his Spirit, through his Word, through his angel, or even through theophany. But the appropriation and understanding of this revelation require the inspiration of the human subject or person who receives it. Long ago this distinction was proposed by James Orr.[18] He argues that therefore inspiration may include the making of records of divine acts of revelation. This may even take permanent or authoritative forms. He comments, "Those who produce the record possess in an eminent degree the Spirit of the revelation."[19] Revelation, he argues, lies in the *provision* of truth about God; inspiration lies in the *use* made of it. The most delicate question on these matters which confronted Israel

---

15. T. C. Vriezen, *An Outline of Old Testament Theology* (Oxford: Blackwell, 1962), p. 249.

16. Eichrodt, *Theology of the Old Testament,* vol. 2, p. 58.

17. Eichrodt, *Theology of the Old Testament,* vol. 2, p. 59.

18. James Orr, *Revelation and Inspiration* (London: Duckworth, 1909), esp. pp. 155-74.

19. Orr, *Revelation and Inspiration,* p. 156.

was that of true and false prophecy. This *claim* to be inspired by the Spirit remained only a *claim* until it was tested and verified.

George Montague sees the Spirit "as the instigator and the animator of prophecy."[20] An early example of inspired prophecy occurs perhaps in Numbers. Although some date parts of Numbers later, there is archaeological and other evidence that the story of Balaam (Num. 22–24) rests on an early tradition. Numbers depicts this non-Israelite prophet as defying Balak of Moab by blessing Israel, when King Balak had hired him to curse Israel. Num. 24:2 declares, "The Spirit of God came upon him" (Balaam), and he uttered his oracle as "one who heard the words of God" (22:4). This finds a parallel in Num. 23:16: "The LORD . . . put a word into his mouth." This is a clear example of the Spirit of the Lord's revealing words of God, and inspiring the prophet. This theme develops into the Spirit's inspiring both the prophets and Scripture in later passages and in Judaism.

The reference in Isa. 11:1-2 appears to associate "wisdom" gifts with the anointing of a ruler whom many Christians regard as a Messianic figure: "A shoot shall come forth from the stump of Jesse, and a branch shall grow out of his roots. The Spirit of the LORD shall rest on him; the Spirit [perhaps spirit] of wisdom and understanding, the Spirit [spirit?] of counsel and might. . . ." However we define the figure who is envisaged, as a Messiah or a king on David's throne in historical terms, or as Christ in Christological terms, this figure receives the Spirit permanently. Indeed, this figure suggests a possible plurality of fulfillments. He will vindicate the poor and oppressed (v. 4), and will bring in a cosmic vision of peace, justice, and well-being or salvation (11:6-10). Clearly this refers to his restoration of the remnant of God's people (v. 11). "Spirit" occurs four times, although in vv. 4-5 the word may be anthropological, to mean "quality" or "mind-set" of wisdom, or it may be God's Agent, "the Spirit who gives wisdom." Isa. 28:6 repeats "Spirit [or spirit] of justice" (Hebrew *rûach mishpāṭ*, and Isa. 32:15 speaks of the pouring out of the Spirit, who will bring justice and peace.

Among human prophets, however, there soon emerged the need to distinguish between true and false *claims* to prophecy in the name of the Spirit of the Lord. This issue comes to light in the complex story of Micaiah ben Imlah in 1 Kings 22:11-28. Micaiah claimed, "Whatever the LORD says to me, I will speak" (22:14). His message appears to be, "Go up and triumph" (v. 15). But when Ahab presses him, he admits, "I saw all Israel scattered. . . . These have no master" (v. 17). In vv. 21-22 "a spirit" says, "I will entice him. . . . I will go out and be a lying spirit in the mouth of all his prophets" (repeated in v. 23). Finally, Zedekiah replies, "Which way did the Spirit of the LORD pass from me to speak to you?"

---

20. George T. Montague, *The Holy Spirit: The Growth of a Biblical Tradition* (Eugene, OR: Wipf & Stock, 1976), p. 45.

and the king put Micaiah in prison (22:24, 27). In his definitive book on this subject, *Prophecy and Discernment,* Moberly discusses the Micaiah passage for some twenty pages.[21] It occurs in a sequence of passages which largely depict Elijah's confrontations with King Ahab. Ahab depends on the direction of a prophetic voice (22:1-4). Ramoth-gilead is a disputed frontier town, near the Golan Heights, which Syria and Israel still dispute. The story follows that of Naboth's vineyard, which may alert the reader to Ahab's greed for territorial gains.

The decision was virtually taken, so the question for Ahab was a pseudo-question. But Jehoshaphat does not want simply to rubber-stamp the king's decision, so for him the question is genuine. The four hundred prophets (of Baal?) confirm Ahab's decision. The king already knows that Micaiah does not simply rubber-stamp his policies. The scene is set for a drama like that of Washington, DC, or Westminster, England. Micaiah must face the public stage. When the king asks his question (22:15a), he at first gives the required answer (v. 15b). But both Ahab and the prophet know that it is not what he believes. This comes in v. 17, and warns of disaster. But the prophet's sarcastic answer has caught the king off-guard. It is similar to Nathan's seductive strategy before David (2 Sam. 12:1-7). He avoids simply stating the obvious. The conclusion of this "indirect communication" is clear: the Lord has decreed disaster, as declared by the heavenly court. This God-centered aspect conveys the theological meaning. Zedekiah intervenes as a leader of the court prophets, but Micaiah does not flinch. He has won the contest "between self-will and integrity," as well as its fulfillment.[22]

The problem of false prophecy again occurs in Deuteronomy. The whole subject concerns Deut. 18:9-22. But the conclusion in 18:20-22 carries the utmost challenge to anyone who claims to speak in God's name today. If the prophet is a "true" prophet, "I will put my words in the mouth of the prophet" (v. 18). But v. 20 reads: "Any prophet . . . who presumes to speak in my name a word that I have not commanded the prophet to speak — that prophet shall die." Verse 22 repeats that if he speaks "a word that the LORD has not spoken, the prophet has spoken presumptuously." In the broader context, Moses is described as a prophet (Hebrew *nābhî'*), and in later Judaism and in Calvin he becomes preeminently the prophet, passing God's words to the people. Moberly calls him "the model for Israel's other prophets," and says that he is exercising a ministry which is "explicitly based upon his proximity to God."[23] But Deut. 18:9-22 pictures people's bewilderment when "they had no easy way of knowing which prophet was telling the truth."[24] Deut. 18:15-22 depicts such a case. This

---

21. R. W. L. Moberly, *Prophecy and Discernment,* Cambridge Studies in Christian Doctrine (Cambridge: Cambridge University Press, 2006), pp. 109-29.

22. Moberly, *Prophecy and Discernment,* pp. 125 and 128.

23. Moberly, *Prophecy and Discernment,* pp. 8 and 9.

24. Moberly, *Prophecy and Discernment,* p. 17.

dilemma persists until New Testament times, when the Church must "weigh what is said" (1 Cor. 14:29), or "test" the words of prophets (1 Thess. 5:21).

The ease with which false prophets can claim to speak in the name of the Lord may largely account for the relatively few references to the Spirit of God in eighth- and seventh-century canonical prophets. A partly alternative argument is that "their sayings were collected and eventually published under their name."[25] This would not preclude their appealing to speak by the Spirit. The first of the "writing" prophets, Amos, virtually omits any reference to the Spirit of God, but stresses the ordinariness of his vocation (Amos 1:1). Hosea also prefers to speak of the "word" rather than of the Spirit. In Hos. 4:19 *rûach* means "wind," and in 4:12 and 5:4 the term is used anthropologically to mean "mind-set." The Isaiah of Isaiah 1–39, who is usually said to be contemporary with Micah, does not use "Spirit" to describe his own inspiration. J. E. Fison captures the mood of the classical prophets when he comments, "There is all the difference in the world between 'hearing the word of the Lord' and working yourself up into an ecstasy of mystical rapture."[26]

Micah prophesied in Judea and the South, while Amos and Hosea ministered to Israel in the North. Like Amos, his emphasis was especially ethical and social. Yet he did lay claim to inspiration by the Spirit of God. He acknowledged the power and deceptiveness of false prophets "who lead my people astray" (Mic. 3:5). He declared, "The seers shall be disgraced" (3:7). But this does not prevent Micah from asserting: "But as for me, I am filled with power, with the Spirit of the LORD, and with justice and might, to declare to Jacob his transgression" (Mic. 3:8). The appeal to the Spirit of God, however, is conjoined with the consequent concern for justice and righteousness. This is a vital condition.

A century later, in the seventh century, the Spirit is virtually absent from Jeremiah. Jeremiah attacks false prophecy frequently (Jer. 2:8; 5:13, 31; 6:13; 14:11-16; 23:9-40; 28:1-17). These prophets "lead my people astray" (23:32), and they "prophesy lies in my name" (23:25). "I did not send them" (v. 32); "I did not send the prophets. . . . I did not speak to them, yet they prophesied" (v. 21). "The prophets are prophesying lies in my name" (14:14). Montague comments, "Never before have we met such a strong opposition of word to spirit . . . ; later in Paul we will find a trace of this Jeremian reaction . . . (1 Cor. 14:13-19)."[27] Jeremiah has visions (Jer. 1:11-14), but normally attacks them. His emphasis remains on "the word of the LORD" (2:1; 7:1; 14:1), while "visions" may denote "interpreting ordinary objects" (an almond tree, or a boiling pot) *as* part of a divine message (Jer. 1:11, 13). For the rest, in Jer. 51:11 "spirit" may simply denote "mind-set,"

25. Montague, *The Holy Spirit*, p. 33.

26. J. E. Fison, *The Blessing of the Holy Spirit* (London and New York: Longmans, Green, 1950), p. 67.

27. Montague, *The Holy Spirit*, p. 43.

as in "the LORD has stirred up the spirit of the Medes." Vriezen actually claims: "The major prophets never connect revelation with the operation of the Spirit, except Ezekiel (once) and Deutero-Isaiah."[28]

Yet in spite of terrible and widespread abuses, God continues to speak through prophets, even if the more reflective prophets show misgivings about the phenomenon. The lesson to be learned is that we should approach "prophecy" with openness but also with extreme caution. When we examine Paul, we shall consider carefully whether Paul understands the term in the sense in which it is widely understood today.

1.5. Remaining Themes:
Effects, Creativity, Life, and the Derived or Shared Spirit

Our examination of prophecy and inspiration adds point to our earlier claim that, like the wind blowing a field of corn, or shaking trees, we see the wind only *by its effects,* and likewise we see the Spirit in terms of visible effects. Thus if a prophet claims to reveal what is patently false, or what conflicts with God's will or earlier revelation, we shall not accept his claims. Isa. 7:2, as we noted, declares: "The heart of his people shook, as the trees of the forest shake before the wind." As chaff is blown out of the wheat, "You shall winnow them, and the wind shall carry them away" (Isa. 41:16). Under the Spirit's transcendence, we could not avoid seeing the Spirit as creative. He does not represent a human aspiration, but that on which humans are dependent, as they are for their creation. Increasingly this will lead in the Bible to the Spirit's role in transformation and the new creation.

Similarly, we have in effect already perceived aspects of the work of God's Spirit as *life-giver.* Ezek. 37:1-14, with its vision of the valley of dry bones, offers an instructive example. The bones were "very dry" (v. 2). By his Spirit, God takes these lifeless, long-dead bones and causes them to become a living person, with flesh and skin (v. 6). "They lived, and stood on their feet, a vast multitude" (v. 10). The Lord says, "I am going to open your graves, and bring you up from your graves" (v. 12). This is all because "I will put my Spirit within you, and you shall live" (v. 14). Not for nothing does Jürgen Moltmann call his book on the Spirit *The Spirit of Life.*[29]

One gap in what we have considered so far concerns applying further the *derived or shared gift of the Spirit, which we have already noted in connection with Moses.* The "seventy elders" of Num. 11:16-25, we saw, "derive" this gift from Moses. The gift is given through Moses. He complains about the "burden" of

---

28. Vriezen, *Old Testament Theology,* p. 250.
29. Jürgen Moltmann, *The Spirit of Life: A Universal Affirmation* (London: SCM, 1992).

leading such a large number of people. We noted, "The LORD . . . took some of the Spirit that was on him [Moses] and put it on the seventy elders; and when the Spirit rested upon them, they prophesied" (Num. 11:25). Similarly, Joshua derives his gift of the Spirit through Moses and the laying on of hands (Deut. 34:9). Likewise, Elisha "derives" his share of the Spirit of God from Elijah: "The Spirit of Elijah rests on Elisha" (2 Kings 2:15; cf. 2:9, 13-14). Christians in a later era will derive their gift of the Holy Spirit from Christ's anointing by the Spirit of God, just as their sonship is directly derived from Christ as the Son of God (Gal. 4:4-7; Rom. 8:9-11; cf. 8:26-27). This makes these Old Testament passages especially significant for Christians. Many would see this as also prefigured in the language of the Servant Songs. In Isa. 42:1, 5, we encounter the first of the Servant Songs. The Servant is "my chosen, in whom my soul delights; I have put my Spirit upon him." Charles Cranfield observes, "The words of the *bath-qôl* (the voice from heaven at Jesus' baptism) are reminiscent of Isa. 42:1" (in Mark 1:11).[30] Matt. 12:18 includes (in Greek) *ho agapētos mou eis hon eudokēsen hē psychē mou,* "my Beloved, with whom my soul is well pleased," and adds, "I will put my Spirit upon him" (NRSV); and Matt. 3:16-17 speaks of the Spirit descending and anointing Jesus, while the voice from heaven exclaims, "This is my Son, the Beloved, with whom I am well pleased." Luke's parallel in Luke 3:22 has almost identical words. The conclusion in Isa. 42:7, "to open the eyes that are blind, to bring the prisoners from the dungeon," is taken up on the lips of Jesus in Luke 4:18-19. Both Isa. 42:1-7 and the Gospels show how God's chosen Agent acts and ministers through the anointing of the Spirit. It embraces both Jesus Christ and corporate Israel, from a canonical perspective.

The reference to the Spirit is not in conflict with other Servant Songs (Isa. 49:1-6, 50:4-9, and 52:13–53:12), although these contain an abundance of Messianic language, and the ability of the Servant is regularly ascribed to God himself (Isa. 50:4-5, 7-9; 53:10, 12). Yet Isa. 61:1-3 is startling: "The Spirit of the Lord GOD is upon me, because the LORD has anointed me; he has sent me to bring the good news to the oppressed, to bind up the broken-hearted, to proclaim liberty to the captives, and release to the prisoners; to proclaim the year of the LORD's favor . . . ; to give them [those who mourn] a garland instead of ashes. . . ." In Luke 4:17-19 Jesus explicitly quotes from Isaiah. It is a composite quotation from Isa. 40:3-5 and Isa. 61:1-2. L. T. Johnson claims, "Luke offers here a mixed citation from the LXX of Isa. 61:1, 58:6, and 61:2."[31] I. H. Marshall comments, "The functions of the Old Testament figure are now fulfilled in Jesus, who has been anointed by the Spirit for this purpose."[32]

30. C. E. B. Cranfield, *The Gospel according to Saint Mark* (Cambridge: Cambridge University Press, 1963), p. 54.

31. Luke T. Johnson, *The Gospel of Luke,* Sacra Pagina (Collegeville, MN: Glazier, 1991), p. 79; cf. Joel B. Green, *The Gospel of Luke,* NICNT (Grand Rapids: Eerdmans, 1997), pp. 209-13.

32. I. Howard Marshall, *The Gospel of Luke,* NIGTC (Grand Rapids: Eerdmans, 1978), p. 183.

Isaiah 63:10-14 also associates the Spirit of God with God's past deeds for the people of Israel. 63:10 explains that Israel's rebellion "grieved his Holy Spirit." This is of the utmost importance. In using the word "grieved" (the Holy Spirit; Hebrew *wᵉʿiṣᵉbhû ʾeth-rûach qādᵉshô;* Greek LXX, *parōxynan to pneuma to hagion autou*), this implies a personal or suprapersonal Agent since a *force* or sheer *power* cannot be *grieved*. Second, this is one of only three references in the Old Testament with the explicit double term "Holy Spirit." The Hebrew, *rûach qōdhshᵉkā,* "your Holy Spirit," also occurs in Ps. 51:13(11), this time referring to the community of Israel, while Isa. 63:10-11 refers to the Holy Spirit within the individual. Usually, however, "Spirit of the LORD" occurs without further qualification, although in Dan. 4:8 he is the "Spirit of the holy God." Isa. 63:14, again, refers to "the Spirit of the LORD" providing security for Israel in the wilderness. Isa. 59:21 speaks of "my Spirit" in a speech from God, who will "not depart" and is therefore no temporary endorsement, but who acts as the Spirit to sustain the covenant, or God's terms concerning his relationship with Israel.

One other important feature concerns prophetic promises about the eschatological or future New Age. This occurs especially in Jeremiah 31 and in Joel 2. Jer. 31:31 promises a new covenant whose law is written "on their hearts" (v. 33), but it does not explicitly appeal to the work of the Spirit. Joel 2:28 is explicitly quoted by the apostle Peter on the Day of Pentecost in his first sermon: "I will pour out my Spirit on all flesh; your sons and your daughters shall prophesy, your old men shall dream dreams, and your young men see visions" (Acts 2:17). Joel declares, "Even on the male and female slaves, in those days, I will pour out my Spirit" (2:29). The term "all flesh" denotes "everyone" without distinction, even if Luke's idiom, in which he follows the Septuagint, denotes "all types of people." The allusion to dreams and visions, and to the darkening of the earth, sets these events in a cosmic and apocalyptic context. The event constitutes the beginning of the new creation, which is an earth-shaking event. "The sun shall be turned to darkness, and the moon to blood" (v. 31) is standard apocalyptic imagery for the dawning of the last days, or of the new creation. The hearers or readers would understand the imagery to mean that it was a major event in the world's history, of genuinely cosmic proportions. Hence the apostle Peter may repeat the imagery (Acts 2:20) without suggesting an event that concerns astronomy. Such events also indicate that this "was in no sense the work of men: it is solely the work of God."[33] The gift of the Spirit of God comes as both judgment and grace, for "everyone who calls on the name of the LORD shall be saved" (Joel 2:32).

To conclude this chapter: we may acknowledge that many uses of *rûach* are *anthropological,* denoting the human spirit, especially in the Wisdom literature (Prov. 11:13; 15:13; 16:18; 18:14; 29:23; Eccl. 1:14, 17; 2:11, 17; 3:21; 4:4, 6; 10:4; Job 7:11;

---

33. Johannes Weiss, *Jesus' Preaching of the Kingdom of God.*

10:12). But the very different uses of *rûach* should not be confused. Although the Spirit functions as an intermediary with God, like Wisdom and the Word, for the most part the Spirit of God is a *transcendent* influence on humans "from without." The least that we can say is that even in the Old Testament the Spirit is "the Beyond who is within." This radically affects our notions of "spiritual" and "spirituality," as the New Testament material will confirm. Second, even where specific gifts are given to *individuals,* this is for the benefit of the whole community. This, too, will be confirmed by the New Testament. Third, to seek the Spirit, or to hear the Spirit, is *to seek and hear God.* This will be confirmed by later Trinitarian doctrine. Other features include holiness, revelation, creativity, and life. But the feature most akin to the New Testament is the principle of *a derived or shared gift.* In the New Testament, all Christians possess the Spirit of God because they are in Christ and share his Messianic anointing. The center of the stage in the New Testament is the *Christ* to whom the Spirit witnesses (John 16:13). At the very least, in time this focus will embrace *the whole Trinity* — Father, Son, and Holy Spirit.

Many late-twentieth- and early-twenty-first-century writers have amplified some of these points. But we have postponed referring to them in this chapter for two reasons. First, we wanted to avoid the use of too many footnotes at this early stage; second, we want to consider their comments in the context of their own writings. Hence we will consider particular issues further in Part III.

2

The Spirit in Judaism

2.1. Introduction: Practical Themes

Because the situation and themes of Judaism between the Testaments are, like those of the Old Testament, varied and complex, we shall begin again with a general summary, but especially with Christian readers in mind, who may be looking for the practical thrust of this section. Otherwise we shall endeavor to keep this chapter as short as we can, without undue oversimplification.

First, it is often mistakenly argued that Judaism expected the Spirit to be silent during the period. Many, however, argue the contrary, that this is almost entirely based on a misunderstanding of a single text, namely *Tosefta Soṭah* 13:2-4. This passage apparently states: "When Haggai, Zechariah, and Malachi, the last of the prophets, died, the Holy Spirit ceased [from] Israel. Nevertheless, a *bath-qôl* [literally, 'daughter of the voice'] was heard by them. . . . they heard a *bath-qôl* saying, 'There is a man here who is worthy of the Holy Spirit.'" This man, it is suggested, was Hillel, and he enables the Spirit to be present again. At best, we may conclude that a single text of perhaps the third or fourth century A.D., whose significance is disputed, can hardly be decisive, and indeed many other texts in Judaism suggest a different conclusion.

In general, three themes seem to emerge from the Old Testament, which are also taken up in the New Testament. (1) First, in the Dead Sea Scrolls (see below) 1QS 8:15-16 takes up Neh. 9:30 and Zech. 7:12 to suggest that the Spirit was active in inspiring the *prophets of the Old Testament* and the study of the Law. *Jubilees* 31:12 conveys a similar perspective. (2) Second, the Holy Spirit begins to be associated more distinctly with *holiness* or purification. Some debate whether the Spirit is seen as the cause or the effect of purification. (3) Third, the *community* becomes a clearer focus of the Spirit's activity, especially in the Dead Sea Scrolls (1QS 3:7-8), though it is not always clear that this denotes the Spirit of God.

On the other hand, in *Greek-speaking Judaism* (discussed below) the Spirit of God becomes much more *immanent,* or overlaps with the rational spirit in human beings. This characterizes much Greek philosophy, rather than Paul or the rest of the New Testament. Considerable contrasts emerge between Philo and Paul, and many popular assumptions today perhaps owe more to this "Hellenistic" thought about the Spirit than to Paul and the New Testament.

2.2. The Settings, Purposes, and Range of Judaism between the Testaments

Jewish literature between the two Testaments takes two broad forms. The older titles for these two groups of writings were once those of "Palestinian" and "Hellenistic" Judaism. But Martin Hengel and many others agree that these are unsatisfactory terms. Both streams of thought and culture interpenetrate and influence each other along a spectrum. Yet at the same time we can give clear examples of these two trends at each end of the spectrum. Ben Sirach, for example, in our Apocrypha, closely follows Proverbs; and much rabbinic literature follows conservative or "Palestinian" traditions. At the opposite end of the spectrum, Philo of Alexandria and the pro-Roman Flavius Josephus are deeply concerned to show positive attitudes toward the Greco-Roman world and are saturated with Greek philosophy and culture. They are largely loyal to Judaism, but the distinctive Judaism of the Diaspora. Some common attitudes can be found in the bold speech of the Greek-speaking Stephen in Acts 7.

Many Jewish writings of the period fall between these two extremes. The Wisdom of Solomon, also in the Apocrypha, is soaked in Greek concepts like those of Philo. 4 Maccabees is heavily influenced by Greek thought, as is much of the Pseudepigrapha. The Dead Sea Scrolls, discovered at Qumran from 1948 onward, represent a sect of Judaism in Palestine dating largely from the first century B.C. into the first century A.D. Within the apocalyptic literature stands the anti-Roman *Psalms of Solomon,* which awaits victory "over Latin men." In the book of Judith, Judith acts like one of the Old Testament judges, similarly to resist foreign rule. On the other hand, *1 Enoch* retains a form of eschatology akin to the Old Testament. The *Testaments of the Twelve Patriarchs* includes some varied outlooks, but has Christian additions.

Two prominent bridges between the two Testaments are found in the Wisdom tradition and in apocalyptic traditions. In the Wisdom tradition the conservative book the Wisdom of Ben Sirach (known also as Ecclesiasticus) comes from the second century B.C. It often looks back to Proverbs. Wisdom is highly prized as a preexistent gift of God, at times virtually a divine attribute. It (or she) may often be regarded as the Agent of God, in place of the Spirit. Wisdom also becomes identified with the Law. Ben Sirach is written for Jews who live in a Hellenistic culture. Often "spirit" denotes mind-set, as in "filled with the spirit of understanding" (Sir. 39:6). Here this reflects on a scribal calling. Ben Sirach also often focuses on human capacities. The scribe is a sage. There is a hint of the Old Testament debate about false prophecy in "Dreams have deceived many. . . . Without such deceptions the law will be fulfilled" (Sir. 34:7-8). Like Ezra, the scribe is to transmit the pure tradition and law. John Levison declares, "Ben Sirach . . . gives no credence to those who allegedly attain knowledge through divination, omens, and dreams (34:5)."[1] But the inspiration of the canonical prophets is not doubted. Ben Sirach speaks of "the prophet Isaiah, who was great and trustworthy in visions" (Sir. 48:22), and of Ezekiel, "who saw the vision of glory, which God showed him" (49:8). Wisdom, rather than the Spirit, however, usually mediates the Scriptures to the Jews.

The first-century writing, Wisdom of Solomon, also addresses Jews who live in an alien Hellenistic culture. But in other respects it differs radically from Ben Sirach. Where Ben Sirach is conservative, but has an optimistic view of providence like Proverbs, Wisdom of Solomon is more radical, soaked in Greek concepts as Philo was, and more aware of struggles in life, like Job and Ecclesiastes. It may reflect Roman rule in Egypt. It denounces idolatry (Wis. 14:8, 12, 24-27, which has affinities with Rom. 1:18-32). It looks to the past and to the future, and even has traces of Platonic dualism.

In the Judaism of the Diaspora firmly rooted in the Greco-Roman world, the key sources remain the Septuagint, Wisdom of Solomon, 4 Maccabees, and especially Philo of Alexandria (c. 20 B.C.–A.D. 40 or 45) and Flavius Josephus (A.D. 37–c. 100). Philo produced up to forty treatises (published in the Loeb Library in twelve volumes). He was loyal to Diaspora Judaism but was saturated in Greek culture and philosophy, including Plato and Stoicism. He sought to interpret the Torah or the Law by explaining it in terms acceptable to Greeks and Romans. Yet there are resonances with Paul and John. God's Agent in creation is the Logos rather than the Spirit, although God is "Spirit" in the sense of nonmaterial transcendence. Philo is careful to avoid anthropomorphisms. The mediating figure between the spiritual, transcendent God and humankind is the rational mind, although Philo also believed that a "holy spirit" dwelt within humankind (Philo, *Allegorical Interpretation* 1:31-42). The Spirit inspired Bezalel (Exod. 31:3) and "is diffused in its fullness everywhere" (*On Giants* 27). Like the Stoics, Philo saw *pneuma* as all-pervasive, although he also explicitly distanced himself from Stoicism. This stands in contrast to Paul in 1 Cor. 2:12, who sees the Holy Spirit as distinct from the Stoic "world-soul," but as "proceeding from God" (Greek, *to pneuma to ek theou*). We might describe his general view of Spirit as immanent.

---

1. John R. Levison, *The Spirit in First-Century Judaism* (Boston and Leiden: Brill, 2002), p. 259.

2.3. *Rûach* (Spirit) in Aramaic-Speaking Judaism and *Pneuma* in Greek-Speaking Judaism

The Wisdom of Solomon uses the terms "holy" and "spirit" together three times in *hagion pneuma paideias,* but not to denote the Holy Spirit. Here the phrase denotes "a holy and disciplined spirit" (NRSV), or a kind of mind-set (Wis. 1:5). Although Hatch and Redpath list twenty occurrences of *pneuma* in their *Concordance to the Septuagint,* only two or perhaps three clearly denote the Spirit of the Lord rather than a human disposition (Wis. 1:7).[2] This verse may anticipate what Paul says of Christ: "The Spirit of the Lord . . . holds all things together" (Wis. 1:7; Col. 1:17). The second passage is Wis. 12:1, where the writer speaks of God's love of his creation and its providential preservation, and declares, "For your immortal Spirit [NRSV, lowercase 'spirit' once again] is in all things." *This is "panentheism" rather than pantheism.* But the Spirit is immanent rather than, here, transcendent. However, Montague argues, "Man holds his life-breath precariously as a gift from God (Ps. 104:29). . . . The breath-life never ceases to be God's. On loan to man during his earthly life (Wis. 15:16), it will return to its author at man's death."[3]

A third probable reference to the Holy Spirit of God occurs in Wis. 9:17: "You have given wisdom, and sent your Holy Spirit from on high." This almost anticipates Paul in 1 Cor. 2:10-13, where Paul contrasts earthly wisdom with the wisdom of God revealed by the Holy Spirit. Yet Wisdom remains the major figure (Wis. 7:7-30). There is in Wisdom a spirit (mind-set?) that is "intelligent, holy, unique, manifold, subtle, mobile, clear, unpolluted, distinct, invulnerable, loving the good, keen, irresistible, beneficent, humane, steadfast, sure, free from anxiety, all-powerful, overseeing all" (Wis. 7:22-23). It is ambiguous whether this is a God-given human disposition or at times the divine Spirit, for the writer calls this "a pure emanation of the glory of the Almighty . . . , a spotless mirror of the working of God" (7:25-26). Not only does Wisdom share many of God's own distinctive qualities, but some of these are also ascribed to God's Word: "Your all-powerful Word leaped down from heaven, from the royal throne" (Wis. 18:15). Wisdom, Word, and Spirit may all denote God in action. For the most part, however, *rûach* denotes human dispositions. By the time of the New Testament there has become a parallel between the mediation of the divine Word and the mediation of the divine Spirit.

We suggested that *apocalyptic* writings formed a second bridge between the two Testaments, alongside Wisdom literature. One such writing concerns parts

---

2. Edwin Hatch and Henry A. Redpath, *A Concordance to the Septuagint* (Athens: Beneficial Books, 1977), vol. 2, p. 1152.

3. George Montague, *The Holy Spirit: The Growth of a Biblical Tradition* (Eugene, OR: Wipf & Stock, 1976), p. 102.

of *1 Enoch,* most of which can be dated during the second century B.C. Many uses of "spirit" are simply anthropological, referring to a human disposition (*1 Enoch* 13:6). The term may even denote spirits of the dead (*1 Enoch* 22:5-12). When the word denotes "evil spirit," this may mean a disposition or an entity (*1 Enoch* 15:10; 39:8; 60:4). Sometimes "the spirits" denotes angelic beings and action (*1 Enoch* 39:9-13; 60:6, 8, 25), but in *1 Enoch* 106:17 we find a contrast between "according to the flesh" and "according to the spirit" (or Spirit). A similar range of meanings can be found in the *Testaments of the Twelve Patriarchs,* often dated 109-106 B.C. in the time of Hyrcanus, and probably first written in Hebrew by a Pharisee. Most frequently "spirit" denotes a human disposition (*Testament of Simeon* 6:5; *Testament of Judah* 16:1; *Testament of Reuben* 3:5; *Testament of Levi* 2:3; 18:7). *Bath-qôl* (daughter of the voice) occurs in *2 Baruch* 8:1; 13:1; 22:1; *Jubilees* 17:15; and *1 Enoch* 65:4. Some compare it with the voice of God at the baptism and transfiguration of Jesus (Mark 1:11; 9:7; John 12:28).

The *Psalms of Solomon* are usually dated in the time of the Roman general Pompey, around 50-40 B.C. These psalms are molded by Old Testament passages, but attack foreign aggression. The task of an apocalyptic figure, who is King and "Son of David," is to purge Jerusalem from foreign oppressors, especially "from all Latin men." He is anointed by the Spirit of God to perform this task: to be "shepherd of the flock" and to purify Jerusalem. An explicit reference to his anointing by the Holy Spirit comes in *Psalms of Solomon* 17:37. The book is pro-Pharisaic. It also has affinities with 2 Esdr. 3-14, which is also known as 4 Ezra or the Ezra Apocalypse (Esdras is the Greek name for the Hebrew *Ezra*). The other chapters are probably post-Christian. It relates visions and includes a vision of a Messianic figure who emerges from the depths of the sea, flies on the clouds, and is identified as the Lion of Judah from the race of David. This figure comes "at a time appointed" (2 Esdr. 13). Baruch also has many detailed Messianic expectations, and it may date from the first century A.D. *2 Baruch* 21:4 speaks of making firm the height of heaven by the Spirit.

In Rabbinic Judaism we return to a more frequent emphasis on the Spirit of God. Sjöberg writes, "In the Rabbis there is also a sense of the link between the Holy Spirit and a life which is obedient to God. Here the gift of the Spirit is especially viewed as a reward for a righteous life."[4] Sjöberg cites Rabbi Nehemiah as commenting on Exod. 15:1: "He who undertakes a commandment in faith is worthy that the Holy Spirit should rest on him" (*Mekilta Exodus* 15:1, a Tannaitic midrash on Exodus). Rabbi Acha declares, "He who sacrifices himself for Israel will receive . . . the Holy Spirit" (*Numbers Rabbah* 15:20, a rabbinic midrash on Num. 11:16). By contrast, Paul in Galatians argues that the Holy

---

4. Erik Sjöberg, "*Rûach* in Palestinian Judaism," in *TDNT,* vol. 6, p. 383 (cf. pp. 375-89 for Sjöberg's article). Cf. W. D. Davies, *Paul and Rabbinic Judaism* (London: SPCK, 2nd ed. 1955), p. 219.

Spirit precisely is *not a "reward"* for righteousness but the *cause* of it (Gal. 3:1-5). Similarly Martin Luther saw the Radical Reformers like those at Münster undermining Paul's doctrine of grace by their call for radical holiness. Thus among the rabbis we find the saying, "When Jacob turned to self-indulgent grief, the Holy Spirit departed from him" (*Genesis Rabbah* 91:6, a rabbinic midrash on Gen. 42:1). Rabbi Gamaliel II is said to have "been seen by the Holy Spirit," that is, been inspired by the Spirit (*Lev. Rabbah* 37:3).

A second major theme in Rabbinic Judaism is that the canonical prophets were inspired by the Holy Spirit. Many speak of "the spirit of prophecy" (*Jubilees* 25:14; 31:12). Moreover, just as they saw the Spirit inspiring the Scriptures of the past, so equally, Davies comments, "We cannot doubt that the Rabbinic Judaism of the first century would have regarded the Messianic Age or Age to Come as the Era of the Spirit."[5] Sometimes the Spirit is spoken of in personal terms. To quote Sjöberg once again, "There are many instances of the Spirit speaking, crying, admonishing, sorrowing, weeping, rejoicing, comforting."[6] As we shall note in Paul, these personal terms are used alongside "dynamistic" terms such as "fill, shine, appear." We shall argue that the two together function like Ian Ramsey's "models and qualifiers" to signify together that the Spirit is *suprapersonal,* not subpersonal, let alone impersonal, like a mechanical force. For the most part, however, there is not a huge amount on the Spirit. The rabbis are also silent about the term "spiritual."[7]

Although the rabbis emphasized the inspiration of Scripture by God's Spirit, many saw this postcanonical period as one of absence of the Spirit, although we noted that this was based on a misunderstanding. Nevertheless, often the *bath-qôl* (or voice from heaven) and perhaps the *Shekinah* (radiance, shining, or presence, of God) did duty for the Spirit.[8] Yet there are many exceptions to this generalization. Some stress the absence of the spirit after Haggai, Zechariah, and Malachi (*Tosefta Soṭah* 13:2; Babylonian Talmud *Yoma* 21b; Babylonian Talmud *Sanhedrin* 65b of Rabbi Akiba). Sjöberg insists, however, "The Rabbis did not keep strictly to the idea that the Spirit is no longer to be had."[9] Other features of rabbinic theology include a multiplicity of references to the human spirit and a few references to the Spirit's cosmic function: "You sent forth your Spirit, and [he] formed them" (Jdt. 16:14; cf. 2 *Baruch* 21:4). Most surprising is what Sjöberg calls "the autonomy of the Spirit," or his independent choice of action. Sjöberg also claims, "The Spirit proceeds from God himself."[10]

It remains to consider the Dead Sea Scrolls as a further example of Palestin-

5. Davies, *Paul and Rabbinic Judaism,* p. 216.

6. Sjöberg, "*Rûach* in Palestinian Judaism," in *TDNT,* vol. 6, p. 387.

7. S. Schlechter, *Some Aspects of Rabbinic Theology* (London: Black, 1909), p. 144.

8. Roy A. Stewart, *Rabbinic Theology* (Edinburgh: Oliver & Boyd, 1961), pp. 39-43.

9. Sjöberg, "*Rûach* in Palestinian Judaism," in *TDNT,* vol. 6, p. 386.

10. Sjöberg, "*Rûach* in Palestinian Judaism," in *TDNT,* vol. 6, p. 388.

ian sectarian Judaism. Perhaps the three major writings of the Dead Sea Scrolls may be the *Manual of Discipline* (also called the *Rule of the Community;* 1QS), the *Thanksgiving Hymns* (1QH), and the *War Scroll* (1QM), although numerous other texts exist, often as commentaries or Old Testament books. The modern discovery of the Scrolls began in 1947-48 from a cave near Qumran. Eventually more than nine hundred Scrolls were recovered from eleven caves, mostly in Hebrew. The earliest go back to the third century B.C., but many date from the middle of the first century A.D. They were largely written on site, and represent a sect of first-century Judaism distinct from the Pharisees, Sadducees, or Zealots. The Community lived near Qumran from around 140 B.C. to A.D. 70.

The *Manual of Discipline* or *Rule of the Community* reflects a community of the "last days" who lived under a strict discipline "until there shall come a prophet and the Messiahs of Aaron and Israel" (1QS 9:11), that is, a priestly and kingly Messiah. If "and" is explanatory, the Messiah is also a prophetic figure. This would correspond to Calvin's famous three offices of Christ as *prophet, priest, and king.* God's Spirit is a "holy" Spirit. God will sprinkle upon the Messianic figure a "Spirit of truth" (1QS 4:20-21), a phrase which later appears on the lips of Jesus in John's Gospel.

The *Thanksgiving Hymns* likewise speak of the holiness of the Spirit (1QH 7:6; 9:32; 12:1; 13:19; 14:15; 16:11-12; 17:17). In the *Damascus Document* God will give to the Messiah power to make the Spirit of holiness known to the community or the remnant (CD 2:12). The Spirit will cleanse the community (1QS 3:6-8; 1QH 16:12). It is well known that two spirits in humankind are found in 1QS 3:13–4:26. These are "the spirit of truth" and "the spirit of error" (cf. esp. 4:16).[11] Qumran, or the Scrolls, reflects the kind of dualism found in John between light and darkness, and truth and error, formerly thought to reflect only the Greek influence of Plato and later thought, or, in Bultmann's case, Gnosticism. Like many parts of the New Testament the Scrolls suggest that the Spirit has been given, and can still be further sought. The Spirit of holiness (or Holy Spirit) is already active in the whole community, and his work is continuing and progressive, not once for all.[12]

2.4. Further Themes relating to the Holy Spirit in Philo, Josephus, and the Mishnah

We have already noted the *"immanentalist"* view of the Spirit found in Philo, in contrast to the Old Testament and Paul. The mediating figure between the spir-

---

11. See A. R. C. Leaney, *The Rule of Qumran and Its Meaning* (London: SCM, 1966), pp. 34-56.

12. See George J. Brooke, *The Dead Sea Scrolls and the New Testament* (London: SPCK, 2005); and Géza Vermès, *The Complete Dead Sea Scrolls in English* (London: Allen Lane, 1997).

itual, transcendent God and humankind is the *rational mind,* although Philo also believed that a "holy spirit" dwelt within humankind in an immanental or all-pervasive way (Philo, *Allegorical Interpretation* 1:31-42). However, he repeats many Old Testament passages. He asserts the example of inspiration that we have noted: the Spirit inspired Bezalel (Exod. 31:3); but he also sees the Spirit as "diffused in its fullness everywhere" (*On Giants* 27). Like the Stoics, he saw *pneuma* as *all-pervasive.* This stands in contrast to Paul in 1 Cor. 2:12, who sees the Holy Spirit as distinct from the Stoic "world-soul" but as "proceeding from God" (Greek, *to pneuma to ek theou*).

Philo repeatedly sees the Spirit as Agent of *the inspiration of the Old Testament* (*On the Life of Moses* 2:191; 1:277; *On the Virtues* 217–19). He follows much of the Old Testament text. In Philo *pneuma* may sometimes denote "air" or "wind" (Philo, *On Giants* 22; *Allegorical Interpretation* 42). But he also associates the Spirit with the *Logos* as the rational principle, often within human beings (Greek, *logikon pneuma; That the Worse Attacks the Better* 80-84), and saw the rational soul as providing a close analogy with God (*On the Special Laws* 1:171). However, he was reluctant to adopt Stoic concept uncritically, and even introduces "an overt polemic against the Stoics," rejecting the notion that *spirit* in humankind is "a particle of ethereal substance" (*On Planting* 18).[13] All the same, Philo expends great effort to adhere to the philosophy of Plato in his biblical interpretation, including the myth of the ascent of the soul in Plato's *Phaedrus* as a vision of the intelligible world.[14] Levison speaks of the pivotal role of Platonism in Philo's argument.

Philo speaks of the prophet as being completely overborne by the Spirit. According to Philo, "The Divine Spirit puts such words as he pleases in our mouths and such discourses as we are not conscious of," with reference especially to Balaam (cf. also Josephus, *Antiquities* 8:4:3). R. Birch Hoyle declares, "The Greek words for the prophetic state are matched in Hellenism."[15] On the other hand, in Part III we shall note Christopher Forbes's rejection of such parallels in the New Testament.

In *On Giants* 19–55 Philo interprets the story of the giants in Genesis 6, in which references to the spirit (or Spirit) are rooted in the biblical account. But *spirit* tends to be the "souls" of demons and angels (*On Giants* 6). Yet the spirit as "soul" blurs into a concept of the Spirit of God when Philo considers the gift of the Spirit to Bezalel in Exod. 31:3. Levison shows how complex his relation to Stoicism and to Plato becomes. Philo considers the ascent of the mind also in *On Planting* 18–26. In contrast to Greek-speaking Judaism, the Judaism of the Holy Land or "Palestinian Judaism" tended to preserve a sharper distinction

---

13. Levison, *The Spirit in First-Century Judaism,* p. 148.
14. Levison, *The Spirit in First-Century Judaism,* p. 155.
15. R. Birch Hoyle, *The Holy Spirit in St. Paul* (London: Hodder & Stoughton, 1967), p. 206.

between the human spirit and the Spirit of God. Spirit and angels tended to represent respectively "internal" and "external" agents of God.

We may call attention to the fact that, in spite of his normal name, the writer called "Pseudo-Philo" is much less "Greek" than Philo. He is the anonymous author of *Liber Antiquitatum Biblicarum,* now known as Pseudo-Philo. He writes of Gideon, "He put on the Spirit of the Lord" in his military exploits with his three hundred men (*Liber Antiquitatum Biblicarum* 36:2). This relates to Judg. 6:34 and 7:14. Levison comments, "Philo and Pseudo-Philo share the conviction that the spirit of God can produce enormous effects upon Israelite leaders."[16]

Flavius Josephus also ascribes *the inspiration of prophecy* to the Spirit of God. He is aware of the phenomenon of false prophecy, and asserts, "You shall know whether he (the self-proclaimed prophet) is a true prophet and has the form of the Divine Spirit" (*Antiquities* 8:408). Even the meaning of prophecies or their interpretation may be inspired (*Jewish War* 3:351-53). "Prophecy" and its inspiration probably mean the exposition of revealed truth, as later in Thomas Aquinas and others. On 1 Sam. 16:13 Josephus notes that David prophesied by the Spirit (*Antiquities* 6:166). Normally, however, as Levison argues, Josephus is keen "to omit references to the Spirit."[17]

Concerning the word "spirit" or "Spirit," Josephus can use *pneuma* to denote "wind" (*Jewish War* 4), "the breath of life" (*Antiquities* 1:1), the seat of *feeling* or *passion* (*Antiquities* 6:9), "demon" (*Jewish War* 6:3), or the "Spirit of prophecy" (*Jewish War* 1:2:8).

We have referred only occasionally to the Mishnah and the Talmud. The Mishnah was not completed until the end of the second century A.D., and the written Talmud belongs even later; but both contain traces of an earlier oral tradition and translation. Both postdate the New Testament as far as the written text is concerned. But the Mishnah presents two points which are of special interest. First, the Holy Spirit leads to the *resurrection* of the dead, as Paul also argues in Rom. 8:11. Second, the Mishnah reemphasizes that the gift of the Spirit does not *bring about* purification or righteousness; the Spirit is given *in response to* righteousness. Paul *dissents from* such a view, especially in Gal. 3:1-5. This brings us to examine Paul's theology of the Holy Spirit in Chapter 3.

Erik Sjöberg comments on the Spirit in Rabbinic Judaism by arguing that there is the sense of "the link between the Holy Spirit and a life which is obedient to God." Nevertheless, "Here the gift of the Spirit is viewed as a *reward* for a righteous life."[18] The Spirit, he argues, is the *result* of a righteous life; not, as in Paul, the *basis* of a righteous life. If we may digress to consider the postbiblical

---

16. Levison, *The Spirit in First-Century Judaism,* p. 97.

17. Levison, *The Spirit in First-Century Judaism,* p. 133.

18. Sjöberg, "*Rûach* in Palestinian Judaism," under "*Pneuma,*" *TDNT,* vol. 6, p. 383 (my italics).

world, Martin Luther objected to the pietism of the Radical Reformers on the ground that their extreme concern for obedience had unwittingly undermined precisely his call for righteousness by grace through faith alone. Even if we take into account what is known as "covenantal nomism" and the "New Look" on Paul, which emphasizes grace in Jewish piety, there is pause for thought in Sjöberg's warning. Nevertheless Judaism in the first century was immensely varied, and it might be misleading to select one theme about the Holy Spirit.

2.5. The Spirit in Hellenism, Especially in Stoicism, and Its Influence on Wisdom and through Judaism on Luke

There can be no doubt about the influence of the Stoics' use of *pneuma* on the book of Wisdom. *Pneuma* may sometimes be regarded as warm air, or as the soul of the world, from which Paul explicitly distances himself in 1 Cor. 2:10. Wisdom speaks of "the 'out-raying' [NEB 'effluence'] of the pure splendor of the Almighty Himself" (Wis. 7:25).[19] Cicero sees all elements of the universe "contained in harmony by one divine and connected spirit" (*On the Nature of the Gods* 2:7:19). In the end we reach the conclusion argued by Eduard Schweizer that in Hellenism and Stoicism *spirit* is often thought of as *substance*, a subtle energy or force, often diffused throughout the universe. Since this was stock-in-trade in Paul's day, Hoyle asserts: "It is significant in Paul's use that he never applies 'spirit' to natural phenomena."[20] Yet *pneuma* in Stoicism also denoted "reason." Seneca declared, "Reason is common to both gods and men; . . . if its power and spirit be present in the body of a person, such a one is equal to the gods. . . . we are . . . members of him" (Seneca, *Epistles* 22:27-30). Further, Seneca declares, "God is in you, . . . a holy spirit is resident in us, . . . a guardian of both what is good and what is evil in us" (*Epistles* 41:1). Even if he may sometimes use Stoic terminology, Paul does not use Stoic content.

As we shall see in more detail in Part III, Max Turner, and to less extent Robert Menzies, appeal to Intertestamental Judaism to explain the prominence of prophecy and inspired speech in Luke-Acts.[21] Turner also notes that the Septuagint goes further than the Hebrew text in emphasizing God's creative activity.[22] But for the most part he cites numerous references in the Targums which attribute charismatic revelation to the Spirit. From the *Targum Pseudo-Jonathan* he

---

19. Hoyle, *The Holy Spirit in St. Paul*, p. 220.

20. Hoyle, *The Holy Spirit in St. Paul*, p. 221.

21. Max Turner, *Power from on High: The Spirit in Israel's Restoration and Witness in Luke-Acts* (Sheffield: Sheffield Academic, 1996), esp. pp. 62-66 and 86-104; and Robert Menzies, *Empowered for Witness: The Spirit in Luke-Acts* (Sheffield: Sheffield Academic, 1994), which is focused more narrowly on prophecy than is Turner.

22. Turner, *Power from on High*, p. 107.

cites the gloss on Gen. 27:5; 27:42; 30:25; 31:21; 35:22; 37:33; 42:1; and 43:14.[23] In Palestinian Judaism he cites 1 Enoch 91:1; 4 Ezra 14:22; Jubilees 31:12; 1QS 8:16; and CD 2:12. He notes that in the example of Bezalel (Exod. 35:30-31) Targum Pseudo-Jonathan adds: "the Spirit of prophecy from before the Lord."[24] He concludes: "The category 'charismatic wisdom' emerges as the second most frequent gift of the Spirit in the Targum tradition."[25] We may dispute the direct influence this has on Luke, but his case remains convincing in relation to Judaism. In the case of Paul, to cite a different example, Paul uses analogical language between a human and God in 1 Cor. 2:11-12, as the Stoics and Wisdom did (Wis. 13:5), but the twist he gives to the analogy by speaking of "the Spirit who [comes forth] from God" (to pneuma to ek tou theou, v. 12) makes it clear that Paul distances himself from Wisdom and the Stoics.[26] We return to Turner in Part III.

Meanwhile, we may note that Turner also derives an emphasis on both the miraculous and the ethical or transforming from the Targums. In Gen. 6:3 the Masoretic Hebrew text reads, "My spirit will not always abide with [or contend with] man," but Targum Pseudo-Jonathan adds: "Did not I put my Holy Spirit in them that they might perform good deeds? But behold their deeds are evil."[27] The Neofiti Targum refers to their evil deeds and weak flesh. Testament of Simeon 4:4 refers to Joseph not only as a prophet, but as "a good man, one who had within him the Spirit of God" (cf. also Testament of Benjamin 8:1-3). Qumran refers to the Holy Spirit, who "upholds" the believer (1QH 7:6-7; cf. 17:25-26), and we may also compare the two spirits of truth and error in the Manual of Discipline (1QS 3:18–4:26). The "Holy Spirit" (1QS 4:21) purifies, probably on the basis of Ezekiel 36. Messianic allusions from Isa. 11:1-4 can be traced in 1 Enoch 49:2-3; Psalms of Solomon 17:38; 18:7; and 1QSb 5:25. In this respect Turner believes that Eduard Schweizer and Hermann Gunkel have been misleading.[28] Even the Intertestamental Jewish writings occasionally have soteriological and ethical references to the Spirit of God. Some of the sources cited, however, may reflect a date in the Christian era.

---

23. Turner, Power from on High, p. 93.
24. Turner, Power from on High, p. 95.
25. Turner, Power from on High, p. 96.
26. Hoyle, The Holy Spirit in St. Paul, p. 239; cf. p. 260.
27. Turner, Power from on High, p. 123.
28. Turner, Power from on High, p. 133.

3

The Holy Spirit in the Synoptic Gospels

In the first three Gospels, or the Synoptic Gospels, Mark and Luke each have their distinctive concerns about the Holy Spirit, as well as agreement about basic themes. Much of the literature on the Spirit quantifies explicit references to the Spirit in different ways, so I have classified three different uses of *pneuma* to allow us to see genuine references to the Holy Spirit, on the basis of the Greek concordance edited by Moulton and Geden.[1]

Mark, generally acknowledged to be the earliest Gospel and written shortly after the major epistles of Paul, has six clear references to the Holy Spirit (four of these use *pneuma hagion*, "Holy Spirit"). Thirteen refer to "unclean" or "dumb" spirits (usually *pneuma akatharton*), and three seem to refer to the human spirit. Luke includes seventeen or eighteen references to the Holy Spirit (depending on MS readings; often *pneuma hagion*), about eleven references to "unclean" or "evil" spirits, and about four to the human spirit. Matthew has eleven references to the Spirit of God, or to the Holy Spirit; about three or four to unclean spirits, and about three to the human spirit. I have examined the Greek phrases which provide the context in each case.

3.1. The Baptism and Messianic Temptations of Jesus

All of the first three Gospels agree, however, that Jesus' baptism and temptations, as well as his ministry up to the cross, *occurred in the power of the Holy Spirit*. Mark 1:10 reads: "As he was coming out of the water, he saw . . . the Spirit descending like a dove on him"; Matt. 3:16 is a close parallel; and Luke has: "I

---

1. W. F. Moulton and A. S. Geden, *A Concordance of the Greek Testament* (Edinburgh: T&T Clark, 2nd ed. 1899), pp. 819-20.

baptize you with water. . . . He shall baptize you with the Holy Spirit and fire" (Luke 3:16), and "Jesus also had been baptized and was praying, . . . and the Holy Spirit descended upon him in bodily form [Greek, *sōmatikō*] like a dove. And a voice came from heaven, 'You are my Son; with you I am well pleased'" (Luke 3:21-22). C. K. Barrett represents the consensus view when he comments: "It is essentially the solemn appointment of the Messiah to his office, the installation of the Son of God."[2] Luke T. Johnson adds: "For Luke it is the same 'Holy Spirit' that has already been at work earlier in the story (1:15, 35, 41, 67; 2:25, 26). . . . Luke . . . emphasizes the physical reality of the event."[3]

The Messianic temptations are initially instigated by the Holy Spirit, as a testing or trial of the Messianic vocation of Jesus. Mark 1:12-13 vividly declares, "And the Spirit immediately drove him out [Greek, *euthys to pneuma auton ekballei*] into the wilderness. He remained in the wilderness for forty days, tempted [Greek, *peirazomenos*] by Satan." Matt. 4:1-2 has: "Then Jesus was led up by the Spirit into the wilderness to be tempted by the devil. He fasted forty days and forty nights." Luke 4:1-2 reads, "Jesus, full [Greek, *plērēs*] of the Holy Spirit, returned from Jordan, and was led by the Spirit in the wilderness, where for forty days he was tempted by the devil." As Turner observes, "'Full of the Holy Spirit' is a Lukanism, normally characterizing an endowment of some duration . . . to mark the person concerned as one in whose life the Spirit was regularly and powerfully felt."[4]

In Mark the activity of Jesus in the power of the Holy Spirit is implied rather than explicitly stated. For example, the question asking by what power Jesus casts out demons, and the scribal charge that this is done by the power of Beelzebul, lead to the statement: "Whoever blasphemes against the Holy Spirit can never have forgiveness" (discussed below; Mark 3:29). Matthew is only slightly more explicit than Mark: "If it is by the Spirit of God that I cast out demons, then the kingdom of God has come to you" (Matt. 12:29). Luke, however, is explicit and emphatic. He writes, "Then Jesus, filled with the power of the Spirit [Greek, *en tē dynamei tou pneumatos*], returned to Galilee" (Luke 4:14). When he read from Isaiah in the synagogue, Jesus applied the passage to himself: "The Spirit of the Lord is upon me, because he has anointed me to bring good news to the poor. He has sent me to proclaim release to the captives, the recovery of sight to the blind, . . . to proclaim the year of the Lord's favor" (Luke 4:18-19).

While all three Synoptic Gospels recount the baptism and temptations, Matthew and Luke also stress the role of the Holy Spirit in the conception and

2. C. K. Barrett, *The Holy Spirit and the Gospel Tradition* (London: SPCK, 1958), p. 115.

3. Luke T. Johnson, *The Gospel of Luke,* Sacra Pagina 3 (Collegeville, MN: Glazier/Liturgical Press, 1991), p. 69.

4. Max Turner, *Power from on High: The Spirit in Israel's Restoration and Witness in Luke-Acts,* JPTSS 9 (Sheffield: Sheffield Academic Press, 1996), p. 202.

birth of Jesus. Matthew asserts, "She [Mary] was found to be with child from [Greek, *ek*] the Holy Spirit" (Matt. 1:18). Ulrich Luz comments on Matt. 1:20, "The reference to the Holy Spirit, already familiar from v. 18, is repeated. This refers to the creative intervention of God through the Spirit, and not to the Spirit as a second partner for Mary."[5] Luke has more detail. The angel Gabriel is sent by God to address Mary with these words: "The Holy Spirit will come upon you, and the power of the Most High will overshadow you" (Luke 1:35). Luke also recounts that Elizabeth was "filled [Greek, *eplēsthē*] with the Holy Spirit" (Luke 1:41) to give birth to John the Baptist. Luke's next reference to the Holy Spirit comes in the narrative about Simeon. Simeon looks forward to the fulfillment of God's promises to Israel, "and the Holy Spirit rested on him. It had been revealed to him by the Holy Spirit that he would not see death before he had seen the Lord's Messiah. Guided by the Spirit, Simeon came into the temple," and saw Jesus (Luke 2:25-27). The encounter with Simeon invites three references to the Spirit by Luke.

The most important events in the Messianic theology of Jesus are not only the conception and birth of Jesus but even more clearly the baptism of Jesus, which all four Gospels agree in recounting (cf. John 1:32-34). Many nineteenth-century scholars called this event "the anointing of Christ," or sometimes "the unction of the Spirit."[6] Smeaton is entirely correct to say that Jesus was empowered by the Spirit, although he is on dated and speculative ground when he claims that the Spirit mediated communication between Jesus' deity and "his manhood." (But see further below in this chapter, under heading 3.)[7] He is surely right, however, when he asserts, "The visible descent of the Holy Spirit, not only for the sake of the Jews and of the Baptist, but for a testimony to Christ himself (Matt. 3:16), took place while Jesus [in Luke] was praying to the Father, probably with a view to obtain the Spirit . . . (Lk. 3:21)."[8]

As we have already gathered from Johnson, it is characteristic of Luke to add "in bodily form" to indicate a more-than-subjective account of the baptism. Luke typically recounts events in the real, external world, just as in Acts he underlines the visible, institutional character of the Church. The "dove" may also signify the new creation that belongs to the new age and new world, as the dove did after the flood (Gen. 8:8-12; cf. Gen. 1:2). Turner describes Luke's appeal to the agency of the Holy Spirit as a "metaphorical way of referring to the inception of a specific new activity."[9] Matthew, Mark, and Luke have the phrase "descending like a dove." Matthew alone addresses the problem of why Jesus

---

5. Ulrich Luz, *Matthew 1–7: A Commentary* (Edinburgh: T&T Clark, 1990), p. 120.

6. George Smeaton, *The Doctrine of the Holy Spirit* (London: Banner of Truth, rpt. 1958, from 1882 ed.), pp. 116-36, and esp. pp. 118 and 120.

7. Smeaton, *The Holy Spirit*, p. 126.

8. Smeaton, *The Holy Spirit*, p. 129.

9. Turner, *Power from on High*, p. 47.

needed to receive baptism (Matt. 3:14-15). The phrase "to fulfill all righteous-ness" may seem obscure, but, in C. K. Barrett's language, the reference shows Je-sus "as moving in the same circle of prophetic and eschatological concepts as the Baptist."[10] "Through his [John's] baptism, the penitent became one of the *prepared* people of God," and Jesus stood in solidarity with God's prepared peo-ple (my italics).[11]

All three Gospels narrate the voice from heaven (Greek, *phōnē ek tōn ouranōn*), which is "exactly similar to that which is frequently described in the Rabbinical literature in the words *bath-qôl*, 'daughter of the voice,'" as we saw in Chapter 2 on Judaism.[12] This can be a substitute for the Word of God or the Spirit of God. Matthew focuses on the *word*, while Luke often focuses on the *Spirit*. On the other hand, this voice may reflect the rabbinic notion of the sound of a bird, in which case it may be linked in all three Gospels with the dove. The content of the communication by the voice or sound from heaven was "You are my Son, the Beloved [Greek, *ho huios mou ho agapētos*]; with you I am well pleased" (Mark 1:11); or "This is my Son, the Beloved, with whom I am well pleased" (Matt. 3:17; Luke 3:22; although in the NRSV and in many MSS Luke follows Mark). The Greek wording is identical, apart from the pronouns. Here both the Holy Spirit and the Word testify to the Messianic status and empower-ment of Jesus, and firmly establish his Messianic vocation. As the Son of God, he also represents Israel.

The Holy Spirit then "drives" (Greek, *ekballei*; Mark 1:12) or "leads" (Matt. 4:1) Jesus into the wilderness, while Luke uses the expression "full of the Holy Spirit" (Greek, *plērēs pneumatos hagiou*, Luke 4:1). There Jesus finds his Messi-anic status and vocation tested, in the form of temptations or testing (Greek, *peirazomenos*), by the devil (in Matthew and Luke) or by Satan (in Mark). Since so much is often made of the phrase "Spirit-filled," we may note, along with Turner's earlier comment, that the regular meaning of Luke's word *plērēs* is "containing within itself all that it will hold," or "being complete and nothing lacking."[13] Likewise *plēroō* means "to fill up," "to complete," or "to fulfill," as the verb *pimplēmi* also does. The Holy Spirit provokes questioning *not* to do *evil*, but to aim at God's goal in easier, self-chosen *ways*: to take shortcuts to the *kind* of Messiahship which falls radically short of the will of God. Jesus could win a following by spectacular acts, or even by means which Satan, rather than God, would choose. Again there is a dual combination of Word and Spirit, as Jesus, "full of the Holy Spirit," also quotes Scripture in response to each temptation (Matt. 4:4 and Luke 4:4; Matt. 4:7 and Luke 4:8; Matt. 4:10 and Luke 4:12).

10. Barrett, *The Holy Spirit and the Gospel Tradition*, p. 35.

11. Barrett, *The Holy Spirit and the Gospel Tradition*, p. 33; cf. Turner, *Power from on High*, pp. 188-201.

12. Barrett, *The Holy Spirit and the Gospel Tradition*, p. 39.

13. Danker, in BDAG, pp. 826-27.

We must not assume that the temptations of Jesus ended at that point. Luke recounts, "The devil . . . departed from him *until an opportune time*" (Luke 4:13; Greek, *achri kairou*). The Epistle to the Hebrews asserts, "We have one who in every respect [Greek, *kata panta*] has been tested as we are, yet without sin" (Heb. 4:15). As long ago as 1889, B. F. Westcott pointed out, "Only One who is sinless has experienced the greatest intensity of temptation, for only such a person has not yielded before the last and greatest strain."[14] Hebrews adds that throughout his incarnate life Jesus offered "prayers and supplications with loud cries and tears" (Heb. 5:7).

3.2. The Messianic Ministry of Jesus

It is utterly clear that both Word and Spirit played a decisive role in Jesus' work as Messiah. It is when we come to his healings, exorcisms, teaching, and miracles that theologians and commentators make different assumptions, or at least place their emphasis on different phenomena. We have noted that in Mark, after decisive references to the Holy Spirit in the baptism and temptations, *spirit* becomes confined to allusions to "unclean spirits" from Mark 3:11 virtually to the end, except for a probable reference to the spirit in a person in Mark 14:38: "The spirit is willing, but the flesh is weak." It is possible but doubtful whether this refers to the Holy Spirit.

Matthew is similar. Matt. 5:3 refers to the "poor in spirit." Matt. 8:16, 10:1, and 12:43 refer to unclean spirits. But Matt. 10:20 has "not you who speak, but the Spirit of your Father speaking through you," and Matt. 12:28 has the famous "If it is by the Spirit of God that I cast out demons," in contrast to Luke's unexpected and probably older parallel, "by the finger of God" (11:20). Matt. 12:18 also has a reference to the Servant Songs of Isaiah: "I will put my Spirit upon him, and he will proclaim justice to the Gentiles," immediately after "This is my servant [Greek, *ho pais mou*] . . . with whom my soul is well pleased." In Matt. 22:43, "David by the Spirit" (NRSV; "in spirit," KJV, AV) repeats the traditional Jewish view of the inspiration of the word of God. Matt. 26:41 ("the spirit is willing") is parallel to Mark 14:38 and is ambiguous.

Luke, once again, has a more explicit interest in the Holy Spirit than Matthew and Mark. Luke 2:40 has "favor of God" in the NRSV, although the Greek *charis* also means "grace," or "goodwill." The best MSS do not have "Spirit," as in the KJV/AV. However, Luke 1:80, "The child grew, and became strong in spirit," could perhaps be a reference to the Holy Spirit. More significant are Luke 4:14, "Then Jesus, filled with the power of the Spirit, returned to Galilee,"

---

14. B. F. Westcott, *The Epistle to the Hebrews: The Greek Text* (New York and London: Macmillan, rpt. 1903), on 4:15.

and the quotation from Isaiah in the synagogue, "The Spirit of the Lord is upon me, because he has anointed me to bring good news to the poor . . . release to the captives . . . sight to the blind . . . the year of the Lord's favor" (Luke 4:18-19; partly from Isa. 42:1, but mainly from Isa. 61:1). G. W. H. Lampe describes this as one of the "two great discourses" (the other being Peter's discourse at Pentecost) of Luke-Acts, especially on the Spirit.[15] Since this is a synagogue service, Lampe is also right to say that in Luke the Holy Spirit is associated with both *prayer* and the *word of God* in the church or congregation. He comments, "The reading of the prophecy and the announcement of its fulfilment in the mission of Jesus serve as a prologue to the whole of the rest of St. Luke's work."[16] Otherwise Luke, like Mark and Matthew, does not explicitly say very much about the Holy Spirit, in spite of Turner's arguments, except in Luke 11:13, where the gift of the Holy Spirit belongs to the context of prayer (Luke 11:1-13).

These two facts, the role assigned by Lampe to Luke 4:18-19, and the relative silence for the rest of the Gospel, lead to what look like diametrically opposite views held by two distinguished New Testament specialists. James D. G. Dunn discusses Luke's use of Isa. 61:1 in 4:18-19, and also calls Jesus "a charismatic figure."[17] Under this heading Dunn discusses his miracles (often Greek, *dynameis*), his "supernatural power," his authority (Greek, *exousia*), his prophetic office, and whether he was "an ecstatic." He admits that relevant evidence of this last remains "minimal."[18] Nevertheless he concludes that the consciousness of the Holy Spirit inspiring and empowering him "was basic to his mission."[19] On the other hand, C. K. Barrett includes in his book *The Holy Spirit and the Gospel Tradition* a chapter entitled "Why Do the Gospels Say So Little about the Spirit?" and concludes: "Jesus acted under the necessity of a divine constraint. Lack of glory and a cup of suffering were his Messianic vocation, and *part of his poverty was the absence of all the signs of the Spirit of God.* They would have been inconsistent with the office of a humiliated Messiah."[20] Barrett and J. E. Fison argue that Jesus deliberately withheld explanatory allusions both to his Messiahship and to the Holy Spirit until he had lived out their meaning in his everyday incarnate life.

How can such distinguished writers appear to hold these very different

---

15. G. W. H. Lampe, "The Holy Spirit in the Writings of St. Luke," in *Studies in the Gospels: Essays in Memory of R. H. Lightfoot*, ed. D. E. Nineham (Oxford: Blackwell, 1967), p. 159; cf. pp. 159-200.

16. Lampe, "The Holy Spirit in Luke," in *Studies in the Gospels*, p. 171.

17. James D. G. Dunn, *Jesus and the Spirit: A Study of the Religious and Charismatic Experience of Jesus and the First Christians as Reflected in the New Testament* (London: SCM, 1975), p. 68; cf. pp. 54 and 68-92.

18. Dunn, *Jesus and the Spirit*, p. 85.

19. Dunn, *Jesus and the Spirit*, p. 88.

20. Barrett, *The Holy Spirit and the Gospel Tradition*, p. 158 (my italics); cf. pp. 140-62; J. E. Fison, *The Blessing of the Holy Spirit* (London: Longmans, Green, 1950), pp. 81-109.

conclusions? Dunn is supported by the quotation of Luke 4:18-19 on the Holy Spirit. When Jesus performs a mighty work, some invite an old-fashioned and mistaken Christology in order to assume that this is the "divine nature" of Jesus at work. But as Dunn rightly asserts, Jesus relied on trust in God and in the Holy Spirit. J. A. T. Robinson has in any case done much to restore a biblical emphasis on the true humanness of the earthly Jesus.[21] Nevertheless Barrett receives support from the temptation narratives and elsewhere. These are instigated by the Holy Spirit, but in each case the more spectacular "self-glorifying" way is renounced, in favor of the hard path of the will of God and *kenōsis,* or self-emptying. There is undoubtedly truth in Barrett's and Fison's claim that references to the Spirit had to be relatively few before the resurrection and glorification of Jesus Christ. But there is also truth in the claims of Dunn and Turner that Jesus is seen, through his exorcisms and deeds of power, as the Bearer of the Spirit and as what they call a "charismatic" figure. Each picture needs to be carefully qualified by the other. To ask in what sense both are right would provide an excellent seminar or exam question. Dunn's conclusions should be accepted only in the light of Barrett's careful Christological warning.

This is all the more striking when we recall Luke's special interest in the Holy Spirit. One moral is to note that it is more important for the Spirit to *work* in the everyday life of Jesus than constantly to *talk* about it as a doctrine or theory. Barrett has yet more to say on this subject. He not only sees a parallel with silence or secrecy about the Messiahship of Jesus before the resurrection, and silence about the Spirit. He also notes that the great canonical or "writing" prophets appeal to the Spirit relatively seldom, and are even reticent about the word "prophet." This is in contrast to the earliest $n^e bh\hat{i}$'$\hat{i}m$ in the Old Testament (cf. Mic. 3:8; Jeremiah, Ezekiel).[22] On the other hand, Turner draws on the recognized importance of the Spirit's inspiration of *prophecy* in Judaism and the Intertestamental writings. In this he is supported by Roger Stronstad and Robert Menzies.[23]

Barrett also argues that most of Jesus' exorcisms "occur in Mark," and that we must distinguish what is distinctive from material in rabbinic and pagan sources. Barrett argues for discontinuity with Judaism, where Turner argues for influence and continuity. Those who suffer as "demoniacs" are usually "in a very grievous state."[24] Jesus would have appeared to the sufferer as "a 'pneumatic' figure . . . with authority."[25] Nevertheless, "The unique element in the

---

21. John A. T. Robinson, *The Human Face of God* (London: SCM, 1973).

22. Barrett, *The Holy Spirit and the Gospel Tradition,* pp. 143-52.

23. Turner, *Power from on High,* pp. 82-138; Roger Stronstad, *The Charismatic Theology of Saint Luke* (Peabody: Hendrickson, 1984); and Robert P. Menzies, *Empowered for Witness: The Spirit in Luke-Acts* (Sheffield: JSOT, 1994). Differences between them are discussed in Part III.

24. Barrett, *The Holy Spirit and the Gospel Tradition,* p. 55.

25. Barrett, *The Holy Spirit and the Gospel Tradition,* p. 57.

exorcisms of Jesus is that they are special signs of God's power and his King-dom."[26] The word *dynamis,* similarly, may not only denote miracle, but also represent God, as eschatological power, or the power of the Holy Spirit.[27] All in all, however, on one side we may assert, with J. E. Fison, Barrett, and the Fourth Gospel, "the self-effacement" of the Holy Spirit; on the other, we may see these exorcisms as the inbreaking of the Kingdom of God, and of the com-ing of the New Age.[28] The Gospel writers cannot help understanding the work of Jesus in the anticipated light of the resurrection, as can be seen especially from John. The ambiguity is no more puzzling than the tension created by "the Kingdom of God is here in Jesus," and "the Kingdom of God is near but future," since Jesus will complete his work only after the cross and the resur-rection. We argue in Chapter 6 (on gifts of healing in Paul's letters) that one of the main arguments for physical healing is the eschatological breaking in of the Kingdom of God; while one of the best explanations for apparent *lack* of healing, when God so chooses, is the "not yet" aspect of the coming of the Kingdom of God as still future. Both the present and future aspects of a dual or overlapping eschatology deserve emphasis. We have addressed these ques-tions in the context of hermeneutics.

3.3. Further References to Jesus' Messianic Experience of God: Prayer, Intimacy, and Son to Father

There is, however, a further related aspect that invites almost the same degree of debate. Dunn seeks to substantiate his case about Jesus' possession of the Holy Spirit by citing not only his deeds of power but also his life of prayer, his broader experience of God, and his relation as Son to his Father. This comes under the heading "Jesus' more private experience of God."[29] Dunn is certainly right to say that this becomes important "for *our* faith in God" (his italics).[30] He also cites the concerns with this on the part of Adolf von Harnack and Adolf Deissmann. All four strata of the Synoptic tradition emphasize this. In Matt. 11:17 and parallels the temple is a house of prayer (quoting Isa. 56:7). Dunn cites the "Q" tradition of the exhortation to ask, to seek, and to knock (Matt. 7:7; Luke 11:9-13). Gethsemane (Mark 14:32-42) provides a profound example of Je-sus' dependence on prayer.[31]

Dunn rightly includes a long section on the use of "Abba" in the personal

26. Barrett, *The Holy Spirit and the Gospel Tradition,* p. 62.
27. Barrett, *The Holy Spirit and the Gospel Tradition,* pp. 71-77.
28. Fison, *The Blessing of the Holy Spirit,* pp. 11, 22, 27, 72, 93, 107-8, 138-40, and 199-200.
29. Dunn, *Jesus and the Spirit,* p. 11.
30. Dunn, *Jesus and the Spirit,* p. 13.
31. Dunn, *Jesus and the Spirit,* p. 17.

prayers of Jesus.[32] "Abba" (dear Father) is preserved in Mark 14:36, and is distinctive to the prayers of Jesus. It is then found on the lips of Christians in Rom. 8:15 and Gal. 4:6, when the Holy Spirit explicitly makes actual for believers what it is to have the same attitude toward, and relationship with, God as Father. They directly derive this from Christ. Dunn comments, "Jesus' calling on God as 'Father' was *the language of experience rather than a formal address*" (his italics).[33] Many scholars associate this emphasis on the uniqueness of "Abba" with Joachim Jeremias, but later experience disappointment when they learn that his approach is open to question.[34] Dunn affirms his general approach, but admits that its uniqueness may have been exaggerated. He brackets together Jesus' "sense of *sonship* and his consciousness of *spirit*" (his italics).[35] "Jesus believes himself to be empowered by the Spirit and thought of himself as God's son."[36] The allusion to Ps. 2:7 (cf. Luke 3:22, Western Text) suggests that "consciousness of sonship and consciousness of the spirit" are two sides of the one coin.[37] Dunn asserts, *"The gift of the Spirit was understood to be Jesus' adoption as Son"* (his italics).[38]

This theme certainly affirms Dunn's argument in his *Baptism in the Holy Spirit*. To be made a son of God presupposes reception of the Holy Spirit; to receive the Holy Spirit means to be made a son of God (Rom. 8:9).[39] But to what extent, if at all, does this read back Christian experience onto the Person of Jesus? We earlier dismissed George Smeaton's nineteenth-century argument that the close intimacy between Jesus and God the Father was due to this being through his "divine nature," and therefore did not need explicitly to appeal to the experience of the Holy Spirit.[40] But even if we are uncomfortable today with talk about what each "nature" of Christ achieved, is there a valid point behind Smeaton's language? Certainly if we are allowed for a moment to compare the Fourth Gospel, the intimacy with the Father does not seem to depend on any explicit appeal to the Holy Spirit. To repeat: this is true without qualification of all Christians, but is Christ Jesus exactly in this position?

The point can be debated, or even perhaps answered, for according to Hebrews Jesus was "in every respect" tempted or tested as we are (Heb. 4:15). J. A. T. Robinson, as we have noted, rightly insists that the earthly Jesus was fully

---

32. Dunn, *Jesus and the Spirit*, pp. 21-40.

33. Dunn, *Jesus and the Spirit*, p. 22.

34. Joachim Jeremias, *New Testament Theology*, vol. 1: *The Proclamation of Jesus* (London: SCM, 1971), pp. 61-68.

35. Dunn, *Jesus and the Spirit*, p. 62.

36. Dunn, *Jesus and the Spirit*, p. 63.

37. Dunn, *Jesus and the Spirit*, p. 66.

38. Dunn, *Jesus and the Spirit*, p. 65.

39. James D. G. Dunn, *Baptism in the Holy Spirit* (London: SCM, 1970), p. 95 and throughout.

40. See p. 35 of this chapter.

human, and any human being depends on the Holy Spirit for intimacy with God. But Jesus does not spell this out with emphasis. Even Dunn concedes "a reticence on Jesus' part to speak often or openly about his experience of God."[41] If we were allowed to look retrospectively at the Synoptic Gospels through the eyes of Christian tradition in the Church Fathers, we might say that the Holy Spirit is involved wherever the Father and the Son are active. The Spirit partici- pates in the fellowship between the Father and the Son, or between Jesus and God. We do not flatly disagree with Dunn, but wish to show more caution on this issue. The debate between Dunn and Turner, on one side, and Barrett and Fison, on the other, needs qualification of what is asserted by what is ques- tioned. It would assist the present discussion. We should expect that issues about the Spirit would interact with issues about Christology.

Do Max Turner, Robert Menzies, and Roger Stronstad press this argument further than Dunn? In one sense their arguments are perhaps less controversial on this particular point, for their concern is mainly with the empowerment of Jesus by the Holy Spirit, and this is not disputed. If we may refer to the Christol- ogy of Hebrews once again, the writer to the Hebrews makes it plain that even Jesus had to learn not only obedience but also *trust* (Heb. 2:13). But how is "trust" possible if what Smeaton calls his "divine nature" remains an innate ca- pacity within the earthly or incarnate Jesus? Jesus did indeed depend on the Holy Spirit for his acts of power and his resistance to Messianic testing. We might interpret some texts a little differently in Turner's chapter 7, "The Prom- ise of the Baptist," although we reserve a fuller discussion of Turner for Part III.[42] But the two chapters "The Empowering of the Messianic Son" and "Jesus Anointed with the Spirit" seem to accord broadly with our view.[43] In Part III we also discuss some reservations, which we share with Turner, about the work of Menzies and Stronstad.

3.4. Other References to the Holy Spirit in the Synoptic Gospels

(1) The *saying of Jesus about blasphemy against the Holy Spirit* (Mark 3:28-30; with parallels in Matt. 12:31-32 and Luke 12:10) causes perplexity and anxiety to very many today. In Mark the operative Greek word is *blasphēmēsē*, where Mat- thew and Luke use the same word but with grammatical variants. Luke has *blasphēmēsanti*, and Matthew re-constructs the sentence to place the noun in 12:31 *(blasphēmia)*, but simply refers to whoever "speaks against the Holy Spirit"

---

41. Dunn, *Jesus and the Spirit*, p. 67.

42. Turner, *Power from on High*, pp. 170-87.

43. Turner, *Power from on High*, pp. 188-266; cf. Max Turner, *The Holy Spirit and Spiritual Gifts Then and Now* (Carlisle: Paternoster, 1996), pp. 19-35.

(eipē logon kata tou pneumatos tou hagiou) in 12:32. According to Danker, *blasphēmeō* means "to speak in a disrespectful way that demeans, denigrates, maligns," or "to revile, slander, or defame"; the noun *blasphēmia* has a similar meaning.[44] Grimm-Thayer agrees, suggesting "to speak reproachfully, to revile, to slander."[45] But what does this mean in its Synoptic context?

Some interpreters believe that the original context in Mark 3:28-30 was different because the context in Luke 12:10 is different. But Matthew repeats Mark's content, connecting the saying with the false accusation that Jesus casts out demons by the prince of demons. Mark begins the saying with *'amēn,* used in the Old Testament to express the validity of such an utterance as a warning or curse, equivalent to "truly." In the New Testament it introduces a solemn and weighty affirmation. Since Jesus carried out his exorcisms in the power of the Holy Spirit, "to blaspheme against the Holy Spirit" clearly denotes calling what is good "bad." Those who do this have twisted what is good and what is evil to their own advantage.[46] It is difficult to see how a person who has *utterly distorted and confused good and evil* still has *the capacity to repent.* Hence this may indicate the "internal" consequences of such an attitude. It is as if to say, "If you stubbornly insist on justifying *evil* by regarding it as *good,* or if you demean or slander the *good* by calling it *evil,* how can you ever *repent, and thereby be forgiven?*" The Church of England Doctrine Commission, of which I was then a member, expresses it thus: "The saying stands as a warning against a wilful and deliberate manipulation of good and evil, by which evil is called 'good' and good is called 'evil' . . . there is no way out of the vicious circle that has been erected."[47]

It is well known in pastoral ministry that anyone who is *worried* by this saying is *thereby* showing signs of grace, and the beginnings of the work of the Spirit in their lives. If their stubborn obstinacy were absolute, they simply would not worry about it. Jesus is clearly referring to discounting good by calling it evil, which in this case is to ascribe evil to the work of the Holy Spirit. For most Christians, the saying comes as a warning against overly hasty judgments, or against jumping to mistaken conclusions. Regarding the Lukan context, Joel Green writes, "For Luke blasphemy of the Holy Spirit refers to apos-

---

44. Danker, BDAG, p. 178.

45. Joseph H. Thayer, *A Greek-English Lexicon of the New Testament* (Edinburgh: T&T Clark, 1901), p. 102.

46. Cf. Charles E. Cranfield, *The Gospel according to St. Mark* (Cambridge: Cambridge University Press, 1963), pp. 139-43; and William Lane, *The Gospel of Mark,* NICNT (London: Marshall, Morgan and Scott, 1974), pp. 144-46; R. T. France, *The Gospel of Mark: A Commentary on the Greek Text,* NIGTC (Grand Rapids: Eerdmans, 2002), pp. 178-79. On the history of reception, see Ulrich Luz, *Matthew 8–20: A Commentary* (Minneapolis: Fortress, 2001), pp. 206-10.

47. The Church of England Doctrine Commission, *We Believe in the Holy Spirit* (London: Church House Publishing, 1991), p. 184.

tasy in the face of persecution."[48] But the Markan meaning captures the original sense. Lindsay Dewar, perhaps over-simplistically, calls this "the falsification of conscience."[49]

(2) *The guidance of the Holy Spirit in moments of crisis* (Mark 13:11; Matt. 10:19-20; Luke 12:12; cf. Luke 21:14-15). Mark 13:11 predicts persecution but asserts, "When they bring you to trial, . . . do not worry about what you are to say; but say whatever is given you at that time, for it is not you who speak, but the Holy Spirit." Once again, Matthew is very similar. Like Mark, Matthew has "do not be anxious"; "it will be given you in that hour"; and "it is not you who speak, but the Spirit of your Father . . ." (rather than "Holy Spirit"). Luke's broad parallel in Luke 21:12 speaks of persecutions, but not of the Spirit. Luke's closer parallel is Luke 12:11-12, which reads, "For the Holy Spirit will teach you in that very hour what you ought to say." Barrett discusses the originality of the sayings.[50] Charles B. Cranfield thinks that Mark is the more primitive form, in contrast to Barrett.[51] Mark has *to pneuma to hagion,* and Matthew has *to pneuma tou patros hymōn.*

In Mark this is one of only three references to the Holy Spirit after the Prologue. It anticipates the Johannine references to the Paraclete (John 15:26-27; 16:8-11). This might also be one of the few references genuinely to link the Holy Spirit with "spontaneity." However, R. T. France warns us that the words refer to an emergency or crisis, and do not encourage "lazy preachers."[52] (A student who allegedly relied on "inspiration" received the tart reply from his tutor: "That's not inspiration; that's desperation!") In Matthew this is the only place where the Spirit is promised to the disciples. In his "History of Reception" Ulrich Luz points out that John Chrysostom and Thomas Aquinas warn us "that God's promise is valid for the preacher only if he has no time for preparation; 'he must not tempt God when he has had time for reflection.'"[53] H. B. Swete concludes, "It guarantees to Christian confessors, in the moment of need, the presence of an Advocate within"; it is the "given" of the Paraclete doctrine found in the Fourth Gospel.[54] Dewar adds, however, "There is no reason to question the authority of the present saying."[55] Again, the saying occurs in all three Synoptic Gospels.

(3) *The links between the Spirit of God, exorcisms, and the arrival of God's Kingdom or rule* (Matt. 12:28). This passage reads, "If it is by the Spirit of God that I cast out demons, then the kingdom of God has come to you." Luke, we re-

---

48. Joel B. Green, *The Gospel of Luke,* NICNT (Grand Rapids: Eerdmans, 1997), p. 484.

49. Lindsay Dewar, *The Holy Spirit and Modern Thought* (London: Mowbray, 1959), p. 19.

50. Barrett, *The Holy Spirit and the Gospel Traditions,* pp. 130-32.

51. Cranfield, *The Gospel according to St. Mark,* p. 400.

52. France, *The Gospel of Mark,* p. 517.

53. Luz, *Matthew 8–20,* p. 90.

54. H. B. Swete, *The Holy Spirit in the New Testament* (London: Macmillan, 1921), p. 122.

55. Dewar, *The Holy Spirit and Modern Thought,* p. 21.

call, has "finger of God" in place of "Spirit of God" (Luke 11:20). This comes as a surprise, given Luke's special interest in the Holy Spirit. "Finger" is like the biblical term "hand of God" or "arm of God," which denotes God's power. Luz argues from the probability that Luke's version may be earlier, and calls Matthew's use of "Spirit" "redactional."[56] If so, this again raises C. K. Barrett's question about the relative paucity of references to the Holy Spirit in the Synoptic Gospels. Barrett's question, in fact, was raised early in the twentieth century. Griffith Thomas had raised it in 1913, and answered it not by appealing to a "lack of glory and a cup of suffering" as the Messianic vocation of Jesus, but to "the immediacy of His communion with the Father," following Winstanley.[57] They argue that Jesus therefore did not *need* to speak of his endowment with the Messianic Spirit, since it was transparent.

Both Matt. 12:28 and Luke 11:20 use the Greek verb *ephthasen* to indicate the coming or arrival of the Kingdom of God. Norman Perrin comments, "These exorcisms are the signs of victory in the decisive battle against the power of Satan."[58] He points to parallels in the *War Scroll* of Qumran (1QM 6:6; 12:7), which looks for God's intervention to bring in the New Age.

(4) *The Father's gift of the Holy Spirit to those who ask* (Luke 11:13). Once again, this is in the context of *prayer*, and is *distinctive to Luke*. Matthew has "give good things" in place of "Holy Spirit" (Matt. 7:11). The majority of New Testament specialists see Matthew as earlier, and Luke as spelling out the saying in accordance with his understanding of the Holy Spirit. It is difficult to imagine why "Holy Spirit" should be changed to "good things." Montague links this with the Pauline tradition in Rom. 8:15; 8:26-27; and Gal. 4:6, which we shall discuss in a later chapter on Paul.[59]

(5) *Postresurrection commands and promises: two postresurrection sayings.* One saying is peculiar to Matthew, and the other is found only in Luke. The Great Commission of Matt. 28:19, "Make disciples of all nations, baptizing them in the name of the Father, the Son, and the Holy Spirit . . . ," is widely considered to be "the expression of later reflection or revelation."[60] Some attribute it to Matthew's special interest in the community or church. But the Trinitarian formulation of the baptismal rite soon became established. It occurs, for example, in the *Didache,* which is either late first century or early second century (*Didache* 7:1 and 3). Christian baptism in Paul and in Acts is in the name of

---

56. Luz, *Matthew 8–20,* p. 200.

57. W. H. Griffith Thomas, *The Holy Spirit of God* (London and New York: Longmans, Green, 1913), p. 57; and Edward W. Winstanley, *Spirit in the New Testament* (Cambridge: Cambridge University Press, 1910), pp. 128-29.

58. Norman Perrin, *The Kingdom of God in the Teaching of Jesus* (London: SCM, 1963), p. 171.

59. George T. Montague, *The Holy Spirit: The Growth of a Biblical Tradition* (Eugene, OR: Wipf & Stock, 1976), p. 259.

60. Dunn, *Jesus and the Spirit,* p. 129.

Christ alone. John Nolland, however, argues that the language of this passage is "well rooted in earlier language in Matthew's narrative," including making disciples and God as Father.[61] He looks to Matthew's special emphasis on the Fatherhood of God, and to the activity of the Holy Spirit at the baptism of Jesus Christ. Nolland's case is not implausible.

One of the more thorough discussions that invite a positive answer to the question of the authenticity of the verse is that by Arthur W. Wainwright.[62] He first considers the textual arguments against authenticity, concluding that these are "not convincing."[63] He then considers in turn the literary and historical arguments. The arguments from historical factors largely depend on the witness of Acts to baptism in the name of Christ only. Why should the earliest churches disregard the command of the risen Christ? It has been argued in reply that the one who baptizes may have used the threefold name, while the confession by the candidate concerned only the pledge of total loyalty to Christ as Lord (1 Cor. 12:3). But Wainwright rejects this as lacking evidence. More important, perhaps, is early evidence of the threefold name from Justin and apocryphal writings. In the end Wainwright asserts the authenticity of the text as Matthew's, but doubts whether Jesus himself uttered these words. If he is right, at least they have canonical authority.

(6) *Luke 24:49 and "power from on high."* Although Luke 24:49 does not speak of the Holy Spirit explicitly, it does refer to the Father's promise. This is a clear allusion to Pentecost, and looks forward to Acts. Acts 1:4 also speaks of "the promise of the Father." Luke Johnson observes: "Luke uses such prophecies at critical junctures in his narrative as a means of interpreting for the reader the story which follows. . . . Prophecies at the end and beginning of the Gospel are equally important as clues to the narrative's meaning. Jesus' promise of a 'power from on high' (Luke 24:49) enables the reader" to see the ascension and Pentecost "not as a departure."[64] In this passage "I am sending" (Greek, *apostellō*) reminds the reader both of the "sending" of prophets and of "sent" apostles.[65]

3.5. Four Possible Conclusions

Four repeated themes, among many others, emerge from a study of the activity of the Holy Spirit in the Synoptic Gospels. Three are far from exhaustive. *First,*

---

61. John Nolland, *The Gospel of Matthew: A Commentary on the Greek Text*, NIGTC (Grand Rapids: Eerdmans, 2005), pp. 1268-69.

62. Arthur W. Wainwright, *The Trinity in the New Testament* (London: SPCK, 1962), pp. 238-41.

63. Wainwright, *Trinity*, p. 239.

64. Johnson, *The Gospel of Luke*, p. 16.

65. Johnson, *The Gospel of Luke*, p. 403.

the anointing and equipping of Jesus by the Holy Spirit is a vital and indisputable starting point. All three Synoptic Gospels stress this at his baptism and Messianic temptations, which represent his Messianic call and testing. Matthew and Luke also stress the Spirit's work in the conception and birth of Jesus, and especially Luke in his entire ministry, including exorcisms and deeds of power.

Second, the Gospels are restrained in their relative silence about the Spirit for multiple reasons, including the cross, set out by Barrett and Fison. Nevertheless this should be *qualified by the concrete examples of the power of the Spirit* such as exorcisms and deeds of power, as discussed by Dunn and Turner. This may be because of what Fison calls the Holy Spirit's "self-effacement," or because the Messianic vocation entails humiliation, "the absence of the signs of the Spirit," and the way of the cross. Mark is dominated by the shadow of the cross. The first eight chapters flash by at a rapid narrative time; the narrative slows after Peter's confession; and the passion narrative occurs as if in slow motion — all to show that the cross is the goal of Christ's life. Luke uses the journey motif geographically from Galilee to the cross outside Jerusalem. The outpouring of the Holy Spirit is kept back until the New Age of Pentecost. On the other hand, there can be no doubt that the mighty deeds of Jesus are performed through the agency and power of the Holy Spirit. Jesus thus fulfills in himself the prophetic expectation of a king or messiah who will be anointed by the Spirit in an unprecedented way; but he also fulfills the apocalyptic stream of hope that God himself will bring about the new creation, although in the Synoptic Gospels this is God acting decisively through the Holy Spirit and Jesus Christ.

Third, although Dunn makes out a very good case for seeing parallels between Jesus' experience of prayer and intimacy with God as Father and his dependence upon the Spirit (to the extent of calling him "charismatic"), *the need for caution here remains a matter of further discussion* and debate. How far should we press this? Although the earthly Jesus did depend on the Holy Spirit, his status as the Son of God, even in his earthly form, suggests a level of uniqueness which demands the use of very careful language. This must occur whenever Christology relates to language about the Holy Spirit, even in the Synoptic Gospels.

Fourth, Jürgen Moltmann does not shrink from seeing this as a narrative of God's Trinitarian work. He writes, "In the power of the Spirit he [Jesus] drives out demons and heals the sick. . . . This energizing power of God is given him not for himself but for others."[66] Thus, while the Gospels clearly show monotheism and not tritheism, all three Persons of the Holy Trinity are involved in the Person and work of Christ. Moltmann adds: *"The New Testament talks about God by proclaiming in narrative the relationships of the Father, the Son and the Spirit, which are relationships of fellowship and are open to the world"* (his

---

66. Jürgen Moltmann, *The Spirit of Life: A Universal Affirmation* (London: SCM, 1992), p. 61.

italics).[67] This remains true of the Synoptic Gospels, in which *narrative* reveals truth about the Holy Spirit and, less directly, about the Holy Trinity. In view of pleas for more attention to the Trinitarian frame not least in relation to Pentecostal and Renewal circles (often pleas from within those groups), this must remain a focus of attention, even though it is more explicit among the Church Fathers than in the New Testament.

---

67. Jürgen Moltmann, *The Trinity and the Kingdom of God: The Doctrine of God* (London: SCM, 1981), p. 64.

4

The Holy Spirit in Acts

The Acts of the Apostles is structured around mission and the outreach of the Apostolic Church, and recounts the expansion of the gospel from Jerusalem to Rome. Some years ago Werner Kümmel proposed a classic fivefold structure for Acts which has hardly been bettered. He perceives "a division into five geographically determined sections in accordance with the *missionary commission* (Acts 1:8)."[1] These are Acts 1:15–8:7: centered on Jerusalem; 8:4–11:18: centered on Samaria and the coastal region; 11:19–15:35: centered on Antioch and the Antiochene mission; 15:36–19:20: centered on lands around the Aegean Sea; and 19:21–28:31: from Jerusalem to Rome. This shows Luke's purpose more clearly (until perhaps very recently) than the traditional division of chapters 1–12, the expansion from Jerusalem to Antioch, centered mainly on *Peter;* and chapters 13–28, from Antioch to Rome, centered mainly on *Paul.*

Even when persecutions and setbacks arise, these serve only to promote the expansion of the Church. Thus, after a first threat, "They let them go, finding no way to punish them because of the people" (Acts 4:21), and the Church preached "with all boldness" (4:29). Later, "A severe persecution began, . . . and all except the apostles were scattered. . . . Now those who were scattered went from place to place, proclaiming the word" (Acts 8:1, 4). Ronald R. Williams produced a small commentary that carried the subtitle "Nothing Can Stop the Gospel."[2] The outpouring of the Holy Spirit and subsequent references to the Spirit owe much significance to this mission framework.

Nevertheless Beverly Roberts Gaventa has more recently argued that although this seems to take the form of a story or account of the history and *expansion of the Church,* Luke's overriding preoccupation is with *God,* the *plan of*

---

1. Werner G. Kümmel, *Introduction to the New Testament* (London: SCM, 1966), p. 108.
2. Ronald R. Williams, *The Acts of the Apostles,* Torch Commentary (London: SCM, 1953).

God, the *will of God,* and the *purposes of God.*[3] The Holy Spirit empowers the Church, and "the Word of God" denotes the content of the gospel (Acts 13:7, 44; 16:32). Although her concern is primarily theological, Gaventa does not underplay the importance of history, for God, God's Spirit, and God's Word operate *through* human means, not least, in Acts, through Paul. Hence God's purposes in salvation history remain primary. She cites the importance of such terms as *boulē theou,* the will or purpose of God. Peter's speech on the Day of Pentecost draws on the prophecy of Joel, for the God of Israel is the God of the Church. It was once a convention to underplay the historical aspect, especially following the works of Ernst Haenchen and Hans Conzelmann.[4] But more recently I. Howard Marshall and F. F. Bruce in Britain, Joseph Fitzmyer and Beverly R. Gaventa in America, and Martin Hengel in Germany have done much to turn this tide, so that Acts is no longer approached as *either* history *or* theology, but as *both* theology *and* history.[5] God works *in* and *through* history.

It so happens that the theme of God's working through history and through human agents constitutes a central theme of both classical Pentecostalism and the Renewal Movement. They readily recognize that Luke-Acts constitutes for them a key founding document; in contrast to this, they argue, mainline or "orthodox" writers grant more privilege to Paul and perhaps to John. Hence, later in this book, we need to give special consideration to Pentecostal and Renewal writers. Explicitly from within the Pentecostal Movement Robert Menzies and Roger Stronstad have become New Testament specialists who have written extensively on Luke-Acts. Max Turner, who is not a Pentecostal but is both deeply committed to the Renewal Movement and a New Testament specialist, has also written much on Luke-Acts. Gordon Fee is perhaps the most respected New Testament scholar from within Pentecostalism, but his magisterial book *God's Empowering Presence* (1994 and 1995) is largely limited to Paul.[6] In

3. Beverly Roberts Gaventa, *The Acts of the Apostles,* Abingdon New Testament Commentaries (Nashville: Abingdon, 2003), esp. pp. 25-60.

4. Ernst Haenchen, *The Acts of the Apostles: A Commentary* (Oxford: Blackwell, 1971); and Hans Conzelmann, *The Theology of Luke* (London: Faber; and New York: Harper & Row, 1961) and the Hermeneia volume *Acts of the Apostles* (Minneapolis: Fortress, 1987).

5. Joseph A. Fitzmyer, *The Acts of the Apostles,* Anchor Bible Series (New Haven: Yale University Press, 1998); Martin Hengel, *Acts and the History of Earliest Christianity* (London: SCM, 1979); I. Howard Marshall, *Luke: Historian and Theologian* (Exeter: Paternoster, 1970 and 1989); F. F. Bruce, "Commentaries on Acts," *Epworth Review* 8 (1981): 82-87.

6. Max Turner, *Power from on High: The Spirit in God's Restoration and Witness in Luke-Acts,* JPTSS 9 (Sheffield: Sheffield Academic, 1996) and *The Holy Spirit and Spiritual Gifts Then and Now* (Carlisle: Paternoster, 1996), pp. 36-56; Robert P. Menzies, *The Development of Early Christian Pneumatology with Special Reference to Luke-Acts* (Sheffield: Sheffield Academic, 1991) and *Empowered for Witness* (Sheffield: Sheffield Academic, 1984); Roger Stronstad, *The Charismatic Theology of Saint Luke* (Peabody: Hendrickson, 1984); Gordon D. Fee, *God's Empowering Presence: The Holy Spirit in the Letters of Paul* (Carlisle: Paternoster, 1995, and Peabody, MA: Hendrickson, 1994).

Part III we shall note the huge growth of Pentecostal theology and some Pentecostal or Renewal writers, and increasing interest in serious academic concerns as witnessed not only by the work of Fee, Turner, Menzies, and Stronstad but also such writers as Veli-Matti Kärkkäinen, Frank Macchia, Amos Yong, and Mark J. Cartledge, as well as contributors to the *Journal of Pentecostal Theology* (20 numbers since 1991), and its Supplement series (about 34 vols. to date).

4.1. The Day of Pentecost and the Outpouring of the Spirit

Although much of Luke's theme concerns the Church, Luke insists that it is not a purely human institution, like a network or club. In the call and conversion of Paul, the heavenly voice asks, "Why do you persecute *me?*" (Acts 9:4; 22:7; and 26:14). But just as surely as Christ identifies himself with his Church (as J. A. T. Robinson stresses), so from the start the Church comes into existence only by receiving the creative life of the Holy Spirit (Acts 1:8; 2:1-36).[7] Succeeding events in the life of the Church are directed by the Holy Spirit (e.g., Philip's encounter with the Ethiopian on the road to Gaza, Acts 8:29, 39). Praise, prayer, teaching, and the common breaking of bread and fellowship all proceed in response to the gift of the Spirit at Pentecost (Acts 2:42-47). In this sense, Conzelmann's suggestion that this is a construction of Luke, which is not to be repeated but is distinctive to the remote past, does not seem entirely plausible and has recently lost general favor in this form.

Since Peter appeals to the inspiration of the Holy Spirit in the Psalms (Acts 1:16-21; 4:25-26), we may assume that the timing of the Day of Pentecost had Old Testament roots. Pentecost was the Greek name for the Hebrew and Jewish Festival of Weeks, which came about fifty days or seven weeks after Passover (Lev. 23:15-16; Deut. 16:9-10; cf. Exod. 23:14-17; 34:18, 22-24). The two terms are identified as implying each other in Tob. 2:1 and 2 Macc. 12:31, as well as in Philo (*On the Special Laws* 2:30) and Josephus (*Jewish War* 2:42-44; *Antiquities* 17:254-55). It became the second in importance of the three Jewish festivals, but was also a holiday celebrated with joy and with crowds of pilgrims in Jerusalem. Ernst Lohmeyer's theory of an "earliest" Christian community in Galilee (perhaps alongside the Jerusalem community) invites a helpful critical reply from Dunn.[8] Pentecost also signified the end of the reaping season, which completed the "Passover sheaf offering." Hence Philip Loyd, followed by J. H. E. Hull, suggests that for Luke "the work of the Resurrection was com-

---

7. John A. T. Robinson, *The Body: A Study in Pauline Theology* (London: SCM, 1952), pp. 55-58.

8. James D. G. Dunn, *Jesus and the Spirit: A Study of the Religious and Charismatic Experience of Jesus and the First Christians as Reflected in the New Testament* (London: SCM, 1975), pp. 136-39.

pleted when the disciples by the descent of the Holy Ghost were made members of the Lord's risen Body."[9]

This would match Dunn's suggestion that we should not divide Pentecost too sharply from the resurrection appearances, including the appearance "to more than 500 brothers and sisters at one time" (1 Cor. 15:6).[10] Moreover, this suggests an easier compatibility with "the Johannine Pentecost" in John 20:19-20 than is usually or often imagined: "Jesus breathed on them, and said to them, 'Receive the Holy Spirit'" (John 20:22).

Although H. B. Swete may be less explicit than Hull, he nevertheless makes two points about the Day of Pentecost. He writes, "It is easy to see the appropriations of such a day for the coming of the Divine Gift which is the firstfruits of the spiritual harvest"; and second, "Among the later Jews the Pentecost was kept as the anniversary of the giving of the Law. . . . The Holy Spirit came to write on men's hearts the perfect law of liberty."[11] He adds, however, that we must be cautious about this second point, for it is far from certain that this aspect of Pentecost goes back as early as the apostolic age. All the same, Jerusalem would have been thronged by joyous pilgrim-visitors at that time.

When the apostles and other Christians were "all together in one place" (Acts 2:1), the Holy Spirit was "poured out" upon them, accompanied by various signs of observable phenomena. (1) The signs or phenomena were audible, with "a sound like the rush of a violent wind" (2:2). Luke uses *ēchos* for "sound" (rather than *phōnē*), which is often used to indicate theophanies in the LXX (Exod. 19:16; 1 Sam. 4:5). On the other hand, Paul also uses the verb *ēcheō* to suggest mere noise (1 Cor. 13:1). (2) The accompaniments are also visible: "Tongues, as of fire, appeared . . . and . . . rested on each of them" (Acts 2:3). Fire is an image or metaphor of judgment (Isa. 5:24; *1 Enoch* 14:8-13; Luke 3:16), and would recall John the Baptist's saying, "He will baptize you with the Holy Spirit and fire" (Luke 3:16). In both the revelation to Elijah in the cave on Horeb and the vision of Ezekiel by the river Chebar, the combination of wind and fire accompanied a theophany (1 Kings 19:11-12; Ezek. 1:4).[12]

Luke then recounts in Acts 2:4, "All of them were filled [Greek, *eplēsthēsan pantes*] with the Holy Spirit, and began to speak with other *(heterais)* languages, as the Spirit gave them ability." The NIV retains "other tongues" *(heterais glōssais)*, with languages as a marginal alternative, while NAB and NJB simply have "languages." Were these "languages," as might be suggested in a context of "foreign" mission? Or if this constitutes a reversal of Babel, might

---

9. Philip Loyd, *The Holy Spirit in Acts* (London: Mowbray, 1957), p. 28; J. H. E. Hull, *The Holy Spirit in the Acts of the Apostles* (London: Lutterworth, 1967), pp. 50-51.

10. Dunn, *Jesus and the Spirit*, pp. 140-46.

11. Henry B. Swete, *The Holy Spirit in the New Testament* (London: Macmillan, 1909, rpt. 1921), p. 68.

12. Swete, *The Holy Spirit in the New Testament*, pp. 71-72.

these rather be "unintelligible sounds," which is what Paul usually means by *glōssa*?

There are strong arguments on each side. One clear argument *against* foreign *languages* is that the Christians are accused of being drunk (Acts 2:13). Some subsidiary arguments include the notion that "other" *(heterais)* tongues might denote strange or unfamiliar speech, as in 1 Corinthians 12–14, and that the main impact in the non-Christian world comes in the form of Peter's explanatory speech (Acts 2:14-36 and 37-41). Max Turner argues that the tongues are not evangelistic, for "It is Peter's preaching which communicates the gospel."[13] Bruce sees here a form of speech "beyond his [the speaker's] conscious control, . . . a gift . . . valued by the Corinthian Church."[14] Janet Everts Powers writes in the *Journal of Pentecostal Theology* that there is "no biblical evidence" for seeing tongues as a *missionary* gift; in Acts they "preach in the vernacular, not tongues."[15] Such a view, she argues, would give hostage to the "cessationist" view of B. Warfield. Further, although some describe the point as "banal," it can be argued that most Diaspora Jews would speak and understand Greek, especially since most Jews of the Dispersion were urban or city dwellers, who normally did not live in remote rural areas.[16] Dunn sees the phenomena as glossolalia.[17]

The traditional and earlier view that the Spirit-filled Christians spoke foreign languages goes back at least to John Chrysostom.[18] Hull comments, "Luke does not seem to have thought that the 'other tongues' at Pentecost were *glossolalia*. . . . Luke appears to wish us to conclude that it was foreign tongues, foreign languages, that were spoken at Pentecost."[19] He admits, however, that some of the Church Fathers thought that this was a miracle of hearing rather than of speaking. Luke writes that the crowd was bewildered "because each one heard them speaking in the native language of each. . . . How is it that we hear, each of us, in our own native language?" (Acts 2:6, 8). Kirsopp Lake and others see the languages as a reversal of Babel, which could have been a lectionary reading for Pentecost. Lake comments, "It is clear that . . . 'other tongues' [are] 'other languages.'"[20] There also existed a Jewish tradition that everyone heard the Law in their own language.

13. Max Turner, *The Holy Spirit and Spiritual Gifts Then and Now* (Carlisle: Paternoster, 1996), p. 223.

14. F. F. Bruce, *The Book of Acts* (Grand Rapids: Eerdmans, and London: Marshall, Morgan & Scott, 1965), p. 57.

15. Janet Everts Powers, "Missionary Tongues," *JPT* 17 (2000): 40; cf. pp. 39-55.

16. Hull, *The Holy Spirit in Acts*, p. 62, criticizes this view.

17. Dunn, *Jesus and the Spirit*, pp. 148-49 and 152.

18. Chrysostom, *Commentary on Acts*, Homily 4 (*NPNF*, ser. 1, vol. 11, pp. 28-29).

19. Hull, *The Holy Spirit in Acts*, p. 61.

20. Kirsopp Lake, "The Gift of the Spirit on the Day of Pentecost," in *The Beginnings of Christianity,* ed. F. J. Foakes-Jackson and Kirsopp Lake, vols. 1-5 (London: Macmillan, 1920-33), vol. 5 (1933), pp. 111-20, esp. 114-15.

One of the strongest and least compromising advocates of the "foreign languages" view is Donald A. Carson. He insists, "In Luke's description of the utterances on the day of Pentecost we are dealing with *xenoglossia* — real, human languages never learned by the speakers."[21] He dismisses the compromise suggestion of C. G. Williams that the "gibberish" or tongues of ecstasy were intertwined with occasionally recognized words from foreign languages. He also declares, "It goes beyond the text to argue that this was a miracle of hearing rather than of speech."[22] Finally, he addresses the accusation of drunkenness. He argues that if three thousand people repented after Peter's sermon (Acts 2:41), the original crowd was probably larger, and some did not hear their own tongue. Aramaic-speaking Jews, he concludes, "found *nothing* intelligible in the utterances" (his italics).[23] For they would not know the languages listed by Luke. Many were filled with the Holy Spirit, and spoke in foreign languages, but Carson adds, "it does not follow that that is the normative New Testament stance. . . . Paul flatly denies that all speak in tongues" (1 Cor. 12:30).[24]

The interpretation of Acts 2 is made all the more difficult because respected scholars differ in their interpretation. Years before Carson wrote, no lesser New Testament and Greek scholar than H. B. Swete argued that everyone in the crowd could have understood "either a dialect of Aramaic or the colloquial Greek which was spoken everywhere. . . . In what language was St. Peter's long speech delivered?"[25] Moreover, "Acts does not affirm that the speakers spoke in the tongues of several nationalities . . . but only that the hearers so interpreted their utterances *(ēkouon heis hekastos . . . akouomen)*. It is a subjective effect, . . . not an objective fact."[26] Montague agrees: "It would seem, thus, that there was a miracle of hearing."[27]

We cannot be certain about Luke's intention. But in favor of the possibility of *glossolalia,* in addition to the arguments above, is the unique event of transformation and crises that Luke recounts. At such moments considerable nervous energy is discharged. This is not to give a "psychological" explanation to a miracle, perhaps to a miracle of hearing, but as we observe from Gerd Theissen's *Psychological Aspects of Pauline Theology* and also from Krister Stendahl, moments of acute disturbance and new beginnings encourage what Stendahl calls "high-voltage" experience, and what Theissen sees as the removal

---

21. Donald A. Carson, *Showing the Spirit* (Grand Rapids: Baker, 1987), p. 138.

22. Carson, *Showing the Spirit,* p. 138.

23. Carson, *Showing the Spirit,* p. 139.

24. Carson, *Showing the Spirit,* p. 142.

25. Swete, *The Holy Spirit in the New Testament,* p. 73.

26. Swete, *The Holy Spirit in the New Testament,* p. 381.

27. George T. Montague, *The Holy Spirit: The Growth of a Biblical Tradition* (Eugene, OR: Wipf & Stock, 1976), p. 281.

of inhibitions or censors of the subconscious.[28] Dunn correctly notes: "The epochal significance of Pentecost raises the whole course of salvation-history to a new plane. . . . In one sense, therefore, *Pentecost can never be repeated* — the new age is here, and cannot be ushered in again. But *in another sense . . . the experience of Pentecost can and must be repeated* in the experience of all who would become Christians."[29] The event was earth-shattering. It is not surprising that Peter used apocalyptic language: "portents in the heavens above, and signs on the earth below; blood and fire. . . . The sun shall be turned to darkness, and the moon to blood . . ." (Acts 2:19-20). Beverly Roberts Gaventa concludes that several themes overlap, including that of Babel, but that the key theme concerns God and the community, and the rejection of "the individualistic self-preoccupation that often passes itself off as spirituality."[30]

In this sense, Pentecost was *initiatory*. It initiated the birth and era of the Church. Hence the missionary context of Pentecost is fulfilled by the commissioning and empowering of the Church. This poses a complex answer to the question, "Is this the baptism of the Spirit?" J. H. E. Hull writes clearly: "The promise made by Jesus that his disciples would be baptized with the Holy Spirit (Acts 1:5) was realized on the Day of Pentecost when 'they were all filled with the Holy Spirit.' . . . 'To be filled' appears to be only a stylistic variant of the metaphor 'to be baptized,' which can also mean 'to be soaked, to be saturated.'"[31] But many reject this meaning.[32] Part of the answer to this dilemma seems to be that *as a Church* they experienced a *communal initiatory baptism with the Spirit;* but *as individuals,* whatever experiences they had, or were yet to have, Luke agrees with Paul that "baptism with the Holy Spirit" applies to "becoming a Christian," not to some subsequent experience. Swete admits that Luke's Pentecost is one of the most difficult events to interpret.[33] Yet, he states: "In the history of the Church, her baptism with the Spirit was at hand."[34] Dunn observes, "The Church properly conceived did not come into existence until Pentecost."[35]

F. Dale Bruner describes Pentecost as a unique *communal* "baptism with the Holy Spirit." He calls the event "this paradigmatic announcement of the

---

28. Gerd Theissen, *Psychological Aspects of Pauline Theology* (Edinburgh: T&T Clark, 1987), pp. 59-80, and 96-114; Krister Stendahl, *Paul among Jews and Gentiles* (London: SCM, 1977 and Philadelphia: Fortress, 1976), pp. 109-24.

29. James D. G. Dunn, *Baptism in the Holy Spirit: A Re-examination of the New Testament Teaching on the Gift of the Holy Spirit in Relation to Pentecostalism Today* (London: SCM, 1975), p. 53 (my italics).

30. Beverly Roberts Gaventa, "Pentecost and Trinity," *Interpretation* 66 (2012): 5; cf. pp. 5-15.

31. Hull, *The Holy Spirit in Acts,* p. 65.

32. Lindsay Dewar, *The Holy Spirit and Modern Thought* (London: Mowbray, 1959), p. 43.

33. Swete, *The Holy Spirit in the New Testament,* p. 72.

34. Swete, *The Holy Spirit in the New Testament,* p. 65.

35. Dunn, *Baptism in the Holy Spirit,* p. 51.

baptism of the Holy Spirit."[36] It fulfills the "promise" (Greek, *epangelia*) made in Luke 24:49 and Acts 1:4 and 2:33 of this "free gift" *(dōrea)* from God. Acts 1:8, Bruner argues, sets out the "contents" which govern the Acts narrative: the Spirit is given in Jerusalem, Samaria, and to the nations of the world. He rightly notes that the Holy Spirit comes *from above, not from within* (Luke 24:49), which, as we shall see, is vital for popular notions of "spirituality." Moreover, the baptism in or with the Holy Spirit enables witness to Christ: "baptism of the Holy Spirit is the power of Christocentricity."[37] Pentecost brings a complete "filling" with the Spirit, which is neither partial nor conditional. Bruner insists that "other tongues" denotes "foreign languages" in Acts 2 at Pentecost, whereas this is not the case at Caesarea (Acts 10) or Ephesus (Acts 19). According to Acts 2:4, the pouring out of the Holy Spirit is "not asked for."[38]

Bruner insists that Word and Spirit are closely associated together. For it is Peter's sermon (Acts 2:14-36) that is "the center of Luke's attention; . . . not spiritual ecstasy but a Christian sermon."[39] He then concludes this section by asserting that "incorporation into Christ grants the Spirit," as also in Paul.[40] Pentecost portrays "baptism of the Holy Spirit," but "there is no record in Acts of men praying that they might receive the Holy Spirit."[41] This stands in contrast to Mark Cartledge's description of a "third wave" charismatic Renewal meeting (discussed below), in which leaders "invite" the Holy Spirit to fall upon the meeting.

Very recently (2010) Arie Zwiep has shed further light on the event of Pentecost in Acts 2. He rightly sees it as a "barrier-breaking" event.[42] However, he also sees as "the crucial question" whether Luke considered "the fiery baptism with the Spirit announced by John to be *fulfilled* at Pentecost" (his italics).[43] He concedes that it is difficult to deny that the outpouring of the Spirit at Pentecost is not only the definitive and final fulfillment of eschatological promises and expectations, but also "an anticipation . . . of traditional eschatological promises."[44] The language of Acts 2:19-20 is explicitly apocalyptic: "the sun turned to darkness and the moon to blood." It ushers in a new age. But rightly Zwiep stresses the universal, cosmic, and corporate aspect of apocalyptic. Several

---

36. Frederick Dale Bruner, *A Theology of the Holy Spirit: The Pentecostal Experience and the New Testament Witness* (Grand Rapids: Eerdmans, 1970), p. 157.

37. Bruner, *A Theology of the Holy Spirit*, p. 161.

38. Bruner, *A Theology of the Holy Spirit*, p. 164.

39. Bruner, *A Theology of the Holy Spirit*, p. 165.

40. Bruner, *A Theology of the Holy Spirit*, p. 169.

41. Bruner, *A Theology of the Holy Spirit*, p. 171.

42. Arie W. Zwiep, *Christ, the Spirit and the Community of God*, WUNT 2.293 (Tübingen: Mohr, 2010), p. 116.

43. Zwiep, *Christ, the Spirit*, p. 108.

44. Zwiep, *Christ, the Spirit*, pp. 108-9.

times he dissents from Robert Menzies for describing Pentecost as an event experienced by a succession of individuals: "to be experienced (at least potentially) by every individual believer."[45] Insofar as the event is a baptism, it is the community that is involved: a "dynamic community in which faith in Christ bridges ethnic and social barriers."[46] Zwiep might have clinched this argument against Menzies by citing Tom Holland and perhaps Oscar Cullmann on the corporate nature of baptism, and Charles F. D. Moule and Alan Richardson on baptism as an anticipation of the Last Judgment. This material is documented when we look further at Zwiep at the end of Part III. Zwiep, therefore, offers a strong rejoinder to claims concerning the separation in time between coming to faith and a "second blessing" such as baptism in the Spirit, at least insofar as this is based on an individualistic understanding of Pentecost. This is not to deny that there may be subsequent experiences; it is to deny that Acts 2 should be interpreted in this way.

4.2. Pentecostal and Renewal-Movement Interpretations of Acts: Prophecy, Empowerment, and a Variety of Views

Max Turner follows Hans von Baer in seeing Pentecost not only as empowerment for witness to Christ but also *as inspirer of prophecy,* largely on the basis of a careful scrutiny of expectations in Intertestamental Judaism. Further, most Pentecostals interpret "when the Holy Spirit has come upon you" (Acts 1:8) as promising an experience *subsequent to incorporation into Christ or coming to faith.* This experience used to be called "the second blessing" in many circles. Increasingly this is disputed by some within Pentecostalism, but it remains the position of "classical Pentecostalism."

The classical Pentecostal view is well discussed in Gary McGee's volume of essays, *Initial Evidence,* which recounts the views of Edward Irving, Charles Parham, William Seymour, and Robert Menzies, as well as suggesting "New Directions."[47] David Dorries gives an emphatic "yes" on whether Edward Irving, whom we consider in our chapter on the nineteenth century, saw tongues-speech as initial evidence of baptism in the Spirit.[48] Charles Parham, generally regarded as the founder of Pentecostalism in about 1901-3, whom we discuss in Part III, believed in "Holy Spirit baptism evidenced by speaking in tongues."[49] Cecil Robeck insists that William J. Seymour, Pentecostalism's second or co-

---

45. Zwiep, *Christ, the Spirit,* p. 111.

46. Zwiep, *Christ, the Spirit,* p. 138.

47. Gary B. McGee (ed.), *Initial Evidence: Historical and Biblical Perspectives on the Pentecostal Doctrine of Spirit Baptism* (Eugene: Wipf & Stock, 1991), pp. 41-95 and 219-34.

48. David W. Dorries, in *Initial Evidence,* ed. McGee, pp. 48-52.

49. James Goff, in *Initial Evidence,* ed. McGee, p. 69.

founder, "initially believed that the ability to speak in tongues was evidence of Spirit baptism, just as Parham thought," but later "found it more difficult . . . to maintain Parham's position."[50] The understanding of tongues-speech is now a moving and varied set of beliefs.

At a recent conference of Pentecostals held in 2006, partly sponsored by the John Templeton Foundation, Veli-Matti Kärkkäinen reported that some 40 percent of Pentecostals did not claim to speak in tongues. In his book *Pneumatology,* moreover, he provides an interpretation of Acts which seems close to that of most New Testament scholars, including James Dunn.[51] Frank Macchia, who was also a speaker at this conference, and whom we also discuss in Part III, proposed that tongues-speech could probably be equated with "sighs too deep for words" in Rom. 8:26.[52]

On the basis of extensive interviews and questionnaires among both Pentecostals and adherents of the Renewal Movement, Mark Cartledge concludes that, whereas in classical Pentecostalism tongues-speech was seen as the "initial evidence" of baptism in the Spirit, this phenomenon has increasingly come to be seen today as an expression of praise and prayer. Cartledge writes: "First, *glossolalia* finds its primary context within prayer. . . . Second, charismatic socialization is a factor. The theory which states that *glossolalia* is a learnt experience has considerable support from the data. . . . Third, direct charismatic activity is a factor. . . . There is conceptual overlap between prayer and worship, and between prayer and spiritual battle."[53]

In 2006 Cartledge edited a volume of essays entitled *Speaking in Tongues,* to which Max Turner, Frank Macchia, David Hilborn, and others have contributed (also indirectly, by reference, Robert Menzies). Turner writes on Acts and Paul; Macchia compares Babel in Genesis 11 with Acts 2; David Hilborn considers an approach in the light of pragmatics and H. P. Grice on implicature; Margaret Poloma introduces a sociological perspective; and Cartledge assesses each contribution in the light of the "Third Wave" or "New Wine" Renewal Movement. The documentation is substantial. Turner considers the "initial evidence" movement at one end of the spectrum, and the "cessationist" theory at the other. He insists that Luke himself understood the phenomenon of tongues as actual unlearned foreign languages. He comments: "He would hardly be inclined to suggest that the apostolic band merely . . . babbled ecstatically and

50. Cecil M. Robeck, in *Initial Evidence,* ed. McGee, p. 88.

51. Veli-Matti Kärkkäinen, *Pneumatology: The Holy Spirit in Ecumenical, International, and Contextual Perspective* (Grand Rapids: Baker Academic, 2002), pp. 30-32.

52. Frank D. Macchia, "Sighs Too Deep for Words: Toward a Theology of Glossolalia," *JPT* 1 (1992): 47-73; cf. "Groans Too Deep for Words: Towards a Theology of Tongues as Initial Experience," *Asian Journal of Pentecostal Studies* 1 (1998): 149-73.

53. Mark J. Cartledge, *Charismatic Glossolalia: An Empirical-Theological Study* (Aldershot U.K., and Burlington, VT: Ashgate, 2002), pp. 215-16.

incomprehensibly."[54] The content of the tongues in Luke was *ta megalia tou theou*, "mighty deeds of God," although Luke uses *megalynō* in Acts 10:46 and 19:17 to denote simply "praise to God." On the other hand, in Acts 10:46 and 19:6 there is no indication that the tongues were languages. These have "strong parallels with the Pentecostal experience."[55] But in these instances the content is not clear.

Frank Macchia believes that to view Pentecost as a simple reversal of Babel (as famously J. G. Davies did) is inadequate; it is merely a "one dimensional" view, lacking deeper ideas.[56] Tongues can be liberating, as Paul argues in Romans 8, and also ecumenical. Neil Hudson traces the phenomenon to Parham, Seymour, Alexander Boddy, and the beginnings of Pentecostalism, and to a later period of self-evaluation and even division. Yet he concludes: "Speaking in tongues continued to be a marker of Pentecostalism," and this also applied to "the charismatic renewal movement, which began in 1960."[57] James K. A. Smith sees tongues as a "resistance discourse" especially for the poor or oppressed. David Hilborn calls on linguistics and pragmatics to show that tongues can be communicative, but with two constraints: they communicate primarily with God; and as H. P. Grice observes in his theory of implicature, meaning may be implied, not stated, from its behavioral context. Further, from J. L. Austin's speech-act theory, he argues that different kinds of effects are more at issue than purely inner states or feelings alone. In terms of speech acts "Glossolalia serves . . . primarily as an 'ostensive sacramental act' [and] is hardly to be denigrated as such."[58]

Robert Menzies, to whom Turner refers, is perhaps the most explicit today in adhering to the classical Pentecostal position that tongues constitute "initial evidence" of "baptism in the Holy Spirit."[59] Finally, Cartledge observes the actual practice among the "Third Wave" or "New Wine" charismatic gatherings of some five thousand to eight thousand people. In their main evening meeting they program a period of songs, a sermon, a time of "prayer ministry" (with "words of knowledge"), and "the Spirit is invited to come upon the whole congregation" or "publicly invoked in tongues."[60] Very clearly there is a social ele-

---

54. Max Turner, "Early Christian Experience and Theology of Tongues," in *Speaking in Tongues,* ed. Mark J. Cartledge (Milton Keynes: Paternoster, 2006), p. 5.

55. Turner, "Early Christian Experience," in *Speaking in Tongues,* ed. Cartledge, p. 7.

56. J. G. Davies, "Pentecost and Glossolalia," *JTS* 3 (1952): 228-31; and Frank Macchia, "Babel and Tongues," in *Speaking in Tongues,* ed. Cartledge, p. 43; cf. pp. 34-51.

57. Neil Hudson, "Strange Words and Their Impact on Early Pentecostals," in *Speaking in Tongues,* ed. Cartledge, p. 79.

58. David Hilborn, "Glossolalia as Communication," in *Speaking in Tongues,* ed. Cartledge, p. 137; cf. pp. 111-46.

59. Robert Menzies, "Evidential Tongues: An Essay on Theological Method." *Asian Journal of Pentecostal Studies* 1 (1999): 111-23.

60. Cartledge, "The Practice of Tongues," in *Speaking in Tongues,* ed. Cartledge, p. 210; cf. pp. 206-34.

ment behind the practice. It is embedded within a tradition of understanding. Cartledge comments: "Hilborn argues that, although tongues-speech may appear to be spontaneous, its acceptance and legitimisation is dependent on shared assumptions about its 'propriety, frequency and divine origin.'"[61] He further comments that this attracts those who enjoy a social form of spirituality.

Max Turner, who is not a Pentecostal but an advocate of Renewal in the charismatic sense, confirms what we have noted, namely, that the Acts of the Apostles constitutes *foundational*, or what he called "crunch," material for Pentecostalism.[62] Hence a balanced study must take full account of further claims about the interpretation of Acts. Prior evaluations of Luke may determine whether the three episodes in Acts 8, Acts 10, and Acts 19 (discussed below) constitute "exceptions" or "norms" in relation to what Luke and Paul believe about the Holy Spirit. In his book *The Holy Spirit and Spiritual Gifts* (1996) Max Turner tends to regard these events, certainly with Pentecost itself, as "paradigmatic"; as models or blueprints for all or later times. On the other hand, in *Power from on High* (also 1996) he seems to show more caution about declaring each of these four events "paradigmatic."[63] He calls these "prototypical gifts."[64] Just as much to the point is Turner's belief that Luke owes much to Intertestamental Judaism and a Jewish emphasis on the Spirit of prophecy. He takes Peter's explanation of the phenomena of Pentecost not simply as a promise of the Spirit for all kinds of people (Acts 2:17) but also, as we have noted, as a narrower reference to prophecy. Yet Turner is far less explicit and "narrow" than Robert Menzies. Indeed, the latter specifically responds to Turner on this point.[65] While Turner brackets with "prophecy" healing minds and deeds of power, Menzies retains prophecy in a narrow sense.

In fact, Turner categorizes this as witness *to Christ*, which, as we have noted, constitutes a theme which features in the Paraclete discourses of John (John 16:13-14). He has little difficulty in seeing "power for witness" in Acts 1:8; 2:22, 37-38; "mighty works" in Matt. 4:23; or "wonders" in Acts 2:43 (cf. Acts 5:15). Many would agree. It is not so much "Spirit-baptism" here which invites controversy, for he has rightly cited Acts 1:7-8 (v. 8, "you will be baptized with the Holy Spirit"), which is corporate and initiatory, unlike misinterpretation of 1 Cor. 12:13, which is often understood as a "gift" subsequent to faith. Frederick Danker does include "power, might, strength, force" in his first heading.[66] But Danker also observes that the underlying meaning is that of *"capability"* or *"effectiveness,"* as Barth often translates the word. These terms are more subtle

---

61. Cartledge, "The Practice of Tongues," in *Speaking in Tongues*, ed. Cartledge, p. 219.
62. Turner, *The Holy Spirit and Spiritual Gifts Then and Now*, pp. 36-56.
63. Turner, *Power from on High*, pp. 357 and 360.
64. Turner, *Power from on High*, p. 349.
65. Turner, *Power from on High*, pp. 348-57.
66. Danker, in BDAG, p. 262.

than "power," which suggests the brute force of steam or electricity in the Industrial Revolution, with its quasi-causal, quasi-mechanical overtones. When we consider Pentecostalism in a later chapter, we shall encounter "power evangelism," which at first sight does not seem to harmonize with Jesus' use of parables as "indirect" communication, his reticence to perform "signs," and his relationships of love.

Danker further explains that "capability" denoted "ability to carry out something."[67] This may include deeds which seem "remarkable," to which the name "miracle" is often attributed. As we have noted, this may be acceptable as meaning that divine action may sometimes transcend known cause-and-effect in the natural world, but not as a dualist term to divide divine action into two categories.

A further difficulty arises from Turner's insistence, on the basis of Acts 19:2, that the Holy Spirit is given *after* faith.[68] How, then, can the Spirit be the *cause* of faith? But especially in the face of Baer's criticisms, he soon dissociates himself from perceiving faith as "effort." He writes that other conditions are not required in addition to faith, but "as an expression of faith."[69] Arie Zwiep's argument about individuals and community in baptism also remains relevant. Further, from within Pentecostalism today there are a variety of attitudes toward tongues. In Part III we shall consider Gordon Fee's views. Meanwhile he notes that tongues are "only one among many manifestations of the Spirit."[70]

It remains true, however, that many of the aspects of the ministry of Jesus, given as a capacity by the Holy Spirit, characterize the early Church in Acts. Moreover, Turner does not dismiss mainline scholarship. He describes his own position as that of "mediator" between Menzies (or traditional Pentecostalism) and James Dunn.[71] In his assessment of the meaning of Pentecost there is much concerning which we cannot "be sure."[72] This kind of openness on both sides of the debate will lead us forward, to the benefit of the Church today.

This discussion does, however, leaves us with at least three questions, to which we shall return later.

(1) In spite of very much serious work on Luke-Acts, who is right about Luke's over-all intention? Is he primarily the narrator of events which occurred at particular places and times in a *unique, unrepeatable* way, or does he seek to offer *a model or paradigm* for Christians of all time, or later generations? Although we should not go as far as Conzelmann in calling this an idealized age, not to be repeated, we cannot be blind to all of his arguments. In practice the

---

67. Danker, in BDAG, p. 263.
68. Turner, *Power from on High*, p. 362.
69. Turner, *Power from on High*, p. 362.
70. Fee, *God's Empowering Presence*, p. 214.
71. Turner, *Power from on High*, p. 79.
72. Turner, *Power from on High*, p. 357.

second, or "Restorationist," view is characteristic of classical Pentecostalism, but increasingly some contemporary Pentecostals argue that Luke was not writing a blueprint for subsequent generations.

(2) In spite of claims to the contrary, does Pentecostal zeal for renewal and purity risk that which invited Luther's complaint about the radical Reformers? Is there more than a hint of receiving the Holy Spirit when faith, obedience, and prayer are *first* offered? Or does the Spirit himself *originate and cause* faith, obedience, and prayer? Was Luther right in claiming that the "radical" Reformers unintentionally undermined Paul's doctrine of justification by pure *grace* through faith? We shall return later to this subject. Again, we encounter differences within the Pentecostal and Charismatic Movement. Max Turner and Frank Macchia, for example, are more concerned than Robert Menzies and J. R. Williams to find "middle ground" or openness.

(3) Much may depend on what is meant by "baptism in the Holy Spirit." Macchia regrets the decline in the use of the term among Pentecostals, and proposes a much broader and more inclusive meaning of the term than in the classical Pentecostalism of Parham or Seymour.[73] He regrets as a "problem" the revivalist influence of the Holiness Movement, which transformed "Wesley's more process-oriented understanding of sanctification into a high-voltage crisis experience."[74] It is difficult not to regret that the "Third Wave" of the *Renewal Movement* does not appear to be marked by such *self-critical* and creative thinking as Macchia, Kärkkäinen, and others manifest among Pentecostals. As we have noted, they do not diverge hugely on the interpretation of Acts, whereas many Holiness Movement writers and Restorationist exponents may be said to do so.

4.3. Is Pentecost Unique in View of the Events
Which Concern the Samaritans, Cornelius, and the Ephesians
(Acts 8:14-24; 10:17-48; and 19:1-7)?

Those who argue that Pentecost was decisive for *all* Christians have to face the fact that Luke recounts subsequent outpourings of the Holy Spirit, accompanied by phenomena like those of Pentecost, on at least three important occasions: in Samaria (Acts 8:17), on Cornelius the Roman centurion (10:44-46), and on some of the Ephesians (19:6-7). These three events in fact belong to five episodes of the gift of the Spirit (the others occur in 4:31 and 9:17, the call and conversion of Paul). But these three events invite considerable discussion be-

---

73. Frank D. Macchia, *Baptized in the Spirit: A Global Pentecostal Theology* (Grand Rapids: Zondervan, 2006), esp. pp. 19-60.

74. Macchia, *Baptized in the Spirit*, p. 30.

cause many (probably most New Testament specialists) regard them as "the three classic exceptions" to a Lukan norm, whereas many in the Pentecostal or Renewal tradition claim that such a view depends on critical presuppositions, and that these should be taken at their face value as norms in certain situations.

Some interpreters despair of accurate exegesis, and suggest that everything depends on the glasses through which we choose to read the text, whether these be Pentecostal or traditional. They invoke the well-known principle in hermeneutics of holding presuppositions or a "pre-understanding" which controls our exegesis. Such a theme is said to derive from Rudolf Bultmann.[75] But most of those specialists in hermeneutics who speak of preliminary understanding (or pre-understanding or presuppositions) also rightly appeal to the "Hermeneutical Circle" originated by Friedrich Schleiermacher and Martin Heidegger, whereby a to-and-fro between text and interpreter leads to a refinement and correction of "presuppositions" until good exegesis becomes possible. Bultmann and Hans-Georg Gadamer do not refuse to negotiate and revise "pre-understanding" in the light of the text. As I have urged elsewhere, the word "presuppositions" should be avoided as conveying a disastrous impression to those who do not wish to negotiate, under cover of a pretentious appeal to "hermeneutics." Pentecostals and radical critical scholars who do this are not alone; many in Liberation Theology mask a selective exegesis by the same means, as sometimes do traditionalists. We develop these points further in Chapter 6, the second chapter on Paul.

(1) We turn, first, to the *Samaritans,* where some find a difficulty not only with the Pentecost-like reception of the Holy Spirit but also with the connection between this gift and the laying on of hands (Acts 8:17). Frank Macchia declares, "The Samaritans are filled with the Holy Spirit at the laying on of hands by the representatives of the Jerusalem Church."[76] In the case of Cornelius, the Holy Spirit was not given by the laying on of hands, so Griffith Thomas observes, "It is essential to study all the instances."[77] In his earlier book on the Spirit, James Dunn calls this episode "The Riddle of Samaria," and for a long time "the chief stronghold of Pentecostal . . . and Catholic alike."[78] As it stands, it appears to contradict Rom. 8:9 and other Pauline passages, to the effect that being a Christian and receiving the Holy Spirit are the same. One is impossible without the other. Yet Luke seems to imply that there were those who had Christian faith who subsequently received the Holy Spirit. The Samaritans "had accepted the word of God" (Acts 8:14); but "as yet the

75. Rudolf Bultmann, "Is Exegesis without Presuppositions Possible?" in Rudolf Bultmann, *Existence and Faith: Shorter Writings* (London: Collins, Fontana ed., 1964), pp. 342-51.

76. Macchia, *Baptized in the Spirit,* p. 166.

77. W. H. Griffith Thomas, *The Holy Spirit of God* (London and New York: Longmans, Green, 1913), p. 276.

78. Dunn, *Baptism in the Holy Spirit,* pp. 55-72, and p. 35; cf. pp. 131-86.

Spirit had not come upon any of them; they had only been baptized in the name of the Lord Jesus" (8:16).

The complexity of this situation is shown by Dunn's discussion and dismissal of four or five views, which were designed to clarify the verses.[79] He then seems to favor Geoffrey Lampe's view that virtually everything hinges on the unique status of Samaria as "a turning-point in the missionary enterprise."[80] After all, Acts 1:8 has the Great Commission: "You shall be my witnesses in Jerusalem, in all Judea and Samaria, and to the ends of the earth." Many, therefore, see an epoch-making event, first in the case of Jews in the region of *Jerusalem;* second, in the case of Hellenized Jews *in Samaria;* and then, third, "to the ends of the earth," represented by the *Roman* centurion *Cornelius.* To be sure, after twenty centuries the event may seem difficult to explain: Dunn speaks of "the riddle of Samaria," Bruner calls this "the Samaritan puzzle," and Montague calls Acts 8:16 "the puzzling verse 16."[81] But a major key is the hostility between Jews and Samaritans, and the unexpected surprise is that they should receive the Holy Spirit too. The event needed confirmation, perhaps, by some physical, observable evidence, at least given Luke's cultural concern for the Hellenistic world.

The first five chapters of Acts recount the work of the Holy Spirit and of the earliest Christian community in Jerusalem. But in 6:1 we hear of Greek-speaking Jews (the "Hellenists") as a distinct group, for whom seven leaders with Greek names are appointed to supervise relations with the Aramaic-speaking Jewish widows with whom they are in conflict (Acts 6:1-6). Then 6:8–7:60 recounts Stephen's arrest and speech. Acts 8:1 recounts the crucial event of "severe persecution" that overtook the Christians. It had the profound effect that "those who were scattered" carried the gospel to Judea and Samaria (8:1, 4). Indeed, "Philip went down to the city of Samaria and proclaimed the Messiah to them" (8:5). Empowered by the Spirit, he both proclaimed the gospel and enacted "signs," including healings and exorcisms (8:6-9, 12-13).

The "puzzle" or "riddle" is that the Samaritans believed the gospel and were baptized, but "as yet the Spirit had not come upon any of them" (Acts 8:16). However, Acts makes it entirely clear that to avoid the danger of a fragmented Church, "When the apostles at Jerusalem heard that Samaria had accepted the word of God, they [corporately] sent Peter and John to them . . . that they might receive the Holy Spirit" (Acts 8:14-15). Some scholars adopt an anachronistic interpretation, and read back into the earliest era that Peter and John acted as bishops on behalf of the episcopal college of Jerusalem to administer "confirmation." But Dunn and the majority of scholars reject such an interpretation.

79. Dunn, *Baptism in the Holy Spirit,* pp. 56-62.

80. Dunn, *Baptism in the Holy Spirit,* p. 62; and Geoffrey W. H. Lampe, *The Seal of the Spirit: A Study of the Doctrine of Baptism and Confirmation in the New Testament and the Fathers* (New York and London: Longmans, Green, 1951), pp. 70-72.

81. Bruner, *A Theology of the Holy Spirit,* p. 175; Montague, *The Holy Spirit,* p. 292.

The visit of Peter and John and their laying on of hands in practice constituted a visible and tangible act displaying the *unity* of the one Church, and the *solidarity* of the Jerusalem apostles with Samaria. Macchia is broadly right, but makes the laying on of hands seem disproportionately important. In modern times we declare the four "marks" of the Church in the ecumenical creeds: the Church is "one, holy, Catholic, and apostolic." This act of Peter and John safeguarded the oneness, catholicity, and (many would argue) the visibly apostolic nature of the Church. Bruner rightly argues that Samaria was both a bridge to be crossed and a base to be occupied. It was a "bridge to be crossed, because Samaria represented the deepest of clefts; the racial-religious." It was "a base to be occupied, because the Church no longer resides in Jerusalem or among Jews alone, but becomes a mission."[82] This was the first step of advance beyond Judaism to the world.

(2) This step is confirmed when we turn to the *Cornelius episode* of Acts 11:15, 17. In both cases the faith status of those involved concerned *both* the word of God *and* the Holy Spirit. When he explains the Cornelius event to others, Peter says, "The Holy Spirit fell upon them just as it [he] had fallen on us at the beginning [i.e., at Pentecost]. . . . God gave them the same gift that he gave us" (11:15, 17).[83] Montague comments, "The aorist *pisteusai (epi)*, used here, always in Acts means the decisive act of faith, by which one becomes a Christian."[84] In this episode there is no mention of baptism or of the laying on of hands. The momentous event of the inclusion of the Gentiles, represented by Cornelius, may be seen as a milestone of "catching up" to what Christian Jews had experienced. It is crucial that each radical new step in the expansion of the Church to all the world is perceived as expressly initiated by the Holy Spirit as the Spirit of Jesus Christ. The Holy Spirit instructs Peter, virtually against his inclination or will (Acts 10:19; 11:12), and the Holy Spirit falls upon the Gentile converts while Peter is preaching (10:44). F. Dale Bruner notes that Peter refers to the "baptism of the Spirit" as he explains to the Church the events that occurred in Caesarea. But "it is not a doctrine which Acts teaches for the on-going church, since the phrase occurs only at the crisis initiations of the Jews and of the Gentiles into the church."[85] Acts constantly stresses that the source behind the admission of the Gentiles is God, to whom the Church gave glory (11:18).

Peter confirms this in his second account at the Council of Jerusalem in Acts 15. The cleansing, coming-to-faith, and gift of the Holy Spirit depict a single event. Only in some rabbinic literature is there any notion that the gift of

---

82. Bruner, *A Theology of the Holy Spirit*, p. 175.
83. Montague, *The Holy Spirit*, p. 293.
84. Montague, *The Holy Spirit*, p. 293.
85. Bruner, *A Theology of the Holy Spirit*, p. 195.

the Spirit *follows* what in Christian thinking he initiates. Lindsay Dewar described the Cornelius event as "plainly unique — a Gentile Pentecost."[86] The Pentecostal "reply" emerges further in Part III.

4.4. Paul's Reception of the Holy Spirit in Acts

The Holy Spirit in Acts brings about each new step in the Church's mission. As Montague reminds us, on the mission to the Gentiles, "Despite Peter's resistance (Acts 10:14), he is instructed by the Spirit to co-operate in this new direction. . . . The decision of the Antioch community to undertake the evangelization of Asia Minor was clearly the Spirit's initiative."[87] Acts 13:1-3 reads: "Now in the church at Antioch there were prophets and teachers. . . . While they were worshiping the Lord and fasting, the Holy Spirit said, 'Set apart for me Barnabas and Saul for the work to which I have called them.' Then after fasting and praying they laid their hands on them and sent them off." The Holy Spirit also on occasion told them where they should not go: "They went through the region of Phrygia and Galatia, having been forbidden by the Holy Spirit to speak the word in Asia" (Acts 16:6). On a second occasion they attempted to go to Bithynia, "but the Spirit of Jesus did not allow them" (Acts 16:7).

In the case of Paul's call, at first sight there appears to be an interval between Paul's encounter with the exalted Lord Jesus and the words and action of Ananias, "Brother Saul, the Lord Jesus, who appeared to you on your way here, has sent me so that you may regain your sight and be filled with the Holy Spirit" (Acts 9:17; cf. 9:4-7). Turner observes: "A traditional Pentecostal position (defended recently by Ervin) argues 9:17 must refer to Paul's 'baptism in the Spirit' because he is already fully converted either in the Damascus Road event itself (where he acknowledges Jesus as 'Lord,' 9:5) or at least immediately after it."[88] Turner replies that this is an "oversimplification," not least because *Kyrios* ranges between "Lord" and "sir" in Hellenistic Greek. It does not denote a Christological confession here. He agrees with Dunn that the Ananias experience "completes" the experience on the road to Damascus. Dunn insists: Paul "never speaks of his conversion as such; the resurrection appearance is never cited as the beginning of his Christian faith and life . . . the emphasis lies on the *commissioning*" (my italics).[89]

This does not entirely dismiss the Pentecostal interpretation, however, for

86. Dewar, *The Holy Spirit and Modern Thought*, p. 54.
87. Montague, *The Holy Spirit*, p. 295.
88. Turner, *Power from on High*, p. 375; H. M. Ervin, *Conversion-Initiation and Baptism in the Holy Spirit: A Critique of James D. G. Dunn, "Baptism in the Holy Spirit"* (Peabody: Hendrickson, 1987), pp. 73-78.
89. Dunn, *Jesus and the Spirit*, p. 110.

Robert Menzies also sees Acts 9:13-17 as a commissioning account.[90] He and Turner both see the experience as one of empowerment, especially for mission, or as the empowering presence of God, to use Fee's term. This may be argued on the basis of such Old Testament passages as Isa. 22:4-16; 26:12-18. Turner, however, still speaks of "the general account of this whole conversion-and-calling process."[91] The laying on of hands, he argues, concerns chiefly the *healing* of Paul's blindness alone. Moreover, "*filled* with the Spirit" seems to mean more than conversion alone, but here "power to fulfil the commission he has just received as Christ's witness."[92] We may compare this with Swete's comment, "While all believers, whether Jews or Gentiles, received the Spirit, some received him as the Spirit of prophecy and 'prophesied.'"[93]

Silas, Agabus, some from the church at Antioch, and some from Ephesus (Acts 19:6) provide example of prophets. Prophets, as Swete argues, were held in high esteem, second in rank only to apostles. But whether "prophecy" *always* meant messages from *within* a congregation rather than applied apostolic or ministerial preaching is not entirely clear. No doubt it could include this, but that it cannot involve more is often assumed rather than argued with evidence. Certainly Paul was a prophet; yet he communicated the gospel most often by rational reflective argument, as Günther Bornkamm explains, and not by a prophetic "Thus says the Lord."[94] His status as a prophet is discussed by K. O. Sandnes.[95] Further detailed arguments to this effect have been put forward by Ulrich Müller, David Hill, Helmut Merklein, and Thomas Gillespie, although they refer mainly to Paul's epistles rather than to Acts.[96]

Gillespie is largely confined to 1 Corinthians, and Merklein to Paul, while Müller argues that prophecy is *preaching the gospel,* either for judgment or for salvation, with special reference to Revelation 1–3. Nevertheless Hill urges regarding Acts: "Although in the book of Acts prophecy, as an eschatological power of the Spirit, is a possibility for any Christian — else what would the ful-

90. Menzies, *Development of Early Christian Pneumatology,* pp. 260-63.

91. Turner, *Power from on High,* p. 376.

92. Turner, *Power from on High,* p. 378.

93. Swete, *The Holy Spirit in the New Testament,* p. 99.

94. Günther Bornkamm, *Early Christian Experience* (London: SCM, 1969), pp. 30-35; cf. pp. 29-46.

95. K. O. Sandnes, *Paul — One of the Prophets? A Contribution to the Apostle's Self-Understanding,* WUNT 2.43 (Tübingen: Mohr, 1991).

96. David Hill, *New Testament Prophecy* (London: Marshall, 1979), esp. pp. 110-40 and 193-213; Hill, "Christian Prophets as Teachers or Instructors in the Church," in *Prophetic Vocation in the New Testament and Today,* ed. J. Panagopoulos (Leiden: Brill, 1977), pp. 108-30; Ulrich B. Müller, *Prophetie und Predigt im Neuen Testament* (Gütersloh: Mohn, 1975); Helmut Merklein, "Der Theologe als Prophet: Zur Funktion prophetischen Redens im theologischen Diskurs des Paulus," *NTS* 38 (1992): 402-29; and Thomas W. Gillespie, *The First Theologians: A Study in Early Christian Prophecy* (Grand Rapids: Eerdmans, 1994).

filment of Joel's promise mean? — it is mainly associated with certain leaders who exercise the gift as a ministry in the Church."[97] He considers the groups from Antioch, from Ephesus, Agabus, Barnabas, and Paul, concluding that prediction was certainly not their main function, but the characteristics of applied pastoral preaching. He cites Earle Ellis as arguing that exposition of Scripture was an important part of their ministry. J. W. Doeve also argues for the genuineness of a sermon in Acts 13:1. The modern charismatic Renewal or Renewal claims are, as Zwiep argued about Spirit-baptism, *more individualistic* and less corporate than Acts or the New Testament implies.

An additional key problem now arises. Many in the Renewal Movement often seem to imply that the Holy Spirit does not *inspire* people through ordinary processes of *reflection* and *reason*. This seriously devalues the arguments of Paul's epistles and his sermon at Thessalonica (Acts 17:1-9), which includes "arguing" and "persuasion" (17:2 and 4) but also implies a dualism of divine action. Wolfhart Pannenberg asserts: "If . . . the preacher desires to convince his audience [by] power of judgment, then the Holy Spirit becomes effective through his words and arguments. Argumentation and the operation of the Spirit are not in competition with each other. *In trusting in the Spirit, Paul in no way spared himself thinking and arguing*" (my italics).[98]

As the mission in Acts proceeds, further moments of decision and opportunity require the guidance of the Holy Spirit. Acts 15:28 provides a further example: "It seemed good to the Holy Spirit and to us . . . ," with reference to the epoch-making Council of Jerusalem. In the third account of Paul's call (Acts 26:16-18) Paul alludes to God's call to serve "as a witness . . . to open the eyes of those to whom I am sending you, to turn them from darkness to light." Montague sees the background to this in Isa. 42:7, which recalls the call of prophets: "In Luke's eyes, then, Paul is a prophet."[99] However, Montague goes further. Jer. 1:7-8 recalls the call of Jeremiah; Isa. 42:1-4 suggests the mission to Gentiles; Isa. 61:1-2 is applied by Luke to Jesus. In Acts Luke applies it to Paul, and Paul's ministry and call reflect the mission of Jesus, who was seen as the preeminent prophet. Paul's willingness to face death in Jerusalem, where he is chained (Acts 21:33), where his life is endangered (Acts 21:30-36), and where he is brought before the high priest (Acts 22:30), follows the pattern of the passion of Jesus. It is only because of the earlier commission to reach "the ends of the earth" (Acts 1:8) that Rome, rather than Jerusalem, provides the climax of Acts and the goal of the Holy Spirit's plan for the Church. In Turner's words, the Holy Spirit is *"the driving force within Lucan salvation history"* (his italics).[100]

---

97. Hill, "Christian Prophets as Teachers," in *Prophetic Vocation*, ed. J. Panagopoulos, p. 124.
98. Wolfhart Pannenberg, *Basic Questions in Theology*, vol. 2 (London: SCM, 1971), p. 35.
99. Montague, *The Holy Spirit*, p. 298.
100. Turner, *The Holy Spirit and Spiritual Gifts*, p. 37.

As a postscript to Acts, we may ask a question which concerns many today, but which Luke does not seem to answer clearly. In Hull's words, can we reach a conclusion about "the preconditions necessary for the gift of the Holy Spirit"? Hull concludes that any theory "must be of a tentative nature," especially since the role of the laying on of hands remains controversial.[101] Mark Cartledge's description of "Third Wave" Renewal Ministry as *"inviting"* the Holy Spirit to fall upon a congregation may perhaps seem surprising and a little inappropriate when we compare this with the Acts narratives. Luther reminds us that nothing should undermine the purity of sheer grace, as any attempt to manipulate the coming and presence of the Holy Spirit might do among those to whom he has come. Luther has in mind particularly some of the medieval mystics and Radical Reformers. It is customary to avoid reading Luke through the lenses of Paul. This is right. But we may doubt, especially if "Luke" was the traveling companion of Paul, whether he substantially differed from Paul in his view of the primacy of grace, not least because it was also the teaching of Jesus.

101. Hull, *The Holy Spirit in Acts*, p. 101.

5

Key Themes in Paul

5.1. Eight Basic Themes in the Epistles of Paul

(1) The work of the Holy Spirit is *Christ-centered*. Paul exclaims: "No one can say 'Jesus is Lord' except by the Holy Spirit" (1 Cor. 12:3). "God has sent the Spirit of his Son into our hearts, crying, 'Abba! Father!'" (Gal. 4:6). This is the word that Jesus had used. Admittedly this is even clearer in John, where he explicitly states: "He [the Spirit] will not speak on his own *(aph' heautou)*. . . . He will glorify me" (John 16:13-14). Without commenting yet in more detail on distinctions between the Persons of Christ and the Holy Spirit, who are also distinct, James D. G. Dunn concludes that in the light of Rom. 8:9-11, 1 Cor. 12:4-6, and other passages, "Paul's experience of Christ and the Spirit were one, and . . . Christ was experienced through the Spirit."[1] D. E. H. Whiteley calls the Holy Spirit "the hallmark of the Christian."[2]

Although some Pentecostals and adherents of the Renewal Movement have been accused of being Spirit-centered, the more thoughtful emphatically reject this. In the words of Gordon Fee, perhaps the most scholarly of Pentecostals: "The Spirit is none other than the Spirit of Christ."[3] The Pentecostal writer Frank Macchia writes: "The Spirit . . . binds us to Christ through the proclaimed gospel."[4] Even the gifts of the Spirit are not ends in themselves, but point beyond themselves to Christ and to the common good of the Church.

---

1. James D. G. Dunn, *Baptism in the Holy Spirit: A Re-examination of the New Testament Teaching on the Gift of the Spirit in Relation to Pentecostalism Today* (London: SCM, 1970), p. 148.

2. D. E. H. Whiteley, *The Theology of St. Paul* (Oxford: Blackwell, 1964; 2nd ed. 1971), p. 124.

3. Gordon D. Fee, *God's Empowering Presence: The Holy Spirit in the Letters of Paul* (Milton Keynes: Paternoster, 1995, and Peabody, MA: Hendrickson, 1994), p. 545.

4. Frank D. Macchia, *Baptized in the Spirit: A Global Pentecostal Theology* (Grand Rapids: Zondervan, 2006), p. 72.

Karl Barth observes in this context: "What we are really concerned with is not phenomena in themselves, but with their whence? And whither? To what do they point?"[5]

(2) Paul is emphatic that *every Christian* receives the Holy Spirit, whether or not the believer concerned "deserves" the Spirit. This, as we saw in Chapter 2 on Judaism, stands in opposition to Rabbinic Judaism. Many argue that it also stands in contrast to the implications of the Radical Reformers and to certain "Holiness" movements, both of which we examine in Part II. Paul asserts, "Because you are children, God sent the Spirit of his Son into our hearts, crying, 'Abba! Father!'" (Gal. 4:6). Paul also expresses this in negative terms: "Anyone who does not have the Spirit of Christ does not belong to him" (Rom. 8:9). Many Pentecostals today accept that this is Paul's view, even if a number dissent that it is found in Luke-Acts. Dunn argues that this verse rules out the possibility *both* of a non-Christian's possessing the Spirit *and* of a Christian's *not* possessing the Spirit.[6] Again, while some in the Holiness and Pentecostal Movements may still dispute this, toward the end of this section we cite some insightful comments of Fee, Macchia, Amos Yong, and Veli-Matti Kärkkäinen in reply to this.

(3) The third main point in Paul is that, as in the Old Testament, the Holy Spirit constitutes *both* a special gift given to *a chosen individual* to perform particular tasks, and a gift poured out either over the *community of all God's people,* or within the framework of God's purposes for the *whole community.* These two features coexist and overlap in Paul. On the one hand, the Spirit allots his gifts "to each one individually, just as the Spirit chooses" (1 Cor. 12:11); on the other hand, these gifts are "for the common good" (12:7). Albert Schweitzer defines the Spirit as "the life principle of his [Christ's] personality, which Christ then shares with all his people who are 'in Christ.'"[7] The Holy Spirit constitutes the *basis* of union with Christ. However, Floyd Filson comments rightly, "*It is likewise true that chosen individuals are given the Spirit for special tasks. But this does not mean that some are left without the Spirit. Each is given the Spirit"* (my italics).[8] The Old Testament scheme is still relevant in the New Testament.

(4) A fourth main point concerns the Holy Spirit as Agent of the *resurrection,* and the timing of the gift of the Holy Spirit. Paul nowhere suggests that the Spirit was not active before Pentecost. Nevertheless he shares with pre-Pauline apostolic testimony (including Peter's) that the Holy Spirit is given in a fresh way after the "eschatological" turning point of the last days, ushered in by Christ's resurrection.[9] When "God through the Holy Spirit raised Jesus from

5. Karl Barth, *The Resurrection of the Dead* (London: Hodder & Stoughton, 1933), p. 80.

6. Dunn, *Baptism in the Holy Spirit,* p. 95.

7. Albert Schweitzer, *The Mysticism of Paul the Apostle* (London: Black, 1931), p. 165.

8. Floyd V. Filson, *The New Testament against the Environment* (London: SCM, 1950), p. 78.

9. Anders Eriksson, *Traditions as Rhetorical Proof: Pauline Argumentation in 1 Corinthians* (Stockholm: Almqvist & Wiksell, 1998), pp. 74-80 and 217-22.

the dead" (Rom. 8:11), this constituted *a cosmic act,* which created *a new era.* It fulfilled Old Testament promises concerning "the last days." W. D. Davies believes that this is so important that he writes, "The Pauline doctrine of the Spirit, then, is only fully comprehensible in the light of Rabbinic expectations of the Age to Come as an Age of the Spirit and of the Community of the Spirit."[10]

(5) Fifth, the *preaching of the gospel* is thus "more than human." In the earliest document of the New Testament, Paul declares in 1 Thess. 1:5: "The gospel came to you not in word only, but also in power and in the Holy Spirit and with full conviction." He exhorts the Thessalonians in 1 Thess. 5:19: "Do not quench the Spirit." We might be tempted to call this "supernatural," for it is *more than* natural. But there are certain problems with this word, as we shall see in due course. The Pauline doctrine of the Holy Spirit is fundamentally Christ-centered or derived from Christ; communal as well as individual; and eschatological, or associated with the resurrection of Christ and the New Age, or the more than natural. Friedrich Horn also places special emphasis on 1 Thess. 4:1-10, 5:19, and 5:23 for Paul's earliest assertions about the Holy Spirit.[11] He separates the early teaching in 1 Thessalonians on sanctification and prophecy from the middle and later Paul, seeing later developments as entirely due to "enthusiasm" at Corinth and to controversy about "Judaizing" and the Law. Hence the developments in 1 Corinthians, Galatians, and Romans become mainly reactive and circumstantial.[12] But such a hard-and-fast chronological development in Paul and even Horn's dating of Galatians remain open to question, as we argue in Part III of this book.

(6) Sixth, the Spirit is "Holy" most of all in the sense that, in Gordon Fee's words, the Holy Spirit brings the *power and presence of God himself.*[13] This entails an emphasis on the *otherness* or *transcendence* of God, and on the *more-than-natural* character of his action through the Holy Spirit. In the Old Testament Joel explicitly saw the pouring out of the Spirit on "all flesh" (or in Luke, as often in the LXX, "all kinds of flesh") as a predicted event of the last days (Joel 2:28-29). Paul expresses this transcendence in his distancing the Spirit from "the spirit of the world" in 1 Cor. 2:12, where by contrast the Holy Spirit proceeds from God (Greek, *to pneuma to tou ek theou*).

J. E. Fison relates this aspect to the *holiness* of the Spirit. He comments, "*Qōdeš* [holy] is something . . . reserved to . . . the living God of the Hebrews. . . . A parallel term is *ḥērem,* which is something . . . reserved for Yahweh [Jehovah]. . . . The flesh stands for this world, the natural world of man; and

10. W. D. Davies, *Paul and Rabbinic Judaism* (London: SPCK, 2nd ed. 1955), p. 217.

11. Friedrich W. Horn, *Das Angeld des Geistes: Studien zur paulinischen Pneumatologie* (Göttingen: Vandenhoeck & Ruprecht, 1992), pp. 121-60.

12. Horn, *Das Angeld des Geistes,* pp. 160-274.

13. Fee, *God's Empowering Presence,* pp. 5-9.

with this is contrasted the other world . . . of which the spirit is the token."[14] Without this emphasis, Fison urges, we can suffer from "an over-emphasis upon the morality of God and an under-emphasis upon his mystery, . . . rendering him . . . innocuous, but also . . . impotent."[15] We have avoided the term "supernatural," not because we doubt the point which often lies behind the word, but because, as we stated in Chapter 4, it often implies a dualistic understanding of the world sometimes characteristic of the Enlightenment, which ironically those who use it often seek to avoid. "More-than-natural" denotes that for which explanations reach beyond an empirical causal chain.

(7) The *eschatological* dimension also articulates the sense of *futurity and purpose.* The Holy Spirit transforms us into our future destiny; into that which God destines us to become. In the present life Christians enjoy the "firstfruits" of the Holy Spirit, or that of which more is to come (Rom. 8:22-23). Paul speaks of God's "giving us his Spirit in our hearts as a first installment" (2 Cor. 1:22; Greek, *dous ton arrabōna tou pnematos*). In the last few years Friedrich Horn, Gordon Fee, and Finny Philip have all drawn attention to this aspect.[16] Philip calls attention to Old Testament material in Ezek. 36:26-27; 37:1-14; Isa. 32:9-20; 44:1-5; and Joel 3:1-2, and in Intertestamental writings to *Jubilees, 4 Ezra,* and Qumran.

Frederick Danker translates *arrabōn* as *"payment of part of a purchase price in advance; first instalment, deposit, down payment, pledge."*[17] The KJV/AV has "earnest of the Spirit." In Rom. 8:23 Paul exclaims, "We ourselves, who have the first fruits of the Spirit, groan inwardly while we wait for adoption, the redemption of our bodies." This time the Greek word is *tēn aparchēn tou pneumatos.* Danker translates this as *"first fruits, first portion"* of any kind.[18] It is a pledge of more of the same quality or kind to come. The word *arrabōn* is also used in 2 Cor. 5:5: God "has given us the Spirit as a *guarantee.*" In this eighth chapter of Romans, Paul relates the gift of the Holy Spirit to the future reward of creation (Rom. 8:21). Hermann Gunkel and Neill Hamilton are among the many who emphasize this aspect.[19] Hamilton urges, "The centre of gravity lies in the future. . . . 'He who sows to the Spirit will of the Holy Spirit reap eternal life'" (Gal. 6:8).[20]

(8) Finally, the Holy Spirit has been seen in the Old Testament and Judaism

---

14. J. E. Fison, *The Blessing of the Holy Spirit* (London and New York: Longmans, Green, 1950), pp. 43 and 44.

15. Fison, *The Blessing of the Holy Spirit,* p. 47.

16. Horn, *Das Angeld des Geistes,* pp. 385-87; Fee, *God's Empowering Presence,* pp. 287-96 and 572-75; and Finny Philip, *The Origins of Pauline Pneumatology: The Eschatological Bestowal of the Spirit,* WUNT 2.194 (Tübingen: Mohr, 2005), pp. 18-20 and 164-225.

17. Danker, in BDAG, 3rd ed., p. 134.

18. Danker, BDAG, p. 98.

19. Hermann Gunkel, *The Influence of the Holy Spirit* (Minneapolis: Fortress, 2008), p. 82; and Neill Q. Hamilton, *The Holy Spirit and Eschatology in Paul,* Scottish Journal of Theology Occasional Paper 6 (Edinburgh: Oliver & Boyd, 1957), pp. 19-21.

20. Hamilton, *The Holy Spirit and Eschatology in Paul,* p. 19.

as *prophetic* and *revelatory*. Paul appropriates these themes, although we discussed in the last chapter on Acts the more-than-popular scope of the word "prophetic" in the New Testament. The prophetic is part of the revelatory role of the Holy Spirit. We need not repeat our previous arguments to the effect that David Hill, Ulrich Müller, Helmut Merklein, and Thomas Gillespie argue for a broader concept of prophecy, which includes applied preaching, even if it also includes more spontaneous revelations. Paul himself, we noted, was a prophet, who frequently used reflection and argument rather than oracular utterance. Together with the Old Testament, the Intertestamental literature, Jesus, and the apostolic witness, Paul saw the Holy Spirit as also Inspirer of the Scriptures, and as having a clear revelatory function (1 Cor. 2:6-16). The difference from the Jewish writing is the Christocentric conclusion: "we have the mind of *Christ*" (1 Cor. 2:16).

Apart from its Christ-centered application, much of Paul's language, as we noted, reflected Old Testament and Rabbinic Judaism. He writes, "Among the mature we do speak wisdom, . . . God's wisdom. . . . These things God has revealed to us through the Spirit. . . . For . . . no one comprehends what is truly God's, except the Spirit of God" (1 Cor. 2:6, 10, 11). Then in the last verse of chapter 2, Paul distinctly defines the wisdom and revelation of the Spirit as "the mind of Christ," in contrast to claims to hear or to possess the Spirit which are not focused on Christ and do not reflect the mind-set of Christ.

In selecting the above eight themes as "basic" or as "main points" in Paul, we may be accused of making a subjective judgment, although in broad terms they can be found also in the first three Gospels, in John, and in Acts. The Christ of John, as we shall note, asserts, "He [the Paraclete or Holy Spirit] will glorify me, because he will take what is mine, and show it to you" (John 16:13-14). "He [Christ] will baptize you with the Holy Spirit. . . . The Spirit descended . . . on him" (Mark 1:8, 10). In Luke: "The Spirit is upon me because he has anointed me to bring good news to the poor . . ." (Luke 4:18; Isa. 61:1). Peter, inspired by the Spirit, preached Jesus (Acts 2:17, 22-28, 30-33, 38). The Holy Spirit is *Christ-centered*. In the early years of the twentieth century some Pentecostals might be accused of being "Spirit centered," but most Pentecostals now seek to redress this imbalance. Whether it remains a problem for some "Third Wave" adherents of the Renewal Movement remains a pertinent question.

The only other theme over which any dispute could arise concerns the second, that every Christian receives the Spirit, for without the Spirit the believer would never become united with Christ (Rom. 8:9; 1 Cor. 12:3). Many Pentecostals follow Gordon Fee, Frank Macchia, Amos Yong, and Veli-Matti Kärkkäinen in adopting a "Christocentric" rather than "Holiness Movement" approach. Fee describes the Holy Spirit as "the identity marker of the converted."[21] Macchia

---

21. Gordon D. Fee, *Paul, the Spirit, and the People of God* (Peabody: Hendrickson, 1996), p. 88.

writes, "The problem is that the revivalist influence on the Holiness Movement caused it to transform John Wesley's more process-oriented understanding of sanctification into a high-voltage crisis experience . . . as . . . a renewal for worldly or lazy Christians."[22] Amos Yong attempts to deobjectify Christian encounter with the Holy Spirit within a Trinitarian frame, appealing to Rom. 8:9 and to N. Q. Hamilton.[23] Kärkkäinen declares: "Paul's pneumatology is christologically founded . . . (Rom. 8:9; Gal. 4:6. . . . It is only through the Spirit that the believer is able to confess that 'Jesus is Lord' (1 Cor. 12:1-3). . . . It is the gift of the Spirit that makes one a Christian (Rom. 8:9)."[24] All four are leading Pentecostals. Although Yong may currently be no longer explicitly such, he retains the respect of Pentecostals and has close relations with them.

It is hardly necessary to find examples of the Holy Spirit being *more than natural* or *beyond nature* in the two Testaments. C. H. Powell comments, "[The Spirit] does not belong to him whose native sphere is that of *bāśār* (flesh)."[25] Other features and themes, that of future orientation, the New Age, and eschatology, are everywhere apparent. Oscar Cullmann writes of the whole New Testament witness, "The Holy Spirit is nothing else than the anticipation of the end in the present."[26] Fison expressed the converse of the same point: "The Holy Spirit is the key to the Christian doctrine of the End."[27] Finally, the Spirit is universally regarded as the source of inspiration, revelation, and wisdom, both in the Old Testament, Judaism, and the rest of the New Testament.

Various themes in Paul require further discussion or expansion. A partial ambiguity marks some of Paul's language about the Spirit; we need to inquire further about the Spirit's relation to Christ; we need to explore the "gifts" of the Spirit, including "the utterance of knowledge," "the utterance of wisdom" (NRSV translation), faith, gifts of healing, "the working of miracles" (NRSV translation), and other gifts in 1 Cor. 12:8-10, as well as those listed in 1 Cor. 12:28-30, which include teachers and "forms of assistance" (NRSV), and Eph. 4:11. In the next chapter we shall consider more controversial issues such as tongues-speech and the personhood of the Holy Spirit.

22. Macchia, *Baptized in the Spirit,* pp. 30-31.

23. Amos Yong, *Spirit–Word–Community: Theological Hermeneutics in Trinitarian Perspective* (Aldershot, Hants, U.K., and Burlington, VT: Ashgate, 2002), p. 227.

24. Veli-Matti Kärkkäinen, *Pneumatology: The Holy Spirit in Ecumenical, International, and Contextual Perspective* (Grand Rapids: Baker Academic, 2002), p. 32.

25. Cyril N. Powell, *The Biblical Concept of Power* (London: Epworth, 1993), p. 26.

26. Oscar Cullmann, *Christ and Time: The Primitive Christian Conception of Time and History* (London: SCM, 1951), p. 72.

27. Fison, *The Blessing of the Holy Spirit,* p. 4.

5.2. Ambiguities of Language in Paul about the Divine and Human Spirit

"Spirit" possesses a wide range of meanings, especially as we take into account those from Stoicism and Judaism with which Paul's converts might already have become familiar.[28] We stated at the beginning that we would spell "Spirit" with a capital *S* when the word denoted the Spirit of God, and a lowercase *s* when the term denoted the spirit in humankind, in spite of the NRSV's consistently using a lowercase *s* for most uses of "spirit" or "Spirit." In Greek we cannot trace a difference. Uncial manuscripts are wholly in capitals, while minuscule manuscripts generally use lowercase letters only, except for later editions. This gives rise to a variety of English translations.

One such example is Rom. 12:11, in which the Greek is *tō pneumati zeontes*. The KJV/AV translates this "be fervent in spirit"; the RSV has "be aglow with the Spirit"; the NRSV returns to "be ardent in spirit"; the New Jerusalem Bible has "an eager spirit." Both uses, we saw, are evident in the Old Testament. A similar difference occurs in Rom. 1:4, where the NRSV has "according to the spirit of holiness"; the New Jerusalem Bible, I think rightly, has "in terms of the Spirit and of holiness"; and the KJV/AV has "according to the spirit of holiness." In 2 Cor. 4:13, the traditional versions read "spirit of faith." P. E. Hughes interprets it as "spirit of faith," on analogy with "spirit of gentleness" in 1 Cor. 4:21; but Victor Furnish comments, "It is preferable . . . to read this as a reference to the [Holy] Spirit with whom faith comes."[29]

Paul often refers to the human spirit, but this is not the *primary* reference of *pneuma*. One of the most abused passages is his reference in 1 Thess. 5:23 to "body, soul, and spirit." Paul prays that God may make the readers holy "through and through." Many nineteenth-century exegetes, and many in earlier centuries, debated whether this constituted an example of "trichotomy," the division of the human person into three "parts": body, soul, and spirit.[30] Origen extended this verse to denote the "bodily" or historical significance of a text (or person); the "moral" meaning, corresponding to the soul; and a "spiritual" meaning, corresponding to the spirit.[31] But the verse means simply: "May God sanctify you through and through" or "wholly," as most commentators recognize. Tertullian calls this "the entire substance of man" (Tertullian, *On the Resurrection of the Flesh*, 47). John Calvin speaks of the "whole" per-

28. R. Birch Hoyle, *The Holy Spirit in St. Paul* (London: Hodder & Stoughton, 1927), pp. 175-274.

29. Victor P. Furnish, *2 Corinthians*, The Anchor Bible (New York and London: Doubleday, 1984), p. 258.

30. Anthony C. Thiselton, *1 and 2 Thessalonians Through the Centuries*, Blackwell's Bible Commentaries (Oxford: Wiley-Blackwell, 2011), pp. 162-75.

31. Origen, *First Principles* 4.1.21 (*ANF*, vol. 4, p. 370).

son.[32] It is the same kind of use as "My soul magnifies the Lord, and my spirit rejoices in God my Savior" (Luke 1:46-47), which denotes the whole self, as when we say, "Put your heart and soul into it!"

The allusion in 2 Thess. 2:2 not to be alarmed "either by spirit or by word or by letter" (NRSV) is also capable of more than one interpretation. Most commentators refer "spirit" to "an ecstatic utterance or spiritual revelation," as Ernest Best does.[33] But does this mean "inspired by the Spirit"? Or since *pneuma* has no definite article, does this anarthrous form suggest "a lying spirit," or even a heightened human spirit? 1 Cor. 5:3, "absent in body . . . present in spirit," is also perhaps ambiguous. It probably means "human spirit" in contrast to the physical limitations of location, but it might well mean "made present with the church" by the action of the Holy Spirit. From the nineteenth century to the late 1950s it was almost unanimously taken to mean "in spirit" in a non-bodily sense. Today many, if not most, take it to refer to the Holy Spirit. I have discussed this in detail elsewhere.[34]

It is possible that 1 Cor. 14:14-15 has some ambiguity. Probably "my spirit prays" (v. 14) could be anthropological: the human spirit. But the parallel, "I will pray with the spirit" (v. 15), may refer either to the human spirit or to the Holy Spirit. It may mean: "my deepest spiritual being" *(tō pneumati)*, repeated twice; but Paul may mean that even the work of the Holy Spirit involves, rather than excludes, the use of intelligence, or the mind. Again, elsewhere I offer three pages of discussion.[35] Similarly 1 Cor. 14:32, "The spirits of the prophets are subject to the prophets" (NIV, "to the control of the prophets"), is probably a reference to the human spirit, but it is not out of the question that Paul speaks with their language, as if to say: "Inspiration by the Spirit" does not give you carte blanche to speak forever!

On the whole Romans and Galatians usually speak about the Holy Spirit with less ambiguity (except for Rom. 12:11, discussed above), but Col. 2:5 is parallel to 1 Cor. 5:3: "absent in body, . . . I am with you in spirit." If Ephesians is Pauline, it is like Romans and Galatians. The NRSV, however, suggests an ambiguity in 1 Tim. 3:16: "revealed in flesh, vindicated in spirit." Yet when we compare Rom. 1:4, it becomes apparent that for Paul, whatever the "flesh" may suggest, the Holy Spirit vindicates Jesus Christ by raising him from the dead as Son of God. "Spirit of power and love" in 2 Tim. 1:7 could refer to a human disposi-

---

32. John Calvin, *1 and 2 Thessalonians* (Wheaton, IL, and Nottingham, U.K.: Crossway, 1999), p. 63.

33. Ernest Best, *The First and Second Epistles to the Thessalonians* (London: Black, 1972), p. 279; Earl J. Richard, *First and Second Thessalonians*, Sacra Pagina (Collegeville, MN: Glazier, 1995), pp. 324-25.

34. Anthony C. Thiselton, *The First Epistle to the Corinthians: A Commentary on the Greek Text*, NIGTC (Grand Rapids: Eerdmans, 2000), pp. 390-92.

35. Thiselton, *The First Epistle to the Corinthians*, pp. 1111-13.

tion, especially in parallel to "spirit of cowardice," but the context refers to "the laying on of my hands," so it might refer to the Holy Spirit.

At all events, little that is absolutely crucial depends on these interpretations. That is why we called them "partial or marginal ambiguities." No doubt Paul often uses *pneuma* to refer to the human spirit or to a human disposition. But his primary concern is with the action of the Holy Spirit, and these "ambiguities" simply require care and caution.

5.3. Further Detailed Discussion on the Holy Spirit and Christ

A high proportion of passages in Paul show that the work of the Holy Spirit remains above all Christ-centered. (This becomes even clearer in John, as we noted.) Such is the Spirit's concern to throw the spotlight onto Jesus Christ, or to glorify Christ, that Fison calls the Holy Spirit "self-effacing." He asserts this at least eleven times.[36] The primary thrust is that the Spirit points not at himself, but at Christ. We may well be suspicious of "Spirit-centered" movements. A second point, shared with Karl Barth, is that sometimes prominent "media" of the Spirit or "experience" of the Spirit may reduce us into confusing the Holy Spirit himself with noisy claims about the Spirit. This could become an idolatrous confession.[37] We noted Karl Barth's comment about the goal of gifts of the Spirit in 1 Corinthians 12–14. Third, Fison argues, if we identify the Holy Spirit with external phenomena or media, we shall not only replace the Holy Spirit's "self-effacement" with "self-advertisement" but also be reduced into assuming that the Spirit is a "quasi-material external fluid substance," or force, rather than a Person.[38] "His testimony will always be a self-effacing witness to Jesus Christ."[39]

In Stoicism and in Greek thought the reverse was the case. R. B. Hoyle insists that in these circles, the word (spirit) was heard on every side.[40] Thus Paul is at pains to reduce the scope of the term "Spirit" to the life of those who are "in Christ," rather than see it as a general and sweeping term for "spirituality" and "spiritual," as if the term meant "relating to human religious aspiration," as it is often used (following the Greek sense) today. Hoyle declares: "In Paul's usage it is always God who gives or imparts it [him]."[41] Thus in one direction Paul asserts that the Holy Spirit is the basis of union with Christ, or of being Christian. He declares, "No one can say 'Jesus is Lord' except by the Holy Spirit"

---

36. Fison, *The Blessing of the Holy Spirit*, pp. 11, 22, 27, 72, 93, 107, 138, 140, 175, 177, and 199.
37. Fison, *The Blessing of the Holy Spirit*, p. 22.
38. Fison, *The Blessing of the Holy Spirit*, p. 72.
39. Fison, *The Blessing of the Holy Spirit*, p. 93.
40. Hoyle, *The Holy Spirit in St. Paul*, pp. 180-85; cf. also pp. 175-85 and 199-297.
41. Hoyle, *The Holy Spirit in St. Paul*, p. 182.

(1 Cor. 12:3). Yet, conversely, Christians derive their share of the Holy Spirit from "being in Christ." Paul writes: "You have received a spirit [NRSV; better, "the Spirit"] of adoption. When we cry, 'Abba! Father!' [the word Jesus used], it is that very Spirit bearing witness . . . that we are children of God, . . . joint-heirs with Christ" (Rom. 8:15-17). Similarly, in Galatians Paul explicitly states, "Because you are children, God has sent the Spirit of his Son into our hearts, crying 'Abba! Father!'" (Gal. 4:6). Paul would hardly have used the Aramaic *Abba* when addressing a Greek-speaking audience, unless it was to make the point that through the "Spirit of his Son" Christians take the attitude of Christ to God.

One of the most discussed texts in Paul which seems to identify Christ with the Spirit is 2 Cor. 3:17: "Now the Lord is the Spirit." No modern New Testament specialist thinks that the verb "is" denotes absolute *identification*. Paul is *not* saying that Christ and the Holy Spirit are the same person. Possibly a few of the Greek Fathers may have implied this, but *Paul is not speaking of identity or ontology.* Too many passages treat Christ and the Holy Spirit as *two distinct persons* for this to be possible. For example, "The Spirit bear[s] witness . . . that we are children of God, . . . joint-heirs with Christ" (Rom. 8:16-17). Most modern scholars follow George Hendry and Vincent Taylor in calling "is" an *exegetical "is,"* equivalent to *significat* or "denotes."[42] "Lord," Hendry explains, refers to the "Lord" of the preceding sentence (2 Cor. 3:16), which is clearly an echo of Exod. 34:34. Thus, as Vincent Taylor also asserts, it means: "Now *kyrios in the passage I have just quoted* denotes the Spirit, and where the Spirit of the Lord is, there is liberty."[43] After discussing alternatives, Jürgen Moltmann and James Dunn reach the same conclusion.[44]

H. P. van Dusen insists that the explicit and indissoluble link between the Holy Spirit and Christ constitutes "the most original contribution of Paul to the Christian conception of the Holy Spirit, if not to the Christian faith in its entirety."[45] Van Dusen may exaggerate the uniqueness of this emphasis, for John's Gospel undoubtedly also stresses it. But in the sense that Paul is probably the first to make it so explicit, this comment has its place.

One of the most emphatic passages comes in 1 Cor. 2:4-15. There Paul portrays the Holy Spirit as empowering the preaching of the gospel (v. 4), and the source of Christian wisdom (vv. 6-7) and revelation (vv. 10-11). This Holy Spirit communicates the very mind of God (vv. 12-14), and is not to be confused with

---

42. George S. Hendry, *The Holy Spirit in Christian Theology* (London: SCM, 1966), p. 24.

43. Vincent Taylor, *The Person of Christ in New Testament Teaching* (London: Macmillan, 1958), p. 54.

44. Jürgen Moltmann, *The Spirit of Life: A Universal Affirmation* (London: SCM, 1992), pp. 101-2; James D. G. Dunn, *The Theology of Paul the Apostle* (Edinburgh: T&T Clark, 1998), pp. 421-22.

45. Henry P. Van Dusen, *Spirit, Son and Father* (New York: Scribner, 1958), p. 66.

the immanent Stoic "world-soul" (v. 12). He is the transcendent Holy Spirit who comes forth from God (Greek, *to pneuma to ek tou theou*, v. 12). The "ordinary" person (Greek, *psychikos*) does not receive the Spirit of God (v. 14). Unless, as a very few argue, vv. 15-16 are the response of a Corinthian "pneumatic" group that Paul quotes, the Holy Spirit gives discernment (v. 15), or (against the political correctness of the day) discrimination. Paul reaches the climax in v. 16: what Paul's argument means is that "we have the mind of Christ." The beginning of v. 16, "But [Greek, *hēmeis de*] we have . . ." may suggest that *Christlikeness* as a key effect or visible sign of the Spirit is even more important, or no less important, than the wisdom of the Spirit. The Greek *de* is a weaker contrastive than *alla*, but it may mean: "As for us, on the other hand. . . ." Be that as it may, a *Christ-centered focus and disposition* sum up what defines this "spirituality."

There are several passages in Paul where the Holy Spirit is parallel with Jesus Christ. One such occurs in 1 Cor. 6:11: "You were washed, you were sanctified, you were justified, in the name of the Lord Jesus Christ and in the Spirit of our God." Later it will accord with Christian doctrine to state that all Persons of the Holy Trinity are involved in every redemptive and saving act of God. But at this very early stage Paul simply asserts that cleansing, setting apart as holy, and putting right with God (perhaps with others) come about through Jesus Christ and the Holy Spirit. A similar parallel arises from the whole of 1 Corinthians 15, where sharing in the resurrection is seen as sharing in Christ's resurrection, yet the "body," or mode of being, of the resurrection is a "spiritual" body (v. 44), that is, a mode of existence animated and controlled by the Holy Spirit.[46]

We have already mentioned the explicit statement in 1 Cor. 12:3: "No one can say 'Jesus is Lord' except by the Holy Spirit." The first half of v. 3, however, causes great puzzlement to many: "No one speaking by the Spirit of God ever says 'Let Jesus be cursed!'" Margaret Thrall, W. Schmithals, and J. Weiss think that this can be said by some who enjoy such ecstatic frenzy that words tumble out unnoticed by the brain. Alternatively, some see this as a hostile slogan sometimes used by Jews, or demanded in a persecution contest, in contrast to "Caesar is Lord." W. C. van Unnik has suggested that it is rejection of the purely earthly Jesus who bore our "curse" on the cross, without the further necessary expression of faith in his resurrection. I used to favor this third view, even as late as 2000, when I wrote my commentary on the Greek text. Shortly after this, however, I became convinced by the proposal of Bruce Winter, who reads not the passive ("Jesus be cursed") but the active ("Jesus grants a curse").[47] For the Greek text simply reads *Anathema Iēsous*, with no explicit verb. An active verb is

---

46. Thiselton, *The First Epistle to the Corinthians*, pp. 1275-81; and N. T. Wright, *The Resurrection of the Son of God* (London: SPCK, 2003), pp. 352-54.

47. Bruce Winter, "Religious Curses and Christian Vindictiveness, 1 Cor. 12–14," in Winter, *After Paul Left Corinth* (Grand Rapids: Eerdmans, 2001), pp. 164-83.

supplied in the light of the discovery of some twenty-seven ancient "curse" tablets made of lead and unearthed near Corinth, fourteen of them on or near Acrocorinth in pagan temples. Some pagans prayed to their deities to "curse" rivals in business, in love, in litigation, or in sport. Winter suggests that Paul is most probably alluding to this: such a phenomenon as asking Jesus to curse a rival cannot be "of the Holy Spirit."[48] This sounds entirely convincing. The Holy Spirit will inspire only Christ-like attitudes and obedience to Christ as practical Lord and Master. Christians "belong to" Christ, as slaves "belong to" their lord.

The passage 1 Cor. 12:4-7 also involves a close parallel between Christ and the Spirit, and at the same time a further parallel with God the Father. Hence Athanasius and Basil of Caesarea, as well as other Church Fathers, refer to this passage emphatically for establishing a Trinitarian doctrine.[49] We shall therefore postpone these verses until the next chapter. 1 Cor. 12:13 similarly offers an implicit parallel between the Holy Spirit and Christ by speaking of baptism (usually the baptism of allegiance to Christ, 1 Cor. 1:12-13; Rom. 6:3-11). But since some interpret this baptism as a special subsequent experience of "baptism in the Holy Spirit," this discussion must also be postponed, under more controversial issues.

2 Corinthians contains not only the crucial verse in 3:17, but also the well-known "grace" in 2 Cor. 13:13, with its Trinitarian parallels that we shall consider in the next chapter. We also find connections between apostles, whose ministry is focused on Christ, and the Holy Spirit (2 Cor. 6:6), just as in 1 Cor. 12:8-11 gifts of the Spirit are for the benefit of the whole Church as the body of Christ (1 Cor. 12:27-28). We have looked at Gal. 4:6-7, which sees the Holy Spirit as actualizing the sonship of Christians as derived from Christ's Sonship.

Romans 8 sets the work of the Holy Spirit in the context of those who are "in Christ Jesus" (8:1). Again, Rom. 8:14-17 sees the Spirit as actualizing the Sonship of Christ. We have set out sufficient examples from Paul to show that the work of the Holy Spirit focuses on Jesus Christ, just as it does in John and elsewhere.

5.4. Further Detailed Discussions:
The Spirit, the Future, and the Inspiration of Scripture

We have already noted the passages in which the Holy Spirit is understood as a *"deposit"* or *"down payment" of a future yet to come* (2 Cor. 1:22; Greek, *arrabōn,* a

---

48. Anthony C. Thiselton, *1 Corinthians: A Shorter Exegetical and Pastoral Commentary* (Grand Rapids: Eerdmans, 2006), pp. 192-94.

49. Michael A. G. Haykin, *The Spirit of God: The Exegesis of 1 and 2 Corinthians in the Pneumatomachian Controversy in the Fourth Century,* Supplements to *Vigiliae Christianae* 27 (Leiden and New York: Brill, 1994).

"guarantee"). The term also occurs in 2 Cor. 5:5 (also *arrabōn*). But we have yet to consider Rom. 8:11, Rom. 8:17-27, Gal. 3:2, and Eph. 1:13, all of which, many writers argue, place the center of gravity on the Spirit's work in the future. Further, because the reception of the Holy Spirit by every Christian, or by all Christians, was prophesied as an eschatological event, numerous passages underline this "universal" aspect. Eduard Schweizer sums up the point: the Holy Spirit is "a guarantee of the reality of what is to come."[50] He urges that *pneuma* as a sign of what is to come, expressed especially by *aparchē*, "firstfruits," and *arrabōn*, "deposit," is common to Paul and early Christian eschatology. We have already referred to the more recent work of Friedrich Horn, *Das Angeld des Geistes* (1992); Gordon Fee, *God's Empowering Presence* (1994); and Finny Philip, *The Origins of Pauline Pneumatology* (2005), all of which enlarge upon this theme.

In Rom. 8:11 the Holy Spirit is clearly the instrument or Agent of Christ's resurrection (Greek, *ho egeiras ek nekrōn Christon Iēsoun*) who will give life (Greek, *zōopoiēsei*) to our mortal bodies. Charles Cranfield understands the genitive to mean "by the agency of."[51] He then heads the passage Rom. 8:17-30, "The Indwelling of the Spirit — the gift of hope."[52] He sees this passage as a close parallel with Galatians 3–4 and Romans 4. All speak of "inheriting" what lies in the future (esp. Gal. 4:7 and Rom. 4:13). Heirship is associated with sonship. In the present there remains an element of suffering and struggle; but the final consummation will be one of glory (8:18). "The revelation of our sonship is still in the future."[53] Hence Paul speaks of "confident expectation," or says that "the creation waits with eager longing" (NRSV; Greek, *apokaradokia;* cf. Phil. 1:20, where it is also associated with hope). The creation (Greek, *hē ktisis*) includes all humankind, angels, and nature, and it holds its breath in anticipation of the revelation in the future of the glory of the children of God as "the whole magnificent theatre of the universe."[54] The term for "wait with eager longing" is made up of *apo* — intensive, and *karadokein*, "to outstretch the head or neck," and means *"craning its neck,"* or, in colloquial English, *"to wait on tiptoe."*[55] Meanwhile, until the future denouement, the whole creation *"groans together"* (Greek, *systenazei*) in labor pains (v. 22).

If the climax were already present, Paul declares, we could not *hope* for it (v. 24). But in this present interim period the Holy Spirit is active, nurturing prayer and hope (vv. 26-27). At the same time this is only the firstfruits (Greek,

---

50. Eduard Schweizer, *"Pneuma,"* etc., in *TDNT,* vol. 6, pp. 422-24; cf. Eduard Schweizer, *Bible Key Words: Spirit of God* (London: Black, 1960), p. 64.

51. C. E. B. Cranfield, *The Epistle to the Romans* (Edinburgh: T&T Clark, 1975), p. 392.

52. Cranfield, *Romans,* p. 403.

53. Cranfield, *Romans,* p. 409.

54. Cranfield, *Romans,* p. 414.

55. See J. H. Thayer, *Greek-English Lexicon of the New Testament* (Edinburgh: T&T Clark, 4th ed. 1901), p. 62.

aparchē) of the Spirit (v. 23), that is, a foretaste and a guarantee of the greater reality in the future, or a pledge of the fuller gift to come. N. Q. Hamilton observes, "The gift of the Spirit in the present is to be understood as only the beginning of the harvest proper, which will occur in . . . the future age."[56] Paul speaks of "inheriting" five times: 1 Cor. 6:9, 10; 1 Cor. 15:50; Gal. 5:21; and Eph. 5:5 (Greek, *klēronomein*).[57] Yet in part the Holy Spirit is also a present possession; Christian believers already "walk" by the Holy Spirit (Gal. 5:25) and have the "mind" of the Holy Spirit (Rom. 8:5-6). They are "led by the Spirit" (Rom. 8:14).

This eschatological gift means that the Holy Spirit is given to all Christians, not just to some. We noted that Whiteley calls the Holy Spirit "the hallmark of the Christian."[58] "Jesus is Lord" is the confession of faith of all Christians, but it cannot be made without the Holy Spirit (1 Cor. 12:3). Every "son" of God has the Holy Spirit (Rom. 8:15-16). Christians know what is revealed by the Spirit (1 Cor. 2:10). All Christians constitute the temple of God, both as each individual and as a community (1 Cor. 6:19; 3:16). All receive the promise of the Spirit through faith (Gal. 3:14). In contrast to rabbinic theology, Scripture teaches that the Spirit is not a "reward" for a good life. Rom. 5:5 is sometimes called "the Pauline Pentecost," where through the Spirit "God's love is poured into our hearts."

Finally, the Holy *Spirit's inspiration of the Old Testament "Scripture"* remains the *common* teaching of Judaism, the New Testament, and the Church Fathers. In the Pauline corpus, this becomes most explicit in the Pastoral Epistles, even if a number of writers dispute this authorship. The NRSV translation, "All Scripture is inspired by God" (2 Tim. 3:16), conveys the Greek *theopneustos,* which John Calvin interpreted as its human authors' not speaking "of themselves, but as organs of the Holy Spirit."[59] On the other hand, William Mounce and others understand the Greek word to mean "straight from God."[60] The word does not occur elsewhere in the Greek Bible, but Mounce argues that it is a rejection of the false claim in Ephesus that Scripture did not come from God. H. B. Swete comments, "'Spirit' suggests 'inspiration.'"[61] He points out that in 2 Pet. 1:21 "the Prophets are said to have spoken as they were borne along *(pheromenoi . . .)* by the Holy Spirit."[62] This comes from Judaism and from Jesus: David spoke in the

---

56. Hamilton, *The Holy Spirit and Eschatology in Paul,* p. 19.

57. James D. Hester, *Paul's Concept of Inheritance: A Contribution to Paul's Understanding of Heilsgeschichte* (Edinburgh: Oliver & Boyd, 1968).

58. Whiteley, *The Theology of St. Paul,* p. 124.

59. John Calvin, *The Second Epistle of Paul to the Corinthians; The Epistles of Paul to Timothy, Titus and Philemon* (Edinburgh: St. Andrew's Press, 1964), p. 330.

60. William D. Mounce, *Pastoral Epistles,* Word Biblical Commentary, vol. 46 (Nashville: Nelson, 2000), p. 570.

61. Henry B. Swete, *The Holy Spirit in the New Testament* (London: Macmillan, 1909, rpt. 1921), p. 328.

62. Swete, *The Holy Spirit in the New Testament,* p. 329.

Holy Spirit (Mark 12:36). Swete adds that a Holy Spirit which moved a David or an Isaiah could not have failed to move a Paul or a John.

In the major epistles Paul seems more concerned about the inspiration of the Holy Spirit for his communication of the gospel. Indeed, from the beginning he claims, "The gospel came to you not in word only, but also in power [effectiveness?] and in the Holy Spirit" (1 Thess. 1:5). His speech and proclamation, he tells the Corinthians, were "not with plausible words of wisdom, but with a demonstration of the Spirit" (1 Cor. 2:4). In 2 Cor. 3:13-18 Paul's point is that the Holy Spirit will remove any blindness that hinders the communication of Scripture. It can hardly be imagined that Paul holds a different doctrine of the Spirit's inspiration of Scripture from that which most of Judaism presupposed.

5.5. Gifts of the Holy Spirit Clearly Based on Context and Exegesis

Paul introduces his chapters on the use of the gifts of the Holy Spirit (1 Corinthians 12–14) with the warning (on the negative side) that to curse rivals in love or business would be incompatible with claims to possess the Spirit or his gifts; and (on the positive side) that living out the lordship of Christ in daily life would constitute a mark that the Holy Spirit is actively working (1 Cor. 12:1-3; see above). It is not to be confused with the frenzy of "inspiration" in Hellenistic religion, or with worshiping "idols that could not speak," as if worshipers have to produce the spiritual phenomena themselves from their side (12:2).

After this foundational introduction Paul points out (lest the Corinthians should be "uninformed," v. 1) that the purpose of gifts to chosen individuals is to benefit the *whole community:* "To each is given the manifestation of the Spirit *for the common good*" (Greek, *pros to sympheron*, 12:7). There are indeed *varieties* of gifts (Greek, *diaireseis de charismatōn*, 12:4), but the gifts are given for a common purpose and goal. Paul addresses the Corinthians' question *peri de tōn pneumatikōn* (1 Cor. 12:1), which can be translated *either as* "concerning spiritual people" *or as* "concerning spiritual things," *not* in terms of *their* word, *pneumatikoi* (spiritual people) or *pneumatika* (spiritual things), but as *charismata (free gifts)*, which Paul spells out in vv. 4-11.

Jürgen Moltmann writes, "Call and endowment, *klēsis* and *charisma* belong together. . . . Every Christian is a charismatic . . . *I would not call them 'supernatural,'* over against the 'natural' charismata, . . . for practically speaking, what believers do is to put their natural gifts at the service of the congregation" (my italics).[63] He continues, "The rule for the community of Christ's people has to be *unity only in diversity,* not unity in uniformity."[64]

---

63. Moltmann, *The Spirit of Life,* pp. 180 and 183.
64. Moltmann, *The Spirit of Life,* p. 183 (his italics).

Certainly Paul stresses both unity and diversity, but does either of these have precedence over the other? Dale Martin observes, "In 12:4-11 Paul continually stresses unity in diversity in order to overcome divisiveness owing to different valuations being assigned to different gifts, with tongues as the implied higher-status gift."[65] Harrington also stresses unity of source.[66] Others, however, stress the *diversity* of the gifts. But probably Martin is convincing in this context, and the Trinitarian frame in vv. 4-7 seems to clinch the fact that God is one (1 Cor. 8:6) even if the Father activates the gifts; the Son is served as Lord through these gifts; and the Holy Spirit apportions or distributes the gifts (12:4-5). The words *the same* constantly recur. Yet within the unity and variety, the gift totally commits its recipients to total self-involvement in receiving and using the gift. Jean-Jacques Suurmond declares, "It is not so much a matter of *having* a gift as of *being* a gift" (his italics).[67]

We shall not yet consider every gift that Paul mentions. Those that invite controversial interpretations will be postponed to the next chapter. Here we shall consider most of the gifts listed in 1 Cor. 12:8-10, and those listed in 12:28-30, Rom. 12:6-8, and Eph. 4:11-12. Compared with the intense interest and concern generated by this subject, the gifts feature very little in the rest of the New Testament. This is not to underrate their importance, for only 1 Cor. 11:17-34 and 10:16-17 provide systematic teaching on the Lord's Supper. We may be thankful for misunderstandings in the earliest Church, for they provide the occasion for teaching on themes which may otherwise have been the subject of oral communication to the churches, then lost for subsequent generations. Nevertheless these are not the main topics in Thessalonians, Galatians, 2 Corinthians, Philippians, or other epistles.

(1) Logos sophias *or "utterance of wisdom" (NRSV): an agreed proposal.* The phrase translated "the *utterance* of wisdom" (NRSV) is the first gift to be mentioned in 1 Cor. 12:8, followed by "utterance of knowledge." These can hardly be identical, for the second is given "to another."

Mark Cartledge describes how these gifts are popularly understood and operate when he recounts the conduct of evening worship in "Third Wave" charismatic Renewal meetings, after the style of John Wimber or David Pytches. He describes how "words of knowledge" are "relayed from two or three people on stage" to some five thousand to eight thousand people "in a fairly prescribed Wimber model" in 2005.[68] Both *logos sophias* and *logos gnōseōs* are

---

65. Dale B. Martin, *The Corinthian Body* (New Haven: Yale University Press, 1995), p. 87.

66. D. J. Harrington, "Charisma and Ministry: The Case of the Apostle Paul," *Chicago Studies* 24 (1985): 245-57.

67. Jean-Jacques Suurmond, "A Fresh Look at Spirit-Baptism and the Charisms," *The Expository Times* 109 (1998): 105; cf. pp. 103-6.

68. Mark J. Cartledge, "The Practice of Tongues," in *Speaking in Tongues: Multi-Disciplinary Perspectives,* ed. Mark J. Cartledge (Milton Keynes: Paternoster, 2006), p. 209; cf. pp. 206-34.

translated "word of . . . ," although *logos* in this context almost certainly conveys "communication, statement, formulation, assertion, declaration," or even per-haps "reckoning" or "reflection."[69] Anyone who has compared 1 Corinthians with the rest of the New Testament and Pauline epistles will see that these terms represent a technical usage borrowed from the Corinthians themselves, which Paul perhaps modified.[70] *Sophia,* "wisdom," for example, occurs *sixteen times* in 1 Corinthians alone, compared with eleven in all the other Pauline epistles, in-cluding Ephesians. *Sophos,* "wise," occurs *eleven* times in 1 Corinthians only, compared with five times in all other epistles, almost all in Romans.[71] In view of the contrast between divine and human wisdom in 1 Cor. 1:18–4:21, many re-fer it to "God's plan of salvation."[72] James Dunn, Simon J. Kistemaker, Wolfgang Schrage, S. Schatzmann, and others all relate it to God's saving deed *in the crucified Christ* and his revelation on the cross.[73] In their context in 1 Cor. 1:18–4:21, it would surely be banal to conceive these gifts as private words about a medical or psychological condition, unrelated to the gospel.

If this were not enough, we need to consider the special function of *wisdom* and *knowledge* in the Old Testament, Judaism, and the New Testament. I briefly examined the use of "wisdom" in the Old and New Testaments and in Judaism in two articles published recently in *Theology.* Clearly "wisdom" refers to "charac-ter," "disposition," and "trained judgment," which are not "spontaneous" or in-tuitive gifts.[74] In these two articles I have argued that wisdom equips us for the complexities of practical life, and is not to be confused with knowledge or infor-mation. God is indeed the source of wisdom (Hebrew, *ḥokmâ;* Greek, *sophia*), but often he gives it through education and through the community. Hans-Georg Gadamer expounds the difference between wisdom and knowledge, especially through Gambattista Vico, Thomas Reid, and the pietist F. C. Oetinger.[75] Wis-dom is not simply concerned with knowing facts, but with trained critical judg-ments and character; with *phronēsis* rather than even *Sophia.* It is "totally differ-ent from theoretical reason."[76] Gerhard von Rad, like Vico, speaks of "learning from experiences which proved true over a long series of generations."[77] The Wis-

69. Danker, BDAG, 3rd ed. 2000, pp. 599-601.

70. Stephen M. Pogoloff, *Logos and Sophia: The Rhetorical Situation of 1 Corinthians* (Atlanta: Scholars Press, 1995), pp. 97-172.

71. W. F. Moulton and A. S. Geden, *A Concordance of the Greek Testament* (Edinburgh: T&T Clark, 1899), pp. 898-99.

72. S. Schatzmann, *A Pauline Theology of Charismata* (Peabody: Hendrickson, 1987), p. 36.

73. Thiselton, *First Epistle to the Corinthians,* p. 939; cf. pp. 938-44.

74. Anthony C. Thiselton, "Wisdom in the Old Testament and Judaism," *Theology* 114 (2011): 163-72, and "Wisdom in the New Testament," *Theology* 115 (2011): 260-68.

75. Hans-Georg Gadamer, *Truth and Method,* 2nd Eng. ed. (London: Sheed & Ward, 1989), pp. 9-30.

76. Gadamer, *Truth and Method,* p. 23.

77. Gerhard von Rad, *Wisdom in Israel* (London: SCM, 1972), p. 79.

dom literature often uses aphorisms, gnomic sayings, paradoxes, and so on, transmitted often by the community. Wisdom readily accepts correction and draws on the past (Prov. 15:2, 7, 31; Job 15:18). Ben Sirach and the Wisdom of Solomon continue respectively the outlook of Proverbs and of Ecclesiastes. Wisdom relates to such practical matters as knowing when to speak, honoring parents, the use and danger of riches, prayer and giving, hard work and idleness, and maintaining good health.

In the New Testament Jesus often uses aphoristic sayings, pithy sentences, gnomic utterances, and parables and analogies, especially in the so-called Q sayings of Matthew and Luke. Practical wisdom occurs in James in relation to teaching, humility, justice, sincerity, discipline, and integrity (Jas. 3:13-18), and is given especially by God (Jas. 1:5-8). There are parallels, for example, with Jesus on swearing and keeping one's word (Jas. 5:12; Matt. 5:33-37).[78] Paul draws a contrast between the self-seeking "wisdom of the world" cultivated at Corinth, and the Wisdom of God shown mainly through Christ and the cross (1 Cor. 1:18–2:16). At times the cross points to, or brings about, a reversal of values.

Is it conceivable that Paul should suddenly switch the meaning of wisdom when he comes to 1 Cor. 12:8? His initial teaching on wisdom in chapters 1–4 would be fresh in their minds, and Jewish believers would be aware of "wisdom" in Proverbs, Ecclesiastes, Job, and Judaism. "A word of wisdom" (Greek, *logos sophias*) does not mean a "word" but a unit of language, such as a sentence or a speech, or a discourse, divinely "given," but addressed to the practicalities of life in the light of Christ and the cross. *Logos* has an enormous semantic range.[79] In limited situations it *could* be a spontaneous expression of a long-standing disposition, but it need not be. Indeed, when the Holy Spirit inspired Bezalel to special feats of craftsmanship (Exod. 35:30; 36:1-2; 37:1), we can hardly imagine that *craftsmanship* did not involve *training and practice*. We recall Moltmann's reluctance to characterize gifts as "supernatural" and "natural." For *God* no less *inspired* it if it involved *reflection and judgment,* or even the help of others. In my larger commentary I suggested equally the *subjective* genitive "articulate utterance *deriving from* [God's] wisdom," *or* the *objective* genitive "articulate utterance *about* [God's] wisdom."[80] *Sophia,* to repeat, was a catchphrase in Corinth (cf. 1 Cor. 1:17, 19, 20, 21, 22, 24, 30; 2:1, 4, 5, 6, 7, 13; 3:19). As we stated, it is used sixteen times in this one epistle, with only two further uses in the four major epistles of a roughly similar date (Rom. 11:33 and 2 Cor. 1:12).

(2) Logos gnōseōs *or "utterance of knowledge" (NRSV): a new proposal.* "Word of knowledge" (Greek, *logos gnōseōs;* v. 8) commands no exact consensus

---

78. P. J. Martin, *James and the Q Sayings of Jesus* (Sheffield: Sheffield Academic, 1991), esp. pp. 188-89; and Ben Witherington, *Jesus the Sage: The Pilgrimage of Wisdom* (Minneapolis: Fortress, 2000).

79. Thiselton, *The First Epistle to the Corinthians,* p. 143.

80. Thiselton, *The First Epistle to the Corinthians,* p. 938; cf. pp. 142-45.

about its precise difference from "word of wisdom." But *gnōsis* appears regularly in 1 Cor. 8:1, 2, 3, 7, 10, 11, if we include its verbal form. It also occurs in Rom. 11:33; 15:14; 1 Cor. 1:5; 12:8; 13:2, 8; 14:6; 2 Cor. 2:14; 4:6; 6:6; 8:7; 10:5; 11:6; Phil. 3:8; and Col. 2:3, of the widely accepted Pauline epistles. *Gnōsis* very often has negative nuances ("knowledge inflates; love builds," 1 Cor. 8:1), and the gradual process of "coming to know," implied by the verb, is more welcome to Paul than the more complacent noun *gnōsis*, "the knowledge that I have achieved." We should therefore be cautious about its exact boundaries in relation to wisdom. In 1 Cor. 8:1-6, however, the word combines some discomfort with *basic creedal knowledge of the one God*. It seems to be the most intellectual of the gifts. If used without pastoral sensitivity, in 1 Corinthians it can unsettle believers. Here it definitely is a "gift," a *charisma*.

The nearest equivalent today might be "knowledge of basic Christian truths," or even creedal affirmations. Today this has become all the more important when many believers pay less attention than they should to Christian doctrine. Doctrine need not be dry and divisive. It requires hard intellectual work no less than prayer. But it constitutes a gift of the Holy Spirit for the health, well-being, and authenticity of the Church. Philip Carrington, Vernon Neufeld, and others have spoken and written of catechetical instruction even in the era of the New Testament.[81] If Paul thought instruction and argumentation were unimportant, he could have spared himself a lot of trouble, as Pannenberg has commented. I have argued at length for the importance of doctrine elsewhere.[82] In the end, there is no compelling reason why a "communication of knowledge" could not amount to *instruction in the basic truths of the gospel, perhaps for baptismal candidates*, alongside the gifts of *teaching* and *apostleship*. We may not be absolutely and utterly certain of this, but it seems by far the most probable meaning. It may seem self-contradictory to place a "new" proposal under "clear" exegesis, but on exegetical grounds this does appear to be a "clear" interpretation.

It may be difficult to think ourselves into Paul's situation in a generally first-generation Church. On the one hand, Paul undoubtedly saw more scope for congregational participation. In this sense Moltmann argues, "Our regular, mainline church services display a wealth of ideas . . . in their sermons, but are poverty-stricken in their forms of expression, and offer no opportunity at all for spontaneity. . . . [They are] one big mouth and a lot of little ears."[83] He argues that mainline churches and "charismatic" renewal groups need each other.

---

81. Philip Carrington, *The Primitive Christian Catechism: A Study in the Epistles* (Cambridge: Cambridge University Press, 1940); Vernon H. Neufeld, *The Earliest Christian Confessions* (Leiden: Brill, and Grand Rapids: Eerdmans, 1963), pp. 1-33 and 42-68.

82. Anthony C. Thiselton, *The Hermeneutics of Doctrine* (Grand Rapids and Cambridge: Eerdmans, 2007), pp. xvi-xx, 72-74, 126-34.

83. Moltmann, *The Spirit of Life*, p. 185.

On the other hand, however, even at this early date, Paul defines some of these *charismata* as giving rise to *office:* "Are all apostles? Are all prophets? Are all teachers?" (1 Cor. 12:29). More particularly "God has appointed in the Church first apostles, second prophets, third teachers, . . . forms of assistance [Greek, *antilēmpseis,* probably administrators] . . ." (1 Cor. 12:28). To recognize the force of Moltmann's comment should still allow for caution in so generalizing about the gifts that we move from one extreme to the other.

By the date of Ephesians these have become distinct, recognized offices: "The gifts he gave were that some would be apostles, some prophets, some evangelists, some pastors and teachers, to equip the saints . . ." (Eph. 4:11-12). Yet later, by the time of the Pastoral Epistles, formal criteria for appointment as bishop (or overseer) and deacons (1 Tim. 3:1-13; Tit. 1:5-9) have emerged.[84] The wisdom-speech and knowledge-speech, therefore, might often come from prophets or teachers respectively. But the Church was even then in process of development, especially in A.D. 53. We can imagine Paul bewailing that in the future *some* churches would listen only to an ordained ministry, while *other* churches would invite the less ordered swing to constant "spontaneous" speeches from an assembled congregation. Paul might well have encouraged an orderly norm accompanied by the freedom for exceptions, as indicated by the Holy Spirit. The Church of England has attempted some form of compromise in its "Fresh Expressions," where radical developments may occur but still under disciplinary monitoring by the bishop. Catholic Renewal processes often reflect the same kind of compromise.

(3) *The third "gift" of 1 Corinthians 12:8-9: "faith."* *Faith* comes third in this list of gifts, although we must not forget the "list" in 1 Cor. 12:28-31 and elsewhere. Virtually every commentator asserts that this does *not* denote the faith of justification, since not every Christian will be given it, but every Christian is justified by grace through faith. The Greek uses *heterō,* "to another," that is, to one who might not be given other gifts but is especially singled out for this gift from the Holy Spirit.

Paul uses the word "faith" in a multiplicity of ways. He sometimes speaks of "the obedience of faith" (Rom. 1:5), to the extent that Rudolf Bultmann claims that Paul conceives of faith as obedience. He comments, *"Paul understands faith primarily as obedience."*[85] He sees a parallel between "your faith is proclaimed in all the world" (Rom. 1:8) and "your obedience is known to all" (16:19). He suggests that when Paul says in 1 Thess. 1:8: "Your faith in God has gone forth everywhere," this must refer to the converts' obedience. 2 Cor. 9:13, he claims, describes faith as "obedience in acknowledging the Gospel of

---

84. See Mounce, *Pastoral Epistles,* pp. 152-212 and 385-93.

85. Rudolf Bultmann, *Theology of the New Testament,* vol. 1 (London: SCM, 1952), p. 314 (his italics).

Christ."[86] Bultmann, however, does not suggest that *every* occurrence of "faith" in Paul denotes "obedience." Faith is also "the radical renunciation of accomplishment," which belongs more closely to justification by grace in contrast to "works."[87] In his article on faith *(pistis)* in Kittel and Friedrich's *Theological Dictionary*, he distinguishes between the different contexts of (1) common apostles' teaching; (2) the contrast with Judaism; (3) the contrast with Gnosticism; and other contexts.[88]

None of these meanings, however, fits Paul's use in his account of gifts of the Holy Spirit. Indeed, in the *Two Horizons* I argued that it would be misleading to speak of "the essence" of faith in the Pauline letters, for what faith *is* can be answered only in the light of the theological or pastoral issue at stake, and dispositions that respond to circumstances. Faith is a "polymorphous" concept.[89] An analogy would be the words "to try." To try to lift a heavy object would not match the meaning of "to try" to sleep, or "to try" to play the piano. What "to try" consists in is determined by *what* we are trying to do. Hence justifying faith is the appropriation of God's promise of *grace by all Christians.* To live out this faith is seen in obedience. However, when Paul says, "We walk by faith, not by sight" (2 Cor. 5:7), he is speaking of *trust* in contrast to full knowledge. Yet again, in Gal. 1:23 "faith" means simply "Christianity." But in 1 Cor. 13:2 "faith that can move mountains" seems to be a *special gift* given to some, but not all, Christians, similar to that in 1 Cor. 12:9. Bornkamm asserts, "The nature of faith is given in the object to which faith is directed."[90] Conzelmann thinks that in the list of gifts of the Spirit faith has to do with the miraculous.[91] But we have already noted Moltmann's reasons for reserve about overly neat divisions between natural and supernatural, not least as imposing a modern way of thinking onto Paul.

In this special context we must bear in mind that none of the nine gifts of the Spirit in 1 Cor. 12:8-10 are primarily for the individual alone, but for the congregation. We can readily see how a congregation may pass through times of fear, pressure, or despondency when one or two of its number may display *a glad, even daring, confidence in God's sovereignty, mercy, and leading,* with the result that the whole congregation is lifted up and reenergized by those one or two gifted individuals. Their trust, confidence, and optimism become contagious, and a gift of the Spirit *through them to the whole congregation.* Where

---

86. Bultmann, *Theology of the New Testament,* vol. 1, p. 315.

87. Bultmann, *Theology of the New Testament,* vol. 1, p. 316.

88. Bultmann, "*Pisteuō*; faith," in *TDNT,* vol. 6 (1968), pp. 217-22.

89. Anthony C. Thiselton, *The Two Horizons: New Testament Hermeneutics and Philosophical Description* (Grand Rapids: Eerdmans, and Exeter: Paternoster, 1980), pp. 407-10.

90. Günther Bornkamm, *Paul* (London: Hodder & Stoughton, 1972), p. 141.

91. Hans Conzelmann, *1 Corinthians: A Commentary,* Hermeneia (Philadelphia: Fortress, 1975), p. 209.

some experience faintheartedness, *the buoyant, robust, gift of faith* to an individual may *reanimate* them.

(4) *Apostles, teachers,* antilēmpseis *("forms of assistance," NRSV),* kybernēseis *("forms of leadership," NRSV), pastors, donors and others.* The remaining gifts of the Spirit in 1 Cor. 12:9-10 involve not only exegesis but also hermeneutics. They are radically open to interpretations which transcend such issues as context, grammar, syntax, and the meaning of words — in other words, what constitutes the substance of exegesis. We may regret this, as most New Testament specialists would do. But if we are to take account of their reception in the ecumenical Church, there are many who go beyond this, whether they are rationalists who doubt the currency of miracles, or Pentecostals or Renewal enthusiasts who hold various views of healing, prophecy, and "kinds of tongues" in Paul. We consider these in the next chapter, together with wider questions about the personhood of the Holy Spirit. We shall also comment on Pentecostal or charismatic hermeneutics.

Meanwhile we may return with some relief to gifts and offices in 1 Cor. 12:28-30, which include apostles, teachers, *antilēmpseis,* translated as "forms of assistance" in the NRSV, and *kybernēseis* translated as "forms of leadership" in the NRSV. Other gifts in 1 Cor. 12:28-30 relate to deeds of power, to prophets, to tongues, and to healing, which belong to Chapter 6. Rom. 12:6-8 includes dispositions such as "givers" (NRSV; Greek, *metadidous*), and the gifts which we have mentioned. Eph. 4:11 adds evangelists and pastors to apostles and prophets.

We are familiar with apostles and teachers, although apostle thrusts us into ecclesiological controversy. An apostle denotes one whom God has sent (Greek, *apostellō*). But Paul clearly intends the term to denote more than this, as his question in 1 Cor. 9:1 indicates: "Am I not an apostle?" Whereas Luke sees the term as denoting primarily one of the Twelve, Paul associates the term with both God's calling and being a witness to the resurrection of Christ (1 Cor. 9:1b; 15:8-10). James Dunn writes: "Paul's own perception was of apostles appointed to found churches (1 Cor. 9:1-2), limited in the scope of their commission," not as holding "a universal office."[92] There is no hint in Paul of any institutional or mechanical notion of apostolic succession. We may also compare Gal. 1:13–2:21.[93]

Some stress that to be an *apostle* is a mark of authority. Karl Rengstorff emphasizes this.[94] Ernst Käsemann and Jürgen Moltmann urge the extent to which the apostle is an authentic witness to Christ: "Christian Identity" is found in "an act of identification with Christ."[95] The most persuasive, in our

---

92. Dunn, *The Theology of Paul the Apostle,* p. 540.
93. J. Christiaan Beker, *Paul the Apostle* (Edinburgh: T&T Clark, 1980), p. 45.
94. Karl L. Rengstorff, *"Apostolos,"* in *TDNT,* vol. 1, pp. 407-47.
95. Jürgen Moltmann, *The Crucified God* (London: SCM, 1974), p. 19.

view, is the view of Chrysostom, Schrage, and Crafton, that apostleship points away from the self to Christ and to others, and is therefore a sign of humility.[96] In my larger commentary on 1 Corinthians I set out and documented eight distinct approaches.[97] This does not detract from Paul's sometimes speaking of the foundational role of apostles. Hence in 1 Cor. 12:28 he writes: "First apostles, second prophets, third teachers; then deeds of power." He reinforces this by asking: "Are all apostles?" (expecting the answer "No"). In this sense it is arguable that apostleship is perhaps unrepeatable.

"Teacher" is one of the few terms with a transparent match with what the term means today. Rom. 12:7 says that the teacher *(ho didaskōn)* fulfills this calling "in teaching" *(en tē didaskalia)*. Danker translates this verb as "to provide instruction in a formal or informal setting," and this noun simply as "teaching."[98] This meaning is also well attested in Plato, Philo, and Polycarp. Today there seem to be two quite opposite needs in the Church as a whole: some suffer from undue clericalism, and need more lay ministry; others need a better-informed and trained *teaching* ministry. I have been astonished when some lay people commented with obvious surprise after a sermon: "We really *learned* something today!" Paul stresses the need for both prophets and teachers, and sees both as inspired by the Holy Spirit. To suggest that the Spirit works only through "spontaneous, unprepared, and unreflective" discourse would have astonished Paul, and denigrated his epistles as merely human thoughts.

The modern translations of *antilēmpseis* ("forms of assistance," NRSV) and still more of *kybernēseis* ("forms of leadership," NRSV) in 1 Cor. 12:28 would be less easy. The NRSV is near, but hardly captures the punch of the terms. Often the rather colorless words or phrases "helps" (AV), "helpers" (RSV), or "those able to help others" (NIV) do useful service for *antilēmpseis*. But it would rightly resonate better with the Church today to translate *antilēmpseis* as "kinds of administrative support." Admittedly Danker renders it "helpful deeds."[99] Indeed, the verb *antilambanō* normally means simply "to assist," "to come to the help of," or "to commit oneself to share." "Administrative support" may be too narrow and specific. But in view of the part played by church administrators today, it may be helpful to spell out that administrators are gifted by the Holy Spirit, and that a "spontaneous administrator" is a contradiction in terms! In point of fact, Danker renders the next word *kybernēsis* as "administration," as does the NIV.[100] But Moulton and Milligan translate the

96. J. A. Crafton, *The Agency of the Apostle*, JSNTSS 51 (Sheffield: Sheffield Academic, 1991), pp. 53-103.

97. Thiselton, *The First Epistle to the Corinthians*, pp. 666-73.

98. Danker, BDAG, pp. 240-41.

99. Danker, BDAG, p. 89.

100. Danker, BDAG, p. 573.

usual use in the papyri (often contemporary with Paul) of *kybernētēs* as "steersman" or "pilot," and *kybernēsis* as "guiding" or "piloting."[101] In a church situation often strategic decisions have to be made. My belief is that "church strategist" or, better, the "gift of strategic thinking" would best do justice to this gift. We need the gift of the Holy Spirit to avoid short-termism.

In Romans *charisma* occurs six times, but of *prophecy, ministry, teaching, exhorting, being a generous donor,* and having a so-called "cheerful compassion" (Rom. 12:6-8) all spring from a settled disposition or habits of character, other than perhaps prophecy, so that meaning by itself remains debatable. As Charles Cranfield points out, *diakonia,* "ministry," can have both a wider meaning (service to God or to the Church) and a narrower one (service to the needy). He sees it as approximating the work of a deacon.[102] Joseph Fitzmyer agrees that either the broader or narrower term is possible, although he suggests "table service" for the latter.[103] Recently the research of John Collins on "deacon" has added to its complexity, and he and Danker suggest that "deacon" may denote "assistant" or "deputy," especially to a bishop or presbyter in some contexts, or even "intermediary."[104] "Ministry" may be taken as practical service of various kinds. "Exhorter" *(ho parakalōn)* clearly overlaps with teacher in its goal, as Cranfield argues, but is one of the very few terms which allow for *either public or private, corporate or individual, exhortation.*

"Donor" translates *ho metadidous.* The verb *metadidonai* denotes the distribution of what is one's own (as in LXX, Luke, and Ephesians), but Cranfield, following Calvin, argues that this term in Romans may allow for a distribution of what *others* hold in common.[105] If this is correct, the two terms which resonate best with church life today would be either "donor" or "church treasurer." It is not anachronistic to suggest either of these terms. We know that in the context of the Roman Empire such men as Erastus and Babbius Philinus erected monuments or provided public inscriptions which celebrated their donations of buildings to cities, for the Erastus and Babbius monuments can still be seen at ancient Corinth today.[106] Benefaction was an important part of the life of the wealthy. Alternatively or additionally, most churches, as today, would appoint a trusted person to oversee their donations, gifts to the poor, and expenses. *Cheerfulness* is often mentioned with giving: "God loves a cheer-

---

101. James H. Moulton and George Milligan, *The Vocabulary of the Greek Testament* (London: Hodder & Stoughton, 1952), p. 363.

102. Cranfield, *Romans,* vol. 2, pp. 621-22.

103. Joseph A. Fitzmyer, *Romans,* Anchor Bible (New York: Doubleday, 1992), p. 648.

104. John N. Collins, *Deacons and the Church* (Leicester, Gracewing, and Harrisville: Morehouse, 2002).

105. Cranfield, *Romans,* vol. 2, p. 624.

106. Donald Engels, *Roman Corinth* (Chicago: University of Chicago Press, 1990), pp. 68-69; Bruce W. Winter, "The Public Honouring of Christian Benefactors," *JSNT* 34 (1988): 87-103.

ful giver" (2 Cor. 9:7, KJV/AV). But it constitutes a disposition or stable virtue; it is not "spontaneous," any more than the others.

In Eph. 4:11 most of the gifts of the Holy Spirit are repeated from 1 Corinthians or Romans. After enumerating apostles and prophets the writer introduces the new terms of "evangelists" *(hoi euangelistai)* and "pastors" *(hoi poimenai)*, before resuming "and teachers." Danker simply translates *euangelistēs* as "proclaimer of the gospel" or "evangelist."[107] It derives from the verb *euangelizō*, "to bring good news," or "to proclaim the message of salvation" (which Danker gives as the two usual meanings), or the noun *euangelion*, "gospel." In its nonmetaphorical form *poimēn* denotes "shepherd." But it easily comes to be extended, even in nonreligious Greek, to denote "guardian," "protector," or "leader." Danker approves of "pastor" for Eph. 4:11. Clearly the emphasis falls upon pastoral work; but in view of its extended usage as guardian or leader, the usual meaning today cannot be excluded, and depends on other arguments, such as whether the writer envisages multiple or single presbyters in a church.

It is noteworthy that the lists of charismata move into Paul's major concern for love, not only in 1 Cor. 12:31, which is well known, but also in Rom. 12:8-10. He immediately concludes his list of gifts through the exalted Christ with "Let love be genuine; . . . love one another with mutual affection." Eph. 4:11 even repeats the context of 1 Corinthians: "to equip the saints . . . for building up the body of Christ" (4:12). In 1 Cor. 8:1b, knowledge puffs up or inflates, whereas love builds up the community. Paul would not have been unduly surprised that so much more debate and striving, and many more books are devoted to "spiritual gifts" than to learning to love. He would simply recall Corinth, and reflect: "Nothing has changed!"

107. Danker, BDAG, p. 403.

6

Further Gifts of the Spirit and More Controversial
Themes That Involve Hermeneutics

6.1. The Need for Hermeneutics for the Remaining Gifts of the Spirit

In the previous chapter we considered themes relating to the Holy Spirit in Paul in which his meaning can be determined with straightforward exegesis. We have explored the meanings of words, their grammar and syntax, Paul's context of thought, and, where necessary, the arguments of specialist biblical scholars. The present chapter, by contrast, raises issues that are more complex and more controversial, which involve not only questions of meanings, contexts, and Pauline theology but also the area which has come to be known widely as *hermeneutics,* or interpretation in the very broadest sense.

Few would dispute that when we come to such issues as the work of the Holy Spirit in healing, miracles, prophecy, tongues-speech, and "baptism in the Spirit," much depends (to use a phrase often employed in Pentecostal circles) on the lens through which we see and read the text. This also becomes a live issue for secular historians and positivist scholars, as well as for Pentecostals and adherents of the Renewal Movement. Historically it also raises questions of judgment about the Personhood of the Holy Spirit.

It would be short-sighted and inappropriate to avoid considering the impact of Pentecostal and Renewal thinkers. After all, the sheer numbers and the huge following of the Pentecostal Movement throughout the world, especially in Latin America, Africa, and Asia, but also in America and Europe, make it more than a force to be reckoned with. We discuss the explosion of Pentecostalism and the Renewal Movement in Part III, and argue for sympathetic dialogue, as well as some mutually critical debate, with the "mainline" churches and scholarship. What causes me deep concern is the recent emergence of three appeals, arguments, or devices now popular among many Pentecostal writers.

(1) The first concerns the unfortunate word "presupposition." In popular

terms this recalls conservative students of various kinds thirty or more years ago, who became famed for responding to less conservative or "liberal" lecturers with the comment: "You have your presuppositions, and I have mine; it is inevitable that we see things differently." The problem with the word "presupposition" is that it appears to promote an opt-out clause from genuine dialogue.[1] It suggests that *presuppositions* are forever *fixed,* and incapable of initiating *negotiation or dialogue.* Each side, it is suggested, is firmly wedded to theirs. Clark Pinnock, Roger Stronstad, and numerous Pentecostal writers, as well as such scholars as Oscar Cullmann, use this term.[2] Stronstad appeals, as I did in *The Two Horizons* ten years earlier, to Bernard Lonergan's warning against "the empty head." This is reasonable if we are speaking of central creedal concerns, and Stronstad appeals to those who bring "saving faith" to the text as a presupposition. But often more than this is involved. I know of no biblical scholar who cannot enter into dialogue at a major society of mainline biblical scholars simply because he has "saving faith" as a presupposition.

Over the last thirty years many have advocated replacing the word "presuppositions" with the word "horizons," as I did in my first major book, *The Two Horizons* (1980).[3] *Horizons are capable of movement and expansion.* It has been a serious disaster that Rudolf Bultmann's famous essay "Is Exegesis without Presuppositions Possible?" uses the German word *Voraussetzung,* which does mean *presupposition* or *assumption,* even if Heidegger and others more properly use *Vorverständnis,* preliminary understanding.[4] A better English translation would be "preliminary understanding." I have argued for this, and explained my reasons, in my *Hermeneutics* (2009).[5] Schleiermacher, Heidegger, Bultmann, and Gadamer constantly argue that a preliminary understanding provides a starting point or way into the text, which constantly undergoes *revision, correction, and adjustment, in the light of the text.*[6]

(2) Second, many of the Pentecostal and Renewal concerns about the

---

1. Even the latest essay on "Pneumatic" Hermeneutics still uses "presupposition"; see Kevin L. Spawn and Archie T. Wright, *Spirit and Scripture: Exploring a Pneumatic Hermeneutic* (London: T&T Clark International/Continuum, 2012), p. 5; though, later, they also use "horizons."

2. Roger Stronstad, "Pentecostal Experience and Hermeneutics," in *Enrichment Journal* (formerly a paper at the 20th Annual Meeting of The Society of Pentecostal Studies, Dallas, November 1990).

3. Anthony C. Thiselton, *The Two Horizons: New Testament Hermeneutics and Philosophical Description* (Grand Rapids: Eerdmans, 1980).

4. Rudolf Bultmann, "Is Exegesis without Presuppositions Possible?" in Bultmann, *Existence and Faith: Shorter Writings of Rudolf Bultmann* (London: Collins, Fontana ed., 1964), pp. 342-51; German, *Glauben und Verstehen* (Tübingen: Mohr, 1965-85), vol. 3, pp. 142-50.

5. Anthony C. Thiselton, *Hermeneutics: An Introduction* (Grand Rapids: Eerdmans, 2009), pp. 13-16.

6. For example, Martin Heidegger, *Being and Time* (Oxford: Blackwell, 1962), p. 194; German, p. 153.

reader's or readers' *experience* fairly find parallels with secular *Reader-Response theory* in literary studies and hermeneutics. I have argued in detail that in such a careful and cautious form as we find in Wolfgang Iser this can facilitate genuine engagement with the text, and we have to take account of both text and performance or actualization.[7] But in the hands of Stanley Fish, David Bleich, Norman Holland, and others the rights of the text can become unduly compromised in favor of prior attitudes held by the reader.

Bleich, Holland, and Fish slide into what I called at the time "socio-pragmatic" hermeneutics. Whatever promotes the good of the reading community becomes the criterion of truth. Rorty dismisses a critique which is offered from outside the community. All interpretation, Fish argues, is *constituted* by the community of readers: "The reader's response is not *to* the meaning; it *is* the meaning."[8] If the reader, in effect, *creates* the meaning, how can anyone from outside the privileged community challenge or question it? When Richard Rorty, the postmodern philosopher, declares imperialistically that there are "no givens," what does this say about the cross or the work of the Holy Spirit?[9]

Again we return to Stronstad's paper, cited above. The whole burden of his article is that "experience also enters the hermeneutical enterprise at the beginning of the task; that is, as a presupposition, and not merely as a certification/verification."[10] But this raises two main problems. We have rehearsed the first, namely, the difference between "presupposition" and "preliminary understanding" or "horizon." The second is the difference between an *experience* and a *conceptual* name or *conceptual* description of that experience. This is admirably illustrated by the term "baptism in the Spirit." If only it were the case that the Pentecostal horizon *was* the *experience* that is too often called by that name! *But to decide upon a name or term is not an experience,* but a *cognitive and conceptual* decision what to call it. I can identify with and respect what Pentecostals call "baptism in the Spirit," with some cognitive provisos about sequence and timing. But I cannot agree that on grounds of "presuppositions" Stronstad can rightly identify this term with the experience which he claims lies behind it, at least if he wants to be true to Paul. It is a bad case of Reader-Response theory which has become out of hand.

(3) The third line of argument or unfortunate device used by many recent

7. Anthony C. Thiselton, *New Horizons in Hermeneutics: The Theory and Practice of Transforming Biblical Reading* (Grand Rapids: Zondervan, and London: Harper-Collins, 1992), pp. 58-79 and 516-57.

8. Stanley Fish, *Is There a Text in This Class? The Authority of Interpretive Communities* (Cambridge, MA: Harvard University Press, 1980), p. 3.

9. Thiselton, *New Horizons*, pp. 546-50.

10. Stronstad, "Pentecostal Experience and Hermeneutics," *Enrichment Journal,* November 1990, p. 3.

Pentecostals emerges in the recent stream of literature on Pentecostal hermeneutics. It takes the form of appealing directly to *postmodern* hermeneutics. For example, Kenneth Archer states in the *Journal of Pentecostal Theology*, "Pentecostalism must have a postmodern accent."[11] I am aware that as important a writer as Michael Welker finds positive resources on the Holy Spirit in this direction.[12] We consider Welker in Part III, and I do not reject everything in postmodernism, especially its reaction to the standardization of knowledge.[13] But I am less inclined to fragmentation and pluralism than Michael Welker seems to be. In my view, it undermines the very identity of Pentecostalism and the Renewal Movement. Admittedly this approach has the attraction for some Pentecostals of appearing to call on a highly sophisticated theory of hermeneutics. But Pentecostals have seriously studied and published on hermeneutics only over the last twenty-five years or so, and it is overly hasty at this stage to try to cash in on postmodern hermeneutics until there has been adequate time to grasp the seductive nature of the postmodern secularism which such hermeneutical approaches conceal.

This becomes most blatant in two ways. (a) First some appeal to *incommensurability*, ultimately derived from Thomas Kuhn's work in philosophy of science, whereby there is no shared criterion for deciding between two viewpoints or "paradigms," as Kuhn calls them.[14] A number of writers use the word "paradigm" outside its context in philosophy of science to defend a method of biblical interpretation.

(b) Second, and much worse, consequences become more disastrous when this appeal to an incompatibility of views is harnessed to an explicit postmodernism of the kind expounded by Jean-François Lyotard as "pagan" or more specifically in terms of what he calls *"the differend."*[15] Lyotard uses "pagan" to denote a plurality which has departed from "monotheism" of a single "meta-narrative" of world history; he uses "differend" to denote two effectively irreconcilable positions concerning which *no one can arbitrate* because any "negotiation" or even dialogue would disguise the use of *force* or strength by one side over against the other. This postmodern device provides a shortcut which bypasses the whole attempt of hermeneutics to provide the kind of dialogue

11. Kenneth J. Archer, "Pentecostal Hermeneutics: Retrospect and Prospect," *JPT* 8 (1996): 80; cf. pp. 63-81.

12. Michael Welker, *God the Spirit* (Minneapolis: Fortress, 1994), pp. 28-48.

13. For a brief balance sheet see Thiselton, *Hermeneutics: An Introduction*, pp. 327-48.

14. Thomas S. Kuhn, *The Structure of Scientific Revolutions* (Chicago: University of Chicago Press, 1st ed. 1962; 2nd ed. 1970); Kuhn, *The Essential Tension* (Chicago: University of Chicago Press, 1977).

15. Jean-François Lyotard, *The Differend* (Manchester: Manchester University Press, 1990); and Lyotard, *The Postmodern Condition* (Manchester: Manchester University Press, and Minneapolis: University of Minnesota Press, 1984).

which leads to mutual understanding. It completely ignores Emilio Betti's observation that hermeneutics promotes tolerance, patience, and respect for "the other," and should therefore be taught in all universities.

These remain the three key difficulties. But a fourth difficulty of a different nature inevitably arises from the open acknowledgment that Pentecostals do not agree, or, to cite Spawn and Wright, maintain a "broad" approach on the nature of Pentecostal hermeneutics. Gordon Fee and Max Turner, for example, openly say that they are first and foremost New Testament scholars who are also Pentecostals (in Fee's case) or advocates of Renewal (in Turner's case). Gordon Fee maintains: "It is simply not possible to show that Luke *intended* to teach an experience of the Spirit as subsequent to conversion. . . . Clearly descriptive history in Acts must not be translated into normative experiences for the ongoing church" (his italics).[16] Similarly, in the very recent book *Spirit and Scripture,* the main concern seems to be to retain a close relationship between Spirit and Word, which is shared by many who would not clearly identify themselves as Pentecostals or advocates of the Renewal Movement. Many writers share the conviction that God acts in the physical world and in all reality. In other words, they, too, believe in the credibility of miracles in principle.[17] Howard Ervin argued long ago that the prevailing weakness of hermeneutical conversation consisted in presuppositions whereby "the supernatural manifestations of the Holy Spirit must appear as mythological."[18] But such scholars as Joel Green, Telford Work, and Daniel Trier all believe that God works in the world, and use the term "theological interpretation" to identify their work.[19] With perhaps more variable success Mark Bowald and Jens Zimmermann also follow this path.[20]

It is easy to select such a scholar as Philip Davies, and use him as a representative of "the" historical-critical method (as if there were only one), and then ignore such writers as B. F. Westcott, J. B. Lightfoot, and, in our own day, Walter Moberly, Christopher Seitz, Francis Watson, N. T. Wright, and many others in this tradition. Francis Watson rightly launches a blistering attack on

16. Gordon Fee, *Gospel and Spirit: Issues in New Testament Hermeneutics* (Peabody: Hendrickson, 1991), pp. 94-96.

17. Spawn and Wright, *Spirit and Scripture,* esp. pp. 3-144.

18. Howard Ervin, "Hermeneutics: A Pentecostal Option," in *Essays on Apostolic Themes: Studies in Honor of Howard M. Ervin,* ed. Paul Elbert (Peabody, MA: Hendrickson, 1985), pp. 11-25; and earlier comments in *Pneuma* 3 (1981): 11-25.

19. Joel B. Green, *Practicing Theological Interpretation* (Grand Rapids: Baker Academic, 2011); Telford Work, *Living and Active: Scripture in the Economy of Salvation* (Grand Rapids: Eerdmans, 2002); and Daniel Trier, *Introducing Theological Interpretation of Scripture: Recovering a Christian Practice* (Grand Rapids: Baker Academic, 2008).

20. Jens Zimmermann, *Recovering Theological Hermeneutics* (Grand Rapids: Baker Academic, 2004), and Mark A. Bowald, *Rendering the Word in Theological Hermeneutics* (Grand Rapids: Baker Academic, 2007).

the illusion of supposed value-neutral secular scholarship.[21] It is scarcely surprising, then, that Robert Menzies, a well-known Pentecostal biblical scholar, insists: "The hermeneutics of evangelicalism has become our hermeneutic."[22] In his recent debate with James Dunn the hermeneutical issue turned largely on whether Dunn had interpreted Luke in the light of Paul.

Meanwhile in 1990 the twentieth annual meeting of the Society for Pentecostal Studies was wholly devoted to hermeneutics, and then published in *Pneuma*.[23] Clearly serious divergences within Pentecostalism exist. Kenneth Archer writes of interpretation which is "rigidly literal" in classical Pentecostalism. He refers to the example of the longer ending of Mark, which is lacking in Sinaiticus and Vaticanus, very early manuscripts. This was regarded as inauthentic by Eusebius and Jerome, and viewed as non-Markan by virtually all experts on style and text. It includes the handling of poisonous snakes, which is often seen as a model for today, in spite of these difficulties.[24] Donald Dayton argues that Pentecostals read the New Testament "through Lukan eyes, especially with the lenses provided by the Book of Acts."[25] Walter Hollenweger declares, "The Pentecostals and their predecessors based their views almost exclusively on the Gospel of Luke and the Acts of the Apostles."[26]

Arguably these last examples are not strictly hermeneutical in the broadest sense. But it is therefore more serious, especially when we come to look at miracles and healing that Hollenweger more recently comments on Pentecostalism and even more on "Third Wave Renewal": "They see the world as a cosmic and moral duality. There is no room for the natural. Everything is either divine or demonic."[27] In this broad vein, William Menzies explicitly dissents from a narrower method, which he sees in David Cartledge. He attacks not only the "latter rain" movement in Pentecostalism, but also openness "to a high degree of subjectivity in what he calls a 'Pentecostal hermeneutic.'"[28] Menzies argues that this opens the door to a power struggle in the movement. This is precisely what we shall see in Part III in the earliest history of Pentecostalism.

---

21. Francis Watson, *Text, Church and World: Biblical Interpretation in Theological Perspective* (Edinburgh: T&T Clark, 1994), pp. 1-14.

22. Robert Menzies, "The Essence of Pentecostalism," *Paraclete* 26 (1992): 1.

23. *Pneuma* 3 (1990), Fall issue.

24. Kenneth J. Archer, "Pentecostal Hermeneutics," *JPT* 8 (1996): 65.

25. Donald W. Dayton, *Theological Roots of Pentecostalism* (Grand Rapids: Baker Academic, 1987), p. 23.

26. Walter J. Hollenweger, *The Pentecostals* (Peabody: Hendrickson, 1972), p. 336.

27. Walter J. Hollenweger, "Critical Issues for Pentecostals," in *Pentecostals after a Century: Global Perspectives on a Movement in Transition,* ed. Allan H. Anderson and Walter J. Hollenweger, JPTSS 15 (Sheffield: Sheffield Academic, 1999), p. 180; cf. pp. 176-96.

28. William W. Menzies, Review of *The Apostolic Revolution;* and David Cartledge, *The Apostolic Revolution: The Restoration of Apostles and Prophets in the Assemblies of God in Australia* (Chester Hill: Paraclete Institute, 2000), p. 175.

However, Pentecostalism has one huge advantage over the "Third Wave" of the Renewal Movement. After approximately one hundred years, it has developed an *impressive self-criticism.* There is scarcely any "academic" query that we might wish to make which cannot find parallels among Pentecostals themselves. We can gain access to such criticism either by reading the books of Frank Macchia, Veli-Matti Kärkkäinen, Gordon Fee, and many others, or by reading letters and blogs on the web under "Pentecostal Theology Worldwide." This contains a predictable mix of the trite and anecdotal with some very serious insights and reservations or questions about what many take for granted. We might wish that "Third Wave" charismatic Renewal advocates had had time and energy to engage in comparable self-criticism. This may be the difference between a hundred and ten (or more) years of history and about thirty-five.

We are also faced with the difficulty that many special studies of healing focus on the early days of Pentecostal teaching or even the Holiness Movement, before much sustained reflection on hermeneutics. Certainly most Pentecostals in the earliest years were oblivious to hermeneutics. Kimberly Ervin Alexander, for example, aims to present what "the first decade of the Pentecostal Movement" believed and practiced, but the related section on hermeneutics shows little understanding of the advanced issues of the subject beyond the often repeated issue of seeing texts through a given "lens."[29] We examine this twice in Part III.

In this part, which is devoted to biblical teaching, we have not yet offered a full critical survey of Pentecostal and Renewal hermeneutics. In Part III we specifically consider the hermeneutics of Amos Yong's *Spirit–Word–Community.* We shall also consider Roger Stronstad's work and Max Turner's work on Luke-Acts in *Power from on High* and other books. We have outlined enough of the live issues today to allow us to proceed with an examination of Paul's theology of gifts of the Holy Spirit that concern healing, "deeds of power" or "miracles," "prophecy," speaking in tongues, and claims about "baptism in the Spirit" in 1 Cor. 12:13.

6.2. Gifts of Healing and "the Working of Miracles" (NRSV)

(1) *Gifts of healing* (NRSV) translates the Greek *charismata iamatōn,* where "healings" is in the plural, probably to denote "kinds of healings."[30] The Greek idiom is like the English, where people speak of cheeses or fruits to convey *kinds*

---

29. Kimberly Ervin Alexander, *Pentecostal Healing: Models in Theology and Practice* (Dorset, Blandford Forum: Deo, 2006), pp. 5 and 27-36.

30. See Thiselton, *The First Epistle to the Corinthians,* NIGTC (Grand Rapids: Eerdmans, 2000), pp. 946-56, on the generic force of the plural.

of cheese or kinds of fruit. This gift of various kinds of healings does not appear in the list in Rom. 12:6-8 and Eph. 4:11. The more usual Greek word is *therapeuō*, which occurs forty times in the Gospels and Acts, but Paul does not use it; he seems to prefer an alternative word. Paul refers to healing only in 1 Cor. 12:9, 28, and 30. In 2 Cor. 12:8 God does not appear to "heal" him of his "thorn in the flesh" (or "sharp physical pain") at all, except to enable him to find sufficiency in God. His arrival in Corinth "in weakness" (1 Cor. 2:3) might refer to illness, as some claim, but this cannot be verified. Collins argues, Paul "does not claim for himself the gift of healing."[31] On the other hand, Max Turner believes that healing would have been among the "signs and wonders" with which Paul preached (Rom. 15:18-19; 1 Cor. 2:2-5; 1 Thess. 1:5).[32]

Probably most writers associate *healings* with the gift of faith just mentioned in the same verse. But this invites caution. While we must not impose modern reactions onto Paul, a constantly troubling pastoral problem arises when some Christians claim that they have prayed for healing with genuine faith, but God has not been pleased to heal them or the one for whom they prayed. If faith becomes a high-profile *condition* of healing, for believers of genuine faith it may seem *to exacerbate* the problem of suffering. Further, what place is also given to corporate faith, or to faith within a prayerful community?

We must return to Paul's use of the plural "healings." Schrage thinks that it might refer back to traditions of the healings of Jesus.[33] On the other hand, the Pentecostal writer Donald Gee insists (surely rightly) that "kinds of healings" should "not preclude . . . the . . . work of medical healing."[34] Similarly, Bengel argued that this gift of healing neither excluded the miraculous nor excluded "natural remedies" (Latin, *per naturalia remedia*).[35] Godet, Meyer, Robertson and Plummer, Carson, and Schatzmann all follow T. C. Edwards and Hollenweger in understanding the Greek text as including normal, natural cures as well as direct interventions from God.[36] In 1 Tim. 5:23 Timothy is to seek heal-

---

31. R. F. Collins, *First Corinthians*, Sacra Pagina (Collegeville, MN: Glazier/Liturgical Press, 1999), p. 454.

32. Max Turner, *The Holy Spirit and Spiritual Gifts Then and Now* (Carlisle: Paternoster, 1996), p. 252.

33. W. Schrage, *Der erste Brief an die Korinther*, EKKNT 7/3 (Neukirchen: Neukirchener Verlag, 1999), vol. 3, p. 151.

34. Donald Gee, *Spiritual Gifts in the Work of the Ministry Today* (Springfield, MO: Gospel Publications, 1963); and Gee, *Concerning Spiritual Gifts* (Stockport: Assemblies of God, 1928, 3rd ed. 1937).

35. J. A. Bengel, *Gnomon Novi Testamenti* (Stuttgart: Steinkopf, and London: Dulau, 1866), p. 652.

36. F. Godet, *Commentary on St. Paul's First Epistle to the Corinthians*, 2 vols. (Edinburgh: T&T Clark, 1886), vol. 2, p. 197; H. A. W. Meyer, *Critical and Exegetical Handbook to the Epistles to the Corinthians*, 2 vols. Edinburgh: T&T Clark, 1892), vol. 1, p. 364; A. Robertson and A. Plummer, *First Epistle to the Corinthians*, ICC (Edinburgh: T&T Clark, 2nd ed. 1914), p. 110; Don Carson,

ing of the stomach by avoiding a dubious water source and instead drinking wine. Surprisingly, in a volume of some thousand pages on gifts of the Spirit, Gordon Fee comments on kinds of healings, "What this refers to needs little comment."[37] Hollenweger, supported by Arnold Bittlinger, declares: "The whole distinction between natural and supernatural is outdated, both scientifically and theologically, and can no longer be seriously advocated."[38] We shall discuss his comments further shortly.

Paul would have known that in oral tradition Jesus was credited with exorcisms and healings. But he would also have known that Jesus accepted the constraints of poverty, suffering, and humiliation. The whole emphasis on the gifts of the Spirit is that these are indeed *gifts, as God wills and chooses*. We have argued above that we must avoid *an artificial dualism of "natural" and "supernatural,"* as if to imply that the action of God is restricted to one of these two areas alone. All things are possible for God, whether this is a sheer "spontaneous" gift, or God's working through human skills, expertise, and training. The latter are no less "gifts of grace." As Peter Mullen observes, Francis McNutt's claim that "it is always God's normal will to heal" comes from a very *different world of thought from Paul's*.[39] To invoke a Pentecostal or Renewal "lens" simply does not do justice to Paul's own experience, as he records it. In Pauline terms, this view would imply a wholly *realized eschatology*.

A joint statement, "Gospel and Spirit," collected by Kilian McDonnell as one of many ecumenical documents in 1980, declares, "All wholeness, health and healing come from God. We do not therefore regard 'divine healing' as being *always* miraculous. We look forward to the resurrection, knowing that only then shall we finally and fully be freed from sickness, weakness, pain, and mortality"; we must not imply "that it is sinful for a Christian to be ill" (my italics).[40] In 2000 the Church of England published a Report, *A Time to Heal,* which ran to over 400 pages and included among its members John Gunstone, author of *Live by the Spirit.*[41] This concluded: "The healing ministry should be

---

Showing the Spirit (Grand Rapids: Baker, 1987), pp. 174-75; and Siegfried Schatzmann, *A Pauline Theology of Charismata* (Peabody, MA: Hendrickson, 1987), p. 37.

37. Gordon Fee, *God's Empowering Presence: The Holy Spirit in the Letters of Paul* (Carlisle: Paternoster, 1994), p. 168.

38. Walter J. Hollenweger, *Der 1 Korintherbrief, eine Arbeitshilfe zur Bibelwoche* (Kingmünster: Volksmissionarisches Amt der Pfälzischen Landeskirche, 1964), p. 25; and Arnold Bittlinger, *Gifts and Graces: A Commentary on 1 Corinthians 12–14* (London: Hodder & Stoughton, 1967), p. 70.

39. Peter Mullen, in *Strange Gifts? A Guide to Charismatic Renewal,* ed. David Martin and Peter Mullen (Oxford: Blackwell, 1984), p. 100; cf. pp. 97-106.

40. "Gospel and Spirit: A Joint Statement," documented in K. McDonnell (ed.), *Presence, Power and Praise: Documents on the Charismatic Renewal,* 3 vols. (Collegeville, MN: The Liturgical Press, 1980), vol. 2, p. 305; cf. pp. 291-306. McDonnell includes Anglican, Methodist, Catholic, and Reformed documents.

41. John Gunstone, *Live by the Spirit* (London: Hodder & Stoughton, 1984).

given the weight appropriate to its importance as a gospel imperative, in the recruitment, selection, and training of ordinands, [and] in . . . lay training. . . . the Church of England should co-operate with Churches . . . in the support and encouragement of the healing ministry worldwide."[42] Although I expressed regret to General Synod that this Report did not explicitly address those who felt that, in spite of their faith, they had not transparently received "healing," the Report does presuppose "limitation and illness," and the need for pastoral care in depression, disability, and long-term psychiatric illness.[43]

We must also be bold and honest enough to question some of the anecdotal accounts of healings, which seem at first sight often to be exaggerated. Tom Smail, who is associated with the Renewal Movement and was formerly Director of the Fountain Trust in England, stresses that John Wimber's "Vineyard" Fellowship and "Third Wave" charismatics are often guilty of this. He writes: "The rhetoric about miraculous healing far exceeds the reality. The testimonies to healing do not appear to be of the same order as the miracles of the New Testament."[44]

At the same time we must distinguish Paul's expectations about the gift of healing from practices today. The clear markers in Paul are that God gives gifts though the Spirit of various kinds of healing (without ranking the kinds); that these gifts follow the practice of Jesus, of which he must have been aware; and that in some cases, as in his own (2 Cor. 12:8-9), God's free choice did not entail healing, in spite of prayer. The only hermeneutical question left is the view raised by Benjamin Warfield's "cessationism." Cessationists see healing miracles in the ministry of Jesus as peculiar to the era of the coming of the Kingdom of God in the Person of Jesus.[45] But Paul does not appear to qualify the gift of healing in 1 Corinthians in this way. The strongest argument against "cessationalism" is the eschatological one. Pentecostals from the very beginning appealed to the apocalyptic Coming of Christ, and saw healing and "miracles" as the inbreaking of the Kingdom of God.

We must not deny this in principle. But early Pentecostals, unlike their successors today, failed to see the twin polarity of "now" and "not yet." Insofar as the Kingdom is here, we may expect acts of healing. But insofar as it pleases God not to bring in the End wholly before the Return of Christ, it should not cause undue dismay when God chooses to declare: "Not yet." Some years ago

---

42. *A Time to Heal: A Contribution to the Ministry of Healing: A Report for the House of Bishops* (London: Church House Publishing, 2000), pp. 284-85.

43. *A Time to Heal,* pp. 127-52.

44. Tom Smail, with Andrew Walker and Nigel Wright, *The Love of Power or the Power of Love: A Careful Assessment of the Problems of the Charismatic and Word-of-Faith Movements* (Minneapolis: Bethany House, 1994), p. 43.

45. Jon Ruthven, *On the Cessation of the Charismata: The Protestant Polemic on Postbiblical Miracles* (Sheffield: Sheffield Academic, 1993), attempts a reply.

Oscar Cullmann wrote definitively on this issue. He declared: "The Holy Spirit is . . . the anticipation of the end of the present. . . . Man is that which he will become only in the future."[46] Meanwhile, Christians *still sin and still die;* hence, although "The Spirit even now at times invades the area of physical life, in healings of the sick," this is "a redemptive action which comes to its *full* expression *only in the future*" (my italics).[47]

(2) *Effective deeds of power (usually translated "miracles").* The fifth gift is termed by the NRSV, NJB, and AV/KJB "the working of miracles" (Greek, *energēmata dynameōn*). But the actual word "miracles" is not in the Greek. The Greek means "workings of powers." I have translated it "effective deeds of power."[48] For one thing Karl Barth persuasively argues that "power" in 1 Corinthians denotes what is *effective* against any obstacle.[49] Moreover, in 12:6 the NRSV translates the Greek *diaireseis energēmatōn* as "varieties of *activities*," and *ho autos theos ho energōn ta panta in pasin* as "the same God who *activates* all of them [the gifts] in everyone" (my italics). John Calvin doubts whether either v. 6 or v. 9 refers to miracles. He observes, "I am inclined to think that it is the power *(virtutem)* which is exercised against demons and also hypocrites."[50] Again, it denotes "effective working." H. Thielicke sees it as effective power against "ungodly forces," which may mean demons.[51]

Power has in some quarters become almost an obsessional quality after the Industrial Revolution. But there is a real problem if it is construed as brutish physical force or its equivalent in the spiritual realm. As in the situation at Corinth, this may appeal especially to the disempowered, weak, vulnerable, or oppressed. In 1 Cor. 12:28 the NRSV and most translations render the Greek "deeds of power." But in 12:29 the word is changed to "miracles" in the question: "Do all work miracles?" In v. 28 the Greek reads simply *dynameis*, "power"; more strikingly v. 29 reads *mē pantes dynameis*; "Surely all are not powers, are they?" The translators *assume* that *dynameis*, "powers," *must* mean "miracles" in v. 29, but not in v. 28.

However, we have already read Hollenweger's wise comment that to use the term today, after the legacy of Deism and the Enlightenment, implies a "God of the gaps" and a dualist view of the world. He urged, as we noted and quoted, that the distinction between natural and supernatural is scientifically and theologically outdated (his words). He continues: "Scientifically it is no

---

46. Oscar Cullmann, *Christ and Time: The Primitive Christian Conception of Time and History* (London: SCM, 1951), pp. 72 and 75.

47. Cullmann, *Christ and Time*, p. 76.

48. Thiselton, *The First Epistle to the Corinthians*, p. 952.

49. Karl Barth, *The Resurrection of the Dead* (London: Hodder & Stoughton, 1933), p. 18.

50. John Calvin, *First Epistle to the Corinthians* (Edinburgh: Oliver & Boyd, 1960), p. 262.

51. Helmut Thielicke, *The Evangelical Faith,* 3 vols. (Grand Rapids: Eerdmans, 1974-82), vol. 3, p. 79.

longer possible to delineate the boundaries of what was called 'natural.' . . . From the theological standpoint as well, it is irresponsible to describe the supernatural as a breaking through of natural laws."[52] Bittlinger agrees with this point.

Danker gives the first meaning of the singular *dynamis* as "potential for functioning in some way, *power, might, strength, force, capability*."[53] The second half of the first meaning is "specifically the power that works wonders," for which in the New Testament he cites Matt. 14:2, Mark 6:14, Acts 10:38, Rom. 1:4, 1 Cor. 12:28-29, and Gal. 3:5. The second meaning is "ability to carry out something, ability, capability," while the third meaning is "a deed that exhibits ability to function powerfully, deed of power, miracle, wonder"; and a fourth meaning includes "resource." Finally, it may also mean "the capacity to convey thought" (see below on the "interpretation" of tongues).[54] The verb *dynamai* denotes primarily "the possession of capability for experiencing or doing something."[55] The adjective *dynatos* conveys "being competent," "being capable." Paul would not here have used the noun *dynastēs*, for it generally refers to a person in a high position, ruler, or sovereign.

Recently Craig S. Keener has published a definitive, two-volume, exhaustive study of miracles (2011).[56] Richard Bauckham describes it on the dust jacket as "a uniquely — indeed staggeringly — extensive collection of comparative material, . . . a very strong challenge to methodological scepticism about the miraculous to which so many New Testament scholars are still committed"; and Amos Yong again describes it as "exhaustive research." Keener comments near the beginning: "It is extraordinarily naive to pretend that eyewitnesses, including sincere eyewitnesses, do not offer . . . claims [about miracles]."[57] He discusses evidence for the miracles of Jesus and the reports of Paul. He observes: "Paul anticipated noticeable miraculous phenomena in the Christian communities (1 Cor. 12:9-10, 28-30; Gal. 3:5)."[58] In his chapter 2, Keener considers claims about miracles outside Christianity, and compares these with the Gospels, looking at healing sanctuaries, Asclepius shrines, holistic medicine,

---

52. Hollenweger, *Der 1 Korintherbrief, eine Arbeitshilfe zur Bibelwoche*, pp. 25-26; Bittlinger, *Gifts and Graces*, pp. 70-71, quotes Hollenweger with approval.

53. Danker, BDAG, p. 262.

54. Danker, BDAG, p. 263.

55. Danker, BDAG, pp. 261-62; Joseph H. Thayer, *Greek-English Lexicon of the New Testament* (Edinburgh: T&T Clark, 4th ed. 1901), pp. 158-60; James H. Moulton and George Milligan, *The Vocabulary of the New Testament Illustrated from Papyri and Non-Literary Sources* (London: Hodder & Stoughton, 1930), pp. 171-72, are even clearer. *Dynamis* hardly ever means "miracle" in the papyri, for which a different word, *dynamos*, is used.

56. Craig S. Keener, *Miracles: The Credibility of the New Testament Accounts*, 2 vols. (Grand Rapids: Baker Academic, 2011).

57. Keener, *Miracles*, vol. 1, p. 4.

58. Keener, *Miracles*, vol. 1, pp. 30-31.

and pagan miracle workers. He concludes, "Understanding how miracle workers were viewed in the first century helps us appreciate the context of miracles in early Christianity."[59]

Understandably enough, Keener moves on to discuss David Hume's well-known argument that miracles break natural laws and are contrary to nature, and traces its effect in philosophy. Surprisingly I cannot find references to Augustine's anticipation of this critical objection by suggesting that, far from being "against nature" *(contra naturam)*, miracles are "beyond" what we know of nature (*praeter naturam; Reply to Faustus the Manichaean*, 26:3). Nevertheless he brings to bear a battery of more recent writers, concluding, "Hume's argument . . . should appear even less persuasive in a twenty-first century multicultural context than it appeared in his own day."[60] Over much of the rest of his book, Keener cites testimony of postbiblical miracles from Asia and Latin America, and the healing of specific diseases, including blindness and spirit-possession.

We may return to Paul without embarrassment that healing sometimes involves miracles. But do the Greek terms which Paul uses place the primary emphasis on what most call the "supernatural"? We are not contesting that these terms may *include* the performing of miracles, but simply whether *miracles* carry the *primary* emphasis, excluding notions of effective action or *competence.* Prophets and preachers may be effective at applying the gospel and at applying truth; teachers may be effective at expounding and communicating truth. But might a congregation or church still need those who are competent and effective in following through and sustaining a number of tasks for the church, as well as perhaps at times performing a miraculous deed? Indeed, the list in 1 Cor. 12:8-10 omits two important gifts which are cited in 12:28. The Greek terms are *antilēmpseis* and *kybernēseis,* about which we commented above. The NRSV, we saw, renders the first "forms of assistance," and the AV/KJV renders it "helps," and Danker suggests "helpful deeds." But Bittlinger writes, "According to recently discovered papyri the Greek word for administration *(antilēmpsis)* was a technical term in the field of banking and referred to the chief accountant. In other words, here we are concerned with the *administration of money. . . . Kybernēsis* (leading or *piloting* duties) . . . refers to . . . the *'manager,'* so to speak" (my italics).[61] Danker renders it "administration."[62] In both of my commentaries I argued that these two terms must imply *administration.* In my larger commentary I argued that *kybernēs* meant one who could strategically *steer* the church. We may therefore tentatively argue not that "mir-

59. Keener, *Miracles,* vol. 1, p. 65.
60. Keener, *Miracles,* vol. 1, p. 169.
61. Bittlinger, *Gifts and Graces,* p. 70.
62. Danker, BDAG, p. 573.

acle" is *wrong,* but that in this context it is *too narrow* and directs attention *away* from Paul's main point.

This appears all the more convincing when we note again that the plural need not be a numerical plural but a *generic* one, denoting kinds of effective power, depending on the need and related *task.* I have expanded this argument in greater detail in my commentary on the Greek text. To cite *helps* as a parallel *(antilēmpseis)* may mean helping administration with royal petitions (*Paris Papyri* 26:40; first century B.C.), administering such medical aids as bandages (Hippocrates, *In the Surgery,* 743) and the like.[63] This may well include the *ability to formulate strategies* which pilot the church through stormy seas.[64]

6.3. The Gift of "Prophecy" and "Discernment of Spirits"

(1) *Paul and the meaning of prophecy.* We shall comment on a modern evaluation of this phenomenon when we consider the Pentecostal and Charismatic Renewal Movements in Part III of this study. Here our aim is to arrive at what Paul actually meant by these two phenomena. Our conclusion may invite controversy, but it is intended to engage with exegetical literature and with Paul himself.

"Prophecy" *(prophēteia)* occurs in Rom. 12:6; 1 Cor. 12:10; 13:2; 14:6; and 1 Thess. 5:20; cf. 1 Tim. 4:14. The verb "to prophesy" *(prophēteuō)* occurs in 1 Cor. 11:4, 5; 13:9; 14:1, 3, 4, 5, 24, 31, 39. Everyone agrees that its primary purpose is to *build up* the community (Greek, *oikodomeō,* 1 Cor. 14:4, 17; cf. 8:1; 10:23; the noun *oikodomē* occurs in 1 Cor. 14:3, 5, 12, 26; cf. 3:9). Most interpreters, including Danker, agree that the term "to prophesy" also means "to encourage" or "to bring comfort."[65] The noun *prophēteia* relates to interpreting the will of God (Rom. 12:6; 1 Cor. 12:10), while the verb *prophēteuō* especially relates to proclaiming the revealed word and, sometimes, to predict. The noun *prophētēs* means one who proclaims inspired revelation.

At this point controversy arises. We may recall that Paul lays claim to this title for himself. Philipp Vielhauer and K. O. Sandnes both associate Paul's own apostolic commission to build up the Church (Gal. 1:15-16; cf. Jer. 1:5, 10) with the prophet's call to plant and to build (1 Cor. 3:6, 10).[66] But, more controversially, is this achieved by a *creative reinterpretation* of Scripture, or by "sponta-

---

63. Thiselton, *The First Epistle to the Corinthians,* pp. 1019-21; cf. pp. 952-56.

64. Thiselton, *The First Epistle to the Corinthians,* pp. 1021-22.

65. See two extended notes in Thiselton, *The First Epistle to the Corinthians,* pp. 956-70 and 1087-94; and Danker, BDAG, pp. 889-91.

66. P. Vielhauer, *Oikodomē: Das Bild vom Bau in der christlichen Literatur vom Neuen Testament bis Clemens Alexandrinus* (Karlsruhe: Harrassowitz, 1940), pp. 77-98; and K. O. Sandnes, *Paul — One of the Prophets?,* WUNT 2.43 (Tübingen: Mohr, 1991).

neous" charismatic utterances, or by applied pastoral preaching of the gospel *kērygma*?

(a) E. Earle Ellis, to a lesser extent G. Stählin, most Pentecostals, and many in the Renewal Movement follow the first view. This has the advantage of seeing it as the interpretation of Scripture as well as charismatic utterance, rather than only as a quasi-ecstatic utterance on analogy with its understanding in Greek cults. The interpretation of Scripture in the synagogues, Ellis urges, "is a key feature of the missions of Barnabas, Paul and Silas."[67] So far, so good. But Ellis also develops the notion that prophetic interpretation is "pneumatic" exegesis. However, in the first section of this chapter we saw what a huge range of meanings "pneumatic" interpretation could have. In one sense it could denote simply biblical interpretation based on belief in the living God, who acted in the physical world. In another sense it could denote a highly subjective understanding based almost entirely on past and present experience, akin to Reader-Response theories in the secular literary world. Ellis sees this as the key difference between the prophet and the teacher. But Christopher Forbes and É. Cothenet remain unconvinced about such a "free" interpretation as Ellis imagines.[68] We shall look at the work of Forbes more closely in Part III. A classic adage about the Old Testament prophets is that they were reformers, rather than innovators, and David Aune maintains that there was significant continuity with prophetic speech in the Old Testament.[69] If both Scripture and Christ formed the bedrock against which prophecy was tested, it remains uncertain how "pneumatic" or "free" exegesis could be tested, any more than the "prophecy" against which the canonical or writing prophets protested. As we observed when discussing the hermeneutics of Fish and Rorty, we cannot test their claims *outside* a given community. It is not for nothing that, after the fire of the major epistles, Paul as an older man (many would say, a Pauline disciple) saw that urging the need for teaching and reflection might curb too great an appeal to "experience" (Tit. 2:1-10; 1 Tim. 1:3; 3:2; 4:13; 5:17; 2 Tim. 3:13-14).

(b) A more serious issue concerns whether prophecy must necessarily be "spontaneous." James D. G. Dunn, Max Turner, and Christopher Forbes come near to supporting this view as proven. In Dunn and Turner this is almost a circular argument, as if to respond to God's clear initiative and revelation somehow implied a contrast with that which had its origin in human reflection or

---

67. E. Earle Ellis, "The Role of the Christian Prophet in Acts," in E. E. Ellis, *Prophecy and Hermeneutic in Early Christianity* (Grand Rapids: Eerdmans, 1978), p. 132; cf. pp. 23-62 and 129-45.

68. Christopher Forbes, *Prophecy and Inspired Speech in Early Christianity and Its Hellenistic Environment*, WUNT 2.75 (Tübingen: Mohr, 1995), p. 235; and É. Cothenet, "Les prophètes chrétiens comme exégètes charismatiques de l'écriture," in *Prophetic Vocation in the New Testament and Today*, ed. J. Panagopoulos, NovTSup 45 (Leiden: Brill, 1977), pp. 77-107.

69. David E. Aune, *Prophecy in Early Christianity and the Ancient Mediterranean World* (Grand Rapids: Eerdmans, 1983), p. 195.

thought. Max Turner writes, "For Paul, prophecy is the reception and subsequent communication of spontaneous, divinely given *apokalypsis* (revelation)."[70] James Dunn insists, "It does not denote a previously prepared sermon. . . . It is a spontaneous utterance," citing 1 Cor. 14:30.[71] Dunn's main arguments for this are that prophecy cannot be "summoned" to order, and that a first prophet is to stop speaking if another prophet receives a revelation (1 Cor. 14:30). Christopher Forbes also argues that, in contrast to preaching, "revelation [to prophets] is normally spontaneous."[72]

Forbes's insertion of the word "normally" moves toward a less speculative view. We do not deny that prophecy may *sometimes* be "spontaneous." But we shall shortly consider further the views of Gillespie, Müller, and Hill that "prophecy" denotes applied pastoral preaching, in most or at least many cases. In this section on Paul, the issue turns on how God acts within the world and in human beings. It reflects the old science-and-religion question of whether God miraculously acts *against* nature, or *through* or even *beyond* nature, as we considered in relation to miracles and healing. We argued, for example, that gifts of healing could *include* God's acting through medical doctors or natural processes, and not always by dramatic intervention. Bengel, Hollenweger, and others affirmed this. We saw that "administration" constitutes a genuine gift of the Holy Spirit, while "spontaneous administration" constitutes a contradiction in terms. The Holy Spirit clearly gives administrative gifts over time and training. The "spontaneous" view not only goes too near to what is popularly called the *"Deus ex machina"* view, but also raises questions about how far Paul, Luke, and other biblical writers were "inspired as prophets" when they planned and thought out their writings.

The "spontaneous" view would also wreck the attempt to defend the divine inspiration of the Bible or Scripture. It would play into the hands of those who maintain that because Scripture shows all the marks of human composition, style, vocabulary, and historicity, it thereby cannot be inspired by God. But classical theism has always rejected this "Deist" and rationalist view. Nineteenth-century writers such as Westcott, Lightfoot, and Hort saw no contradiction between intelligent, thoughtful criticism and self-criticism and openness to divine action in the origins and content of the Bible.

Again, this does not imply that prophecy can *never* operate *against* the will or the expectations of the prophets. Jeremiah could bear prophetic burdens which *ran against* his inclinations; but for the *most* part he *thought them through.* As a tailpiece, we must also dissent from Dunn's appeal to 1 Cor. 14:30.

---

70. Max Turner, "Spiritual Gifts, Then and Now," *Vox Evangelica* 15 (1985): 10; cf. pp. 7-64.

71. James D. G. Dunn, *Jesus and the Spirit* (London: SCM, 1975), p. 228; cf. pp. 205-300; and *The Theology of Paul the Apostle* (Edinburgh: T&T Clark, 1998), pp. 552-64 and 580-98.

72. Forbes, *Prophecy and Inspired Speech*, pp. 229 and 236.

The "second" prophet may already have *thought through a disclosure or revelation* from God. But as the "first" prophet began to wander into self-indulgent homily, or even into self-deception, distraction, or error, the second prophet would feel impelled to want to interrupt, in order to make a relevant, God-given point. This does not mean, for Paul, that most Christian discourse takes the form "Thus says the Lord." Paul *usually uses rational argument,* and it is pure speculation to imagine that he does not expect his converts and churches to do the same. Günther Bornkamm comments, "The style of the Pauline sermon is just *not that of the revelation-speech* but of the diatribe. . . . The hearer [is] a *partner in a dialogue*" (my italics).[73] Would Paul, then, regard *preaching* or *writing* as the same genre as *prophecy?*

(c) This brings us to the claims to David Hill, Ulrich Müller, Thomas Gillespie, and others. They argue that for Paul *prophecy* often denotes "applied pastoral preaching."[74] We introduced these writers when we considered "prophecy" in Acts. The *effect* of prophecy is certainly similar to that of a sermon or proclamation of the gospel in 1 Cor. 14:25: "After the secrets of the unbeliever's heart are disclosed, that person will bow down before God and worship him, declaring, 'God is really among you.'" The secrets of the heart concern a person's largely unconscious attitudes to God. Unlike *teaching,* prophecy has the aim of a subsequent turning to God. "Secrets" cannot refer in 1 Corinthians 14 to some medical condition which the prophet diagnoses, as in some popular "Renewal" circles today; nor to an improper relationship; nor to some purely "domestic" matter in the church; at least, hardly ever, and never as an expected norm. David Hill observes, "The congregation will learn only when what they hear is intelligible, coherent . . . expressed *in sustained utterance.*"[75]

This in turn signifies, Hill urges, "pastoral preaching which, by its very nature, offers guidance and instruction to the community."[76] Gillespie and Müller see it as primarily *paraklēsis,* "exhortation," and *paramythia,* "consolation."[77] Müller (and later Forbes) argues that the false notion that *ecstasy* evidences inspiration comes largely from the Greeks, and perhaps also from the non-writing, noncanonical prophets. We do not need to rehearse this argument again. Forbes and others have argued convincingly against it, as we shall note in Part III. We are on more secure ground to stress that Paul insists that it is "for

73. Günther Bornkamm, "Faith and Reason in Paul," in Bornkamm, *Early Christian Experience* (London: SCM, 1969), p. 36; cf. pp. 29-46.

74. David Hill, *New Testament Prophecy* (London: Marshall, 1979), esp. pp. 110-40 and 193-213; Ulrich B. Müller, *Prophetie und Predigt im Neuen Testament* (Gütersloh: Mohr, 1975); and Thomas W. Gillespie, *The First Theologians: A Study in Early Christian Prophecy* (Grand Rapids: Eerdmans, 1994), throughout.

75. Hill, *New Testament Prophecy,* p. 123.

76. Hill, *New Testament Prophecy,* p. 114.

77. Gillespie, *The First Theologians,* p. 25.

upbuilding, . . . encouragement and consolation" (1 Cor. 14:3), which *involves the mind* (1 Cor. 14:13-19).[78] Müller insists that it includes "repentance speech" *(Bussrede)* and "exhortation speech" *(Mahnrede),* and is "emphatically ordered."[79] It preaches and applies *the truths of the gospel.* Gillespie, whose work on prophecy in Paul is probably more thorough and comprehensive than most, associates both 1 Thess. 5:20-21 ("Do not despise the words of prophets, but test everything") and Rom. 12:6 ("prophesy, in proportion to faith") with the gospel: *prophecy is an expression of the gospel.*[80] Again, it is not a private message about individual situations. We do not doubt that this has a pastoral place; but are "private revelations" what Paul or Luke thinks of as "prophecy"?

Gillespie comments that prophecy is the only work of the Holy Spirit listed in 1 Cor. 12:8-10, 28-30; Rom. 12:6-8; and Eph. 4:11, all of which enumerate gifts not for a domestic few, but for the common good of all *(pros ton symphoron).*[81] That the context of prophecy is the *whole worshiping community,* Gillespie concludes, is seen in Paul's exhortation in 1 Cor. 14:1: "Strive for the spiritual gifts, especially that you may prophesy." This "assumes the [whole] church at worship."[82] Thus, while 1 Cor. 14:1-12 set out the *criterion of intelligibility* for prophecy, 14:13-19 *apply* "the criterion of the *believing community,* and . . . verses 20-25 *apply the criterion of the outsider or unbeliever* who might be present in the worship assembly" (my italics).[83] Gillespie concludes that this prophecy denotes the proclaiming of the *gospel from God to the whole church,* not some "horizontal" communication to an individual. Even in the Old Testament, "the prophetic announcement of the promise is thus the equivalent of the pre-proclamation of the gospel . . . of judgement and grace."[84]

(d) Finally we may consider C. M. Robeck's contention that prophecy is addressed only and strictly to believers.[85] We might have thought that 1 Cor. 14:25 would be sufficient to dispel such a theory. His main point is that prophecy should not be confused with proclamation. But Müller shows that the combination of judgment and grace in prophecy belongs to the whole "proclamation" to both believers and unbelievers.[86] It is indisputable that 1 Cor. 14:24-25 presupposes a Christian congregation which welcomes outsiders or unbelievers. Hill comments, "By including intentionally outsiders and non-believers . . .

---

78. Müller, *Prophetie und Predigt,* pp. 14 and 24.

79. Müller, *Prophetie und Predigt,* p. 26.

80. Gillespie, *The First Theologians,* p. 63.

81. Gillespie, *The First Theologians,* p. 117.

82. Gillespie, *The First Theologians,* p. 129.

83. Gillespie, *The First Theologians,* p. 132.

84. Gillespie, *The First Theologians,* pp. 135 and 136.

85. C. M. Robeck, "The Gift of Prophecy in Acts and Paul," *Studia Biblica et Theologica* 5, no. 2 (1975): 39-54; cf. no. 1, pp. 15-38.

86. Müller, *Prophetie und Predigt,* pp. 24-26; cf. pp. 12-46.

Paul demonstrates . . . the missionary function of the word, even of the inspired prophetic word spoken in worship."[87] When we consider postbiblical writers, we will see in Part II that Augustine, Thomas Aquinas, Calvin, Estius, Matthew Henry, John Wesley, and James Denney regard prophecy in Paul as the public preaching of the word of God, or applied exposition of Scripture.

As a tailpiece, in addition to liberating the term to *denote a broader and more solemn, gospel-centered discourse or utterance,* we must be aware of how easily "prophecy" can be *manipulated as a power tool.* Many who might regard an action as unnecessary or foolish have been browbeaten to agree to what claims to be a prophecy *from God.* This possibility that prophecy can be abused is not in itself an argument about Paul's meaning. But it is significant that many see the divisions at Corinth in terms of *a power struggle.* L. L. Welborn has twice argued this. He writes of 1 Corinthians 1–4: "It is a power struggle, not a theological controversy, that motivates the writing of 1 Corinthians 1–4."[88] *Eris* (strife) and *zēlos* (jealousy) in 1 Cor. 3:3 are exactly the right words for a power struggle, and Paul nowhere favors the theology of one group against the others, including the "I am for Paul" faction.

(2) *"Discernment of spirits."* Paul declares, "Do not despise the words of the prophets, but test everything" (1 Thess. 5:20-21). In this context the gift of evaluating, assessing, discerning, or disseminating what is "of the Holy Spirit" is not only vital but also accords with the precise meaning of *diakrisis* and *diakrinō* in 1 Cor. 11:29: "not discerning the Lord's body." The meaning of *diakrinō* in 1 Cor. 4:7 is probably, "What distinguishes you?" (NRSV, "Who sees anything different in you?").

G. Dautzenberg argues that here the term means "to interpret," largely on the basis of the Dead Sea Scrolls. In Qumran *diakrinō* may reflect the Hebrew *pēsher* to mean the interpretation of a prophecy.[89] He concludes, however, that in 1 John 4:1-6 it probably means the testing of prophecy, where we also have "test the spirits to see whether they are from God." Like Qumran, 1 John 4:6 distinguishes between "the spirit of truth" and "the spirit of error." *Didache* 11:7 discourages "examining" one who speaks in the Spirit (Greek, *ou peirasete oude diakrinete*), probably at the end of the first century. Yet the *Didache* continues, "Not everyone who speaks in a spirit is a prophet, except he has the behavior of the Lord" (*Didache* 11:8). Helmut Merklein follows Dautzenberg.[90]

---

87. Hill, *New Testament Prophecy,* pp. 123-24.

88. L. L. Welborn, "Discord in Corinth," in L. L. Welborn, *Politics and Rhetoric in the Corinthian Epistles* (Macon, GA: Mercer University Press, 1997), p. 7; cf. pp. 1-42; and Welborn, *Paul, the Fool of Christ: A Study of 1 Corinthians 1–4* (London and New York: T&T Clark, 2005).

89. G. Dautzenberg, "Zum religionsgeschichtlichen Hintergrund der *diakriseis pneumatōn* (1 Kor. 12:10)," *Biblische Zeitschrift* 15 (1971): 93-104.

90. H. Merklein, "Der Theologe als Prophet: Zur Funktion prophetischen Redes im theologischen Diskurs der Paulus," *NTS* 38 (1992): 402-29.

Wayne A. Grudem, however, dissents from Dautzenberg. In his view the plural *pneumatōn* denotes respectively evil spirits and the Spirit of God. An evil spirit may inspire a false interpretation of prophecy or wholesome teaching. Hence *diakrisis* would mean "distinguishing." "Testing," he argues, is inadequate.[91] Ernst Fuchs has a similar view, but sees the "distinguishing" as on the one hand from a purely human spirit, and on the other from the Holy Spirit of God.[92] This would accord with Paul's emphatic *to pneuma to ek tou theou* in 1 Cor. 2:12. James D. G. Dunn surely insists rightly that this all implies a weighing, distinguishing, and *evaluating.* This may be what is at issue in the notorious "silence of women" passage (1 Cor. 14:33-36). It is unnecessary to suggest that this is an interpretation. The immediate context is prophecy. Perhaps a woman cries, "My husband cannot be a prophet. If you only knew . . . !" Hence Paul bans domestic feuds in such a serious situation. Antoinette Wire's argument about "Corinthian Women Prophets" adds force and plausibility to such a hypothetical reconstruction.[93]

6.4. The Gifts of the Spirit: Speaking in Tongues

Before we consider further controversial issues, three preliminary points come directly from the New Testament text. First, Paul does not speak of tongues, or *glossolalia,* as a single, *uniform* phenomenon. In 1 Cor. 12:10 he speaks of "kinds" or "species" of tongues (Greek, *genē glossōn*). Second, in 1 Cor. 14:2 Paul explicitly declares, "Those who speak in a tongue do not speak to other people, but to *God.*" This may distinguish Paul from Acts. It is possible that in a miracle of hearing, rather than of speaking, people overheard the apostles addressing God. But most scholars interpret the speaking in tongues as addressed to those who witnessed it. Certainly Paul contrasts prophecy as *from* God with speaking in tongues as addressed *to* God. Third, Paul insists that tongues as such cannot "edify" or "build up" fellow Christians in the way that prophecy can, "unless [someone] interprets [them]." It is notable, however, that the Greek simply reads *ei mē diermēneuē* (1 Cor. 14:5), that is, there the words for "someone" (Greek, *tis*) and for "them" do *not* occur in the Greek text (cf. 1 Cor. 14:6-9).

The third point, however, introduces controversy. The key verse here is 1 Cor. 14:4: "Those who speak in a tongue *build up themselves,* but those who prophesy build up the church." Philipp Vielhauer insists that Paul's deliberate

---

91. Wayne A. Grudem, *The Gift of Prophecy in 1 Corinthians* (Washington, DC: University Press of America, 1982), pp. 58-60.

92. Ernst Fuchs, *Christus und der Geist bei Paulus* (Leipzig: Hinrichs, 1932), pp. 36-48.

93. Antoinette C. Wire, *The Corinthian Women Prophets: A Reconstruction* (Minneapolis: Fortress, 1990), pp. 135-58.

use of *oikodomeō*, "to build up," implies that "to build up oneself" amounts to self-affirmation, self-sufficiency, self-indulgence, or egoism.[94] Similarly, W. Schrage links 14:4 with 1 Cor. 10:24, "Do not seek your own advantage."[95] But Gordon Fee argues, "The edifying is not self-centeredness, but the personal edification of the believer that comes through private prayer and praise."[96] Fee's view derives from John Chrysostom (*1 Corinthians*, Homily 35:1). It may be that the two views can be reconciled. Since Paul urges that speaking in tongues is strictly private, not public (1 Cor. 14:6-19), it may be that tongues can be of value to the individual in private (hence: "I would like you all to speak in tongues"; 14:5); but in *public* the tongue-speaking becomes *self-indulgent* (14:4). Some, of course, would argue that "interpretation" plays a role here; but we shall consider later what "interpretation of tongues" probably means.

Now that we have cleared some ground, we may survey critically various theories about what speaking in tongues *(glossolalia)* amounts to. Although speaking in tongues today may assist sensitivity in interpreting Paul, we should not ascribe to Paul experiences of today, without further ado. To do so would risk circular argument.

(1) One of the earliest theories about the nature of speaking in tongues is known as *xenolalia,* or speaking in other languages. This view was known in early Pentecostalism and associated with their missionary outreach. In spite of objections, some ascribe this view to Luke in Acts 2:5-21, although many New Testament specialists argue that the Jewish hearers whom Luke describes would all know Greek, as W. L. Knox and J. Weiss maintain. Conversely, Knox argues that it is most unlikely that any Jew of the Dispersion would have understood the native dialects that survived in the remote regions of the Middle East, since the Jews of the Dispersion were almost entirely city dwellers. Nevertheless Luke may have the reversal of the confusion at Babel in view.

Certainly Luke is concerned with missionary expansion. Max Turner declares in the volume on tongues by Mark J. Cartledge, "In Paul's view, the *glōssai* are most probably languages of some kind, not merely ecstatic shouts."[97] Again in one of his own books, Max Turner similarly writes, "There is no doubt that Luke considers the Pentecost phenomenon, which he designates as *heterais glōssais lalein* (to speak with other tongues), to be *xenolalia,* that is, the speaking of actual foreign languages."[98] Luke was concerned with the missionary spread

94. Vielhauer, *Oikodomē*, pp. 91-98.

95. Schrage, *Der erste Brief an die Korinther*, vol. 3, p. 388, nn. 62 and 63.

96. Gordon D. Fee, *The First Epistle to the Corinthians* (Grand Rapids: Eerdmans, 1987), p. 657; and Fee, *God's Empowering Presence*, p. 219.

97. Max Turner, "Early Christian Experience and Theology of Tongues — A New Testament Perspective," in *Speaking in Tongues: Multi-Disciplinary Perspectives*, ed. Mark J. Cartledge (Milton Keynes: Paternoster, 2006), p. 12.

98. Turner, *The Holy Spirit and Spiritual Gifts*, p. 222.

of the gospel (although most village centers in the Roman Empire spoke Greek or Latin), and perhaps saw Pentecost as a reversal of Babel.[99] Frank Macchia recognizes that Luke sees some contrasting relationship with Babel, but also believes that sheer contrast is "one-dimensional, lacking deeper and complex ideas implied by a more differentiated comparison."[100] But does *Paul* regard the phenomena in this way?

This was perhaps the predominant opinion before the modern era. Irenaeus states that "Those who have received the Spirit of God . . . through the Spirit speak all [kinds of] languages" (*Against Heresies,* 5:6:1; *ANF,* vol. 1, p. 531). The content is his exposition of the work of the Holy Spirit, in which he famously calls Christ and the Spirit "the [two] hands of God." Such a view is ascribed to Origen, though I cannot find such a passage. Indeed, in *On First Principles,* 2:8:2 he seems to regard speaking in tongues as mindless (1 Cor. 14:15, "I will pray with the spirit," in contrast to "with the understanding"; *ANF,* vol. 4, p. 287). Indeed, in *Against Celsius,* 7, he refers to "fanatical and quite unintelligible words, of which no rational person can find the meaning" (*ANF,* vol. 4, p. 614). John Chrysostom stresses the cessation of tongues, but urges that this provides no proof "that they were done then" (*Homily on 1 Corinthians,* 6; also *NPNF,* ser. 1, vol. 12, p. 31). The Spirit is primarily a proof of apostleship (*Homily on 2 Corinthians,* 12; *NPNF,* ser. 1, vol. 12, p. 338).

In Cyril of Jerusalem, however, the gift of speaking languages becomes explicit, although he refers primarily to Acts 2. He believes that the Galilean Peter or Andrew spoke Persian or Median, and took many years to learn to speak Greek well. But, he says, "The Holy Spirit taught them many languages at once, languages which all their life they never knew" (*Catechetical Lectures,* 17:16; *NPNF,* ser. 2, vol. 7, p. 128). Hilary of Poitiers seems to imply that "interpreted tongues" may communicate foreign languages (*On the Trinity,* 8:30; *NPNF,* ser. 2, vol. 9, p. 146). Augustine ascribes "other tongues" to Acts 2, but seems to restrict this to "the extension of the first beginnings of the church" (*Answer to the Letters of Petilian the Donatist,* 2:32:74; *NPNF,* ser. 1, vol. 4, p. 548; and *On Baptism, Against the Donatists,* 3:16; *NPNF,* ser. 1, vol. 4, p. 443).

We can trace other views in Thomas Aquinas and in Peter Lombard. Erasmus then asserts that this gift is given in order that it may be spoken in various languages (Erasmus, *Opera Omnia: Epistola Pauli ad 1 Corinthios Prima,* vol. 6 [Leiden, 1705], p. 898; Latin, *ut idem variis linguis loquatur*). Similarly, John Calvin refers to *interpreted* tongues, but in relation to Acts 2:1-10. He writes, "Interpreters translated foreign languages into native speech."[101] Even in the nine-

---

99. Frank Macchia, "Babel and the Tongues of Pentecost: Reversal or Fulfilment? — A Theological Perspective," in *Speaking in Tongues,* ed. Mark J. Cartledge, pp. 34-51.

100. Macchia, "Babel," in *Speaking in Tongues,* ed. Mark J. Cartledge, p. 43.

101. John Calvin, *First Epistle to the Corinthians* (Edinburgh: Oliver & Boyd and St. Andrews, 1960), p. 263.

teenth century Charles Hodge saw tongues as linguistic translation.[102] Today we can find this view in the scholarly work of J. G. Davies, Robert Gundry, and Christopher Forbes.[103] Forbes asserts, "I am confident that Paul, like Luke, understands *glossolalia* as the miraculous ability to speak unlearned human and (possibly) divine or angelic languages."[104] At a more popular level, Dennis and Rita Bennett cite 1 Cor. 14:21, "By people of strange tongues and by the lips of foreigners I will speak to this people," although they concede that private prayer or praise is the main use of tongues. They state: "The tongue may be language known to the unbeliever."[105]

In complete contrast, Cyril G. Williams asserts, "That the Corinthian phenomenon is not *xenoglossia* seems clear from 1 Cor. 14:10-11."[106] Paul states in 1 Cor. 14:11: "If I do not know the meaning of the sound, I will be a foreigner to the speaker, and the speaker a foreigner to me." *Glossolalia* does *not* denote *cognitive communicative* speech between people. Paul's analogy between tongues and a language that conveys nothing to the hearer leaves no room for doubt. According to Williams, it "clears away any vestige of doubt that he [Paul] thinks of the gift of tongues as miraculous speaking in unlearned tongues."[107] Cheryl Bridges and the Pentecostal writer Frank Macchia observe, "That Paul understood tongues-speaking as *xenolalia* seems unlikely, since in 1 Corinthians 14 he nowhere assumes that a natural understanding of the gift is possible."[108] Some insist that this applies only to *uninterpreted* tongues. But, first, we shall consider what the "interpretation of tongues" denotes under a separate heading; second, if tongues are *not* to be exercised in *public*, interpersonal communication would not seem to apply. For the present we must at the very least postpone the question of the status of "interpreted" tongues. Meanwhile Cyril Williams, again, comments, "I discover no compelling reason to abandon the widely held view that the Corinthian phenomenon is unintelligible glossolalia . . . attended by uncontrolled behaviour."[109]

---

102. Charles Hodge, *The First Epistle to the Corinthians* (London: Banner of Truth, 1958), p. 248.

103. J. G. Davies, "Pentecost and Glossolalia," *JTS* 3 (1952): 228-31; Robert H. Gundry, "Ecstatic Utterances (N.E.B.?)," *JTS* 17 (1966): 299-307; and Christopher Forbes, *Prophecy and Inspired Speech*, pp. 60-64.

104. Forbes, *Prophecy and Inspired Speech*, p. 64.

105. Dennis and Rita Bennett, *The Holy Spirit and You* (Eastbourne: Kingsway, 1974), pp. 93-95.

106. Cyril G. Williams, *Tongues of the Spirit* (Cardiff: University of Wales Press, 1981), p. 31.

107. Williams, *Tongues of the Spirit*, p. 222; cf. Cyril G. Williams, "Speaking in Tongues," in *Strange Gifts 2: A Guide to Charismatic Renewal*, ed. David Martin and Peter Mullen (Oxford: Blackwell, 1984), pp. 79-82.

108. Cheryl Bridges and Frank Macchia, "Glossolalia," in *The Encyclopedia of Christianity*, vol. 2 (Grand Rapids and Cambridge: Eerdmans, 2001), p. 413; cf. pp. 413-16.

109. Williams, *Tongues of the Spirit*, p. 30.

Janet Everts Powers sympathetically considers the early Pentecostal belief that tongues-speech was speech in foreign languages because it belonged to the missionary mandate of the Church. She admittedly addresses Acts 2 rather than Paul, but comments that she finds "no Biblical evidence" for using tongues-speech as a mission-related phenomenon of communication, whether in Paul or elsewhere.[110] They preached the *gospel in the vernacular.* Moreover, in a communication age, she claims, this view delivers a hostage into the hands of the "cessationists," who would see it as an appropriate gift only in the pre-modern world. If tongues have anything to do with mission, she concludes, "Tongues are a sign that believers have been empowered by the Holy Spirit."[111]

In addition to these exegetical and theological issues, the well-known work of William J. Samarin, especially in *Tongues of Men and Angels,* applied *linguistic criteria* to tape recordings of *glossolalia* to discover that, while it exhibited analogies with *baby talk* or magical incantations, it bears the characteristics of a *definite specific language only superficially as a pseudo-language.*[112] He described it as "only a facade of language." There are admittedly numerous anecdotal accounts of appearing to speak in natural languages.[113] It is difficult for the nonspecialist inquirer or theologian to assess these, but Samarin, a linguist from the University of Toronto, remains adamant that in linguistic and anthropological terms this has not been adequately assessed in social-scientific or linguistic terms in such a way as to suggest *xenolalia.* This is presumably why Mark Cartledge has put together a volume recently of biblical, linguistic, political, psychological, and sociological perspectives.[114] He has also explored church groups in some half-dozen countries. He would reply to objections that people seem to recognize merely syllables which seem to fit a given language. He mentions also the work of Felicitas Goodman, who approached the phenomena from an anthropological perspective, declaring that it was trancelike behavior, which would exclude *xenolalia.*[115] But many who speak in tongues would be reluctant to accept her findings.

(2) At the very opposite end of the spectrum of interpretation, we may distinguish *ecstasy or ecstatic utterance.* The New English Bible favored this translation of speaking in tongues, although Robert Gundry has attacked it.[116] Ecstatic experience may be expressed in sublinguistic noise, akin to laughing, crying, or

---

110. Janet Everts Powers, "Missionary Tongues?" *JPT* 17 (2000): 39-55.

111. Powers, "Missionary Tongues?" *JPT* 17 (2000): 53.

112. William J. Samarin, *Tongues of Men and Angels: The Religious Language of Pentecostalism* (New York: Macmillan, 1972).

113. Ralph W. Harris, *Spoken by the Spirit: Documental Accounts of "Other Tongues" from Arabic to Zulu* (Springfield, MO: Gospel Publishing House, 1973).

114. Cartledge (ed.), *Speaking in Tongues.*

115. Felicitas Goodman, *Speaking in Tongues: A Cross-Cultural Study of Glossolalia* (Chicago: University of Chicago Press, 1972).

116. Gundry, "'Ecstatic Utterance' (N.E.B.?)," *JTS* 17 (1966): 299-307.

clapping, when a person longs to give expression to that which is beyond human words. Many have cited Paul's references to the indistinct sounds of music (1 Cor. 14:7-9), which give an ambiguous signal or are analogous to "speech that is not intelligible" (14:9). They also appeal to his reference to "speaking like a child" (1 Cor. 13:11, where "child" [Greek, *nēpios*] may denote "infant," "baby," or "a very young child," in contrast to NRSV, "child," in general).[117] It may well mean baby talk, especially in the light of becoming adult and putting an end to "childish things" (13:11). Hence in 14:20 Paul says, "Do not be children [Greek, *paidia*] in your thinking; rather, be infants in evil [Greek, *nēpiazete*], but in thinking be adults [Greek, *teleioi*, 'mature']."

Then follows the verse which Dennis and Rita Bennett think refers to translating foreign languages, "By people of strange tongues and by the lips of foreigners I will speak" (14:21). Paul looks back to Isa. 28:11-12.[118] But this refers to the coming of the Assyrians and to God's way of punishment, and C. D. Stanley and many other Pauline specialists see the significance of this entirely differently than Dennis and Rita Bennett.[119] All around them, exiled and fallen Israel will hear "strange tongues," and will feel *alienated and homesick*. Paul then sees this as *inappropriate for the hearing of Christians*, who should be comfortable, welcome, and "at home" in their own church. Tongues are thus a sign "for unbelievers" (14:22), that is, *Christians should not be put in the position of those who do not believe and who suffer divine punishment*. I have expounded this more fully elsewhere.[120] In addition to all this, when someone speaks in tongues, the "mind is unproductive" (1 Cor. 14:14). No one can say "Amen" to the utterance (14:16). Whereas "prophecy" will lead to a change of heart, the confession that "God is really among you" (14:25), in the case of "tongues" unbelievers and outsiders who enter the church will say "that you are out of your mind" (14:23; Greek, *mainesthe*, "be out of one's mind, be mad, or be raving").[121] In Luke's terms, would not "babble" mean the reversal of Babel?

(3) We have considered all but one of the main views of tongues-speech. However, in my commentary on the Greek text I have set out three more views, two of which have little support, and a third which deserves consideration.[122] The first is that tongues constitutes angelic speech. Earle Ellis and G. Dautzenberg argue for this view, and Ben Witherington has some sympathy with it. It depends on parallels with Qumran, *Jubilees*, and selected Jewish apocalyptic literature (cf. *Jubilees* 25:14; *Testament of Job* 48:1–50:3; *1 Enoch* 40 and 71:11).

---

117. Danker, BDAG, p. 671.

118. Bennett, *The Holy Spirit and You*, p. 94.

119. C. D. Stanley, *Paul and the Language of Scripture*, SNTSMS 64 (Cambridge: Cambridge University Press, 1992), pp. 197-205.

120. Thiselton, *The First Epistle to the Corinthians*, pp. 1120-22.

121. Danker, BDAG, p. 610.

122. Thiselton, *The First Epistle to the Corinthians*, pp. 970-88.

Wayne Grudem and E. B. Allo, however, reject this as speculative, and reflecting a Montanist belief. The second view sees tongues as reflecting liturgical, archaic, or rhythmic phrases. F. Bleek advocated this view in 1829, followed by C. F. G. Heinrici some sixty years later. Today it might be linked with Dale Martin's view of tongues as an indicator of status, but it is not widely favored, and criticized as speculative. We pass, therefore, to consider the third view.

(4) In effect this view draws on that of Gerd Theissen on the importance of the unconscious in Paul, which we consider in detail in Part III.[123] It is often said that Pentecostals dismiss any "psychological" explanation. But Theissen writes primarily as a theologian. He genuinely considers Paul's concerns about "the secrets of the heart," which, since Freud, we have come to call the unconscious. God's love is poured into our hearts through the Holy Spirit (Rom. 5:5), to reshape those sins and habits of which we may be unaware. Sin and sanctification are not just conscious matters. It is now well known that the Pentecostal Frank Macchia sees Rom. 8:26 as an example of "tongues": "The Spirit intercedes with sighs too deep for words. And God, who searches the heart, knows what is in the mind of the Spirit, because the Spirit intercedes for the saints according to the will of God" (Rom. 8:26-27).[124] This also resonates with the important article by Krister Stendahl in which he accepts that glossolalia may mean a release of inhibitions and experience of freedom (as Ernst Käsemann also does).[125] Stendahl's main caveat, however, is that mature Christians would find "high voltage" religion unhealthy if it became a permanent practice.

We shall look at this fourth contribution in more detail in Part III when we consider Theissen and Macchia among late-twentieth-century and twenty-first-century writers. It is not incompatible with other views.

6.5. The Personhood of the Holy Spirit

When we ask about features of the doctrine of the Holy Spirit most distinctive to Paul, we find that these, too, tend to generate controversy. Three issues still clamor for attention. (1) Paul came to see the Holy Spirit as God's Personal Agent, but his approach is not exactly the same as in John, and remains open to debate. (2) There are possible Trinitarian implications in Paul's epistles. Athanasius and Basil made extensive use of 1 Cor. 12:4-7, as well as of 1 Cor. 2:14-16 and 2 Cor. 13:13. (3) When he speaks of "being baptized in (or with) the Holy Spirit" (1 Cor. 12:13), some refer to this as the experience of becoming a Chris-

---

123. Gerd Theissen, *Psychological Aspects of Pauline Theology* (Edinburgh: T&T Clark, 1987).

124. Frank D. Macchia, "Groans Too Deep for Words," *Asian Journal of Pentecostal Studies* 1 (1998): 149-73.

125. Krister Stendahl, "Glossolalia — the New Testament Evidence," in his *Paul among Jews and Gentiles* (London: SCM, 1977), pp. 109-24.

tian, while others believe that it denotes an experience subsequent to that of becoming a Christian. Further, is this the same experience as that to which the Gospels allude (Mark 1:8)?

First, on the Personhood of the Holy Spirit, we have to face the fact that the majority of people, even often Christians, refer to the Holy Spirit as "it," and nurture the concept of a powerful force, perhaps on the analogy of steam or of electricity, in operation. It is an oddity of Christian preaching and education that this is so widespread. Two factors in the past contributed to this, one spurious and one genuine. On top of this, the Spirit is often separated from God in what, at best, would be a kind of tritheism.

First, Paul Feine (1859-1933) of Breslau and Halle belonged to the "History-of-Religions School," and claimed that the ancient world did not know our strict concept of *person*. The ancient world, he claimed, could use only circumlocutions such as name, face, soul, body, and so on. Rudolf Bultmann claims, "The Spirit may be called the power of futurity."[126] Yet Paul speaks of personal activities of the Spirit such as coming alongside us to help (Greek *synantilambanetai,* Rom. 8:26), which Lindsay Dewar calls "a strongly personal word."[127] Whether the Greeks have a specific *word* for *person* is irrelevant to whether they could have a *concept* of *person*. James Barr calls this the word-concept fallacy. He writes, "Vocabulary grids themselves are ultimately irrelevant. The abstracting . . . of the 'vocabulary grids' may be the fundamental fallacy. . . . Theological thought . . . has its characteristic linguistic expression not in the word individually, but in the word-combination or sentence," that is, in how the word is *used*.[128] Clearly if English, unlike Russian, does not have special *words* for light blue and dark blue, this does spell confusion on the day of the Oxford vs. Cambridge boat race, for this does not inhibit our having *concepts* of light blue and dark blue. Likewise we should not argue, Barr suggests, that the French are more "erotic" because they call most objects masculine or feminine, or the Turks unaware of gender because their words lack a gender distinction! We are considering accidents of grammar and vocabulary.

Barr rejects drawing inferences from grammatical gender, which is the product of contingent accident and convention, to the gender of personal identity. Barr asserts, "A grammar does not strictly follow linguistic method."[129] It is an accident of convention that "spirit" *(rûach)* in Hebrew is feminine, and "spirit" *(pneuma)* in Greek is neuter. It does not suggest that Greeks viewed children as subpersonal merely because *teknon,* "child," is neuter. God and the Holy Spirit transcend the human genders, so that both "masculine" and "femi-

---

126. Rudolf Bultmann, *Theology of the New Testament,* vol. 1 (London: SCM, 1952), p. 335.

127. Lindsay Dewar, *The Holy Spirit and Modern Thought* (London: Mowbray, 1959), p. 71.

128. James Barr, *The Semantics of Biblical Language* (Oxford: Oxford University Press, 1961), pp. 38 and 233.

129. Barr, *The Semantics of Biblical Language,* p. 96.

nine" qualities are ascribed to them, as biblical passages about fatherly and motherly qualities apply to them.

A greater difficulty stems from a second factor, that Paul often speaks of the Holy Spirit as if he were merely a *fluid or liquid*. Bultmann calls this "dynamistic thinking," and uses as examples, "giving" the Spirit, "pouring out" or "supplying" the Spirit (Rom. 5:5; 2 Cor. 1:22; 5:5; 1 Thess. 4:8), and passages in which "Spirit" seems synonymous with "power."[130] This, he says, constitutes a contrasting and *different* formulation from the "animistic" one, which uses more personal language. *But this does not mean that the Holy Spirit is a subpersonal force.* Personal language is used. For example, the Spirit "bears witness with our spirit that we are children of God" (Rom. 8:16). The Spirit "searches everything" and "comprehends what is truly God's" (1 Cor. 2:10-11).

The problem is that *"personal" words alone* might imply that Holy Spirit is a "person" *in the same sense as human beings*. By *qualifying* personal language with "dynamistic" language, Paul suggests that the Spirit is *more than personal, not less than personal. He is suprapersonal.* He proceeds from God as the kind of Person that God is. We should not dream of calling *God "it,"* or a *force*. To do so would be demeaning to God, and since humans are created in God's image, thereby to demean humanity.

Nor should we interpret the personal or the "dynamistic" language concerning the Holy Spirit *in isolation from each other.* Ian Ramsey has conclusively shown that virtually all language about God borrows "models" from ordinary language, and "qualifies" these models in such a way that *both together* communicate truth about God in a unique and distinctive way. For example, God is not simply "a cause" of the world, but its "first cause"; he is not merely "wise," but "infinitely wise." Hence the terms "first" and "infinitely" serve to *qualify* the models "cause" and "wise."[131] It is the same with language about the Holy Spirit. Personal or "animistic" language provides the model; "dynamistic" language provides a crucial qualifier. The result is not that the Holy Spirit is subpersonal, let alone impersonal. The dual language shows together that he is *suprapersonal. He is more*, but *not less*, than a human person. *He is suprapersonal in the same sense as God is suprapersonal.*

6.6. The Holy Spirit and the Holy Trinity

Many New Testament scholars are reluctant to find a doctrine of the Trinity in Paul or in the New Testament as a whole. But many go to the very brink of ad-

---

130. Bultmann, *Theology of the New Testament*, vol. 1, pp. 155 and 156.

131. Ian T. Ramsey, *Religious Language: An Empirical Placing of Theological Phrases* (London: SCM, 1957), pp. 61-71; cf. pp. 49-89.

mitting it. D. E. H. Whiteley, for example, argues that the parallels between the Father, the Son, and the Holy Spirit in 1 Cor. 12:4-6 and 2 Cor. 13:13 ("the grace of our Lord Jesus Christ . . .") suggest what he calls "traces of a Trinitarian ground-plan."[132] The Spirit is clearly distinct from God the Father in Gal. 4:6: "God has sent into our hearts the Spirit of his Son"; and in Rom. 5:5: "God's love has been poured into our hearts through the Holy Spirit that [who] has been given to us" (probably the "divine passive," i.e., "given by God"). We find the same clear distinction between God and the Spirit in Rom. 8:27: "God . . . knows the mind of the Spirit"; and 1 Cor. 2:11-12: "No one comprehends what is truly God's except the Spirit of God." All four "major epistles" witness to the point.

The same distinction marks the relation between the Holy Spirit and Christ. The most striking example is Rom. 8:11: "The Spirit of him who raised Jesus from the dead. . . . He who raised Christ . . . will give life to your mortal bodies also through his Spirit. . . ." But there are others. In Gal. 3:13-14 Paul declares, "Christ redeemed us . . . so that we might receive the promise of the Spirit." In 1 Cor. 12:4-6, "the same Spirit" is associated with "varieties of gifts"; "the same Lord" is associated with "varieties of services"; and "the same God," with "varieties of activities." We have already cited 2 Cor. 13:13: "The grace of the Lord Jesus Christ, the love of God, and the communion [or joint-share] of the Holy Spirit be with all of you." Again, all four major epistles support one another.

Yet Whiteley seems reluctant to take this further in his study of Paul. Similarly, even James Dunn prefers to speak of Pauline and early Christian experience, which "may have played a significant part in the development of a Trinitarian conception of God," rather than go further.[133] He prefers to speak of "this confusing welter of imagery . . . of conceptuality being stretched" in which Christological reflection and inherited monotheism largely overshadow any Trinitarian formulation.[134] He does indeed speak of "triadic" texts, and rightly concludes, "The character of Jesus' ministry had become the defining character of the Spirit. . . . This would have provided an invaluable test, . . . the character of Jesus."[135] Dunn's reluctance to go further rests on New Testament monotheism, which the first generation of Christians would be reluctant to surrender, both because monotheism is confessed in early Christian creeds (1 Cor. 8:4-6) and because debates about God with Jews would have left little alternative option.

Admittedly Dunn and Whiteley go further than most. Can we say more than J. Christiaan Beker, namely, "Paul has only an incipient doctrine of the Trinity (1 Cor. 12:4-11; 2 Cor. 13:13). . . . We must therefore not read later developments into Paul. Paul's 'Trinitarian' construct is apocalyptic-monarchic (1 Cor.

---

132. D. E. H. Whiteley, *The Theology of St. Paul* (Oxford: Blackwell, 1964; 2nd ed. 1971), pp. 128-29.

133. James D. G. Dunn, *The Theology of Paul the Apostle* (Edinburgh: T&T Clark, 1998), p. 264.

134. Dunn, *The Theology of Paul*, p. 265.

135. Dunn, *The Theology of Paul*, p. 263.

15:28), that is, Christ and the Spirit function as apocalyptic heavenly 'associates' of God — not unlike Irenaeus' concept of Christ and the Spirit as God's 'hands.' We can say that Paul was moving towards a fuller Trinitarian conception. . . . Yet . . . Paul does not have a full Trinitarian scheme."[136]

While we should be cautious about dissenting from Whiteley, Dunn, and Beker, there is still more to be said. We may cite three further factors. The first is the extent to which Origen, Athanasius, Basil the Great, and perhaps Gregory rely on an exegesis of Paul for their formulation of a doctrine of the Holy Trinity, believing that it represents Paul's view. The second is the exposition of the Holy Trinity, especially in Jürgen Moltmann and Wolfhart Pannenberg, who insist that it is better to extrapolate from the *narrative* of the New Testament, or, as they would say, "from below." This then suggests the construction of later models and analogies, which may not be as explicit in the New Testament itself. This approach is utterly convincing. L. Hurtado has also demonstrated that at least "Binitarianism" *depends on Paul's inherited monotheism, as reconfigured,* not on a denial of it.[137]

Looking first at the Church Fathers, these writers were not constructively "adding to" the Pauline material, but were under the impression that they were explicating what was already Pauline (or sometimes Johannine). In the first century Clement coordinates the actions of the Father, the Son, and the Holy Spirit. He writes, "As God lives, and the Lord Jesus Christ lives, and the Holy Spirit, who are at once the faith and the hope of the elect" (*1 Clement* 58). Stanley Burgess comments, "The Bishop's letter reveals that nothing has been added to the New Testament doctrine of the Spirit."[138] As is well known, Tertullian (c. 160–c. 225) formulated an *explicit doctrine* of the Trinity. He writes, for example, "I testify that the Father and the Son and the Holy Spirit are inseparable from each other . . . and that they are distinct from each other. . . . The Father is the entire substance [*substantia*, Being], but the Son is a derivation and portion of the whole, . . . so He showed a third degree [of distinctness] in the Paraclete. . . . They are distinct in personality" (Tertullian, *Against Praxeas,* 25; also in *ANF,* vol. 3, p. 621; and *Against Praxeas,* 7–9; *ANF,* vol. 3, pp. 602-3). In the first reference Tertullian is not merely opposing a "heresy"; he quotes John 14:10, 11, 16; 16:14; 17:1, 11, "I and the Father are one" (John 10:30). In the second passage he quotes 1 Cor. 2:11. He genuinely appeals to Paul and to John.

In about 229-30 Origen wrote *On First Principles,* offering the first systematic treatise on the Holy Spirit by a Greek author. Again, like Tertullian, he draws on John and Paul. He declared that the apostles "handed down that the

136. J. Christiaan Beker, *Paul the Apostle: The Triumph of God in Life and Thought* (Edinburgh: T&T Clark, 1980), p. 200.

137. L. W. Hurtado, *Lord Jesus Christ* (Grand Rapids: Eerdmans, 2003), pp. 48-53 and 64-78.

138. Stanley M. Burgess, *The Holy Spirit: Ancient Christian Traditions* (Peabody, MA: Hendrickson, 1984), p. 18.

Holy Spirit is associated with the Father and Son in honor and dignity," and spoke of "matters which ought to be examined from the Holy Scriptures" (*On First Principles*, 1, Preface 4; also in *PG*, vol. 11, cols. 117-18A).[139] In *On First Principles* 1:3, he develops the joint naming of the Father, the Son, and the Holy Spirit in liturgical expressions, which Basil of Caesarea later expounds as of central importance for all Christians. In *On First Principles*, 1:3:4, Origen insists, "All knowledge of the Father is obtained by revelation of the Son through the Holy Spirit," citing 1 Cor. 2:10, and, further, rejects the view that the Holy Spirit was "not yet" at any time, adding, "For if this were the case, the Holy Spirit would never be reckoned in the unity of the Trinity, i.e., along with the . . . Father and His Son" (1:3:4; also in *ANF*, vol. 4, p. 253).

Throughout, Origen refers to Paul. In *On First Principles*, 1:3:5, Origen asserts: "Regeneration by God to salvation has to do both with the Father and Son and Holy Spirit . . . with the co-operation of the entire Trinity" (also in *ANF*, vol. 4, p. 253). Again in the next section he quotes 1 Cor. 12:3: "No one can say that Jesus is Lord, but by the Holy Spirit"; and 1 Cor. 12:4-7: "There are varieties of gifts, but the same Spirit; . . . the same Lord; . . . the same God." Paul clearly states that "the power of the Trinity is one and the same" (Origen, *On First Principles*, 1:3:7; *ANF*, vol. 4, p. 255). These declarations of Paul establish "the Unity of the Father, and of the Son, and of the Holy Spirit" (1:3:8). We might cite other passages in Origen, but for the present we simply point out that the purpose of those which we have cited is not speculation, nor even "development," but Origen's attempt to reflect Paul faithfully.

Athanasius of Alexandria (c. 296-373) received a letter from his friend Serapion, the Bishop of Thmuis, while he was in the desert fleeing Constantius, which informed him of a group in his Diocese which held derogatory views of the Holy Spirit. In 358-59 he replied in his *Epistle to Serapion*, confronting those whom he called "Tropici" in *Epistle to Serapion*, 1–4:7. Athanasius insists that the Holy Spirit cannot be a created being, for this would make the Trinity consist of Creator and creature (*Epistle to Serapion*, 1:21-27; also in *PG*, vol. 26, cols. 581A-593C). But the Holy Trinity is indivisible (*Epistle to Serapion*, 1:2; 1:29). In 1:28 Athanasius writes: "There is, then, a Triad, holy and complete, confessed to be God in Father, Son and the Holy Spirit, . . . all creative, . . . in nature indivisible, and its activity is one. The Father does all things through the Word and the Holy Spirit. Thus the unity of the Holy Triad is preserved." He insists that this truth was taught by the apostles; he does not see this as independent of Scripture. He depends especially on 1 Cor. 12:4-6 and 2 Cor. 3:13 and 13:13. Michael Haykin concludes, "Athanasius is thus led to state the co-inherence of the three Persons in their unified activity."[140] Haykin shows repeatedly that the conclu-

---

139. *ANF*, vol. 4, p. 240.

140. Michael A. G. Haykin, *The Spirit of God: The Exegesis of 1 and 2 Corinthians in the*

sions and formulations of Athanasius are driven by a sober exegesis of 1 and 2 Corinthians. We shall consider this further in Part II.

In 365, Basil of Caesarea (Basil the Great, c. 330-79) undertook a brief exposition of the doctrine of the Holy Spirit in *Against Eunomius*. He was called by his bishop, Eusebius of Caesarea, to study and write to defend orthodoxy rather than pursue his ascetic life, and in 372 he succeeded Eusebius as bishop. Like Athanasius, he had to contend with those who devalued the Holy Spirit, a group largely led by Eunomius and based especially in Sebaste. Michael Haykin well sums up his similarities with, and differences from, Athanasius. He declares, "Whereas Athanasius' focus is on the inseparable nature of the triune God, Basil's emphasis is placed on the natural holiness of the Spirit, . . . holy without qualification."[141] Haykin adds, "Basil argues that the Spirit must be accorded the same honour and glory as the Father and the Son."[142]

For Basil, the threefold *Gloria* held a special, decisive place, as did baptism in the threefold Name. As we might expect, 1 Cor. 2:10-11, ". . . no one comprehends what is truly God's except the Spirit of God," played a dominant role for Basil (Basil, *Against Eunomius*, 3:4; *On the Holy Spirit*, 24:56). The Holy Spirit sets in motion "the imitation of Christ" (*On the Holy Spirit*, 15:35). That the Holy Spirit is revelatory, eternal, and Trinitarian is for him explicitly Pauline; it is not a later "development" from Paul. We shall return to Athanasius and to Basil later in Part II.

Our second argument is that, in contrast to Beker and Dunn, some scholars are prepared to go further in seeing the Trinity in the New Testament. Arthur Wainwright, for example, states: "The Spirit was often described in language which suggested that he was a person closely related to God. . . . There is abundant evidence that the Spirit was regarded as a personal being, who was capable of experiences of grief and approval. . . . Paul . . . speaks of the Spirit as if he were a person. The Spirit is grieved, bears witness, cries, leads, and makes intercessions."[143] Yet just as Christ can represent God, can speak with his authority, and with him be regarded as uncreated or as "no creature," this is hardly less so in the case of the Holy Spirit. Certainly both come from God (2 Cor. 5:19-21; 1 Cor. 2:10-16). Yet there is a difference of function between them (1 Cor. 12:4-7). Wainwright interprets the Greek of Phil. 3:3 (*hoi pneumati theou latreuontes*) as "'who worship the Spirit of God,' since *latreuein* regularly construes the object of worship in the dative case."[144]

Pneumatomachian Controversy of the Fourth Century, Supplements to *Vigiliae Christianae* 27 (Leiden and New York: Brill, 1994), p. 95.

141. Haykin, *The Spirit of God*, p. 38.

142. Haykin, *The Spirit of God*, p. 44.

143. Arthur W. Wainwright, *The Trinity in the New Testament* (London: SPCK, 1962), pp. 100-101.

144. Wainwright, *The Trinity in the New Testament*, pp. 227-28.

Wainwright admits that explanations of the Trinity do not develop until the age of the Church Fathers. But this argument cuts both ways. Paul did not have explanations of the Trinity on his agenda when he wrote his letters. But this does not mean that he did not presuppose or imply it. For example, if we do not reject Ephesians as "non-Pauline" or not by a close Pauline disciple, Eph. 4:4-6 alludes to "one Spirit, . . . one Lord, . . . one God."[145]

We move to our third point, namely, the *"narrative"* approach to the Holy Trinity, especially in Moltmann, in Pannenberg, and most recently in the Catholic writer Eugene F. Rogers. Moltmann admits that "the dogma of the Trinity stands at the end of the theological labours of the patristic period over the concept of God."[146] But he also asserts that Liberal Protestants have made an "irreconcilable contradiction" out of the doctrine. A key statement is as follows: *"The New Testament talks about God by proclaiming in narrative the relationships of the Father, the Son and the Spirit, which are relationships of fellowship and are open to the world"* (Moltmann's italics).[147] God the Father constitutes the substance of Jesus' preaching of the Kingdom, or reign, of God. Conversely, "God sent his own Son in the likeness of sinful flesh" (Rom. 8:3-4).[148] Seen as a whole, the "history of the Son" means: "the Father sends the Son through the Spirit. The Son comes from the Father in the power of the Spirit. The Spirit brings people into the fellowship of the Son with the Father."[149]

The "abandonment" by God of Jesus on the cross, when God seems to be silent, underlines the *differentiation* between the Persons of the Trinity. But "the One who is forsaken and cursed . . . is still the Son."[150] "Here the innermost life of the Trinity is at stake, yet this remains "the common sacrifice of the Father and the Son, [which] comes about through the Holy Spirit."[151] We see the glory of God "in the face of Jesus Christ" (2 Cor. 4:4), and Christ was raised through the activity of the Holy Spirit (Rom. 1:4; 8:11; 1 Cor. 6:14). In the resurrection of Jesus "the Father raises the dead Son through the life-giving Spirit; the Father enthrones the Son as the Lord . . . ; the risen Son sends the creative Spirit from the Father to renew heaven and earth."[152] Moltmann finds the scheme Father–Spirit–Son in the death and resurrection of Christ; the scheme Father–Son–Spirit in the sending of the Spirit; and the scheme Spirit–Son–Father in the eschatological consummation.

---

145. Wainwright, *The Trinity in the New Testament*, p. 259.

146. Jürgen Moltmann, *The Trinity and the Kingdom of God: The Doctrine of God* (London: SCM, 1981), p. 61.

147. Moltmann, *The Trinity and the Kingdom*, p. 64.

148. Moltmann, *The Trinity and the Kingdom*, p. 72.

149. Moltmann, *The Trinity and the Kingdom*, p. 75.

150. Moltmann, *The Trinity and the Kingdom*, p. 80.

151. Moltmann, *The Trinity and the Kingdom*, pp. 81 and 83.

152. Moltmann, *The Trinity and the Kingdom*, p. 8.

The participation of the whole Trinity in creation, redemption, and eschatology is clear. This is not counter to Paul's monotheism inherited from Judaism, for it is a carefully qualified monotheism, in contrast to monotheism "in its purest form" in Arianism.[153] This has nothing to do with shamrocks or with mathematical or numerical formulas, especially since the Church Fathers rejected this "numerical" approach to the Trinity as a crass misunderstanding of "three" and "one."

Wolfhart Pannenberg similarly speaks of "the beginnings of the doctrine of the Trinity" in the New Testament.[154] But even in the New Testament we see "God's fatherly goodness" and God as *Father* as *"much more than metaphor"* (my italics).[155] On the lips of Jesus, "Father" became a proper name for God. Paul presents Jesus as "Son," for example, in Rom. 8:9-16, 1 Cor. 12:4-6, and 2 Cor. 13:13. Believers share in the Sonship of Christ. The Holy Spirit performs a correlative work, although he is not yet "a separate hypostatic entity."[156] Paul, unlike the Greeks, does not ask questions about Being, Substance, Entities, or Hypostases. If this is why we should hesitate to see in Paul "a doctrine of the Trinity," this may be technically correct, except that since Paul never approached God in this way, it hardly detracts from seeing the Trinity in Paul. Only in an anachronistic sense can we deny that Paul is a "Trinitarian" thinker.

Eugene Rogers discusses the New Testament's narrative account of the Holy Trinity with particular reference to the baptism of Jesus.[157] However, he uses narratives from creation, from the annunciation, from the incarnate life of Jesus, and from the resurrection and the ascension of Christ, to expound the point further.[158] He even implies a brief suggestion, although not fully amplified as especially in Paul Ricoeur, that a narrative is the genre that *precisely exhibits a person in terms of what personhood entails.*[159]

Even in terms of later doctrine, Paul goes nowhere near to "modalism"; and the charge of "subordinationism" rests mainly on 1 Cor. 15:28: "The Son will also be subjected to the One who put all things in subjection under him, so that God may be all in all," but also on 1 Cor. 3:23 and 11:3. There are very particular reasons for this in the situation of 1 Corinthians. It is no accident that all

153. Moltmann, *The Trinity and the Kingdom*, p. 133.

154. Wolfhart Pannenberg, *Systematic Theology*, vol. 1 (Grand Rapids: Eerdmans and Edinburgh: T&T Clark, 1991), p. 259.

155. Pannenberg, *Systematic Theology*, vol. 1, pp. 259-61.

156. Pannenberg, *Systematic Theology*, vol. 1, p. 269.

157. Eugene F. Rogers, *After the Spirit: A Constructive Pneumatology from Resources outside the Modern West* (London: SCM, and Grand Rapids: Eerdmans, 2006), pp. 136-63.

158. Rogers, *After the Spirit*, pp. 98-134, 172-99, 200-212.

159. Rogers, *After the Spirit*, p. 457; cf. Paul Ricoeur, *Time and Narrative*, 3 vols. (Chicago: University of Chicago Press, 1984, 1985, and 1988); and Ricoeur, *Oneself as Another* (Chicago: University of Chicago Press, 1992).

three passages come in 1 Corinthians, namely, 3:23, "Christ belongs to God," and 11:3, "God is the head of Christ." In my larger commentary on 1 Corinthians, I have drawn attention to James Moffatt's explanation that in many Greek cults "God" or Zeus appeared as a remote and shadowy deity, in contrast to the cult-Lord, who was a familiar and more approachable figure.[160] Asclepius, Serapis, and similar cult deities were in danger of eclipsing the supreme god as the central deity. This may even have been a parallel failing of the "Christ" group in 1 Cor. 1:12. Neil Richardson points out that there are "clusters" of passages peculiar to 1 Corinthians which stress the sovereignty or rule of God, for example, 1 Cor. 1:26-28, 30; 2:4, 5, 11, 12, 14; 3:6, 7, 9, 23; 8:6; 11:30).[161]

The narrative of Jesus, which involved God the Father and the Holy Spirit, would be the oral tradition which Paul presupposed.[162] We can see the explication in Paul's epistles. We conclude that Paul bequeathed a clearly Trinitarian theology of the Holy Spirit, even if others spoke of the Spirit as a "hypostasis" only later.

6.7. A Further Note on Baptism in the Holy Spirit

We have already indirectly examined claims about "baptism" in the Spirit in our previous chapter. We also discuss the term in Part III. We noted, and agreed with Dunn's comment that every Christian receives the Spirit, for without the Spirit the believer would never become united with Christ (Rom. 8:9; 1 Cor. 12:3). We saw that many Pentecostals follow Gordon Fee, Frank Macchia, and Veli-Matti Kärkkäinen in adopting a "Christocentric" rather than "Holiness Movement" approach. To repeat: Fee describes the Holy Spirit as "the identity marker of the converted."[163] Macchia writes, "The problem is that the revivalist influence on the Holiness Movement caused it to transform John Wesley's more process-oriented understanding of sanctification into a high-voltage crisis experience . . . as . . . a renewal for worldly or lazy Christians."[164] Kärkkäinen declares: "Paul's pneumatology is christologically founded . . . (Rom. 8:9; Gal. 4:6). . . . It is only through the Spirit that the believer is able to confess that 'Je-

---

160. Anthony C. Thiselton, *The First Epistle to the Corinthians: A Commentary on the Greek Text,* NIGTC (Grand Rapids: Eerdmans, 2000), pp. 328-29, 811-22, and esp. 1236-40.

161. Neil Richardson, *Paul's Language about God,* JSNTSS 99 (Sheffield: Sheffield Academic, 1994), pp. 114-19 and 303-4.

162. See G. N. Stanton, *Jesus of Nazareth in New Testament Preaching,* SNTSMS 27 (Cambridge: Cambridge University Press, 1974), pp. 86-116; and Richard Bauckham, *Jesus and the Eyewitnesses: The Gospels as Eyewitness Testimony* (Grand Rapids: Eerdmans, 2006), pp. 1-289.

163. Gordon D. Fee, *Paul, the Spirit, and the People of God* (Peabody, MA: Hendrickson, 1994), p. 88.

164. Frank D. Macchia, *Baptized in the Spirit* (Grand Rapids: Zondervan, 2006), pp. 30-31.

sus is Lord' (1 Cor. 12:1-3). . . . It is the gift of the Spirit that makes one a Christian (Rom. 8:9)."[165] All three are leading Pentecostals.

Why, if these thinkers do not appear still to accept the time sequence and precise meaning of "baptism in the Spirit" in classical Pentecostalism, does Macchia still regard it as a key identity-marker of Pentecostalism?[166] Macchia and Kärkkäinen want both to preserve what is distinctive to Pentecostalism and yet also to enter upon the ecumenical stage. Macchia writes: "In the broader context of the New Testament, Spirit-baptism is a fluid metaphor surrounded by ambiguous imagery that suggests broader boundaries pneumatologically than Spirit empowerment."[167] He even agrees with "mainline" scholars that 1 Cor. 12:13 concerns incorporation into Christ. He says that Dunn's emphasis on the Spirit "as the hallmark of Christian identity (the 'nerve center' of the Christian life) seems compelling."[168] He also notes that in Luke baptism in the Spirit is more "charismatic" than in Paul. This becomes a central factor not only in Pentecostalism, which is theologically growing, but also in the "Third Wave" Charismatic Renewal Movement, which, with a few exceptions, seems to have settled into what some might call satisfaction, or others might suggest even complacency.

In "mainline" Christianity there is plenty of room for *repeated endowments* of the Holy Spirit, particularly as increased consecration and as endowment for particular tasks. In an Episcopal church, no one would dream of insisting that we cannot pray for an anointing of one who is to be ordained bishop on the ground that he has already received the Holy Spirit, either when he became a Christian or when he was ordained priest.

Here is where we must return to hermeneutics, and to the difference between "experience" and traditional Pentecostal and Renewal ways of conceptually articulating, naming, and describing this experience. Provided that it is not the "second blessing," the problem is that of claiming that it is *the right name in Paul or the rest of the New Testament. It is not the experience, but the name or label for it that is in question.* I do not think that any amount of hermeneutical wriggling will answer this. Even to say, "We want to keep the term, but recognize that it is not Paul's usage" would help the ecumenical vision which Macchia and Kärkkäinen creditably serve. We consider their work further in Part III.

---

165. Veli-Matti Kärkkäinen, *Pneumatology: The Holy Spirit in Ecumenical, International, and Contextual Perspective* (Grand Rapids: Baker Academic, 2002), p. 32.

166. Macchia, *Baptized in the Spirit*, pp. 21-28.

167. Macchia, *Baptized in the Spirit*, p. 14.

168. Macchia, *Baptized in the Spirit*, p. 39.

7

The Holy Spirit, the Paraclete, in the Johannine Writings

7.1. John in Relation to Luke-Acts and Paul

It is customary to view the Fourth Gospel in two parts. These are often called the Book of Signs (John 1:19–12:50); and the Book of the Passion (John 13:1–20:31).[1] The most distinctive teaching in John concerns the five sets of sayings about the Paraclete in John 14–16 (John 14:15-17; 14:25-26; 15:26; 16:7-11, and 16:12-15).[2] Attached to this is the post-resurrection "Johannine Pentecost," namely, John 20:22-23: "He [Jesus] breathed on them, and said to them, 'Receive the Holy Spirit. . . .'" In the first twelve chapters, John the Baptist declares, "I saw the Spirit descending from heaven like a dove, and it remained on him. . . . He on whom you see the Spirit descend and remain is the one who baptizes with the Holy Spirit" (John 1:32-33). Three events are then recounted: the private conversation with Nicodemus, which includes the new birth (3:1-15); the private conversation with the Woman of Samaria (4:1-42); and the public declaration at the Feast of Tabernacles (7:38-39, "He said this about the Spirit").[3]

The assessments about the relation of these Johannine passages to the Holy Spirit in Luke-Acts vary dramatically. Alasdair Heron regularly comments, "Like the Synoptics and Acts, the Fourth Gospel speaks of the Spirit in Jesus' life

---

1. C. H. Dodd, *The Interpretation of the Fourth Gospel* (Cambridge: Cambridge University Press, 1953), pp. 289-390; cf. Dodd, *The Historical Tradition in the Fourth Gospel* (Cambridge: Cambridge University Press, 1963), pp. 21-151 and 152-232; more recently, Max Turner, *The Holy Spirit and Spiritual Gifts Then and Now* (Carlisle: Paternoster, 1996), p. 76.

2. Henry B. Swete, *The Holy Spirit in the New Testament* (London: Macmillan, 1909, rpt. 1921), pp. 147-68.

3. Cf. Lindsay Dewar, *The Holy Spirit and Modern Thought* (London: Mowbray, 1959), pp. 27-41.

and ministry."[4] The Holy Spirit *remains* on Jesus; he gives the Spirit *"without measure"* (3:34-35); he will *baptize* with the Holy Spirit; the Spirit gives *life* (6:63); and the Paraclete will come when Jesus is glorified.[5] James Dunn offers a broadly similar view, but with significant modifications. He writes, "John's account could . . . dovetail chronologically into the Acts narrative," provided that 14:16, 26; 15:26; and 16:7 refer to a later sending of the Spirit, "following Jesus' final return to the Father after his various appearances to the disciples. . . . The promised baptism of the Spirit (1:33) could easily be referred to as the unrecorded Pentecost."[6] John's treatment of religious experience, he writes, "is notable for its freshness and vigour."[7]

On the other hand, many other assessments are radically different. Eduard Schweizer writes, "Jesus is not represented as a pneumatic. His inspired speech and His miracles are nowhere attributed to the Spirit. The path taken by Luke does not satisfy John."[8] Ernest F. Scott insists, "His thought has certainly nothing in common with that of the primitive Church."[9] Because John emphasizes that Jesus and God the Father are one, he even argues: "He has no need of the supernatural gift [of the Spirit], since he is of divine nature."[10] Joseph E. Fison similarly argues, "Scott is in a sense correct; the Spirit is unnecessary and irrelevant. . . . [*The Spirit*] *effaces himself, and advertises Jesus:* 'He will not speak of his own [Greek, *aph' heautou*]. . . . He will glorify me' (Jn. 16:13, 14)" (my italics).[11] Concerning his promise for the future Jesus declares, "*I* will come to you" (John 14:3; 14:18). The Holy Spirit is "self-effacing"; the "tokens of his presence" are not noise and wind as such, but an authenticity which goes beyond human capacities and understanding, and resists any attempt at "control and manipulation."[12]

Fison would not see outright contradictions here, but an attempt by John to put a different side to a reality which is too one-sided in Luke-Acts. Even Max Turner comments, "The portrayal of the Spirit in the Fourth Gospel has many interesting points of similarity and dissimilarity with that in Luke-Acts. . . . Un-

---

4. Alisdair Heron, *The Holy Spirit* (London: Marshall, Morgan & Scott, 1983), p. 51.

5. Heron, *The Holy Spirit*, pp. 51-53.

6. James D. G. Dunn, *Baptism in the Holy Spirit: A Re-examination of the New Testament Teaching on the Gift of the Spirit in Relation to Pentecostalism Today* (London: SCM, 1970), p. 177; cf. p. 178.

7. James D. G. Dunn, *Jesus and the Spirit: A Study of the Religious and Charismatic Experience of Jesus and the First Christians as Reflected in the New Testament* (London: SCM, 1975), p. 356; cf. pp. 350-57.

8. Eduard Schweizer, *"Pneuma, pneumatikos,"* in *TDNT*, vol. 6, pp. 438-39; cf. pp. 438-44.

9. Ernest F. Scott, *The Spirit in the New Testament* (London: Hodder & Stoughton, 1924), p. 196; cf. pp. 193-208.

10. Scott, *The Spirit in the New Testament*, p. 194.

11. Joseph E. Fison, *The Blessing of the Holy Spirit* (London and New York: Longmans, Green, 1950), p. 137.

12. Fison, *The Blessing of the Holy Spirit*, p. 140.

like Luke, he nowhere attributes liberating acts of exorcism or healing to the Spirit."[13] He has power, above all, to *reveal* God. Finally, George Montague sums up the crux of the problem. He writes, "While Luke is interested in the charismatic explosion of the Spirit in tongues, prophecy, and healing, John is more interested in the relation of the Spirit to the power over sin, . . . founded on a word of Jesus and the gift of the Spirit."[14]

How are we to account for at least this recognized difference and emphasis? Many would point out that it is only one of numerous differences in style and content. (1) In the Synoptic Gospels the most striking feature of the teaching of Jesus is his use of *parables;* in John there are either none, or, at most, two, and the style of teaching is that of *meditative discourses.* (2) The central content of the Synoptists, namely, the *Kingdom or reign of God,* occurs only three times in John, and is, according to Davey, largely replaced by the idea of *eternal life.*[15] (3) Whereas the Synoptic Gospels portray the baptism and temptations of Jesus and his *humanity* or human life, John depicts Christ's "unfailing dependence upon, and immediate experience of, God His Father. . . . In John the *divinity of Christ* with its native glory is in the centre of the picture and overshadows all else."[16] (4) Many claim that Johannine *chronology* is theologically motivated. The best-known examples concern the Cleansing of the Temple (John 2:14-17; Mark 11:15-17; Matt. 21:12; Luke 19:45) and the observance of the third Passover (Mark 14:12; Matt. 26:17; Luke 22:7; John 13:1; 18:28; 19:14). (5) Many stress the role of *symbol and dualism* in John. John contrasts God and the world (John 8:23; 8:42; 8:47), light and darkness (3:19-20; 12:36), and truth and falsehood. Bultmann and others used to attribute this to Hellenism or Gnostic influences, but the same contrasts have been found in the Dead Sea Scrolls since their discovery in 1948.

Yet these five different ways or approaches all derive their distinctiveness from John's overriding concern to proclaim Christ, to bring the believer into a greater appreciation of Christ, or to preach Christ to the world. Colleen Conway writes, "Everything in the Gospel of John concerns Christology. Indeed that in itself makes it distinctive."[17] Even though it is now unfashionable to speak too much of "Christological titles," there is a progressive unveiling of Christological titles or confessions in John. We find "Lamb of God" and "Son of Man" (John 1:29, 51), "Son of God" (John 5:19-24), and Bread of Life (John 6:35), and in response to the resurrection appearance of Christ, Thomas's cli-

---

13. Turner, *The Holy Spirit and Spiritual Gifts,* p. 57; cf. pp. 57-102.

14. George T. Montague, *The Holy Spirit: The Growth of a Biblical Tradition* (Eugene, OR: Wipf & Stock, 1976), p. 363.

15. J. Ernest Davey, *The Jesus of St. John* (London: Lutterworth Press, 1958), p. 10.

16. Davey, *The Jesus of St. John,* p. 12 (my italics).

17. Colleen M. Conway, "Gospel of John," in *The New Interpreter's Dictionary of the Bible,* 5 vols. (Nashville: Abingdon, 2008), vol. 3, p. 357; cf. pp. 356-70.

mactic confession, "My Lord and my God!" (John 20:28). There is no "Messianic secret," as W. Wrede saw in Mark, but a direct confession of Christ. In place of miracles are "signs" (Greek, *sēmeia*) that point beyond the natural, empirical, realm (John 2:1-11 onward to 11:12-44). John's Prologue (John 1:1-18) presents Christ as God's "Word" or *logos* from "the beginning" (John 1:1), who was both "with God," "God," and Creator (John 1:1-3). Christ the *logos* is the source of life and light (John 1:4), who is also the Judge "who sheds light upon" (Greek, *ho phōtizei*), which "enlightens [NRSV] everyone" (John 1:9).[18] Hans Conzelmann sees "light" *(phōs)* as revelation, which embraces all aspects.[19] The term in the Prologue for "lived among us" (NRSV, John 1:14), Greek, *eskēnōsen en hēmin,* is often compared with Wisdom's "pitching a tent" (Sir. 24:8), suggesting that Christ is presented here as preexistent Wisdom as well as Word (Prov. 8:23-24).

This emphasis on the centrality of Christ in John serves partly to explain Fison's point about the "self-effacing" character of the Holy Spirit in John. The Spirit himself testifies to Christ and glorifies Christ, not primarily himself. In this sense, John may stand as a conscious correction to those communities who are centered on the Holy Spirit. Since the Spirit is "another paraclete" or "another 'comforter'" in continuity with Christ, and since Christ declares, "I will come to you," in the Person of the Spirit, it is arguable that in John Spirit-centeredness is no different from Christ-centeredness. But John distinguishes between the Spirit as means and Christ as end. Moreover, what is implicit in the narratives of the Synoptic Gospels and in the theology of Paul becomes explicit in John, namely, an anticipation of a doctrine of the Holy Trinity. The problem of the relation between the Holy Spirit or the Paraclete and Jesus Christ becomes softened and better defined if its theological basis is perceived to be Trinitarian. We address this further in Part II of this book.

In John the seeds of this development can be seen, for example, in references to Jesus being "from God" (John 3:2; 6:46; 8:42; 9:33; 13:3; 16:27), and that to honor the Son is to honor the Father (John 5:22-23). Jesus is not only "the light of the world" (John 8:12) but also "the resurrection and the life" (11:25). Elsewhere in the New Testament God alone is the source of the resurrection, through the Spirit (Rom. 8:11). As "the true vine" (15:1) Jesus fulfills all that God could be to Israel. The aim of the Fourth Gospel, E. K. Lee declares, is "to prove that the God of being and history was revealed in Jesus Christ. Heaven and earth meet in him."[20] The term *monogenēs,* used of Jesus' relation to this Father,

18. This is controversial. Against Barrett and others Raymond Brown defends the traditional view, largely on the basis of v. 7. See Raymond E. Brown, *The Gospel according to John,* 2 vols., Anchor Bible (New York: Doubleday 1966 and 1971), vol. 1, p. 9. Frederick Danker lists both meanings in Danker, BDAG, p. 1074, but "sheds light upon" appears in 1 Cor. 4:5 decisively.

19. Hans Conzelmann, *"Phōs,"* in *TDNT,* vol. 9, p. 351; cf. pp. 310-58.

20. Edwin K. Lee, *The Religious Thought of St. John* (London: SPCK, 1950), p. 59.

exhibits more than the word "only" (NRSV) or "only begotten" (KJV/AV) might imply (John 1:14, 18; 3:16, 18). It includes the notion of *"an only child who is especially dear to its parents."*[21] Danker uses the English equivalent *"unique,"* or, in John, *"uniquely divine as God's Son, and transcending all others"* (my italics).[22] Martin Luther called John "the one, fine, true, and chief Gospel," because it focused on *Christ* more than the other three appeared to do, and because it concentrated more on his discourses than on his miracles.[23]

7.2. The Holy Spirit in John 1–12

As a preliminary, we may note that, according to Charles H. Dodd, all of John's references to the Spirit would have been fully familiar to Greek readers. He lists, for example, six familiar meanings: (1) *pneuma* as wind (John 3:8, "the Spirit blows where he wills"); (2) its psychological or anthropological use (11:33; 13:21, "he was troubled in spirit"); (3) the Spirit of truth (14:17; 15:26; 16:13, "the Spirit of truth, . . . he will guide you into all truth"); (4) the association of the Spirit with life (6:63, "the Spirit is the giver of life"); (5) the Spirit is thereby the medium of rebirth (3:5, "unless a man be born from above"); and (6) "God is Spirit" (4:24), for which Dodd insists that to render it "God is a spirit" is "the most gross perversion of the meaning. . . . [For] there is no trace in the Fourth Gospel of the vulgar conception of a multitude of *pneumata.*"[24]

Dodd cites numerous uses from Hellenistic sources which would have been familiar to a Greek-speaking readership. These include words which roughly correspond with the above sequence: "wind" or "air in motion" (Philo, *That the Worse Attacks the Better,* 83); "the soul," or the anthropological use (Philo, *That the Worse Attacks the Better,* 80; *On Flight and Finding,* 134); "Spirit of truth" (Philo, *On the Life of Moses,* 2.265); "giver of life" (*Corpus Hermeticum* 9:9). Many Greek writers, however, "were confused and uncertain about [the] precise ontological status" of God as Spirit.[25] Dodd's citations include more Greek sources than Philo and the *Corpus Hermeticum.* He is interested to show John's concern to reach Greek readers readily.

In their commentary on John, J. N. Sanders and B. A. Mastin argue that readers would probably have equated the Spirit with the Logos until they grasped the epoch-making effects of the incarnation of the Logos: "The Logos and the Spirit were virtually indistinguishable before the Incarnation (cf. Jn.

---

21. Lee, *The Religious Thought of St. John,* p. 65.

22. Danker, BDAG, p. 658.

23. Martin Luther, *Luther's Works* (St. Louis: Concordia, 1959), vol. 35, p. 362, and *Luther the Expositor* (companion volume), p. 60.

24. Dodd, *The Interpretation of the Fourth Gospel,* pp. 223-26.

25. Dodd, *The Interpretation of the Fourth Gospel,* p. 219.

7:39)."[26] They note that in spite of the neuter gender of *pneuma* in grammar, John calls the Spirit "him," "thus indicating that the Spirit is as personal as the Logos, and not just an impersonal force (cf. John 16:13)," where John uses *ekeinos*.[27] Dunn, similarly, declares, "For John, and for Paul, the Spirit has ceased to be an impersonal divine power."[28]

In common with the Synoptic Gospels, although he does not record the baptism of Jesus, John recounts the "descent" of the Spirit in John 1:32-34, asserts that the Holy Spirit "descends and remains" (Greek, *katabainon kai menon*) on Jesus, who is the One who will "baptize in the Holy Spirit" (*ho baptizōn en pneumati hagiō*, v. 33). Fison comments, "The Fourth Gospel speaks of the Baptist's witness to the abiding presence of the Spirit upon Jesus at His baptism and therefore naturally of the Lord's own promise of His abiding presence with the Church."[29] Every New Testament writing sees the Holy Spirit as God's gift, who is derived through Christ's anointing.

The First Epistle of John is explicit on this matter: "You have been anointed [Greek, *hymeis chrisma echete*] by the Holy One. . . . The anointing that you received from him abides in you" (*to chrisma ho elabete ap' autou menei en hymin*, 1 John 2:20 and 27). Some point out that this does explicitly mention the Holy Spirit, and understand "the anointing" to refer to the truth of the gospel. But *to chrisma* (the anointing) regularly denotes anointing by the Holy Spirit both in the LXX and in the New Testament (Luke 4:18, of Jesus himself). Danker argues that *chrisma* in 1 John 2:20, 27 is "usually taken to refer to the Holy Spirit."[30]

The verb *chriō*, "to anoint," "to anoint oneself," "to smear," or "to rub" in early usage, gives rise to the nouns *Christos*, "anointed one," and *chrisma*, "anointing."[31] The Old Testament exhibits a history of the regal anointing of a king (1 Sam. 9:16; 10:1; 24:6), the high priest as "the anointed" (Lev. 4:3, 5, 16; Dan. 9:25-26), and anointed prophets (1 Kings 19:16). It is inconceivable that this anointing is not by the Spirit of God. *The difference in the Johannine writings is that this anointing is derived from Christ, and is permanent.* The Dead Sea Scrolls explicitly use the phrase "anointed by the Spirit" of the two Messianic figures to which they refer as anointed "at the end of days" (1QS 9:11; CD 12:23-24; 14:19; 20:1; 4QTest 9-13; 14:20; 4QFlor 1:11). The priestly and kingly Messiah remain distinct *until Jesus Christ is anointed as Prophet, Priest, and King by the*

---

26. J. N. Sanders and B. A. Mastin, *The Gospel according to St John* (London: Black, 1968), p. 96.

27. Sanders and Mastin, *St. John*, p. 96.

28. Dunn, *Jesus and the Spirit*, p. 351.

29. Fison, *The Blessing of the Holy Spirit*, p. 100.

30. Danker, BDAG, p. 1090.

31. Walter Grundmann and Marinus de Jonge, "*Chriō, Christos, chrisma*," in *TDNT*, vol. 9, pp. 493-580.

Spirit. These three categories became especially important in John Calvin's Christology. Eventually *Christos* effectively became a proper noun or name.

Much of the Synoptic and Pauline teaching about the Holy Spirit is absent from the Gospel of John. There is no temptation account. *Healings are fewer, and exorcisms are absent.* Fison asserts: *"There is no sign whatever that Jesus spoke with tongues or was caught up into any particular heaven or paradise"* (my italics).[32] Yet Dunn insists that John does not wholly share in the "fading of vision" which he associates with the 80s and 90s, in which he dates John on the subject of the Holy Spirit. He concludes: *"The distinctive essence of Christian experience lies in the relation between Jesus and the Spirit"* (his italics).[33]

Each of the "signs" points to the significance of *Christ;* and each points also to his passion, cross, and resurrection or glorification. Yet distinctively Jesus in John speaks of the new birth, or of being born from above (*anōthen*, John 3:3), or of being born "of water and the Spirit" (*ex hydatos kai pneumatos*, 3:5). Jürgen Moltmann resists the translation "born again" or even "reborn," especially in view of modern use, and insists that the terms "new" birth and "birth from above" make the point better than the words of John or Jesus express at face value.[34] An alternative meaning for *anōthen* (3:3) is "from above," and H. B. Swete, Max Turner, and the NRSV favor this translation.[35] It harmonizes with 3:31, "The one who comes from above is above all." Danker gives both meanings in his *Lexicon*, with "from above" associated with John 3. However, since Nicodemus replies about birth "a second time" (John 3:4), John may well intend a play on both meanings, "anew" and "from above," although probably not "again."

Here "water and Spirit" (John 3:5) do not denote two separate baptisms, but a "unitary event" which involves both purification from sin and being born anew by the Spirit from above.[36] It is parallel with Paul's language about becoming "a new creation" (2 Cor. 5:17; Greek, *kainē ktisis*). It shows that the beginning of the Christian life is due to the activity of the creative Holy Spirit, as in Paul, and concerns new creation, not mere reformation, as with John the Baptist. The action of the Holy Spirit is mysterious and transcends control, manipulation, or prediction, for it is like the wind, which "blows where it chooses, and you hear the sound of it, but do not know where it comes from or where it goes" (3:8).

---

32. Fison, *The Blessing of the Holy Spirit*, p. 100.

33. Dunn, *Jesus and the Spirit*, p. 358.

34. Jürgen Moltmann, *The Spirit of Life: A Universal Affirmation* (London: SCM, 1992), p. 145.

35. Turner, *The Holy Spirit and Spiritual Gifts*, p. 68; Danker, BDAG, p. 92; Swete, *The Holy Spirit in the New Testament*, p. 131.

36. This is not quite the view that "water is the outward, visible sign" of the inner work of the Spirit (Swete, *The Holy Spirit in the New Testament*, p. 133), as if to narrow the reference to water baptism; cf. Turner, *The Holy Spirit and Spiritual Gifts*, p. 68.

In the same chapter, but following the closing of the discourse (3:1-21), a dialogue with John the Baptist ensues. The prediction that Jesus will baptize with the Spirit is, in effect, expanded. The testimony and words of Jesus, it is asserted, are "the words of God, for he [God] gives the Spirit [to Jesus] without measure . . . and has placed all things in his hands" (John 3:34-35). George Beasley-Murray explains that Jesus can speak the words of God "since the Father has given him the Spirit 'without measure,' and the Spirit to the Jew is supremely the Spirit of prophecy. The saying of R. Aha (*Leviticus Rabbah* 15:2) is often cited: 'The Holy Spirit, who rests on the prophets, rests on them only by measure.'"[37] He adds that the immeasurable gift of the Spirit to Jesus "corresponds to the perfection of the revelation through him."[38]

In John 4 the dialogue with a peasant Samaritan stands in contrast to the previous one with a learned Jew. But in both cases the issue turns on Christ and his provision. Here Jesus offers "living water" (John 4:10) which, once drunk, abolishes thirst forever (4:13-14); indeed, the recipients find that this water "will become in them a spring of water gushing up to eternal life" (John 4:14). Living water in the Greek of the time denotes "fresh, flowing water," in contrast to stale, stagnant water from a cistern which can be stored. The reference to the Holy Spirit is not explicit, although the water of life is later related to the Holy Spirit in *Targum Isaiah* 44:3 and elsewhere. The whole discourse is a classic of irony and double meaning to John. Jesus promises water forever thirst-quenching; the Samaritan woman replies, "Then, I won't need to keep carrying a bucket here!" (v. 15). Jesus offers water as he sits by the well; the Samaritan woman replies, "But you have no bucket from which to draw the water!" (v. 11). Is the woman portrayed as unintelligent or cheeky to the Jew who overcomes all conventions (v. 9) by speaking with her? Normally we might hesitate to equate this well of living water (a contradiction in terms) with the Holy Spirit. But John carefully uses layers of meaning. (A further example concerns "eating": the disciples urge Jesus to eat; Jesus replies that his "food" is to do God's will, 4:31-34.) Moreover, similar language about "flowing water" occurs in John 7:37-38, with the comment: "He said this about the Spirit" (7:39).

It is not easy to determine what the statement "God is Spirit" (without the definite article") means in John 4:24. We noted that Dodd emphatically rejected "God is a spirit," and Jürgen Moltmann agrees with Dodd. The context suggests that worship of God *transcends physical locations* such as Gerizim, "this mountain," or Jerusalem (John 4:20), which constituted a burning issue between Jews and Samaritans. It may be an oblique reference to worship from the heart "in spirit and in truth" (v. 24). Or, again, it may combine levels of meaning,

---

37. George R. Beasley-Murray, *John*, Word Biblical Commentary 36 (Nashville: Nelson, 2nd ed. 1999), p. 53.

38. Beasley-Murray, *John*, p. 54.

whereby divine action in the world is seen as light, love, and Spirit (cf. 1 John 1:5; 4:8). At all events, the main focus is Jesus, who by the Spirit can give the dynamic gift of ever-running, or ever-flowing, "water." This may refer to the "true" or authentic worship which accords with the Person and work of Christ. The passage has been used of the Spirit for many centuries. Moltmann comments, "Through the Holy Spirit, God's eternal life brims over . . . and its overflowing powers and energies fill the earth."[39]

This passage also links with John 7:37-39. On the last day of the Festival of Booths, Jesus cried out, "Let anyone who is thirsty come to me. . . . As the scriptures have said, 'Out of the believer's heart shall flow rivers of living water.'" John comments: "Now this he said about the Spirit, which believers in him were to receive. For as yet there was no Spirit, because Jesus was not yet glorified" (7:37-39; some MSS have variant readings). It is clear that the emphasis in John is on coming to *Jesus,* through whom the Holy Spirit is yet to be given, but is promised. The saying reflects Isa. 55:1, "Ho, everyone who thirsts, come to the waters. . . ." Most writers believe that water-drawing took place on each of the seven days of the Festival, and the joyous nature of the Festival (like a modern Christmas) reflected Isa. 12:3: "With joy you will draw water from the wells of salvation."[40] Brown suggests a number of Old Testament passages, including Ps. 78:15-16, Isa. 43:20, Ezek. 47:1-11, and Zech. 14:8, although the quotation does not exactly correspond with the Hebrew Masoretic text or the LXX. Zech. 14:8 had predicted that living waters would flow out of Jerusalem; and Ezek. 47:1 saw a river flow underneath the temple. Some MSS soften "there was no Spirit" by reading "the Spirit was not yet given." Clearly the Old Testament writers were familiar with the Spirit, but not yet with the "pouring out" of the Spirit in the last days. Raymond Brown points out that at least three sets of MSS suggest three ways of reading and understanding this verse. The first and most usual is Christological: Jesus is the source of an ever-fresh supply; the second is that the believer becomes the source of water ("from within him shall flow rivers of living water," the punctuation for which is supported by the manuscript P[66], Origen, many of the Greek Fathers, K. Rengstorf, and E. Schweizer); the third leaves a greater degree of vagueness. Everything points to the glorification of Christ as the mediate source of this communal bestowal of the Spirit. The passage is reminiscent of Rev. 22:17: "Let him who is thirsty come; let him who wishes take the water of life without price" (cf. Rev. 22:1).

John once again uses *imagery.* Flowing, ever-fresh water is the best image he can find for describing the experience of the Holy Spirit. Both this passage and the book of Revelation use everyday phenomena to depict spiritual reali-

---

39. Moltmann, *The Spirit of Life,* p. 176.

40. Cf. Beasley-Murray, *John,* p. 113; and Brown, *The Gospel according to John,* vol. 1 (London: Chapman, 1971, and New York: Doubleday, 1966), pp. 320-25.

ties.[41] It is as disastrous to interpret John with wooden literalism as it is to do so with Revelation. On the other hand, symbol should not be interpreted too narrowly. For example, while most writers insist that John 3:5 must be "baptismal" and that John 6:35-59 must be "eucharistic," I am not fully convinced by their arguments. John is "sacramental" in the broad sense of seeing the everyday as symbolic of deeper truths; but whether he wanted to recall the Church from too narrow a preoccupation with the two dominical sacraments demands further reflection. After all, no one seems adequately to explain the omission of overt reference to the baptism of Jews and to the institution of the Eucharist. I remain open to arguments on both sides, but am not sure that the majority view can be taken for granted. The immediate point, however, concerns the use of imagery about the Spirit. This may contribute to preserving much of his transcendence and mystery, in contrast to Luke's preference to recount visible phenomena. The other key point remains the centrality of Jesus Christ in John.

7.3. The Holy Spirit, the Paraclete, in John 14–16 and 20

A huge amount of discussion relates to the unity or integrity of the last discourses in John. The word "paraclete" (Greek, *paraklētos*) does not occur elsewhere in John. Hans Windisch argued that all the *paraclete* passages are secondary insertions by a later editor (John 14:15-17, 26; 15:26-27; 16:5-15).[42] He argued that not only did they reflect a distinctive vocabulary but also that, if they were removed, the earlier text of John would flow on as a coherent unit. Barnabas Lindars points out, however, that even if this is true of 14:15-17 and 26, it can hardly be argued for chapters 15 and 16.[43] Windisch's argument that John seeks to *replace* the Synoptic Gospels in any case remains open to question.

The first Paraclete saying, in John 14:15-18, explicitly equates the Paraclete (v. 16) with the Spirit (v. 17). The meaning of the Greek *paraklētos* is widely debated. Since the verb *parakaleō* strictly means "to call alongside" (to help), Danker gives the first meaning of the noun as *"helper, mediator, intercessor, or one who appears on another's behalf."*[44] He cites numerous Greek examples from all periods. Earlier, around 1950, Johannes Behm had stressed the legal context, suggesting the translation "advocate" or "defending counsel," claiming that this meaning was "widespread," alongside that of "helper."[45] However, Kenneth

---

41. See Anthony C. Thiselton, *Life after Death: A New Approach to the Last Things* (Grand Rapids: Eerdmans, and London: SPCK, 2012), ch. 11.

42. Hans Windisch, *Johannes und die Synoptiker* (Leipzig: Hinrichs, 1926), pp. 147-49.

43. Barnabas Lindars, *The Gospel of John*, New Century Bible Commentary (London: Oliphants, 1972), p. 468.

44. Danker, BDAG, p. 766.

45. Johannes Behm, *"Paraklētos,"* in *TDNT*, vol. 5, p. 809; cf. pp. 800-814.

Grayston has reservations about its supposed legal context.[46] G. R. Beasley-Murray agrees with Danker and Grayston that "it never became a technical term (unlike the Latin *advocatus,* meaning a professional legal adviser)," and he feels that the law court aspect is "clear in 16:8-11."[47] Swete and Turner therefore accept "Advocate." Turner writes, "'Advocate' may thus regularly provide the best translation . . . and indeed Rabbinic Judaism came to use *p*^e*raqlit* (a loan word) for 'advocate' (cf. *Pirqe Aboth* 4:11)."[48] But he also recognizes that others prefer "comforter" (J. G. Davies), "exhorter" (C. K. Barrett), and "Helper" (R. Bultmann).[49] E. F. Scott argues that this may reflect a play on the different meanings.[50] One writer suggests that it is most accurate to leave the word untranslated as *Paraclete.*

Whatever we decide, the key point in the first two sayings is that, as Heron expresses it, "the same vocabulary is used to describe Jesus Christ himself as the Holy Spirit."[51] John 14:18 declares, "*I* will not leave you orphaned, *I* am coming to you." Swete expresses this differently, "The Spirit was sent to reveal the Son."[52] This "truth," Swete adds, goes beyond a mere recovery of the Lord's words. The Spirit witnesses to the character of Christ, to show *Christ* to his people. The very phrase "another paraclete" (*allon paraklēton,* John 14:16) demonstrates the intimately close relation between the Spirit and Christ. Even as "the world" rejected Christ, so it will reject the Holy Spirit (v. 17, "is not able to receive"). Dunn regards this point as crucial. He writes, "The Spirit . . . continues the presence of Jesus. . . . It is implied in the . . . parallelism between the ministry of Jesus and that of the 'Paraclete.' . . . Both come forth from the Father (John 15:26; 16:27-28); both are given and sent by the Father (John 3:16-17; 14:16, 26); both teach the disciples (6:59; 7:14, 28; 8:20; 14:26); both are unrecognized by the world (John 14:17; 16:3)."[53]

John 14:26, "The Paraclete [NRSV, 'Advocate'], the Holy Spirit, whom the Father will send in my name, will teach you everything, and remind you of all that I have said to you," constitutes the key point in Franz Mussner's argument about two distinct layers of Johannine teaching. He sees the apostolic teaching of the past transposed into the Johannine editor's present. The original witness

---

46. Kenneth Grayston, "Paraclete," *JSNT* 13 (1981): 67-82.

47. Beasley-Murray, *John,* p. 256.

48. Turner, *The Holy Spirit and Spiritual Gifts,* p. 77; Swete, *The Holy Spirit in the New Testament,* p. 149.

49. J. G. Davies, "The Primary Meaning of *Paraklētos,*" *JTS* 4 (1953): 35-38; C. K. Barrett, "The Holy Spirit in the Fourth Gospel," *JTS* 1 (1950): 1-15; and Rudolf Bultmann, *Theology of the New Testament* (London: SCM, 1952 and 1955), vol. 1, pp. 164-83 and vol. 2, pp. 1-92.

50. Scott, *The Spirit in the New Testament,* pp. 199-200.

51. Heron, *The Holy Spirit,* p. 52.

52. Swete, *The Holy Spirit in the New Testament,* p. 153.

53. Dunn, *Jesus and the Spirit,* p. 350.

of John "saw" Jesus made flesh and his works (John 1:4; 1:34; 4:42; 6:40; 20:29). But, according to Mussner, the Johannine Paraclete "reveals" more of Christ, but this time the exalted Christ, from the postresurrection perspective. Hence Mussner asserts both the historical reliability and theological vision of John, except that the "historical" Christ is "projected" and re-presented from a spiritual perspective.[54] He draws on H.-G. Gadamer for levels of meaning, writing: "The 'Johannine problem' is chiefly a hermeneutical one. Considerable light and help can be had from . . . Martin Heidegger . . . and . . . Hans-Georg Gadamer."[55] Hence Jesus says, "I still have many things to say to you, but you cannot bear them now. When the Spirit of truth comes, he will guide you into all the truth . . ." (John 16:12-13). Thus the Paraclete sayings become the key to a number of critical questions about John.

G. R. Beasley-Murray, however, comments: "Mussner appears to have overstated his case."[56] This is because he drives a wedge between the earthly, historical Jesus and the Christ of faith, appealing to the Holy Spirit for such a two-level meaning. Others have approached the Synoptic Gospels in the same way. It is an irony that a more extreme form of criticism, in the shape of Ernst Käsemann's appeal to the words of "early Christian prophets" and "sentences of Holy Law," attributes the same kind of authority to prophets as we find among some fundamentalist Christians.[57] Admittedly some allowance must be made for the difference between fragments of tradition and reflective interpretation.[58] Dodd sees a combination of the two in the words of John the Baptist (John 1:29, 36) and the dialogue with Nicodemus (John 3:1-15 and 16-21). Arguably, the Jesus of history and the Christ of faith remain closer together, as Dunn insists. Moreover, the test of the possession of the Holy Spirit is conformity to the tradition of Jesus' sayings (14:15-17, "keep my commandments"; 15:27, "from the beginning"; 16:13, "will not speak on his own, but will speak whatever he hears"; cf. 1 John 4:1: "do not believe every spirit, but test the spirits . . ."). In addition to this, we must take account of work on oral traditions behind the Fourth Gospel, first by Gardner-Smith, then by Robert Kysar and Raymond Brown, and most recently by Donald A. Carson and Richard Bauckham.[59] In a

54. Franz Mussner, *The Historical Jesus in the Gospel of St. John*, Quaestiones Disputatae 19 (London: Burns & Oates, 1967), pp. 45-46.

55. Mussner, *The Historical Jesus in the Gospel of St. John*, p. 8.

56. Beasley-Murray, *John*, p. 11.

57. Ernst Käsemann, "Blind Alleys in the 'Jesus of History' Controversy" (featuring an attack on Jeremias) and "Sentences of Holy Law in the New Testament," in *New Testament Questions of Today* (London: SCM, 1969), pp. 23-65 and 66-81.

58. Cf. C. H. Dodd, *Historical Tradition in the Fourth Gospel* (Cambridge: Cambridge University Press, 1963).

59. P. Gardner-Smith, *St. John and the Synoptic Gospels* (Cambridge: Cambridge University Press, 1938); Robert Kysar, *The Fourth Evangelist and His Gospel* (Minneapolis: Augsburg, 1975),

general sense, however, Xavier Léon-DuFour is right to suggest, "The reading of the Gospel . . . consists. . . . in developing a deeper understanding of the present in the light of the past."[60]

To return to the Paraclete sayings, following Dunn, Max Turner well comments, "The coming Spirit . . . mediates the presence of the Father and of the glorified Son to the disciple."[61] He conveys the personal presence of Jesus. Both Jesus and the Spirit are teachers. Turner observes, "John insists on this historical anchor. The Paraclete's task is not to bring *independent* revelation."[62] The saying in John 15:26-27 confirms that the Spirit goes forth or "proceeds" from the Father (Greek, *To pneuma . . . ho para tou patros ekporeuetai*). Later, the Cappadocian Fathers rightly insisted that neither the Son nor the Spirit was *created;* the Son was *begotten,* and the Spirit *proceeds* from the Father, as our creeds bear witness. The Paraclete also bears witness to *Christ* (15:26); he does not speak of himself (*aph' heautou,* John 16:13; i.e., on his own initiative or his own authority).

The sayings in chapter 16 speak of exchanging the visible but local presence of Christ for the invisible but universal presence of the Holy Spirit. His further ministry is to "convict" (Greek, *elenxei*) the world of sin, righteousness, and judgment (John 16:8-11). This is very close to Paul's thought, that through the Spirit of "prophecy" (preaching?) "the secrets of the unbeliever's heart are disclosed, [and] that person will bow down before God and worship him, declaring, 'God is really among you'" (1 Cor. 14:25). E. F. Scott rightly comments on John 16:8-11: "Confronted by the holy community in which the divine power is manifestly working, the world will be brought to a sense of its wickedness and unbelief."[63]

Scott adds, "The world will grow conscious that over against it there is a righteousness to which it must give account."[64] Hence these Paraclete sayings speak of "the Spirit of truth" at least three times (John 14:17; 15:26; 16:13). Swete speaks of "the sinfulness of refusing to believe on Jesus."[65] C. K. Barrett argues that in this context, with *elenchō, paraklētos* may have the sense of "prosecuting counsel." "Truth" will ensure that the world is presented with an authentic verdict of judgment.

---

p. 45; Dodd, *Historical Tradition in the Fourth Gospel,* p. 423; Donald A. Carson, *The Gospel according to John,* Pillar New Testament Commentary (Grand Rapids: Eerdmans, 1991), pp. 49-67; and Richard Bauckham, *Testimony of the Beloved Disciple* (Grand Rapids: Baker Academic, 2007).

60. Xavier Léon-Dufour, "Towards Symbolic Understanding of the Fourth Gospel," *NTS* 27 (1981): 446; cf. pp. 439-56.

61. Turner, *The Holy Spirit and Spiritual Gifts,* p. 80.

62. Turner, *The Holy Spirit and Spiritual Gifts,* p. 83.

63. Scott, *The Spirit in the New Testament,* p. 201.

64. Scott, *The Spirit in the New Testament,* p. 202.

65. Swete, *The Holy Spirit in the New Testament,* p. 158.

Jesus now turns from the operation of the Holy Spirit to the *world*, to that which influences the *disciples* (John 16:12-15). The Spirit will "guide you into all truth" (v. 13), and will not speak "on his own" (Greek, *aph' heautou*), translated as "of his own accord" in the NJB and "on his own authority" in the NEB. What v. 13 expresses negatively, v. 14 expresses in positive terms: "He will glorify me, because he will take what is mine and declare it to you." As with Paul, John's view of the Holy Spirit is Christ-centered. "Spirit of truth" is a well-known phrase in the Dead Sea Scrolls (1QS 3:17-19; 1QS 4:23-24), which leads us to dismiss Bultmann's theory that this phrase reflects Gnostic or Hellenistic dualism. Throughout the Paraclete sayings, John is using the masculine word *paraklētos*. But *to pneuma* is neuter; and the Hebrew *rûach* happens to be feminine. We have urged that the Spirit is a Person in Paul and John, and that, as we have noted, James Barr insists that the accident of *grammatical* gender has nothing whatever to do with the actual *personal* gender of the Holy Spirit.[66] The Spirit, like God, *transcends gender*, which is a phenomenon of the human world of created beings.

We have briefly commented on "the Johannine Pentecost" of John 20:22 (cf. 20:19-23). It ties the experience of the Holy Spirit more closely to Jesus Christ than even Luke-Acts. The breath of Jesus animates and vitalizes the disciples as his postresurrection gift. The act of breathing (Greek, *enephysēsen*) is preceded by the commission: "As the Father has sent me, so I send you" (v. 21). The bodily Christ gives both authority to Christ's mission and a living, vital Spirit to empower, direct, and actualize it.

7.4. The Johannine Writings: The Gospel and Epistles of John

By considering the Gospel according to John alongside the Johannine Epistles I do not imply anything about their respective authorship. Whatever we conclude about authorship, the fact remains that these documents express similar themes. Despite valiant attempts by H. P. V. Nunn, James Moffatt, and others to argue that John the Apostle, the son of Zebedee, was the author of the Fourth Gospel, only a few still support this view.[67] Irenaeus mediates an early tradition which points in this direction. But the Gospel nowhere names its writer, and even "the Beloved Disciple" has been variously identified and is not necessarily the author.[68] Many believe that the author was the Elder or Presbyter John, and some also argue that he is the author of the Johannine Epistles. But many also

66. James Barr, *The Semantics of Biblical Language* (Oxford: Oxford University Press, 1961), pp. 39-40.

67. H. P. V. Nunn, *The Son of Zebedee and the Fourth Gospel* (London: SPCK, 1932).

68. Floyd V. Filson, *Who Was the Beloved Disciple?* (London: Marshall, Morgan & Scott, 1977), p. 29.

insist that the writer of this Gospel is unknown to us. The sons of Zebedee are not mentioned in the Gospel of John, except in the appendix at John 21:2. The Beloved Disciple appears five times, but not until John 13:23. An extended discussion relating to these issues about the Gospel of John came earlier in this chapter, when we discussed Franz Mussner's interpretation of John 14:26: "The Holy Spirit . . . will teach you everything. . . ." J. Estlin Carpenter seeks to bring together the book of Revelation and the Gospel of John, and writes extensively on "the Johannine Writings," but he leaves aside any question about authorship and date.[69] To enter into this debate would take us away from our subject, and involve extensive discussion of style, vocabulary, grammar, and syntax, as well as other matters.

In the case of both the Gospel and 1 John, F. W. Horn observes, "The Spirit manifests itself [himself] . . . *not* in ecstatic or charismatic phenomena, but in the area of the proclamation of the word, specifically in remembrance (John 14:26), doctrine (14:26), imitation (16:13), and prediction (16:13)" (my italics).[70] Similarly, Schweizer observes, "The unusual nature of the gifts of the Spirit is not emphasized."[71] On the other hand, both Horn and Schweizer note that, in common with the Fourth Gospel, 1 John also recognizes that the Spirit prompts the confession that "Jesus Christ has come in the flesh [and] is from God" (1 John 4:2). This also comes close to Paul's expression of the criterion of Spirit-possession as prompting the confession "Jesus is Lord" (1 Cor. 12:3). Hence 1 John declares, "Do not believe every spirit, but test the spirits to see whether they are from God. For many false prophets have gone out into the world" (1 John 4:1; discussed further below). More like Paul than Luke, Montague argues, "the first norm of testing is conformity to the traditional faith . . . John's formula . . . stresses the incarnation."[72] Both the Epistles and the Gospel of John emphasize the relation between the Holy Spirit and *truth* (1 John 5:6). 2 John 9 states: "Everyone who does not abide in the teaching of Christ, but goes beyond it, does not have God." Similarly, John 16:13 urges, "When the Spirit of truth comes, . . . he will not speak on his own. . . . He will glorify me."

Stephen Smalley gives special attention to two passages on the Holy Spirit in 1 John. In 1 John 2:20 the NRSV translates: "But you have been anointed by the Holy One, and all of you have knowledge."[73] The Greek is *chrisma echete*: "you have a consecration" (Smalley), or "you have an anointing." He believes that this represents a play on words between *chriō*, "to anoint," and *Christos*.

---

69. J. Estlin Carpenter, *The Johannine Writings: A Study of the Apocalypse and the Fourth Gospel* (London: Constable, 1927).

70. F. W. Horn, "Holy Spirit," in *The Anchor Bible Dictionary*, 5 vols. (New York: Doubleday, 1992), vol. 3, p. 277; cf. pp. 260-80.

71. Schweizer, *"Pneuma,"* in *TDNT*, vol. 6, p. 448.

72. Montague, *The Holy Spirit*, p. 336.

73. Stephen S. Smalley, *1, 2, and 3 John* (Waco: Word, 1984), pp. 104-8.

Chrisma appears only here and at 2:27 in the whole New Testament. If it were to mean "act of anointing," it could not be "had" or "possessed." Westcott and Marshall interpret it to mean "means of anointing," namely, anointing oil.[74] But according to Smalley, the anointing could be either literal or figurative. The Old Testament background suggests that the meaning is *consecration* (Exod. 29:7; 30:25; 40:15; Dan. 9:26). In Isa. 61:1 the Spirit of the Lord anointed the Servant of the Lord to preach good news (cf. Acts 10:38). Hence Smalley concludes that this in effect refers to the gift of the Spirit. If we press the possible double meaning, the Gnostics may have used the same term to denote "initiation into knowledge."

The second passage is 1 John 4:1-6, which combines a rejection of worldliness as true children of God with six references to "spirit" or to the Spirit of God (4:1, 2, 3, and 6).[75] The writer warns the readers against an attitude which is anchored in a society which does not know God. They must resist such seductions and enchantments in the conflict between worldly delusion and divine truth. Hence they must "not believe every spirit, but test the spirits to see whether they are from God" (4:1). The second part of v. 1 explains that the reference is to false prophecy. The contrast is expressed in v. 2: "By this you know the Spirit of God: every spirit that confesses that Jesus Christ has come in the flesh is from God." As in the Gospel of John, the primary work of the Spirit is to witness to Christ; a second entailment may be the work of "prophecy" (see above, on Paul). Verse 3 resumes the discussion of "antichrists" (alone in the New Testament, but prominent in the Fathers) from 2:18, 22. Smalley comments: "Those who claim to be inspired must be 'tested,' to see if the spirit they reflect belongs to God."[76]

Dokimazō denotes to put to the test (cf. 1 Thess. 5:21). "Spirits" (plural) may reflect the Spirit of truth and the spirit of error, not a multiplicity of spirits, as in the writings of Qumran.[77] As in the Old Testament, false prophecy was sufficiently widespread to give rise to the regular term *pseudoprophētēs*.[78] In vv. 2-3 the word for "confess" *(homologei)* reminds us of Paul's criterion concerning the Holy Spirit in 1 Cor. 12:3, the early confession of Christ as Lord. The dualism between the world and God or the Spirit of God, and between falsehood and truth, reflects another characteristic theme of the Gospel according to John.

---

74. B. F. Westcott, *The Epistles of St. John: Greek Text with Notes* (Abingdon, Berkshire: Marcham Manor, and Grand Rapids: Eerdmans, 1966), p. 73; and I. Howard Marshall, *The Epistles of John*, NICNT (Grand Rapids: Eerdmans, 1978), p. 153.

75. Smalley, *1, 2, 3 John*, pp. 214-32.

76. Smalley, *1, 2, 3 John*, p. 218.

77. Marshall, *Epistles of John*, p. 204; and Rudolf Bultmann, *A Commentary on the Johannine Epistles*, Hermeneia (Philadelphia: Fortress, 1973), pp. 61-62.

78. Cf. R. W. L. Moberly, *Prophecy and Discernment* (Cambridge: Cambridge University Press, 2006).

1 John 5:6 takes up the theme of the Spirit of truth as witness, which is also prominent in the Fourth Gospel. The Spirit testifies in the present to Jesus and to his oneness with God. His coming in the flesh probably denotes its saving significance, not just the bare fact. The water and blood need not refer to the two dominical sacraments, but to the historical events of the baptism of Jesus, his cross, and his commission and empowerment, which involved the Spirit. This most naturally reflects the meaning of v. 6. Although 1 John is a "practical" epistle, clearly the witness of the Spirit is not unrelated to the importance of true doctrine. H. B. Swete concludes: "The Spirit of Christ is known by the witness which He bears to Christ. A secondary test . . . is to be found in readiness to accept the testimony of the authorized teachers of the truth. No man who was taught by the Spirit of Christ could reject the witness of His duly accredited messengers."[79]

---

79. Swete, *The Holy Spirit in the New Testament*, p. 269.

8

1 and 2 Peter, Hebrews, James, Jude, and Revelation

Of the writings in the New Testament not yet discussed, 2 and 3 John contain no references to the Holy Spirit, and 1 Peter probably has the most (eight uses of *pneuma*, "spirit," and two of *pneumatikos*, "spiritual"). In these writings we find several parallels with Paul. The Epistle to the Hebrews, which constitutes a major theological document alongside Paul and John, has twelve references to *pneuma*: four clear references to the Holy Spirit, one or two ambiguous references, and some references to "spirit" alluding to angels or to the human spirit. James, 2 Peter, and Jude have little more than one reference each. However, the book of Revelation has some eighteen uses of *pneuma*, of which some refer to prophecy, and some to the Spirit of God.[1]

8.1. 1 Peter

It is generally agreed that 1 Peter constitutes a homily or letter to those who have recently become Christians and have been, or are about to be, baptized. Some have called it a baptismal homily. Estimates of its probable date vary considerably from 63 to 112. It was written to churches in the northern part of Asia Minor to encourage them to endure persecution patiently, especially in the light of Christ's suffering and redeeming work. It also explores the theme of hope. Many scholars detect a number of parallels with other New Testament writings. While F. W. Beare accounts for this in terms of dependence and therefore assigns to it a late date, E. G. Selwyn, E. Lohse, J. N. D. Kelly, Ernest Best, John Elliott, and É. Cothenet account for these parallels in terms of dependence on a common (perhaps very early) Christian tradition. C. E. B. Cranfield repre-

---

1. W. F. Moulton and A. S. Geden, *A Concordance of the Greek Testament* (Edinburgh: T&T Clark, 1899), pp. 823-24.

sents a judicious view of its authorship. He gives eight significant reasons why it is difficult to see Peter as its author, but fully recognizes that if Silvanus (1 Pet. 5:12) was responsible for the Greek vocabulary and style, the traditional view is not impossible. He concludes, "The question is not yet settled."[2]

(1) The address describes its readers as "chosen and destined by God the Father and sanctified by the Spirit [Greek, *en hagiasmō pneumatos*] to be obedient to Jesus Christ, and to be sprinkled with his blood" (1 Pet. 1:2). The theme of *sanctification* runs from the earliest New Testament writings, such as 1 Thessalonians, to later literature. The Greek phrase *en hagiasmō pneumatos* occurs not only here but also in 2 Thess. 2:13. Here the work of the Holy Spirit also relates directly to Christ's work on the cross.

(2) 1 Peter's second reference concerns the work of the Holy Spirit in *inspiring the Old Testament prophets,* but the Spirit is also explicitly called "the Spirit of Christ" (1 Pet. 1:11). As in Paul, this Old Testament inspiration serves "not themselves, but you" (v. 12, i.e., Christians newly come to faith). Moreover, the Spirit, even then, was testifying to the sufferings of Christ. Yet 1 Peter also sees the Holy Spirit as enabling a *present proclamation* of the gospel: the same Holy Spirit "*brought you good news by the Holy Spirit* sent from heaven — things into which angels long to look!" (1 Pet. 1:12). The deepest knowledge of Christ's sufferings "for us" is reserved for forgiven and renewed sinners; angels can only stand and stare as they marvel.

(3) While the allusion to "the beauty of a quiet spirit" in 1 Pet. 3:4 clearly denotes the human spirit, nevertheless 1 Pet. 3:18, "made alive in the Spirit," probably refers to Christ's resurrection by the *Holy Spirit,* as does Rom. 1:4. It is unclear on what ground Swete understands this reference "clearly to be the human spirit of the Lord."[3] He further appeals to "the spirits in prison" in v. 19. But Ernest Best rightly refers to the Pauline parallel in Rom. 1:3-4 (cf. 1 Tim. 3:16) and comments, "The contrast is not between two parts of man's nature . . . (a contrast which is on the whole foreign to the N.T.), nor between two parts in Christ, . . . nor is it possible to mean that Christ went in bodiless fashion to preach to the 'spirits' (v. 19). When Spirit is opposed to flesh in the New Testament the opposition of divine Spirit to human existence is intended."[4] F. W. Beare sees this as "a liturgical stock phrase" alluding to Rom. 4:17; 8:11; 1 Cor. 15:22.[5] This would imply a reference to the Holy Spirit, but he goes back to "spheres of existence." J. N. D. Kelly speaks of Christ's "heavenly, spiritual sphere of existence, considered as divine Spirit."[6]

---

2. C. E. B. Cranfield, *1 and 2 Peter and Jude* (London: SCM, 1960), p. 16.

3. Henry B. Swete, *The Holy Spirit in the New Testament* (London: Macmillan, 1909, rpt. 1921), p. 262.

4. Ernest Best, *1 Peter,* New Century Bible Commentary (London: Oliphants, 1971), p. 139.

5. F. W. Beare, *The First Epistle of Peter* (Oxford: Blackwell, 1961), p. 143.

6. J. N. D. Kelly, *The Epistles of Peter and Jude* (London: Black, 1969), p. 151.

It is not our purpose to try to unravel the complexities of 1 Pet. 3:19, widely understood as "a proclamation to the spirits in prison." Clement of Alexandria (*Stromata* 6:6:44-46) takes the verse to refer to Christ's descent to hell on Holy Saturday before his resurrection. *Spirits* are then seen as Noah's sinful contemporaries (Ignatius, *To the Magnesians* 9:2; Justin, *Dialogue*, 72:4). Augustine assigned the preaching to the preexistent Christ (*Letters*, 164:14-17). The commentators exhaust themselves on grammar and syntax, and on textual criticism. Many conclude that the "spirits" are rebellious angels, partly on the basis of *1 Enoch* 10–16, Bar. 56:12-13, *Jubilees* 5:6, and the Dead Sea Scrolls. Best concludes, "The development of the doctrine of the descent into Hell . . . does not greatly assist the understanding of our passage. . . . The apocalyptic writings on the basis of Gen. 6:1-6 depict a group of angels (or spirits) who fell at the time of Noah."[7] Rendel Harris, followed by Edgar Goodspeed and James Moffatt, made the brilliant suggestion that the text originally read "Enoch" as the one who preached, but few today accept Harris's theory. The text seems to tell us that Christ preached in the Spirit to those who perished in the flood, or to those who were rebel angels, but does not specify when or how. Beare observes, "The passing reference to the Descent scarcely deserves the attention it has received, at least in a commentary on this epistle."[8]

Cranfield, however, considers it to be overly hasty to dismiss notions of the descent of Christ. He remarks, "The idea of a descent of Christ into Hades is to be found elsewhere in the New Testament. It occurs in Acts 2:27, 31; Rom. 10:6-8; Eph. 4:8-10."[9] Acts 2:31 declares, "He was not abandoned to Hades"; Rom. 10:7 asks, "'Who will descend into the abyss?' (that is, to bring Christ up from the dead)." Eph. 4:9 asks: "When it says, 'He ascended,' what does it mean but that he also descended into the lower parts of the earth?"

One interpretation, which is not widely favored, understands Christ's preaching through his eternal existence in the Spirit to the spirits *now* in prison as mediated through the lips of the antediluvian Enoch. Rendel Harris proposed that "Enoch" had accidentally been omitted from the MS after "in which" and before "also." This may seem far-fetched until we recall that *1 Enoch* 17–36 (cf. *1 Enoch* 18:12-14) tells of Enoch's journey to the underworld. Coupled with notions of New Testament writers seeing Christ as active in the Old Testament, this interpretation may have more appeal than at first sight.[10] Although he does finally accept this solution, Kelly expounds it plausibly; indeed, he spends nearly twenty pages on this complex verse.[11] He points out that while Liberal Protestants favor the notion of Christ's descent into Hades as a "second chance"

7. Best, *1 Peter*, pp. 145-46.

8. Beare, *The First Epistle of Peter*, p. 145.

9. Cranfield, *1 and 2 Peter and Jude*, p. 104.

10. Anthony T. Hanson, *Jesus Christ in the Old Testament* (London: SPCK, 1965).

11. Kelly, *The Epistles of Peter and Jude*, pp. 146-64.

theology, it lost favor with the Fathers for the very same reason.[12] Kelly extracts from this difficult passage the key theme of the resurrection of Christ within the framework of the Holy Spirit as life-giver and Christ's victory over hostile and fallen powers, both of which encourage new Christians under persecution or oppression.

(4) 1 Pet. 4:14 refers explicitly to "the Spirit of God . . . resting upon you." Here the Spirit is associated with Christ and with glory. This matches Kelly's exposition of 3:18-20. The whole context serves to encourage believers to endure steadfastly. The Greek *anapauetai* comes from Isa. 11:2 (LXX): "The Spirit of God shall rest upon him," which fits well with John 1:32 and with Paul. Ernest Best paraphrases the complex syntax by suggesting that "though judged at death in the sphere of the flesh according to human standards, they might live in the sphere of the Spirit as God lives."[13] 1 Pet. 4:6 may refer to living in the Spirit, but the allusion is not clear. If 1 Peter is genuinely "baptismal," the writer explains that the principles operating in Christ's death and resurrection will apply to their baptism.

When we put these references together, we see that 1 Peter is close to Paul in associating the gift of the Holy Spirit with Jesus Christ and the glory of his finished work. 1 Peter may well be a letter or homily written to those who have recently become Christians and are now under persecution. Those who call it "a baptismal homily" probably go further than the evidence specifically warrants, but their view is certainly possible.

8.2. 2 Peter, James, and Jude

(1) *2 Peter* has only one clear reference to the Holy Spirit. It affirms the traditional teaching that the declarations of *the Old Testament prophets* are confirmed by the Spirit, who inspired them. The well-known verse reads: "No prophecy ever came by human will, but men and women moved by the Holy Spirit spoke from God" (2 Pet. 1:21). Swete notes that the nearest parallel comes in the Pastoral Epistles: "All Scripture is 'God-breathed'" (*pasa graphē theopneustos*, 2 Tim. 3:16). Prophecy is not the invention of a human will, as when Jeremiah would have preferred not to speak the prophecy that God gave. Like the warning in 1 John 4:1-3, it is a warning against false prophecy (2 Pet. 2:1-22). False prophets "twist [texts] to their own destruction, as they do the other scriptures" (2 Pet. 3:16). Again, as in 1 Peter, this verse comes close to Paul: spiritual things are interpreted by the Spirit (1 Cor. 2:9-15). We have also noted the reference to false prophets in 1 John.

---

12. Kelly, *The Epistles of Peter and Jude*, p. 153.
13. Best, *1 Peter*, p. 158.

(2) *James.* Jas. 4:5 states "that the Scripture says, 'God yearns jealously for the Spirit that he has made to dwell in us.'" The Greek is probably transitive (*katōkēsen*, "made to dwell"), although it might be intransitive ("dwelt"). The phrase *pros phthonon* is adverbial, denoting "yearning jealousy." Swete paraphrases: "The Spirit of Christ in us longs after us, but jealously, with a love which resents any counteracting force such as the friendship of the world."[14] This rightly implies the personhood of the Holy Spirit. It is parallel to "Do not grieve the Holy Spirit of God" (Eph. 4:30). James states that *too much friendly pre-occupation with the world provokes the Holy Spirit in us to jealousy.* Nevertheless God gives more grace to overcome this. George Montague argues that God's "jealousy" is precisely that of the Old Testament over against the *ba'alîm:* God "does not want it [the Spirit of life] to be shared with false gods or values."[15] Peter Davids argues, "James has a wisdom pneumatology, for wisdom in James functions as the Spirit does in Paul."[16] This might help to explain the paucity of explicit references to the Spirit, since James is a typical "wisdom" writing, with its short, gnomic sayings.

(3) *The Letter of Jude* has only one chapter, and it presents parallels with 2 Peter, especially between 2 Pet. 2:1–3:3 and Jude 4-18. Many writers believe that one is dependent on the other. Some believe that both used a common source, but there are strong arguments against this.[17] The one reference to the Holy Spirit occurs in two parts in Jude 19-20: "worldly people, devoid of the Spirit, . . . are causing divisions"; and "Build yourselves up . . . ; pray in the Holy Spirit." If these "worldly people" *(psychikoi)* had claimed to be "spiritual," the writer is expressly denying this, in parallel to 1 Cor. 3:1-3 (and 1 Cor. 2:14-16). Kelly insists that this is indeed the case: some wrongly claimed the self-description *pneumatikoi* or "spiritual," and regarded other faithful believers as "ordinary" or "not spiritual" *(psychikoi),* thereby dividing the community as well as promoting elitism.[18] Because Jude uses the very rare word *apodiorizein* for "cause divisions," he is doing more than simply making a general statement that such people are devoid of the Spirit. The second clause is even closer to Paul and to 1 Corinthians. 1 Cor. 8:1; 14:4 speaks of edification or "building," and Rom. 8:26-27 and 1 Cor. 14:15 speak of the Holy Spirit as the inspirer of prayer. It is too often forgotten that the Holy Spirit, not the worshiper alone, initiates prayer. It is helpful to keep in mind that the problems at Corinth were not peculiar to that church alone.

---

14. Swete, *The Holy Spirit in the New Testament*, p. 257.

15. George T. Montague, *The Holy Spirit: The Growth of a Biblical Tradition* (Eugene, OR: Wipf & Stock, 1976), p. 311.

16. Peter H. Davids, *The Epistle of James: A Commentary on the Greek Text* (Grand Rapids: Eerdmans and Carlisle: Paternoster, 1982), p. 56.

17. Cranfield, *1 and 2 Peter and Jude*, pp. 145-46.

18. Kelly, *The Epistles of Peter and Jude*, p. 284.

8.3. The Epistle to the Hebrews

Hebrews is one of the most powerful writings of the New Testament, ranking in its theological sophistication and originality with Paul and John, in spite of its anonymity. Since at least the time of Origen, it has been admitted that only God knows who the writer was. Many interpreters suggest that this writer could have been Priscilla, partly because of its learning and Alexandrian style and vocabulary, and partly because the suppression of a female name would be understandable. Nevertheless, in spite of Luther's advocacy, we cannot move from possible or even plausible to certain. It is clearly not Pauline. Where Paul focuses on the resurrection of Christ, Hebrews sees his exaltation in terms of his ascension; where Paul speaks of reconciliation with God, Hebrews speaks of access into God's presence; where Paul speaks of justification, Hebrews speaks of the finished work of Christ as High Priest. Whereas Paul usually has large blocks of theology, followed by large blocks of practical exhortation (e.g., Rom. 1–11 and Rom. 12–16), Hebrews alternates shorter theological passages with short practical or hortatory ones. Nevertheless many themes overlap. These include the covenant and the Holy Spirit. Some commentators see Hebrews largely as a sermon, with the last section, including chapter 13, added to make it a letter.

At first sight, it may seem surprising that the Holy Spirit does not feature more prominently. B. F. Westcott argues: "The action of the Holy Spirit falls into the background . . . from the characteristic view which is given of the priestly work of Christ," and Swete agrees with this verdict.[19] A number of references to "spirit" refer either to the human spirit (Heb. 4:12; 12:23), or to angels (1:7, 14), or are ambiguous (9:14; 12:9). All the same, there are at least four clear references to the Holy Spirit.

(1) The first occurs in 2:4, where this passage takes its place among hortatory sections. Heb. 2:1 uses the positive didactic notion of paying attention and the negative nautical metaphor of "not drifting away from one's course" *(pararyōmen)*. The nautical metaphor conveys slipping away, or lethargy (cf. 5:11; 6:11-12).[20] Drifting "drains away" faith. Hence the readers must pay attention to the "signs and wonders" which accompany the testimony of God, to which is added "gifts of the Holy Spirit, distributed according to his will." This verse is clearly parallel with 1 Cor. 12:4-11. The passage also stresses the authenticity and urgency of the message to which "signs and wonders and various miracles" bear witness, together with "gifts [plural] of the Holy Spirit" (v. 4). It also has affinities with 1 Thess. 1:5 and 1 Cor. 2:4-5, except that Paul here men-

---

19. B. F. Westcott, *The Epistle to the Hebrews: The Greek Text* (London and New York: Macmillan, 3rd ed. 1903), p. 331; and Swete, *The Holy Spirit in the New Testament*, p. 249.

20. A. Vanhoye, *Homilie für haltbedürftige Christen* (Regensburg: Pustet, 1981), on this verse.

tions the Holy Spirit without miraculous signs (cf. 1 Cor. 14:25). Signs and miracles are more prominent in Luke-Acts, as "evidence of the truth of the gospel."[21]
"Signs and wonders" *(sēmeia kai kerata)* is a standard phrase used in Exod. 7:3
and Deut. 4:34; 6:22; 7:19, for example.

(2) The second unambiguous occurrence comes in Heb. 6:4, where the
theme is again *moving ahead without falling back,* or retracing old ground. The
readers must not compromise the complete and once-for-all nature of Christ's
work with constant repetitions of where they began. F. F. Bruce and William
Lane refer the six elements of "the foundation" to catechetical instruction.[22]
Verses 4-5 speak of "those who have once been enlightened, and have tasted the
heavenly gift, and have shared in the Holy Spirit, and have tasted the goodness
of the word of God and the powers of the age to come." Such people, Hebrews
asserts, cannot be "restored again to repentance . . . [if they] then have fallen
away." These verses have given rise to endless distracting debate, which we seek
to avoid. The issue about whether a Christian can fall away is not the author's
main concern here; nor does it impinge on his reference to the Holy Spirit.[23] He
stresses the ongoing character of the Christian life. Hugh Montefiore comments, "Apart from apostasy, no retrogression is possible in the Christian
life. . . . The only way of recovering lost ground is to forge ahead."[24] F. F. Bruce
comments, "Continuance is the test of reality. . . . He is not questioning the perseverance of the saints."[25] Participating in the Holy Spirit involves tasting the
powers of the new age, in accord with Peter's sermon on the Day of Pentecost.

The logic of these difficult verses is that one would never have come to
faith at all without the Holy Spirit; therefore, humans cannot undo the work of
God. But the writer wants his readership to see the seriousness of threatened
apostasy: they are not to be complacent about their status. To fall away is as un-
thinkable as "crucifying again the Son of God and . . . holding him up to contempt" (v. 6). The writer insists that *either* Christian faith is forever on the move
and progressing *or* appearances can mislead, and those who consider apostasy
may not possess genuine faith. Those who engage with Christianity at a purely
superficial level without the Spirit are likely to be inoculated against it.

(3) The third unambiguous two passages provide an affirmation of the *traditional view of the inspiration of Scripture:* "As the Holy Spirit says, 'Today, if
you hear his voice . . .'" (Heb. 3:7; cf. Ps. 95:7-11). Once again, this comes in one

---

21. William L. Lane, *Hebrews,* 2 vols., Word Biblical Commentary 47A (Dallas: Word, 1991),
p. 40.

22. Lane, *Hebrews,* vol. 1, pp. 140-41; F. F. Bruce, *The Epistle to the Hebrews* (Grand Rapids:
Eerdmans, 1964), p. 112.

23. Donald A. Hagner, *Hebrews* (Peabody, MA: Hendrickson, 1990/1995), p. 92.

24. Hugh Montefiore, *A Commentary on the Epistle to the Hebrews* (London: Black, 1964),
p. 104.

25. Bruce, *Hebrews,* p. 118.

of the practical "warning" blocks, or *parenesis,* in contrast to the more "theological" ones. As Lane points out, this formula of introduction to the quotation is common to many Jewish sources.[26] This view is repeated in Heb. 10:15-16: "The Holy Spirit also testifies to us [through Jeremiah], . . . 'This is the covenant: . . . I will remember their sins and their lawless deeds no more'" (Heb. 10:15-17; cf. Jer. 31:31, 33-34).

(4) The fourth reference occurs in Heb. 10:29, which speaks of "those who have spurned the Son of God, profaned the blood of the covenant . . . and outraged the Spirit of grace" *(to pneuma tēs charitos enybrisas).* The verb expresses the *hubris* of apostasy, as an insult to the holy presence.[27] Heb. 10:29 belongs with 6:4-6 in arguing for the logical impossibility of genuine Christians profaning "the blood of the covenant" and outraging "the Spirit of grace."

Evidently some Christians seriously considered relapsing into the protection of Jewish faith in the face of persecution. If this should ever happen, the writer urges, there remains "a fearful prospect of judgment, and a fury of fire that will consume the adversaries" (v. 27). "The Spirit of grace" has shown his utter generosity. This phrase may allude to Zech. 12:10 (LXX), as Otto Michel and William Lane suggest. Either Christians must persevere and go forward, or, even in the face of such generosity, they suggest that their faith is not genuine; for how can one who is genuine "insult" the Spirit of grace in this way? Lane sets out a visual comparison between 10:26-31 and 6:4-8.[28]

The most ambiguous passage in Hebrews is perhaps 9:14, which reads: "How much more will the blood of Christ, who through the eternal Spirit [Greek, *dia pneumatos aiōniou*] offered himself without blemish to God, purify our conscience from dead works to worship the living God!" Swete believes that "eternal Spirit" is "overbold; . . . it is safer not to connect the term definitely with the Holy Spirit, or with our Lord's human spirit . . . but to take the words in a more general and non-technical sense."[29] Lane, however, declares: "He [Christ] had been divinely empowered. . . . A reference to the Spirit is appropriate in a section under the influences of Isaiah, where the Servant of the Lord is qualified for his task by the Spirit of God (Isa. 42:1; 61:1; see F. F. Bruce)."[30] Montague and Montefiore reject this interpretation, but it seems convincing.[31] The NRSV, REB, NIV, and KJV/AV accept this view and translate the Greek as "the eternal Spirit."

As a final comment, we suggest that the occurrence of only four or five references to the Holy Spirit in such a major theological work as Hebrews raises a

---

26. Lane, *Hebrews,* vol. 1, p. 84.

27. Swete, *The Holy Spirit in the New Testament,* p. 250.

28. Lane, *Hebrews,* vol. 2, pp. 296-97; cf. pp. 289-99.

29. Swete, *The Holy Spirit in the New Testament,* p. 252.

30. Lane, *Hebrews,* vol. 2, p. 240.

31. Montague, *The Holy Spirit,* pp. 316-17; Montefiore, *The Epistle to the Hebrews,* pp. 154-55.

question about those who seem to claim that a genuine Christian will speak constantly about the Holy Spirit. On the other hand, the themes of Hebrews are the high priesthood of Christ and access to God through the finished work of Christ, and this demonstrates the extent to which the prominence or absence of given themes depends on the aims of the particular author and the specific needs of the first readers.

8.4. The Revelation of John

As I have pointed out elsewhere, there are three overlapping conditions (apart from the Holy Spirit's guiding) for understanding this complex book.[32] Indeed, it is part of the Spirit's leading to bring home the importance of these conditions. First, the writer is steeped in Old Testament allusions and imagery. For example, he would never have imagined that anyone would interpret the "seven" spirits (Rev. 1:4; 3:1; 4:5; 5:6), the seven stars (Rev. 1:20), or the "seven horns" (Rev. 5:6) numerically. The number "seven" occurs fifty-four times in this book. Often Ezekiel and sometimes Daniel hold the key to interpreting given passages. Second, John writes as both a prophet and an apocalyptist. If we had been first-century Jews, we should at once have recognized many of his otherwise obscure images as standard tools of apocalyptic writers of the time. In my youth I held the theory that he concealed his meaning for protection against persecution. But many have shown that this theory is impossible because some of its language is openly provocative. The symbols would be well known from such writings as Daniel, *1 and 2 Enoch,* and many other apocalyptic writings, some from the Old Testament. Third, it is crucial to recognize how often John uses symbols, and more than one level of meaning. Here is a point of contact with the Fourth Gospel, although in the Gospel they are used less frequently.

Umberto Eco is one of many who have rightly distinguished between a "closed" text, which conveys a straightforward "factual" meaning, and an "open" text, which is rich in suggestive metaphors and allusions that offer more possibilities of interpretation, as poetry often does, but which demands sophisticated and careful interpretation. Revelation uses much of this second kind of text. George Caird comments on Rev. 1:15 (the vision of the Son of Man), "To compile . . . a catalogue [of qualities] is to unweave the rainbow. John uses his allusions not as a code in which each symbol requires separate and exact translation, but rather for their evocative and emotive power. This is not photographic art."[33] Montague compares reading Revelation with being witnesses to

32. Anthony C. Thiselton, *Life after Death: A New Approach to the Last Things* (Grand Rapids: Eerdmans, and London: SPCK, 2012), pp. 193-203.

33. George B. Caird, *The Revelation of St John the Divine* (London: Black, 1966), p. 25.

a dream sequence.[34] With this in mind, we can proceed to John's passages on the Holy Spirit.

(1) Rev. 1:4, 3:1, 4:5, and 5:6 speak of *"the seven spirits of God."* But is this the Holy Spirit? Mounce believes that the writer uses seven spirits here partly in view of the "seven churches" to whom he writes (1:4), and partly in analogy with the seven eyes of the Lamb, where in 4:5 the imagery may reflect Zech. 4:2b, 10b.[35] H. B. Swete holds that this phrase refers to the seven angels of the Presence in Tob. 12:15, but in response he points out that these "seven spirits" appear between the eternal Father and the glorified Christ, which would be "unsuitable even for the highest of created spirits."[36] George Caird, however, comments, *"John uses the number seven as a symbol of completeness or wholeness."*[37] Even the "seven" local churches probably indicate "the church at large."[38] David Aune sees the key to the meaning in its use in Qumran.[39] Montague understands this as "the prophetic Spirit."[40] As in much apocalyptic literature, *seven* in Revelation has symbolic, not numerical, significance. John speaks of "seven eyes" (Rev. 5:6), as does Zech. 3:9; seven seals (Rev. 5:1, 5; 8:1); seven stars (Rev. 1:16, 20; 2:1); seven lamps (Rev. 4:5); seven angels (Rev. 8:2, 6; 15:6); seven trumpets (Rev. 8:2); seven thunders (Rev. 10:3, 4); and seven heads (Rev. 12:3; 13:1; 17:9).

(2) The Seer next uses the phrase *"in the Spirit"* (Rev. 1:10; 4:2; 17:3; 21:10). Swete describes this as "a state of mental exaltation" when the seer becomes "conscious of sights and sounds which to other men are invisible and inaudible," like the "ecstasy" of prophetic insight.[41] He sees this as identical with experience of the prophetic Spirit in Rev. 19:10: "To be a true prophet is to witness to Jesus."[42] Montague agrees that this phrase "in the Spirit" denotes being "caught up in the prophetic state."[43] Yet he adds that most of the revelations in the central part of Revelation are by angels. The function of the Spirit and that of angels may overlap here.

David Aune points out that in all four passages the word *pneuma* has no definite article.[44] But he retracts any suggestion that this is significant, because the article may be omitted with nouns which follow a preposition. But in spite

---

34. Montague, *The Holy Spirit*, p. 321.

35. Robert H. Mounce, *The Book of Revelation*, NICNT (Grand Rapids: Eerdmans, and London: Marshall, Morgan and Scott, 1977), pp. 69-70.

36. Swete, *The Spirit in the New Testament*, p. 273.

37. Caird, *The Revelation of St John*, p. 14.

38. Caird, *The Revelation of St John*, p. 15.

39. David E. Aune, *Revelation*, 3 vols. (Dallas: Word, 1997-98), vol. 1, p. 33.

40. Montague, *The Holy Spirit*, pp. 322-23.

41. Swete, *The Holy Spirit in the New Testament*, pp. 276-77.

42. Swete, *The Holy Spirit in the New Testament*, p. 278.

43. Montague, *The Holy Spirit*, p. 323.

44. Aune, *Revelation*, vol. 1, p. 83.

of this, and the peculiarity of the Seer's grammar, he concludes, "There is no reason for understanding any of these four passages as references to the Spirit of God." Instead, to him the phrase means that the Seer's revelatory experiences were "not in the body" but in the spirit. This might apply more readily to Rev. 17:3: "he carried me away in the spirit," which is also similar to 21:10. But this would be a departure from much of normal New Testament usage, although in this book the Seer often uses distinctive syntax and vocabulary. Aune translates Rev. 4:2 as "I was in a prophetic trance," so some translations leave open whether the reference is to the Spirit of God.[45]

Swete's statement, "There is no trace in the Apocalypse of any such *abuse* of prophetic powers as is implied in St. Paul's account of the assemblies at Corinth," seems surprising (my italics).[46] The church at Thyatira is warned about "that woman Jezebel, who calls herself a prophet, and is teaching and beguiling my servants . . ." (Rev. 2:20). Further, the beast of Rev. 13:11-18 "performs great signs. . . . it deceives. . . . This calls for wisdom. . . ." This is likely to refer to false prophecy. Indeed, "the mouth of the false prophet, . . . performing signs" occurs in 16:13-14, as in 19:20 ("the false prophet who had performed . . . the signs by which he deceived those who had received the mark of the beast"). Finally, Rev. 20:10 speaks of the demise of "the beast and the false prophet." There is a clear affinity with 1 John 4:1-3: "Do not believe every spirit, but test the spirits . . . ; for many false prophets have gone out into the world. . . . This is the spirit of the antichrist. . . ."

Caird translates the phrase "in the Spirit" in Rev. 1:10 as "I fell into a trance," and suggests, "It must have been Domitian's new insistence on the worship of the reigning emperor that provided the stimulus for his [John's] visions."[47] Mounce also calls this "existential openness to the Spirit of God."[48] To hear "a loud voice like a trumpet" (v. 10), he explains, means that there is no possibility of misunderstanding, because the voice is a clear and unmistakable sound, like the sound of a trumpet. Here, therefore, is a point of contact with Luke-Acts on prophecy and in the guidance of the churches.

(3) In Rev. 11:11 the NRSV has "the breath of life from God entered them," but the Greek has *pneuma*, which might be translated, "The Spirit of life from God entered them." The NRSV and NIV have chosen to translate *pneuma* as "breath." Clearly the passage alludes to Ezekiel 37, especially 37:10, where NRSV translates Ezek. 37:9 as "breath," and 37:14 as "Spirit." But Mounce and Aune prefer "breath" for Rev. 11:11, even if "Giver of life" constitutes a major theme of the Holy Spirit.[49] It may be either here. In Rev. 13:15, however, *pneuma* denotes

---

45. Aune, *Revelation*, vol. 1, p. 283.

46. Swete, *The Holy Spirit in the New Testament*, p. 277.

47. Caird, *The Revelation of St John*, pp. 19 and 23.

48. Mounce, *The Book of Revelation*, p. 76.

49. Mounce, *The Book of Revelation*, p. 228; Aune, *Revelation*, vol. 2, pp. 623-24.

"breath." Rev. 16:13-14 also denotes an evil or demonic spirit (cf. Rev. 18:2). This is linked with the (probably) symbolic "three": the dragon, the beast, and the false prophet.

(4) It is entirely different in the case of Rev. 14:13. This begins: "I heard a voice from heaven," and continues: "Yes, says the Spirit, they will rest from their labors." Here the traditional Jewish and Christian theme of the Spirit as inspirer of prophecy applies to the Seer. The Nestle-Aland text reads *nai, legei to pneuma,* where *nai* could also be translated "Amen" or "truly."[50] The Spirit of prophecy also occurs in Rev. 19:10: "The testimony of Jesus is the Spirit of prophecy" (NRSV) or, perhaps more clearly, "The prophetic spirit proves itself by witnessing to Jesus" (NAB). George Montague declares, "Prophecy occupies a central place in Revelation."[51]

(5) The last explicit reference to the Spirit in Revelation is: *"The Spirit and the bride say, 'Come'"* (Rev. 22:17). The most remarkable point is the reproduction of the Spirit's yearning in the life of the Church, the Bride. The Holy Spirit reproduces his own longing for the Return of Christ (cf. 22:20) in the cry of the Church. Here is a strong link with Pauline and Johannine teaching. Moreover, all apocalyptic stresses the reality of the unseen world, as well as using symbol. The language about living water, which we noted in John, appears in Revelation. John writes, "The angel showed me the river of the water of life . . . flowing from the throne of God and of the Lamb" (Rev. 22:1) and the tree of life "for the healing of the nations" (22:2). Montague, for one, links this with the "pouring out" of the Spirit in Isa. 32:15, Acts 2:17, and Rom. 5:5 ("the Pauline Pentecost"), as well as "the fountain of water" in John 7:38-39.[52] Although references to the Holy Spirit in Revelation are remarkably few, there are distinct points of contact with other New Testament writings. Even John's so-called dualisms of "above" and "below" and "Spirit and flesh" (John 3:6, 31) have their counterpart in Revelation.

Elsewhere I have tried to show how much of the symbolism of Revelation helps us to see how the ever-fresh, ongoing, ever-new work of the Holy Spirit shapes the life of heaven, alongside the work of God the Father and God the Son.[53] I have also tried to show how the Holy Spirit may make enhanced perceptions and new experiences possible.[54] The Spirit will more than satisfy every longing and hunger. We cannot claim that teaching about the Holy Spirit constitutes an explicitly central theme in Revelation, any more than it does in Hebrews, let alone James, 2 Peter, and Jude. Nevertheless Revelation conveys the themes of the prophetic Spirit, the affirming or longing Spirit, and the "seven"

50. Aune, *Revelation,* vol. 2, p. 839.
51. Montague, *The Holy Spirit,* p. 322.
52. Montague, *The Holy Spirit,* pp. 330-32.
53. Thiselton, *Life after Death,* pp. 204-15.
54. Thiselton, *Life after Death,* pp. 197-203.

spirits or sovereign and omnipresent Spirit.[55] Almost all of these writings contain at the very least incidental references to the Holy Spirit, which are often unplanned and uncontrived, and which therefore shed further light on the life of the earliest Church.

---

55. Montague, *The Holy Spirit*, pp. 322-28.

PART II

The Holy Spirit through the Centuries

9

The Apostolic Fathers and Early Christian Apologists

9.1. The Apostolic Fathers: The Inspiration of the Holy Spirit

The Apostolic Fathers or subapostolic writings belong to the so-called "tunnel" period between the New Testament and the early apologists and Church Fathers. Some even go back to the first century. *1 Clement* may be dated as early as c. 96. The other subapostolic writings, Ignatius, the *Didache,* Polycarp, the so-called *Epistle of Barnabas,* and *The Shepherd* of Hermas, belong mainly to the early or middle part of the second century. On the whole they reiterate such central teachings of the New Testament as the death and resurrection of Christ and his genuinely physical incarnation. Clement of Rome, for example, asserts: "He [Christ] bore the sins of many, and for their sins he was delivered up" (*1 Clement* 16:14; cf. 26:1-2 on the resurrection). Ignatius insists that Jesus Christ was truly man and truly God: he "ate and drank, . . . was truly crucified, . . . truly raised from the dead" (Ignatius, *To the Trallians* 9:1-2). Yet some material is foreign to the New Testament: Rahab was saved for "her faith and hospitality" (*1 Clement* 12:1). What, then, can be said of their view of the Holy Spirit?

Burns and Fagin may surely overstate the case when they observe: "References to the Holy Spirit were rare, and limited to his gift of inspiration."[1] Admittedly about half of their references to the Spirit concern the Holy Spirit's inspiration of the Old Testament, and sometimes of New Testament material, and several concern prophetic inspiration in the present. Only when we compare them with Paul and Luke-Acts do those references seem relatively few. Compared, however, with Hebrews, the General Epistles, and Mark or Matthew, the difference does not seem huge. These writings speak with sufficient

1. J. Patout Burns and Gerald M. Fagin, *The Holy Spirit: Message of the Fathers of the Church* (Wilmington: Glazier, 1984), p. 17.

regularity about inspired prophets, however, to warrant Harnack's controversial comment that "prophecy" was needed only until the close of the New Testament canon.[2] Even some Pentecostals associate this era with "the early rain," and their own era with "the latter rain" of Old Testament prophecy (discussed in Part III). Our method in this section is to trace *the main themes* of the subapostolic writings, to avoid an unduly fragmented picture of their work.

(1) *The inspiration of the Old and New Testaments. 1 Clement* 13:1 declares, "Let us do what is written, for the Holy Spirit says, 'Let not the wise man boast himself in his wisdom . . .'" (Jer. 9:23-24; 1 Cor. 1:31). Clement also declares that Christ came with humility: Christ "was humble-minded, as the Holy Spirit spoke concerning him. For it says, 'Lord, who has believed our report . . . ?'" (Isa. 53:1-12; *1 Clement* 16:2-3; Greek, *kathōs to pneuma to hagion peri autou elalēsen*). He continues, "You have studied the Holy Scriptures, which are true, and given by the Holy Spirit" (Greek, *dia tou pneumatos tou hagiou, 1 Clement* 45:2).

Ignatius (c. 107) in his seven authentic letters shares the same view of the inspiration of the Old Testament, although his view of the inspiration of the New Testament material is stronger and more explicit. He argues that the three-fold ministry of bishop, presbyter, and deacon *(syn tō episkopō . . . presbyterois kai diakonois . . .)* was established by the mind of Christ "according to his own will by the Holy Spirit *(tō hagiō autou pneumati)*" (Ignatius, *To the Philadelphians*, Preface).

The *Didache,* which is an early manual of church instruction, is probably from the early second century and is full of quotations from the New Testament (e.g., *Didache* 1:3-5 quotes the Sermon on the Mount extensively, including Matt. 5:39, 41, 44, 46, 47, 48; 7:12; Luke 6:30-33). Baptism in the threefold name of the Father, the Son, and the Holy Spirit (*Didache* 7:1 and 3) reflects Matt. 28:19, either directly or from current practice. Polycarp, bishop of Smyrna (martyred in 155), has one extant letter, to the church at Philippi. He extensively quotes from 1 Peter and other New Testament literature, but mentions the Holy Spirit more in the context of moral conduct than inspiration (Polycarp, *To the Philippians* 5:3) and speaks of being "well versed in the scriptures" (12:1).

The trend is reversed in the *Epistle of Barnabas* (between c. 98 and c. 150), where the author explicitly associates the inspiration of the Holy Spirit with Abraham, Moses, and other Old Testament figures. This is all the more remarkable because this is an anti-Jewish document attacking a literalist reading of the Old Testament by Jewish readers. The *Epistle* quotes from Ezekiel, applying the text to "those whom the Spirit of the Lord foresaw . . ." (*Barnabas* 6:14; Ezek. 11:19; 36:26). "Barnabas" writes, "'They who are afar off shall hear . . . ,' and 'Circumcise your hearts, says the Lord.' Again the Spirit of the Lord prophesies, 'Who is he that will live forever? . . .'" (*Barnabas* 9:1-2; Ps. 33:13; Isa. 33:13; Jer. 4:4;

---

2. Adolf von Harnack, *History of Dogma*, vol. 2 (New York: Russell & Russell, rpt. 1938), p. 53.

7:2, 3). On Moses in Deuteronomy: "Moses spoke in the Spirit" (*Barnabas* 10:2; Deut. 4:1-5). The author writes, "Moses received these doctrines [Greek, *dogmata*] concerning food, and thus spoke of them in the Spirit; but they [the Jews] received them as really referring to food" (*Barnabas* 10:9; Lev. 11:29). He concludes, "Moses received from the Lord the two tables, written by the finger of the hand of the Lord in the Spirit" (*Barnabas* 14:2; Exod. 31:18; Greek, *en pneumati*). Concerning Abraham he writes, "Abraham, who first was circumcised, did so looking forward in the Spirit to Jesus" (*Barnabas* 9:7). He declares, "Jacob saw in the Spirit a type of the people of the future" (*Barnabas* 13:5; Gen. 48:13-19).

Hermas remained a layman, a former slave from Rome. His book, *The Shepherd* (Greek, *Ho Poimēn*), claims to be a series of visions in which at least the fifth is dictated by an angel in the guise of a shepherd. He recounts five visions, twelve "mandates," and ten parables or "similitudes." It is probably dated in the middle of the second century. It urges the necessity of penance. It is possible that Hermas thinks of the Holy Spirit as the Teacher and Sanctifier of believers (*Similitude* 25:2). Swete argues, "It is still the age of ecstasy and prophecy."[3] Hermas shows more eagerness to speak of the inspiration of contemporary prophets than of Scripture.

(2) *Prophetic inspiration in the present.* Inspiration is the most frequent activity of the Spirit in *1 Clement*. But Clement does not seem to refer to contemporary prophets as such, unless, as we believe, the term "prophets" includes *preachers.* Burgess cites *1 Clement* 42:3 as providing an example of "inspiration . . . in everyday life."[4] But this passage speaks of "the word of God," and states: "They went forth in the assurance of the Holy Spirit, preaching the good news that the Kingdom of God is coming. They preached from district to district . . ." (Greek, *euangelizomenoi*, v. 3; and *kēryssontes*, v. 4). Indeed, Burgess cites the passage in which "the Holy Spirit was poured out in abundance on you all" in the past (*1 Clement* 2:2; cf. 1:1-3). He declares, "The Holy Spirit calls us," but this is *through Christ* (*1 Clement* 22:1; cf. Ps. 34:11).

Ignatius has less reservation about seeing himself as inspired by the Holy Spirit. He writes, "For even if some desired to deceive me after the flesh, the Spirit is not deceived, for it [he] is from God" (Ignatius, *To the Philadelphians* 7:1). However, he states in the same passage: "Give heed to the bishop and to the presbytery and deacons" as also "God's own voice," spoken by him. Hence it is not clear whether this is the Spirit of prophecy or the Spirit who equips believers for church office, perhaps at ordination. He refers elsewhere to the Holy

---

3. Henry B. Swete, *The Holy Spirit in the Ancient Church: A Study of Christian Teaching in the Age of the Fathers* (London: Macmillan, 1912), p. 23.

4. Stanley M. Burgess, *The Holy Spirit: Ancient Christian Traditions* (Peabody, MA: Hendrickson, 1984), p. 17.

Spirit, but especially as the Spirit of redemption or salvation. Similarly, Polycarp, his near contemporary, may speak of the Holy Spirit in sanctification, sustaining power, and doxology, but I cannot find a reference here to prophecy.[5]

The *Didache* uses the word "prophet." It states: "Every true prophet who wishes to settle among you is 'worthy of his food'" (*Didache* 13:1; cf. Matt. 10:10; 1 Cor. 9:13-14). The prophet is distinct from the teacher (v. 2; Greek, *prophētēs*, v. 1; *didaskalos*, v. 2). But how wide or how narrow was the ministry of a prophet? The *Didache* also states: "Suffer the prophets to hold Eucharist as they will" (*Didache* 10:7). Were these presidents of the Eucharist, or prophets, or both? If "prophet" could mean "preacher," did they preside because they preached, or preach because they presided? Or is this merely a later question? In *Didache* 13:3 the "prophets" *(prophētai)* "are your high priests *(archiereis)*." Yet in *Didache* 11:3-12, which concerns "Apostles and Prophets," the role appears to be *charismatic*. For if an itinerant prophet stays "three days, he is a false prophet" (*pseudoprophētēs*, v. 5). "If he asks for money, he is a false prophet" (v. 6). But contrary to Paul, the *Didache* urges, "Do not test or examine any prophet in a spirit" (Kirsopp Lake's translation; perhaps in the Spirit, *en pneumati*, v. 7; cf. 1 Cor. 14:29b and 1 Thess. 5:21, "test everything"). The *Didache* continues: "Not everyone who speaks *en pneumati* is a prophet" (v. 8). The difference between a true and false prophet can be seen from his *behavior* (Greek, *apo tōn tropōn*, v. 8). On the other hand, Kirsopp Lake's translation, "in a spirit," would fit v. 12: "Whoever shall say in a spirit *(en pneumati)*, 'Give me money,' ... you shall not listen to him" (*Didache* 11:12).[6] Swete concludes, "The *Didache* is the earliest post-apostolic writing that gives any account of a charismatic ministry."[7]

In the *Epistle of Barnabas* the writer comes near to Origen's notion of "spiritual" exegesis, and perhaps even to what many regard as "charismatic" hermeneutics today. When Moses said, "You shall not eat swine" (Lev. 11:7) *"in the Spirit,"* he means, "You shall not consort ... with *men who are like* swine" (*Barnabas* 10:2-3). Similarly, Ezekiel's prophecy about "hearts of flesh" (Ezek. 36:26), uttered by virtue of the Spirit, is spoken "because he [the Lord] was going to be manifest in the flesh and to dwell among us" (*Barnabas* 6:14). The temple has a new meaning, for the "temple built with hands ... was full of idolatry. ... [The Lord] himself prophesying in us [speaks of] a spiritual temple being built for the Lord" (*Barnabas* 16:7-8, 10). It is easy to see how "spiritual exegesis can move between reflecting a legitimate typology, as in the third example, and a clumsy imposing of an alien context and meaning, as in the first and second ex-

---

5. The doxological allusion is recounted in Eusebius, *Church History* 5:15.

6. Kirsopp Lake, *The Apostolic Fathers*, 2 vols. (London: Heinemann, and Cambridge, MA: Harvard University Press, 1965), vol. 1, p. 327.

7. Swete, *The Holy Spirit in the Ancient Church*, p. 20.

amples. "Charismatic exegesis" shares this precarious situation, and we discuss it further in Part III.

The Shepherd of Hermas recounts the "rapture" or seizing of Hermas when he is carried by the Spirit through a wilderness, and the heavens are opened (*Vision* 1:1:3 and 2:1:1). He warns his readers against false prophecy. In the *Similitudes* or *Parables,* the Shepherd, or angel of repentance, "came and said to me: I wish to show you all things that the Holy Spirit, who spoke with you in the form of the Church, showed to you. For that Spirit is the Son of God" (*Similitude* 9:1:1). Hermas saw "the building of the tower . . . by an angel . . . by the same Spirit" (*Similitude* 9:1:2). The five visions, twelve mandates, and ten parables reflect the kind of material that we read of in the visions of the prophet Ezekiel, or the prophet John in Revelation. Yet the Holy Spirit does not feature often explicitly, although prophetic vision is presupposed throughout.

9.2. Other Aspects of the Work of the Holy Spirit in the Apostolic Fathers

1 Clement is primarily concerned about *unity* within the church at Corinth. Hence it begins with examples of jealousy and disruption in the case of Cain and Abel (*1 Clement* 4:1-6); of Jacob and Esau (4:7-9); of Nathan (4:12); and of others, beseeching the church to "gaze on the blood of Christ" and to hear "the Holy Spirit concerning repentance" (8:1). Repentance entails praying, "Take not thy Holy Spirit from me. . . . Strengthen me with thy governing Spirit" (18:11). For God says: "The Spirit of the Lord is a lamp searching the inward parts" (21:2). He calls us "through his Holy Spirit" to desire life (22:1-2). He asks: "Why are there divisions . . . among you? Or have we not one God, and one Christ, and one Spirit of grace — poured out upon us?" (46:5-6). The apostles preached "in the assurance of the Holy Spirit" (42:3), and they appointed bishops and deacons, "testing them by the Spirit" (42:4).

One of the most famous analogies about the Holy Spirit comes in Ignatius's *Epistle to the Ephesians* 9. Believers are "made ready for the building of God our Father, carried up to its heights by the engine of Jesus Christ, that is, the cross, and using the rope of the Holy Spirit" (*To the Ephesians* 9:1; Greek, *schoiniō chrōmenoi to pneumati tō hagiō*). This may appear labored and overly mechanistic, but it remains memorable and suggestive. Its implicitly Trinitarian formula does not do violence to the work of the Father, the Son, or the Spirit. All the people are stones of the living temple of God. Later, Calvin, Barth, and others would stress that the cross has to be appropriated and applied through the work of the Holy Spirit. In the same letter Ignatius writes, "Our God, Jesus the Christ, was conceived by Mary . . . as well as of the seed of David as of the Holy Spirit" (Greek, *ek spermatos men Daveid, pneumatos de hagiou, To the*

Ephesians 18:2). Polycarp, anticipating Basil, gives glory to the Holy Spirit together with the Father and the Son (Greek, *di' hou kai sun autō kai pneumati hagiō hē doxa,* as recounted in Eusebius, *Church History* 5:15).

We have noted already that the *Didache* speaks of baptism twice "in the name of the Father, Son, and Holy Spirit" (*Didache* 7:1-3). The Trinitarian formula stresses both the unity and distinction of the Trinity here. Virtually all the other references to the Spirit relate to prophecy and inspiration. But the relation between "charisma" and "office" remains ambiguous. Certainly charismatic itinerant prophets exist. But do those who *permanently* serve churches experience charismatic gifts independently of an assigned church *office?* Or does God endow those appointed to office with *gifts for this task?* On occasion, we have urged, "prophet" may include "preacher"; the same answer might not apply to every occasion.

The Epistle of Barnabas usually refers to the Spirit in the context of a distinctively Christian interpretation of the Old Testament. Some speculate that this begins the Alexandrian tradition represented by Origen. But the letter also refers to descending to the water of baptism "full of sins and foulness," and ascending from the water "having hope in Jesus in the Spirit" (*en tō pneumati, Barnabas* 11:11). Further, the call of God comes to "those whom the Spirit prepared" (*Barnabas* 19:7). This appears to suggest that faith in Christ is not a human work, but one which the Holy Spirit initiates. This epistle also refers to the body as "the vessel of the Spirit" (Greek, *to skeuos tou pneumatos, Barnabas* 7:3; 11:9).

The Shepherd of Hermas remains mainly in the realm of prophecy. A prophet who does not possess the Spirit is "empty" (*Mandate* 11:3), and speaks only "according to the desires of men" (11:6). But the difference between a true and false prophet is seen "by his life: test the man who has the Divine Spirit" (11:7). The Spirit is one of truth, "free from lies" (*Mandate* 3:2). Hermas comes close to the prohibition "Grieve not the Spirit" (Eph. 4:30) when he warns that folly and evil can "crush out the Holy Spirit" (*Mandate* 10:2). One of the most distinctive utterances comes in *Similitudes* 5:6:5: "The Holy Pre-existent Spirit, who created the whole creation, God made to dwell in flesh . . . , walking . . . in holiness and purity." This may appear to ascribe creation to the Spirit.

This study of the subapostolic writings shows how unwise it is to generalize about this era. The inspiration of Scripture by the Holy Spirit has multiple attestations. But we should show caution about generalizing concerning the relation between the charismatic experience and church order. *1 Clement* is very different from the *Epistle of Barnabas* or the *Shepherd* of Hermas. The relation between cause and effect with reference to office and charisma in Ignatius remains ambiguous, except that nothing can "cause" the Spirit; we should avoid preconceived theories about charisma and order. It may be that God gives gifts for particular tasks; but each passage needs to be interpreted on its own merits. Clement of Rome and Ignatius in their different ways urge the importance of unity and order. Hermas may appear eccentric and mystical to many, but some of the Church Fathers valued his writings as almost equivalent to Scripture, even if others held a contrary view.

9.3. The Early Christian Apologists

The apologists include Aristides, Justin Martyr, Tatian, Athenagoras, Theophilus, and others. They addressed their defenses of the Christian faith in some cases to the emperor, but mainly to an educated Roman readership. They spanned the second century from about 120 or 130 to 200 or 220. They sought to gain a fair and positive hearing for Christian faith, and often engaged with Greek philosophy or Jewish attacks.

(1) *Aristides,* together with Quadratus, is thought to represent the first of the apologists. Some date the apology of Aristides c. 124. In this case it would be an apology to the Emperor Hadrian. But most date it after 138 when Antoninus Pius succeeded Hadrian. Before 1878 his work was known only indirectly through Eusebius and Jerome, but in the nineteenth century Armenian and Syrian translations of his work came to light. The single reference to the Holy Spirit in Aristides concerns the incarnation: Jesus came down from heaven, he states, in the Holy Spirit for our salvation (Aristides, *Apology,* 15; Greek, *en pneumati hagiō*). In this sense the Spirit initiates salvation through Christ.

(2) *Justin Martyr,* the most widely known apologist, came to faith c. 130 and wrote his *Dialogue with Trypho* in c. 135, engaging with the claims of Judaism. In c. 155 he addressed his *First Apology* to Emperor Antoninus Pius from Rome, and in 161 he wrote his *Second Apology* to the Roman senate. He claims a wide philosophical knowledge, and considers the hypothesis put by his dialogue partner: "Will the mind of men see God at any time, if it is uninstructed by the Holy Spirit?" (Justin, *Dialogue with Trypho,* 4; *ANF,* vol. 1, p. 196).

Later in the *Dialogue* Trypho objects to the words "The Spirit will rest on him" (Christ) (John 1:32). Justin, however, notes that "the Spirit will rest on him" comes from Isa. 11:2 (*Dialogue,* 87; *ANF,* vol. 1, p. 243). Justin argues that Christ is preexistent "filled with the powers of the Holy Spirit," and "became incarnate" (*Dialogue,* 87). Jesus, he argued, "needed nothing" but nevertheless relied on "the grace of the Holy Spirit's power" (*Dialogue,* 87). He then quotes from Acts 2:17 and Joel 2:28, "I will pour out my Spirit on all flesh" (*Dialogue,* 87). Justin asserts that it is now "possible to see among us women and men who possess the gifts of the Spirit of God; as it was promised" (*Dialogue,* 88; *ANF,* vol. 1, p. 243). Further, Justin writes, "The Holy Spirit lighted on him [Jesus] like a dove, as the apostles . . . wrote" (*Dialogue,* 88; Mark 1:10). In *Dialogue,* 39, there is an implicit reference in Christ's "ascending . . . to give gifts to men, which include wisdom, prophecy, understanding and knowledge" (*ANF,* vol. 1, p. 214).

In *1 Apology* Justin argues a different set of issues, seeking to present Christian faith *as rationally acceptable.* He refutes the charge of "atheism," arguing that Christians worship "the true God, the Father of righteousness." Moreover, they also worship "the Son . . . and the prophetic Spirit [whom] . . . we adore, knowing them in reason and truth" (*1 Apology*, 6; *ANF*, vol. 1, p. 164). Interestingly, he brings together the Holy Spirit, prophecy, and rationality or reasonableness, *not ecstatic consciousness.* This is hammered home in *1 Apology*, 13, which speaks of being "sober-minded," recognizing that God has "no need of streams of blood and libations and incense." Indeed, "we reasonably worship him. . . . He is the Son of the true God . . . , holding him in the second place and the prophetic Spirit in the third . . ." (*1 Apology*, 13; *ANF*, vol. 1, pp. 166-67). The remaining reference to the Holy Spirit in the *1 Apology* affirms the inspiration of Scripture: "The Holy Spirit of prophecy taught us this, telling as by Moses that God spoke thus" (*1 Apology*, 44; Deut. 30:15, 19; *ANF*, vol. 1, p. 177).

(3) *Tatian* was Justin's pupil and came from Assyria, although Hellenistic by education. His expertise was in rhetoric rather than philosophy or indeed theology, and Swete comments that his teaching on the Spirit "is undoubtedly much off the track of contemporary Christian opinion."[8] He is said to have founded the ascetic, rigorist sect of the Encratites in A.D. 172, and distanced himself from the Church. Much of his work is immoderate. He includes little material on the Holy Spirit, and what there is constitutes a distinctive advance on other apologists and the subapostolic writings. He recognizes that human beings as such are not immortal, but may become so if they are united with the *Spirit of God* (Tatian, *Oration against the Greeks*, 13). He also argues that not all can receive the Spirit (1 Cor. 2:14), but only those who live righteously and obey wisdom, who are armed with the breastplate of the heavenly Spirit (*Against the Greeks*, 16). Tatian, however, speaks of the Spirit as the "envoy" or *"ambassador"* of God (*Against the Greeks*, 15).[9]

(4) *Athenagoras* addresses his defense (or *Legatio*), *Embassy on Behalf of Christians*, to Emperor Marcus Aurelius and his son Commodus (176-80). He refutes the popular charge of atheism, stating that Christians believe in the God who created all things by his Word and who *holds them together by the Spirit* who comes from him (*tō par' autou pneumati*, Athenagoras, *Embassy*, 6). It is not unreasonable or irrational, he argues, that God should beget a Son who is his Word both in concept and action. Such a notion is not absurd (*Embassy*, 10). Athenagoras gives a remarkably early account of the *Trinity*: the Father, Son, and Holy Spirit are one "by the unity and power of the Spirit" *(henotēti kai dynamei pneumatos).* God is no more "separate" from the Son than a mind is

---

8. Swete, *The Holy Spirit in the Ancient Church*, p. 40.

9. Danker, BDAG, p. 361; cf. Swete, *The Holy Spirit in the Ancient Church*, p. 41, who suggests "ambassador" or "deputy."

separate from the word which it speaks; and he is no more separate from the Holy Spirit than a ray of the sun, or a "flowing forth," is separate from the sun (*aporreon kai epanapheromenon hōs aktina hēliou; Embassy,* 10:3; or Migne, *PG,* vol. 6, col. 909B).[10] Athenagoras further declares, "We affirm that God and his Word or Son and the Holy Spirit are one in power," with the Son as God's Word and Wisdom and the Spirit as "an out-flowing from him [God] as light from fire" (*aporrasia hōs phōs apo pyros to pneuma, Embassy,* 10). The Spirit unites God the Father, the Son, and the Spirit (*Embassy,* 12).

Athenagoras has been credited by some with a second treatise, *The Resurrection of the Dead.* This also aims to show that Christian belief is reasonable and compatible with philosophical inquiry. We cannot be certain, however, that this second treatise comes from Athenagoras. He is probably the ablest of the apologists, and he holds together the importance of the Holy Spirit and rational, philosophical inquiry. There is certainly nothing incompatible with its biblical roots about his exposition of the Holy Spirit.

(5) *Theophilus* was Bishop of Antioch. He argued that the Christian doctrine of creation was more rational and convincing than the immoral myths of the Greco-Roman pantheon of Olympian deities. He saw the logos as both the mind or intelligence of God the Father and its external embodiment in the created order. He called divine thought *logos endiathetos;* and divine creation, *logos prophorikos.* He identified the Holy Spirit with God's wisdom, declaring that God the Father created all things through his Word (the Son) and his Wisdom (the Spirit) in accordance with Ps. 33:6 (*To Autolycus,* 1:7). Specifically Theophilus says that the *Spirit* moved on the waters (Gen. 1:2) with *life-giving, effective,* or *anointing* power (2:13).[11] He declares, "The whole creation *(hē pasa ktisis)* is embraced *(periechetai)* by the Spirit of God, and the Spirit who embraces *(to pneuma to perichon)* is himself embraced with creation by the hand of God *(hypo cheiros theou,* 1:5)."[12] This rightly points to an immanental aspect, but without any hint of pantheism. God, Word, and Wisdom represent a triad: Theophilus uses the term *trias,* which Lampe catalogues as (1) the number *three;* (2) *a group of three,* (a) in general; (b) the Trinity, a triad of divine Persons, citing Theophilus, *To Autolycus,* 2:15 (Migne, *PG,* vol. 6, col. 1077B) before Hippolytus and others.[13] Yet since Theophilus also uses man, or human being, as a fourth term within a *tetraktus,* Swete doubts whether this is a full formulation of the Trinity.[14]

10. Geoffrey W. H. Lampe (ed.), *A Patristic Greek Lexicon* (Oxford: Clarendon, 1961), p. 509, where *epanapherō* may mean "throw back again" or "direct one's thoughts."

11. Danker, BDAG, p. 386, includes under *epipherō,* "to bring about, to add something on top of something, or to bestow."

12. Lampe (ed.), *A Patristic Greek Lexicon,* p. 1065: *"periechō,"* "to embrace, to surround"; middle, *"be wrapped up in."*

13. Lampe (ed.), *A Patristic Greek Lexicon,* p. 1404; cf. pp. 1405-7.

14. Swete, *The Holy Spirit in the Ancient Church,* p. 47.

Theophilus, however, follows his predecessor in regarding the Holy Spirit as the Spirit who inspired the prophets of the Old Testament. The Spirit had insight into the future, and Theophilus believes that these prophets and even the Evangelists were "Spirit bearing" or "inspired" *(pneumatophoroi)*. Theophilus writes, "Men of God, carrying in them the Holy Spirit and becoming prophets, being inspired and made wise by God, became God-taught, wise and righteous. . . . They are predicting pestilences and famines . . ." (*To Autolycus*, 2:9; Migne, *PG*, vol. 6, col. 1064A; *ANF*, vol. 2, p. 97).[15] It is notable that among the apologists Justin and Athenagoras are explicitly theological in their work on the Holy Spirit. Moreover, none of the apologists speaks of the Spirit as a created being, which would be implied by the English word "it."

---

15. Lampe (ed.), *A Patristic Greek-English Lexicon*, p. 1106, and *ANF*, vol. 2, p. 97.

10

The Ante-Nicene Fathers

10.1. Irenaeus against the Background of the Gnostics

Irenaeus became Bishop of Lyons in A.D. 180, and often receives the accolade "the first theologian of the Church." As J. B. Lightfoot has insisted, he is especially significant in expressing both the Eastern and Western traditions of the Church, and having oral links with the apostles through Polycarp. He grew up in Asia Minor, was a student in Rome, and became presbyter and subsequently bishop in Lyons. It is important to trace back the "rule of faith," in the form of the tradition of the Church, to the public legacy of the apostles. He regards Mark, for example, as the interpreter of Peter the apostle.

Nevertheless the main writing of Irenaeus, *Against All Heresies,* remains primarily an attack on the Gnostics, and we can fully understand his exposition of particular theological themes as a response in large measure to Gnostic speculations. His shorter work, *The Demonstration of the Apostolic Preaching,* was discovered only in modern times, and is less explicitly targeted against Gnostic "heresy." Some see Gnosticism as an alien system which infiltrated the Church; others argue that it was aberrant teaching that arose within the Church. It is mainly a second-century phenomenon, and by the end of the century it had become separated increasingly from the Church.

The two main tenets of Gnosticism were, first, its view of creation as the work of the Demiurge or God of the Old Testament, in contrast to the true God who was virtually beyond thought and language. Hence much of the interest of Irenaeus about the Holy Spirit concerned his work in creation. The second main tenet of Gnosticism, as the name implies, was that of *gnōsis* ("knowledge") as revelation. Hence Irenaeus saw the Holy Spirit's role in *revelation* and *wisdom,* first, from *God,* not of human devising; second, as a *growing process* rather than as a complete possession. Notably in the New Testament, especially in Paul, the noun *gnōsis* may lead to self-inflation and pride (noun, as in 1 Cor. 8:1), whereas coming to be known by God and "knowing" as I have been known (verbal form) remains a growing process culminating in the *future*. Irenaeus is true to Paul, and he also represents "the tradition" or "rule of faith" as a *public* transmission of knowledge, not a *private* one, as in *gnōsis* (e.g., *Against Heresies*, 1:10:1; *ANF*, vol. 1, p. 330).

Irenaeus explicitly attacks the three Gnostic systems of Valentinus, Basilides, and Marcion, who have been known to us since ancient times mainly through the writings of Irenaeus and Tertullian. In 1945-46, however, more than forty further Gnostic texts came to light in Coptic, and these in turn confirm and develop our understanding of Gnosticism. Marcion is distinctive in contrast to some Gnostic systems, and Tertullian directs his attack specifically at Marcion. The main point here is that this targets Irenaeus's work on the Spirit in a specific direction. These are some of his main themes:

(1) *Creation.* Irenaeus declares: "God is the Creator of the world," as "all the Scriptures" testify, and as the whole Church celebrates, "one God, the Maker of heaven and earth. . . . The Universal Church, moreover, . . . has received this tradition from the apostles" (*Against Heresies*, 1:9:1; *ANF*, vol. 1, p. 368). Scripture testifies: "I am God, and besides me there is no other" (Isa. 46:9; *Against Heresies*, 1:9:2). Irenaeus refutes the notion that "Monogenes," as one of the emanations of God, begat Christ and the Holy Spirit (*Against Heresies*, 1:12:7; *ANF*, vol. 1, p. 372). *Christ and the Holy Spirit are of the same order of being as God.* Indeed, "God . . . moulded by his hands, that is, by the Son and Holy Spirit, to whom also he said, 'Let us make man'" (*Against Heresies*, 4, Preface 4; Gen. 1:26; *ANF*, vol. 1, p. 463). *The Son and the Spirit as the two hands of God* provides a memorable metaphor for their distinctness but inseparability from God. Later, in book 4, Irenaeus asserts: "The Word, namely the Son, was always with the Father; and . . . Wisdom also, which is the Spirit, was present with him and anterior to all creation" (*Against Heresies*, 4:20:3; *ANF*, vol. 1, p. 488). This makes it utterly clear that *the Holy Spirit is not a creature*, preexisting creation, and is distinct from the Son and inseparable from the Father.

Irenaeus quotes Prov. 8:27-31 at length to show that Wisdom and the Holy Spirit are "from everlasting. . . . When he prepared the heaven, I was with him" (*Against Heresies*, 4:20:3). But how could Christ and the Spirit be manifestations of a Demiurge (4:20:4)?

(2) *The Holy Spirit anointed Christ for his incarnate ministry.* In opposition to some Gnostic notions that "Christ" descended upon the man Jesus, Irenaeus argues in *Against Heresies* 3, chapters 17 and 18, that it was the Holy Spirit who descended upon Jesus, as the apostles taught. He quotes Mark's testimony that "the Spirit of God as a dove descended upon him; this Spirit, of whom it was declared by Isaiah, 'And the Spirit of God shall rest upon him' (Isa. 11:2), . . . and again, 'The Spirit of the Lord is upon me, because he has anointed me' (Isa.

61:1). That is the Spirit of whom the Lord declares, 'For it is not you who speak, but the Spirit of your Father who speaks in you' (Matt. 10:20)" (Irenaeus, *Against Heresies*, 3:17:1; *ANF*, vol. 1, p. 444). A little later he repeats, "the Spirit of God . . . descended upon the Lord . . . , 'the Spirit of wisdom and understanding, the Spirit of counsel and might' . . ." (Isa. 11:2; *Against Heresies*, 3:17:3; *ANF*, vol. 1, p. 445). The Gnostics here "set aside the Spirit altogether" (3:17:3).

Chapter 18 continues the argument. The chapter begins by stressing the reality of the bodily incarnation, in opposition to the Gnostics, and also the Virgin Birth and the resurrection (*Against Heresies*, 18:3; *ANF*, vol. 1, p. 446). Irenaeus then distinguishes between "He who anoints, He who is anointed, and the unction itself with which he is anointed. And it is the Father who anoints, but the Son who is anointed by the Spirit, who is the unction, as the word declares by Isaiah, 'The Spirit of the Lord is upon me, because He has anointed me' (Isa. 61:1)" (*Against Heresies*, 3:18:3). These chapters form only two of a number of places where Irenaeus makes this point. He also recounts the baptism of Jesus, when "the heavens were opened, and he saw the Spirit of God, as a dove, coming upon him" (*Against Heresies*, 3:9:3; *ANF*, vol. 1, p. 423).

(3) *The Holy Spirit, revelation, and Scripture.* Irenaeus rejects the Gnostic notion that knowledge *(gnōsis)* can be fully achieved in the present, let alone by some private tradition. This becomes prominent in the argument of book 2, chapter 28. Even revealed knowledge gradually grows like a child (*Against Heresies*, 2:18:1; *ANF*, vol. 1, p. 399). Even Scripture does not "give us explanations" of everything, although "the Scriptures are indeed perfect, since they were spoken by the Word of God and his Spirit" (2:18:2). What transcends our knowledge "we must leave to God" (2:18:2). Scripture speaks of the Nile, but not about where it rises. The "diversified utterances" of Scripture can still be heard as "one harmonious melody" (2:18:3). *To claim to receive "unspeakable mysteries" is "presumptuous"* (2:18:6). For example, only the Father knows the day and hour of judgment (Mark 13:32; *Against Heresies*, 2:18:6; *ANF*, vol. 1, p. 401). He dismisses the "private" "gnōsis" of Valentinus, Marcion, and Basilides (2:18:6). Irenaeus endorses Paul's assertion that "the Spirit . . . searches all things" (1 Cor. 2:11). Nevertheless, the Spirit gives "diversities of gifts, differences of administrations, and diversities of operations" (1 Cor. 12:4-6), not a conveyance of all knowledge (2:18:7). Now we know only in part "and prophesy in part" (1 Cor. 13:9; 2:18:7).

(4) *Irenaeus correctly relates revelation and the Holy Spirit to eschatology.* Irenaeus writes: "We do now receive a certain portion of the Holy Spirit . . . , preparing us for incorruption, being little by little accustomed to receive and hear God; which the apostle terms 'an earnest,' that is, a part of the honor which has been promised by God" (*Against Heresies*, 5:8:1; *ANF*, vol. 1, p. 333). He continues: "This earnest, therefore, thus dwelling in us, renders us spiritual even now. . . . 'For you are not in the flesh, but in the Spirit, if so be that the Spirit of God dwells in you' (Rom. 8:9)." In the present the Holy Spirit evokes the cry

"Abba, Father" (Rom. 8:15), but this is not the same as being raised to see God "face to face" (*Against Heresies,* 5:8:1). Irenaeus expounds further "the earnest of the Holy Spirit" (5:8:2-4), contrasting it with the presumption of the Gnostics and their private revelation. They twist Paul's passages about the Holy Spirit (*Against Heresies,* 5:9:1-4; *ANF,* vol. 1, pp. 334-35).

(5) *The prophetic Spirit.* Following the Apostolic Fathers and the apologists, Irenaeus retains a belief in the Holy Spirit as *inspirer of prophecy,* especially in the Old Testament. This is less prominent, however, than in earlier writers, and emerges largely in opposition to the Gnostic claim that inspiration had a non-Christian source when it initiated Old Testament material. A genuine disciple "who receives the Spirit of God" will discuss the one God of both Testaments (*Against Heresies,* 4:33:1; *ANF,* vol. 1, p. 506). Elsewhere Irenaeus argues: "For the preaching of the Church is everywhere consistent, and continues to be on an even course, and receives testimony from the prophets, the apostles, and all the disciples . . . by the Spirit of God" (*Against Heresies,* 3:24:1; *ANF,* vol. 1, p. 458; Migne, *PL,* vol. 7, col. 966B). Prophecy is not given by human beings, such as a magician, but by the "Divinely bestowed power of prophesying where and when God pleases" (1:13:4; *ANF,* vol. 1, p. 335; Migne, *PL,* vol. 7, col. 585A). But Irenaeus rejects "irrationality," as do the apologists (*Against Heresies,* 5:8:3; *ANF,* vol. 1, p. 534). *The "where and when" of prophecy, I believe, should not exclude either charismatic spontaneity or prepared, reflective preaching.*

Irenaeus has a few further passages on the Holy Spirit in the Church and the Spirit of holiness in a believer, but we have outlined the major themes. The Spirit is important to Irenaeus, not least in his engagement with Gnosticism. The Holy Spirit is God's Creative Wisdom, through whom God made the world; who anointed Christ for his work of redemption; and who comes to believers as an earnest of their inheritance.

10.2. Clement of Alexandria

Clement's dates are probably c. 150–c. 215. He became a pupil of Pantaenus in Alexandria, and became a head of the catechetical school in c. 190. The works which survive include *An Exhortation to the Greeks* (the *Protrepticus*); the *Instructor (Paedogogos);* eight books of the *Miscellanies* or *Stromata; Extracts from Theodotus* (a Valentinian Gnostic); and various fragments. He sought to steer a middle path between Christianity and Gnosticism, and saw Christianity as the fulfillment both of the Old Testament and of Greek philosophy. He strives to present Christianity as a suitably *rational* and sophisticated religion, not merely as piety for the ignorant. By drawing on Gnosticism and middle Platonism, he presents Christian faith as the religion of the "Christian Gnostic."

Alexandria was probably the second largest and most prosperous city in the Roman Empire, after Rome itself. It was a strong intellectual center, attracting the speculations of Hellenistic Judaism, Gnosticism, Neoplatonism, and many exotic religions and philosophies. Clement was born and died roughly ten years earlier than Tertullian of Carthage. He went part of the way with the Gnostics in his use of negative theology, in which God is beyond human thought and language. He also shared the Gnostic view that the redeemed all possess the Spirit and are "spiritual."

(1) *Possession of the Holy Spirit, or "spirituality" and gifts of the Spirit.* Clement does not accept the Gnostic view that all believers are "spiritual" without qualification. In the *Instructor* he carefully examines Paul's argument in 1 Cor. 3:1-2. Even believers may be childish or immature: Paul fed them with milk (*Instructor*, 1:6; *ANF*, vol. 2, p. 218). This is "the beginning of faith in Christ" (1:6). Here he even cites Homer in alleged support. He quotes Paul: "I could not speak to you as to spiritual people . . . , but to babes in Christ" (1 Cor. 3:1). Yet "he called those who had already believed on the Holy Spirit spiritual, and those newly instructed and not yet purified, carnal" (1:6). "For where there is envy and strife, are you not carnal?" (1 Cor. 3:3). Yet "faith with baptism is trained by the Holy Spirit" (1:6; *ANF*, vol. 2, p. 217).

True "spirituality," Clement observes in *Miscellanies,* comes largely with *experiences of the gifts of the Spirit as enumerated in 1 Cor. 12:7-11,* which he quotes in full. Kilian McDonnell and George Montague make much of this kind of evidence in the Fathers, especially in relation to Tertullian, in the course of considering whether the early eight centuries of the Church offer evidence of expecting a "baptism of the Holy Spirit" in its initiatory rite of baptism.[1] Clement considers the Gnostic claims about "the perfect man," which is a state in Christianity reserved for the future (*Miscellanies*, 4:21; *ANF*, vol. 2, p. 453). "The manifestation of the Spirit" entails such qualities as "the word of wisdom by the Spirit, . . . faith through the same Spirit, . . . healing, . . . miracles, . . . prophecy, . . . discernment of spirits, . . . diversities of tongues, . . . interpretation of tongues. . . . All these works by the same Spirit . . ." (1 Cor. 12:7-11; *Miscellanies,* 4:21; *ANF*, vol. 2, p. 434). These are not "the common virtues" but gifts of the Spirit. Homer, similarly, speaks of the gifts of God. Clement quotes Paul, "If we live by the Spirit, let us walk in the Spirit" (Gal. 5:25; *Institutes*, 3:12; *ANF*, vol. 2, p. 294, and *Miscellanies*, 5:6; *ANF*, vol. 2, p. 452).[2]

(2) *The inspiration of the Holy Spirit.* Clement speaks briefly of the inspiration by the Spirit of Old Testament prophets. For example, "The Holy Spirit, uttering his voice by Amos, pronounces the rich to be watched on account of

---

1. Kilian McDonnell and George T. Montague, *Christian Initiation and Baptism in the Holy Spirit: Evidence from the First Eight Centuries* (Collegeville, MN: Liturgical Press, 1991), pp. 94-105.

2. For further examples, see Geoffrey W. H. Lampe (ed.), *A Patristic Greek Lexicon* (Oxford: Clarendon, 1961), pp. 1104-5, under *"pneumatikos."*

their luxury" (Amos 6:4, 6; *Instructor,* 2:2; *ANF,* vol. 2, p. 245). He writes: "It was God who promulgated the Scriptures by his Son" (*Miscellanies,* 5:14; *ANF,* vol. 2, p. 464). "Man . . . it is written in Genesis, partook of inspiration. . . . The Holy Spirit inspires him who has believed" (5:14; *ANF,* vol. 2, p. 465). Clement follows Justin, Irenaeus and others.

(3) *The Spirit and degrees of union with God.* Clement does not entirely discard the Neoplatonic and Gnostic concepts of emanation and divine hierarchy. Hence, after stating that the Holy Spirit "inspires" believers (*Miscellanies,* 5:13; *ANF,* vol. 2, p. 464), he turns to Plato and to the Stoics, seeing the best among Jewish and Greek philosophers as "the silver," but Christians as those "with whom he [God] has mingled the regal gold, the Holy Spirit, the golden" (5:14; *ANF,* vol. 2, p. 467; *tēn chrysēn* is strictly supplied). Christians are thus an amalgam in which union with the "gold" of the Holy Spirit comes about by degrees. McDonnell and Montague would probably see this as an "actualization" of baptism.

A similar metaphor occurs in *Miscellanies,* 7:2, where "the minutest particle of steel is moved by the Spirit . . . over many steel rings; so also, attracted by the Holy Spirit, the virtuous are added by affinity to the first abode, and the others in succession down to the last" (*ANF,* vol. 2, p. 525). The language is necessarily obscure to most readers today, since it presupposes concepts drawn from Gnosticism and Stoicism. Yet behind the attempt to speak in Gnostic terms, a biblical faith struggles to find expression. Clement writes: "As wine is blended with water, so is the Spirit with man" (*Instructor,* 2:2; *ANF,* vol. 2, p. 242). This occurs in a chapter on drinking wine, which also alludes in colorful terms to the blood of Christ and the Eucharist. The Spirit, Clement declares, is "the energetic principle of the Word, as blood is of flesh" (2:2).

(4) *The Spirit, the Logos, and the Trinity.* Clement is so eager to present Christianity as a fulfillment of the best in Greek philosophy that he purports to find anticipation of the Trinity in Plato's *Timaeus.* Plato, he says, calls God "the Father" and Creator of all good things. A second order of Being is "the good." By the third, "I understand nothing else than the Holy Trinity to be meant, for the third is the Holy Spirit, and the Son is the second" (*Miscellanies,* 5:14; *ANF,* vol. 2, p. 468). The Son of God as *Logos,* or creative rational principle, is central to Clement, but often in conjunction with the Spirit, as Word and Wisdom, although "Christ himself is Wisdom," and Wisdom is the goal of philosophy (*Miscellanies,* 6:7; *ANF,* vol. 2, p. 494). He declares: "The Holy Spirit . . . comes to [a human person] through faith" (*Miscellanies,* 6:16; *ANF,* vol. 2, pp. 511-12).

10.3. Tertullian against the Background of Montanism

Tertullian (c. 160–c. 220) was born, educated, and practiced law in Carthage, North Africa. Much of his work attacks the Gnostics, Marcion, and Praxeas, but between c. 196 and c. 212 he produced probably more than any third-century Christian writer on a variety of subjects. More than thirty of his works survive, and he is the first Christian writer to write extensively in Latin. His philosophical works include his *Treatise on the Soul,* while his theological works include *On the Flesh of Christ, On the Resurrection of the Flesh,* and *Against Praxeas.* His apologetic works contain *The Apology* and works on martyrdom; his polemical or controversial writings include his five books *Against Marcion;* and his didactic books are made up of moral treatises such as *On Idolatry, The Shows, On Repentance,* and *On the Veiling of Women.* He also wrote a number of miscellaneous works.

Tertullian was converted from paganism to Christianity by 197, and at once attacked pagan superstition in *The Apology.* He stressed the distinctive nature of the faith and its difference from pagan culture. His famous saying "What has Athens to do with Jerusalem?" did not mean a repudiation of all philosophy; indeed, his view of the soul draws much from Stoic philosophy. But he was rigorous on Christian thought and life, tending toward asceticism. This rigorous attitude and his interest in eschatology probably attracted him to Montanism and to his emphasis on the immediacy of the Holy Spirit or the Paraclete, and to prophecy. The precise date of Tertullian's turn to Montanism is not certain, but most scholars estimate this as between 203 and 207, halfway through his writings. He regarded the Bishop of Carthage as too lenient, and bordered on perfectionism and the notion of a "pure" Church. He was also fiery and passionate in his controversial or polemical works.

(1) *Montanism and the immediacy of the Holy Spirit.* Montanus began to prophesy either in 172 (according to Eusebius, *Church History,* 16) or else in 156-57 (according to Epiphanius, *Refutation of All Heresies,* 48:1).[3] He expected a speedy outpouring of the Spirit on the Church, and his message was one of apocalyptic expectation and preparedness for the End. Two women disciples, Prisca and Maximilla, joined him, and the movement spread from Phrygia to North Africa. The movement *called themselves "Spirit-filled"* or *pneumatics,* and labeled the mainline or Catholic Church *"psychicals"* or "ordinary people." Tertullian did not hold every tenet of the movement, but he was attracted by its emphasis on the immediacy of the Holy Spirit, its rigor and asceticism, and its separation from the world, along with its indifference to "order" in the Church. The followers of Montanus called their movement "the new prophecy." It was in large measure a reaction against formalism and bureaucracy in the Church.

The "Paraclete" was the vehicle of Montanist prophecy and revelation, and in the view of the mainline churches such prophecy was ecstatic and usually frenzied. The major problem for the rest of the church was the extravagant and exclusivist claims of the New Prophecy. They believed that through them the

3. McDonnell and Montague, *Christian Initiation,* p. 107.

Paraclete spoke for the last time, that is, before the descent of the New Jerusalem. Maximilla declared, "After me, no prophet more, but the End."[4]

Evaluations of Montanism vary dramatically. Tertullian saw the New Prophecy as an authentic call to a lax Church which was obsessed with formal office. The New Prophecy seemed to represent what he had always championed. Even John Wesley in later life saw it as an authentic call to holiness and experience. A number of feminists (including Christine Trevett, cited below in n. 4) perceive it as valuing the positive role of women. On the other hand, Eusebius recounts that they were "elated and not a little puffed up, . . . forgetting . . . the Lord, . . . seducing spirits, . . . estranged from the true faith. . . . They talked wildly, unreasonably, and strongly. . . . The arrogant spirit taught them to revile the entire universal Church under heaven: . . . the spirit of false prophecy . . . heresy . . . expelled from the Church" (Eusebius, *Church History*, 5:16; *NPNF*, ser. 2, vol. 1, pp. 231-32). One hundred years ago, Henry Gwatkin wrote: "Just as the Gnostics referred everything to man, so the Montanists referred everything to God. . . . They degraded [inspiration], the one [Gnosticism] to the goddess 'human reasoning,' the other [Montanism] to a magic power overriding human nature. . . . The failure of Montanism did much to discredit every form of prophecy. . . . *It threw even preaching into the background for a thousand years.*"[5] Tertullian did not admit that Montanus, Prisca (or Priscilla), and Maximilla had set themselves against the Church. It may be argued that within the North African Church they were forerunners of the Donatists, and later of the "left-wing" Radical Reformers, whom Luther called "the fanatics," and in some measure the more extreme of the Puritans.

(2) *The extent of Tertullian's pre-Montanist writings.* It is not easy to be certain in a number of cases which of Tertullian's many writings are clearly *pre-Montanist.* There is general agreement, however, that his work *On Baptism* was written before his Montanist era. Here he offers what many today would call a "sacramental" view of the Holy Spirit, namely, his blessing of baptismal water. He writes, "The Spirit of God, who hovered over [the waters] from the beginning (Gen. 1:2), would continue to linger over the waters of the baptized" (Tertullian, *On Baptism*, 4; *ANF*, vol. 3, p. 670). The source of the water does not matter: "all waters, . . . after invocation of God, attain the sacramental power of sanctification, for the Spirit immediately supervenes from the heavens, . . . sanctifying them from himself" (ch. 4). By contrast, the water ceremonies of the pagans, including those of Isis and Mithras, are of no avail (ch. 5). They are a "spurious imitation of the Divine Spirit" (ch. 5). It is not, however, *in* the water

---

4. Ronald E. Heine, *The Montanist Oracles and Testimonia* (Macon, GA: Mercer University Press, 1989), pp. 163-69. Christine Trevett, *Montanism: Gender, Authority and the New People Prophecy* (Cambridge: Cambridge University Press, 1996), offers a feminist and positive evaluation.

5. Henry M. Gwatkin, *Early Church History to* A.D. *313*, 2 vols. (London: Macmillan, 1912), vol. 2, pp. 77 and 94 (my italics).

that we are cleansed, but the preparatory action of the Holy Spirit is what cleanses (ch. 6; *ANF*, vol. 3, p. 672). When we have been baptized, "a blessed unction" occurs (ch. 7), like "the dove of the Holy Spirit" (ch. 8; *ANF*, vol. 3, p. 673). McDonnell and Montague argue that Tertullian places baptism in the context of the communion of Christians.[6]

It is also widely agreed that Tertullian's *On Prescription against Heretics* belongs to his pre-Montanist period. This includes a summary of an early creed, which he calls "this rule of faith." It expresses belief "that there is only one God, . . . the Creator of the world, who produced all things out of nothing through his own Word. . . . This Word is called his Son . . . ; [he was] heard . . . in the prophets" (*On Prescription against Heretics*, 13; *ANF*, vol. 3, p. 249). The Son was "brought down by the Spirit and power of the Father into the Virgin Mary, was made flesh, . . . went forth as Jesus Christ, . . . was crucified. . . . He rose again on the third day" (ch. 13). After his glorification he sent "the Holy Spirit to lead such as believe, [and] will come with glory" (ch. 13). *The Holy Spirit, then, is active in the conception, birth, and incarnation of Jesus Christ,* and is sent in place of Christ to guide believers. The main elements of the Conciliar Creeds are here.

(3) *The Post-Montanist writings.* It is not surprising that it is difficult to classify the writings after Tertullian's turn to Montanism, for Tertullian did not "convert" to Montanism but saw it largely as representing what he earlier stood for. Praxeas had virtually identified the Father and the Son. Hence *Against Praxeas* expounds a theology of the Trinity. In this context he explores the Paraclete in the Farewell Discourses of the Fourth Gospel, especially, in effect, John 14:16, 20 and 16:14. The Paraclete is called "another Comforter," but "another" distinguishes him from Christ, while affirming his close relation to Christ (*Against Praxeas*, 25; *ANF*, vol. 3, p. 621). He continues, "These three are one [Latin, *unum*] essence, not one Person, as it is said, 'I and my Father are one [*unus*, John 10:30].'" Neither the Son nor the Holy Spirit is separable from the Father in the way in which emanations in Valentinus would be: "God sent forth his Word, as the Paraclete also declares, just as the root puts forth the tree, the fountain, the river, and the sun ray" (*Against Praxeas*, 8; *ANF*, vol. 3, p. 603). "The Spirit indeed is third from God and the Son, just as the fruit of the tree is third from the root" (ch. 8).

In chapter 4 of this treatise Tertullian writes the epoch-making statement which is the basis of the Western (in contrast to the Eastern) creeds. He declares, *"I believe the Spirit to proceed* from no other source than *from Father through the Son"* (my italics; *Against Praxeas*, 4; *ANF*, vol. 3, p. 599). In a subsequent passage he asserts, "God was pleased to renew his covenant with man in such a way that his Unity might be believed in . . . through the Son and the Spirit . . ." (*Against Praxeas*, 31; *ANF*, vol. 3, p. 627). In chapter 7 he states that

6. McDonnell and Montague, *Christian Initiation*, p. 111; cf. pp. 106-21.

Montanus, Prisca, and Maximilla were initially acknowledged by the Bishop of Rome, but later urged "false accusations against the prophets, . . . insisting on the authority of the bishop, predecessor in the See. . . . Praxeas did a twofold service to the devil at Rome: he drove away prophecy . . . ; he put to flight the Paraclete, and crucified the Father" (*Against Praxeas*, 1; *ANF*, vol. 3, p. 597).

Tertullian's treatise *On Monogamy* fully reflects a Montanist outlook. Montanists banned remarriage, even after the death of a partner. The Church discouraged it, but permitted it. Tertullian firmly shares the Montanist rigor. The Church, he argues, calls this "a heresy," but thereby "find themselves compelled to deny the Paraclete" (*On Monogamy*, 2; *ANF*, vol. 4, p. 59). He asserts, "*The psychics [ordinary Christians] . . . receive not the Spirit. . . .* [T]he things which are of the flesh will please them as being contraries of the Spirit" (Gal. 5:17; *On Monogamy*, 2; my italics). The issue of divorce and remarriage would occur "until the Paraclete began his operations, [when] the Spirit may vanquish the flesh" (*On Monogamy*, 14; *ANF*, vol. 4, p. 71).

Tertullian's treatise *On the Soul* borrows much from Stoic concepts of a quasi-material "soul." Its significance for Christian theology lies in its being the first formulation of *traducianism*, the notion that sin, or original sin, can be passed to descendants; God does not freshly create new souls *de novo*. Tertullian suggests: "Reasoning has taught us its [the soul's] corporeal nature . . . [and] seeing that we acknowledge spiritual *charismata* or gifts, we too have merited the attainment of the prophetic gift. . . . We have now among us a sister . . . favored with sundry gifts of revelation, which she experiences in the Spirit by ecstatic vision. . . . She converses with angels, and sometimes even with the Lord; she both sees and hears mysterious communications. . . . She says, 'There has been shown to me a soul in bodily shape'" (*On the Soul*, 9; *ANF*, vol. 3, p. 188). He describes the soul which reaches a state of rest or repose which is not natural to it as achieving "*ecstasy, in which the sensuous soul stands out of itself*, in a way which even resembles madness" (Latin, *amentiae instar; On the Soul*, 45; *ANF*, vol. 3, p. 223; my italics). God, who promised his Spirit, sends *dreams* of various kinds "even when in an ecstatic condition" (*On the Soul*, 47; *ANF*, vol. 3, pp. 225-26). Fasting may have a role in encouraging dreams (ch. 48). He concludes: "We, however, desire dreams from God" (ch. 49; *ANF*, vol. 3, p. 227).

We can be reasonably sure about the relation of the books that we have cited to Montanism. The early works show a reasonably orthodox approach to the Holy Spirit. The "post-Montanist" writings begin with Trinitarian developments, but seem to become more extravagant in their claims. From one point of view, namely, that of the Renewal Movement or Pentecostalism, Stanley Burgess calls Tertullian "the Church's first important Pentecostal theologian."[7]

---

7. Stanley M. Burgess, *The Holy Spirit: Ancient Christian Traditions* (Peabody, MA: Hendrickson, 1984), p. 63.

McDonnell largely shares the verdict, but also points out: "The disappearance of prophetic charisms . . . seems to be related to the rise of Montanism."[8] On one side, he defends and develops an orthodox doctrine of the Holy Trinity, and the sanctification of believers through the living Spirit. On the other side, he defends some utterances of *"the new prophecy,"* which many regard as unconvincing and irrational, and stoutly defends "ecstatic experience," which not all Pentecostals wish to defend. He did at one time allow for God's love toward the "less honorable members" of the Church (1 Cor. 12:23; *On the Resurrection of the Flesh,* 9; *ANF,* vol. 3, p. 352). He argued that "the body cannot feel gladness at the trouble of any one member" (1 Cor. 12:26; *On Repentance,* 10; *ANF,* vol. 3, p. 664). No doubt his passion and commitment remain impressive, but not his extremism. Like Montanism itself, this provoked a reaction from which the Church in general was slow to recover. He certainly encouraged the "distribution of gifts" of the Spirit among the faithful (1 Cor. 12:4-12; *On Baptism,* 20; *ANF,* vol. 3, p. 679). But as we have seen, Tertullian denies the Pauline maxim that every Christian has received the Holy Spirit (Rom. 8:9). McDonnell concludes: "Given Tertullian's aggressive, passionate, style, it cannot be a matter of surprise that Cyprian and Hilary would distance themselves, that Jerome and Augustine would condemn him."[9]

10.4. Origen against the Background of Alexandrian Scholarship

Origen (c. 185–c. 254) was born in Egypt, probably in Alexandria, into a Christian family, and received a Christian education. In his early years he sought martyrdom during a period of persecution (c. 202), and led a rigorously ascetic life. From c. 218, in his mid-thirties, to 230, when he was ordained priest, he devoted his life to writing for the sake of the Church. A wealthy friend, Ambrosius, provided him with stenographers and copyists. Epiphanius alleges that there were up to six thousand of these writings, but today only a small proportion survives. His works were of four kinds: on textual criticism and translation; on biblical exegesis; on Christian doctrine; and on prayer and practical disciplines for the Christian life.

(1) In the first category, textual criticism, Origen spent many years on *The Hexapla,* giving six parallel columns: the Hebrew text of the Old Testament, a transliteration of the Hebrew into Greek letters, the Septuagint, and the respective translations of Aquila, Symmachus, and Theodotion. All except fragments of the Septuagint, copied by Eusebius, remain. (2) Works of biblical exegesis included consideration of difficult passages, and sermons or homilies. The homi-

---

8. McDonnell and Montague, *Christian Initiation,* p. 106.
9. McDonnell and Montague, *Christian Initiation,* p. 121.

lies on John are most widely known today. (3) Origen's chief doctrinal work was his *On First Principles* (Latin, *De Principiis*, or Greek, *Peri Archōn*). His books *Against Celsus (Contra Celsum)* also provided an *apologia* or defense as a criticism of the faith voiced by Celsus. (4) His practical works included his writing *On Prayer* and his *Exhortation to Martyrdom* (now published in English in more than one edition).[10] A collection of extracts from his writings by Basil of Caesarea and Gregory of Nazianzus appeared under the title *Philocalia*, in the late fourth century.

In geographical terms, Rome, Carthage, and Alexandria had now become the most important cities of Christendom, taking the place of Ephesus and cities of Asia Minor. Here Origen found fertile soil for his scholarship. Pagans and unbelievers attended his lectures. According to Gwatkin's classic verdict, "Origen was beyond comparison the greatest scholar and the greatest teacher of his time."[11] He sought to expose prejudices and confusions in the tradition of Socrates, and placed education of the time on a new footing. Even the pagan Porphyry admired his scholarship and knowledge of Greek literature, except that, as he saw it, Origen sold his intellect to Christianity! Even his Sunday services were educative to all. He no longer permitted rhetoric to come before philosophy, and in Alexandria all this had a ready hearing. He sought to provide "healthy nourishment" for famished souls.

Origen produced his main doctrinal work, *On First Principles,* probably between 220 and 230, dividing systematic theology into four areas. After defining the task of theology in his Preface, book 1 considers the *nature and oneness of God* (against Marcion, Valentinus, and the Gnostics). He expounds the doctrine of the Holy Spirit in book 1, chapter 3. Book 2 examines *humanity and the cosmos,* including the Fall and redemption by Jesus Christ, including resurrection and judgment. Book 3 considers the cosmic struggle of good and evil, including *God, freedom, and evil.* Book 4 includes the interpretation of *Scripture, with its postulated "three senses"* (*On First Principles,* 4:1:11). In the background stands the relation between Christian faith and philosophy.

On First Principles, 1:3, then, provides the most succinct and systematic view of Origen's thought about the Holy Spirit. We may briefly outline ten themes, which are developed further in other writings of Origen. (1) Against the Gnostics, Origen affirms that one Holy Spirit *inspired* both Testaments of Scripture. Scripture was "inspired by the Holy Spirit," both Gospels and Epistles, and the law and the prophets, "according to the declaration of Christ himself" (*On First Principles,* 1:3:1; *ANF,* vol. 4, p. 252). "What the Holy Spirit is, we

10. Rowan A. Greer (ed.), *Origen: An Exhortation to Martyrdom, Prayer, and Selected Works,* Classics of Western Spirituality (London: SPCK, and New York: Paulist, 1979); see also John J. O'Meara (ed.), *Origen: Prayer and Exhortation to Martyrdom,* Ancient Christian Writers 19 (New York: Paulist Press, 1954, rpt. 1979).

11. Gwatkin, *Early Church History to A.D. 313,* vol. 2, p. 198.

are taught in many passages of Scripture" (1:3:2, cf. 2:7:1). (2) Origen establishes in several ways the close relationship between the *Holy Spirit and Christ.* He "descended upon Christ" at Christ's baptism, and Jesus Christ breathed upon his apostles after his resurrection, "saying, 'Receive the Holy Spirit'" (John 20:22; 1:3:2). (3) It is *by the Spirit that Christians can call Christ "Lord."* Origen quotes 1 Cor. 12:3, "No one can call Jesus Lord, save by the Holy Spirit."

(4) *Baptism,* Origen argues, *remains "not complete except by . . . the Trinity"* (*On First Principles,* 1:3:2). This is why baptism involves an appeal to the three-fold name of God. He exclaims, "Who is not amazed at the exceeding majesty of the Holy Spirit, when he hears . . . [about him] who is guilty of blasphemy against the Holy Spirit . . . !" (1:3:2). (5) *We cannot prove from Scripture that the Spirit was "made" or "created"* (*creatura; On First Principles,* 1:3:3). This point will be expressed more decisively by Athanasius and Basil. (6) *The Holy Spirit is the Spirit of revelation.* Origen writes: "All knowledge of the Father is obtained by revelation of the Son through the Holy Spirit" (1:3:4; *ANF,* vol. 4, p. 253). He quotes Paul in 1 Cor. 2:10, "'God has revealed them to us by the Holy Spirit'; for He also cites the Paraclete sayings in John: 'The Spirit, the Comforter [the Paraclete], . . . will teach you all things . . .'" (1:3:4). It is foolish, he suggests, to think of the Spirit as ignorant.

(7) *The Holy Spirit brings "unceasing sanctification"* (*On First Principles,* 1:3:8; *ANF,* vol. 4, p. 255). He makes believers "purer and holier" and gives "increasing sanctification" (1:3:8). Christians derive "existence from God the Father; secondly, their rational nature from the Word; thirdly, their *holiness from the Holy Spirit.* . . . sanctified by the Holy Spirit, . . . made capable of receiving Christ, . . . [who is] the righteousness of God" (1:3:8; my italics). (8) *This does not diminish the Spirit's role in giving gifts* (1 Cor. 12:8; *On First Principles,* 1:3:8). (9) *The Holy Spirit works "with the cooperation of the entire Trinity"* (1:3:5). Indeed, we cannot obtain salvation otherwise: "It is impossible to become partaker of the Father or the Son without the Holy Spirit" (1:3:5; *ANF,* vol. 4, p. 253). Origen asserts: "The power of the Trinity *is one and the same*" (my italics, 1:3:7; *ANF,* vol. 4, p. 255). Hence Paul declares in 1 Cor. 12:4-7: "There are diversities of gifts, but the same Spirit; . . . the same Lord; . . . the same God. . . ." All the gifts are "for the common good" (1 Cor. 12:7). The Holy Spirit belongs to "the unity of the Trinity. . . . He had always been the Holy Spirit" (1:3:4). (10) *The Spirit is life-giver.* "He breathed into his face the breath of life" (Gen. 2:7; John 20:22). God pours out his Spirit on all flesh (Joel 2:28; *On First Principles,* 2:7:2; *ANF,* vol. 4, p. 285).

Origen's further teaching on the Holy Spirit can be found in less systematic form in *On Prayer,* to a smaller extent in his *Exhortation to Martyrdom,* and in his *Commentary on John,* as well as elsewhere. He probably began book 1 of his *Commentary on John* in 231-32 in Alexandria, but completed it later in Caesarea, with book 32 in 248. Origen underwent two periods of persecution: under

Septimius Severus in 202, when Origen's father was martyred, and in 250 under Decius, four years before his death. In the latter he was arrested, severely tortured, and finally released. Rowan Greer observes, "The absolute loyalty of the Christian martyr holds a persuasive power to bring pagans to a vision of the truth."[12]

In his work *On Prayer* Origen follows the argument of Paul in Rom. 8:26-27 that "the Spirit Himself makes special intercession with God with sighs too deep for words. . . . The Spirit intercedes for the saints according to the will of God" (*On Prayer,* Preface 3).[13] The Spirit "intensifies the petition" (Preface 3). The verse in 1 Cor. 14:15, "I will pray with the Spirit, but I will pray with the mind also," is linked with the Romans 8 passage (*On Prayer,* Preface 4). For "the Spirit searches everything, even the depths of God" (1 Cor. 2:10; Preface 4). The Spirit, Origen observes, enables us "to think and speak rightly of so great a subject" (Preface 6).[14] Many of these passages have special importance for Pentecostals and those in the Renewal Movement. Burgess declares: "Spiritual gifts . . . are still in operation in the Church of Origen's day."[15] He cites especially *Against Celsus,* 7:8; *ANF,* vol. 4, p. 614: "There are still traces of his presence in a few who have had their souls purified by the gospel," and a companion reference which perhaps represents a misprint. But whether this reference genuinely implies charismatic gifts some may doubt.

Origen considers the standard objection to prayer that since God knows our needs, prayer becomes supposedly superfluous (*On Prayer,* 5:1-6). He also addresses other supposed objections, for example, that it compromises human freedom (*On Prayer,* 6:1-5). But Scripture, he replies, gives many reasons to pray. These include "the love of neighbour. . . . 'If one member suffers, all suffer together . . .'" (1 Cor. 12:26; *On Prayer,* 11:2).[16] He again appeals to the action of the Holy Spirit in Rom. 8:26-27 (*On Prayer,* 14:5).[17] Then he cites the example of the Lord's Prayer (18:1-3, 19-30).

In *An Exhortation to Martyrdom* the main emphasis falls again on *the Spirit and prayer.* Origen speaks of one "who prayed in the Spirit for the children whom the martyrs left behind" (*On Martyrdom,* 38).[18] He urges, "Become worthy of becoming one with the Son and the Father and the Holy Spirit" (39).[19] In his *Commentary on John,* Origen addresses the difference between a "literal"

12. Greer, "Introduction" to *Origen,* p. 5.

13. Greer, *Origen,* p. 84.

14. Greer, *Origen,* p. 86.

15. Stanley M. Burgess, *The Holy Spirit: Ancient Christian Traditions* (Peabody, MA: Hendrickson, 1984), p. 76.

16. Greer, *Origen,* p. 102.

17. Greer, *Origen,* p. 111.

18. Greer, *Origen,* p. 69.

19. Greer, *Origen,* p. 70.

meaning, for example, of the cleansing of the temple, and "spiritual interpreta-tions," for example, of the entry into Jerusalem (*John*, book 10, pp. 123-96).[20] The "spiritual meaning" requires "the mind of Christ" (1 Cor. 2:16 and 12; 10:172).[21] This is "because the Holy Spirit came upon the Lord" (10:173).[22]

In summarizing and assessing Origen's teaching on the Holy Spirit, we may perhaps distinguish three points. First, he affirms *all the traditional themes of his predecessors*. For example, the Spirit intimately cooperates, or works to-gether with, the Father and the Son, and has inspired both Testaments as the one Spirit. Second, numerous writers argue that he *has developed the doctrine of the Holy Spirit to the point of departure at which Athanasius could take it up* in the following century. Third, there remains some *ambiguity about whether he believes or implies that only the "worthy" can receive the Spirit*. But he does not intend this to be understood in the way in which a minority of Pentecostals or some in the Renewal Movement might be tempted to use it. This use would be different from the situation of which Origen observes, "The Spirit of God is taken away from all who are unworthy" (*On First Principles*, 1:3:7; *ANF*, vol. 4, p. 254). On the other hand, the Holy Spirit is a power "in which all are said to have a share, who have deserved to be sanctified by His grace" (1:1:3). On the Trinity, Michael Haykin concludes: "The text emphasizes Origen's belief that, while the Son and the Spirit belong within the divine sphere, they are *definitely inferior to the Father*. . . . [But] this inferiority may be only economic and not ontological" (my italics).[23]

10.5. Hippolytus, Novatian, and Cyprian

None of these thinkers approaches the theological stature of Tertullian or Origen, and they can be discussed more briefly. To some extent they anticipated the Donatist controversy in the second half of the third century and the fourth century, namely, the issue about a "pure church." Much of their work on the Holy Spirit concerned the Trinity, and they wrote less on practical issues than Origen.

(1) *Hippolytus* (c. 170–c. 236). Hippolytus obviously precedes Origen in chronological terms. He was a presbyter in Rome, according to Eusebius, and was exiled to Sardinia in 235, where he died as a martyr in 236. He was passion-ate but inflexible. He opposed Callistus and Urban for the bishopric of Rome,

---

20. Ronald E. Heine (ed.), *Origen; Commentary on the Gospel according to John, Books 1-10* (Washington, DC: Catholic University of America Press, 1989), pp. 262-99.

21. Heine, *Origen*, p. 294.

22. Heine, *Origen*, p. 294.

23. Michael A. G. Haykin, *The Spirit of God: The Exegesis of 1 and 2 Corinthians in the Pneumatomachian Controversy of the Fourth Century* (Leiden and New York: Brill, 1994), p. 16.

although some argue that he was not an antibishop, but that different bishops had oversight over different regions. Allen Brent argues this case, at least up to the time of Novatian.[24] Nevertheless Hippolytus was uncompromising and polemical, and his main work is *Refutation of All Heresies*. He attacked not only Gnosticism, following the example of Irenaeus, but also a modalist or Sabellian approach to the Trinity. He particularly attacked Noetus of Smyrna, who "alleged that Christ was the Father Himself, and that the Father was born, suffered, and died" (*Against the Heresy of One, Noetus*, 1; *ANF*, vol. 5, p. 223). The Scriptures assert that there is one God; yet the Father raised up the Son as a distinct Person, and the apostle Paul declared: "He shall also quicken your mortal bodies by the Holy Spirit, who dwells in you" (Rom. 8:11; *Against Noetus*, 2:4; *ANF*, vol. 5, p. 225).

In spite of his presiding over what most regard as a "sectarian" church, Hippolytus saw the Holy Spirit as a guardian of church order. He writes, "The Holy Spirit [was] bequeathed to the Church, which [i.e., whom] the Apostles in the first instance received [and] have transmitted to those who have rightly believed" (*Refutation of All Heresies*, Preface 5; *ANF*, vol. 5, p. 10). He certainly regards Montanism as "heresy," and Priscilla and Maximilla as "wretched women" who claimed to be prophetesses, "They are seduced into error" (*Refutation of All Heresies*, 10:21; *ANF*, vol. 5, p. 147). Noetus is linked with these "silly women," and "Callistus corroborated the heresy of these Noetians. . . . For Spirit, as the Deity, he says, is not any *being* [his italics] different from the Logos" (10:23; *ANF*, vol. 5, p. 148). In other words, *the Holy Spirit constitutes a distinct Being.*

Hippolytus composed his work *The Apostolic Tradition* in about 215 in Rome, mainly to preserve second-century practices which were in danger of neglect or misuse. Much of the work is lost, but fragments are preserved in a Latin palimpsest and some Eastern MSS.[25] In this he lays down criteria and qualification for appointment as a *bishop* (*Apostolic Tradition*, 2) and the *order of his consecration or ordination* (3–6). Next he turns to *elders* or *presbyters* (7), and deacons (8). He recognizes the ordination of those bishops for whom the *threefold Gloria* is used (3:6, 4:11, and 6:4), and *the prayer for the Holy Spirit* (3:3), as well as Communion and Unction (5:1-2). The prayer for elders includes, "Impart the Spirit of grace . . . filled with your Spirit" (7:2, 4). The concern for *office* is clear: only the bishop can ordain or make a deacon (8:5). The *deacon's* ordination includes, "Give the Spirit of grace and earnestness" (8:11), and the *Trinitarian doxology* (8:12). *A widow and a reader* are appointed by name but *not or-*

24. Allen Brent, *Hippolytus and the Roman Church in the Third Century* (Leiden: Brill, 1995).

25. Bernard Botte, *La Tradition Apostolique*, Sources Chrétiennes (Paris: Editions du Cerf, 1984); and Gregory Dix, *The Treatise on the Apostolic Tradition of St. Hippolytus of Rome, Bishop and Martyr* (London: Alban, 1992).

dained (10:1-5; 11). Similarly, a *subdeacon* is *not ordained* (13). Reference is made to "gifts" among the laity: healing (14), marriage (15:6), and "secular" occupations (16:1-11), with "teaching" as a special category (18–19). Hippolytus then considers baptism, including that of children: "If there are any children who cannot answer for themselves, let their parents answer for them" (21:4). "I renounce Satan" and "I believe . . ." form part of the vows, including "Do you believe in the Holy Spirit?" (21:17).

There follows a section remarkably like confirmation, where the bishop lays his hand on the baptized, and anoints them (*Apostolic Tradition*, 21:19-22). Holy Communion appears to follow (21:27-33). An exhortation to do good works follows that (21; 38), together with further prayer and hymns (22:11). A catechumen cannot take part in the Lord's Supper (27:1). Elders and deacons meet daily *where the bishop appoints* (39:1-2). Times of prayer are prescribed (41:5-18). What seems perhaps unduly puzzling is the claim of Stanley Burgess that "*The Apostolic Tradition* opens with a reference to a now lost work entitled *peri charismatōn*" ("On *Charismatic* Gifts"; my italics).[26] Dix and Botte appear to translate this as simply "spiritual gifts." We may include *administration and trained dispositions* in this list. Even in 1 Corinthians 12–14, as we saw in Part I, not all "gifts" are "charismatic" in the accepted sense.[27] Clearly Hippolytus was mainly concerned with *order and office,* for which he *includes prayer for the Holy Spirit.* Nevertheless, a case can be made for the general *substance* of Burgess's assessment, subject to qualification.

(2) *Novatian* (c. 250, possibly c. 210–c. 280). Novatian was a presbyter at Rome, which adopted a rigorous stance towards those who lapsed in the Decian persecution, and was eventually excommunicated by the church at Rome. Nevertheless his work *On the Trinity* developed Tertullian's theology, and he defended a two-natures Christology. Some regard him as *a bridge between Tertullian and Augustine* in the later church. He corresponded with Cyprian.

In *On the Trinity* Novatian devotes the first eight chapters to God the Father, and broadly chapters 9–23 to God the Son, including his humanity. Chapters 24–31 address Christology further, and, in places, the doctrine of the Holy Spirit. In chapter 24 he affirms the role of the Spirit in the *virginal conception of Christ:* "The Holy Spirit shall come upon you . . ." (Luke 1:35). In chapter 28 he refers to John 14:26, "The Advocate, that Holy Spirit whom the Father will send, . . . will teach you." In chapter 29 he refers to the promise in Joel 2:28 and in Acts 2:17: "I will pour out my Spirit . . . ," and the word of Jesus Christ: "Receive the Holy Spirit" (John 20:22). He is also *"the Spirit of truth"* (John 14:16-17; ch. 29; *ANF,* vol. 5, p. 640). The Holy Spirit is not "new" since he is also "in the prophets and in the apostles" (ch. 29). The Spirit makes possible "different kinds of

26. Burgess, *The Holy Spirit: Ancient Christian Traditions,* p. 81.
27. See above on gifts of the Spirit in Paul.

offices" in the Church (ch. 29). It is clear that Novatian is referring to Old Testament prophets, not New, when he asserts: "He is therefore one and the same Spirit who was in the prophets and apostles, except that in the former he was occasional, in the latter, always. . . . In the former distributed with reserve, in the latter all poured out; in the former, sparingly, in the latter liberally bestowed" (*On the Trinity,* 29; *ANF,* vol. 5, p. 640). Novatian then expounds the work of the Paraclete in the Farewell Discourses (e.g., John 14:16-17; 15:26; 16:13).

Novatian next discusses *gifts of the Holy Spirit:* "prophets in the Church, . . . teachers, . . . tongues, . . . healing, . . . wonderful works, . . . discrimination of spirits, . . . powers of government, . . . charismata" (1 Cor. 12:7-11; *On the Trinity,* 29; *ANF,* vol. 5, p. 641). But "the source of the entire Holy Spirit" remains *in Christ.* . . . The Holy Spirit dwells affluently in Christ" (ch. 29). Paul insists, *"He who has not the Spirit of Christ is none of his"* (Rom. 8:9). The Spirit gives new birth, but this is "in Christ." The Spirit is then *"the pledge of a promised inheritance . . .* who can make us God's Temple" (*On the Trinity,* 29; my italics). He is the *Spirit of sanctification,* for "we have not received the spirit of the world, but the Spirit who is of [proceeds from] God" (1 Cor. 2:12). Novatian quotes: "The Spirit of the prophets is subject to the prophets" (1 Cor. 14:32), and "No one ever calls Jesus anathema" (1 Cor. 12:3). Almost predictably he includes Jesus' saying about blasphemy against the Holy Spirit (Matt. 12:32), with an eye on discipline and rigor. He concludes with two chapters on the Trinity.

Novatian's other, much shorter, extant treatise is *On the Jewish Meats,* in which he "spiritualizes" Jewish blood laws and makes an attack on "luxury." Concerning *On the Trinity,* 29, Swete declares, "No passage in ante-Nicene literature is more rich in the New Testament doctrine of the work of the Spirit."[28] Burgess, almost predictably, uses the present tense of Novatian to argue for the continuance of charismatic gifts in Novatian's time, although he concedes that this may be "the extended present."[29] His case is certainly arguable, but the distinction between charisma and office is not always easy to make, and the least that we can say is that the Holy Spirit remains crucial for Novatian in the actualization and performance of offices and gifts. But clearly he does not believe in a "second," decisive blessing.

(3) *Cyprian of Carthage* (d. 258). Cyprian, who was previously a pagan rhetorician, was converted to the Christian faith in c. 246. Within two years he became Bishop of Carthage. He had a good knowledge of Scripture and of Tertullian's writings. The Decian persecution in late 249 had brought about large-scale apostasy. Cyprian was forced to flee, but he returned in 251. As persecution slackened, many sought rehabilitation in the churches. In spite of Jesus'

---

28. Henry B. Swete, *The Holy Spirit in the Ancient Church: A Study of Christian Teaching in the Age of the Fathers* (London: Macmillan, 1912), pp. 108-9.

29. Burgess, *The Holy Spirit: Ancient Christian Traditions,* p. 79.

assertions to Peter about limitless forgiveness, Cyprian wrote *On the Lapsed* (c. 251; *ANF*, vol. 5, pp. 437-47) against the readmission of lapsed Christians who sought to be restored. The problem was complicated by the fact that, in accordance with tradition or convention, some confessors had already agreed to this readmission, whereas Cyprian insisted that only the bishop could decide on their status. Novatian of Rome shared his attitude toward the lapsed. Both at Rome and at Carthage rival candidates for the episcopate took opposite views. In the light of a split church in both places, Cyprian wrote his treatise *On the Unity of the Church* (c. 251; *ANF*, vol. 5, pp. 421-29). He saw the Church as held together above all *by the episcopate*. Then in 252 a horrific plague occurred, which Cyprian saw as a sign of death to the world. It prompted him to write two further treatises, *To Demetrianus* (*ANF*, vol. 5, pp. 457-65) and *On Morality* (*ANF*, vol. 5, pp. 469-75). Factionalism began to spread for a variety of reasons, including controversy about the validity of particular baptisms. Stephen, Bishop of Rome, and Cyprian, Bishop of Carthage, were caught up in controversy about baptism and "papal" claims. Cyprian died in 258, after what many would regard as deep involvement in church politics. The persecution of Emperor Valerian may have precipitated his death, which was regarded as that of a martyr.

Cyprian's other writings included *Testimonia* (c. 248), a collection of biblical texts; *On the Dress of Virgins* (c. 249; *ANF*, vol. 5, pp. 430-36), dealing with the glory and honor of virginity; and *On the Lord's Prayer* (c. 252; *ANF*, vol. 5, pp. 447-57). His voluminous correspondence (*Epistles; ANF*, vol. 5, pp. 275-409) involves many of his controversies. Most of his work on the Holy Spirit concerns baptism and baptismal rites, and the Spirit as the exclusive possession of the Church. Although all believers receive the Spirit, *that gift may "decline" or become "degenerate"* if we dishonor God by compromise rather than facing martyrdom (*On the Lord's Prayer*, 11; *ANF*, vol. 5, p. 450). Martyrs, by contrast, are *"full of the Holy Spirit"* (69:14; *ANF*, vol. 5, p. 451; my italics). He writes: "The Holy Spirit came as a dove, a simple and joyous creature . . . acknowledging the concord of peace" (*On the Unity of the Church*, 9; *ANF*, vol. 5, p. 424).

Finally, we must consider the claims of Stanley Burgess, who asserts: "Bishop Cyprian is strongly charismatic, although he thinks that the bishop has the sole claim to prophetic gifts."[30] There can be no doubt that the second part of the sentence is wholly correct. Cyprian speaks of "priestly authority and power," the priest being "obeyed," the bishop as "the ruler of the church," and so on (*Epistle* 54, *To Cornelius*, 5-7; *ANF*, vol. 5, pp. 340-41). He asserts, "The Lord chose apostles, that is, bishops and overseers, while apostles appointed for themselves deacons" (*Epistle* 64, *To Rogantius*, 3; *ANF*, vol. 5, p. 366). However, the passages of text for which he claims the term "charismatic" say little more

---

30. Burgess, *The Holy Spirit: Ancient Christian Traditions*, p. 85.

than that Cyprian speaks of "visions" in the same way that we might think of the "visions" of John Bunyan, Jeremiah and Ezekiel, or the author of Revelation.[31] Burgess widens the definition of "charismatic." Many people might prefer to use some such term as "open to the Holy Spirit."

Once again, we have argued that "prophecy" as such is *not always or necessarily charismatic* unless we *exclude* reflective revelation, applied preaching, or similar modes of speech. What is clear is that Cyprian had an overblown, virtually "sacramental," "High Church," or "Catholic," concept of the episcopate, and that, like many who were nevertheless passionate men of God, he interpreted his own access to God's counsels especially highly. That said, the main concern of Novatian seems to have been more for *church office* than for *charismatic gifts*. The relative paucity of his references to the Holy Spirit, in contrast to references to the bishop, the priest, or the Church, appears to confirm this. Burgess's appeal to "a prophetess" who acted "as if filled with the Holy Spirit" proves only the second part of his sentence, namely, the authority of the bishop. For her "wonderful and portentous things" merely "deceived one of the presbyters . . . and a deacon, so that he had intercourse with that same woman" (*Epistle* 74, *To Firmilian*, 10; *ANF*, vol. 5, p. 398; Burgess's translation). Cyprian seems to have provided less clarity and teaching on the Holy Spirit than Hippolytus or Novatian, or certainly Origen and Tertullian. But he constitutes a link in the chain of Ante-Nicene Fathers.

---

31. Cyprian, *Epistle 7, To Martyrs and Confessors*, 3–7 (*ANF*, vol. 5, pp. 286-87).

The Post-Nicene Western Fathers

This chapter may be read in the light of another recent article in which I brought together the conclusions of the Post-Nicene Western or Latin Church Fathers on the Holy Spirit, especially in 1 Corinthians 12, with research on this chapter in recent New Testament scholarship.[1] However, for general purposes this eleventh chapter stands on its own.

11.1. Hilary of Poitiers

Hilary (c. 312-67/68) was a convert from paganism, and was elected Bishop of Poitiers c. 350. The pre-Arian Constantius exiled him c. 355-60, where his theology became profoundly influenced by Athanasius and the Eastern Church, and he became familiar with the Arian controversy. He defended orthodoxy at the Council of Seleucia. He made use of Origen's work, owed much to Tertullian, and was celebrated as the ablest Western or Latin theologian of the time, perhaps even exceeding Athanasius. He attempted to mediate between the orthodox "of the same being as the Father" *(homoousion)* and "of like substance" (*homoiousion*), encouraging both parties to unite against Arianism. And he was thoroughly familiar with the biblical writings. Indeed, Kilian McDonnell, following J. P. Brisson, describes him as "the very first exegete in the West before Ambrose and Augustine to produce an important exegetical study."[2]

Hilary's main work, *On the Trinity,* extended to twelve books (A.D. 362)

1. Anthony C. Thiselton, "The Holy Spirit in the Latin Fathers with Special Reference to Their Use of 1 Corinthians 12 and This Chapter in Modern Scholarship," *Communio Viatorum* 53 (2011): 7-24.

2. Kilian McDonnell and George T. Montague, *Christian Initiation and Baptism in the Holy Spirit: Evidence for the First Eight Centuries* (Collegeville, MN: The Liturgical Press, 1991), p. 134.

and was originally entitled *On the Faith*. He argued that the Father and Son are one *(unus)*. "No difference is revealed to sever them; their unity [does] not . . . contradict their distinct existence" (*On the Trinity*, 7:2; *NPNF*, ser. 2, vol. 9, p. 126). The Holy Spirit "is joined with Father and Son" (Gal. 4:6; 1 Cor. 2:12; Rom. 8:9; *NPNF*, ser. 2, vol. 9, p. 60). To reject "the word *homoousion*" is absurd when we confess "one God from whom are all things" and "one Christ our Lord, through whom are all things. . . . One source of all, One the Agent through whom all things are created. . . . In the Spirit she [the Church] recognizes God as Spirit . . ." (4:6; *NPNF*, ser. 2, vol. 9, p. 72). Hilary defended the *deity of the Holy Spirit* in the West, while Athanasius defended it in the East.

Hilary continues: "The Father and the Son are one in nature, honor, [and] power," and Jesus speaks of "the Spirit of truth who proceeds from the Father" (John 15:26; *On the Trinity*, 8:19; *NPNF*, ser. 2, vol. 9, p. 142). Hilary writes, "The Paraclete Spirit comes from the Father or from the Son. . . . He is both sent by him [Christ] and proceeds from the Father" (8:20). "Such a unity admits no difference" (8:20). "He shall not speak of himself. . . . He shall glorify me" (John 16:12-15). "The Spirit of truth is sent from the Father by the Son" (8:20). The issue which divides the Eastern Church from the Western is virtually solved by Hilary. Do we say, "proceeds from the Father and the Son"? Or do we say, "from the Father"? If Father and Son are truly one, there is a sense in which it does not matter. Hence Paul can say in Rom. 8:11: "The Spirit of him who raised up Christ . . . shall quicken your mortal bodies because of his Spirit, who dwells in you" (8:21).

In *On the Trinity*, 8:28-30, Hilary discusses 1 Cor. 8:1-11 and 12:3, 4-7. He quotes v. 3, "No one in the Spirit of God calls Jesus *anathema*" (v. 3), which he takes to mean in effect, "calls Christ a creature." To serve a creature (in effect, idolatry) is to become accursed. To call him Lord is to recognize his divine nature, which entails possessing the Holy Spirit (*NPNF*, ser. 2, vol. 9, p. 145). In *On the Trinity*, 8:29, Hilary enumerates the gifts of the Holy Spirit in 1 Cor. 12:4-10. First he notes the Trinitarian logic of vv. 4-7: "the same Spirit; . . . the same Lord; . . . the same God," but related respectively to gifts, service, and sovereignty. Second, he lists the gifts enumerated in vv. 8-10. He amplifies these in 8:30 (*NPNF*, ser. 2, vol. 9, p. 146). "Wisdom makes utterance . . . heard. . . . Knowledge comes from God-given insight." Faith relates to "believing the Gospel" (8:30).

The gift of healings (plural) includes "the cure of diseases," so that we may "bear witness to his grace." We note that Hilary does not restrict "healing" to "supernatural" gifts, or exclude medical means. However, he next includes "miracles," which denote "the power of God." "*Prophecy*" *means* "*our understanding of doctrine*" *and being* "*taught*" *by God*. Discernment of spirits distinguishes speech from "a Holy or perverted spirit." "Kinds of tongues" (generic and plural) is a "sign of the gift of the Holy Spirit," and "interpretation of tongues" is given so that believers are "not imperilled through ignorance, since the interpreter of a tongue explains the tongue to those who are ignorant of it." McDonnell suggests that according to Hilary these gifts should not be left dormant; but this does not imply that every gift is given to every Christian.[3]

Hilary concludes in 8:31 with the summary in 1 Cor. 12:11, including "as he [God] wills." All three Persons of the Holy Trinity are involved. There is "One Spirit" and "One Divinity" (8:32). In his treatise *On the Synods* he attacks a basic blunder of the Arians that "Father" and "Son" do *not* mean that "the Father [is] older than the Son, nor the Son younger than the Father" (*On the Synods*, 11:29; *NPNF*, ser. 2, vol. 9, p. 11). Later he declares, "The Lord who was to send the Holy Spirit was himself born of the Holy Spirit" (32:85; *NPNF*, ser. 2, vol. 9, p. 27). He also asserts, "I must also deny that this name of 'creature' belongs to your Holy Spirit, seeing that he proceeds from You" (i.e., God) (*On the Trinity*, 12:55; *NPNF*, ser. 2, vol. 9, p. 233). He gives a second, more concise treatment of 1 Cor. 12:1-3 and 4-11 in 8:34. He also considers 1 Cor. 12:12, 28 in 8:33, where he comments, "the power to help government by the prophets. . . ."

Hilary also expounds the baptism of Jesus and the descent of the Holy Spirit at some length. McDonnell comments: "The primary effect of Jesus' own baptism in the Jordan is the imparting of the Spirit joined to divine sonship."[4] He then draws the inference that Christian initiation is "likewise the imparting of the Spirit."[5] But it is doubtful whether all other writers would endorse this leap of logic.

The unity and diversity of the Church reflect the unity and diversity of God. Other writings include commentaries on Matthew and the Psalms. Together with Ambrose (but excluding Augustine), he is the most articulate theologian of the Western Fathers. Some have called him "the Athanasius of the West." Henry Swete asserts, "Hilary's general treatment of the doctrine of the Trinity is Eastern rather than Western. He is influenced by Origen, and he anticipates the Cappadocians. . . . His theology has more affinity with that of Basil and Gregory of Nyssa than with that of Tertullian; from the dogmatic tone of the Roman Damasus he is far removed. With Athanasius Hilary has much in common."[6] He also affirms, in the light of the Old Testament and his philosophical background: "The Spirit has no limits. . . . I will not trespass beyond that which human intellect can know about your Holy Spirit, but simply declare that he is Your Spirit" (*On the Trinity*, 12:56; *NPNF*, ser. 2, vol. 9, p. 233). Burgess comments, "Hilary's formula is *ex Patre per Filium*. The Spirit is *through (per)* Him through Whom are all things (i.e., the Son), and from *(ex)* Him from Whom are all things (i.e., the Father). . . . His views are consistent

---

3. McDonnell and Montague, *Christian Initiation*, p. 145; cf. pp. 139-57.

4. McDonnell and Montague, *Christian Initiation*, p. 142.

5. McDonnell and Montague, *Christian Initiation*, p. 142.

6. Henry B. Swete, *The Holy Spirit in the Ancient Church: A Study of Christian Teaching in the Age of the Fathers* (London: Macmillan, 1912), p. 303.

with [Western] *filioque* doctrine."[7] Nevertheless we have suggested that, in accordance with his character and the oneness of God, he would not necessarily reject the Eastern formulation.

11.2. Ambrose of Milan

Ambrose (c. 339-97) was born at Trier, the son of a senior Roman official, the Praetorian Prefect of Gaul. He received a Christian upbringing and classical education, which included rhetoric. He followed an administrative career, including legal practice and then becoming Governor, in effect, of Milan. On the death of a previous bishop of Milan, Auxentius, Ambrose was elected Bishop of Milan in 374 by popular acclamation (Ambrose, *On the Duties of Clergy*, 1:4). He was at the time not even baptized, but his rise through the ranks of clergy, including ordination as priest, is said to have taken only eight days. After his election as Bishop he became an inspiring, popular, and effective preacher, a good administrator and strategist, and a fervent defender of orthodoxy. He was concerned about what today is called "public" theology, corresponding with emperors and both church and secular politics. Whereas Hilary was less hostile to the "semi-Arians" (those who defended *homoiousia, of like being* with God), Ambrose marked out semi-Arians for special attack.[8] He also defended church order and the unity of the Church. He encountered political and ecclesiastical struggles but won by learning, oratory, competence, energy, and political wisdom. He drew on the Eastern theology of Basil, as well as his own learning. Like Basil he produced three books, *On the Holy Spirit*.[9] In 381 Milan became the governmental head of Italy, and the Western court moved to Milan, which opened further opportunities for Ambrose.[10] Emperor Gratian (375-383), a committed Christian, invited Ambrose to write a treatise for him in defense of orthodoxy.

In book 1 of *On the Holy Spirit* Ambrose first gives a "spiritual" interpretation of the Gideon narrative, in which moistening the threshing floor is a type of the Holy Spirit, poured out on the Gentiles (*On the Holy Spirit*, 1:1-8). Next he argues that "The Holy Spirit is not among, but above, all things" (1:1:19, *"non inter omnia, sed super omnia spiritus sanctus est"*; Eng. *NPNF*, ser. 2, vol. 10, p. 96). "The Spirit searches the deep things of God" (1 Cor. 2:10). "For since the Spirit is

---

7. Stanley M. Burgess, *The Holy Spirit: Ancient Christian Traditions* (Peabody, MA: Hendrickson, 1984), p. 169.

8. D. H. Williams, *Ambrose of Milan and the End of the Nicene-Arian Conflicts* (Oxford: Oxford University Press, 1995); B. Ramsey, *Ambrose* (London: Routledge, 1997).

9. Otto Faller, *Sancti Ambrosii Opera, pars nona* (Vindobonae: Hoelder-Pichler-Tempsky, 1964), includes the Latin text and critical introduction.

10. N. B. McLynn, *Ambrose of Milan: Church and Court in a Christian Capital* (Berkeley: University of California Press, 1994).

of God and is the Spirit of His mouth, how can we say that the Spirit is included among all things?" (1:1:23). "He is not of the fellowship of creatures" (1:1:26; *non esse socium creaturae; NPNF*, ser. 2, vol. 10, p. 97; cf. 1:2:27). In chapter 4 of book 1, Ambrose argues, "The Spirit of God is the same as the Holy Spirit," and he cites 1 Cor. 12:3, "No one speaking in the Spirit of God says 'Anathema' to Jesus, and no one can say 'Lord Jesus,' but in the Holy Spirit. The Apostle calls him the Spirit of God" (1:4:56, *Nemo in spiritu dei loquens dicit anathema Jesu . . .*; Eng. *NPNF*, ser. 2, vol. 10, p. 101).[11] *Ambrose repeatedly urges that the Holy Spirit is not a creature;* not a thing (today, not an "it"), but a being who is *of God.*

Second, in book 1, the Holy Spirit is the same Spirit as the One who spoke through *prophets in Scripture and through the apostles.* Many passages imply the action of the Spirit when this is assumed, not explicit (*On the Holy Spirit,* 1:3:32; *NPNF*, ser. 2, vol. 10, p. 98). He asserts, "Both apostles and prophets received that one Spirit. . . . For we have all drunk of one Spirit" (1:4:61; *unum spiritum et apostoloi et prophetae . . . quia unum spiritum potavimus; NPNF*, ser. 2, vol. 10, p. 101).[12] God also anointed Jesus of Nazareth with the Holy Spirit (1:9:101; *Iesum a Nazareth, quomodo unxerit eum deus spiritu sancto; NPNF*, ser. 2, vol. 10, p. 107).[13] This all contributes to Ambrose's insistence that God the Father, Jesus Christ, and the Holy Spirit are one, and one unique order of being. He writes, "Who then can dare to say that the Holy Spirit is separated from the Father and Christ?" (1:6:80; *audet dicere discretum a deo patre et Christo esse spiritum sanctum; NPNF*, ser. 2, vol. 10, p. 103).[14]

Third, in book 1, Ambrose shows that the diverse gifts of the Holy Spirit do not detract from *his oneness with God,* who is a perfect unity. Ambrose cites the promise of Jesus "to baptize in the Holy Spirit" (Acts 1:5), but this stands in parallel with the initiatory "baptized in the body itself into one Spirit" (1 Cor. 12:13; *On the Holy Spirit,* 3:45; *baptizamini in spiritu sancto . . . in ipso corpore in unum spiritum baptizati sumus; NPNF*, ser. 2, vol. 10, p. 99).[15] The Spirit's "diversities of gifts" has nothing to do with a crowd of creatures, but comes from the one God (1:3:49). "Apostles and prophets received that one Spirit . . . 'all drank of one Spirit' (1 Cor. 12:13), . . . who cannot be divided" (1:4:61; *qui non queat scindii; NPNF*, ser. 2, vol. 10, p. 101). The *inseparability* of the Father, the Son, and the Spirit is proved a second time from 1 Cor. 12:3, "For no one says 'Lord Jesus,' except in the Holy Spirit" (1:11:124; *Nemo enim dicit dominum Iesum nisi in spiritu sancto; NPNF*, ser. 2, vol. 10, p. 109).[16]

The second book of *On the Holy Spirit* begins by showing the gift of the

---

11. Faller, *S. Ambrosii Opera,* 9, p. 39.
12. Faller, *S. Ambrosii Opera,* 9, p. 41.
13. Faller, *S. Ambrosii Opera,* 9, p. 59.
14. Faller, *S. Ambrosii Opera,* 9, p. 48.
15. Faller, *S. Ambrosii Opera,* 9, p. 33.
16. Faller, *S. Ambrosii Opera,* 9, p. 68.

Spirit to Samson in a way that is parallel to the treatment of the Gideon narrative in book 1. Again, the power of the Holy Spirit is the same as God's power
through the Son. Ambrose, however, follows Basil in recognizing that the *Holy
Spirit is to be worshiped and glorified, though not in isolation from the Father and
the Son.* This thought may be relevant when we consider aspects of the Pentecostal and Renewal Movements. The relation of the Spirit to Christ, for example, becomes critical in Paul's assertion: "The Lord is the Spirit" (2 Cor. 3:17; *On
the Holy Spirit,* 2:1:18; *NPNF,* ser. 2, vol. 10, p. 117). Ambrose also alludes to Isa.
11:2, where the Spirit of counsel falls on the Messiah figure (2:2:20). He repeats,
"The Kingdom of the Father, Son, and Holy Spirit [is] one" (2:2:25).

Various gifts of the Holy Spirit receive mention. For example: "the Holy
Spirit is *life,*" and exclusively the Giver of eternal life (*On the Holy Spirit,* 2:3:26-
27). This is no "separate work" from that of the Father and the Son (2:4:29, 31).
The Spirit is *Creator* (2:5:32). The earth exists only with "the operation of the
Holy Spirit" (2:5:35). The Spirit also was at work in the virginal conception of
Jesus (2:5:38; *NPNF,* ser. 2, vol. 10, p. 119). Mary was found "with child of *(ex)*
the Holy Spirit" (Greek, *ek pneumatos hagiou;* Latin, *ex Spiritu Sancto;* 2:5:41,
42). Further, "the Holy Spirit is eternal" (2:6:51; *aeternus est*). The Spirit is also
"the Author of the grace of the Spirit" (2:7:64). Ambrose again refers to 1 Cor.
12:3, "No one can call Jesus Lord, except by the Holy Spirit," to refute any notion
that the Spirit is in subjection to the Father and the Son (2:8:73). He cites 1 Cor.
8:6 to the same effect (2:9:85). Ambrose adds, "Many things are done through
the Holy Spirit," for example, "the word of wisdom" (2:9:99; *NPNF,* ser. 2, vol.
10, p. 127). However, many of these gifts and graces "suit either the Father or the
Son or the Holy Spirit" (2:9:100).

Ambrose next states: "How clearly did the Holy Spirit express his own
power! First, . . . He inspired him who was *praying . . .*" (*On the Spirit,* 2:10:102;
NPNF, ser. 2, vol. 10, p. 128). More explicitly, "The Spirit glorifies the Son, as the
Father glorifies Him, but the Son of God also glorifies the Spirit" (2:11:121;
clarificat ergo et spiritus filium . . . et spiritum clarificat dei filius).[17] He is not
"weak" who causes this reciprocal glorifying. Ambrose continues: "The Father,
Son, and Holy Spirit are of one nature *(naturae)* and one knowledge" (2:11:125).
Again, the Spirit is not a created thing (p. 125). The Pauline passages about
speaking in tongues (1 Cor. 12:10 and esp. 14:2) prove the intimate closeness of
Spirit and Father, because the tongues-speaker *speaks to God* (14:2; 2:12:131); and
shall not speak "from Himself" (Latin, *a se;* John 16:13), hence remains close to
Christ. "The Spirit is not . . . separated, but speaks what he hears *(sed quae audit
loquitur).* This unity is "eternal" *(sempiternae,* 2:12:137), and "the Spirit is said to
hear from the Father" (2:12:138).[18]

---

17. Faller, *S. Ambrosii Opera,* 9, p. 133.
18. Faller, *S. Ambrosii Opera,* 9, p. 137.

At this point Ambrose cites his fullest exposition of the Trinitarian basis of the gifts of the Holy Spirit in 1 Cor. 12:4-7: "There are diversities of gifts, but the same Spirit, diversities of ministrations *(divisiones ministeriorum sint)*, but the same Lord; and diversities of operations *(operationum)*, but the same God *(idem autem Deus)* . . . not severances of the Trinity *(non separationes sunt trinitatis;* 2:12:138; *NPNF,* ser. 2, vol. 10, p. 132).[19]

"The work of one and the same Spirit" also occurs in Ambrose, *The Christian Faith,* 2:6:48, where he emphasizes God's freedom of action. Hence on the basis of the unity of the Spirit with the Father and Son, the gifts of the Spirit are set out: "To one is given through the Spirit a word of wisdom *(per spiritum sermo sapientae),* to another a word of knowledge *(alii sermo scientiae)* . . . to another faith *(alteri fides),* to another the gift of healings *(alii gratia curationum in uno spiritu),* to another the working of miracles *(alii operatio virtutum),* to another prophecy *(alii prophetia),* to another discerning of spirits *(alii discretio spirituum),* to another diverse kinds of tongues *(alii genera linguarum),* to another the interpretation of tongues *(alii interpretatio sermonum).* And one and the same Spirit *(unus atque idem spiritus)* works these, dividing to each as He will" *(dividens singulis prout vult;* 1 Cor. 12:8-11).[20] In all acts the Father, the Son, and the Spirit work together and are inseparable. The Latin formulation well harmonizes with the interpretation of this biblical passage in Part I, chapter 8.

The theme of union or unity certainly connects together 1 Cor. 12:1-11 with 12-31, in which the body is a unity with many members or limbs (Greek, *melē;* 12:12). In 12:13 it also explains the context of the action of the Spirit in Christian baptism as a sacrament of unity, as entry into "one body." There is even empathy between the foot and the hand, and the ear and the eye: "If one member suffers, all suffer together" (Greek, *sympaschei*) (1 Cor. 12:26). No one can say, "I have no need of you" (v. 21).

The Latin text usefully suggests several nuances. *Ministratio* may mean "ministry of *service*," matching *Dominus,* "Lord." *Operatio* may denote "operation" or "action," which corresponds to Paul's Greek *energēmatōn* (v. 6). *Sermo* denotes "speech," "discourse," or "saying," which matches Paul's Greek *logos sophias . . . logos gnōseōs* (v. 8). Greek *pistis* has many meanings but is as varied as *fides* (v. 9). *Curationum* is rightly in the *plural,* as the Greek is, and is probably generic, denoting different "kinds of healing," like kinds of fruits or cheeses. But *curatio* is broader than the Greek, denoting not only "healing" but also "care," "attention," or "management." It may well, therefore, include natural remedies as well as unexpected or unexplained ones, as Bengel and many others indicate. *Operatio virtutum* may denote the "action of ability or effectiveness,"

---

19. Faller, *S. Ambrosii Opera,* 9, p. 141.

20. The allure to faith *(fides)* is taken up in *Concerning Repentance,* 1:11:48 (*NPNF,* vol. 10, p. 537), where the emphasis concerns "differences of gifts."

without implying a dualism of the miraculous and natural, as if God acted in separate ways. *This dualism owes more to Deism, the Enlightenment, and the Industrial Revolution than to Paul. Discretio* denotes both "discrimination" and "separation," which translate the Greek *diakriseis*. Paul's Greek *genē glōssōn* becomes *genera linguarum*. This rightly allows for "kinds" or "species" of tongues, while *lingua* simply denotes "tongue" or "language," like *glōssa. Interpretatio sermonum* denotes making intelligible what is otherwise unintelligible, where *interpretatio* may mean either "interpretation" or "translation," or even "broad explanation" of a term.[21]

Ambrose then repeats: "The Holy Spirit is of one will and operation with God the Father" (*On the Holy Spirit*, 2:12:142), and enumerates the gifts again (2:12:143), using the same Latin words (1 Cor. 12:8-10). This second time, however, he amplifies *prophecy*, referring to the prophecy of Agabus in Acts 21:11 about the Jews of Jerusalem who seek to bind Paul, using the prophetic sign of the girdle (2:12:145). He then proceeds to 1 Cor. 12:28, where God appoints apostles, prophets, teachers, and other gifted ministries (2:12:149). The Latin uses the same words with others: *apostolous . . . prophētas . . . doctores . . . virtutes gratiam curationum opitulationes, gubernationes, genera linguarum. . . .*[22] *Teachers* can hardly have a *spontaneous, "charismatic" gift*, since *teaching* implies *training*, preparation, and practice. *Opitulatio* simply denotes "assistance" or "helps," but is more likely to be *administrative or pastoral* than charismatic. *Gubernatio* normally denotes "management," but in view of the alternative meaning, "helm" or "rudder," and with *gubernator* denoting "pilot" or "steersman," it might well denote a "church strategist," as Ambrose himself was gifted to be. This well fits the Greek *kybernēseis* (v. 28). Verses 29-30 may have delighted Ambrose: you cannot do *all* of these things. He writes, "The whole of the divine gifts cannot exist in each several man" (i.e., in one individual, 2:12:150). The gifts are distributed to different people and orders of ministry (2:12:151). (This may confirm our reservation about McDonnell's general comment above on gifts in Hilary.) This also concludes book 2.

Book 3 of *On the Holy Spirit* focuses largely on the Spirit's anointing of Christ, and on the joint ministry of Christ and the Spirit in the mission of the Church. Ambrose reiterates that the *three Persons of the Trinity are one in being, will, and holiness.* He refers to the verse "The Spirit is upon me" (Luke 4:18), and to the action of the Holy Spirit in the apostles as well as prophets (*On the Holy Spirit*, 3:1:1-8). The Spirit is called "the finger of God" (Luke 11:20), which indicates *his inseparability and divine nature* (2:3:11-16). *The Father, the Son, and the Spirit all share in the sanctification of the believer* (3:4:25-28). He connects the

---

21. Leo F. Stelten, *Dictionary of Ecclesiastical Latin* (Peabody, MA: Hendrickson, 1995), pp. 137 and 311.

22. S. Faller, *S. Ambrosii Opera*, 9, pp. 145-46.

"word of wisdom" with the prophet, especially in communicating the gospel truth that God will judge the world (3:6:38; *NPNF,* ser. 2, vol. 10, p. 140). The Spirit also brings moral character (3:6:41-43), and will punish the Antichrist (3:7:44). "The Spirit is the sword of the Word" (3:7:45). "The Spirit of the Lord is the very Spirit of God" (3:9:54). "Where the Spirit is, there also is Christ" (3:9:55). This sentence is as important as ever today, when some (but far from all) "charismatics" talk as if *everything* was from the *Spirit alone,* or address the Spirit alone. Ambrose confirms the point with reference to John (3:10:63-68). Again, for at least the third or fourth time, he cites 1 Cor. 12:3, "No one can call Jesus Lord, but in the Holy Spirit" (3:11:70; *nisi in spiritu sancto*). He repeats this verse again in 3:22:167.

Next Ambrose insists "God is worshiped in Spirit, for the Spirit is also worshiped" (*On the Holy Spirit,* 3:11:81). Like Basil he insists that worship and glory are given to the whole Trinity. The Church is God's temple, in which the Spirit dwells (3:12:90; 1 Cor. 3:16; 6:19). Believing must therefore be holy (3:14:94-97). For "The Father is holy, the Son is holy, and the Spirit is holy" (3:16:109). Ambrose cites many passages from the New Testament to show that the Father, the Son, and the Holy Spirit *share together in every stage of salvation* (3:19:132-52). He concludes, "It is now possible *(licet)* to recognize the oneness of the majesty and rule *(unitatem maiestatis et regni . . . cognoscere)* in the Father, the Son, and the Holy Spirit" (3:22:165).

Ambrose has produced a rich, sophisticated, and relevant treatise on the Holy Spirit. Swete describes his work as that of "a strong and practical mind." It is quite remarkable that, plunged suddenly and reluctantly into episcopal office, he observes, "With me learning and teaching must go on simultaneously, for I had no time to learn till I became a teacher" (Ambrose, *On the Duties of the Clergy,* 1:4, though cited by Swete as 1:1; Swete's translation, *NPNF,* ser. 2, vol. 10, p. 1).[23] His biblical knowledge was very wide, and he also studied Athanasius, Basil, and Didymus of Alexandria. The result was a masterpiece. He was also instrumental in the conversion of Augustine.

Ambrose includes what, in effect, anticipates some themes in *On the Holy Spirit* in *On the Christian Faith.* In 1:4:31, he urges, "There is one Spirit, all holy . . . one Baptism in the name of the Trinity" (*NPNF,* ser. 2, vol. 10, p. 205). He writes, "Christ was sent by the Father and his Spirit; . . . by the Spirit also he [Christ] is sent" (*On the Christian Faith,* 2:9:75). "There is one Holy Spirit" (1 Cor. 12:11), who is "eternal" (4:8:92). But the context is not in the first place *teaching* on the Holy Spirit as such, but attacking the themes of Arianism.

---

23. Swete, *The Holy Spirit in the Ancient Church,* p. 318 and p. 316.

11.3. Augustine of Hippo

Augustine (354-430) was born in a small town in North Africa, the son of a devout Christian mother, Monica. While studying rhetoric in Carthage, he was troubled by intellectual difficulties concerning the Christian faith, and became a Manichean. Over some ten years, however, he became disillusioned with Manichean teaching. On accepting an appointment in Milan, he heard Ambrose preach, and was greatly impressed both by his rhetoric and his Christian content. He continued to study Plotinus and Porphyry, but in 386 he decided (or was called) to abandon secular hopes, and on the Eve of Easter 387 was baptized by Ambrose as a Christian convert. He moved first to Rome, and then to Africa, where he was ordained priest. In 395 he became co-adjutor bishop, and on the death of Valerius he became Bishop of Hippo, until his death in 430.

Augustine produced a vast literature. It fills no fewer than fourteen volumes in Latin in J-P. Migne's series *Patrologia Latina* (vols. 32-45), and in his *Retractions* he reviewed the ninety-three works that he regarded as important. His writing was not primarily systematic or innovative, but consisted largely of responses to specific problems. *The Confessions* constitutes his most widely read work, and the *Enchiridion* or *Handbook*, written some twenty years later, is perhaps the second. *The Enchiridion* is the nearest that we have to a summary of his teaching. His writings against the Manicheans, against the Pelagians, and against the Donatists, as well as *On the Holy Trinity*, are supplemented by five hundred sermons, many commentaries or homilies, about three hundred letters, and *The City of God*.

The *Anti-Manichean Writings* come among the early writings, when Augustine was defending himself against the charge of Manicheism on his appointment as Bishop. These include his treatise *On Free Will* (c. 395) in three books. He attacked their teaching that sin was involuntary. By contrast, Augustine saw sin as a choice of *will*, resulting in a state of *character*. Sinfulness or sin constitutes a *habit or disposition*, not a mere succession of acts. This is later reflected in *The Confessions* (c. 397-401). In these he recounts the part played by Rom. 13:13-14, "Put on the Lord Jesus Christ, and make no provision for the flesh," in his conversion (*Confessions*, 8:29). Book 7 also recounts his growing disillusion with the Manichees. *On the Two Souls: Against Manichees* (c. 392-93) belongs to the early writings.

Augustine's doctrinal work *On Christian Doctrine* first appeared in three books in 397, but the fourth book appeared in 426, after nearly thirty years of reflection. His deepest theological thought can be found in his theological treatise *On the Trinity* (between 399 and c. 423). Although the Arian controversy was officially resolved in 381, questions still remained about the Holy Spirit. For this Augustine drew on the Eastern Fathers, especially Gregory Nazianzus. Rather than "persons" of the Trinity, Augustine tends to speak of "mind," or a thinking, willing self and self-revelation or will, as also reflected in human consciousness. The third most theological work is perhaps *The City of God* (413-26), which expounded a theology of history when Rome began to fall against the Goths. The two "Cities" were those of God and humankind, with parallel but different courses. The Church and Christians belong to the City of God. The fall of Rome was not due to secession from pagan deities, or to the limitations of God. *The Enchiridion* was written c. 421-22.

The *Donatist Controversy* raged in North Africa, where Cyprian had advocated a "pure Church" outlook. The *Donatists* believed that sacraments depend on the worthiness of the minister. Augustine attacked Donatism in a number of writings, especially in *On Baptism* (c. 400), and the mistaken notion of a "pure" church has still given rise to many needless divisions and power struggles today.

Another group of writings attacked *Pelagianism* (from c. 412–c. 425). These included *On the Grace of Christ* (c. 418), *On Original Sin* (c. 418), various letters (c. 418), *On Marriage and Concupiscence* (c. 419), *Against Two Letters of the Pelagians* (c. 420), and *On Grace and Free Will* (c. 425). Again, the controversy about the sovereignty and priority of grace motivates many theological issues today.

Many remaining volumes include numerous letters, sermons, commentaries, and moral and pastoral treatises. For example, *The Exposition of the Psalms* (396-420), *On the Sermon on the Mount* (c. 394), and especially *On the Gospel of John* (408-20) were particularly influential. Augustine is also relevant today as expositor, ethicist, and pastor.

Augustine's writing on the Holy Spirit is scattered among a number of volumes. In *On the Trinity* (in fifteen books) he considers the Holy Spirit in relation to the Holy Trinity, insisting that the Spirit is one with God and even constitutes the *bond of mutual love* between the Father and the Son. In *On the Trinity*, 6:5:7, he declares, "The Holy Spirit consists in the same unity of substance *(in eadem unitas substantiae)* and in the same equality *(et aequalitate consistit).*[24] He continues that this union may be of holiness or love, and Father, Son, and Spirit "are God, one alone *(deus unus, solus)*, great, wise, holy, blessed. . . . That communion itself is consubstantial and co-eternal *(consubstantialis et coaeterna).*" It might be friendship, "but it is more aptly called love *(caritas)* . . . God is love *(caritas)*" (*On the Trinity*, 6:5:7). This expresses the heart of *On the Trinity.*

Augustine repeatedly emphasizes that God is one. This not only relates to the monotheism of the New Testament (1 Cor. 8:1-6) but also to the tendency in some (not all) charismatic or Pentecostal circles today *to isolate the Spirit in prayers and worship*. Augustine declares, "The Trinity is called one God, great, good, eternal, omnipotent, and we cannot 'except' the Son or the Spirit, or call the whole Trinity 'Son' or, 'in its entirety, the Holy Spirit'" (*On the Trinity*,

---

24. W. J. Mountain (ed.), *S. Aurelii Augustini, De Trinitate*, 2 vols., CCSL (Turnholt: Editores Pontificii, 1968), p. 135; also J-P. Migne, *PL*, vol. 42, col. 928; Eng., *NPNF*, ser. 1, vol. 3, p. 100.

5:11:12; *NPNF*, ser. 1, vol. 3, p. 93). Elsewhere in this treatise he asserts, "The Holy Spirit . . . is neither of the Father alone, nor of the Son alone, but of both . . . a *mutual love,* wherewith the Father and the Son *reciprocally love one another*" (15:17:27; *NPNF*, ser. 1, vol. 3, p. 215; my italics).

The *Treatise* illustrates this unity by using an *analogy with a human person.* Augustine writes, "Memory, understanding, will, are not three lives, but one life; not three minds, but one mind. . . . They are one mind, one essence" *(una mens, una essentia) (On the Trinity,* ser. 1, vol. 3, p. 142). Together they are not a plurality, but a singular entity, namely, Being. It is of great importance that Augustine *rejects* the traditional formulation "three *persons.*" "Person," he claims, is "a genuine name" *(On the Trinity,* 7:4:7). In the case of God, therefore, *"person*" denotes what "is common to them (otherwise they can in no way be so called), just as they are not called three sons [or] . . . three Gods" *(On the Trinity,* 7:4:8; *NPNF*, ser. 2, vol. 3, p. 110; Latin, *persona*).[25] (This rejection of "three Gods . . . three Sons" accounts for what may seem to some to be rather obscure and convoluted language in the "Athanasian Creed.") The image of God, similarly, is not only mind but remembrance, understanding, and love, that is, the image of God reflects the *whole Trinitarian life of God (On the Trinity,* 14:12:15; *NPNF*, ser. 1, vol. 3, p. 191).

Finally, in *On the Trinity* Augustine is explicit on the divisive *Filioque* clause, according to which the Holy Spirit "proceeds from the Father and the Son." The Holy Spirit, he says, "according to the Holy Scriptures, is neither of the Father alone, nor of the Son alone, but of both, and so intimates to us a mutual love" *(nec patris est solius nec filii solius sed amborum; On the Trinity,* 15:17:1).[26] So clear-cut is Augustine that, in contrast to the case of Ambrose, this can be called the *Double Procession* of the Spirit.

It is understandably difficult to find references to the Holy Spirit in *On the Trinity* which fail to point to the unity of God. Augustine cites 1 Cor. 12:7-8 in 13:19:24, but mainly to confirm his argument that the incarnate Christ is a word of knowledge, and the Spirit is a word of wisdom. "A manifestation of the Spirit is given to each person to profit . . . *(datur manifestatio spiritus ad utilitatem; . . . alii . . . sermo sapientiae, alii sermo scientiae . . .*"; Eng., *NPNF*, ser. 1, vol. 3, p. 181). In *On the Trinity,* 3:9:18, he alludes to 1 Cor. 12:10, "To another the discerning of spirits" *(alii diiudicatio spirituum),* but only to stress that if the Holy Spirit is "the finger of God," he is one with God. In 15:19:33 Augustine cites 1 Cor. 12:13, "We have all been made to drink into one Spirit" *(omnes unum spiritum potavimus),* as concerning the relation between Spirit and water, with Jesus as the source of "living water" (John 7:37-39).

Outside *On the Trinity* scattered references to the Holy Spirit frequently oc-

---

25. Mountain, *De Trinitate,* in CCSL, vol. 50, p. 257.
26. Mountain, *De Trinitate,* in CCSL, vol. 50A, p. 501; and Migne, *PL*, vol. 42, col. 1080.

cur. In *Sermon* 21:5, for example, Augustine attacks the Arian belief that "the Holy Spirit . . . was not God, but a creature" (*NPNF,* ser. 1, vol. 6, p. 320). In *Sermon* 55:4, Augustine combines two thoughts. In the Parable of the Importunate Widow (Luke 18:1-8) he encourages the reader that God as Bread will satisfy all their needs. But this leads to analogical reflection on the Holy Trinity. We may receive "three loaves." But these all belong to the one Bread: "That Bread will not come to an end. . . . It is Bread, God the Father, and it is Bread, the Son, and the Holy Spirit co-eternal," all the same, one reality or substance (*Sermon,* 55:4; *NPNF,* ser. 1, vol. 6, p. 431). The Holy Spirit also glorifies Christ, and does not speak "of himself" (John 16:13; Greek, *aph' heautou,* probably "on his own initiative"; but NRSV, "on his own"; *On the Gospel of John, Tractate* 99:2; *NPNF,* ser. 1, vol. 7, p. 381). Again, the context is the Spirit's union with Christ and the Trinity. Augustine draws the same lesson from John 16:13b, "He will speak whatever he hears" (*On the Gospel of John,* 99:5; *NPNF,* ser. 1, vol. 7, p. 383), adding that the Holy Spirit proceeds from both the Father and the Son: "He proceeds also from the Son" (99:6-7). It is similar with 1 Cor. 12:3 (74:1; *NPNF,* ser. 1, vol. 7, p. 333).

In his *anti-Donatist writings,* Augustine does not acknowledge Marcion, Valentinus, Arius, or Eunomius, who are accounted "fleshly," not "spiritual." Yet he asks: "Can it be said that on this account they do not receive the complete sacrament?" He replies, "If the sacraments are the same, they are everywhere complete, even when they are wrongly understood and perverted to be instruments of discord" (*On Baptism: Against the Donatists,* 3:15; *NPNF,* ser. 1, vol. 4, p. 442). "The Holy Spirit is . . . given by the laying on of hands" (3:16). But we should *not expect today* (i.e., *in Augustine's time*), he argues, that those who receive the Spirit "shall forthwith begin to speak with tongues . . ." (*On Baptism,* 3:16; *NPNF,* ser. 1, vol. 4, p. 443). In the present, the criterion is not that of Acts 2, but the Spirit of love and peace. The Spirit gives gifts "to every man severally as he will" (1 Cor. 12:11).

Unity, peace, and church order, including the laying on of hands, are more important than the tongues and prophecy of earlier days. Certainly the list of gifts (1 Cor. 12:4-11) is followed by a section on the body of Christ and unity of the Church, as Augustine expounds in his *Reply to Faustus,* 21:8 (*NPNF,* ser. 1, vol. 4, p. 267; cf. *Reply to Faustus,* 24:2). In *Reply to Faustus,* 29:4, he uses 1 Cor. 12:22-25 to establish that the human body is good, with honorable limbs as members (cf. *The Nature of Good, Against the Manicheans,* 30; *NPNF,* ser. 1, vol. 4, p. 357).

In his *Writings against Pelagianism* Augustine includes a section which sets out the effects of receiving the Holy Spirit as "an ardent desire to cleave to his [man's] Maker, and to burn to enter upon the participation in that true light. . . . 'God's love is shed abroad in our hearts by the Holy Spirit'" (Rom. 5:5; *On the Spirit and the Letter,* 5; *NPNF,* ser. 1, vol. 5, pp. 84-85). Also in his anti-

Pelagian writings, Augustine warns his readers that we can overcome evil not by our own efforts but "by God's Spirit" (Rom. 8:14; *On the Predestination of the Saints,* 22; *NPNF,* ser. 1, vol. 5, p. 508). He adds that "one and the self-same Spirit divides gifts to everyone as He will" (1 Cor. 12:11; *On Predestination,* 22).

As we might expect, he also alludes to the work of the Holy Spirit in *The City of God.* Here he refers to the insufflation of Jesus, or "Johannine Pentecost," when Jesus Christ after the resurrection declares, "Receive the Holy Spirit" (John 20:22), in parallel, says Augustine, to God's breathing in Gen. 2:7. This is a *creative act* of the Creator Spirit, which enables humankind to bear the image of God and to be a rational "soul." This Spirit, once again, is "the Spirit of the Father and the Son, making them the Trinity of Father, Son, and Spirit, not a creature, but the Creator" (*The City of God,* 13:24; *NPNF,* ser. 1, vol. 2, p. 259). Augustine recognizes that *pneuma* is used in a variety of ways, even to denote the human spirit, but here it denotes "uncreated Creator Spirit," as in John 20:22.

In *The Harmony of the Gospels,* 4:10:20, Augustine says again "that to one is given through the Spirit the word of wisdom, to another, the word of knowledge by the same Spirit" (1 Cor. 12:8). The context in *Harmony* is that of the Synoptists, John, and Paul, who will also minister according to the gift that the Spirit has given them (*NPNF,* ser. 1, vol. 1, p. 236). In *The Sermon on the Mount,* Augustine refers to 1 Cor. 12:3, comparing it with those who say "Lord, Lord" but do not enter the kingdom of heaven. Only the Holy Spirit creates the authentic confession (*The Sermon on the Mount,* 2:25:83; *NPNF,* ser. 1, vol. 6, p. 62). Further, only the Holy Spirit can reproduce "the fruits of the Spirit" (Gal. 5:22-23). Augustine cites "the Holy Spirit, who divideth to everyone as He will" (1 Cor. 12:11), as equipping Peter, not least as a writer with authority, perhaps leaving records to Mark (*The Harmony of the Gospels,* 2:21:51; *NPNF,* ser. 1, vol. 6, p. 127).

In his work *On the Gospel of John* Augustine produces another reason why "no man speaks in the tongues of all nations" (Acts 2:5-13; 1 Cor. 12:10; *Tractate* 32:7; *NPNF,* ser. 1, vol. 7, p. 195). He agrees that *"whoso is not of this Church, does not now receive the Holy Spirit"* (my italics). But the historical situation of the earliest Church has changed: "The Church, spread among the nations, speaks all tongues." In his work *On the Psalms,* Augustine sees the gifts of the Spirit in 1 Cor. 12:8-10 as many-sided virtues, which yield to "virtue" and to the four virtues of Plato (*On Psalm 84:1; NPNF,* ser. 1, vol. 8, p. 403). In his exposition of Psalm 144, he stresses the diversity and unity of the gifts of the Spirit (1 Cor. 12:8-10) as a parallel with the two lines of poetic parallelism, "who trains my hands [unity] for war, and my fingers [diversity] for battle" (*On Psalm 144:2; NPNF,* ser. 1, vol. 8, p. 654).

It will have emerged that apart from more scattered references to the Holy Spirit, the central themes of Augustine appear in the work *On the Trinity.* Swete sums up the central point: "The Father does nothing which is not done also by the Son and the Spirit, *the Spirit [does] nothing which is not done by the Father and the Son*" (my italics).[27] He declares, "These three constitute one life, not three lives, one substance, not three substances."[28] The Spirit proceeds from the Father and the Son: *"He is Himself the Love of God"* (my italics).[29] Many other comments are of less systematic significance, but nevertheless also "mark him as one of the most formative pneumatological thinkers of Christian history."[30] It was left to Gregory of Rome to formalize much of Augustine's teaching, as we shall see in due course.

27. Swete, *The Holy Spirit in the Ancient Church,* p. 323.
28. Swete, *The Holy Spirit in the Ancient Church,* p. 331.
29. Swete, *The Holy Spirit in the Ancient Church,* p. 336.
30. Burgess, *The Holy Spirit: Ancient Christian Traditions,* p. 192.

12

The Post-Nicene Eastern Fathers

The Arian controversy, primarily about the deity and eternity of God the Son, was settled as far as Emperor Constantine and many others were concerned, in the Council of Nicea in 325. For some years after Nicea, the Arians, Swete comments, were in no mood to provoke conflict about the Holy Spirit.[1] Nevertheless the years 330-60 proved to be "fruitful," as Swete suggests, for a theology of the Spirit. The beginning of this period is partly dominated by Eusebius of Caesarea in the East; then by Cyril of Jerusalem, who became Bishop of Jerusalem in 350; then supremely by Athanasius of Alexandria, whose *Letters to Serapion* (356 or 359) and other treatises were crucial. Athanasius, in turn, greatly influenced Basil of Caesarea and the other two Cappadocian Fathers in the East, and, less directly, Hilary of Poitiers and Ambrose of Milan in the West.

12.1. Eusebius of Caesarea and Cyril of Jerusalem

Eusebius (260-339), most famous today for his *Ecclesiastical History*, was effectively the court theologian of Emperor Constantine. He may have shared more in common with Arius than many often realize, but he played a major role at the Council of Nicea in 325. In particular he presented the Creed of the Church at Caesarea. After declaring faith in God the Son, who "rose again . . . , ascended . . . , will come again in glory to judge . . . ," Eusebius added: "We believe also in the Holy Spirit; believing each of these [the Trinity] to be and to exist [Greek, *einai kai hyparchein*], the Father truly the Father, and the Son truly the Son, and the Holy Spirit truly the Holy Spirit" (cited in *NPNF*, ser. 2, vol. 1,

---

1. Henry B. Swete, *The Holy Spirit in the Ancient Church: A Study of Christian Teaching in the Age of the Fathers* (London: Macmillan, 1912), p. 166.

p. 16). The purpose of the addition was to exclude Sabellianism, the doctrine that the Father, the Son, and the Holy Spirit constituted only aspects or modes of the One God.

Sabellianism had been revived by Marcellus of Ancyra, and was condemned as a heresy at the Council of Constantinople in 336. Eusebius asserted that the Spirit is "different" (Greek, *heteron*) from the Son, largely on the basis of Christ's words about "another Paraclete." Nevertheless, anticipating Cyril, Athanasius, and Basil, he referred to "the holy and thrice-blessed Trinity," who is "One in substance." Yet, still under the influence of Origen, he also referred to the Spirit as "holding a third rank" (Greek, *tritēn epechōn tēn taxin;* Eusebius, *Preparation for the Gospel,* 7:15). Swete comments, "This is subordinationism in its most outspoken boldness, but it is the subordinationism of Origen rather than of Arius."[2]

Cyril of Jerusalem (c. 315-87). McDonnell states, "No other early writer has given so detailed an account of baptism and the eucharist. Cyril [also] expounded the Person and work of the Holy Spirit, notably in his Catechetical and Mystagogic Lectures delivered to those preparing for Eastern baptism."[3] They were perhaps given in 348, two years before he became Bishop. Lectures 16-17 addressed belief "in one Holy Spirit, the Comforter," largely on the basis of 1 Cor. 12:1, 4, and 8 (*Catechetical Lectures,* 16 and 17; *NPNF,* ser. 2, vol. 7, pp. 115-57). He begins by quoting Matt. 12:32 about "blasphemy against the Holy Spirit" (*Catechetical Lectures,* 16:1-2); expounds 1 Cor. 12:4 in which the Spirit is "a Power most mighty, a Being divine and unsearchable" (1 Cor. 2:10-13); and writes of one Holy Spirit, who spoke in the Old Testament through "the prophets" (16:3). He repeatedly stresses that the Holy Spirit inspired the Scriptures. He writes: "*Let no one separate the Old from the New Testament. . . .* Our hope is in the Father, the Son, and the Holy Spirit" (16:4). Cyril insists: "Let us speak concerning the Holy Spirit nothing but what is written. . . . *The Holy Spirit spoke the Scriptures*" (16:1; my italics). Jesus "would send the Comforter from the Father" (John 14:16; *Catechetical Lectures,* 16:4).

Cyril continues, "He [the Spirit] will not declare his substance with exactness" (*Catechetical Lectures,* 16:5). He rejects Montanism (16:8), but exhorts his hearers, "Let us return to the Scriptures" (16:11). Although the Spirit bestows a variety of gifts (1 Cor. 12:8-10), he is indivisible, and gives "according to his will" (1 Cor. 12:11; *Catechetical Lectures,* 16:12). He lists wisdom, knowledge, faith, prophecy, miracles, and interpretation among these gifts (16:12; *NPNF,* ser. 2, vol. 7, p. 118). He warns his hearers about different uses of "spirit" in Scripture (16:13-16). The Holy Spirit gives revelation and illumination (16:17-18). He also

---

2. Swete, *The Holy Spirit in the Ancient Church,* p. 197.

3. Kilian McDonnell and George T. Montague, *Christian Initiation and Baptism in the Holy Spirit: Evidence from the First Eight Centuries* (Collegeville, MN: The Liturgical Press, 1991), p. 159.

helps us to pray "with groaning that cannot be uttered" (16:20; Rom. 8:26, probably "sighs too deep for words," NRSV). The Holy Spirit can enlighten bishops, priests, deacons, solitaries, and virgins (16:22).

Especially the Holy Spirit may "call to mind what comes from the divine Scriptures" (*Catechetical Lectures*, 17:1; *NPNF*, ser. 2, vol. 7, p. 124). Another list of "gifts of the Spirit," or *charismata*, occurs in 17:4. Cyril cites Rom. 8:9 to the effect that receiving the *Holy Spirit is synonymous with being a Christian* (17:5). The Holy Spirit also initiated the Virgin Birth of Jesus Christ (17:6). He refers, too, to John the Baptist's contrast between water baptism for purification and the promise of Jesus *to baptize "with the Holy Spirit and with fire"* (Matt. 3:11; my italics; *Catechetical Lectures*, 17:8; *NPNF*, ser. 2, vol. 7, p. 126). "God will give the Holy Spirit to all who ask" (17:11; Luke 11:13). Cyril also refers to the insufflation or "Johannine Pentecost" (17:12; John 20:22). He cites the postresurrection promise in Acts 1:5 of being "baptized with the Holy Spirit not many days hence" (17:14), and the speaking with tongues at Pentecost itself (17:16; Acts 2:4). He mentions the prophecy of Joel 2:28, fulfilled in Acts 2:15 (cf. 17:19). He recalls Peter's sermon and apostolic ministry in the power of the Spirit (17:20-22). Then he cites the gift of the Spirit to the Seven in Acts 6:3-7 (cf. 17:24), Philip (17:25), and Paul (17:26) and Barnabas (17:28). The whole of 17:1-38 offers a biblical basis for practical teaching on the Holy Spirit in its varied aspects.

McDonnell warns us that *charisma* in the New Testament includes a variety of gifts. Yet postbiblical Greek extends this variety to embrace "divine and human gifts, [the] gift of the Spirit, baptism, eucharist, endowment of the church, graces, . . . martyrdom, tears, theology."[4] Cyril has six explicit references to 1 Corinthians 12, yet "Cyril is no enthusiast, interested only in charismatic extravaganzas, . . . dazzling miracles, exorcisms by the hundreds."[5] He simply knows, McDonnell argues, that charisms belong to the life of the Church, as he has inherited the tradition from Irenaeus and Eusebius.

Nothing, Cyril asserts, of all things created "is equal in honor to Him" (i.e., the Holy Spirit; 16:23; *NPNF*, ser. 2, vol. 7, p. 121). To quote Swete once more: "Of the work of the Spirit no writer of the fourth century has spoken more fully or more convincingly."[6] Stanley Burgess adds, "As a pastor, Cyril understands the Spirit's gifts to be antidotes for defilement of the believer brought about by wealth, rank, and covetousness."[7] Cyril concludes, "He [the Spirit] tries the soul. . . . The Holy Spirit bestows that which is unseen. . . . All your life long will your guardian, the Comforter, abide with you. *He will care for you, as for his own soldier.* . . . May the very God of all . . . send him forth at this time upon you; and

4. McDonnell and Montague, *Christian Initiation*, p. 166.

5. McDonnell and Montague, *Christian Initiation*, p. 167.

6. Swete, *The Holy Spirit in the Ancient Church*, p. 210.

7. Stanley M. Burgess, *The Holy Spirit: Ancient Christian Traditions* (Peabody, MA: Hendrickson, 1984), p. 108.

by him keep us also, imparting . . . the fruits of the Holy Spirit, love, joy, peace, long-suffering, gentleness, goodness, faith, meekness, temperance, in Christ Jesus our Lord, by whom and with whom, together with the Holy Spirit, be glory to the Father, now and ever" (*Catechetical Lectures*, 17:36-38; *NPNF*, ser. 2, vol. 7, pp. 132-33; my italics; Gal. 5:22-23). McDonnell repeats: "Cyril was no enthusiast. . . . His teaching reflects the range of meanings found in the New Testament and in other Greek authors of the first centuries."[8]

12.2. Athanasius of Alexandria

Athanasius (c. 296-373) is often thought of as the foremost opponent of Arianism in the East. After the death of Constantine, the Arian emperor Constantius forced him into exile in 356. During his shelter in the desert near Alexandria, his friend Serapion, Bishop of Thmuis, wrote to him about a group of Christians who held an inadequate view of the Holy Spirit. Apparently Athanasius called them *"Tropici,"* perhaps on the ground that they interpreted Scripture passages out of context. Michael Haykin includes an extended note on the term, preferring, with W. D. Hauschild, to use the term *"Pneumatomachi."*[9] Athanasius formulated his reply in *The Epistle to Serapion*. This is not included in *NPNF*, ser. 2, vol. 4, but is conveniently provided in translation by C. R. B. Shapland.[10]

Athanasius replies above all that the *Holy Spirit is not a creature;* not a created person or thing (Greek, *ktisma*). G. W. H. Lampe confirms the meaning of *ktisis* as "creature."[11] When we recall that *creatures* or *what has been created* includes angels, humans, animals, and things, *the widespread use of "it" today to denote the Holy Spirit becomes demeaning and even insulting.* We have argued that to call the Spirit a Person does not imply any gender identity, even though by semantic and grammatical accident (as James Barr argues) *rûach* is a feminine noun and *pneuma* a neuter one.[12] Athanasius begins his first letter by declaring that the *Tropici* and Arians commit "blasphemy against the Holy Triad" (*First Epistle to Serapion*, 1).[13] The Arians call Jesus Christ as well as the Holy

---

8. McDonnell and Montague, *Christian Initiation*, p. 173.

9. Michael A. G. Haykin, *The Spirit of God: The Exegesis of 1-2 Corinthians in the Pneumatomachian Controversy in the Fourth Century* (Leiden and New York: Brill, 1994), p. 20, n. 50; cf. W. D. Hauschild, *Basilius von Caesarea: Briefe* (Stuttgart: Hiersemann, 1973).

10. C. R. B. Shapland, *The Letters of Saint Athanasius concerning the Holy Spirit* (London: Epworth, 1951). Substantial extracts are given in Haykin, *The Spirit of God*, pp. 21-24 and 63-98.

11. Geoffrey W. H. Lampe (ed.), *A Patristic Greek Lexicon* (Oxford: Clarendon, 1961), p. 783.

12. James Barr, *The Semantics of Biblical Language* (Oxford: Oxford University Press, 1961), pp. 39-41.

13. Shapland, *Letters*, p. 60.

Spirit "a creature" (*First Epistle to Serapion*, 2).[14] This is evil and false, for the Spirit is the Spirit *of God* (*First Epistle to Serapion*, 1:4).

Athanasius then attacks the group's *method of exegesis.* They ignore the various meanings of "spirit" in Scripture (1:7-8). For example, the meaning of "The Spirit himself bears witness with our spirit . . ." (Rom. 8:16) is quite different from *rûach* or *pneuma* as "wind." The latter is a creature; the former is not (1:7).[15] Yet while "you [the *Tropici*] say that Christ is not a creature, you say that the Spirit is a creature" (1:9). Yet *the Son and the Spirit cannot be separated.* The Holy Spirit is not simply an angel (1:11-12, 14). Moreover, "If he were a creature, he would not be ranked with the Triad. For the whole Triad is one God" (1:17).[16] To isolate the Spirit from the Father and the Son would run counter to Athanasius's claims. There are too many "glib answers" about God and the Spirit (1:18). "When the Holy Spirit is given to us, . . . God is in us" (1:19). "Paul declared that the works he worked by the power of the Spirit were the works of Christ" (1:19).[17]

Like Paul, Athanasius stresses *the transcendence of the Holy Spirit.* He quotes Paul: "We received not the spirit of the world, but the Spirit which is of God" (Greek, *to pneuma to ek tou theou,* 1 Cor. 2:12; *Epistle to Serapion,* 1:22).[18] The Spirit is *the Giver of life* (as in the ecumenical creeds since Constantinople, 381). "He is called a quickening Spirit. . . . He raised Christ from the dead" (Rom. 8:11; *Epistle to Serapion,* 1:23). The Holy Spirit becomes "a well of water springing up into eternal life" (1:23; John 7:38-39). He does not "receive" life, but "gives" it. He also anointed Jesus Christ for his work (1:23; Isa. 61:1).[19] *Christians are the temples of God,* in whom the Spirit dwells (1 Cor. 3:16-17; *Epistle to Serapion,* 1:24). Athanasius continues, "The Spirit is said to be, and is, the image of the Son" (1:24; Rom. 8:29). The Spirit is "proper to the Son and not alien from God" (1:25). He is "from God himself" (1:25). "The Holy Spirit is partaken, and does not partake" (1:27).

The first letter concludes with an appeal to the life and tradition of the Church (*Epistle to Serapion,* 1:28-31). *From the teaching of Jesus and preaching of the apostles* Christians believe that "There is a Triad, holy and complete, confessed to be God in Father, Son, and Holy Spirit" (1:28). "The Church has this foundation of faith" (1:29). As we might expect, Athanasius again cites 1 Cor. 12:4-6: "There are diversities of gifts, but the same Spirit; . . . the same Lord; . . . the same God . . ." (1:30).[20] "This consideration shows that the activity of the Triad is one" (1:31).

14. Shapland, *Letters,* p. 61.
15. Shapland, *Letters,* pp. 77-79.
16. Shapland, *Letters,* p. 103.
17. Shapland, *Letters,* p. 113.
18. Shapland, *Letters,* p. 121.
19. Shapland, *Letters,* p. 124.
20. Shapland, *Letters,* p. 141.

The second, third, and fourth letters constitute largely an abridgment and repetition of the first letter. The Holy Spirit also shares in God's action as *fountain of life,* as wind, and as Wisdom (*Epistle to Serapion,* 2:2). Athanasius refers to Nicea (2:5), and reaffirms: "Our faith is in Father, Son, and Holy Spirit" (2:6).[21] Yet the second and third letters have more on the Arians and God the Son (3:1). However, he also expounds the discourse about the Paraclete in John 15:26 and elsewhere (3:2). He writes, "The Spirit is indivisible from the Son" (3:5), and mentions "The grace . . ." in 2 Cor. 13:13. In the fourth letter he attacks "the shamelessness of the heretics . . . , [who] have a warped mind" (4:1). He exclaims: "If you deny those things which are written [i.e., in Scripture], then you can no longer be called Christians" (4:2).[22] He concludes by speaking of "Jesus Christ our Lord, through whom and with whom to the Father and the Holy Spirit *(syn hagiō pneumati)* be glory and power to all ages of ages" (4:7).[23]

Haykin looks back on his exposition of the *Epistles to Serapion* with the comment: "Athanasius is a theologian steeped in the Scriptures."[24] But in arguing for the divinity of the Holy Spirit, he especially gives an "exegesis of the Corinthian correspondence."[25] Loosely, we may suggest that Haykin groups the content of these letters in the following way: (1) The uncreated Spirit: the Holy Spirit is not a creature (e.g., *Epistle to Serapion,* 1:21; cf. 1 Cor. 2:11-12). (2) The Holy Spirit is of the same order of Being as the incomprehensible, transcendent God (e.g., 1:15; cf. 1 Cor. 2:7-13). (3) He is inseparable from the living God, as the analogies of the fountain and river suggest (Greek, *pēgē* and *potamos;* e.g., 1:19-20; cf. 1 Cor. 10:4 and 12:13). (4) He is the Spirit of sanctification (e.g., 1:22-23; cf. 1 Cor. 6:11). (5) He is the Spirit of unction (Greek, *chrisma* or anointing; e.g., 1:23; cf. 2 Cor. 2:15). (6) He is the indwelling Spirit (e.g., 1:23-24; cf. 1 Cor. 3:16-17). (7) He is the Spirit in the Trinity and the faith of the Church (e.g., 1:28; cf. 1 Cor. 12:4-6 and 2 Cor. 13:13).[26]

H. B. Swete sums up these letters with the comment, "The Spirit of adoption, of wisdom and truth, of power and glory, the Spirit who defies men, making them partakers of the divine nature, must himself be divine and co-essential with God, whose Spirit He is" (Greek, *tou theou . . . idion kai homoousion; Epistle to Serapion,* 1:27).[27] Stanley Burgess adds, "From the Son the Spirit receives His mission to create, to sanctify, and to make divine. . . . The Spirit's relationship to the Son parallels the Son's relationship to the Father."[28]

---

21. Shapland, *Letters,* p. 160.
22. Shapland, *Letters,* p. 181.
23. Shapland, *Letters,* p. 189.
24. Haykin, *Spirit of God,* p. 63.
25. Haykin, *Spirit of God,* p. 67.
26. Haykin, *Spirit of God,* pp. 63-100.
27. Swete, *The Holy Spirit in the Ancient Church,* p. 217.
28. Burgess, *The Holy Spirit: Ancient Christian Traditions,* pp. 118 and 119.

12.3. Basil of Caesarea

Basil (c. 329-379) was about thirty-five years junior to Athanasius, although he died within six years of Athanasius's death. With Gregory of Nazianzus (329-89 or 330-89) and Gregory of Nyssa (c. 330-95), he is known as a Cappadocian Father. Gregory of Nyssa was the younger brother of Basil. Strictly Didymus the Blind (c. 313-98), head of the Alexandrian School, preceded Basil, and he wrote a treatise on the Holy Spirit before 381, which has come down to us through Jerome's Latin version, and three books on the Trinity. Didymus insists that the Holy Spirit is "essentially divine, . . . co-essential and co-equal with God (Greek, *homoousion kai isotimon*)."[29] He was a learned student of the Bible, and was orthodox or Nicene on the theology of the Trinity. Epiphanius (c. 315-403), Bishop of Salamis, was also a staunch defender of Nicea, and deserves mention. But we cannot discuss every thinker, and Basil is usually regarded as in effect the successor of Athanasius on the theology of the Holy Spirit.

Stanley Burgess points out that under the influence of Athanasius the three Cappadocian Fathers emphasized that the Holy Spirit was of the same nature or same being *(homoousios)* as God the Father and the Son, but that in the other direction, under the influence of Origen, they also strengthened the doctrine of the three hypostases.[30] The Trinity was one in Being *(ousia)*, but three in "constitution . . . state of being . . . [what is] pertaining to a person" *(hypostasis)*.[31] Geoffrey Lampe cites and discusses the meanings of *hypostasis* over eight pages or sixteen columns.[32] Their work in the Spirit and the Trinity remained the basis of orthodoxy from the time of the Council of Constantinople in 381. This Council was called by Emperor Theodosius, and reaffirmed Nicea with the addition of a third article of faith on *"the Holy Spirit, the Lord and Giver of life, who proceeds from the Father, who with the Father and the Son together is worshiped and glorified, who spoke by the prophets"* (my italics).[33] This approximates our "Nicene Creed" (strictly Niceno-Constantinopolitan Creed) except that no Western Fathers attended this Council, and the Western Church has always maintained that "the Spirit proceeds from the Father and the Son *(Filioque)*." This is generally known as the Second Ecumenical Council, the first being the Council of Nicea.

Basil was elected Bishop of Caesarea in 370. From 356 he taught rhetoric in Caesarea, was involved with monasteries and asceticism, and built a complex of buildings to meet social needs and for the sick. On his election as Bishop he already had a reputation for his defense of the deity of the Holy Spirit, based in

---

29. Swete, *The Holy Spirit in the Ancient Church*, p. 223.
30. Burgess, *The Holy Spirit: Ancient Christian Traditions*, p. 132.
31. Lampe (ed.), *A Patristic Greek Lexicon*, pp. 1459-61.
32. Lampe (ed.), *A Patristic Greek Lexicon*, pp. 1454-61.
33. *NPNF,* ser. 2, vol. 14, "The Seven Ecumenical Councils," p. 163.

part on his apologetic *Against Eunomius,* written in 364. Michael Haykin comments, "The Pneumatomachian controversy, which dominated much of Basil's episcopacy, compelled Basil to reflect more deeply than ever before on the nature of the Spirit."[34] Eunomius boldly argued that the Holy Spirit was "third" after God the Father and the Son both in dignity and nature, and was actually made by the Son at the instigation of the Father. Basil responded while a presbyter, but his most profound work is *On the Holy Spirit,* written during his episcopate. His *Letters* and *Homilies* provide an additional source.

Some of Basil's *Letters* bear witness to the turmoil in Asia Minor during the 370s. Eustathius, Bishop of Sebaste (300-377), was a close friend of Basil until a breach between them occurred in 372-73 over the Holy Spirit. Eustathius had studied under Arius, and was semi-Arian throughout his life. Basil became concerned about Eustathius's increasing misrepresentation of his views and seductive propaganda throughout Asia Minor (e.g., *Letters,* 130:1, to Theodotus). The production of *On the Holy Spirit* was provoked in 374 when critics questioned the propriety of Basil's use of two doxologies which gave equal honor to the Father, the Son, and the Holy Spirit. He recalls that one gave glory to God the Father "with the Son, together with the Holy Spirit" and "through the Son in the Holy Spirit. . . . I was attacked . . . on the ground that I was introducing something novel" (*On the Holy Spirit,* 1:3; *NPNF,* ser. 2, vol. 8, p. 3).

Two characteristics of this work are (1) that the Holy Spirit should be accorded the same honor and glory as the Father and the Son, *especially in the threefold Gloria;* and (2) that the Spirit is *holy without qualification* and on that ground must be indivisibly one with God, who alone is holy without qualification. Two years after his death, Basil's work was fully recognized in the Council of Constantinople's formulation "the Holy Spirit . . . is worshiped and glorified together with the Father and the Son."

In *On the Holy Spirit,* 2–8, Basil examines different biblical passages about God and the Spirit. He writes: "Scripture varies its expressions as occasion requires. . . . 'Of which' does not always and absolutely . . . indicate the material (Greek, *hylē; On the Holy Spirit,* 4:6; *NPNF,* ser. 2, vol. 8, p. 4). He continues, "'Through whom' is admitted by Scripture in the case of the Father and of the Son and of the Holy Spirit alike" (5:10; *NPNF,* ser. 2, vol. 8, p. 7). The Pneumatomachi assert "that the Spirit is not to be ranked alongside the Son and the Father, but under the Son and the Father" (6:13; *NPNF,* ser. 2, vol. 8, p. 8). Chapters 6–8 argue for the co-equality of the Three, but Basil lays emphasis on Christology. Chapter 9 may or may not have been composed separately, for it differs in tone from chapters 1–8. It refers to the Farewell Discourses in John (*On the Holy Spirit,* 9:22), and to the Spirit as inspirer and life giver.

Chapters 10–27 may well reflect earlier exchanges with Eustathius. Basil be-

---

34. Haykin, *The Spirit of God,* p. 26.

gins, "We must proceed to attack our opponents" (*On the Holy Spirit*, 10:24). Our Lord, he asserts, did "co-join the Spirit with the Father and Himself in baptism" (10:24). At our own baptism we confess "belief in the Father and in the Son and in the Holy Spirit" (11:27). Peter testifies to the *"anointing of Jesus by the Holy Spirit"* (Acts 10:38; *On the Holy Spirit*, 12:28). Paul *similarly associates Father, Son, and Holy Spirit* (13:29). Baptism entails more than the use of water alone (15:34-35). He writes, "The Spirit gives us the earnest of life, . . . having our fruit in holiness. . . . [T]he Spirit pours in quickening power, renewing our souls from the deadness of sin. . . . born again of water and the Spirit" (15:36). He adds: "Through the Holy Spirit comes our restoration to paradise" (15:37; *NPNF*, ser. 2, vol. 8, p. 23). Further, the Holy Spirit gives both prophecy and other gifts. He quotes 1 Cor. 14:24-25; 12:4-6; and 12:10-11: ". . . diverse operations, . . . diversities of gifts; but it is the same God . . ." (16:37). Christians "have their need of holiness from the Spirit" (16:38), while "No one can say 'Jesus is Lord' but by the Holy Spirit" (16:38; 1 Cor. 12:3). To behold the face of God "is impossible without the Spirit" (16:38).

In *On the Holy Spirit*, 17–22, Basil returns to *the co-equality, deity, and glorification of the Spirit*, but this time largely arguing through his bestowal of gifts (19:49). He "makes intercession for us" (19:50; Rom. 8:26-27). Christians are bidden, "Grieve not the Holy Spirit" (19:20; Eph. 4:30). Basil warns his readers that in the Old Testament "They vexed His Holy Spirit; therefore He was turned to be their enemy" (19:50; Ps. 106:32; Mic. 2:7). The Spirit is called "Lord" (21:52; 2 Cor. 3:14-17). In chapter 23 Basil considers the communion of the Holy Spirit and then enumerates more of his qualities, while in chapter 25 he reconsiders the Bible's use of *en* ("in" or "by"). Basil comments, "We find both expressions in use among the faithful; we use both" (25:59; *NPNF*, ser. 2, vol. 8, p. 37).

The remaining chapters (28–30) either repeat many of these points or reflect on the state of the Church in Basil's day. However, Patristic scholars have long debated the status and genre of chapters 9–27. Haykin concludes: "Basil's authorship of the chapter [ch. 9] ought not to be doubted. . . . 10–27 have been a field of controversy among recent scholars."[35] Hermann Dörries argues that the section is retrospectively based on Basil's discussion with Eustathius at Sebaste in 372-73.[36] He distinguishes twenty antitheses in these chapters. We rely entirely on Basil for an account of Eustathius's views. His argument about the probable use of "tachy-graphers," broadly equivalent to shorthand writers, however, is questioned. Henry Chadwick cites the manifesto of Cyzicus as an alternative source of Eustathius's views.[37] Nevertheless, as we look back over the

35. Haykin, *Spirit of God*, pp. 106 and 108.

36. Hermann Dörries, *De Spiritu Sancto: Der Beitrag der Basilius von Plotin* (Berlin: de Gruyter, 1964), pp. 37-38 and 81-90.

37. Henry Chadwick, "Literarische Berichte und Anzeigen: Hermann Dörries, *De Spiritu Sancto*," *Zeitschrift für Kirchengeschichte* 69 (1958): 335-37.

treatise we entirely agree with the verdict of Stanley Burgess: "Basil's grasp of the full range of the Holy Spirit's work in the life of the believer is perhaps the most exceptional in the ancient world."[38]

In his use of 1 Corinthians 12, Basil relates together in a perceptive way the section on gifts or *charismata* (12:4-11) with the section on the body (12:12-30). He observes: "We are members one of another, having gifts differing according to the grace that is given to us" (Rom. 12:5-6). "Wherefore 'the eye cannot say to the hand, I have no need of you, nor again the head to the feet, I have no need of you' (1 Cor. 12:21), but all together complete the Body of Christ in the unity of the Spirit" (*On the Holy Spirit*, 16:61; *NPNF*, ser. 2, vol. 8, p. 38). *No one person receives all the charismata of the Holy Spirit*, but by apportioning his gifts to one and another, the Spirit sustains a unity of *mutual dependence*. A gift of the Spirit is never an end in itself, but is given to benefit others. Burgess comments, "Christian unity exists in the diversity of gifts, the Holy Spirit acting as a whole in parts. . . . He [Basil] also includes earthly goods and services, . . . seeking the common good of the Body."[39]

12.4. Gregory of Nazianzus and Gregory of Nyssa

The remaining two Cappadocian Fathers besides Basil also make points which are relevant to today. *Gregory of Nazianzus* (329/30-390), Basil's close friend, stresses the unity of the Trinity. In other words, we should be cautious about associating the Holy Spirit with specific gifts or prayers while omitting mention of the Father or the Son. He finds a "swarm" of biblical texts which imply the Spirit's deity, and that the Spirit is not simply a "force," or an "it." In the *Trinity*, he argues, *"three" has nothing to do with numbers or a numerical use of the term.* He and Gregory of Nyssa, Basil's younger brother, both stress that the Spirit's deity is seen not primarily in his *"essence,"* but by his *activity*, or "identity of activity," with God. This is broadly the practical or existential approach seen in many modern writers, even in Bultmann and the like.

Gregory of Nazianzus lived in a monastery in Seleucia, but at first reluctantly agreed to be Bishop of the Nicene community in Constantinople. At that time controversy was raging there. In 379 Gregory wrote on the Holy Spirit at the season of Pentecost, at first seeking to sustain a mediating position with the Pneumatomachians. But in 380 he took a bolder line in an oration given in honor of Athanasius. From 380 onward he delivered his five *Theological Orations*, of which Swete and broadly Edmund Hussey call the fifth "this greatest of

---

38. Burgess, *The Holy Spirit: Ancient Christian Traditions*, p. 139.
39. Burgess, *The Holy Spirit: Ancient Christian Traditions*, pp. 140-41.

all sermons on the doctrine of the Spirit."[40] The Greek text is available in A. J. Mason's edition.[41] The fifth oration begins by noting that those who "weary in their disputations concerning the Son . . . struggle with greater heat against the Spirit, . . . being worn out by the multitude of their questions" (*Oration on the Holy Spirit*, 2; *NPNF*, ser. 2, vol. 7, p. 318).

Gregory suggests that, unlike the Sadducees, even pagan Greeks speak of a Mind of the world, even if that Mind is a creature (*On the Holy Spirit*, 4–5). He then begins a strictly logical argument. We have to decide whether the Spirit is *Substance (ousia)* or *Accident* (a contingent being); either he is a *creature (ktisis)* made by God, or he is God. . . . the one belongs to Deity, the other to — anything (*On the Holy Spirit*, 6; *NPNF*, ser. 2, vol. 7, p. 319).[42] Either he is altogether unbegotten or else he is begotten (Greek, *gennēton; On the Holy Spirit*, 7). Many speak of his "proceeding" from God. But "what is Procession?" (*On the Holy Spirit*, 8). This is no easier to define than to call God "Unbegotten." Gregory then defines "of the same substance" with reference to Adam, Eve, and Seth, although "no image" exactly matches the truth (*On the Holy Spirit*, 11).

Gregory then discusses *worship and prayer to the Spirit*. The Holy Spirit intercedes for us (Rom. 8:26) and prays with us (1 Cor. 14:15). He declares, "Therefore to adore or pray to the Spirit seems to me to be simply Himself offering prayer or adoration to Himself" (*On the Holy Spirit*, 12; Greek, *homotimo syndoxazomenos; NPNF*, ser. 2, vol. 7, p. 321).[43] "He is glorified with One of coequal honor" (ch. 12). The *Pneumatomachi* could not call this *tritheism,* or worship of three Gods, for they were themselves *"Ditheists"* if they honored only the Father and Christ (ch. 13). "To us there is One God, for *the Godhead is One,* and all that proceedeth from Him is referred to One, though we believe in Three Persons" (*On the Holy Spirit*, 14; my italics); the Greek, however, simply has *tria ta proskynoumena*. Christians are not polytheists, like ordinary Greeks (chs. 15–16).

No amount of argument will render us "tritheists" (*On the Holy Spirit*, 17). The word "Three" (Greek, *treis . . . tria*) is not here used as to a "number of things." We use *three* "in a different way of so many units, . . . looking . . . at the *quantity*" (ch. 18, my italics; *NPNF*, ser. 2, vol. 7, p. 323).[44] "Three" *(treis)* does not denote numerals, like "three Peters" or "three Johns" (ch. 19). If Scripture is silent on these questions, many passages imply them (ch. 23). Scripture gives a "swarm [Greek, *hesmos*] of testimonies" in which "the Deity of the Holy Spirit

---

40. Swete, *The Holy Spirit in the Ancient Church*, p. 240; cf. M. Edmund Hussey, "The Theology of the Holy Spirit in the Writings of St. Gregory of Nazianzus," *Diakonia* 14 (1979): 224-33.

41. Arthur J. Mason, *The Five Theological Orations of Gregory of Nazianzus* (Greek text; Cambridge: Cambridge University Press, 1899), with notes.

42. Mason, Greek text, p. 153.

43. Mason, p. 160.

44. Mason, p. 168.

shall be shown to all who are not excessively stupid, or else enemies to the Spirit" (ch. 29; *NPNF*, ser. 2, vol. 7, p. 327).

The Spirit is called "the Spirit of God, the Spirit of Christ, the Mind of Christ, the Spirit of the Lord . . ." (*On the Holy Spirit*, 29). The Spirit is "sanctifying, not sanctified; measuring, not measured; sharing, not shared; filling, not filled; containing, not contained . . ." (ch. 29). Blasphemy against the Spirit cannot be forgiven (ch. 30). He is "an eye, a fountain, a river," as God is (ch. 31). Another image is of God as the sun and the Spirit as a ray (ch. 32). We cannot deny him "personality" (ch. 32). Language is inadequate, but I try to persuade all "to worship the Father, Son, and Holy Spirit, the One Godhead and Power" (ch. 33).

The oration *On the Holy Spirit* is the most explicit on this subject, but by no means the only work relevant to it. In his oration *On Pentecost* he argues, "The Spirit shares with the Son . . . both the Creation and the Resurrection. . . . He is the author of spiritual regeneration" (*On Pentecost*, *NPNF*, ser. 2, vol. 7, p. 384). However, we have cited a sufficient number of primary texts to indicate that, after Hilary and Ambrose in the West, and Athanasius in the East, Basil and Gregory bring the doctrine of the Holy Spirit to a climax in the East.

Basil's younger brother, *Gregory of Nyssa* (c. 330-395), also deserves note. He, too, was primarily a solitary ascetic, although he had spent a short period as a rhetorician. He became Bishop of Nyssa at Basil's urging, but much against his will. While the Arian emperor Valens reigned, he was exiled, but he returned as Bishop two years later under the "Nicene" emperor Theodosius in 380. He was invited to assist at the election of a Bishop of Sebaste when Eustathius died, and to his surprise found himself elected as Bishop. He was studious in his activities, and on the subject of the Holy Spirit wrote *On the Trinity*, a treatise *On "Not Three Gods," On the Holy Spirit*, and *Against Eunomius*, in twelve books.

Like Gregory of Nazianzus, Gregory of Nyssa pays special attention to language and to analogy. In *On "Not Three Gods"* (no sections numbered in this six-page treatise; *NPNF*, ser. 2, vol. 5, p. 334) Gregory compares the contrasts between three persons who appear to bear the same name, and the Father, Son, and Holy Spirit who share in the Godhead. In the case of the three with the same name, they are not the same. For three people of the same name may go their separate ways. "But in the case of the divine nature we do *not* similarly learn that the Father does anything *by Himself* in which the Son does not work *conjointly*, or again that the Son has any special operation apart from the Holy Spirit. . . . Every operation . . . has its origin from the Father and proceeds through the Son, and is perfected in the Holy Spirit" (my italics).

Still more distinctive is the approach summed up by Haykin. Haykin writes, "The nature of the Godhead must be based upon the knowledge of its

[sic] activity. . . . The identity of activity indicates the community of nature."[45] He cites Gregory as declaring: "If we perceive that the activity of the Father and the Son and the Holy Spirit is one, . . . it is necessary to infer the unity of their nature" (*On the Trinity*, 6). Elsewhere Gregory states: "The Holy Spirit by the uncreatedness of His nature has contact with the Son and the Father, but is distinguished from them by His own tokens. . . . Joined to the Father by His uncreatedness, He is distinguished from Him again by not being 'Father'" (*Against Eunomius*, 1:22; *NPNF*, ser. 2, vol. 5, p. 61).

Gregory uses many careful *linguistic, philosophical, and conceptual arguments and distinctions.* Much of his work, however, repeats that of Basil and of Gregory of Nazianzus, and we have sought to draw attention to his most creative and distinctive ideas. His work influenced the Council of Constantinople in 381. In Haykin's words, "Gregory [was] a key figure among those bishops of the Council who genuinely sought to convince the *Pneumatomachian* delegation of the error of their ways."[46] Similarly, Burgess concludes that he influenced "its decisions greatly. Ultimately he composed the additions to the Nicene Creed that were sanctioned by the Council. . . . In originality and intellectual ability Gregory was the most gifted of the Cappadocians."[47]

12.5. Philoxenus of Syria

Philoxenus (c. 440-523) became Bishop of Mabbug, or Hierapolis, in 485. He is recognized as one of the leading thinkers of the small but growing Syrian Church. He wrote in Syriac, including thirteen *Discourses on the Christian Life* and numerous letters. He was educated in the theological School of Edessa, and early on championed the cause of monophysite Christology, especially against the Antiochene School. He was also part of the Syrian Monastic Movement. Because Syriac forms a late version or dialect of Aramaic, McDonnell sees him as closer than many of the Greeks to the language and teaching of Jesus.[48]

In his work on the Holy Spirit a pivotal event was the baptism of Jesus. Until his baptism, Philoxenus argues, Jesus lived under the law (*Commentary on the Prologue of John*, 2). But at his baptism Jesus experienced fire *and the Spirit*, and crossed "from the carnal world to the spiritual world" (*Discourse*, 9:274). This "life in the Spirit," however, is one of asceticism and radical self-denial. Following his baptism, the Holy Spirit led Jesus into the wilderness "without beloved friends, . . . without riches, without possessions, . . . accompanied

---

45. Haykin, *Spirit of God*, p. 187.
46. Haykin, *Spirit of God*, pp. 198-99.
47. Burgess, *The Holy Spirit: Ancient Christian Tradition*, p. 144.
48. McDonnell and Montague, *Christian Initiation*, pp. 266-69.

[only] by the Spirit" (*Discourse,* 9:275). The situation changes several centuries after the time of Jesus. McDonnell writes: "What is given at baptism is unfolded and actualized in a long process of maturation."[49] Philoxenus introduces what McDonnell calls a "paradigm." The Christian can experience *three births.* The first birth is that of natural birth into the world; the second birth is that of becoming a Christian by sacramental baptism; the third birth takes the Christian "out of the womb of the world into the *fullness of the Spirit* by self-emptying and the ascetic life" (my italics).[50] Philoxenus asserts: "The world of the Spirit is beyond boundaries, beyond limits" (*Discourse,* 9:343). He explains: "You will only know that you experience happiness, but what that happiness is you will not be able to express" (*Discourse,* 9:289).

McDonnell points out that Philoxenus fused together the ascetic movement and a doctrine of perfection in an experience of the Holy Spirit which many might want to compare with "baptism in the Spirit." His theology is not exactly like that of Pentecostalism because Philoxenus has stated that perfectionism is a gradual, extended process, and it is attained by ascetic discipline. Moreover, he addressed most of his writings to monks in monasteries, and the aspect of "visibility" or "sensation," which does provide a point of contact or overlap, consists not of tongues-speech but of sacramental acts. In his *Letter to Patricius,* Philoxenus *rejects* the claims of Chrysostom and Theodore of Mopsuestia that charismatic gifts belong *only to the past.* He also maintains that all who are Christians do *not possess these gifts* (*Letter to Patricius,* 119 and 120).

A number of writers in the Pentecostal or Renewal tradition claim the origins of their tradition in the early Syrian Church. But the part played by monasticism and the radically ascetic life, by the sacraments, and by gradual steps of extended progress would distance Philoxenus at least from Protestant Pentecostals and the Protestant Renewal Movement, even though there is also an interesting overlap of concerns.

---

49. McDonnell and Montague, *Christian Initiation,* p. 277.
50. McDonnell and Montague, *Christian Initiation,* p. 279.

13

The Earlier Medieval Period

13.1. From Gregory the Great to Alcuin of York

(1) *Gregory of Rome* (c. 540-604) was not strictly a theologian, even though he is called "the last doctor" of the Western Church, together with Ambrose, Jerome, and Augustine. He was an immensely able administrator and pastor, and faithfully transmitted Augustine's theology to the Middle Ages. In some respects he was the last Western Father, but more relevantly to today, he became the first medieval Pope. He founded monasteries, administered finances, and wrote to improve the standards of clergy.

Gregory's well-known work *The Moralia: An Exposition of Job* was written in the monastic *collation,* a daily conference at which the Abbot preached and the monks asked questions. Gregory commented that he often understood Scripture "when I am with my brethren, which, when alone, I could not understand" (*Homily on Ezekiel,* 2:2).[1] In accordance with his threefold or fourfold scheme of biblical interpretation, in addition to historical or "literal" meaning, Gregory saw the moral meaning as a legitimate third meaning: "by the grace of moral instruction, we, as it were, clothe the edifice with an overcast of coloring" (*Preface to the Moralia,* 15). In 590 he became Pope or Bishop of Rome, and at this time wrote his *Forty Gospel Homilies,* followed in c. 593 by twenty-two *Homilies on Ezekiel.*[2] As Bishop of Rome he also produced his *Book of Pastoral Rule,* or *On Pastoral Care: On the Duties and Qualities of Bishops;* fourteen books of *Letters;* and *Four Books of Dialogues on the Lives and Miracles of the Italian Fathers* (593-94).[3]

---

1. Cf. Beryl Smalley, *The Study of the Bible in the Middle Ages* (Notre Dame, IN: University of Notre Dame Press, 5th ed. 1964), p. 32.

2. Gregory the Great, *Forty Gospel Homilies* (Kalamazoo, MI: Cistercian Publications, 1990).

3. Henry Davis, *St. Gregory the Great: Pastoral Care* (New York: Newman, 1950), includes fourteen *Books of Epistles* (*NPNF,* ser. 2, vol. 12, pp. 387-820, and vol. 13, pp. 2-190).

Scattered references occur in most books to the person and work of the Holy Spirit. In the *Moralia* Gregory writes: "When the Lord was made flesh, he was anointed by this oil [i.e., the Holy Spirit] . . . since the Lord was made flesh by the Spirit's mediation, he was anointed with this oil at the very moment when he was created as a man. . . . His ointment is the aroma of the Holy Spirit, who . . . remains on him" (*The Moralia: An Exposition of the Song of Songs*, 14). Here the "literal" meaning is "The odour of your ointments surpasses all performers" (Song of Songs 1:1-3). In book 1, 2:2, Gregory writes, "The Holy Spirit makes its [his] presence known to men not only in the form of a dove, but also in the form of fire. The dove symbolizes simplicity; the fire, zeal, . . . gentleness of spirit, . . . and the zeal of uprightness."[4] This coheres with Gregory's work on Acts 2, on which he comments that the Spirit comes as fire because God is immaterial and indescribable, and Homily 30 of his *Forty Homilies on the Gospels*.

In his *Homily on the Pastoral Office*, 13, Gregory condemns those bishops who try to sell orders for money. If they "confer orders for money, [they] sell the grace of the Holy Spirit." He cites the words of Jesus, "Freely you have received, freely give" (Matt. 10:8). The Holy Spirit from on high is imparted "by the laying on of hands. There are men who undertake the care of souls, and yet they are afraid to lay snares for the flock of the Lord" (*Moralia*, 14). *The best example of the gifts of the Holy Spirit can be seen in Jesus Christ*. Christ was "full of the Spirit of sevenfold grace," as evidenced by Isa. 11:2 and Luke 4:18. In Luke we read, "The Spirit is upon me, because he has anointed me to bring good news. . . ." In Isa. 11:2, "The Spirit of the LORD shall rest upon him, the Spirit of wisdom and understanding, the Spirit of counsel and might, the Spirit of knowledge and the fear of the Lord." Gregory interprets these gifts as being in descending order. *"Wisdom" is the highest gift* (*Moralia*, 2:8:12). The Spirit gives to the Church and to the Christian what he has given to Christ. This is prompted by the "literal" text in Job about resurrection. In his work on Acts, Gregory refers to *various tongues as pointing to the universality of the Church*, and gives a cross-reference to the gifts of the Spirit in 1 Cor. 12:8-10.

On the Person of the Holy Spirit, Gregory teaches the Western and Augustinian view that the Holy Spirit "proceeds *from the Father and the Son*" (*Homily on the Gospels*, 26). In the *Moralia* he also uses a softer version of this, namely, that the Holy Spirit proceeds from the Father "and receives that which is the Son's" (*Moralia*, 5:65 and 27:34). This formula might well have been acceptable to the Eastern Fathers. But the stronger formulation is adopted by the Spanish church, and the East could not accept this formulation. The weaker "acceptable" Greek formulation is *ek tou Patros proerchetai kai en tō huiō diamenei* ("he proceeds from the Father and dwells in the Son"). But the Latin *filioque* clause would soon

---

4. Gregory uses the same two images of dove and fire in his *Forty Gospel Homilies*, Homily 30, Cistercian translation, pp. 242-43.

become part of the Constantinopolitan Creed at Rome and in the West, even if two versions of the Creed existed at Rome up to the time of Charlemagne.

Thus there are two distinct aspects of Gregory's work on the Holy Spirit. Much time is devoted to the *Being, Person, or Procession of the Spirit*, which formed the main legacy to the medieval Church up to Anselm. The other concerns *the gift of holiness* and the work of *the Spirit as the Paraclete*. The Spirit grants wisdom, love, and inspiration. In his *Forty Gospel Homilies* he writes extensively on the Paraclete. He declares, "The Greek word 'Paraclete' means in Latin 'advocate' or 'consoler.'. . . He intervenes before the Father's justice on behalf of the wrongdoings of sinners; he who is of one substance with the Father and the Son is said to plead earnestly on behalf of sinners. . . . Hence Paul says: 'For the Spirit himself pleads for us with unutterable groaning' (Rom. 8:26)" (*Forty Gospel Homilies*, Homily 30; p. 238 of the Cistercian translation). This same Holy Spirit consoles "those grieving over their sins, . . . lifting up their hearts from sorrow and affliction" (Homily 30). The teaching of the Spirit is not simply "human teaching" (Homily 30). In the same homily Gregory sees Pentecost as the reversal of Babel, as many do today. The Holy Spirit is "coeternal with the Father and the Son" (Homily 30; Cistercian translation, p. 240). "The Lord sends fire upon the earth when he enkindles the hearts of the materially-minded with the breath of the Holy Spirit. . . . The Spirit . . . *drives numbness and cold from every heart, fills and warms it to desire its own eternity*" (Homily 30, my italics). Gregory adds: "The true love which fills it torments it to the point of tears" (Homily 30, p. 241).

At the end of his Homily 30, which is mainly on the Holy Spirit, Gregory declares: "I wish to analyze the nature of the Holy Spirit. . . . The Spirit filled a boy who played upon a harp, and made him a psalmist (1 Sam. 16:18); a shepherd and herdsman who pruned sycamore trees and made him a prophet (Amos 7:14-15); . . . a fisherman and made him a preacher (Matt. 4:19); a persecutor, and made him teacher of the Gentiles (Acts 9:1-20); a tax collector, and made him an Evangelist (Luke 5:27-28). What a skillful workman this Spirit is! . . . It [He] *changes a human mind in a moment to enlighten it. . . .* Suddenly it is what it was not" (*Forty Gospel Homilies*, Homily 30, my italics; Cistercian translation, pp. 244-45). He concludes: "Let us love this life-giving Spirit" (Homily 30, p. 246).

Although we cannot ascribe to Gregory any ground-breaking creativity of thought, he remained *faithful to Scripture and to the Church Fathers*, and transmitted this solid legacy to the medieval church. He was practical in applying teaching on the Holy Spirit to the daily life of Christians and clergy, even as he retained the concern of the Fathers with the Being and Procession of the Spirit.

(2) *Pseudo-Dionysius* (probably sixth century) was a monk and mystic in the East, whose name distinguishes him from the Dionysius who was converted by Paul in Acts 17:34. He is also known as Dionysius or Denis the Pseudo-Areopagite. He influenced the medieval East partly by drawing on the Cappa-

docian Fathers, John Chrysostom, and Neo-Platonism, much as Gregory the Great influenced the medieval West by drawing on Ambrose and Augustine. Although he coined the term "hierarchy," this does not denote a graded subordination, as it does today, but the outreach of God's self-manifestation in creation through the divine light of revelation. The purpose of humankind is to be "assimilated to likeness with God as much as possible" (Dionysius, *Celestial Hierarchy*, 3:1). This entails purification, illumination, and perfection or union with God.

Because God is "dazzling light," Dionysius expounded a double method in theology. *Cataphatic theology, or a theology of affirmation* or description, can speak only *about* God. *Apophatic theology, or a theology of negation* or denial, goes further, but cannot formulate what it encounters in positive or descriptive terms. Negative theology stands in stark contrast to frequent present-day "overfamiliarity" with Christ and the Holy Spirit, as if this could be lightly and readily expressed or conveyed in human concepts and language. The limits of our "knowledge" of God are explored in Dionysius's *On the Divine Names*.[5] His equivalent to the standard Western term "sanctification" is "deification": becoming like God, and reaching into the divine nature.

Unfortunately Dionysius's aim was to conceive of Christianity *in Neo-Platonic terms*, mediated by Plotinus. Yet he stresses the Christian doctrine of the Trinity. All three Persons of the Godhead convey light and life. The Father, the Son, and the Holy Spirit are "Lord." But we must be cautious, he urges, about "naming" what is distinctive to each (*On the Divine Names*, 2:2-3). Yet he writes of "the Spirit of the Father and the Son, in whom and through whom gifts of grace are distributed on all things" (Dionysius, *On the Celestial Hierarchy*, 1:1). The Father and the Son are clearly distinguished (*On the Divine Names*, 2:5; Jones's translation p. 121). Dionysius therefore sees the Holy Spirit in cosmic terms, convicting an overly familiar, overly individualistic understanding of the Spirit, and encouraging vision rather than conceptual thought.

(3) *Isidore of Seville* (c. 560-636) ensured clerical education, monastic discipline, and liturgical uniformity in Spain. He presided over the Council of Toledo (633). On the Holy Spirit he is best known for *transmitting Gregory's teaching* and for his permanent endorsement of the *filioque* clause in the Creed on the Procession of the Spirit in the West. He insisted that the Spirit is "consubstantial" with the Father and the Son, and stressed his role as the Giver of holiness. But as Howard Watkin-Jones concludes, "Isidore wrote little on the work of the Spirit."[6]

---

5. Greek, *PG*, vol. 3, cols. 585-976; English, John D. Jones, *Pseudo-Dionysius the Areopagite: The Divine Names and Mystical Theology* (Milwaukee: Marquette University Press, 1980).

6. Howard Watkin-Jones, *The Holy Spirit in the Mediaeval Church: A Study of Christian Teaching concerning the Holy Spirit and His Place in the Trinity* (London: Epworth, 1922), p. 25.

(4) *The Venerable Bede* (c. 673-735) is also largely a *transmitter of Augustine* of Hippo *and of Gregory of Rome.* But in addition to his well-known *Ecclesiastical History of the English People* (731), he wrote a *Commentary on the Acts of the Apostles, Homilies on the Gospels, Excerpts from the Works of St. Augustine on the Letters of the Apostle Paul,* and numerous other works (at least forty-four in all). He entered the monasteries of Wearmouth and Jarrow at the age of seven (680), and from the age of thirty (702), when he was ordained priest, he devoted his life to annotating Scripture. He learned Latin, Greek, and Hebrew. Burgess calls him "the most famous beacon of Christian learning in the early eighth century."[7] Frederick Artz calls him "a man of powerful intellect."[8] His book *On the Nature of Things* was built on the encyclopedic approach of Pliny and Isidore.[9] A study of different speech-patterns inspired his work *The Figures of Rhetoric.* In *On Times* he critically discusses the chronology of the world, and encourages belief in an imminent Last Judgment. In *On the Nature of Things* Bede begins with the Genesis account of creation and "the formation of the world" in seven days.

Bede's commentaries often reproduce Augustine, Ambrose, Jerome, and Gregory. In his *Commentary on John* he insists that the *Holy Spirit is God,* but in view of the rise of Islam as well as because of the New Testament, he also maintains that *God is one and a unity.* The Spirit proceeds from the Father and the Son, and is of one Substance, power, and majesty.[10] In c. 709 Bede wrote his *Commentary on the Acts of the Apostles* (revised in 725-31); his *Commentary on Luke* in c. 709-16; and on Mark in c. 725-30. Arthur Holder comments, "In his interpretation of New Testament miracles, he emphasised inner spiritual conversion more than physical transformation."[11] He allows that miracles took place, but they were more spectacular and *more frequent* "at the beginning of the Church when its faith was young and tender, just as we water a new plant until its roots are established" (Bede, *Commentary on Mark,* my italics).[12] Similarly, Bede writes: "In the earliest times the Holy Spirit fell upon believers, and they spoke in tongues which they had never studied. But nowadays, because the holy Church does not need external signs, whoever believes in the name of Jesus

7. Stanley M. Burgess, *The Holy Spirit: Mediaeval Roman Catholic and Reformation Traditions* (Peabody, MA: Hendrickson, 1997), p. 21.

8. Frederick B. Artz, *The Mind of the Middle Ages* (New York: Alfred Knopf, 3rd ed. 1958), p. 194.

9. Bede, *On the Nature of Things* and *On Times,* trans. with an intro. by Calvin B. Kendall and Faith Wallis (Liverpool: Liverpool University Press, 2010).

10. Watkin-Jones, *The Holy Spirit in the Mediaeval Church,* p. 29.

11. Arthur C. Holder, "Bede and the New Testament," in *The Cambridge Companion to Bede,* ed. Scott DeGregorio (Cambridge: Cambridge University Press, 2010), p. 152.

12. Bede, *In Marci Evangelium Expositio,* ed. D. Hurst, CCSL 120 (Turnhout: Brepols, 1960), p. 645.

Christ . . . gives witness to the Holy Spirit abiding in him" (Bede, *Commentary on the Seven Catholic Epistles*).[13]

Most references to the Holy Spirit, however, seem to concern his Person rather than his work. Bede repeats the procession of the Spirit from the Father and the Son *(filioque)* a number of times, sometimes appealing to the insufflation of the Spirit by the Son as in John 20:22. Again, in the face of Islam, he stresses the unity of God the Trinity.

(5) *Alcuin of York* (c. 735-804) trained at the Cathedral school of York, and then visited Rome in order to share in the creation of a cathedral library. In 781 he met Charlemagne and joined the scholars at his court. In 800 Charlemagne was crowned Emperor of the West by the Pope, which some have described as the most significant event of the Middle Ages. He aimed at "a fusion of Roman, Christian, and Germanic culture."[14] Alcuin stood at the heart of the Carolingian Renaissance, and regarded Charlemagne as his God-given, ideal emperor. He wrote three treatises against Adoptionism, and insisted that *the Holy Spirit was co-equal with the Father and the Son*, although the Holy Trinity remains "one will" and collaborates in *"one operation"* (*Commentary on John* 15:26).[15] In collaboration with Charlemagne, he championed the procession of the Holy Spirit "from the Father and the Son *(filioque).*" He also stressed that the Holy Trinity was of "one Substance, one Nature, one majesty, one glory, one eternity, of the Father, Son, and Holy Spirit."[16] Alcuin also comments: "The Holy Spirit, because he self-exists, is God *(Spiritus sanctus, quod ad se est, Deus est)*; because He is of the Father and of the Son, . . . Holy Spirit" *(quod a Patre et Filio, Spiritus sanctus est)."*

As for the work of the Holy Spirit, Alcuin believed that all baptized people have their sins forgiven, and *receive the Holy Spirit from the Bishop by the imposition of hands* (*per manus impositionem*; Alcuin, *Letters*, 80). This marks an explicit stage in the development of sacramentalism and institutional "order." In another letter Alcuin writes of the Paraclete, who was sent by the Father and the Son (Alcuin, *Letters*, 111). He adds, "The Lord baptizes in the Holy Spirit by forgiving sins through the grace of the Holy Spirit."[17] The *Letters* are a helpful source on the work of the Holy Spirit; on his Person, Alcuin addressed a short work, *On the Procession of the Holy Spirit*, to Charlemagne.

Jaroslav Pelikan observes: "Alcuin saw in Charlemagne Augustine's ideal Christian emperor, the *felix imperator*," in accordance with *The City of God*.[18]

---

13. Bede, *In Epistolas VII Catholicas*, ed. D. Hurst (Turnhout: Brepols, 1983), pp. 198-99.

14. Artz, *The Mind of the Middle Ages*, p. 195.

15. Watkin-Jones, *The Holy Spirit in the Mediaeval Church*, p. 44.

16. Alcuin, *Commentary on John* 16:14-15.

17. Watkin-Jones, *The Holy Spirit in the Mediaeval Church*, p. 45.

18. Jaroslav Pelikan, *The Christian Tradition*, vol. 3: *The Growth of Mediaeval Theology (600-1300)* (Chicago: University of Chicago Press, 1978), p. 49.

Pelikan also points out that for Alcuin the theology of the Church Fathers "was the only reliable guarantee of believing correctly and thereby attaining salvation."[19] Alcuin's work *On the Faith of the Holy Trinity* largely reproduces the approach of Augustine of Hippo, Gregory of Rome, Ambrose, and Jerome. His influence with Charlemagne ensured the transmission of these ideas to the medieval church.

13.2. From Scotus Erigena to Anselm, Rupert, and Abelard

(1) *Scotus Erigena* (c. 812–c. 890). Johannes Scotus Erigena witnessed the final flowering of the Carolingian Renaissance and the beginnings of the scholastic period. Like Pseudo-Dionysius, he uses Neo-Platonism and the notion of a "World-Idea" in his study of God, the world, and the Holy Spirit. He sees no division between theology and philosophy. What is more, he seeks a completely rational explanation of the Christian message in Scripture. Because Augustinian theology dominated the medieval Western tradition, he wrote *On Predestination,* in which he argues that no one is compelled to do evil, for strictly God has no foreknowledge of "what is not." But he closely followed Pseudo-Dionysius and the Neo-Platonic tradition, in which emanation plays a major role. Like Pseudo-Dionysius, he distinguishes between the mystery of the incomprehensible God and the world, but he nevertheless does restrict divine activity to the "supernatural," as is evident in his *Division of Nature* (c. 865). Nevertheless *he was condemned by the Church for pantheism* in 1210. He translated and commented on not only Pseudo-Dionysius and Boethius but also Gregory of Nyssa and produced a commentary on John.

We have included Erigena because he is, as some claim, probably "the one most important philosophical thinker to appear in Latin Christendom between Augustine . . . and Anselm."[20] He also writes on *the Trinity.* He declares that *the Spirit proceeds from (ex) the Father through (per) the Son,* and that the Father, Son, and Holy Spirit are *co-essential and co-eternal.* Watkin-Jones devotes a chapter to him, but Erigena is more interested in the *cosmic* nature of the Holy Spirit than in his work in the Church.[21] He does not hesitate to criticize some of the Church Fathers. Because of his equal concern for philosophy and rationality, and for the apophatic theology of Pseudo-Dionysius, Watkin-Jones cites him as "the father of Western mysticism as well as of rationalism."[22] He resists any trivial demystification of the Holy Spirit.

19. Pelikan, *The Christian Tradition,* vol. 3, p. 46.

20. Eugene Fairweather, "Erigena, John Scotus," in *The Encyclopaedia of Philosophy,* ed. Paul Edwards, 8 vols. (New York: Macmillan, 1967), vol. 3, pp. 44-45.

21. Watkin-Jones, *The Holy Spirit in the Mediaeval Church,* pp. 61-67, ch. 7.

22. Watkin-Jones, *The Holy Spirit in the Mediaeval Church,* p. 67.

(2) *Photius* (c. 810–c. 890) requires consideration. Until recently many Western writers criticized him, although Burgess calls him "certainly the most prolific writer of the ninth-century Byzantine intellectual renaissance."[23] He was elected Bishop or Patriarch of Constantinople, but suffered intermittent deposition and reinstatement through Court and Church intrigue. His best-known work is the massive *Bibliotheca*, which consists of extracts and summaries of 280 volumes of the Church Fathers, including a number of their biblical commentaries. He also wrote *On the Mystagogy of the Holy Spirit*, in which he consistently defends *the Eastern view of the single procession of the Holy Spirit* from God the Father alone.

Photius argues that "He will receive from that which is mine" (John 16:14) explicitly does not assert "from me," and the vast majority of the Church Fathers *supported the single Procession of the Spirit*. He acknowledges that Ambrose, Jerome, and Augustine constitute "minority" exceptions. Anticipating Jürgen Moltmann today, Photius believed that the equality of the Trinity is best preserved *by the single Procession*. Moltmann writes, "With the introduction of the *filioque* into the Nicene-Constantinopolitan Creed, the Spirit was considered as subordinate to the Son, . . . the Son being put ahead of the Spirit. . . . Remodeling will only be possible, however, *if we once again remove the* filioque *from the Western Creed* . . ." (my italics).[24] Photius *passionately* defends this point, arguing that even Leo the Great of Rome taught the single Procession of the Spirit. Some argue that his uncompromising *hard-line stance set back the possibility of an agreed formula between East and West* for many centuries.

Nevertheless Andreas Andreopoulos argues, "It is hard to deny a political dimension to the views of Rome and Constantinople concerning the procession of the Holy Spirit, as they were expressed in the ninth century."[25] But he also sees this division as owing much to ecclesiology. The iconoclastic controversy had polarized "independent" monasticism and the Episcopal Church. Photius was seen by many as an outsider imposed on the Church by the emperor. Hence he had to work hard to gain the trust of the monks and conservatives within the Church. There were many confrontations of power, some concerning a theology of images, which had been fundamental to the East. In this disarray, Photius became entangled with a party of extremists. The controversy about the procession of the Spirit became, in this context, "a challenge to an understanding of the catholicity of the Church."[26] In the discussions between

---

23. Stanley M. Burgess, *The Holy Spirit: Eastern Christian Traditions* (Peabody, MA: Hendrickson, 1989), p. 49.

24. Jürgen Moltmann, *The Spirit of Life: A Universal Affirmation* (London: SCM, 1992), p. 71.

25. Andreas Andreopoulos, "The Holy Spirit in the Ecclesiology of Photios of Constantinople," in *The Holy Spirit in the Fathers of the Church*, ed. D. Vincent Twomey and Janet E. Rutherford (Dublin: Foursquare, 2010), p. 151; cf. pp. 151-63.

26. Andreopoulos, "The Holy Spirit," in Twomey and Rutherford, *The Holy Spirit in the Fathers*, p. 156.

East and West, Photius largely recapitulated Cappadocian theology. He refused to leave open any system of theology, even if a new context suggested it. This goes a long way toward explaining his inflexibility on this subject.

(3) *Anselm of Canterbury* (c. 1033-1109). Watkin-Jones observes, "The tenth century yielded no writer of importance in connexion with the Doctrine of the Spirit."[27] In the eleventh century, however, Lanfranc (1005-89) not only wrote on the Holy Spirit and held influence over William the Conqueror, but also taught Anselm, who would succeed him as Archbishop of Canterbury in 1093. Anselm stressed the unity of God, and the unity of faith and reason. His earliest work, *Prayers and Meditations,* was written during the peace which he experienced during his days as a monk at Beck. He addressed the *Meditations* to a daughter of William the Conqueror in 1072.[28] In about 1077 Anselm produced the *Monologion* and the *Proslogion.* The *Monologion* concerns the qualities of God and reflects Augustine's *On the Trinity.* The *Proslogion* concerns the Being of God and is a more independent work, arising from prayer addressed to God.

In his book on Anselm, Karl Barth asserts, "In this book on Anselm I am working with a vital key, if not the key, to an understanding of that whole process of thought that has impressed me more and more . . . as the only one prayer to theology."[29] *Proslogion* 2–4 concerns proof of the *existence* of God, while *Proslogion* 5–26 concerns the *nature* of God. We may recall what we observed about Pseudo-Dionysius when we read Barth's words: "For Anselm, 'to believe' does not mean simply a striving of the human will *towards* God, but a striving of the human will *into* God, and so a *participation* . . . in God's mode of Being" (my italics).[30] He adds, *"Credo ut intelligam,"* by which he means: "It is my very faith itself that summons me to knowledge."[31] To believe is not illogical or irrational, and Anselm holds firmly to the necessary relation between theology and prayer.

This is not the place to unravel what philosophers call Anselm's formulation of the ontological argument for the existence of God. Many other authors do this, including Barth and Southern, with special regard to the context in Anselm.[32] Anselm's masterpiece, *Cur Deus Homo,* was probably written after 1093, when he became Archbishop, and shows in a masterly way how *the incarnation of Christ is closely bound up with his atoning work.* The atonement depended on Christ's being truly God and truly man.

We have not yet touched specifically on Anselm's doctrine of the Holy Spirit. This first emerges in the *Monologion,* which partly reflects Augustine's

27. Watkin-Jones, *The Holy Spirit in the Mediaeval Church,* p. 68.

28. Cf. R. W. Southern, *Saint Anselm: A Portrait in Landscape* (Cambridge: Cambridge University Press, 1990), pp. 91-137.

29. Karl Barth, *Anselm: Fides Quaerens Intellectum* (London: SCM, 1960), p. 11.

30. Barth, *Anselm,* p. 17.

31. Barth, *Anselm,* p. 18.

32. Southern, *Saint Anselm,* pp. 127-37.

On the Trinity. The Holy Trinity is a self-expression of God, "three Persons in one Substance," in which the Spirit is co-eternal with the Word (Anselm, *Monologion,* 32). He continues: "The Spirit possesses in every respect the 'attributes' [or character] of the Father and the Son. . . . *The whole Father (totus Pater) is present in the Son and the common Spirit*" (*Monologion,* 58-59; my italics). Following Augustine, Anselm sees the Trinity as memory, understanding *(intelligentia),* and love *(amor).* In his *On the Faith of the Trinity* he attacks the tritheism of Roscellin (c. 1050-1130), stressing the essential unity of the Trinity. He argues, "If the Holy Spirit were incarnate, as the Son was incarnate [which is unthinkable], the Holy Spirit would be Son of Man. Therefore there would be two Sons in the Trinity" (*On the Faith of the Trinity,* 5).

This may help to solve the puzzlement of a number of Christians today who may be asked to recite the so-called Athanasian Creed, probably dating from medieval times. They would recite: "So there is one Father, not three Fathers; one Son, not three Sons; one Holy Ghost [Spirit], not three Holy Spirits." The Book of Common Prayer, still legal in England, places the Athanasian Creed or *"Quicunque Vult"* after Evening Prayer under the title "At Morning Prayer," and directs its recital thirteen times a year. It is about three pages long, but today is seldom used. I recall in childhood that this notion of "three Fathers" caused much puzzlement, but it can be understood only in the context of Athanasius's technical concerns of the time. In his work *On the Procession* Anselm urged the use of the *filioque* clause. But he produced nothing on the work of the Holy Spirit comparable to his magisterial *Cur Deus Homo* on the incarnation and work of the Son in relation to the honor and governance of God the Father.

(4) *Rupert of Deutz* (c. 1075-1129). Rupert in his younger years was a monk in the Benedictine Abbey of St. Lawrence in Liège. He was appointed Abbot of Deutz, near Cologne, in about 1120. Stanley Burgess calls him "the most prolific writer of all twelfth-century Western churchmen," including extensive theological treatises.[33] He forms a bridge between the death of Anselm and the emergence of Bernard of Clairvaux, Peter Abelard, and Hugo of St. Victor. His works include *On the Trinity and Its Works* (c. 1114) and biblical commentaries on Matthew, John, the Apocalypse, and the Minor Prophets. Rupert sought to ascribe distinctions between respective "works" to each divine Person: *creation* is ascribed to the Father; *redemption* to the Son; and *renewal* or restoration to the Holy Spirit (*On the Holy Trinity and Its Works,* 21:126). This still lingers in the Book of Common Prayer, but many other writers insist that all persons of the Trinity are active in all these actions. Similarly, Rupert ascribes life to the Father, wisdom to the Son, and love to the Holy Spirit. Likewise God the Father is seen in the early period of creation; the Son, from the fall to his death and resurrec-

---

33. Burgess, *The Holy Spirit: Mediaeval Roman Catholic and Reformation Traditions,* p. 37.

tion; and the Holy Spirit from the incarnation and the anointing of Christ to the Last Judgment. These are expounded respectively in parts 1, 2, and 3 of *On the Holy Trinity*.

There is much in Rupert that seems to anticipate the contemporary Pentecostal and Charismatic Movements. These movements are also concerned to emphasize distinctive works and gifts of the Spirit, whereas most of the earlier Fathers had seen *all* creative, redemptive, and sanctifying gifts as a *cooperative work of one God in the Trinity*, whose "works" could not be easily separated. Conversely, whereas many of the earlier writers had focused simply on the Being, Status, and Procession of the Holy Spirit, Rupert stresses the "works" of the Trinity, as many or most modern writers do. Rupert still defends and champions the Western doctrine of double procession: the Spirit proceeds from the Father and the Son. Part of the arbitrariness of assigning distinct "works" to each Person of the Holy Trinity is seen in Rupert's correlating "wisdom" with the Son and "love" with the Spirit, when in his *Commentary on Revelation* he calls "wisdom" the highest of seven gifts of the Spirit.

(5) *Peter Abelard* (also Abailard, 1079-1142). Watkin-Jones represents many when he calls Abelard "the most thought-provoking writer and teacher of his time."[34] He was of lively and independent mind, and lectured in Paris to large audiences. But tragedy befell him in two forms: first, his love affair with Héloise caused him to retire to monastic life in c. 1117; second, he was condemned without a hearing of his views at the Council of Soissons (1121), and later was denounced by Bernard of Clairvaux (1140). Eventually he was reconciled with Bernard, but these events must have scarred both him and his writings. It is also a pity that in modern thought he is often regarded as voicing an overly general and unsatisfactory criticism of Anselm's brilliant work on the atonement.

Abelard's *Exposition of the Epistle to the Romans*, for example, was never meant to be a fully fledged "answer" to Anselm. Hence its exegetical inadequacies, especially on Rom. 3:19-26, are all too apparent. R. S. Franks comments, "He has reduced the whole process of redemption to one single, clear, principle, viz. the manifestation of God's love to us in Christ."[35] It is also the case that Abelard is often portrayed as a Rationalist, in contrast to Bernard of Clairvaux. E. R. Fairweather asserts, "He manifests intransigent confidence in our reason, which is lacking in Anselm."[36] But Abelard also composed his *Hymn for Saturday Vespers*, where he writes: "O what their joy and their glory must be, those endless Sabbaths the blessed ones see! Crown for the valiant: to weary ones rest; God shall be all, and in all ever blest."[37]

34. Watkin-Jones, *The Holy Spirit in the Mediaeval Church*, p. 91.

35. R. S. Franks, *The Work of Christ* (London: Nelson, 1962), p. 146.

36. Eugene R. Fairweather (ed.), *A Scholastic Miscellany: Anselm to Ockham* (London: SCM, and Philadelphia: Westminster, 1956), pp. 224-25.

37. Represented in Fairweather (ed.), *A Scholastic Miscellany*, pp. 298-99.

In philosophy Abelard distinguished between words and things, formulating a "Conceptualism" that tried to compromise between Realism and Nominalism. Universals are not merely constructions of the mind. Hence, like others, he rejected Roscellin's notion of the Trinity as "a diversity of Persons," or "three substances." Abelard spoke of "a singularity of majesty," or of unity (Abelard, *Christian Theology*, 1:8; 3:60). *In the deeds of Jesus "the entire Trinity was present"* (*Christian Theology*, 50; my italics).[38] So emphatic was Abelard in his *rejection of tritheism* that some even accused him of *modalism*, its opposite. The Persons of the Trinity, he argued, were co-equal and co-eternal. Yet there are three Persons, not one Person. He attributes wisdom especially to the Church, and love especially to the Spirit (Abelard, *Introduction to Theology*, 10).[39]

13.3. The Medieval Mystics: Bernard of Clairvaux, Hildegard, and Richard of St. Victor

(1) *Bernard of Clairvaux* (1090-1153). Bernard entered an austere new monastery at the age of twenty, but shortly afterward took thirty of his friends to found a monastery at Clairvaux, of which he became Abbot. Under his leadership Clairvaux became the mother house of the Cistercian order. He urged strict obedience to monastic vows. He is widely known for his emphasis on contemplation, rest, and the mystical life, especially as it came to flourish in the twelfth century. Love *(caritas),* or charity, stands at the heart of Bernard's teaching, and he wrote especially on humility and "degrees of love."

In his work *On the Love of God* he spoke of "four degrees of love." In the first degree, a human being begins to seek God "through faith as something necessary. . . ." "Man begins by loving God, not for God's sake, but for his own." He loves God to the second degree. In the second degree "he loves purely and without self-interest. . . . [God] grows sweet, and thus by tasting how sweet is the Lord, he passes to the third degree, so that he loves God now . . . for Himself. . . . I know not if the fourth degree is obtained in its perfection by any man in this life" ("The Four Degrees of Love," in Bernard, *On the Love of God*, chs. 8, 9, and 10).[40] But the second, third, and fourth degrees of love are *made possible by the Holy Spirit,* the Giver of love.

Bernard's first work was *On the Steps of Humility and Pride*, which largely summarized the rule of Benedict. *On Loving God* traces the pilgrimage of the soul, especially the growth of love. His sermons on the Song of Songs represent

38. Cf. Pelikan, *Christian Tradition: Mediaeval Theology*, p. 265.

39. Cf. David Luscombe, *The School of Peter Abelard: The Influence of Abelard's Thought in the Early Scholastic Period* (Cambridge: Cambridge University Press, 2008).

40. Reprinted in Ray C. Petry (ed.), *Late Mediaeval Mysticism*, LCC (London: SCM and Philadelphia: Westminster, 1957), pp. 61, 62, and 64-65.

perhaps his fullest work; in them he treats the Song of Songs as an allegory of Christ's love for the Church. He spent eighteen years until his death on these eighty-six sermons. The hymn "Jesus, the Very Thought of Thee," is attributed to Bernard, together with "Jesus, Thou Joy of Loving Hearts" and "O Sacred Head Sore Wounded." Bernard's rich devotional language has substantial theological content. He follows Augustine in understanding the Holy Spirit as proceeding from the Father and the Son; he refuses to isolate the Person and work of the Spirit as the bond of love between the Father and the Son. A Christian believer cannot know the Father or the Holy Spirit without acknowledging the Son (*On Loving God,* and *Sermons on the Song of Songs,* Sermon 20:1).

In *Sermons on the Song of Songs* Bernard expounds God's love as "tender, wise and strong" (Sermon 20:3). Conversely, he urges, "Learn to love him [Christ] tenderly, . . . wisely, to love him with a mighty love" (20:4). He writes: "Delight yourself in Christ. . . . Let the Lord Jesus be to your heart sweet and pleasant" (20:4). Whence does this love arise? "It is the Spirit that quickeneth; the flesh profits nothing" (John 6:63; 20:7). If love is not pure, it is because we "are not as yet capable of perceiving the things which are of the Spirit of God" (20:7).[41] *It is "not without the Spirit that Christ is loved"* (20:1; my italics). He states: "Such devotion . . . is a gift of the Holy Spirit" (20:8).[42] To love purely requires "an assistance so powerful as that of the Holy Spirit. . . . the fullness of the Spirit . . . distinguishes it" (20:9). "I do not fear because I love, and also am loved; nor could I love unless He first loved me" (Sermon 84:6).[43] Union with God (or the wedding of the Bridegroom and Bride) "comes through the Holy Spirit," who is to be approached with awe.[44]

Further, in his comments on the Holy Spirit Bernard admits that superficially Jesus often speaks of the need to know only the Father and the Son. Nevertheless "the Holy Spirit indeed is nothing else but the love and benign goodness of them both [i.e., the Father and the Son]" (*Song of Songs,* Sermon 8: "The Holy Spirit: The Kiss of the Mouth," 8:4). He continues, "When the bride asks for the Kiss, . . . it is the Son whom she approaches. . . . He reveals himself . . . and this revelation through the kiss, that is, through the Holy Spirit, a fact to which St. Paul bears witness. . . . It is by giving the Spirit, through whom he reveals, that he shows us *himself;* he reveals *in* his gift . . . the revelation which is made through the Holy Spirit" (Sermon 8:5). This accords precisely with what is written today by writers as diverse as Karl Barth and Joseph Fison. Like many others, they both insist that the Holy Spirit bears witness not to himself, but *to Christ;* but the revelation of Christ comes about through and *by the Holy Spirit.*

---

41. *Song of Songs,* in Petry (ed.), *Late Mediaeval Mysticism,* p. 72.
42. *Song of Songs,* in Petry (ed.), *Late Mediaeval Mysticism,* p. 72.
43. *Song of Songs,* in Petry (ed.), *Late Mediaeval Mysticism,* p. 77.
44. Burgess, *The Holy Spirit: Mediaeval Roman Catholic and Reformation Traditions,* p. 54.

This cannot but stand in stark contrast to many practices and formulations of the Pentecostal and Charismatic Movement (see in Part III), where too often the goal of prayer, searching, or quest can sometimes be the Holy Spirit rather than Christ. Bernard of Clairvaux is a key writer on the loving graciousness of the "self-effacing" (to use Fison's term) work of the Holy Spirit, whose reality is never doubted, but who does not push Christ from the center of the stage.

Likewise in Sermon 15, Bernard's theme is "The Name of Jesus." But he cites the activity of the Holy Spirit, poured upon the Church at Pentecost, in revealing the centrality of the name of Christ, and of the Trinity as a whole (15:1-3). Elsewhere he admits that we must "attend to these gift-laden visits of the Holy Spirit" (*Song of Songs*, Sermon 17, "On the Ways of the Holy Spirit . . . ," 17:1); we must "let the Holy Spirit always speak" (17:1), but "toward the praise and glory of our Lord Jesus Christ" (17). The Holy Spirit works two operations: in one, "he leads us to *salvation*"; in the other, "he outwardly *endows us* with serviceable gifts" (Sermon 18, "The Two Operations of the Holy Spirit," 18:1). This "double" understanding, by contrast, does reflect affinities with Pentecostals and some in the charismatic renewal. Nevertheless, these operations of the Spirit are not simply "for our own welfare" (18:2). Like Christ, we must "do the will of my Father . . . [with] a love that is enriching and true" (18:5) and "performed to the praise and glory of our Lord Jesus Christ" (18:6). Eighty-six sermons expound these themes further.

On the relation between the Holy Spirit and Christ and on the effects of the work of the Holy Spirit, Bernard's writings are masterly. Only one issue raises a hesitant, partial reservation. Occasionally he speaks of the need for "greater fervour and increased faithfulness" in *seeking* the Holy Spirit *(Sermon on the Lord's Ascension)*. This is a trap which many who seek increased experience of the Spirit find all too seductive, and which Luther would see in the Radical Reformers as undermining his work of grace. It is as if believers have *first to do* what only the Spirit can give, in order to *plead for more* of the Spirit's presence and blessing. We shall note below that for Luther the "radical" or "spiritual" Reformers seemed to undermine, even if unwittingly, the doctrine of justification by grace through *faith alone*. Yet, for the most part, Bernard usually avoids this pitfall, seeing the Spirit's gifts and presence as decision of sovereign grace.

(2) *Hildegard of Bingen* (1098-1179). Hildegard is thought of as an outstanding twelfth-century mystic, notable for her visions, musical compositions, writings, and reforming preaching. At a young age she was sheltered in a small monastery, which became a convent under the Abbess Jutta in about 1113. In 1136 Jutta died, and Hildegard was elected Abbess in her place. In 1141 she began work on her first writing, *Scivias*, which is short for *Scito vias Domini, Know the Ways of the Lord*. She completed part of the work in 1148. Meanwhile c. 1146, at the age of about forty-eight, she wrote to Bernard of Clairvaux to seek his advice. With modesty she described herself as untrained and uneducated. Yet she claimed *prophetic visions*, was writing, and composed music. Was such activity presump-

tuous, she asked Bernard, or should she continue? Bernard gave her encouragement, and her writings were duly approved at the Synod of Trier (1147-48).

In about 1150 Hildegard moved her nuns to a new monastery at Rupertsberg, near Bingen, and her *Scivias* reached completion. Eight years later she began writing *The Book of Life's Merits* and the *Symphony of the Harmony of Celestial Revelations,* and at around sixty years of age she embarked on several preaching tours. In her first journey she traveled along the Maine to Bamberg; her second journey focused on Trier; the third journey followed the Rhine to Cologne. Her preaching was hugely influential.[45] She attacked lax clergy, urged obedience to monastic rules, and became what Atherton calls "a religious, moral, and political adviser to half of Europe."[46]

Hildegard opposed the dualism of the Cathars. By about 1140 they had become a strong sect in Germany, and by 1200 also in France. They claimed purity to the Church, as the name *Cathari* implies, but became widely known as "heretics," not least because of their opposition to Rome, the sacraments, and belief in the resurrection of the dead, and their claims on behalf of themselves. In advance of Pentecostalism, they claimed to have experienced "baptism in the Holy Spirit," often by a laying on of hands. They became a threat to the Roman Church.

Much of Hildegard's theology was based on her *visions.* Hence we may well expect that much of Hildegard's teaching on the Holy Spirit came through *visual imagery, pictures,* and *analogies.* In the Pentecostal and Charismatic Renewal Movement of today, this would often be called *"being given pictures"* of the Spirit's activity. Often she saw God as a bright light, in which the light itself represented the Father; a flash of light as a temporal event represented the Son; and the fire which was in the light and flashes represented the Holy Spirit (*Scivias,* 2:2).[47] She used analogies of flame, a stone, and red burning fire (*Scivias,* 2:2).[48] However, like some traditions of the Charismatic Movement, she added: "the Father is not without the Son, . . . nor the Father without the Son and the Holy Spirit, nor is the Holy Spirit without them, because the three persons are inseparable" (*Scivias,* 2:2).[49] Could we be permitted to wonder whether "charismatic" women, more than men, are especially prone to, or sensitive to, "seeing pictures" of God's action or the Spirit's action? Others may be in a better position to assess this generalization.

Hildegard also sees the Spirit as life-given, not least at the resurrection of Christ (Hildegard, *Scivias,* 2:1). In baptism the Spirit drives out sin and creates

45. See Mark Atherton (ed.), *Hildegard of Bingen: Selected Writings* (London: Penguin, 2001), pp. x-xi and 199-203.

46. Atherton, *Hildegard,* p. x.

47. Hildegard, *Scivias,* 2:2, on light, appears in Atherton, *Hildegard,* p. 14.

48. Hildegard, *Scivias,* in Atherton, *Hildegard,* p. 26.

49. Atherton, *Hildegard,* p. 28.

faith (*Scivias*, 1:6; 3:2). Believers are those who have touched the "fiery tongues" of the Holy Spirit (*Scivias*, 3:9). She sees gifts of the Spirit in biblical terms (*Scivias*, 3:8), but paints a *"picture"* of a building with "seven white marble pillars . . . supporting a round dome of iron on which stands the wisdom of God."[50] How much this is mere imagination must be asked about this and many similar "pictures." Pauline questions about "unintelligibility" may perhaps arise from her two works, *The Unknown Language* and *The Unknown Alphabet*, since these contain *"private languages."* However, if these are not for communication in the public domain, Paul does not disapprove of "private" language in an individual devotional context. In her life-time many regarded her as a *prophet*, as a "Rhineland Sybil," but what are we to make of her allegorical vision of "the cosmic egg"? This perhaps remains open to question. For some, this will seem like a do-it-yourself Revelation of John; for others it will seem to be given from Beyond (Hildegard, *Scivias*, 1:3).[51]

(3) *Richard of St. Victor* (c. 1123-73) entered the Abbey of St. Victor in Paris in the early 1150s, but before then little is known of him, except that he probably came from Scotland. The Abbey had been founded by Anselm's pupil, William of Champeaux, in 1110, and Gilduin was elected Abbot. He was followed by Hugh of St. Victor (d. 1142), who was a theologian and an exegete who wrote commentaries, as well as a contemplative. In his exegesis he underlined the importance of the historical and "literal" sense.[52] On the other hand he also drew on Pseudo-Dionysius. In 1162 Richard became Prior, but Ernisius became Abbot with disastrous consequences for the Abbey. Two years before his death Richard at last became Abbot, after papal intervention. Groves Zinn asserts: "Richard quickly became the chief exponent of Victorine spirituality, . . . a Biblically based, . . . gifted 'specialist' in mysticism."[53] His works included *The Twelve Patriarchs* and *The Mystical Ark*, probably written between 1153 and 1162, and in later years *On the Trinity*. *The Twelve Patriarchs* offers a tropological interpretation of the twelve sons of Jacob in allegorical form. In spite of Zinn's insistence that the tropological interpretation is "not artificial," few today would see why Rachel stands for Reason, and Leah for Affection (Richard, *The Twelve Patriarchs*, ch. 4 and 5).[54] Admittedly Richard begins with Leah's poor eyesight as a historical meaning, but is this why "she is not ashamed to follow the guidance of sensation?" (ch. 5). Richard continues, "The sons of Jacob from Leah are nothing other than ordered affections" (ch. 7).[55]

---

50. Burgess, *The Holy Spirit: Mediaeval Roman Catholic and Reformation Traditions*, p. 94.

51. Atherton, *Hildegard*, "The Cosmic Egg," pp. 89-90.

52. Smalley, *The Bible in the Middle Ages*, pp. 87-106.

53. Groves A. Zinn (ed.), *Richard of St. Victor: The Twelve Patriarchs. The Mystical Book, Book Three of the Trinity*, Classics of Western Spirituality (London: SPCK, 1979), p. 4.

54. Zinn, *Richard*, pp. 57-58.

55. Zinn, *Richard*, pp. 59-60.

Richard acknowledges the *sovereignty of the Holy Spirit*. "The Spirit flows where he wills" (*The Mystical Ark*, book 3:17).[56] Similarly, without Him, I cannot even say "Jesus is Lord" (1 Cor. 12:3) (3:16).[57] In the fifth stage of contemplation *"any joy . . . is the Holy Spirit,"* and his "fruits . . . are charity, joy, patience, long-suffering and goodness (Gal. 5:22). . . . To one 'a word of wisdom through the Spirit, to another a word of knowledge, to another faith, to another the grace of healing, to another the working of miracles, to another prophecy, to another discretion of spirit" (1 Cor. 12:8-10; *The Mystical Ark*, book 3:24).[58] This is *one of the more genuinely "charismatic" of the medieval writers*. Richard's view of the Holy Trinity is partly in the Augustinian tradition. God is "triune in persons, one in substance" (*The Mystical Ark*, book 4:18).[59] He is the Spirit of both the Father and the Son (4:18). His commentators, however, say that his account of the Spirit and the Trinity is more "personal" than Augustine's.[60] Like Augustine, he uses human analogies, but argues that unselfish love between friends reflects the Holy Spirit as love in its supreme form. Bonaventure followed this approach.

In Richard we find one of the nearest approaches to the "spontaneous" gifts of the Spirit regularly defended in most traditions of Pentecostalism and the Charismatic Renewal Movement today. Richard maintains that "in a flash, as it were, and in God's own time comes the purely gratuitous inrush of divine contemplation."[61] One writer suggests that Richard's use of "contemplation" approximates "the mystical" today. Yet for Richard preparation comes first. After years with Leah, Zilpah, and Bilhah, Jacob's fruitful union with Rachel comes at last, with the birth of Joseph and Benjamin. Richard traces the stages of *imagination*: imagination according to reason, reason according to reason, and what is beyond reason. In practice these are six "stages" of contemplation. The fact that Richard provides a *systematic study of modes of contemplation* may suggest that it is less "spontaneous" than we might have supposed (Richard, *The Way to Contemplation: Benjamin*, Prologue and 1–10).[62] He outlines a similar progression in his *Commentary on Joel* in the verse, "I will pour my Spirit on all flesh. . . ." Here to "dream dreams" denotes *ecstasy*, and *"prophecy" the foretelling* of events. Burgess observes, "Ecstasy *(excessus mentis* or *alienatio*, sometimes *ekstasis)* comes from wonder, triggered by a sudden shock of an *unexpected vision* of God" (my italics).[63] Richard finds fertile soil for his

---

56. Zinn, *Richard*, p. 245.

57. Zinn, *Richard*, p. 244.

58. Zinn, *Richard*, p. 257.

59. Zinn, *Richard*, p. 292.

60. Burgess, *The Holy Spirit: Mediaeval Roman Catholic and Reformation Traditions*, p. 67.

61. Petry, *Late Mediaeval Mysticism*, pp. 82-83.

62. Also Petry, *Late Mediaeval Mysticism*, pp. 96-112.

63. Burgess, *The Holy Spirit: Mediaeval Roman Catholic and Reformation Traditions*, p. 67.

flights of imagination in Ezekiel's vision, although this is anchored in the biblical text.[64]

Finally, in *On the Trinity*, Richard asserts, "No person could be wholly deserving of the love of a divine person if he were not in God. . . . Reason proves that a plurality of persons cannot be lacking in the true divinity. . . . God alone is supremely good. God alone, therefore, is to be supremely loved" (*On the Trinity*, 3:2).[65] "True charity demands a plurality of persons; true unchangeability demands co-eternity of persons" (*On the Trinity*, 3:6).[66]

---

64. Part of the Prologue is translated in Fairweather, *A Scholastic Miscellany*, pp. 321-23.

65. In Fairweather, *A Scholastic Miscellany*, pp. 330-31; cf. Zinn, *Richard*, pp. 374-75.

66. Zinn, *Richard*, p. 379.

14

The Later Middle Ages: From Bonaventura and Aquinas
to Julian of Norwich and Walter Hilton

14.1. Bonaventura (Giovanni di Fidanza)

Bonaventura (1221-74) was a prolific writer, whose piety earned him the title
"Doctor Seraphicus" from Rome. He practiced a rigorous asceticism, and he
became Minister General of the Order founded by Francis of Assisi in 1257. He
drew on the Victorines, Peter Lombard, and the mystics for much of his theology. His doctrine of the Trinity broadly follows Augustine, and more specifically that of Richard of St. Victor. The Holy Spirit is Love mingled *(amor
permixtus),* from the Father and the Son.

In 1234 Bonaventura went to study at the University of Paris, where Alexander of Hales was his regent master in the Franciscan convent. He entered the
Franciscan Order in 1243. In 1273 Pope Gregory X appointed him Cardinal
Bishop of Albano. It is said that he died of "ascetic exhaustion."[1] David
Knowles, an eminent medieval specialist, comments: "With St Bonaventura . . .
we reach one of the true summits of mediaeval theology; the Seraphic doctor
who appears the equal of St Thomas in the *Paradiso* of Dante, . . . a younger
contemporary."[2] Knowles adds, "His genius was precocious, even more than
that of St Thomas."[3]

Bonaventura wrote the *Commentary on the Sentences of Peter Lombard,*
which is usually viewed as his most systematic work, and *Itinerarium Mentis in
Deum (Itinerary* [or *Journey*] *of the Mind into God).* His life of St. Francis
shows his admiration for Francis and disdain for "the wisdom of the world."

---

1. Howard Watkin-Jones, *The Holy Spirit in the Mediaeval Church: A Study of Christian
Teaching concerning the Holy Spirit and His Place in the Trinity* (London: Epworth, 1922), p. 137.
2. David Knowles, *The Evolution of Mediaeval Thought* (London: Longmans, 1962), p. 236.
3. Knowles, *The Evolution of Mediaeval Thought,* p. 240.

His portrayal of the "crucified seraph" with six wings represents six stages of illumination by which the human soul *journeys upward toward God.* It is also the progression of Christian wisdom and the way of "the burning seraphic love of the crucified."[4] God is mirrored in the external world, in which he is present. In the sixth stage of his journey the human person may *contemplate God* as a Transcendent Being who is "The 'Esse' of metaphysics and the gracious . . . Trinitarian God of Christian revelation."[5] After the sixth stage, the seventh becomes *mystical,* culminating in *ecstatic love* and transcending the intellect. Here Bonaventura reflects Pseudo-Dionysius by using the language and theology of symbol where words and language run out (*Itinerary of the Mind,* Prologue 3, Ch. 1:4). Experience and contemplation transcend even symbol. "Contemplative love follows the triple hierarchical modes of purification, illumination, and perfection, or consummate union" (*Itinerary,* 1:7). Bonaventura concludes, "The Holy Ghost (Spirit) effects the soul's re-creation in the image of the Trinity."[6]

God's revelation of himself in creation is further expressed by the concept of *vestigia,* "vestiges, *footprints, or traces*" (Bonaventura, *Itinerary of the Mind,* 1:2). Nevertheless "Prayer is . . . the source and origin of every upward progress that has God for his goal" (*Itinerary,* 1:1). Here Bonaventura explicitly appeals to Dionysius's Mystical Theology. He continues: "By so praying we are led to discern the degrees of the soul's ascent to God. . . . this universe is a ladder whereby we may ascend to God, since among these things (of the universe) some are God's footprints *(vestigia),* some God's image, some corporeal, some spiritual" (*Itinerary,* 1:2).[7] Untroubled contemplation is "a garden of delights" (1:7). He adds, "In our quest of God [we] must first leave aside such sins as deform nature" (1:8). The journey takes us through three points of view — "contemplation, . . . faith, . . . reason . . . — three levels of reality" (1:11-13). Finally, "beyond all human estimation" we discover in God "the beauty of things in respect of their variety of light, figure, and colour . . . the plenitude of things" (1:14).[8]

After the sixth stage, by contrast, the "soul was led to raise its gaze above and beyond itself, seeking, as it were, God's countenance, . . . God in his own reflected light, . . . to contemplate the fruit of the highest principle of all, and Jesus Christ, the Mediator of God and man. Then shall it have contact with spiritual things. . . . By means of Jesus Christ, the Way, the Door, the Ladder, shall their transition be effected, for he is, as it were, the seat of mercy . . ." (*Itinerary,*

---

4. Ray C. Petry (ed.), *Late Mediaeval Mysticism,* LCC (London: SCM, and Philadelphia: Westminster, 1957), p. 127.

5. Petry (ed.), *Late Mediaeval Mysticism,* p. 128.

6. Petry (ed.), *Late Mediaeval Mysticism,* p. 129.

7. The English text appears in Petry (ed.), *Late Mediaeval Mysticism,* pp. 132-41; 1:2 occurs on p. 133.

8. Petry (ed.), *Late Mediaeval Mysticism,* p. 137.

7:1).[9] The desire for this *vision* "comes to him only whose being is inflamed by the fire of the Holy Spirit sent by Christ upon the earth. Hence it is that the 'hidden things' of God were revealed, as the apostle says, by the Holy Ghost" (1 Cor. 2:10; *Itinerary,* 7:4). We must "concentrate on God's gift to man, his Holy Spirit" (7:5). Bonaventura concludes: "Let us, with Christ crucified, pass from this world to the Father" (7:6).

The dimension of epistemology, or human knowing, occurs also in Bonaventura's *Disputed Questions concerning Christ's Knowledge.*[10] In this work he describes knowledge not as bare cognition, but as knowledge *accompanied by* "*eternal light,*" *giving certitude* "in so far as it is the image of God. . . . Certitude of sense is not the same as that of understanding" (3:11). David Knowles argues that Bonaventura has a duality of methods concerning knowledge. At the level of sense perception, he adopts Aristotle's theory of abstraction, by which the object of sense perception is "purified" by abstraction for entry into the intelligence. But at another level, *understanding entails correspondence with reality* by virtue of an *innate light* which is a reflection or image of divine ideas. This light provides the criterion of truth *(regula veritatis).* Hence while there is uncertain knowledge of things, since much depends on the *human* soul, we can have *certain knowledge* of unintelligible truth, for *God* is involved in this knowledge.[11]

There can be little doubt that on the whole *Itinerary of the Mind into God* is Christ-centered, and the goal of the journey is possible because of Christ's work as Mediator. Yet knowledge of God comes through divine Wisdom, *mediated by the Holy Spirit.* Further, Bonaventura emphasized the role of the Day of Pentecost as the birthday of the Church, and stressed the power of the Spirit for mission. However, it is surprising that Burgess calls Bonaventura's use of Eph. 4:11-12 a distribution of "charismatic gifts," since these gifts include *apostleship* and its work of pastor and *teacher,* as well as "prophets" and others.[12] He does not seem to stress the Spirit in the first part of the six stages of advance. But he does speak of the Holy Spirit's sevenfold grace (Bonaventura, *The Tree of Life,* 49), and his work in the *anointing of Christ.* He describes Francis as a person of the Spirit, who has the spirit of prophecy (*The Life of Saint Francis,* 3:6 and 12:12). All this is thoroughly based on the unity of the Holy Trinity. Again the pattern of the Holy Spirit's action is "*the Love with which the Father loves the Son*" (Bonaventura, *Commentary on the Sentences of Peter Lombard,* 11:1; my italics).[13]

9. Petry (ed.), *Late Mediaeval Mysticism,* p. 139.

10. English translation, in part, in Eugene R. Fairweather (ed.), *A Scholastic Miscellany: Anselm to Ockham* (London: SCM, and Philadelphia: Westminster, 1956), pp. 379-401.

11. Knowles, *The Evolution of Mediaeval Thought,* p. 241.

12. Stanley M. Burgess, *The Holy Spirit: Mediaeval Roman Catholic and Reformation Traditions* (Peabody, MA: Hendrickson, 1997), p. 73.

13. Watkin-Jones, *The Holy Spirit in the Mediaeval Church,* p. 139.

14.2. Thomas Aquinas

Thomas Aquinas (c. 1225-74) is best known for his magisterial *Summa Theologiae,* or summary of Christian teaching. He was extremely hard-working, and his writings are nothing short of monumental. Even today Brian Davies comments, "Aquinas has much to offer people who are anxious to think and understand."[14] He was concerned to communicate ideas, but was also committed to prayer, preaching, poverty, and austerity. Davies also observes, "His writings are clearly those of one in love with God and the Word Incarnate."[15]

Thomas Aquinas was born in Aquino, which was between Rome and Naples. From early years he entered a Benedictine monastery, studying both biblical books and classical texts. He then entered the newly founded University of Naples (c. 1239), where his studies included philosophy and Aristotle, and Greek. In c. 1242, against the wishes of his family, he joined the Dominican Order of friars, who were mendicants. Thomas valued most of all Dominican teaching and preaching. His religious superiors sent him to Rome, and then in c. 1244 to Paris. In 1248 he studied further under Albert the Great in Cologne. In 1256 he was licensed to teach in Paris as Professor of Theology.

Thomas, therefore, provides a link between the earlier era of education in the monasteries and the later medieval period of education in the newly founded universities of Paris and Oxford. He commented on the *Sentences* [summaries of doctrine] *of Peter Lombard,* and in 1259 lectured on the Bible and began a series of biblical commentaries, including some on the Pauline epistles and the Gospels. In 1261 he was again recalled to Rome, where he finished writing his book on apologetics, *Summa contra Gentiles,* and other works. At this point he began work on his classic *magnum opus, Summa Theologiae,* composed from c. 1266. This is his major achievement: an encyclopedic study of theology. Part 1 of the *Summa* deals with God as the source of all and as Trinity. Part 2 concerns the way of humanity to its source and goal, including sin and the Fall, virtues and vices, and law and grace. Part 3 has to do with Christ as Redeemer, and the way back to God. The *Summa* remains unfinished. The year before his death, Thomas suffered either a stroke or nervous exhaustion from overwork. The sixty volumes in Latin and English of the Blackfriars edition (1963) provide an analysis of each part and volume on the back of the dust jacket.

On the subject of the Holy Spirit, Thomas considers the Holy Trinity in vols. 6–7 of the Blackfriars edition (*Prima Pars* [part 1], *Quaestiones* 27-43). Here his teaching may be thought of as focusing on two main issues: first, does the Holy Spirit *proceed from the Father and the Son?* Second, may we refer to the *Holy Spirit as "Love"?* The questions are divided into "articles." As usual,

---

14. Brian Davies, *The Thought of Thomas Aquinas* (Oxford: Clarendon, 1992), p. 20.
15. Davies, *Thomas Aquinas,* p. 15.

Thomas generally includes under each article up to about six or seven "Objections" to what he proposes; then usually his "Replies" to the Objections, often beginning "I answer that."

In part 1 (Pars Prima) Qu. 36, Aquinas considers whether the name "Holy Spirit" is genuinely a proper name for a person of the Trinity. He answers "yes," insofar as Scripture warrants it. "There are those who bear witness in heaven, the Father, the Word and the Holy Spirit" (1 John 5:7). This is confirmed by Augustine in On the Trinity, 7:4 (Qu. 36, Art. 1, Reply). However, he adds, one of the two processions in God, "the procession of love," has "no name of its own" (Qu. 36, Art. 1, Reply). In Qu. 36, Art. 2, Thomas concludes: "The Holy Spirit is from the Father and the Son, not made, not created, not begotten, but proceeding" (Qu. 36, Art. 2, Reply; my italics). However, he seeks to formulate a compromise with the Eastern Church. The difference from the West is only one of terminology, not content or substance. "Procession" is used, for example, of "origin" of any kind. A line "proceeds" from a point, "a ray from the sun, a stream from a source" (Qu. 36, Art. 2, Reply). Subsequent Councils of the Church have not implied that an earlier formulation was wrong (Art. 1, Reply to Obj. 2). Articles 3 and 4 expand on this.

In part 1a, Qu. 37, Thomas considers the Holy Spirit as love. Thomas may become unduly technical for today's readers. But we shall summarize his main point. He writes, "The name Love of God can be taken essentially and personally. If taken personally, it is the proper name of the Holy Spirit, as Word is the proper name of the Son" (Qu. 37, Art. 1, Reply). We speak of the Word in three senses, as Karl Barth has urged: as Jesus Christ, as Scripture, and as preaching. Thomas adds a stress on mutuality with the one who receives this Love. Brian Davies explains that "His will receives 'a kind of imprint' of 'the reality loved,' and 'the object loved is present in the lover.'"[16] This accurately paraphrases a lengthy sentence in Thomas, which concludes: "The thing loved is in the lover" (Qu. 37, Art. 1, Reply). He expresses this further in Article 2.

Aquinas further considers God's "giving" of the Holy Spirit in Qu. 38. The word "gift" implies "an aptitude (or capacity) for being given. . . . It would not be given by anyone, unless it was his to give. . . . This must be given it from above. . . . Thus a divine person can 'be given,' and be a 'gift'" (part 1a, Qu. 38, Art. 1, Reply). In Article 2, Aquinas insists, "Gift, taken personally, . . . is the proper name of the Holy Spirit." He asserts: "Gift is properly an unreturnable giving, . . . a gratuitous donation. . . . The Holy Spirit proceeds as love . . . as the first gift (part 1a, Qu. 38, Art. 2, Reply; my italics). Thomas cites Augustine's On the Trinity, 15:26: "By the gift which is the Holy Spirit many particular gifts are portioned out to the members of Christ." None of the gifts of the Spirit can "be called a gift of man, but the gift of God" (Art. 2, Reply to Obj. 3).

---

16. Davies, Thomas Aquinas, p. 206.

In the remaining material of the *Summa Theologiae* Thomas includes several other sections which engage with the *gifts and work of the Holy Spirit*. In *Pars Prima Secundae,* Qu. 28, Arts. 1-7 (vol. 19 of the Blackfriars edition), he discusses the relation of the gifts of the Spirit to virtues or habits of action. In Qu. 70, Arts. 1-3, Thomas considers "the fruit of the Holy Spirit" (Gal. 5:22-23). In *Pars Secunda Secundae,* Qu. 171-73 (vol. 45 of the Blackfriars edition), he discusses the gift, nature, and mode of *prophecy.* In Qu. 176 he considers the grace of the *tongues,* and in Qu. 178, the grace of *miracles.* Thomas provides a general consideration of virtue, and considers this in relation to "gifts" of the Spirit in Qu. 68. He declares that virtue denotes some "perfection of a power" (Qu. 55, Art. 1), or "a good quality of mind by which one lives righteously" (Qu. 55, Art. 4). This denotes what modern philosophers would call "dispositions" or abilities; tendencies or capacities to act in relevant situations. For Aquinas "virtue is a *habitus* which is always for good (Qu. 55, Art. 4). Virtues may be *intellectual* virtues, *practical* intellect, *understanding (intellectus), wisdom (sapientia),* and *prudence (prudentia)* (Qu. 57, Arts. 2 and 4) or *moral* virtues (Qu. 58, Arts. 1-2).

As Gregory stated, "The gift of the Holy Spirit, by entering into the soul, endows it with prudence, temperance, justice, fortitude" (Gregory, *Moralia,* 2:26). In Holy Writ, according to Isa. 11:2-3, virtues are given "that we may do good works, but the gifts [are given] in order to conform us to Christ" (Qu. 68, Art. 1, Reply). To be conformed to Christ requires such virtues as humility and meekness: "I am meek and humble of heart" (Matt. 11:29). First, the gifts of the Spirit to Christ include "wisdom and understanding" (Isa. 11:1-2; Qu. 68, Art. 1). *The Holy Spirit not only gives exceptional gifts but habits of mind that nourish everyday qualities of goodness.* The gifts of the Spirit include the sevenfold gifts given to Christ, and will endure even in heaven (Qu. 68, Arts. 5-6).

In Qu. 70 Thomas turns to *"the fruit of the Holy Spirit"* in Gal. 5:22-23. "Fruit," he asserts, "is the product of a plant when it comes to perfection; . . . the fruit of the Holy Spirit, as of a divine creed" (Art. 1). As Ambrose commented, "They refresh those that have them [the fruit] with a holy and genuine delight" (Ambrose, *Paradise,* 13; Aquinas, *Summa,* Qu. 70, Art. 1, Reply to Obj. 2). Thomas adds: "Among the fruits of the Holy Spirit, we reckon 'charity' wherever the Holy Spirit is given in a special manner . . . since He Himself is love," the highest (Qu. 70, Art. 3; Rom. 5:5). The result of love is joy, and the reflection of joy is peace. "'Peace' is given in the third place" (Art. 3). Then goodness, meekness, and the other virtues follow. The fruit of the Spirit implies that "the Holy Spirit moves in the human mind to that which is in accord with reason, or rather to that which surpasses reason; whereas the fleshly . . . draws man to sensible [of the senses] goods which are beneath him" (Qu. 70, Art. 4).

On Paul's *list of gifts in 1 Cor. 12:8-10,* "utterance of wisdom" and "utterance of knowledge" relate to part 2, Qu. 177, on the grace of using words. Thomas stresses that the gifts are for the benefit of others and the whole Church. He declares, "The gratuitous graces are given for the profit of others. . . . A man speaks so as to be understood, . . . to instruct the intellect, . . . 'to teach'; to move the affections to 'sway' his hearers" (Art. 1). In certain cases, however, to speak "privately" is appropriate (Art. 2). Thomas considers "the grace of miracles" in Qu. 178. He agrees that the word uttered needs to be confirmed "by the working of miracles" (Qu. 178, Art. 1). He quotes Mark 16:20, "confirming the word with signs that followed." But he adds a warning: "some miracles are not true, but imaginary deeds; . . . they delude man" (Art. 2).

Thomas discusses the gift of "prophecy," arguing that prophetic knowledge "differs from perfect knowledge, which we will have in heaven . . . when [prophecy] is made void (1 Cor. 13:10)" (Qu. 173, Art. 1). He adds, "Prophetic vision is not the vision of the very essence of God," and cites Dionysius as seeing by images or mirrors. Prophets may predict from "the book of God's foreknowledge" (Qu. 173, Art. 1, Reply to Obj. 1). Moreover, "Prophetic knowledge pertains most of all to the intellect" (Art. 2). Yet there are exceptions to prophecy involving natural reflection. Thomas writes, "Prophetic revelation takes place in four forms, namely by the infusion of an intelligible light, by the infusion of intelligible species, by . . . pictures of the imagination, and by the natural presentation of sensible images" (Qu. 173, Art. 3). This suggests two comments. First, Thomas does not appear to address the question of *how we know*. Can we know whether what the imagination, or even analogy or pictures, may suggest appears to be *true*. Second, it implies the view that he comments on in 1 Thess. 5:19-20, namely, that *preaching* comes under the usual scope of *prophecy*, while "prophecy" in the popular sense comes under *"exceptional"* examples. He quotes Paul: "The spirit of the prophets is subject to the prophets" (Art. 3, Reply to Obj. 4). Genuine prophecy, he concludes, comes "not from oneself," but from the Holy Spirit (Art. 4).

Finally, under "gifts," Thomas discusses "the grace of tongues" in Qu. 176. He sees the original gift in the New Testament as given in order to preach the faith *"throughout the whole world . . . everywhere"* (Art. 1, my italics). It is a *missionary* vehicle. But "the gift of prophecy surpasses the gift of tongues" (Art. 2). This is because it signifies "'an intelligible truth.' . . . Augustine compares the gift of tongues to an imaginary vision, but prophecy is 'more profitable'" (1 Cor. 14:7-14, 23; Art. 2).

The long sections on virtues and gifts should not obscure the main thrust: the Holy Spirit, as in Augustine, is the bond of love between God the Father and God the Son, and this sets the pattern for *amicitia*, "bonding," which is more but not less than friendship (Qu. 24, Art. 2). The Holy Spirit is mutual love *(amor unitivus duorum)* or *nexus* ("bond") between two persons (Aquinas, *Summa contra Gentiles*, part 4, Qu. 21).[17] To Aquinas, this also implies the

17. Cf. Watkin-Jones, *The Holy Spirit in the Mediaeval Church*, pp. 165-66.

Personhood of the Holy Spirit; as a Person he is one of the three Persons of the Holy Trinity.

14.3. Mystics of the Fourteenth and Fifteenth Centuries: Catherine of Siena and Julian of Norwich

(1) *Catherine of Siena* (1347-80, Caterina di Giacomo di Benincasa). Catherine was remarkable in a variety of ways. She was the twenty-fourth of twenty-five children, born into a poor but devout Catholic family. At seven she vowed her life to God, and at fifteen she cut off her hair in defiance of pressure to marry. At eighteen she became a Dominican nun, and began to live in solitude and silence, leaving her room only for Mass. At twenty-one, however, in 1368, she believed that she had been mystically espoused to Christ. She gave herself to the service of the poor and the sick, serving as a nurse in homes and hospitals. Her mystical experiences became more frequent, and she assumed virtual abstinence from food and sleep. After two years she experienced a "mystical death" in which her body seemed lifeless while her inner self experienced ecstatic union with God. After intervening in serious political affairs both in correspondence and often personally by travel, in 1377 she underwent a still more significant mystical experience. This led to her writing her *Dialogue* (c. 1370-77). She died in 1380 at the age of thirty-three. In 1461 she was declared a Doctor of the Church.

Like Hildegard, Catherine used pictures, images, and metaphors to portray her life with God. This "involved the use of *metaphor. . . . Ladders, castles and dark nights* — all have been employed as ways of describing the indescribable. . . . Catherine adopts the metaphor of a *'bridge'* . . . as . . . the way to heaven" (my italics).[18] She sees the bridge "from heaven to earth. . . . The bridge has three stairs. . . . My Son's nailed feet [God is the speaker] are a stair by which you can climb to his side, where you will see revealed his most innermost heart. . . . The soul . . . is herself filled to overflowing with love. . . . It was raised up when my Son was lifted up on the wood of the most holy cross" (*Dialogue,* 8-11, 10). The bridge, she continues, has walls "moistened . . . with his blood. That is, his Blood has united with the mortar of divinity . . . and with the fire of love. . . . 'How was heaven opened? With the key of his Blood, so that you see that the bridge is walled and roofed with Mercy'" (*Dialogue,* 11). To go under the bridge, rather than over it, cannot be done "without drowning."

Later in the *Dialogue Catherine speaks of the Holy Spirit, who reproves the world.* She begins: "There are three reproofs. One was given when the Holy

---

18. Richard J. Foster and James B. Smith (eds.), *Devotional Classics: Selected Readings* (San Francisco: Harper, rev. ed. 1990), p. 264; cf. pp. 264-70 for further excerpts from *The Dialogue.*

Spirit came upon the disciples, who . . . received the plenitude of the Holy
Spirit. . . . Then the Holy Spirit, who is one with Me and my Son, reproved the
world by the mouth of the Apostles, with the doctrine of My truth" (Catherine,
Dialogue, 20). The second reproof takes place "at the extremity of death, when
My justice will cry to them, 'Rise . . . and come to judgment'" (20). The third
"reproof" relates also to the Day of Judgment and exposes self-deception (*Dialogue*, 23). Meanwhile even those who cross the bridge may be imperfect in love.
Yet: "I love you of *grace*, and not because I *owe* you My love" (*Dialogue*, 42, my
italics).

In one very important sense, Catherine is a *mystic*. She envisages God as
declaring: "Oh, best-beloved, dearest and sweetest daughter, my spouse, rise out
of yourself" (*ekstasis;* Catherine, *Treatise on Prayer*, 18). But she also stresses that
"the eye of the intellect, with the light of the holy faith, . . . is the heart of the
Blood of the Immaculate Lamb" (18). Even those who reach the third stage of
perfection "in the sweet light" also enjoy its gift of *reason* (*Treatise on Prayer*,
20). We may venture to repeat the question that we made about Hildegard: is it
because these two mystics were women that one can count a dozen metaphors
or pictures in a short span of writing? It is not surprising that many of the major Reformers felt unsettled about medieval theology, even at its best; for
Catherine also declares, "The whole of your faith is founded on *obedience*" (*A
Treatise on Obedience*, 2; my italics). Nevertheless, she also stresses the work of
Christ on the cross. She counsels: "Walk by the doctrine of My Word. . . . So
perfectly did He [Christ] repair it (obedience) that no matter how a man may
have spoiled his key [obedience] by his free will, assisted by his grace, he may
repair it" (2).

On the Holy Trinity, Catherine simply follows Augustine and Aquinas in
affirming the procession of the Holy Spirit from God the Father and the Son
(*Dialogue*, 78). She was intensely loyal to the Papacy and the Church. In biblical
terms she makes much of Pentecost in Acts, and appeals for her mystical experiences to Paul's "visions and revelations," and of his being "caught up to the
third heaven — whether in the body or out of the body I do not know" (2 Cor.
12:1-4; *Dialogue*, 83). This is even though Paul seems to set little store by it,
deeming it ironically among those items concerning which "he is a fool to
boast."

Catherine relishes metaphors and pictures, in spite of her similar emphasis
on reason. The bridge may be her most decisive one, but she sees the Holy Trinity as "a deep sea," as "the craftsman," and as light, a fire, a mirror, and flowing
water (*Dialogue*, 167). We may simply speculate whether her "mystical death"
was comparable with the experience of "being slain in the Spirit" in the "Third
Wave" of the Renewal Movement; or, more specifically, in the "Toronto Blessing." We discuss this explicitly in Part III, Chapter 22. She certainly prayed for
and cultivated ecstatic experiences. Her language about the Father as a table,

the Son as food, and the Holy Spirit as "servant and waiter," as well as mother (*Dialogue,* 141), has hints of the modern charismatic hymn "The Servant King." The Spirit is seen as captain of a ship which sails to the port of salvation (*Dialogue,* 158). In her active work of ministry to the sick and poor, and of healing the shocking division within the Western, Roman Church, she appeals to the inspiration of the Holy Spirit. She was valued as a prophet, especially by Pope Gregory XI.

If we include her use of imagination, pictures, and metaphors, as well as her sense of intimacy with God, Catherine appears to anticipate much in the Charismatic Renewal Movement. But her faith also involved extreme asceticism and absolute loyalty to the Pope. In Catherine's call, no one can doubt her devotion and the centrality of Christ crucified and the cross. Indeed, the marked difference from what is often claimed about *some* "Pentecostal" traditions today is that, however much she appeals to the Holy Spirit, without doubt the crucified Christ and God the Father remain no less prominent than the Spirit. In Part III we consider the protest of several writers today, including Tom Smail, about this tendency among some involved in "Third Wave" Renewal.

(2) *Julian of Norwich* (1342-1416). Julian was a Benedictine nun who lived as an anchoress, a solitary who had withdrawn from the world, to devote her life solely to contemplation of God. The Anchorite order is said to have originated in the eleventh century. Her solitary room was situated in the churchyard of St. Julian in Norwich. Her spiritual writings constituted an account of sixteen revelations of Christ, called *Revelations of Divine Love* or *Showings.* [19] These revelations exist in a Shorter and Longer version. The Short Text is said to have been written soon after the occurrence of the revelations in May 1373 at thirty years of age (cf. Elizabeth Spearing, Short Text, 2, in the note below). The Long Text was not finished until after 1393. Presumably in retrospect in her fifties, this includes an account of certain visions which she has omitted from the Short Text, probably because she did not consider that she had fully understood them at the time.

The main focus of the visions concerns the sufferings of Christ, and Julian's participation in them. Almost reflecting the mystical elaboration of the times, Julian writes: "God was showing in spiritual sight, . . . the bodily sight of the plentiful bleeding from Christ's head. . . . The great drops fell down from under the crown of thorns. . . . as they came out they were dark red, for the blood was very thick . . ." (*Revelations,* 7, Long Text, Penguin ed., pp. 50-51). She firmly believed in the Augustinian approach to the Trinity. Her two most distinctive and

---

19. Julian of Norwich, *Revelations of Divine Love,* trans. Elizabeth Spearing (London: Penguin, 1998), provides a translation for today. Cf. also Grace Jantzen, *Julian of Norwich: Mystic and Theologian* (London: SPCK, 2000), on Julian's background, content, theologies, and implications for feminism and other themes or movements.

well-known "revelations," however, are: first, "*I will make all things well;* I shall make all things well . . . ; I can make all things well" (*Revelations*, 15; Penguin ed. p. 23); and (2) "*Our Saviour is our true mother* in whom we are eternally born, and by whom we shall always be enclosed" (*Revelations,* 57; Long Text, p. 136; my italics). Julian writes: "the second Person [of the Trinity] is mother of our essential being . . . , for in our Mother Christ, we profit and grow" (*Revelations,* 58, Long Text, p. 137). The Church is "her loved bride" (58).

This causes perhaps complications for a doctrine of the Holy Trinity, which supposedly reflects or expresses "fatherhood, motherhood and lordship," ascribed respectively to the Father, the Son, and the Holy Spirit, and Christ is also "his own son" (*Revelations* 58, Long Text). We must live in the realm of images rather than of propositions. Julian follows Augustine in seeing the Spirit most characteristically as *love.* She writes, "God Almighty is our father by nature; God all wisdom (Christ) is our mother by nature; along with the love and goodness of the Holy Spirit (Ghost)" (*Revelations,* 58). She adds, "grace works with mercy, . . . a work which belongs to the third Person, the Holy (Spirit) Ghost" (*Revelations,* 58, Long Text). Often the Holy Spirit is "Lord" (*Revelations,* 48, Long Text), having pity and compassion. Yet, as with most of the later Church Fathers, *the work of the Trinity is inseparable.* She writes, "Where Jesus appears, the blessed Trinity is understood" (4). However, the inspiration of prayer remains a special work of the Holy Spirit (*Revelations,* 41, Long Text, p. 106).

Julian is often associated with *Margery Kempe* (c. 1373-1458), from King's Lynne, also in Norfolk, who came to consult her for advice. Margery Kempe also experienced mystical visions, but these were sometimes accompanied by outbursts of emotion and tears, which Julian assured her were a sign of the Holy Spirit. She was more at odds with the institutional church than Julian, especially for *her "self-proclaimed" status as a prophet* and her abandonment of her husband and fourteen children to go on pilgrimage to Jerusalem and to Rome. Her retrospective account of her visions, which includes visions of devils and evil forces, can be found in *The Book of Margery Kempe.*[20] She raises more questions than Julian about the status of a "self-proclaimed" prophet, as some have called her.

14.4. Walter Hilton and *The Cloud of Unknowing*

The Cloud of Unknowing (c. 1390-95) is an anonymous book of contemplative prayer, some suggest by a Carthusian monk, which reflects affinities with the

---

20. Lynn Staley (ed.), *The Book of Margery Kempe, book 1* (Kalamazoo, MI: Medieval Institute, 1996); and John H. Arnold and Katherine J. Lewis, *Companion to the Book of Margery Kempe* (Cambridge: Brewer, 2004).

mystical theology of *Walter Hilton* (c. 1343-96). The title comes from the writings of Pseudo-Dionysius, in his negative or "apophatic" theology, in which God is seen as beyond words. Walter Hilton was a contemporary mystical theologian who wrote especially on the nature of contemplation. In spite of his mystical tendencies, he believed that the earlier mystic Richard Rolle (d. 1349) had gone too far in his "enthusiasm," allowing some common ground with John Wycliffe's Lollards. In this respect he expressed similar attitudes to those of *The Cloud of Unknowing.* Some have speculated that the *Cloud's* reference to "another man" might perhaps denote Walter Hilton.

Hilton's book *The Scale of Perfection* exercised huge influence in the fifteenth century. Perhaps surprisingly the first section is written to an ex-anchoress, to correct and modify her notion of mystical contemplation and to avoid such distortions as a self-constructed, "perverted" doctrine of the Holy Trinity.

Walter Hilton addresses the first part of *The Scale of Perfection* to a "Spiritual Sister in Christ Jesus," and recognizes her "travailing with all the power of your soul to fulfil . . . likeness and seeming." She is "enclosed from the inordinate loves and fears of earthly things" (*The Scale of Perfection,* ch. 1). The second chapter expounds Gregory's distinction between the "active" and the "contemplative" life. Hilton observes, "Contemplative life consists in perfect love and charity . . . and knowledge of God" (ch. 3). Instead there are "three parts" of the contemplative life: "knowing God," which includes "study in holy Scripture, . . . not by the special gift of the Holy Spirit" (ch. 4). The "second part of contemplations lies principally in affection," of which there are two levels (ch. 5). The "higher" includes praying the Pater Noster and other prayers and hymns (ch. 7). "The third sort" includes "both . . . knowing and affecting" (ch. 8), with "burning love" (ch. 9). Paul speaks of it when he says, "we see as in a glass the glory of our Lord, and are changed . . . from glory to glory" (2 Cor. 3:18). Thus far Hilton establishes his credentials as a mystic.

Nevertheless in chapter 10 Hilton recognizes that "visions or revelations or any manner of spirit in body appearing or imagining," such as seeing a fire glowing, "may be good . . . or may be deceivable, wrought by a wicked angel" (*The Scale of Perfection,* ch. 10). Satan may appear as an angel of light, and the devil create counterfeit visions and imaginings. How can we know, he asks, which is which (ch. 11)? (This issue was addressed and probably overly pressed in one direction by Charles Hodge in the nineteenth century; but it seems insufficiently considered today in the other direction by some in the Renewal Movement, in spite of formal recognition of false prophecy.) In spite of the problem, Hilton continues, we should not give up on prayer, or on seeking to know and to love God. But we must pray "with greater diligence in prayer" (ch. 12). Almost as if he anticipated Margery Kempe, Hilton asserts: "Though all the devils of hell appeared in bodily shapes, . . . yet believe them not" (ch. 16). What is needed in contemplation is "humility, firm faith, and an entire strong will and purpose" (ch. 18). He concludes: "Draw all that you see and intend within the truth of the holy church. . . . Do all in the name of the Lord Jesus Christ" (ch. 18; cf. 1 Cor. 10:31).

In *The Scale of Perfection,* part 2, Hilton argues that everyone should understand the measure of his gift. Paul tells us that Christians have a particular gift appropriate for them (ch. 3). The gifted person must exercise humility, not confusion by making extravagant claims. In part 3 he returns to the nature of contemplation. *To desire Christ with a clean heart,* he urges, *is more important than "visions, . . . revelations of angels, . . . songs and sounds to the ear,* all tastes and smellings, . . . all the joys of heaven, . . . *without desire to my Lord Jesus Christ"* (*The Scale of Perfection,* part 3, ch. 3, sect. 2). Part 3, chapters 4–8 expand on the deceptiveness and consequences of sin, including "spiritual sins." The Second Book of *The Scale of Perfection* continues the theme of "reforming in faith and feeling" (book 2, part 2, ch. 1). *Hilton also warns us that a person cannot "suddenly" become "high in grace."* In book 2, part 3, chapter 2, he expounds "how God opens the inner eye of the soul," replacing a false mysticism with true mysticism.

All these injunctions are relevant both to Pentecostal experience and to the Renewal Movement today. Hilton encourages intimacy with God, but places devotion to Christ high above the seeking of visions, prophecy, or "event" experiences. He affirms renewal and contemplation of God, but warns his readers against an arbitrary and untested approach to visions, images, analogies, color, and all the kinds of phenomena that may or may not be authentic in Julian and Hildegard. His background was that of training in the law, and he rejects a version of mysticism that is overly emotional or reflects fuzzy thinking.

The Cloud of Unknowing shares with Hilton a warning against pride and arrogance in anyone who receives "revelations." Chapter 2 enjoins meekness: "What have you merited, thus to be called by our Lord?" It is all "by grace. . . . He is a jealous lover." On the other hand, there are affinities with Pseudo-Dionysius which are not the same as those in Hilton: "Of God Himself can no man think. . . . He may be well loved, but *not thought.* By love he may be got and held, but *by thought, never"* (ch. 6; my italics). On the other hand, the anonymous writer declares, "I would that you weigh each thought and each stirring" (ch. 11). Even if we cannot grasp *God* by thought, we may measure *experience* by thought, and here Hilton would probably agree. Meekness is "a true knowing and feeling of a man's self" (ch. 13). Pride and curiosity can "deceive," and cause some to "leave the common doctrine . . . of the Church" (ch. 56). Almost at the end, the writer claims that "Dennis" (Pseudo-Dionysius) affirms "all that I have said": "the most goodly knowing of God is that which is known by unknowing" (ch. 70). This theology of negation, we may note, is a long way from Eberhard

Jüngel's theme that Christ and the cross make God "thinkable" and "conceivable."[21] We consider this in Part III.

14.5. The Spanish Mystics: Teresa of Avila and John of the Cross

(1) *Teresa of Avila* (1515-82). Strictly, it would take us beyond the Middle Ages (often conventionally dated 500-1500) to consider *Teresa of Avila* and her contemporary and colleague, *John of the Cross*. But the sixteenth-century Spanish mystics continue the broad "mystical" approach, although with a few reforming safeguards. Teresa, a Spanish Carmelite nun, like many women mystics, not only speaks of a journey of a soul but also does so often through autobiography and symbols or "pictures." In 1555 she experienced something like "a second conversion," supposedly to a life of "perfection." Whether this in any way corresponds with the Pentecostal or sometimes also charismatic "baptism in the Spirit," others must judge. By contrast, a radically ascetic life followed this experience. In 1562 she began to write *The Way of Perfection*. Like Hildegard and Julian, she uses pictures and allegories.

Teresa's most famous work is *Interior Castle,* which depicts the journey of the soul outside the castle, passing through "assaults of the devils" (Teresa, *Interior Castle,* 1:13). As the journey and ascent proceed, the soul can experience "several kinds of raptures" (ch. 4:2), which the recipient may be "incapable of describing" (4:6). This is not an "imaginary vision" (4:11), but "a supreme state of ecstasy" (4:18). Finally, in the seventh stage, "the three Persons of the most Blessed Trinity reveal themselves. . . . The three Persons are distinct from one another . . . [but] of one substance, . . . one God" (*The Seventh Mansion,* 1:9). Teresa writes, "He [Christ] and the Father and the Holy Spirit will come and make their abode with the soul" (7:1:9).

Teresa regularly elaborates the imagery of the castle. Each mansion or level "contains many rooms, more rooms, . . . with fair garden fountains, and labyrinths, besides other things: . . . delightful" *(Epilogue)*. But she warns the reader, "You cannot enter all the mansions by your own power" *(Epilogue)*. Her writings are Christ-centered, with relatively little reference to the Spirit, and in this respect she differs from a minority in the Pentecostal and Renewal Movements. But like Hildegard and Catherine of Siena, she made much of *"pictures,"* metaphors, imagery, symbols, and analogies to convey what many would call "revelation," and others might call "imagination." Perhaps these were mixed, sometimes conveying revelation through imagination; but during those years, the Bible and the Church could constrain the limits of what many regarded as truth.

---

21. Eberhard Jüngel, *God as the Mystery of the World* (Edinburgh: T&T Clark, 1983), pp. 111-22 and 220-32.

(2) *John of the Cross* (1542-91). John was ordained priest in 1567, the same year as he met Teresa. They experienced commonality together, and she put him in charge of her Carmelite Order. John established several more orders, and urged reform within the Catholic tradition. His best-known work is *The Dark Night of the Soul*, written when he was imprisoned by opponents of his reform. He writes: "The 'dark night' is when those people lose all the pleasures that they once experienced in their devotional life. This happens because God wants to purify them, and move them on to greater heights. . . . After a soul has been converted to the service of God, that soul is nurtured and caressed by the Spirit" (John, *The Dark Night of the Soul*, 1:1-2). John includes some safeguards against arbitrary or mistaken interpretations of visions or revelations, as Hilton does. Among these are "secret pride," "feelings," and "spiritual greed" to advance, as well as "inordinate fear of impure thoughts." John is realistic about the excesses of "ecstasy." We shall recall some of these warnings when we seek to offer a balanced assessment of the Charismatic Movement today in Part III.

15

The Major Reformers

15.1. Martin Luther and the "Enthusiasts"

With *Martin Luther* (1483-1546) we enter a new era. Many of the medieval monks and mystics saw the Holy Spirit as especially close to those who had climbed the ladder of perfection. James Atkinson wrote, "Luther was far in advance of Tauler and the monks. . . . Here was the beginning of the rediscovery of the priesthood of all believers. Here was the beginning of ideas which emptied the monasteries and convents of monks and nuns and set them seeking normal Christian employment."[1] The Holy Spirit could be the fullest gift to *all, including the most "ordinary," Christians*.

This particular emphasis arose not only from Luther's theology as a whole, but also from his need to oppose two virtually opposite fronts. Regin Prenter, the Lutheran specialist on the Holy Spirit, observes: "It is well known how Luther, after his return from Wartburg, . . . had to fight on two fronts. He had to continue his struggle with the Roman Church. He also had to take up the struggle with the new enthusiastic movements."[2] Luther called these "enthusiasts" *Schwärmer* (enthusiasts, fanatics). They included Nicolaus Storch, Thomas Müntzer, and Andreas Carlstadt. Atkinson comments: "It is not always understood that Luther's worst enemy was not Catholicism, but rather that wild left-wing radicalism identified with fanaticism and 'socialism.'"[3] Veli-Matti Kärk-

---

1. James Atkinson, *Martin Luther and the Birth of Protestantism* (London: Penguin, 1968), p. 86.

2. Regin Prenter, *Spiritus Creator: Luther's Concept of the Holy Spirit* (Philadelphia: Muhlenberg, 1953), p. 205. Cf. also Yves Congar, *I Believe in the Holy Spirit* (New York: Crossroad, 1997), p. 138; also cited in Veli-Matti Kärkkäinen (ed.), *The Holy Spirit and Salvation: The Sources of Christian Theology* (Louisville: Westminster/John Knox 2010), p. 152.

3. Atkinson, *Martin Luther and the Birth of Protestantism*, p. 221.

käinen, the Pentecostal writer, claims that the opposition between Luther and the *Schwärmer* was parallel with that between Calvin and the Anabaptists later.[4] Luther and Calvin, it is argued, kept to a middle road.

(1) *Early years to 1521.* Martin Luther was born in Eisleben in Saxony, and brought up in Mansfeld. His father wanted him to become a lawyer. So he entered the University of Erfurt, southwest of Leipzig. He graduated in 1502, and received his M.A. in 1505. While he was at university, the Dominican Johann Tetzel began to sell indulgences. In doubt about his state before God, Luther entered an Augustinian monastery at Erfurt in 1505, and was ordained in 1507. In 1512 he gained his doctorate in theology, became Professor of Biblical Studies in the new University of Wittenberg, and, with the encouragement of Staupitz, began to write his lectures on Genesis, Romans, and Galatians (1513-16). During this period he underwent his "tower experience," influenced by his work on Psalms and Romans. In 1513 Luther came across the verse: "Deliver me in Thy righteousness" (Ps. 31:1).[5] He recalled that he had "hated" Paul and the idea of righteousness, especially when they came together, as in Rom. 1:16-17. Luther saw that *his* righteousness was nothing, but that *God's* righteousness meant *not judgment but grace* through the righteousness of Christ. This must be received as a gift. He writes: "I began to understand . . . that a just man lives by the gift of God. . . . I felt myself born afresh and to have entered . . . into paradise itself."[6]

In 1517 Tetzel began to sell his indulgences near Wittenberg. This was too much for Luther, who saw this as moneymaking medieval superstition. On October 31 (often celebrated in Protestant churches as Reformation Sunday) he nailed his ninety-five theses on the door of Wittenberg's castle church. It had an explosive effect throughout Germany. The following year, in April 1518, Luther held his Disputation at Heidelberg.[7] In Proposition 21, he urged: "The theologian of glory says bad is good and good is bad. The theologian of the cross calls them by their proper name. . . . God is not to be found except in suffering and in the cross."[8] Toward the end of the year, in October, Luther debated with Cajetan at Augsburg, and in 1519 he participated in another debate with Johann Eck at Leipzig. In 1520 Luther wrote his address to the German nobility. He then received a threatening papal bull, and was invited to the Diet of Worms. At Worms he refused to retract his arguments. Luther burned the bull, and in 1521 he was excommunicated from the Catholic Church.

---

4. Kärkkäinen (ed.), *The Holy Spirit and Salvation,* p. 152.

5. Atkinson, *Martin Luther and the Birth of Protestantism,* p. 76.

6. Cited in Gordon E. Rupp and Benjamin Drewery (eds.), *Martin Luther — Documents of Modern History* (London: Arnold, 1970), p. 6; cf. Atkinson, *Martin Luther and the Birth of Protestantism,* p. 77.

7. Translated in James Atkinson, *Luther: Early Theological Works,* LCC 16 (London: SCM, 1962), pp. 274-307.

8. Atkinson, *Early Theological Works,* p. 291.

The Elector of Saxony kept him in safety in his castle at Wartburg, where he wrote his *Answer to Latomus* and began work on translating the Bible into German.[9] Jacobus Latomus had planned to work against Luther in the Leipzig Disputation with Eck, and Luther now carefully appealed to Scripture, tradition, and reason in response. This concludes Luther's early phase. Other works may be included, such as *On Good Works* and *Concerning the Babylonian Captivity of the Church* (1520). By now Luther was about thirty-seven.

(2) *The Holy Spirit as the Spirit of Holiness and the Trinity.* Regin Prenter, Stanley Burgess, and Veli-Matti Kärkkäinen all make the point that a traditional view, which minimizes Luther's emphasis on the Holy Spirit, has been overtaken in 1953 by work from Prenter, which sheds much more light on Luther's theology of the Holy Spirit.[10] Prenter writes, "The concept of the Holy Spirit completely dominates Luther's theology. In every decisive matter . . . we are forced to take into consideration his concept of the Holy Spirit."[11] It is true that his understanding of the Holy Trinity and of the Spirit within the Trinity continues the orthodox Western approach, especially in Augustine, Bernard of Clairvaux, and Richard of St. Victor. But he also urges that the term "*Holy Spirit*" calls attention to his special work of sanctification. In Prenter's view, the greatest difference between Luther and the enthusiasts "concerned . . . one thing: the exclusive understanding of the Spirit as the Spirit *of God.*"[12] Luther's consistently orthodox doctrine of the Trinity ensured that he kept this in view.

In his *Small Catechism* (1529) Martin Luther asserts: "The Holy Spirit sanctifies me [makes me holy] by bringing me to faith in Christ, so that I might have the blessings of redemption and lead a godly life [sanctification in the wide sense]." He adds that I cannot come to Christ "in my own reason or strength," but through the Spirit. Luther declares, "The Scriptures teach that by this Gospel the Holy Spirit 'enlightened me with His gifts,' that is, He gave me the saving knowledge of Jesus, so that I trust, rejoice, and find comfort in Him." The work of the Holy Spirit, he declares, "is called conversion [being turned] or regeneration [new birth]" (*The Small Catechism*). He further states, "The Holy Spirit sanctifies me in the true faith, that is, by faith He works a renewal of my whole life." But he also urges, "The Scriptures do *not* teach, however, that God will necessarily give all Christians in every time and place *special miraculous gifts.* The Holy Spirit bestows His blessing according to His good pleasure" (*The Small Catechism*, my italics). A very large number of biblical texts or passages follow and confirm each declaration. Luther's theology was saturated by his de-

---

9. Luther, *Answer to Latomus*, is translated in Atkinson, *Early Theological Works*, pp. 308-64.

10. Prenter, *Spiritus Creator;* cf. Stanley M. Burgess, *The Holy Spirit: Medieval Roman Catholic and Reformation Traditions* (Peabody, MA: Hendrickson, 1997), p. 147; and Kärkkäinen (ed.), *The Holy Spirit and Salvation*, p. 153.

11. Prenter, *Spiritus Creator*, p. ix.

12. Prenter, *Spiritus Creator*, p. 288 (my italics).

tailed knowledge of all parts of the Scriptures. This is evident, for example, in Luther's 1532 Sermon on John 15:26-27. The Holy Spirit, he argues, promotes the doctrine of Christ, and of his death and resurrection.

As Kärkkäinen observes, "Similarly to Augustine, . . . Luther took the designation *Holy Spirit* to mean the sanctifying work, as the famous passage from *The Large Catechism* clearly puts it."[13] The Holy Spirit, Luther observes here, "makes us holy. . . . God's Spirit . . . who has sanctified and still sanctifies us. . . . The Holy Spirit must be called *Sanctifier,* the One who makes us holy. . . . He first leads us into this holy community . . . , the church, where he preaches to us and brings us to Christ" (my italics).[14] Luther understands that the Holy Spirit not only sanctifies, but also *gives life.* The Holy Spirit, Luther comments, first has "led you into the holy, catholic, church. . . . In that church he preserves [you] and through it he preaches and brings you [to Christ] through the Word. . . . The Holy Spirit . . . sanctifies me."[15]

Luther has some strong words to say in *The Smalcald Articles* (1537).[16] He states: "God grants his Spirit or grace to no one, except through or with the preceding outward Word, in order that we may be protected against the enthusiasts, i.e., spirits who *boast that they have the Spirit without and before the Word . . . ,* who wish to be acute judges between the Spirit and the letter" (*The Smalcald Articles,* part 3, art. 6, "Of Confession," proposition 4, my italics). Luther concludes this article: "In a word, enthusiasm inheres in Adam and his children" (proposition 8). Luther continues: "It is the devil himself whatsoever is extolled as Spirit without the Word and Sacraments" (proposition 10). "Without the outward Word [men of God] were not holy, much less would the Holy Spirit have moved them to speak . . ." (proposition 10). For where Christ is not preached, "there is no Holy Spirit to create, call, and gather the Christian Church" (Luther, *The Large Catechism,* Creed, art. 3). We could know nothing of Christ, Luther urges, without the preaching of the gospel by the Holy Spirit. Christ has won salvation for us, but it is the Holy Spirit's work to offer and apply this treasure.

One of Luther's characteristic themes about the Holy Spirit is his emphasis on *Anfechtung,* or *an inner conflict* in which the believer is corrected of sin and his or her self-confidence is done away (cf. John 16:8). Prenter observes: "The experience of inner conflict indicates the tyranny of the law in the conscience.

13. Kärkkäinen (ed.), *The Holy Spirit and Salvation,* p. 154; Martin Luther, *The Large Catechism* (Philadelphia: Fortress, 1959).

14. Luther, *The Large Catechism,* part 2, art. 3 of the Creed, paragraphs 35-37; and so cited in Kärkkäinen (ed.), *The Holy Spirit and Salvation,* pp. 154-55.

15. Quoted from Kärkkäinen (ed.), *The Holy Spirit and Salvation,* p. 155.

16. Martin Luther, *The Smalcald Articles,* in *The Book of Concord,* part 3, art. 8, "Of Confession," from *The Triglot Concordia* [German-Latin-English]: *The Symbolical Books of the Lutheran Church* (St. Louis: Concordia, on line); also cited in Kärkkäinen (ed.), *The Holy Spirit and Salvation,* p. 156.

[It] is the place where we may know the Spirit in the school of inner conflict. . . . [In contrast to some of the enthusiasts] it does not consist of psychological self-observation within its spirit."[17] There is no precise English equivalent. The word can denote "trials" sent by God to test believers, or "assaults" by the devil. It may cause despair, but may drive the believer to prayer and Scripture in the power of the Holy Spirit. It constitutes an "assault" on confidence *in the self*, to turn the believer *to the Holy Spirit*. From a different viewpoint, it is part of "dying with Christ," and then being raised with Christ. Both are possible only through the Holy Spirit. But to Luther *Anfechtung* was more of an assault, temptation, or attack than a "psychological eccentricity" of the mystics.[18]

(3) *The "Enthusiasts" and Luther's later writings.* While Luther was in Wartburg (until 1521), Andreas Carlstadt came to Wittenberg, wrote and preached against monastic vows, celibacy, and the Mass, and wore lay clothes. He denounced images and pictures, opposed the baptism of infants, rejected all titles and dignitaries, *ridiculed theological learning, and appealed to the leading of the Holy Spirit as grounds for all this.* Carlstadt's group claimed the direct inspiration of the Holy Spirit, irrespective of what Scripture might teach through the Word and Sacraments. In March 1522 Luther returned to Wittenberg to unmask the "fanatics" *(Schwärmer)*. Atkinson, we saw, commented, "Luther's worst enemy was not Catholicism but rather that left-wing radicalism associated with fanaticism. . . ."[19] Carlstadt's fellow "enthusiast," Thomas Müntzer (1483-1546), thought that a preacher must have a special revelation before preaching the Word, whereas Luther looked to the Scriptures.[20] In effect, Müntzer took over the leadership of the radical movement from Carlstadt in 1523. He claimed to receive *private* supernatural revelation. He urged that all property was to be held in common, and, astonishingly, princes who refused to give up their land were to be killed.[21]

In 1520 Müntzer had moved to Zwickau in Saxony, where he met Nicolaus Storch, a self-proclaimed "prophet," who taught that the Bible was secondary to direct revelation to prophets. Müntzer and Storch (with Thomas Dreschal and Markus Stübner), called the "Zwickau prophets," began to elaborate their own doctrine of the Spirit. In Prague they produced "The Prague Manifesto," which expounded their doctrine of the Holy Spirit as well as believers' baptism and imminent apocalypticism. In December 1521 they returned to Wittenberg. Luther, therefore, left the protection of Wartburg Castle to return to Wittenberg, and delivered a series of sermons which attacked the *Schwärmer*. Müntzer

17. Prenter, *Spiritus Creator*, pp. 207-8; cf. David Scaer, "The Concept of *Anfechtung* in Luther's Thought," *Concordia Theological Quarterly* 47 (1983): 15-30.

18. Atkinson, *Martin Luther and the Birth of Protestantism*, pp. 41-43.

19. Atkinson, *Martin Luther and the Birth of Protestantism*, p. 221.

20. Burgess, *The Holy Spirit: Medieval Roman Catholic and Reformation Traditions*, p. 150.

21. Cf. Atkinson, *Martin Luther and the Birth of Protestantism*, p. 238.

moved away to Allstedt, while Luther remained at Wittenberg, translating Mark, Luke, John, and Romans. In 1522 he commented, "John's Gospel and St. Paul's Epistles, especially that of Romans, and St. Peter's First Epistle, are the true kernel and marrow of all the books."[22] In 1523 Luther wrote "On Secular Power," and in 1524 he re-formulated his views against Carlstadt's and Müntzer's movement in his book *Against the Celestial Prophets* (January 1525). He keenly felt the irony of the "left wing radicals," observing: "All my enemies . . . have not hit me as hard as I have now been hit by our own people." But in 1523-24 Carlstadt was teaching people to empty themselves in passivity *to listen to the Spirit;* he wore a peasant's cloak; destroyed images and crucifixes; advocated polygamy; and rejected the doctrine of the Real Presence at the Eucharist — all under supposed revelation from the Holy Spirit.

Meanwhile Müntzer prepared for a violent outburst, as he held secret intercourse with God. Property was distributed to each according to need. Luther now viewed "the new prophets" *as Satanic.* With Müntzer's encouragement on the basis of "revelations," the peasants and mob rose up, seeing revolt and revolution as God's command. They burned convents and cities in the name of the Lord. Luther called Müntzer "the Arch-devil," and wrote against him. In June 1525 Saxon princes attacked and defeated the forces of Müntzer, some eight thousand men.

Luther entreated the princes to be merciful to those who surrendered. The tragedy was to imagine that all this was *at the instruction of the Holy Spirit.* Most would see it as an event comparable to the rise and fall of Montanism in the early Church.[23] For Luther, *the Spirit and the Word* spoke together with one voice. A pure appeal to the "inner" voice of the Spirit alone led to what many regard as an inconsistent attitude to war and violence. Kärkkäinen quotes Müntzer as writing concerning "the inward word which is heard in the abyss of the soul. . . . Anyone may have a thousand Bibles, but he can say nothing about God which has any validity. . . . The Holy Spirit must direct him. . . . Otherwise his heart will be blind."[24]

Prenter sees this as "a peculiar type of piety different in principle from his [Luther's] own view of Christianity. . . . In his *Treatise against the Heavenly Prophets* Luther says that the real error of the enthusiasts is that they turn the order of God upside down. . . . Outwardly he [God] deals with us in the gospel and in the sacraments, and inwardly in the Spirit and his gifts."[25] Prenter rejects

---

22. Luther, "Preface to the New Testament," in *Works of Martin Luther* (Philadelphia: Fortress, 1943), vol. 6, p. 439; also Rupp and Drewery (eds.), *Martin Luther,* p. 94.

23. For an account of the Peasants' Revolt and its consequences for Luther and Müntzer, see Atkinson, *Martin Luther and the Birth of Protestantism,* pp. 140-45.

24. Thomas Müntzer, *The Second Chapter of David,* in *Collected Works* (Edinburgh: T&T Clark, 1988), p. 240; cited by Kärkkäinen (ed.), *The Holy Spirit and Salvation,* p. 185.

25. Prenter, *Spiritus Creator,* p. 248.

the view that Luther changed his doctrine in the face of the enthusiasts. Nor does he consider that William of Ockham or Duns Scotus exercised undue influence on him. Luther's perspective is "theocentric."[26] Carlstadt tried to make the "gift" of the Holy Spirit into a process of "human devotion, or effort."[27] Hence "this enthusiasm made the Spirit the crown of the piety of the law, *the reward of the perfect,* instead of the source and spring of the gospel" (my italics).[28] The work of the Spirit has Christ and free grace at the center. Luther's realism, Prenter argues, remains a key question about the Holy Spirit for today.[29] Ultimately "enthusiasm" leads to "the true, irrevocable, and terrible end of the way of legalistic pietism."[30]

There are also smaller, detailed differences between Luther and the Radical Reformers. Following Augustine, Luther notes that Müntzer and "the fanatics" seek all of the gifts enumerated in 1 Cor. 12:8-10 and elsewhere. Luther was curious about several. He believed that "healing" may reflect the healings of Jesus, but *generally they do not apply to the present era,* and could sometimes amount to "a magic trick."[31] George H. Williams describes Thomas Müntzer's sermon "before the princes" in 1524 as "the high-watermark of . . . the Revolutionary Spiritualist [movement] directed against Luther."[32] Müntzer complains of Luther and his followers: "They teach . . . that God no longer reveals his divine mysteries to his beloved friends by means of valid visions or audible word. . . . [They] attack the Holy Spirit. . . . They can prattle prettily of faith and brew up a drunken faith. . . . It is clearly written in Acts . . . to attend on visions. . . . Brother Fattened Swine and Brother Life [i.e., Luther] rejects them. . . . The Spirit of God is revealing to many elect . . . a decisive, inevitable, imminent reformation."[33] In other words, it is the enthusiasts who will carry through the Reformation, not Luther.

To be fair, Philipp Melanchthon, Luther's able collaborator, saw more good in the enthusiasts than fired Luther's polemic. But temperamentally Melanchthon was a mediator and reconciler, and he also tried to mediate on the Lord's Supper with Ulrich Zwingli's more radical views. On the other hand, Zwingli had as little time for the enthusiasts as Luther, finding them an embarrassment

---

26. Prenter, *Spiritus Creator,* p. 251.

27. Prenter, *Spiritus Creator,* p. 253.

28. Prenter, *Spiritus Creator,* p. 254.

29. Prenter, *Spiritus Creator,* p. 303.

30. Prenter, *Spiritus Creator,* p. 219.

31. Martin Luther, *Against the Heavenly Prophets,* in *Luther's Works* (St. Louis: Concordia, 1958), p. 142; Martin Luther, *Paul's Epistle to the Galatians* (London: James Clarke, 1953), p. 153.

32. George H. Williams (ed.), *Spiritual and Anabaptist Writers,* LCC 25 (London: SCM, 1957), p. 47.

33. Müntzer, "Sermon Before the Princes," in *Spiritual and Anabaptist Writers,* ed. Williams, pp. 54, 56, and 61.

to his cause. There is much to learn today from Luther's difficult relation with the enthusiasts. *Were they devout pietists and "charismatics," or did they betray Luther's theology of grace?*

15.2. Ulrich Zwingli, Heinrich Bullinger, and Martin Bucer

(1) *Ulrich Zwingli* (1484-1531) is no mere copy of Luther. Their differences were most pronounced in their respective theologies of the Lord's Supper. But on the subject of the Holy Spirit the two were close, except that Zwingli probably stressed Scripture alone as the litmus test of the experience of the Spirit, whereas Luther also valued earliest Christian tradition. Zwingli was born into an educated Swiss family, and he was schooled mainly at Basel and Bern. He graduated in Basel in 1504, gained a Master's degree in 1506, and was ordained priest in that year. In 1516 he became preacher at Einsiedeln, and in 1518 he moved to Zürich's Great Minster, where he began a series of biblical expositions. By 1525 he had preached through the New Testament and turned the Minster, in effect, into a theological college. Here he produced his *The Defence of the Reformed Faith.* [34]

Characteristically Zwingli wrote, "Whether the Spirit of God is with you is demonstrated, above all, by whether his word is your guide, and whether you do nothing except what is clearly stated in the word of God, so that scripture is your master, and not you, masters of scripture."[35] On this issue Zwingli was close to Luther. In fact, he faced the same problems when Andreas Carlstadt and Thomas Müntzer visited Switzerland from Germany, to make common cause with the "Radical Reformers" there, led by Conrad Grebel. Zwingli had no more sympathy with their theology of the Holy Spirit than Luther had, in spite of his having more sympathy with their antihierarchical approach. The most crucial difference from the Radicals was their ranking of the authority of Word and Spirit as against that of primarily the Holy Spirit. Zwingli writes, "Whenever we give heed to the word, we . . . are drawn to him by his Spirit and transformed into his likeness."[36]

Zwingli insists that the believer needs the Holy Spirit to understand and to interpret the Word of God. He moves where he wills (John 3:8), and is active even among pagans. Unlike Luther, however, he looked to theocracy rather than to the two kingdoms of the spiritual and secular readers. His influence extended mainly to Switzerland and to southern Germany, but through Heinrich

34. Huldrych Zwingli, *The Defence of the Reformed Faith* (Allison Park, PA: Pickwick, 1984), from Zwingli's *Writings.*

35. Zwingli, *The Defence of the Reformed Faith,* p. 46; also cited in Kärkkäinen (ed.), *The Holy Spirit and Salvation,* p. 163.

36. Zwingli, *The Defence of the Reformed Faith,* vol. 1, p. 57.

Bullinger (1504-75) also to England and other parts of Europe. Like Calvin, he stressed divine sovereignty and the work of the Spirit in exposing sin. Although they differed on Holy Communion and on attitudes toward the state, Zwingli and Luther were at one in justification by grace and the work of the Holy Spirit.

(2) *Heinrich Bullinger* (1504-75). On Zwingli's death, Bullinger succeeded him as "People's Priest" in Zürich. He did his utmost to hold together Zwingli's Reformed Theology Movement, and in 1536 he took a prominent part in the conference that led to the First Helvetic Confession, as well as fostering good relations with Calvin and leaders of the Church of England.[37] Both he and Zwingli stressed the creative power of the Word of God and the Holy Spirit. To elaborate on this teaching further we would need to repeat much of what has been said already about Luther.

(3) *Martin Bucer* (1491-1551) first entered the Dominican order, but adopted Lutheranism in 1521. However, differences from Luther emerged in 1524, and W. Peter Stephens comments, "He belonged in some measure to three great reformation traditions, Lutheran, Reformed, and Anglican."[38] His theology of Holy Communion, like that of the Church of England, probably stood between Luther's view and Zwingli's. Stephens complains of the unfair neglect of Bucer, at least until recently, and stresses "the centrality of the Holy Spirit" in his theology.[39] This does not mean that he endorsed the approach of the "spiritualists" or "Anabaptists." Quite the reverse: Bucer differed from them in his doctrine of election, of baptism, and of the Holy Spirit. The most extreme "Radical Reformers" believed that the Holy Spirit set them free from the Bible.

In Stephens's words, "The outward word is ineffective until the Holy Spirit persuades the heart, but it is nevertheless through the word that the Holy Spirit works."[40] Like Luther, Bucer sees the Spirit primarily as the bringer of *sanctification.* He comments, "At every point it is the Spirit who is the key to the doctrine of sanctification."[41] Bucer uses the images of water, fire, advocate, and finger of God to drive home the point. He is fire because of his strength to burn up sin. He is water because he causes dry land to be fruitful; he is advocate because he protects Christians; he is the finger of God because he is the Agent and Representative of God himself. But it is clear that Bucer anticipates James Dunn and others in seeing inspiration and renewal by the Spirit as given to *all* who enter the Kingdom of Christ. Like Luther, Bucer sees the danger of self-glorification and the need for *constant dependence on the Holy Spirit.*

---

37. Geoffrey W. Bromiley (ed.), *Zwingli and Bullinger,* LCC 24 (London: SCM, 1955), pp. 40-46 and 283-326.

38. W. Peter Stephens, *The Holy Spirit in the Theology of Martin Bucer* (Cambridge: Cambridge University Press, 1970), p. vii.

39. Stephens, *The Holy Spirit in Bucer,* p. 1.

40. Stephens, *The Holy Spirit in Bucer,* p. 46.

41. Stephens, *The Holy Spirit in Bucer,* p. 74.

The best available English translation of Bucer's writings, which provide a primary source for his doctrine of the Holy Spirit, is that part of "A Brief Summary of Christian Doctrine" that comes in his *Common Places of Martin Bucer*.[42] Under "true repentance" he ascribes knowledge of the plight of sin, repentance, and sorrow for sin to the Holy Spirit.[43] Under "justification," he writes: "He also gives us his Holy Spirit to bring us to a true, complete, and sincere belief in this, his gospel (Acts 16:31; 2 Cor. 4:6, 13-14). Through this belief he draws us to his dear Son (John 6:44) so that we conceive a steadfast trust in his grace and in the redemption of Christ our Lord (Eph. 3:12, 17)."[44] By means of his Word and Spirit he will renew us in his image. Under "Trust in God, hope of eternal life, love of God and our neighbour," Bucer asserts: "We teach that the Holy Spirit, the Spirit of faith (2 Cor. 4:13), produces in all those who are regenerated by him . . . an attitude of sincere trust in God. . . . The Holy Spirit also produces in the children of God a deep love for God, . . . an eager obedience towards all his commandments."[45] The Spirit gives the virtues of a new life. But Christians still sin, in spite of his working in us. We "learn from the divine Scriptures, through the Holy Spirit, . . . and live and abide in him."[46]

Bucer's section on the doctrine of the Holy Spirit ends with concern for the Church, with its "shepherds [or pastors] and teachers, overseers [or bishops] [and] ministers [who not only preach the Word, but are] dispensers of his holy mysteries [the sacraments]."[47] Ministers require prayer and the laying on of hands. They include both pastors and those "whom the Holy Spirit styles overseers [bishops] and elders (Tit. 1:5, 7; Acts 14:23; 20:28)."[48] The Spirit is active in the Sacraments and in confirmation, as well as in discipline and marriage.[49]

In addition to this coherent account from a primary source, the best access to scattered references for our subject remains W. P. Stephens, *The Holy Spirit in the Theology of Martin Bucer*. In addition to his comments made above, Stephens also sees the *Spirit as the inspirer of prayer* (Rom. 8:26-27; cf. Matt. 6:1-13), rather than prayer constituting a merely *human* act, and *love* as the fruit of the Spirit (Gal. 5:22-23). He is less hostile to the Law than Luther, seeing it as an instrument of sanctification as well as that from which Christians, in a different sense, have been freed. Moreover, "the completion of God's purposes lies beyond this life. . . . It will be complete when all sin has been destroyed in us by

---

42. Martin Bucer, *The Common Places of Martin Bucer*, trans. and ed. David F. Wright (Abingdon, Eng.: Sutton Courtenay, 1972), pp. 76-94.

43. Bucer, *Common Places of Martin Bucer*, p. 79.

44. Bucer, *Common Places of Martin Bucer*, p. 79.

45. Bucer, *Common Places of Martin Bucer*, p. 80.

46. Bucer, *Common Places of Martin Bucer*, p. 82.

47. Bucer, *Common Places of Martin Bucer*, p. 83.

48. Bucer, *Common Places of Martin Bucer*, p. 83.

49. Bucer, *Common Places of Martin Bucer*, pp. 84-90.

the Spirit of Christ, and God will be all things in us (1 Cor. 15)."[50] This forward-looking note is a constant one.[51] This will reflect a major emphasis of modern biblical scholarship on eschatology and Spirit.

The Holy Spirit who inspired the Bible also *interprets* it.[52] For Bucer, "understanding" the Bible includes not only recognizing it as the Word of God but also *expounding and applying it* as a student of Scripture, for "no prophecy in scripture is a matter of one's own interpretation." The Spirit has brought into being the whole community of God's people, and interpretation cannot be rightly achieved without reference to what today we should call *"public" tradition.*[53] Bucer, like Luther, speaks of the Holy Spirit also as *calling, equipping, guiding, and using the minister.* In an important reference in his *Commentary on Romans* Bucer not only emphasizes the variety of gifts of the Holy Spirit but also understands them as not restricted to Christians alone.[54] *"The way the gift of teaching is given does not make it any less a gift of the Spirit than prophecy"* (my italics).[55] There are key implications here for the modern "Renewal" or Pentecostal notion that many gifts of the Spirit must be "spontaneous," or independent of thought and study. Some gifts, he argues, depend on the laying on of hands. *Preaching* assists "the living word" by making the written Word effective. Stephens declares, "Bucer described the word that is preached as having three elements: (a) the exposing of sin . . . , (b) the testifying to Christ as Saviour ('will baptize them with fire and the Holy Spirit, that is, renew them to salvation by inspiring a new and divine mind'); and (c) the announcement of judgment."[56]

Finally, the Holy Spirit is active through the Sacraments, as he is through the Word. Stephens comments: "The distinction here between baptism in water and baptism in the Spirit represents primarily a fundamental opposition in Bucer between elect and reprobate, rather than an opposition between outward and inward. There is, therefore, a *distinction* between baptism in water and baptism in the Spirit, not a *separation.* . . . *Baptism with the Spirit is not separated, but only distinguished, from baptism with water"* (my italics).[57] This is clearly a long way from the Pentecostal use of the terms. The Holy Spirit, Bucer asserts, is essentially in the believer. Stephens has been meticulous in supporting every statement about the Holy Spirit in the theology of Bucer with reference to primary sources. The Church of England is often described as "Catholic and Reformed." Many will recognize in Bucer a good representative of the "Reformed" tradition within the

50. Stephens, *The Holy Spirit in Bucer,* p. 99.
51. Stephens, *The Holy Spirit in Bucer,* p. 100. Stephens fully documents his sources.
52. Stephens, *The Holy Spirit in Bucer,* pp. 120-15.
53. Stephens, *The Holy Spirit in Bucer,* pp. 156-66.
54. Stephens, *The Holy Spirit in Bucer,* pp. 185-95
55. Stephens, *The Holy Spirit in Bucer,* p. 186.
56. Stephens, *The Holy Spirit in Bucer,* p. 200.
57. Stephens, *The Holy Spirit in Bucer,* pp. 222 and 223.

Church of England. Since Stephens cites so very many references to Bucer's work, often in German, in this section it has been convenient to refer often to Stephens.

15.3. John Calvin

John Calvin (1509-64), the French Reformer, studied in Paris and Orléans, and read law and classics before turning to theology. In the face of persecution he withdrew to Basle in 1535, and published the first edition of *The Institutes* in 1536. When in the same year he passed through Geneva, G. Farel persuaded him to remain in Geneva to organize the Reformation there, which he undertook to do, until Martin Bucer invited him to Strasbourg in 1538. Here he produced a revised and enlarged edition of the *Institutes* and a *Commentary on Romans* (1539). In 1541 Calvin received an invitation to return to Geneva. Over the next fourteen years he worked at writing numerous commentaries. At the same time, he managed the affairs of the city in accordance with the principles of Reformed theology, as represented by Zwingli and Bucer. He promoted Reformed theology in Geneva and elsewhere, and in 1559 founded the Geneva Academy. He produced a further edition of *The Institutes* in 1545, producing five editions in all, the last in 1559. One factor in Calvin's considerable influence was his systematic, logical, and coherent pattern of thought as expressed in the *Institutes*. Another was his independent writing of many commentaries on the Bible. These remained so faithful to genuine exegetical concerns that many scholars regard these works as the first "modern" commentaries of the Church.

Calvin divided his *Institutes of the Christian Religion* into four parts, of which the first concerns knowledge of God. In part 1, chapter 13, section 14, he asserts "the divinity of the Spirit," and recalls how in Genesis the Spirit hovered over the abyss creatively, and "was at work cherishing the confused mass" (*Institutes*, 1:3:14; Henry Beveridge ed., vol. 1, p. 122).[58] Calvin continues: "We are the temple of God. . . . the Spirit of God dwells in us" (1 Cor. 3:16; 6:19), and quotes Augustine's stress that worship is due to God alone (*Institutes*, 1:13:15; Beveridge ed., p. 123). Yet the Persons of the Trinity are distinct, for example, as "the Word and the Spirit." He cites Gregory of Nazianzus in support (1:13:17; Beveridge ed., p. 125). In spite of his undeserved reputation for dogmatism, Calvin asserts: "I am not sure whether it is expedient to borrow analogies from human affairs to express the nature of this distinction" (1:13:18, p. 126). The Father, the Son, and the Spirit are co-eternal (1:13:18); "the unity of essence is retained" (1:13:20; p. 127). Calvin holds the orthodox Western view of the Holy Trinity.

Part 3 of *The Institutes* concerns "the Mode of Obtaining the Grace of

---

58. John Calvin, *Institutes of the Christian Religion*, 2 vols., trans. Henry Beveridge (London: James Clarke, 1957), vol. 1, p. 122.

Christ," and part 3, chapter 1, shows how the "benefits of Christ" are made available "by . . . the Operation of the Spirit." Calvin writes: "The testimony of the Spirit . . . , twice mentioned, . . . is engraven on our hearts by way of a seal, and thus seals the cleansing and sacrifice of Christ" (*Institutes,* 3:1:1; Beveridge ed., p. 463). He adds: "Believers are 'elect' through *sanctification* of the Spirit unto obedience and sprinkling of the blood of Jesus Christ" (1 Pet. 1:2; 3:1:1; my italics). He also appeals to Christ's *empowerment* by the Holy Spirit: "Christ came provided with the Holy Spirit after a peculiar manner" (1:1:2). He points out that Christ then bestows the Holy Spirit on us, in accordance with the prophecy of Joel 2:28. On this basis, "you are not in the flesh but in the Spirit, if so be that the Spirit of God dwells in you. Now if any man have not the Spirit of Christ, he is none of his [no Christian]" (Rom. 8:9; 3:1:2; Beveridge ed., p. 464). In due course, he says, "He who raised up Christ from the dead will quicken your mortal bodies by his Spirit who dwells in you" (Rom. 8:11; 3:1:2).

In the *Institutes,* 3:1:3, Calvin explicitly considers the titles given to the Holy Spirit. He is called "Spirit of adoption," whereby we cry "Abba, Father"; he is the "earnest" of our future inheritance; "his secret irrigation . . . makes us bud forth and produce the fruits of righteousness"; he is "described as *water;* . . . 'If any man thirst, let him come to me and drink'"; he is *"Oil* and *Unction"* and "receives the name of *Fire,"* *"Fountain,"* and "the *Hand* by which God exerts his power" (Calvin's italics, *Institutes,* 3:1:3; Beveridge ed., pp. 464-65). In many ways Calvin's list anticipates Moltmann's "Metaphors for Experiences of the Spirit," in his *The Spirit of Life.*[59] Yet Calvin continues: "Faith is his principal work. . . . it is only by faith that he brings us to the light of the Gospel" (3:1:4). Here Calvin is close to Luther, and this leads on to his chapter 2, on faith. In particular the Holy Spirit gives "confirmation of the heart, . . . sealing upon our hearts the very promises [of God]" (3:2:36; Beveridge ed., p. 501). This is "the earnest of the Spirit" (2 Cor. 5:5; 3:2:36).

In part 4 of the *Institutes* Calvin repeats the point about faith. In this section he is primarily discussing the Sacraments, but he asserts again: "Faith is the proper and entire work of the Holy Spirit, . . . by whom we recognize God and the treasures of his grace, and without whose illumination our mind is so blind that it can see nothing" (*Institutes,* 4:14:8; Beveridge ed., vol. 2, p. 496). In part 1 Calvin also refers to *inspiration* through the prophets: "The same Spirit, therefore, who spoke by the mouth of the prophets, must penetrate our hearts, in order to convince us that they faithfully delivered the message with which they were divinely entrusted" (1:7:8; Beveridge ed., vol. 1, p. 72). He also refers to the insufflation of the Spirit by Jesus Christ in John 20:22: "When our Lord commissioned the apostles to preach the gospel, he breathed upon them." He con-

---

59. Jürgen Moltmann, *The Spirit of Life: A Universal Affirmation* (London: SCM, 1992), pp. 269-85.

tinues: "By this symbol, he represented the gift of the Holy Spirit, which he be-stowed upon them" (4:19:29; Beveridge ed., vol. 2, p. 644). Calvin also observed, characteristically, "By means of him [the Holy Spirit] we become partakers of the divine nature, so as in a manner to feel his quickening energy within us. Our justification is his work; *from him is power, sanctification, truth, grace and every good thought, since it is from the Spirit alone that all good gifts proceed*" (*Institutes*, 1:13:14; Beveridge ed., vol. 1, p. 123; my italics).

Calvin's commentaries lend support to the declarations in his *Institutes*. On Gal. 5:22-23, he comments: "Nothing but good comes from the Holy Spirit. . . . *Peace* I contrast with quarrels and contentions, *long-suffering* is gentleness of mind. . . . Where the Spirit reigns, the law has no longer any dominion."[60] On Ps. 104:29 he notes, "When he withdraws his quickening Spirit, we die. . . . there is shown a renewing of the world."[61] On gifts of the Spirit in 1 Cor. 12:8-10, he observes, "*Faith* is . . . a particular kind of faith. . . . 'The working of powers *(operationibus virtutum)* is exercised against demons and also hypocrites. . . . *energēma* [denotes] effective working. . . . The prophet is God's messenger to men. . . . Interpreters [of tongues] translated foreign languages."[62] On 1 Cor. 12:4 Calvin comments that "one Spirit" denotes "one essential power of God, from which all his activities proceed."[63] On 1 Cor. 2:4 he understands "demonstration of the Spirit to denote much more than miracles." It denotes "the hand of God stretching itself out to act powerfully through the apostle in every way."[64]

Effectual calling consists in both the preaching of the Word of God and the *illumination and actualization* of it by the Holy Spirit. Calvin stresses the final perseverance of the Christian believer, for "God is faithful. . . . Whatever God begins He carries through to completion"; "'the calling of God is irrevocable' (Rom. 11:29). . . . The Spirit alone is the faithful and sure witness to each person of his election, and on that perseverance depends."[65] However, the Christian believer must combine confidence with "fear and uneasiness." This is not the exact equivalent of Luther's *Anfechtung*, but hints at the same lack of confidence in the self. *The Spirit's testimony to the heart* is often said to be Calvin's most distinctive contribution to a theology of the Holy Spirit.[66]

60. John Calvin, *The Epistles of Paul to the Galatians, Ephesians, Philippians and Colossians* (Edinburgh: Oliver and Boyd, 1965), pp. 105-6.

61. John Calvin, *Commentary on the Psalms of David*, 3 vols. (Oxford and London: Thomas Tegg, 1840), vol. 3, pp. 52-53.

62. John Calvin, *The First Epistle of Paul to the Corinthians* (Edinburgh: St. Andrew's, 1960), pp. 262-63.

63. Calvin, *First Corinthians*, p. 260.

64. Calvin, *First Corinthians*, p. 51.

65. Calvin, *First Corinthians*, p. 23.

66. Cf., e.g., Burgess, *The Holy Spirit: Medieval Roman Catholic and Reformation Traditions*, pp. 165-66.

Owen Chadwick helpfully traces the political significance of Calvin's work. Farel invited him to Geneva because, in addition to his qualities as an exegete and theologian, Calvin was an able organizer, bringing clarity both to his writings and to practical affairs. Admittedly "Calvin was not the absolute ruler of Geneva pictured by legend and his enemies."[67] But he constructed what Chadwick calls "new modes of power," and the authority of a purified ministry. His constitution was not "democratic. . . . The pastors chose pastors."[68] He rejected "libertine" attitudes, and focused on the institutional. In this sense, he would have been as quick to dissociate himself from self-styled, "charismatic" prophets as Luther was. Chadwick concludes, "Calvin's wider influence rested upon the clarity of his theological system and his Biblical exposition."[69] His academy in Geneva became one of the great schools of Protestant thought, and in Geneva, Theodore Beza (1519-1605) became, in effect, his successor. Beza consolidated the institutions founded by Calvin, including the Company of Pastors, the Academy, and the Consistory. Geneva became a new model of society and its religion and theology.

67. Owen Chadwick, *The Reformation* (London: Penguin, 1964 and 1972), p. 87.
68. Chadwick, *The Reformation*, p. 83.
69. Chadwick, *The Reformation*, p. 92.

16

The Seventeenth and Eighteenth Centuries:
From Owen to Edwards

John Calvin had left a legacy of concern about "the heart," among many other things, and Luther had also bequeathed a concern about the believer's personal relation to God. Both saw the initiative of divine grace as the source of gifts and calling, although both saw this also as strictly "under" Scripture. Veli-Matti Kärkkäinen groups together a number of Puritans under "Post-Reformation Renewal Movements," of which he considers Richard Sibbes, John Owen, and Thomas Goodwin as examples, alongside the Baptist John Bunyan. However, Richard Baxter (1615-91), George Herbert (1593-1633), William Laud (1573-1645), John Milton (1608-74), Matthew Poole (1624-79), and Jeremy Taylor (1613-67) all belong to the seventeenth century, and almost equally deserve mention.

16.1. John Owen

John Owen's father was an Oxfordshire vicar, and *John* (1616-83) studied mathematics and philosophy at Queen's College, Oxford University, from the age of seventeen. As a student at university, he later recalls that the Holy Spirit was active in his life. He drew spiritual nourishment from Luther's work on Galatians, the autobiographical reflections of John Bunyan, and his own work in expounding Psalm 130. He became ordained, but in 1637 he was ejected by William Laud's Statutes. In 1646 Owen preached before Parliament, and amid the turmoil of the Civil War preached there again. Oliver Cromwell was sufficiently impressed to invite him to become his chaplain, and he traveled with him to Dublin, where he preached to "a numerous multitude of . . . thirsting people" and assisted Cromwell in the reorganization of the University of Dublin.

Owen was allowed to return to England, now as Dean of Christ Church, Oxford, and then Vice-Chancellor of Oxford University. This was all the more notable in that he was no longer an ordained minister of the Church of England. He labored for the religious and moral well-being of the University, and preached alternate weeks in the city in collaboration with Thomas Goodwin, Head of Magdalene College. He was awarded the degree of Doctor of Divinity by the Oxford senate. Meanwhile he published many treatises, including *The Doctrine of the Saints' Perseverance,* of some 500 pages, and many voluminous writings. When Oliver Cromwell resigned as Chancellor of Oxford, Owen was replaced as Vice-Chancellor. He went into "retirement" in his closing years, but presided over the meeting of ministers and delegates of the Independent Churches, and prepared a confession, often known as the Savoy Assembly. In 1657 he published the devotional treatise *Of Communion with God the Father, Son, and Holy Spirit,* of which the section on the Holy Spirit offers a coherent view of his doctrine of the Spirit. He died in 1683.

From his huge collection of writings, we select Owen's work *The Holy Spirit* (1674) as the major source of his teaching on this subject.[1] Book 1, chapter 1, begins with general principles concerning the Holy Spirit and his work, including a section on 1 Corinthians 12 and spiritual gifts, and sin against the Holy Spirit. Second, in book 1, chapter 2, he considers the names and titles of the Holy Spirit. In book 1, chapter 3, Owen looks at the divine nature and personality of the Holy Spirit. In book 2, chapter 1, he considers the Old Testament. In chapter 2 he begins a consideration of the new creation. In chapter 3 he discusses the relation between the Holy Spirit and Jesus Christ. Book 3 concerns sin and regeneration. Finally, in book 4 he focuses on *sanctification by or through the Holy Spirit.* Book 5 explores the nature and necessity of holiness, with a section on election.

(1) Owen insists that *the gifts of the Holy Spirit* in 1 Cor. 12:1-11 and chapter 14 included gifts that were "extraordinary."[2] But the recipients do not differ from other believers, for "they had nothing, but what they received."[3] None can even confess that Jesus is Lord "but by the Holy Spirit" (1 Cor. 12:3; p. 38). Paul stresses the oneness and unity of all believers through "the one Spirit." The gifts are sheer gifts of grace *(charismata).* Owen lists the gifts of 12:8-10, which are given in response to the prayer of Jesus. He links Jesus' warning about "blasphemy against the Holy Spirit" with "despising or rejecting" the work of the Spirit. He then addresses the gift of "prophecy," warning against "*unduly pretending unto supernatural agitations from God,* when they were really acted [his word] by the devil"; he also warns us of "the *deceits and abuses* which have abounded in all ages of the Church under the pretence of the name and work of

---

1. John Owen, *The Holy Spirit* (Grand Rapids: Kregel, 1954). This is a shortened version of a longer one: John Owen, *The John Owen Collection: A Discourse concerning the Holy Spirit* (Rio, WI: Ages Software, 2004).

2. Owen, *The Holy Spirit,* p. 19; cf. pp. 17-25.

3. Owen, *The Holy Spirit,* p. 20.

the Holy Spirit" (my italics).[4] Owen points out that there were false prophets of many kinds: prophets of Baal, the false prophets who spoke against Jeremiah, and others. 2 Pet. 2:1 refers to "false prophets also among the people." John says, "Believe not every spirit" (1 John 4:1-3).[5] Deut. 13:1-3 and Hebrews are also cited. Moreover, some deny even the personality of the Holy Spirit. But the Spirit, he states, will expose the wickedness of the world.

(2) In book 1, chapter 2, Owen discusses the names and titles of the Holy Spirit. The use of *rûach* and *pneuma* are "very various." But we must search the original texts, as Ambrose and Jerome enjoined. We must set aside, he correctly asserts, the meanings "wind" and "human spirit": "Wherever there is mention of 'the Holy Spirit,' his relation unto the Father and the Son is included therein; for he is the Spirit of God."[6] The term "Holy" denotes that through the Holy Spirit God will sanctify his people. The Father is "fount and origin" of the Trinity; the Son is "from him by eternal generation . . . ; so is the person of the Holy Spirit from him by eternal procession or emanation." He is "*to pneuma to ek tou theou* . . . as a distinct person" (1 Cor. 2:12). He is "the Spirit of his Son sent into your hearts" (Gal. 4:6; 1 Pet. 1:11; Rom. 8:9). Jesus specifically prayed that "he should give another Comforter, even the Spirit of truth" (John 14:16-17). The genuineness of the experience can be seen in the confession that Jesus became truly human (1 John 4:3).

(3) Chapter 3 confirms the divine nature and personality of the Spirit. Owen insists that the Holy Spirit must be understood in terms of the being of God himself.[7] He cites Rom. 11:36 and Heb. 11:6 for the fundamental belief in God and his glory. God is, second, the rule and criterion of all worship. Yet the Holy Spirit is "a distinct, living, powerful, intelligent, divine person."[8] In other words, the doctrine of the Trinity is the frame for his doctrine of the Spirit. Owen adds that it is not the *fact* of the Spirit being joined to the Father and the Son, but *how* he is joined. Baptism in the threefold name is important. Like Luther, he stresses the role of "a visible sign," and cites the example of the dove at the baptism of Jesus, and the example of fire (pp. 44-46).[9] Next, Owen considers the "personal properties" given by the Spirit, such as wisdom and understanding. "Power" is also such a gift, as is teaching. He also appointed apostles and the Seven in Acts 6. Indeed, the Spirit sanctifies the whole people of God as his temple.[10] Throughout this chapter a host of biblical references are cited.

(4) Chapter 4 of the first book continues to describe actions which can be

4. Owen, *The Holy Spirit*, p. 25.
5. Owen, *The Holy Spirit*, p. 52.
6. Owen, *The Holy Spirit*, pp. 37-38.
7. Owen, *The Holy Spirit*, pp. 39-40.
8. Owen, *The Holy Spirit*, p. 41.
9. Owen, *The Holy Spirit*, pp. 44-46.
10. Owen, *The Holy Spirit*, pp. 48-54.

ascribed only to God through the Holy Spirit, but, this time, in the created universe and through "works of nature."[11] The Spirit, Owen urges, works both through nature and through grace. A wide array of Old Testament passages is cited. When Ps. 19:1 speaks of "garnishing the heavens," the Hebrews "understand the galaxy or Milky Way."[12] Yet this also includes the empowerment of the judges (Judg. 3:10; 6:34).

(5) Chapter 5 considers the "dispensation," or pouring out of the Holy Spirit. God sends the Spirit; he pours the Spirit out; he puts the Spirit within. In practical terms, the Spirit "proceeds, comes, falls on men, rests and [can] depart."[13] Numerous biblical texts are cited. The Spirit also "gives authority," comes as a gift of grace (1 Cor. 4:7), and is given for the profit of the Church (1 Cor. 12:7). He grants refreshment like rain upon dry ground. He gives "distributions" *(merismois)* to the Church. "Signs" may include "miraculous work, . . . surprising men with a sense of the presence of God."[14]

Book 2 covers much of the same ground, except that it focuses on the new creation (2 Cor. 5:17). By becoming "a new creation" in terms of covenant grace, this renewed nature entails sanctification and obedience through the Holy Spirit. It involves living out "the seed of God, whereby we are born again."[15] The Holy Spirit increases graces of holiness, *even though believers differ by degrees.* "God works in us both to will and to do his good pleasure" (Phil. 2:13). The Spirit gives us experiences of truth and reality. In this book, Owen also discusses "more occasional" gifts of the Spirit, although without doubt *sanctification* remains the primary gift. Moreover, he observes that the work of sanctification is *progressive.*[16] This work is "secret and mysterious." It may involve "perplexing temptations." *Indeed, there may be "delays" in holiness,* although "occasional" ones.[17] On the other hand, Owen warns us *against undue introspection.* Chapter 3 continues to discuss these themes, considering again regeneration and sanctification. Chapter 4 does likewise, expounding especially *purification from sin.* In chapter 5 of the longer version (only), Owen places all this in the perspective of Christ's atonement. "We are purged and purified from sin by the Spirit of God," but on the basis of the work of Christ revealed in Scripture; "You are washed; you are sanctified; you are justified in the name of the Lord Jesus, and by the Spirit of our God" (1 Cor. 6:9-11). Chapter 6 repeats the theme of sanctification. Righteousness becomes habitual.[18]

---

11. Owen *The Holy Spirit* (here the longer version), p. 119.

12. Owen, *The Holy Spirit* (longer version), p. 122.

13. Owen, *The Holy Spirit,* pp. 61-62 (longer version), p. 133.

14. Owen, *The Holy Spirit* (longer version), p. 151.

15. Owen, *The Holy Spirit* (longer version), p. 450.

16. Owen, *The Holy Spirit* (longer version), p. 461.

17. Owen, *The Holy Spirit* (longer version), p. 468.

18. Owen, *The Holy Spirit* (longer version), pp. 507, 544, and 549.

John Owen's account of the work of the Holy Spirit seems to combine careful references to biblical passages with good commonsense realism and a traditional emphasis on the Holy Spirit and sanctification. Many of his themes become implicit in Chapter 24 below, our Summary and Conclusion. Broadly, he seems to follow Luther, Bucer, and Calvin. His writings are voluminous, although also at times seriously repetitive. He has a broad, positive vision of the Person and work of the Spirit, but often returns to underline a point already made. Owen has numerous writings on a different subject. Two of the best known are *The Death of Death in the Death of Christ* in his *Collected Works*, vol. 10, and *The Doctrine of the Saint's Perseverance Explained and Confirmed* in his *Collected Works*, vol. 11. His *Vindication of the Doctrine of the Trinity* remains relevant to the present subject.

16.2. Jeremy Taylor

Jeremy Taylor (1613-67) was born in Cambridge. Although his origins were humble, he entered Gonville and Caius College at the University of Cambridge in 1626, and graduated in 1630 and 1631. In 1633 he became a Fellow of the College, and shortly afterward Archbishop Laud invited him to preach at Lambeth. With Laud's encouragement or patronage, he became a Fellow of All Souls, Oxford. He became chaplain to Charles I, and served subsequently as a chaplain in the Royalist army. Under Oliver Cromwell he suffered three imprisonments, but was allowed to retire to Wales. After the Restoration in 1660, he was appointed Bishop of Down and Connor, and Vice-Chancellor of Dublin University. He had considerable theological learning, was loyal to the Church of England, and became a writer of many significant works. His most widely influential book was *The Rule and Exercises of Holy Living* (1650). A year later he produced *The Rule and Exercises of Holy Dying*.[19] He also wrote *The Great Exemplar* (1647), on Jesus Christ; a series of sermons; and *The Liberty of Prophesying* (1647).

It might be tempting to underrate or to ignore what his work suggests or implies about the Holy Spirit, because he includes relatively *few explicit allusions* to the Holy Spirit as a Person. Nevertheless, if we take seriously the warning of J. E. Fison and others about the "self-effacing" character of the Holy Spirit, we cannot but see how Taylor lived out in practice the effects of the work of the Holy Spirit in an authentic way. This applies especially to the section in *Holy Living* called "The Practice of the *Presence of God*" (my italics).[20] Gordon

---

19. Jeremy Taylor, conveniently in *Selected Writings*, ed. C. H. Sisson (Manchester: Carcanet, 1990), pp. 42-92 and 93-115 respectively. This edition is used here.

20. Taylor, *Selected Writings*, pp. 58-66.

Fee has shown how closely the Holy Spirit should be seen as the Presence of God. Taylor produces nothing directly on the subject on the same scale as John Owen's vast quantity of words, but his work is no less profound, from the other side of the divide between Independent Puritans and those loyal to the King and the establishment, with genuine zeal for the gospel. It would be a serious mistake to equate the volume of sheer *talk* about the Holy Spirit with the extent to which we authentically *experience* the Spirit.

Taylor begins this section: "God is present in all places. . . . He sees every action, hears all discourses, and understands every thought. . . . 'In Him we live and move and have our being' (Acts 17:28)."[21] Under "manners of divine presence," he writes: "God is especially present in the hearts of His people by His Holy Spirit, and indeed the hearts of holy men are temples in the truth of things, and in type and shadow they are heaven itself."[22] The Holy Spirit, he continues, "by His dwelling there has also consecrated it [the human heart] into a temple (1 Cor. 3:16)."[23] Earlier Taylor comments, "God is everywhere present by his power. He rolls the orbs of heaven with His hand; He fixes the earth with His foot; He guides all creatures with His eye, and refreshes them with His influence."[24] But are not these activities often ascribed to the Holy Spirit, and also to the Trinity? As Gordon Fee calls him, the Spirit is "the Power and Presence of God." Ultimately in heaven we shall walk in God's presence and behold the face of God.[25] We shall see God's beauty, as represented in the fire of the Spirit that is experienced, and in the Spirit's gentleness that refreshes. Taylor writes: "From the same fountain" issue "humility of spirit" and "holy fear and holy love."[26]

Elsewhere in his treatise Taylor speaks of inner conflict, as Luther and Owen do, of redeeming the time, of purity of intention, of "retiring to God in short prayers and ejaculations. . . . God is present at your breathings and hearty sighings of prayer."[27] In the morning, he urges, "when you awake, accustom yourself to think first of God."[28] This again is a work of the Holy Spirit. Taylor includes much of what Aquinas would have called "the virtues": on contentedness, on sobriety, on chastity, on marriage, on patience, on sickness, on toleration. Too often a writer may avoid such practical advice by appealing to the dualist alibi that "that is the work of the Spirit." At every step Jeremy Taylor's practical observations on holiness of life presuppose the Person and work of

---

21. Taylor, *Selected Writings*, p. 58.
22. Taylor, *Selected Writings*, p. 60, sect. 5.
23. Taylor, *Selected Writings*, p. 61.
24. Taylor, *Selected Writings*, p. 59.
25. Taylor, *Selected Writings*, p. 62.
26. Taylor, *Selected Writings*, p. 66.
27. Taylor, *Selected Writings*, p. 45.
28. Taylor, *Selected Writings*, p. 44.

the Holy Spirit. If, for example, the Holy Spirit is the Spirit of truth, Taylor's comments on "humility" have special relevance. He asserts: "Humility does not consist in criticizing yourself, or wearing ragged clothes. . . . Humility consists in a realistic opinion of yourself."[29] "When you do receive praise for something you have done, take it indifferently and return it to God. Reflect it back to God, the giver of the gift."[30]

16.3. Philipp Jakob Spener

The mood of *Philipp Jakob Spener's* (1635-1705) writings differs from that of Owen and Taylor, and he is often ranked as the first of the Pietists, who through August Hermann Francke (1663-1727) influenced the Halle School, and ultimately Count von Zinzendorf (1700-1760) and the Moravians. Indirectly, therefore, through Zinzendorf, Spener influenced John Wesley and Jonathan Edwards. Ernst Käsemann warns us not to belittle Pietism, which still nourishes the Church.[31]

Spener's writings often reflect Luther's concerns, yet also some of the religious and cultural phenomena which accompanied the Radical Reformers and, later, Pentecostalism and the Renewal Movement. In what was perhaps his most important work, *Pia Desideria* (1675), Spener sought to reform Lutheran orthodoxy by urging lay engagement with the whole of Scripture.[32] Spener advocates "a more extensive use of the Word of God among us. . . . I do not disapprove of the preaching of sermons. . . . But I find this is not enough. . . . All Scripture, without exception, should be known by the congregation."[33] He continues that "assemblies would also be held in the manner in which Paul describes them in 1 Cor. 14:26-40. . . . Others who have been blessed with gifts and knowledge would also speak, . . . subject to the judgment of the rest."[34] Spener is considered *a loyal Lutheran,* but one who also wished *further reform.* He speaks often of the Holy Spirit. A contribution from the congregation is helpful "in so far as it accords with the sense of the Holy Spirit in the Scriptures."[35] *Spener did not support those Radical Reformers who placed the Spirit above the Word of Scripture.*

---

29. Richard J. Foster and James Bryan Smith (eds.), *Devotional Classics: Selected Readings* (San Francisco: HarperSanFrancisco, 1993), p. 244.

30. Foster and Smith, *Devotional Classics,* p. 145.

31. Ernst Käsemann, *New Testament Questions of Today* (London: SCM, 1969), p. 4.

32. Philipp Jakob Spener, *Pia Desideria,* conveniently at hand in *Pietists: Selected Writings,* ed. Peter C. Erb (London: SPCK, 1983), pp. 31-49.

33. Spener, *Pia Desideria,* in *Pietists,* ed. Erb, p. 31.

34. Spener, *Pia Desideria,* in *Pietists,* ed. Erb, p. 32.

35. Spener, *Pia Desideria,* in *Pietists,* ed. Erb, p. 33.

Spener fully endorsed Luther's assertion: "*All Christians are made priests* by their Saviour, are anointed by the Holy Spirit, and are dedicated to perform spiritual-priestly acts" (my italics).[36] He urged believers to "die to the world and live as individuals who are to become examples, . . . instructed . . . only in the light of the Holy Spirit."[37] A simpleminded minister is better than "a vain and worldly fool with double doctor's degrees, who is very clever, but has not been taught by God . . . and aided by the Holy Spirit."[38] It is not enough, Spener urges, to hear the Word of God with our outward ear: "we must let it penetrate our heart, so that we may hear the Holy Spirit speak there, that is, with vibrant emotion, . . . feel the sealing of the Spirit and the power of the Word."[39] Thus in *Pia Desideria* he holds *the Word and Spirit together.* Less happily, however, he also speaks of "*feeling*" the Spirit. This stress on feeling became a hallmark of the Pietists, and it has resurfaced in our culture today with a vengeance.

In addition to his manifesto-like *Pia Desideria,* Spener also wrote a number of other works. He produced seventy questions and answers in *The Spiritual Priesthood* (1677), in which he argued that "Christ . . . anoints his believers by his Holy Spirit in the power of which [whom] they may and shall bring sacrifices acceptable to God, pray for themselves and others, and edify themselves and their neighbours."[40] The priesthood of all believers is well expounded over the first thirty-three questions and answers. Then Spener offers prayer that the Holy Spirit will open our understanding as we read Scripture. Further, "the enlightenment of the Holy Spirit, by whose inspiration the Scriptures were first recorded," is needed. "God has promised the Holy Spirit to all who call upon him in simplicity, and therefore not only to the learned."[41] Without the gift of the Holy Spirit, Spener warns, Scripture will profit nothing.[42]

In his work *On Hindrances to Theological Studies* (1680) Spener regularly *contrasts the gift of the Holy Spirit with intellectual cleverness alone.* The student "will not be able to do anything zealously without the proper teacher, namely the Holy Spirit."[43] Nevertheless Spener *rejects* those extreme radical enthusiasts (such as Müntzer) "who await a revelation of the Spirit, and despise the preaching of the divine Word."[44] In 1694 Spener's *The Necessary and Useful Reading of the Holy Scriptures* was published, and indeed in this he argued: "Scripture is a light for our enlightenment, but it is a word of the Spirit. . . . [We must not] sep-

36. Spener, *Pia Desideria,* in *Pietists,* ed. Erb, p. 34.

37. Spener, *Pia Desideria,* in *Pietists,* ed. Erb, p. 42.

38. Spener, *Pia Desideria,* in *Pietists,* ed. Erb, p. 43.

39. Spener, *Pia Desideria,* in *Pietists,* ed. Erb, p. 48.

40. Spener, *The Spiritual Priesthood,* Qu. 1 in *Pietists,* ed. Erb, p. 50.

41. Spener, *The Spiritual Priesthood,* Qu. 34-36, in *Pietists,* ed. Erb, p. 56.

42. Spener, *The Spiritual Priesthood,* Qu. 39, in *Pietists,* ed. Erb, p. 58.

43. Spener, *On Hindrances to Theological Studies,* in *Pietists,* ed. Erb, p. 64.

44. Spener, *On Hindrances to Theological Studies,* in *Pietists,* ed. Erb, p. 69.

arate the Spirit from the Word."[45] In *Resignation* (1715) Spener urges: "We must give ourselves to the Holy Spirit as an empty canvas on which He is to paint."[46]

Spener's approach to the doctrine of the Holy Spirit remained relatively uncontroversial until about 1690. Then a series of debates divided the Lutheran Church into Pietist and Orthodox groups. August H. Francke (1663-1727), a disciple of Spener, held Pietist meetings in Leipzig, and the Movement spread across Germany. Often these gatherings *encouraged ecstatic experiences and visions,* and a series of "prophets" arose. This inflamed division with the orthodox Lutherans. In Halle, Francke established schools and an orphanage, and in spite of Francke's attempts at moderation, *apocalyptic or millenarian hopes* and expectations began to flourish. J. E. and J. W. Petersen advocated "premillennialism" (defined in Chapter 18) and the "restoration of all things." Some urged celibacy and believer's baptism. Readers will perceive many parallels with later Pentecostalism.

Pietism remained influential until at least the mid-eighteenth century. Nicholas Ludwig von Zinzendorf (1700-1760) combined Spener's emphasis on the laity with elements drawn from Luther and Hus, in effect to found the Moravians. This, in turn, became one of the formative influences on John and Charles Wesley. Peter Erb traces the development of eighteenth-century Pietism from Spener through Francke and the Halle School and Gottfried Arnold (1666-1714), Johann Albrecht Bengel (1687-1752), and Friedrich Oetinger (1702-82) to Nicholas Count von Zinzendorf (1700-1760).

16.4. George Fox and the Quakers

George Fox (1624-91) became the founder and leader of the Society of Friends, who claimed to be "friends of Jesus" (John 15:15). "Quaker" was originally a nickname given by others because of such phenomena as "shaking" or "trembling" at the presence of God. George Fox was the son of a prosperous weaver who expressed dissatisfaction with those clergy who were educated at Oxford or Cambridge, and who looked to "theology" rather than "experience" as the basis of religious life. Fox criticized and attacked Christian doctrine, whether biblical, traditional, or explicatory, by logic, inference, and reason. In place of this, he urged *the experience of the community and the "inner light" of the Holy Spirit.* "Quaking" involved not only trembling or shaking, but also such *manifestations of emotional and religious fervor as silence and waiting, emotional outbursts, shouting and laughter, and informal worship without sacraments or a priest or minister.* Fox urged the use of "spiritual gifts" as in 1 Corinthians 12–14. He saw the light of the Holy Spirit in all, whether they were believers or not.

---

45. Spener, *The Necessary and Useful Reading of the Holy Scriptures,* in *Pietists,* ed. Erb, p. 72.
46. Spener, *Resignation,* in *Pietists,* ed. Erb, p. 85.

Fox's *Journal* or *Autobiography* (published in 1694) is a narrative classic, which some have compared with Augustine's *Confessions* or with John Bunyan's *Grace Abounding*. He was born in Mansfield, between Nottingham and Doncaster. From 1656 he wrote around three thousand letters. The *Journal* records Fox's personal *experience*, and *"testimony"* became the primary mode of communication for Fox and the Quakers. In early years he was first apprentice to a traveling shoemaker, and then traveled throughout Leicestershire, Derbyshire, and Nottinghamshire seeking spiritual guidance. He broke from the Church of England. In 1647 he experienced a "revelation" in which he learned that all earthly power was corrupt. Revelations came only through "the inner light" of the Holy Spirit. He appealed to John 1:9, "the light that enlightens every man." However, as C. K. Barrett and others have shown, the Greek of the verse uses *phōtizō*, which usually means *not* "inner" light, but *shedding light upon* all people, exposing them to judgment. This is also a work of the Holy Spirit, as John 16:8 makes clear. George Beasley-Murray adopts a compromise by describing the light as positive or negative, "for salvation and judgment."[47]

Fox underwent periods of imprisonment for his attack on the established church. This was extended when his pacifism led him to refuse to enlist in the Parliamentary Army. In 1651 he was released, and ministered in Yorkshire and Lancashire. He refused to raise his hat to social superiors, and included women and children among his speakers. By 1655 Quakerism had spread to Bristol, London, and elsewhere. After the Restoration in 1660, however, Quakers were regarded, with other Independents, as enemies of the Crown and the Church of England. In the face of persecution, Fox fled to the American colonies, to Ireland, to Holland, and to Germany. In 1673 he was imprisoned at Worcester, and began his *Journal* or *Autobiography*, which was published posthumously in 1694.

The actual words and phrases of Fox's *Journal* are memorable. In "Chapter 2, the First Years of Ministry (1648-49)," he recounts that at Mansfield: "The Lord's power began to shake them. . . . The Lord's power was so great that the house seemed to be shaken. . . . The professors said that it was now as in the days of the apostles."[48] In the next paragraph he tells how soon after "I saw," through the Spirit, the blood of Christ. In chapter 2, he recounts that while defending a woman's right to speak, "I was wrapped up as in a rapture in the Lord's Power."[49] He refuses to call established places of worship "churches," consistently labeling them "steeple houses."[50] He recounts "meetings of Friends . . . gathered to God's teaching by his light, Spirit, and power." People, he urged,

47. George Beasley Murray, *John* (Nashville: Nelson, 2nd ed. 1999), p. 12.

48. George Fox, *The Journal of George Fox* (New York: Cosimo, 2007), p. 13; also *The Journal of George Fox* (Leeds: Pickard, 6th ed. 1836), p. 102.

49. Fox, *Journal,* p. 14 (2007 ed.).

50. Fox, *Journal,* p. 14.

cannot reach "the stature of the fullness of Christ" without "the same power and Spirit" that fell on prophets and apostles.[51] Often he receives personal "revelations" from God, which come through "the Spirit of Truth in the inward parts." Friends seek "fellowship . . . in the Holy Spirit, and sing in the Spirit." Typically in chapter 3 of the *Journal*, he exclaims: "The Lord's power was so mighty upon me, so strong in me, that I could not hold, but was made to cry out and say: 'O no; it is not the Scriptures!' But I told *what it was* [his phrase], namely the Holy Spirit."[52]

Chapter 3 of the *Journal* recounts "The First Taste of Prison, 1648-49." He testifies to his rejection of "worldly" customs, saying: "Many come to see the vanity of that custom of putting off the hat to men." When charged in a court of law, he responded: "Christ says, 'Swear not at all, but let your *yea* be *yea,* and your *nay* be *nay.*'"[53] In contrast to sham "steeple houses," the Friends have "meeting houses." He recognizes only the "invisible" church of believers. He rehearses some apparent exorcisms.

Chapter 4 concerns "A Year in Derby Prison" (1650-51). This begins with another exorcism. Fox recounts how, at the ringing of "steeple-house bell" in Derby, he was moved to tell a distinguished congregation that "their preaching, baptism and sacrifices would never sanctify them. . . . The power of God thundered."[54] But they threw him out. After interrogating him, they committed him to prison for six months. He was charged with "diverse blasphemous opinions."[55] When he proved unrepentant, he was imprisoned for a further six months. Chapter 5 covers 1651-52. Fox was "commanded by the Lord" at Lichfield to cry: "Woe to the bloody city of Lichfield." It is typical of Fox, and perhaps of many later Pentecostals and advocates of the Holiness Movement, that what offended many in the established church was his overrealized eschatology, or *"sinless perfection."* He writes: *"They could not bear to hear victory over sin and the devil; for they could not believe that any could be free from sin this side of the grave"* (my italics).[56]

By contrast, York included "some tender people." Chapter 6 is entitled "A New Era Begins, 1651-52."[57] Fox proclaimed "the day of the Lord," and exhorted his hearers to repentance. Francis Howgell comments, "This man speaks with authority, not as the scribes." As he journeyed north, he was favorably received at Kendal, and significantly he came to enjoy the protection of Margaret Fell, the wife of Leonard or Thomas Fell, a Judge of Ulverstone (paragraphs 24-28).

51. Fox, *Journal*, p. 104 (1836 ed.).
52. Fox, *Journal*, p. 24.
53. Fox, *Journal*, p. 323 (1836 ed.).
54. Fox, *Journal*, p. 30.
55. Fox, *Journal*, p. 31.
56. Fox, *Journal*, p. 32.
57. Fox, *Journal*, pp. 41-76 (2007 ed.).

This became a turning point. In spite of his contempt for "worldly authority," Fox began to benefit from Margaret Fell's protection. He also journeyed to Carlisle in the North.[58]

In 1653 Fox was imprisoned again, as chapter 7 of the *Journal* recounts. However, chapter 8, on the years 1653-54, tells how a high-ranking army officer arranged for an interview with Oliver Cromwell, currently Lord Protector of England. He saw his audience with Cromwell as Christ before Pilate: "I spoke much to him of Truth, . . . and he carried himself very moderately." Fox told him that "Christendom had the Scriptures, but wanted . . . power and the Spirit." Allegedly Cromwell had "tears in his eyes," and invited a further hearing. It is said that Cromwell respected his sincerity and piety, but that he perceived problems in his disruptive activity. In due course Cromwell released him. Fox was less successful in the southern part of England, although he was again imprisoned. Chapter 10 recounts his visit to Wales.

The *Journal* covers twenty chapters, but the flavor and ethos remain the same. Fox tells of the Restoration of Charles II, and two years in America, in the years 1671-73.[59] Much of his narrative reads like a *contrived* parallel with Jesus' narrative in the Gospels. For example, he uses such phrases as "He taught with authority, not as the scribes." He firmly opposed all *doctrine,* as most Quakers do today, and opposed reason and education in favor of "experience." Yet it would be harsh to question his sincerity or the genuineness of *some* alleged revelations, and those who applaud his elevation of heart over head may regret the particular eccentricities which make one doubt so many examples of his being led by an "inner voice" or "inner light." Some might suggest, in regard to the times in which Fox lived, that the living fire of the classical Reformers was beginning to harden into a theoretical and intellectual Protestant orthodoxy, against which he passionately reacted. In this sense one can fully understand his reactions and attacks. Had his opponents held *together Bible and Spirit,* or head and heart, more effectively, perhaps his reaction would not have been so extreme. But he is better understood as an anticipation of Pentecostalism and the Renewal Movement, and as an heir to the Radical Reformers and Pietists.

One writer describes Fox as a successor of the mystics of the Middle Ages, and also as a predecessor of the Methodists of the eighteenth century. The latter verdict is perhaps an exaggeration. Fox, however, did see himself as a reviver of earliest Christianity. He was probably closer to Müntzer than to Luther, and closer to the Anabaptists than to Calvin. In America William Penn (1644-1718) became influential as a statesman and politician in the Quaker tradition. Penn said of Fox, "Above all he excelled in prayer. . . . The most awful, living, reverent

58. Fox, *Journal,* pp. 77-93.
59. Fox, *Journal,* pp. 271-315.

frame I ever felt or beheld, I must say, was his in prayer. And truly it was a testimony he knew and lived nearer to the Lord than other men."[60]

Arguably, over the years, the Quakers became less Christ-centered than Fox. Increasingly they stressed the "inner light" of all people, and an ambiguous or reductive attitude toward the Holy Trinity knocked aside Patristic and medieval approaches to the Holy Spirit. Quakers suffered for their faith both in England and America. In New England forty-seven were banished, and four were even hanged. Their universalism drifted into a liberal latitudinarianism, and their opposition to oaths, tithes, war, infant baptism, and worldly power and titles put them at odds with Lutheranism and to a large extent with Calvinism and the rest of the Church.

16.5. John Wesley

John Henry Newman rightly called the eighteenth century a time "when love grew cold." On the other hand, it is understandable that in the face of such "experience-centered" outlooks as that of George Fox, many would echo the sentiments of John Locke (1632-1704) about the criterion of "reasonableness," against mere force or intensity of conviction. Intensity of conviction is *not necessarily* a sign of the Holy Spirit. Hence Locke felt it necessary to produce his book *The Reasonableness of Christianity as Delivered in the Scriptures* (1695). Yet the eighteenth century as a whole witnessed a rise of formalism and rationalism. It is equally understandable that some should protest in the name of authentic biblical and spiritual faith. Such were the brothers John and Charles Wesley, and more broadly Jonathan Edwards, all born between 1703 and 1707.

John Wesley (1703-91) was educated at Charterhouse School and Christ Church, Oxford, and in 1726 was elected as a Fellow of Lincoln College, Oxford University.[61] He was a clergyman of the Church of England, which he never renounced, and also became part-time Curate at Epworth, Humberside, where his father, Samuel, was Vicar. At Oxford he led a group which fellow students called "The Holy Club" because of their diligence in Christian commitment and ethics. The group also contained the more Calvinist George Whitefield (1714-70). Wesley was also influenced by both Jeremy Taylor's *Holy Living* and William Law's *A Serious Call to a Devout and Holy Life* (1728). Law, for example, carefully distinguished between the formal activity of "saying prayers" and the speech-action of genuinely *praying* (*Serious Call*, ch. 14).[62]

---

60. William Penn, "Preface" to Fox's *Journal*.

61. John Wesley, *Journal* (London: Isbister, 1902), p. xix (edited and abbreviated).

62. William Law, *A Serious Call to a Devout and Holy Life* (London and Toronto: Dent, and New York: Dutton, 1906), p. 165; cf. pp. 162-85.

In 1735 John and his younger brother Charles set out for Georgia, U.S.A., on a missionary enterprise under the auspices of the Society for the Propagation of the Gospel. Partly because of his unsuccessful love affair, which ended in legal action, things did not go well, and he returned to England two years later.[63] He doubted that he possessed "saving faith," and had long conversations with Peter Böhler, the Moravian, about his spiritual state.[64] On Wednesday, May 24, 1738, Wesley awoke at 5 a.m. and read in his New Testament of God's "exceeding great and precious promises" (2 Pet. 1:4). Later he read: "You are not far from the kingdom of God." In the afternoon he went to St. Paul's Cathedral, where he heard the anthem: "Out of the depths have I called to you." In the evening he went "very unwillingly" to a meeting on Aldersgate Street, London, where "one was reading Luther's preface to the Epistle to the Romans," and, he recounts, "I felt my heart strangely warmed. I felt I did trust in Christ, Christ alone, for salvation; and an assurance was given me that he had taken away my sin."[65] Although he was "buffeted with temptations," the next morning his first thought on waking was "Jesus, Master."[66] In the afternoon, Wesley went to St. Paul's Cathedral, where "I could taste the good word of God," and afterward, in spite of doubts, now "had peace with God." On June 7 he traveled to Germany to spend three months visiting the Moravians.

On his return to England, Wesley found that many churches were closed to him, and he followed Whitefield in preaching "to about a thousand persons at Bristol," and then to fifteen hundred colliers in Kingswood, Bristol.[67] He then preached to five thousand. His preaching became partly itinerant, in London, Bristol, and Newcastle. It was in 1739 that he uttered his famous dictum: "All the world is my parish."[68] At Moorfields in London he addressed ten thousand, and writes: "I described the difference between what is generally called Christianity and the true, old, Christianity, which under the new name of Methodism, is everywhere spoken against."[69]

There do not seem to be many explicit references to the Holy Spirit in his *Journal,* but he would have ascribed many of the "phenomena" which he described to the work of the Holy Spirit. He came to believe, for example, in "healing."[70] From 1744 Wesley held conferences of lay preachers, with a legal constitution in 1784. He never wanted them to leave the Church of England, but the Church of England authorities could not in conscience recognize the lay

63. Wesley, *Journal,* pp. 3-28.
64. Wesley, *Journal,* pp. 33-41.
65. Wesley, *Journal,* p. 43.
66. Wesley, *Journal,* p. 44.
67. Wesley, *Journal,* p. 48.
68. Wesley, *Journal,* pp. 54-56.
69. Wesley, *Journal,* p. 61.
70. Wesley, *Journal,* p. 145.

preachers as ordained ministers or priests. In America, Wesley ordained Francis Asbury (1745-1816) as his colleague, and Asbury performed the functions of a Methodist bishop there, alongside Thomas Coke. After his death there remained nearly three hundred preachers and over 71,000 members of the new organization in Britain.

Wesley never abandoned Luther's theme of justification by grace through faith, but it is usually argued that he advocated the pursuit of holiness to the point of "perfection." Unlike Fox, he valued *the Bible, reason, and tradition*. But, as with Fox, "experience" and the supernatural *also* counted for much. He prized the Eucharist or Lord's Supper, and tried to hold together liturgical forms of prayer with extempore prayer. Wesley's theology of the Holy Spirit, like that of his brother, Charles, appears through hymns and sermons rather than his *Journal*. For example, Kärkkäinen cites his Sermon 141, "On the Holy Spirit." Under his third point Wesley writes: "Consider what the Holy Spirit is *to every believer* for his personal *sanctification and salvation*. It is not granted to everyone to raise the dead and heal the sick" (my italics). What is "necessary" is to pass from death to life. True, "The Holy Spirit has enabled men to speak with tongues and to prophesy," but the important thing is to practice "degrees of trust in God and love to men." The Spirit is also "preparation for life in God. . . . The gift of the Holy Spirit looks full to the resurrection."[71]

Many of John Wesley's sermons are online, including Sermon 141, "On the Holy Spirit."[72] He begins with Paul's and Luther's contrast between law and Spirit, citing 2 Cor. 3:17. The Spirit is intimately related to Christ, and "gives life." In part 1 he traces our fall in Adam. Part 2 centers on the Person of Christ. Part 3 in effect bypasses "the extraordinary gifts" of the Spirit to consider what the Spirit is "to every believer." Wesley rightly perceives that in Paul these gifts are *for all believers*. The Holy Spirit awakens minds, which may even bring pain. But joy lies ahead as it did for Christ after his suffering. The fruit of the Holy Spirit is to issue in "holy dispositions," including love. The Spirit also enables death and resurrection with Christ. In his Sermon 55 "On the Trinity," Wesley shows that he is fully aware of the need to tread cautiously and reverently on this holy ground. But he concludes: "I do not see how it is possible for any to have vital religion who denies that these Three are one."[73] In Sermon 10, entitled "The Witness of the Spirit (1)," Wesley expounds Rom. 8:16. But he warns his readers, "How many have resisted this scripture . . . to the destruction of

---

71. Veli-Matti Kärkkäinen, *The Holy Spirit and Salvation: The Sources of Christian Theology* (Louisville: Westminster/John Knox Press, 2010), p. 221.

72. Wesley, "On the Holy Spirit: *Sermon 141*," ed. George Lyons (Nampa, ID: Northwest Nazarene College), from *Christian Classics Ethereal Library* (preached at St Mary's, Oxford, at Whitsun, 1736).

73. Wesley, Sermon 55, "On the Trinity," ed. David R. Leonard, at Northwest Nazarene College, and *Christian Classics Ethereal Library*.

their souls! How many have *mistaken the voice of their own imagination for this witness of the Spirit of God!*" (my italics).[74] He continues: "Who can be surprised if many reasonable men, seeing the dreadful effects of this delusion, [labour to] keep at the utmost distance from it?"[75]

In many ways the *Sermons* and Wesley's *Journal* are complementary. The former shows Wesley's openness to the Holy Spirit's guidance and witness; the latter reveals a commonsense and Trinitarian orthodoxy that provides boundary markers for his doctrine of the Holy Spirit. In an age of rationalism, he saw the need for warmth, passion, and experience, but unlike the earlier enthusiasts and Quakers, he did not at the same time despise the witness of the Bible, the use of reason, and the Patristic traditions of the Church. His younger brother, Charles, also held many of his convictions, most of which he expressed through hundreds of hymns. John remained, however, a loyal member of the Church of England.

Ronald Knox asks whether John Wesley deserves the term "enthusiast."[76] He points out that in Wesley's era, "enthusiasm" was not a precise term. Some defined it as a strong persuasion that one acted under the impulse of the Holy Spirit, without question. George Whitefield, Wesley's companion and sometimes co-worker, admitted: "I have sometimes mistaken nature for grace, imagination for revelation."[77] On the other hand, Bishop Butler addressed to Wesley the well-known accusation: "Sir, the pretending to extraordinary revelations and gifts of the Holy Ghost is a horrid thing, a very horrid thing." Moreover, Wesley stated in 1750 that he was "fully convinced . . . that the Montanists . . . were real, scriptural Christians" who were ridiculed by "dry, formal, orthodox" churchmen. After 1743 the Moravians distanced themselves from Wesley, mainly because of his trend toward "sinless perfection," as well as alleged authoritarianism.

On the other hand, Wesley valued "calm" in the face of violent conversion scenes. In the end, Knox sees the legacy of Wesley as overreliance on "feelings": "All through the *Journal* there is constant mention of dreams, warnings, and strange experiences encountered by the faithful; in all such matters Wesley remained inexhaustibly curious."[78] Nevertheless, we recall that Knox writes with his own agenda. The literature on Wesley is enormous and varied. In the light of so many specialists on Wesley, it would be hazardous and foolish to suggest here any firm conclusion. I have discussed Wesley with some leading Method-

74. Wesley, Sermon 10, "The Witness of the Spirit," from *Christian Classics Ethereal Library,* introductory sect. 1.

75. Wesley, Sermon 10 (as above), introductory sect. 2.

76. Ronald A. Knox, *Enthusiasm: A Chapter in the History of Religion* (Oxford: Clarendon, 1950), pp. 449-54; cf. pp. 422-548 on Wesley.

77. Knox, *Enthusiasm,* p. 450.

78. Knox, *Enthusiasm,* p. 536.

ists, and many regard the charge of "perfectionism" in Wesley as either without foundation, or at least as highly controversial.

16.6. Jonathan Edwards

Jonathan Edwards (1703-58) was born in Connecticut, and is best known for his key role (as well as critical attitude) in the Great Awakening in America of the 1730s and 1740s. He entered Yale at the age of thirteen, graduated in 1720, and received a Master's degree three years later. Although as a youth he had difficulties with the Calvinist stress on the sovereignty of God, he later wholeheartedly accepted the doctrine with "a sense of the glory of the divine being." In 1727 he was ordained to serve in a Congregational church at Northampton, Massachusetts. He is credited with bringing, or at least with leading, a huge revival, which came to be known as the First Great Awakening of the 1730s and 1740s. His church attracted large numbers, and in 1737 he published *A Faithful Narrative of the Surprising Works of God.* However, nine years later, in 1746, he followed this with his *Treatise concerning Religious Affections,* in which he defended not only the emotions and professions of faith released in revival, but also the need for intellectual inquiry and self-criticism. He urged the value of *habits of the renewed will,* and asserted that *some examples* of alleged revival *were not genuine.* As a Calvinist he asserted the value of Christian doctrine; as a philosopher he expounded the *peril of self-deception* and the need for *discernment over "experience."* He wrote much about the Holy Spirit, but also about an *"imagined"* work of the Spirit which was merely due to the wishes of the human heart. Although he defended evangelical revivals, he also stressed the *Bible, reason, and tradition.*

In 1750 his congregation deposed Edwards from his church because of his strict policy of admission to Holy Communion. His grandfather, Solomon Stoddard, whom he succeeded as pastor in 1729, had regarded Communion as "a converting ordinance," whereas Edwards saw it as a sacrament for the believing faithful only. Edwards moved to Stockbridge, also in Massachusetts, and completed his work *The Freedom of the Will* (1754). In 1758, three months before his death, he was elected president of the College of New Jersey (later, Princeton). In that year he fell victim to smallpox. Edwards left voluminous writings, especially if we include his sermons. Nineteenth-century editions usually run to eight volumes; more recent editions run to thirteen volumes.

For the present subject, some of Edwards's sermons provide an excellent summary of his doctrine of the Holy Spirit, but the most relevant major work is probably his *Treatise concerning Religious Affections.*[79] One key section of this

---

79. Jonathan Edwards, *A Treatise concerning Religious Affections,* in *Select Works of Jonathan Edwards,* vol. 3 (London: Banner of Truth, 1959), and *Works of Jonathan Edwards,* vol. 2: *Religious*

work is "Distinguishing Signs of Truly Gracious and Holy Affections." Section 1 discusses "Affections That Are Truly Spiritual." These indeed come from the Holy Spirit, as against operations which may merely *seem* so. Edwards rightly follows the *Pauline* pattern of using *"spiritual" for what issues from the Holy Spirit,* "because they are born of the Spirit and because of the indwelling and holy influences of the Spirit of God." The Holy Spirit may indeed "influence natural man," but not as an indwelling principle.[80] Edwards adds: "Holiness is the nature of the Spirit of God; therefore he is called in Scripture the *Holy Ghost*" (his italics).[81] "He makes the soul a partaker of God's beauty and Christ's joy, so that the saint has truly fellowship *with* the Father, and *with* his Son, Jesus Christ, in thus having the communion or participation of the Holy Spirit" (his italics).[82] These affections arise from influences that are truly divine, and "this is what I mean by *supernatural.*"[83] The natural man is like someone observing honey but never actually tasting it.

Edwards urges that "true" affections are marked by conviction of reality and certainty, not by "opinions." Effective correction is "great, spiritual, mysterious." However, this must also be "*reasonable,* solid, persuasive and a correction of the truth of the gospel" (my italics).[84] The testimony of martyrs is not a mere "opinion," but a "testimony." Edwards stresses that genuine affections arise from one's "own utter insufficiency, despicableness, and odiousness," which "God has abundantly manifested in his Word."[85] Indeed, in a crucial passage Edwards warns us: "There is a *pretended* great humiliation, being dead to the law, and emptied of self, which is one of the most *elated* things in the world. . . . Some, who think themselves quite emptied of themselves, confident that they are abased in the dust, are full . . . with *the glory of their own humility,* and lifted up to heaven with a high opinion of their abasement. Their humility is . . . self-conceited, confident, noisy, assuming humility. . . ."[86]

In section 7 of *Religious Affections* Edwards reiterates that where religious affections are genuine, "such power as this is properly divine, and is peculiar to *the Spirit of the Lord,* [effecting] a remarkable and abiding change in persons" (his italics). If this is absent, even apparent conversion remains "imaginations

---

Affections, ed. John Smith (New Haven: Yale University Press, 2009). Substantial extracts are available in *Jonathan Edwards: Basic Writings,* ed. Ola Winslow (New York: New American Library, 1966), pp. 184-95, and in *An Anthology of Devotional Literature,* ed. Thomas S. Kepler (Nappanee, IN: Jordan Publishing, 2001), pp. 461-72.

80. Edwards, *Religious Affections,* 1:1.
81. Edwards, *Religious Affections,* 1:2.
82. Edwards, *Religious Affections,* 1:2.
83. Edwards, *Religious Affections,* 1:2, also in Kepler, *Anthology,* pp. 461-62.
84. Edwards, *Religious Affections,* 5:1.
85. Edwards, *Religious Affections,* 6:1.
86. Edwards, *Religious Affections,* 6; in Kepler, *Anthology,* p. 464 (my italics).

and pretences, . . . stupid and perverse, unchristian and unsavoury." This is more telling than "the brightest story of experiences."[87] Edwards, however, is realistic about temporary backsliding: "Allowances indeed must be made for the natural temper, which conversion does not entirely eradicate."

The work of the Holy Spirit witnesses primarily to Christ, and Edwards makes this point with sensitivity. He first expounds in general terms what it means to be *holy,* especially in showing "humility, meekness, love, forgiveness and mercy." But he then observes: "These things are especially the character of Christ; so they are all especially the character of Christians. Christians are *Christ-like*" (his italics).[88] Yet he also warns his readers: "There is a pretended boldness for Christ that arises from no better principle than pride." On the other hand, the Spirit also inspires a genuine zeal and fervor, which is *not* marked by bumptious pride. This kind of zeal is gentle and loving. He asserts: "All true saints are of a loving, . . . beneficent temper."

Gracious and genuine affections, Edwards argues in section 9, "soften the heart" and are marked by "tenderness of spirit. . . . Gracious affections . . . turn a heart of stone more and more into a heart of flesh."[89] The Holy Spirit promotes convictions of conscience. In section 10, Edwards sees true, gracious affections as arising in those who have "put on Christ," while "false" affections come often from hypocrites. Claims to exhibit the fruit of the Spirit can sometimes become "disproportionate" to confessions of faith. Another difference lies in the extent to which there is a genuine *longing for God.* True affections are like "the kindling of a flame; the higher it is raised, the more ardent it is."[90] Once again, "false affections deceive."

The *Sermons* of Jonathan Edwards expound his concept of the work of the Holy Spirit further.[91] Kärkkäinen quotes from the sermon "The Work of Redemption." Edwards says, "The sum of all that Christ purchased is the Holy [Ghost] Spirit. [This] is communion with God, which is only having the Spirit. . . . The Spirit is the river of the water of life, which in heaven proceeds from the throne of God and of the Lamb (Rev. 22:1)."[92] In "The Spirit's Operation" the Spirit sanctifies.

Jonathan Edwards's material on the Holy Spirit shows a faithful reflection of the New Testament and Patristic tradition, which is accurate, constructive, and critical. In particular, like Paul, he reserves the biblical use of "spiritual" to

---

87. Edwards, *Religious Affections,* 7; in Kepler, *Anthology,* p. 466.

88. Edwards, *Religious Affections,* 8; in Kepler, *Anthology,* p. 467.

89. Edwards, *Religious Affections,* 9; in Kepler, *Anthology,* p.

90. Edwards, *Religious Affections,* sect. 11; in Kepler, *Anthology,* p. 471.

91. Edwards, *The Sermons of Jonathan Edwards,* ed. Wilson H. Kinnach (New Haven: Yale University Press, 1999); extracts found conveniently in Kärkkäinen, *The Holy Spirit and Salvation,* pp. 236-39.

92. Edwards, *Sermons,* in Kärkkäinen, *The Holy Spirit and Salvation,* p. 236.

denote "of the Holy Spirit" in authentic, Christ-related contexts. He avoids using "spiritual" in the broader and nonredemptive sense. He also accepts the authenticity of what people often call "supernatural" acts of the Holy Spirit, for which he prefers the word *"surprising,"* or "from *beyond,*" or "from *outside man.*" But he is intensely cautious about disentangling the leading of the Spirit from *imagined* visions, voices, or guidance, insisting on "Christ-likeness" as the key criterion of the activity of the Spirit in the heart. He rightly suspects any devaluation of reason, and argues that sheer emotional experience may minister simply to pride.

Many may hold a range of views on other aspects of Christian doctrine. Edwards certainly glories in the absolute sovereignty of God. He works this out in his well-known attack on Arminian theology in *The Freedom of the Will* (1754). Here he defends theological determinism, or what in philosophy is often called *occasionalism,* namely, the view that God is the entire cause of everything. Natural or second causes become mere "occasions" for which God produces an appropriate effect. Creation is a manifestation of God's splendor and beauty. Eschatology and the Last Judgment play a major part in his theology. Although *in this life* we love others enough to have ambiguous thoughts about hell, *in the life to come* believers will become so concerned for God's justice and glory, Edwards maintains, that the negative or punitive effects of the Last Judgment will bring them only joy.[93] This does not alter the case that, on the subject of the Holy Spirit, Edwards seems to rank (perhaps with Luther, Calvin, and Owen) as open and biblical, yet sane and critical.

93. Jonathan Edwards, *Select Works of Jonathan Edwards,* vol. 2: *Sermons* (London: Banner of Truth Trust, 1959), "The End of the Wicked Contemplated by the Righteous," pp. 245-65, esp. p. 255. Cf. also "The Justice of God in the Damnation of Sinners," in *Sermons,* pp. 114-55.

PART III

The Holy Spirit in Modern Theology and Today

17

The Nineteenth Century: The Parting of the Ways

Two reasons suggest that we begin Part III at this point. First, most modern theologies begin with Schleiermacher and Hegel, almost now as a convention. Second, before 1800 most works on the Holy Spirit could be read with profit by Christians of virtually all traditions. The beginnings of a "Pentecostal" or "Renewal" kind of approach found expression in the life and *Journal* of George Fox and the early Quakers, but Fox was simply one man, and communities such as the Quakers were often regarded as on the "fringes" of the tradition of the Christian Church. It was otherwise with John Owen and John Wesley, who maintained a largely traditional view of the Holy Spirit within a firmly Trinitarian framework. Whether Wesley explicitly taught "sinless perfection" remains more controversial than some imply, especially from such occasional sources as his sermons. However, with the dawn of the nineteenth century, writers on the Holy Spirit tended to belong to one of four distinct traditions. We may indeed perhaps distinguish between four or five different approaches to the Holy Spirit.

(1) First, the "mainstream" but largely Liberal line of theological scholarship, as represented by Schleiermacher and Hegel, was heavily influenced by Kant and by the Enlightenment, even if Schleiermacher also reflected his Pietist roots and Romanticism. This tradition remained largely dominant until the first quarter of the twentieth century, with Harnack.

(2) The nineteenth century witnessed to a radically different and more conservative tradition in the resurgence of Calvinism and Reformed Orthodoxy among such writers as Charles Hodge in America, George Smeaton in Scotland, and Abraham Kuyper in the Netherlands. Smeaton and Kuyper explicitly wrote books on the Holy Spirit, Kuyper's running to over 650 pages, while Hodge devoted over fifty pages of his three-volume *Systematic Theology* to the Trinity and the Holy Spirit, and 150 pages to sanctification, regeneration,

and faith. Newman's phrase "the Parting of the Ways" perhaps demonstrates this chasm between Liberalism and a more conservative approach more clearly than his concern about Anglican–Roman Catholic traditions as such.

(3) To a smaller extent a third and even perhaps a fourth kind of approach may be distinguished. A third began to anticipate what in the next century would become the Pentecostal and Charismatic approach. At the beginning of the nineteenth century Edward Irving emphasized "prophecy" and founded the Catholic Apostolic Church. Benjamin H. Irwin later emerged from a Holiness background in America, and sought to revive the eighteenth-century concerns of John Fletcher and his "baptism of fire." Albert B. Simpson also came from an American Holiness background, and promoted an emphasis on all the gifts of the Holy Spirit and Pentecost. Outside Europe and America, there emerged, according to anecdotal accounts, what might be called Pentecostal phenomena in various parts of the globe.

(4) A fourth tradition potentially concerns work within the Roman Catholic Church, although this did seem to touch only marginally on the work of the Holy Spirit. John Henry Newman was the most creative and progressive thinker, who provides an exception. He reacted both against the barrenness and dry rationalism of much nineteenth-century scholarship, and equally against the unstructured, do-it-yourself antiauthoritarianism of multiple "independent" and congregational churches. He was eager to recapture the supernatural reality of the unseen world. The Holy Spirit is like "a sweet perfume" that is pervasive; the movement of the Spirit does not need to be ecstatic: Christians are "consecrated temples." The Holy Spirit "indwelt" believers.

17.1. Friedrich D. E. Schleiermacher

Friedrich Schleiermacher (1768-1834) has been called "the father of modern Protestant theology."[1] His father was a pastor, and he was educated initially among the Moravians, and subsequently at Barby, near Halle. From the beginning he was a Pietist, who spoke of Christ as "My Savior" and regarded preaching as "my proper office." But away from his home environment, at the University of Halle, he felt that at last he could breathe freely. He never abandoned his Pietism entirely, in which "being in a relationship with God" through Christ remained central to him.[2] Gerrish calls him "a liberal evangelical."[3] He was profoundly influenced by Immanuel Kant (1724-1804) and by the Enlightenment.

1. David E. Klemm, *Hermeneutical Inquiry*, 2 vols. (Atlanta: Scholars Press, 1986), vol. 1, p. 55.

2. Friedrich D. E. Schleiermacher, *The Christian Faith* (Edinburgh: T&T Clark, 1989; from 2nd ed. 1830), p. 12.

3. B. A. Gerrish, *A Prince of the Church: Schleiermacher and the Beginning of Modern Theology* (London: SCM, 1984), pp. 18-20.

In the light of Kant's philosophy, he learned to ask *transcendental* questions. Almost equally, for a long period, he was attracted to Romanticism. This stressed *organic processes* rather than *mechanical* ones, and synthesis or unity rather than mere analogies. In his theology and his hermeneutics this led him to stress the "divinatory" (German, *divinatorisch*) and *immediacy*. Dissection or "analysis" (in the literal sense), as his contemporary William Wordsworth saw, can destroy what we seek to understand.

In 1799, in his early thirties, Schleiermacher wrote *On Religion: Speeches to Its Cultured Despisers.*[4] In it he declared: "True religion is a sense and taste for the infinite."[5] There is an implicit allusion to the Holy Spirit when he rejects juggling with the "trappings" of religion rather than with "the holy Being that lies beyond the world."[6] He adds: "Piety cannot be a . . . craving for a mess of metaphysical and ethical crumbs. . . . It is . . . a revelation of the Infinite in the finite."[7] In 1809-10 he produced his *Aphorisms* on *Hermeneutics*. Showing his awareness of the *biblical inspiration by the Holy Spirit,* he wrote: "The customary belief that the Holy Spirit is not to be subjected to the rules of interpretation is simply erroneous."[8] In the second edition of *The Christian Faith* he sees the Holy Spirit as the source and origin of the Church.[9] He asserts: "The Holy Spirit is the union of the Divine Essence with human nature in the form of the common [i.e., shared] Spirit animating the life in common [shared life] of believers."[10] Other works are informative, for example, the long essay *Christmas Eve: A Dialogue on the Incarnation* (1812) and his *Brief Outline on the Study of Theology* (1830).

For most of his life Schleiermacher was both Professor of Theology at the newly founded University of Berlin and also a regular preacher at Trinity Church, Berlin. He tried *to hold together his hermeneutics and living preaching*. In his preaching, he reflects, "How often have I struck up the music of my religion, seeking to move the bystanders!"[11] Karl Barth, an incisive critic, asserts: "Preaching to the congregation to awaken faith was by far the sweetest desire of his life."[12] Yet for all this, there remains a danger that his theology of the Holy Spirit was nearer to *immanentalism* than to the biblical or orthodox Christian

4. Friedrich D. E. Schleiermacher, *On Religion: Speeches to Its Cultured Despisers* (London: Kegan Paul, Trench & Trübner, 1893).

5. Schleiermacher, *Speeches*, p. 39.

6. Schleiermacher, *Speeches*, p. 1.

7. Schleiermacher, *Speeches*, pp. 31 and 36.

8. Friedrich D. E. Schleiermacher, *Hermeneutics: The Handwritten Manuscripts,* ed. Heinz Kimmerle (Missoula: Scholars Press, 1977), p. 67.

9. Schleiermacher, *The Christian Faith*, pp. 533 and 560-81.

10. Schleiermacher, *The Christian Faith*, p. 569.

11. Schleiermacher, *Speeches*, p. 119.

12. Karl Barth, *The Theology of Schleiermacher: Lectures at Göttingen, 1923-24* (Grand Rapids: Eerdmans, 1982), p. xiii.

tradition. He is understandably ambiguous about "experience." His early Piet-ism placed this in the center of the stage. He called himself "a Pietist of a Higher Order" because Kant had exposed how problematic and complex the notion of "experience" was. In his *Critique of Pure Reason* (1781), his *Critique of Practical Reason* (1788), and his *Critique of Judgment* (1790) Kant has shown the extent to which what appears as "experience" is already shaped by the mind *to count as* experience.

Certainly Schleiermacher's central notion was that of "a feeling of utter de-pendence on God" *(Gefühl schlechthinniger Abhängigkeit).*[13] Popular, cheap cri-tiques have reduced this to a stress on "feeling"; but Schleiermacher's concern was to express *dependence on God* which was *utter or absolute,* and a relation of *immediacy.*[14] It is an oversimplification to claim that whereas Kant found the absolute or ultimate only in the moral imperative, and Hegel found it in ratio-nality, Schleiermacher found this in "feeling," for this does not carry as heavy an emphasis as the immediacy of absolute dependence on God. In dogmatic or theological terms this is appropriated through the Holy Spirit. Schleiermacher, like many earlier mystics, declares, "Religion is essentially contemplative"; the focus of contemplation is "not turned . . . to a finite thing," nor to merely ab-stract notions of "a first cause. . . . Religion is not knowledge and science . . . but [again] a revelation of the Infinite in the finite."[15] In *The Christian Faith* he ar-gues, "*Every regenerate person partakes of the Holy Spirit, so that there is no living fellowship with Christ without an indwelling of the Holy Spirit,* and vice versa" (his italics).[16]

To become a *sharer in the Holy Spirit,* Schleiermacher continues, is no differ-ent from having *fellowship with Christ:* "neither in fact *nor in point of time* are the two things to be distinguished."[17] Both entail sonship with God and the lordship of Christ. The outpouring of the Spirit means entry into the common or shared life of the Holy Spirit. (In the twentieth century this emphasis is ably confirmed by L. S. Thornton.)[18] Schleiermacher writes: "This is the work of the Holy Spirit — to bring Christ into memory and glorify Him in us."[19] He adds: "The *leading of the Holy Spirit* is never other than a divine incitement to realize the standard of *what Christ . . . was and did*" (my italics).[20] He adds: "The indwelling of the

---

13. Schleiermacher, *The Christian Faith,* pp. 12-31.

14. John Macquarrie, *Studies in Christian Existentialism* (London: SCM, 1966), pp. 31-42, ex-plains and confirms this point decisively.

15. Schleiermacher, *Speeches,* p. 36.

16. Schleiermacher, *The Christian Faith,* sect. 124, p. 574.

17. Schleiermacher, *The Christian Faith,* p. 574 (my italics).

18. Lionel S. Thornton, *The Common Life in the Body of Christ* (London: Dacre Press, 3rd ed. 1950).

19. Schleiermacher, *The Christian Faith,* p. 576.

20. Schleiermacher, *The Christian Faith,* p. 576.

Spirit of God, . . . the immediate influence of Christ," and the appearance of Christ were the "supernatural foundation of Christianity."[21] "The phenomena of Pentecost . . . bear distinctly enough the mark of the miraculous."[22]

All this must be understood in *corporate or community* terms, as well as in individual terms. *"The Christian Church animated by the Holy Spirit,"* Schleiermacher declares, *"is in the purity, . . . the perfect image of the Redeemer"* (his italics).[23] Yet earlier in *The Christian Faith* and in the *Speeches* Schleiermacher expresses reservations about the "supernatural." Christ is not entirely "supernatural" as if to compromise his genuine humanity.[24] Schleiermacher asserts, "The Redeemer, then, is like all men in virtue of the identity of human nature, but distinguished from them all by the constant potency of His God-consciousness."[25] In the *Speeches* some of his language is *Romanticist and immanental,* such as his reference to "the inner-most springs of my being"; sometimes he speaks of how "miserable love of system rejects what is strange" or "other."[26] In *The Christian Faith* he asserts: "The idea that the divine revelation in Christ must in this respect be absolutely supernatural will simply *not stand the test*" (my italics).[27] However, he wants equally to guard against "Docetism" and "Ebionite" views of Christ. The most that we can say is that this immanental aspect of the Spirit remains ambiguous rather than reductive. It is a modified orthodoxy, in accordance with both Kant and the Enlightenment and Pietism. The Holy Spirit is "an effective spiritual power" who *conveys the immediacy of fellowship with God in Christ.*[28] Schleiermacher was not a pantheist, but, in the words of Claude Welch, "He was plainly seeking a view beyond naturalism and supernaturalism, . . . the archetype for nearly all the later liberal theologies."[29]

17.2. Georg Wilhelm Friedrich Hegel

The life of *Hegel* (1770-1831) was relatively uneventful, after his initial searching. He was educated in Stuttgart, and entered the University of Tübingen in 1788 to study theology as a Lutheran. But he became disillusioned with the Lutheran

---

21. Schleiermacher, *The Christian Faith,* p. 577.
22. Schleiermacher, *The Christian Faith,* p. 578.
23. Schleiermacher, *The Christian Faith,* p. 578; cf. pp. 565-69 and 579-81.
24. Schleiermacher, *The Christian Faith,* pp. 62-68 and 374-424.
25. Schleiermacher, *The Christian Faith,* p. 385.
26. Schleiermacher, *On Religion: Speeches,* pp. 3 and 55.
27. Schleiermacher, *The Christian Faith,* p. 64.
28. Schleiermacher, *The Christian Faith,* p. 272.
29. Claude Welch, *Protestant Thought in the Nineteenth Century,* vol. 1: *1799-1870* (New Haven: Yale University Press, 1972), pp. 79 and 85.

scholasticism of the time, and immersed himself in the philosophy of Kant and Romanticism. He did not go forward to ordination, but taught philosophy at Jena in 1801. In 1818 he became Professor of Philosophy in the newly founded University of Berlin, where he remained as a colleague of Schleiermacher until his death in 1831. His thinking is very complex. *Spirit plays a key role.* But this is not the Holy Spirit of Schleiermacher's *The Christian Faith.* It is a moot point of debate, on which I have held many seminars, whether his view of the Spirit was dictated by theological concerns about God and the Holy Trinity, or whether his view of spirit was dictated by his philosophy of history, in which he sees the work of the Father, in effect, as Thesis, the Incarnate Son and his death as Antithesis, and the Holy Spirit, following the resurrection of Jesus Christ, as Synthesis. *Spirit* became as much a key category for his philosophical theology as *life* did for Wilhelm Dilthey, or *immediacy* did for Schleiermacher.

Hegel and Schleiermacher were utterly different. Hegel saw theology as relating to intellectual inquiry and curiosity about the world, truth, reality, and God; Schleiermacher saw it as providing professional training *for the ministry,* parallel to that in law or medicine, which would ultimately shape a preacher's exposition of the New Testament. One sad event befell Schleiermacher: David Strauss came to Berlin to study under Hegel. Schleiermacher interviewed him in 1831 to tell him of Hegel's death, and offered to teach him. Strauss replied: "But it was for Hegel that I came here!" Nevertheless he stayed.

Hegel produced his classic *Phenomenology of Spirit (Geist)* in 1807, which includes his speculative view of the incarnation and a "ladder" or "pathway" toward philosophy as a crowning or enlightening critical science. In 1812-16 he published his *Science of Logic,* in which this "ladder" is seen as a logical one. In 1817 Hegel published *Encyclopaedia of the Philosophical Sciences;* in 1821, his *Philosophy of the Right;* and posthumously his great Berlin lectures, *Lectures on the Philosophy of Religion.*[30]

In addition to all that has been said, Hegel introduced into philosophy and theology a turning point which was hardly less significant than that of Kant. All knowledge, he urged, was neither purely rational, as in Descartes and Leibniz; nor empirical, as in Locke and Hume; nor even transcendental, as in Kant; it was *historically* mediated by *historical* reason. Historicity, or *historical finitude,* or historical situatedness, determined much of what counts as knowledge. This introduced what Heidegger and Gadamer call *Geschichtlichkeit,* or being historically conditioned. Because people are simply "thrown" into history, then race, class, and upbringing determine what they "count as" knowledge. This leads to *sociology* of *knowledge,* as expressed in the schools of Habermas, Adorno, and others.

---

30. Georg W. F. Hegel, *Lectures on the Philosophy of Religion,* 3 vols. (London: Kegan Paul, Trench & Trübner, 1895); and Hegel, *The Phenomenology of Mind,* Harper Torchbooks (New York: Harper & Row, 1967), remain for our purposes the two most important.

The center of Hegel's system is the premise that God, as the Trinity, "spiritualizes himself in the world-historical process."[31] Kant is insufficiently dialectical, and Schleiermacher is trapped in *subjective* immediacy. Hegel's system has earned the name *objective idealism* in contrast to Kant's *subjective idealism;* it is centered in God, not in humankind. Hegel proposed "a speculative dialectic of identity and difference."[32] Dialectic involves separation or negation and mediation or synthesis. In terms of the world, the finite raises *(erheben)* and "sublates" *(aufheben)* itself into something higher. In terms of God's Being, the Holy Trinity also permits the following dialectic. God, especially God the Father, is eternally "Absolute Spirit." However, the Antithesis of this state is the incarnation and especially the death of Christ. God the Son thus exhibits the principle of *negation* or *antithesis,* by undergoing enfleshment and even death. God differentiates himself in the experience of the Son. God's identity is both himself, as eternal Spirit; and the "other," or "Christ," as he takes flesh. But whereas, in Hegel's view, the Roman Catholic absolutizes the crucified Christ in *a static crucifix,* the *dialectical narrative of the Trinity moves on* to mediation or synthesis. *Christ is raised, and the Holy Spirit is poured out* and given; thus, without annihilating the incarnation, *God again reigns as Spirit.* History has reached the era of the Spirit. In this sense, which is very different from that of most writers, *Hegel sees the Holy Spirit as God's crowning self-revelation.*

Hegel expounds this most clearly at the beginning of vol. 3 of his *Lectures on the Philosophy of Religion.* He begins with "the absolute, eternal Idea . . . in and for itself, God in his eternity before the creation of the world, and outside of the world."[33] What God creates is "otherness or other-Being," which means both "physical Nature and finite Spirit."[34] Thus "the divine Idea unfolds itself in these three forms: 'Spirit is divine history, the process of self-differentiation. . . . The third element is . . . thinking reason, the thought of free Spirit, free only when it returns to itself.'"[35] Hegel adds, "It is possible also to occupy a standpoint at which we do not get beyond the Son and his appearance in time. This is the case in Catholicism."[36] The third part of the process, by contrast, entrusts "the formation of the Spiritual Community, or the third point; it is the Spirit."[37] We move from "outward" religion to "inner." This reveals individuality, person-

31. Peter C. Hodgson, "Georg Wilhelm Friedrich Hegel," in Ninian Smart, John Clayton, Patrick Sherry, and Steven Katz, *Nineteenth-Century Religious Thought in the West* (Cambridge: Cambridge University Press, 1985), vol. 1, p. 84, cf. pp. 81-121. Hodgson's seems to be the best treatment of Hegel.

32. Hodgson, "Hegel," in Smart et al., *Nineteenth-Century Religious Thought,* p. 85.

33. Hegel, *Philosophy of Religion,* vol. 3, p. 1.

34. Hegel, *Philosophy of Religion,* vol. 3, p. 1.

35. Hegel, *Philosophy of Religion,* vol. 3, pp. 2-3.

36. Hegel, *Philosophy of Religion,* vol. 3, p. 103.

37. Hegel, *Philosophy of Religion,* vol. 3, p. 104.

hood, subjectivity, and freedom. The new community is characterized by love: by a "unity which belongs to Spirit."[38] In God as Spirit, God and the world find reconciliation: "all men are called to salvation."[39]

As a system, this has a certain self-contained brilliance. But Hegel usually speaks of "Spirit" rather than "the Holy Spirit," and we can never be sure whether "Spirit" genuinely features as the biblical Holy Spirit, or as part of Hegel's phenomenological and logical system. The one important and positive thing is *the centrality of God as Trinity* and of God *as Spirit,* as well as an emphasis on personhood in the "third stage." In this third stage "love is . . . the Holy Spirit," and is equivalent to Christ's "I am with you always."[40]

In his *Phenomenology of Mind* (better, *Spirit, Geist*), Hegel uses "Spirit" in a variety of ways. He asserts: "Spirit . . . is the ethical life of a nation, . . . ethical life *(Sittlichkeit)*."[41] He continues, "Spirit, in its ultimate simple truth, is consciousness."[42] This is a long distance away from Paul's use of "spiritual." No later than Augustine, we were being warned about the different meanings of "spirit." We cannot but suspect that Hegel has sometimes conflated two meanings. Whatever his philosophical brilliance, he made no claim to be a careful exegete. His even fiercer critic, Søren Kierkegaard, pronounces: "The absolute method, Hegel's invention, is already a difficult issue in logic, indeed a brilliant tautology. . . . But it has also prompted the learner's mind to become distracted."[43]

17.3. Charles Hodge, George Smeaton, and Abraham Kuyper

These three thinkers adopt an entirely different approach from the Liberalism of the nineteenth century. They attempt to revive Calvinism of an orthodox or conservative nature. Schleiermacher and Hegel did not represent mainstream scholarship in England. Indeed, at the very end of the nineteenth century J. B. Lightfoot, B. F. Westcott, and F. J. A. Hort represented the tradition of mainstream Christian biblical scholars, who were also conservative theologians. However, Hodge in America, Smeaton in Scotland, and Kuyper in the Netherlands specifically represented a conservative Calvinism, which inhabited a separate world from that of Schleiermacher and Hegel.

(1) *Charles Hodge* (1797-1871) was ordained to the Presbyterian ministry in 1821, and he taught at Princeton for nearly the whole of his life. He produced

---

38. Hegel, *Philosophy of Religion,* vol. 3, p. 106.

39. Hegel, *Philosophy of Religion,* vol. 3, p. 108.

40. Hegel, *Philosophy of Religion,* vol. 3, p. 107.

41. Hegel, *The Phenomenology of Mind,* p. 460.

42. Hegel, *The Phenomenology of Mind,* p. 462.

43. Søren Kierkegaard, *Philosophical Fragments* (Princeton: Princeton University Press, 1985), p. 78.

commentaries on Romans (1835), Ephesians (1856), 1 Corinthians (1857), and 2 Corinthians (1859), and wrote an influential three-volume *Systematic Theology*, which he began in 1839 but published between 1871 and 1873. He was not a notably original thinker; he actually disparaged original thinking as leading away from orthodoxy, stating proudly concerning Princeton, "A new idea never originated in this Seminary."[44] He championed Calvinism at Princeton, in contrast to his near-contemporary Horace Bushnell (1802-76), who expounded Liberal theology at Yale. His knowledge of theology, however, was not confined to Calvinism in America. In 1826 he studied in Paris for two years; then under Gesenius in Halle; and under Hengstenberg in Berlin. Bushnell, Hengstenberg, and Schleiermacher appear in his *Systematic Theology*, but not Hegel and Kierkegaard.

The Holy Spirit is considered mainly under *"The Spirituality of God"* and *"The Meaning of the Word 'Spirit.'"* He placed this under the heading *"The Holy Spirit: His Nature, Personality, Divinity and Office,"* and he surveyed the history of the doctrine and the Spirit's work of regeneration and sanctification.[45] Hodge also includes a section on "perfectionism" and conflict.[46] On the first section, writers seldom speak of divine "attributes" today, as if God were merely a static Aristotelian object. Hodge then considers *rûach* and *pneuma*, and the meaning of Spirit. We may ignore what he writes about "the soul" and "substance." By today's standards, his linguistic approach lacks precision. To say that spirit is "not matter" largely reaches the heart of the issue, and more readily reflects nineteenth-century idealism.[47] Hodge's work on God as "spiritual" seems to miss the transcendence of the Spirit, although he speaks of a "higher order." He refers to "I am" in Exodus 3, although scholars today largely recognize the Hebrew imperfect as future and dynamic in meaning, suggesting, "I will be what I will be," indicating God's step-by-step revelation of himself. Later in volume 1, under the heading "The Holy Spirit," he returns to the Greek and Hebrew terms for "Spirit."

Hodge introduces the "personality" of the Spirit, rightly enumerating the verbs of action of which he is the subject. His "proof" of the Spirit's personality again turns to the biblical example of his activity. His argument concerning the Spirit's "relation to us, and . . . offices, which none but a person can sustain or perform, has a more modern ring.[48] The Holy Spirit is our teacher, sanctifier, com-

---

44. Paul C. Gutjahr, *Charles Hodge: Guardian of American Orthodoxy* (Oxford: Oxford University Press, 2011), p. 363.

45. Charles Hodge, *Systematic Theology*, 3 vols. (Grand Rapids: Eerdmans, 1946), vol. 1, pp. 376-80, 522-34; vol. 2, pp. 710-32; vol. 3, pp. 31-40, 213-32.

46. Hodge, *Systematic Theology*, vol. 3, pp. 245-58.

47. Hodge, *Systematic Theology*, vol. 1, p. 379.

48. Jürgen Moltmann, *The Spirit of Life: A Universal Affirmation* (London: SCM, 1974), pp. 269-74; Arthur W. Wainwright, *The Trinity in the New Testament* (London: SPCK, 1962), pp. 109-236.

forter, and guide. . . . He calls. . . ."[49] He makes much of a comparison with human
personhood, but does not seem to argue that the Holy Spirit is "suprapersonal,"
that is, more but not less than a human person. He points out that in church tradition there is "little dispute" about the divinity of the Holy Spirit, although it
might be suggested that Athanasius, Hilary, Basil, and Calvin himself offer a more
sophisticated argument. He introduces the sin of blasphemy against the Holy
Spirit (Matt. 12:31) with no reference to context or exegesis as something that
"could not be unless the Holy Ghost were God."[50] He reaches safer ground when
he appeals to 1 Cor. 2:10-11, as many of the Church Fathers do. He concludes,
rightly: "The works of the Spirit are the works of God."[51]

On "the office of the Holy Spirit," Hodge states, "The Holy Spirit is the executive of the Godhead."[52] The Spirit is omnipresent: it is he that causes the grass
to grow. According to Job, "The Spirit of God has made me" (Job 33:4). The Holy
Spirit is also "the source of intellectual life," and has given us a rational nature.[53]
In actualizing the work of redemption, the Holy Spirit inspired the Virgin Birth
(Luke 1:35), and endowed the Messiah "with all the spiritual gifts"; he descended
upon him at his baptism (John 1:32).[54] *Jesus is full of the Spirit,* who remains on
him, and he gives the Spirit "without measure" (John 3:34). He reveals God's
truth, and convinces the world of sin. In the history and development of the
doctrine, the Spirit was "involved in the religious experience of all Christians."[55]
He is life-giving, as we confess in the Nicene-Constantinopolitan Creed. In volume 2 Hodge supplements this with a history of the doctrine of grace.[56] He discusses the Pelagian doctrine, semi-Pelagianism, the Scholastic Period, Trinitarian doctrine, and the Reformed Church and its relation to Lutheranism. He
concludes this by comparing rationalism with "supernaturalism." His single reference to "Hegelianism" is to suggest that it denotes that "What God does, I [the
human person] do; and I do what God does."[57] This, Hodge suggests, is simply
"anti-Christian or anti-theistic."

In volume 3 Hodge asserts that regeneration is wholly an act of God, and
an act of his almighty power. Here, he argues, the Reformed Church stands on
more solid ground than the Lutherans.[58] Regeneration is as much an exclusively divine act as the raising of Lazarus. It is the sheer gift of a new life; a

---

49. Hodge, *Systematic Theology,* vol. 1, p. 525.
50. Hodge, *Systematic Theology,* vol. 1, p. 528.
51. Hodge, *Systematic Theology,* vol. 1, p. 528.
52. Hodge, *Systematic Theology,* vol. 1, p. 529.
53. Hodge, *Systematic Theology,* vol. 1, p. 530.
54. Hodge, *Systematic Theology,* vol. 1, p. 531.
55. Hodge, *Systematic Theology,* vol. 1, p. 532.
56. Hodge, *Systematic Theology,* vol. 2, pp. 710-52.
57. Hodge, *Systematic Theology,* vol. 2, p. 781.
58. Hodge, *Systematic Theology,* vol. 3, p. 31.

quickening by "the things of the Spirit."[59] It is a new birth and a new heart. Similarly, in the Westminster Confession, sanctification is "the work of God's free grace."[60] It is through "the voluntary agency of the Holy Spirit. . . . The effect produced by the Spirit [is] to transcend the power of second causes. . . . The effects of grace [are] the fruits of the Spirit . . . above the sphere of the natural."[61] He concludes, "Predominantly sanctification is referred to the Holy Spirit, as his peculiar work in the economy of redemption. . . . The Spirit dwells in the people of God. . . . The Father and the Son operate through the Spirit."[62]

Granted that in the earlier volumes Hodge writes as an author of his times, in his later work he reflects the kind of system and comprehensiveness that we observed in John Owen. There are some questions today which he does not address, but he adheres to an orthodox exposition of the subject.

(2) *George Smeaton* (1814-89) was ordained in the Church of Scotland in 1839, after study at New College, Edinburgh University. At the Disruption of 1843, with many he entered the Free Church of Scotland, in which he became a professor at Aberdeen in 1854, and Professor of Exegesis in 1857 at Edinburgh. He is widely referred to as a learned and eminent scholar, but also as being modest and unassuming. He was a close friend of Hugh Martin. His book *The Doctrine of the Holy Spirit* appeared in 1892.[63] He also wrote *Christ's Doctrine of the Atonement* and *The Apostles' Doctrine of the Atonement*. His work is Reformed and Calvinistic.[64]

Smeaton's *The Doctrine of the Holy Spirit* has a surprisingly "modern" ring, in the sense of addressing some live issues today. Rightly, his first division addresses the doctrine of the Trinity. In his Part II he discusses the Personality and Procession of the Holy Spirit; his anointing of Christ; his work in revelation, inspiration, regeneration, and holiness; and the Spirit and the Church. Perhaps the Third Part is the most revealing in relation to today: a wide historical survey with relevant assessments and critiques up to the later nineteenth century. The first part is probably strong in its aim but not always convincing in its exegesis. Like the Church Fathers, Smeaton spends much of his time searching for biblical evidence of Trinitarian patterns. Like Hilary, Athanasius, and Basil, he makes use of 1 Cor. 12:1-7, and he draws on the Paraclete Discourses in John 14:16–16:7.[65] But the first thirty or so pages relate to the Old Testament, and many today would call the exegesis patchy.

---

59. Hodge, *Systematic Theology*, vol. 3, p. 33.

60. Hodge, *Systematic Theology*, vol. 3, p. 213.

61. Hodge, *Systematic Theology*, vol. 3, pp. 214-15.

62. Hodge, *Systematic Theology*, vol. 3, p. 216.

63. See John W. Keddie, *George Smeaton: Learned Theologian and Biblical Scholar* (Darlington: Evangelical Press, 2011).

64. George Smeaton, *The Doctrine of the Holy Spirit* (London: Banner of Truth Trust, 1958).

65. Smeaton, *The Holy Spirit*, pp. 44-71.

In the second part of his book, Smeaton begins with the Personality and Procession of the Spirit. He rejects the "Sabellian" tendency to suggest that "the Spirit of God" denotes no more than "God," even if God in action. The Holy Spirit is Teacher, Helper, Advocate, and much more. His Procession is anticipated in John 15:26, "who proceeds from the Father" *(ho para tou patros ekporeuetai)*.[66] He then argues, "The Supreme Deity of the Holy Spirit is clearly established by the procession of the Spirit."[67] He speaks through the biblical prophets and apostles, and "less of himself."[68]

Smeaton then addresses the empowerment of the incarnate Christ by the anointing of the Holy Spirit. He cites his conception, birth, baptism, temptations, ministry, and resurrection. He asserts, "For all his offices, the Lord Jesus received the *unction of the Spirit*" (his italics). "The Spirit . . . interposes his power, *only to execute the will of the Son*" (my italics).[69] This provides both an accurate Christology and a paradigm for Christian believers. Predictably, Smeaton has a chapter on revelation to and inspiration of prophets and apostles by the Spirit. Here he speaks of "supernatural gifts" (Eph. 4:7-11), including prophecy (2 Pet. 1:21; Rev. 19:10).[70] He may include the broader sense of *revelation,* or more *specific* ways such as "extraordinary gifts of the Spirit."[71] But he warns us: "*These extraordinary gifts of the Spirit were no longer needed when the canon of Scripture was closed.* Up to that time, they were an absolute necessity. They are no longer so. Nor is the Church warranted to expect their restoration, or to receive prophetic visions, immediate revelations, or miraculous gifts, either in public or in private, beyond, or besides, the all-perfect canon of Scripture."[72] This is the so-called cessationist view associated with Benjamin Warfield. Smeaton presses home this argument, seeing the Roman Catholic acceptance of miracles as "ingenuous to the Spirit as author of Scripture," and the problem of "self-manifestation."[73]

Chapter 4 of part 2 concerns regeneration, which is "the application of redemption to the individual."[74] In the sayings of Jesus in John this means "being born again . . . of water and of the Spirit" for all believers (John 3:3-6). Smeaton rejects the view that *water* denotes *baptism,* and insists that it denotes *cleansing.* "Spirit" denotes the *Spirit as efficient cause.* With this he links John 16:8-11. The Spirit convicts human beings of sin and judgment; it refers to "the convincing

---

66. Smeaton, *The Holy Spirit,* pp. 101 and 105; cf. pp. 116-36.
67. Smeaton, *The Holy Spirit,* p. 109.
68. Smeaton, *The Holy Spirit,* p. 114.
69. Smeaton, *The Holy Spirit,* pp. 118 and 120; cf. pp. 116-36.
70. Smeaton, *The Holy Spirit,* pp. 137, 139, and 137-61.
71. Smeaton, *The Holy Spirit,* pp. 138-40.
72. Smeaton, *The Holy Spirit,* p. 140 (my italics).
73. Smeaton, *The Holy Spirit,* pp. 140-59.
74. Smeaton, *The Holy Spirit,* p. 162; cf. pp. 162-203.

process of the Spirit."[75] He discusses the respective exegeses of Augustine, Calvin, and Wesley.

Chapter 5 concerns the Spirit of holiness, which comes from "the inhabitation of the Spirit in all true believers."[76] Smeaton quotes Rom. 8:9: the Spirit is given to *all* Christians *as an entailment of union with Christ.* The Holy Spirit also works with "prevenient grace."[77] He argues in favor of the Puritan and Reformed views as against the Lutheran and others. Love becomes the principle of unity in the work of the Spirit, who is "the Spirit of life."[78] The ultimate aim is the formation of "the character of Christ" in Christians.[79] Chapter 6 continues these themes with reference to the work of the Holy Spirit in the Church. Smeaton cites the predictable passages about the temple of the Spirit (1 Cor. 3:16; Eph. 2:22); "The Church [is] animated by the Holy Spirit."[80] The Spirit maintains its unity, inspires its worship and prayer, and empowers it for mission.

Smeaton's concluding Third Division is most illuminating. It involves assessment as well as description of the history of the doctrine. He cites the Apostolic Fathers and early Patristic sources with approval, but approves less of Montanism, unlike Wesley. Montanus was an "enthusiastic Christian of weak mind, but fervent piety and zeal."[81] He speaks of the Montanists' "crude utterances, ecstasies, and prophecies." Smeaton applauds the work of Athanasius, Basil, and Gregory of Nazianzus, and also follows the Western double procession of the Spirit.[82] He notes that interest or concern largely moves from the Person of the Holy Spirit to his work after Photius (c. 867). The Western Church had a clearer stress on grace. He claims, "The principal error of the Semi-Pelagian system consisted in the fact that grace was said to be given according to men's merits."[83] He then asserts, by contrast, "The Reformers . . . began largely to use the phrase 'the work of the Holy Spirit,' instead of the term 'grace.'"[84] He ascribes "synergism," however, to Philipp Melanchthon and the Greek Church. By contrast, "conversion has its efficient cause only in the operation of the Holy Ghost."[85] He therefore prefers to consider the Synod of Dort (1618-19) as a Reformed consensus. "Enthusiasts," he concludes, who include the Quakers, "substitute the Spirit for the word," with "mischievous results."[86]

---

75. Smeaton, *The Holy Spirit*, p. 183.
76. Smeaton, *The Holy Spirit*, p. 208; cf. pp. 204-29.
77. Smeaton, *The Holy Spirit*, p. 211.
78. Smeaton, *The Holy Spirit*, p. 221.
79. Smeaton, *The Holy Spirit*, p. 223.
80. Smeaton, *The Holy Spirit*, p. 232; cf. pp. 230-55.
81. Smeaton, *The Holy Spirit*, p. 265; cf. pp. 256-368.
82. Smeaton, *The Holy Spirit*, pp. 271-91.
83. Smeaton, *The Holy Spirit*, p. 302.
84. Smeaton, *The Holy Spirit*, p. 308.
85. Smeaton, *The Holy Spirit*, p. 317.
86. Smeaton, *The Holy Spirit*, p. 328.

Smeaton praises the Puritans, and surveys the work of Spener, and Jonathan Edwards and the Great Awakening, including with him George Whitefield, John Wesley, and Henry Venn. Edwards had great influence on the nineteenth century, but Finney and the Revivalists tended "to magnify human ability."[87] He asserts: "*As to Irvingism, with its ostentatious parade of supernatural gifts and of extraordinary offices, which have had no real existence since the apostolic age, . . . such a supply of the Spirit as this sect claims could not co-exist with its pomp . . .*" (my italics).[88] Some, even of the Brethren, make a presumptuous claim to be . . . under the presidency of the Holy Spirit."[89] Moreover, "Schleiermacher . . . did not recognize the personality of the Holy Spirit" and is "highly unjust to Biblical Trinitarianism, along with F. C. Baur and David Strauss."[90] He adds: "So-called Christian consciousness is made the arbiter and judge of Scripture."[91] The Holy Spirit provides a steady flame, but in some revivalist sects it is "spasmodic, and fitful, from self and for self."[92] These last polemical comments thoroughly justify our heading: "The Parting of the Ways."

(3) *Abraham Kuyper* (1837-1920). Kuyper was a Dutch Calvinist who studied at Leiden, Utrecht, and Amsterdam. He entered politics, and in 1880 founded the Free University of Amsterdam. He was appointed to be a professor in that University. He published his book *The Work of the Holy Spirit* in 1888, based on a series of articles published from 1871. One of his themes was: "transcendent above nature, God is also immanent in nature." This perhaps recalls our slogan, quoted earlier, that the Holy Spirit is "the Beyond Who Is Within." Benjamin B. Warfield provided the Introduction to the English translation (1900), which runs to over 650 pages. In 1899 Kuyper gave the *L. P. Stone Lectures* in America on Calvinism. Warfield alludes to Smeaton's work and admits that in this light Kuyper's work is not "something of a novelty." This, he claims, is primarily a doctrine of Reformed theology.[93] This suggests that in the light of our treatment of Smeaton, we may offer a briefer discussion of Kuyper.

Kuyper's "volume 1," pp. 3-201, covers predictable themes: creation, re-creation, Holy Scripture, the incarnation, the outpouring of the Spirit, the apostolate, and the Church. Toward the beginning Kuyper lists several Calvinist themes: "the redeemed and the lost"; the glory of God . . . sovereign grace alone"; "the vindication of the counsel of God"; "Man is fallen. . . . the Holy

---

87. Smeaton, *The Holy Spirit*, p. 348.
88. Smeaton, *The Holy Spirit*, p. 355.
89. Smeaton, *The Holy Spirit*, p. 356.
90. Smeaton, *The Holy Spirit*, pp. 358-59.
91. Smeaton, *The Holy Spirit*, p. 363.
92. Smeaton, *The Holy Spirit*, p. 368.
93. Abraham Kuyper, *The Work of the Holy Spirit* (New York and London: Funk & Wagnalls, 1900), pp. xxxiii-xxxv.

Spirit must purify and sanctify him"; and "the work of the Spirit is continuous and perpetual . . . throughout eternity."[94] In one of his most distinctive sections he distinguishes between "indwelling" and "outgoing" works. The latter are apparent in his actions in the world. The former (which we can know only by revelation) require contemplation, "watching and waiting in speechless suspense . . . and prayer," as one contemplates an "architect forming his plans."[95] The purpose of these observations is to stress contemplation of God's eternal decrees and permanent grace.

In chapter 4 Kuyper distinguishes the work of the Holy Spirit from that of the Father and that of the Son: "In every work effected by the Father, Son, and Holy Ghost in common, the power *to bring forth* proceeds from the Father; the power *to arrange,* from the Son; the power *to perfect,* from the Holy Spirit" (his italics).[96] With reference to Col. 1:16 "created by" is distinct from the word "from"; "without him [Christ] not one thing came into being" (John 1:3). Kuyper rightly anchors his account of the Spirit's work *in the Holy Trinity.* In a statement which contrasts with that of some "enthusiastic" circles, he insists, "[The Spirit] effects only that which is invisible and inseparable. This marks all the Holy Spirit's operations."[97] Similarly, creation is ascribed to the Spirit (Job 33:4; Ps. 104:30). The Spirit hovered over chaos. The Holy Spirit also inspires natural talents, including "mechanical arts and official functions."[98] We must not forget that all this is a matter of "gift" and "gift of grace."[99] Kuyper insists, "The work of the Spirit is not confined to the elect. . . . it touches every creature, . . . quickening and sustaining . . . life."[100]

Much of the rest of volume 2 (pp. 56-201) broadly repeats Hodge and Smeaton. The Holy Spirit inspires Scripture, anoints Christ, produces the unity of the Church, and so on. Baptism with the Holy Spirit refers to Pentecost (Acts 1:5; 10:44-45). Kuyper compares the "pouring out" of the Spirit, in contrast to temporary gifts, to being connected to a water main. Here Acts 2 recounts the connection for the Christian Jewish community; and Acts 10 for the Christian Gentile community: "there is an original outpouring in Jerusalem on the day of Pentecost, and a supplementary outpouring in Caesarea for the Gentile part of the Church."[101] The significance of the apostolate is "unique."[102] He addresses the divide in the nineteenth century: *"Let us not forget that the apostles of the*

---

94. Kuyper, *The Work of the Holy Spirit* (abbreviated as *Work*), p. 11.
95. Kuyper, *Work,* p. 13; cf. pp. 14-17.
96. Kuyper, *Work,* p. 19.
97. Kuyper, *Work,* p. 25.
98. Kuyper, *Work,* p. 39.
99. Kuyper, *Work,* pp. 41 and 43.
100. Kuyper, *Work,* p. 46.
101. Kuyper, *Work,* p. 126; cf. pp. 124-26.
102. Kuyper, *Work,* p. 144.

Irvingites completely lack the marks of the apostolate" (my italics).[103] According to Kuyper, the Roman Catholic view of apostolic succession involves "effacing the boundary line between apostles and believers."[104]

Toward the end of part 1 (the first "volume") Kuyper takes a softer line than Hodge or Smeaton. The notion that for eighteen centuries the Church "received no gifts whatever" seems foolish.[105] He even distinguishes between "the *official,* the *extraordinary,* and the *ordinary*" (his italics).[106] He is at one with Hodge in suggesting that "ordinary" ministerial gifts are no less of the Spirit, and worthy of honor, than others. But there are other gifts, such as healing; and in the third category, the Spirit inspires "offices and appoints incumbents."[107]

Kuyper's volume 2 concerns the work of the Spirit in the individual. From the point of view of Calvinist orthodoxy this means a full exposition of the doctrine of grace: image of God and sin; preparatory grace; regeneration, justification, and faith. Sin is not merely the loss of righteousness, but a power. At the commencement of the discussion of regeneration, Kuyper points out the distinction between two senses of the term: "In the *limited* sense . . . regeneration is the *starting point,*" like new birth (his italics).[108] But "in its *wider* sense [it] denotes the entire change by grace effected in our persons, ending in our dying to sin . . ." (his italics).[109]

Volume 3 (or part 3 of the single volume) considers traditional effects of the Holy Spirit: *sanctification, love, and prayer.* Kuyper is *realistic* about the process of sanctification: it *takes time, patience, struggle, and perseverance:* "When on a cold morning the fire does not burn, . . . it is foolish to say, 'Since the fire does not burn, remove it.' . . . To keep from freezing requires *more* fire" (his italics).[110] Sanctification also differs from justification: "Justification acts *for* man; sanctification *inheres in* man" (his italics).[111] Yet sanctification flows from both Christ and the Spirit, not from the Spirit alone. It is a grace inherent in Christ. It is "his form reflecting itself in the soul (or in us)."[112]

In an important chapter (ch. 11 of the third part) Kuyper attacks both the *Pietist* and the *Perfectionist.* Nothing can be worse than spiritual pride. Sanctification remains "a gradual process."[113] It involves *constant conflict.* Kuyper as-

---

103. Kuyper, *Work,* p. 139.
104. Kuyper, *Work,* p. 158.
105. Kuyper, *Work,* p. 186.
106. Kuyper, *Work,* p. 187.
107. Kuyper, *Work,* p. 199.
108. Kuyper, *Work,* p. 293.
109. Kuyper, *Work,* p. 29.
110. Kuyper, *Work,* p. 433.
111. Kuyper, *Work,* p. 446.
112. Kuyper, *Work,* p. 459.
113. Kuyper, *Work,* p. 477.

serts: "Being wedded to the new man before God, he is, by a painful process, yet to die to the old man."[114] Similarly, with a possible glance at Wesley, he insists, "Sanctification itself is not of faith. It has nothing to do with faith," although "a good work must be of faith."[115] It has much to do with self-denial.

Lastly, Kuyper turns to love and to prayer. He speaks primarily of *God's* love, not of love in general, which even enemies show. This is derived from "the Triune Being of God."[116] The Holy Spirit manifests this love to our hearts. This "pouring out of love" is "an ever-continued, never-finished work."[117] Love suffers.[118] The Holy Spirit clearly prays in us and for us (Rom. 8:26-27). This is "a work of His Person *in our own prayers*" (his italics).[119] When we pray for others, this is prayer born of love. Such is the conclusion of Kuyper's 550-page study. He stands in the tradition of Hodge, as Warfield declares, yet he adds many homely and softer remarks of his own. He clearly separates his view from that of Roman Catholics and perhaps more strongly from that of many Pietists and the followers of Irving. Many of his observations still remain relevant to today.

17.4. Edward Irving, Benjamin Irwin, and A. B. Simpson

(1) *Edward Irving* (1792-1834). Irving was born in the southwest part of Scotland, and educated in divinity at the University of Edinburgh. In 1819 he became an assistant minister in Glasgow, and in 1822 he moved to London. In the midst of theological debate, he reacted against much of the traditional theology of the Church of Scotland. He attempted what many regarded as unorthodox innovations in the two areas of Christology and the doctrine of the Holy Spirit. In 1828 there were outbreaks of *speaking in tongues* in the western part of Scotland, and in 1831 in Irving's own church in London. In 1830 his London presbytery had excommunicated him, and Irving and six hundred of his followers were ejected from his own local church in London. Together with Henry Drummond, he formed *the Catholic Apostolic Church,* which was a revivalist group also holding beliefs in the imminent Return of Christ. By 1835 they had appointed twelve "apostles," with prophets, evangelists, pastors, teachers, and "angels," which was the name given to their bishops. Irving was ordained "bishop" in the Catholic Apostolic Church, and its members were popularly known as "Irvingites." After his expulsion from the Church of Scotland, mainly because of his Christology, Irving's health declined, and he died at forty-two.

114. Kuyper, *Work,* p. 479.
115. Kuyper, *Work,* p. 499.
116. Kuyper, *Work,* pp. 513-16.
117. Kuyper, *Work,* p. 532.
118. Kuyper, *Work,* pp. 565-69.
119. Kuyper, *Work,* p. 639; cf. pp. 618-49.

Irving's first book was entitled *Oracles of God: Four Orations* (1823), later published in his *Collected Writings* as the second volume of five.[120] Irving contrasted the intellectual religion of the catechism with the fact that the Bible presented its message more frequently to the heart, to the fancy, to all the faculties of the soul. The religion of the intellect alone became "clear" but superficial. The second part concerns the judgment to come. Neither Presbyterian appeals to the intellect, nor Methodist appeals to emotions, nor Anglican appeals to moral sense, are adequate *alone.* On Christology, Irving suspected that a "sinless" Christ could not reach the depths of humans to redeem them; in some sense Christ must have shared in sinful human nature without actually committing sin. These two possibilities could coexist because of the power of the Holy Spirit. In 1827 Irving preached in effect on baptism in the Spirit in Acts 2:39. Contrary to Hodge and Smeaton, he suggested that sanctification could be an *event* rather than a *process.* Two books have since been written on this subject. One implies that Irving *anticipated Pentecostalism;* the other suggests that he was the *forerunner of the Charismatic Movement.*[121] By contrast, Warfield made an outright attack on Irving.[122] Irving had fallen under the influence of Samuel Taylor Coleridge on imagination and fancy, and of Thomas Carlyle, who detested creeds and dogmas.

Irving established prayer groups to plead for a new outpouring of the Holy Spirit. Many of his followers sought all the gifts of the Spirit in 1 Cor. 12:8-10. He believed that these gifts were "irrevocably removed from the Church."[123] In Scotland, up to a thousand met daily to pray for a restored power of the Holy Spirit. In April 1831, it was claimed that tongues-speaking and prophecy emerged, and Irving defended their authority. In October this occurred in a normal meeting of morning worship, when Irving defended this on the basis of 1 Corinthians 14. Allegedly tongues and the interpretation of tongues occurred at subsequent meetings. After considerable confusion and commotion, in 1832 the Board of Trustees took the issue to the London Presbytery, and the Presbytery removed Irving from his position of leadership. In 1833 he was charged with heresy. Irving then continued a charismatic ministry, first in an independent church, and in due course in association with the Catholic Apostolic Church. In the Catholic Apostolic Church he was declared to be "an angel," or "bishop," and Drummond and Carlyle were declared to be "apostles." Finally, Irving was sent back from London to Glasgow by his church.

120. Edward Irving, *Collected Writings,* ed. G. Carlyle (London and New York: Straham, 1866), vol. 1, *The Catholic Apostolic Church;* vol. 2, *Orations of God.*

121. Charles G. Strachan, *The Pentecostal Theology of Edward Irving* (London: Darton, Longman & Todd, 1973; and Peabody, MA: Hendrickson, 1988); and Arnold A. Dallimore, *Forerunner of the Charismatic Movement* (Chicago: Moody, 1983).

122. Benjamin B. Warfield, *Counterfeit Miracles* (London: Banner of Truth, 1996).

123. Irving, *Collected Writings,* vol. 2, p. 56.

Anecdotal accounts of the disruption abound. Some attribute Irving's early death to rejection by the Church of Scotland; others attribute it to exhaustion after high spiritual excitement, or what Krister Stendahl would describe as "high-voltage religion." F. Dale Bruner traces "the ancestral line of the Pentecostal Movement . . . through . . . the Montanists, . . . the *Schwärmer* of the Reformation period, . . . Quakers, . . . Wesleyan and revivalist movements, . . . interestingly through Edward Irving in England, . . . influentially through Charles Finney in America. . . ."[124] Charles Finney (1792-1876) constitutes an influential source for the Holiness Movement, and is described by Bruner as "the major historical bridge between primitive Wesleyism and modern Pentecostalism."[125] For better or worse, Irving became an important figure for the self-understanding of Pentecostalism.

(2) *Benjamin H. Irwin* (1854). Irwin was a lawyer who became converted in a Baptist church in America. By 1891 he received what has been called "a sanctification experience" through the Iowa Holiness Association. He then studied the writings of John Wesley intensively, together with the writings of John Fletcher, Wesley's successor. Irwin was drawn to Fletcher's "baptism of burning love." From 1892 to 1895 he became a traveling evangelist in the Wesleyan Methodist Church in Kansas, Nebraska, and Iowa. But in 1895 he received what he called "a baptism of fire," and began teaching the need for a "third blessing." He founded "Fire-Baptized Holiness Associations," beginning in Iowa, in which the "third" blessing went beyond justification and sanctification. The "fire baptism" was often accompanied by shouting and manifestations of exuberance.

By 1896 Irwin was preaching at tent revivals in Georgia and South Carolina. But the mainstream of the Holiness Movement eventually disowned the "third blessing." In 1900 Irwin confessed to "open and gross sin," and fell from leadership. Thereafter his life seems to have ended in obscurity. His assistant, Joseph H. King, continued the Movement in Georgia. In 1907 King received "baptism in the Holy Spirit" and tongues in the Azusa Street meeting of Pentecostals, and the church accepted Pentecostalism and the experience of tongues as "initial evidence" of baptism in the Spirit.

(3) *Albert Benjamin Simpson* (1843-1919). Simpson was a Canadian, educated at Knox College, Toronto, and ordained in Hamilton, Ontario, to the Presbyterian ministry. In 1881 he resigned to establish an independent church in New York. He urged the *"fourfold gospel" of Christ as Savior, Sanctifier, Healer, and Coming King,* which became the hallmark of Pentecostals and the "Foursquare Gospel" Movement. He founded the Christian and Missionary Alliance in 1897. He taught the need for "a higher life," and became a prophet in the Holiness Movement.

---

124. F. Dale Bruner, *A Theology of the Holy Spirit: The Pentecostal Experience and the New Testament Witness* (Grand Rapids: Eerdmans, 1970), p. 35.

125. Bruner, *A Theology of the Holy Spirit,* p. 40.

Simpson's "Restorationist" hermeneutic looked forward to the "latter rain" of the Holy Spirit, in accordance with KJV/AV rendering of Joel 2:23. He looked for a new Pentecost of the last days. This aspect helps to explain the eschatological and apocalyptic color of Irving's and others' theology of the Holy Spirit. It need hardly be said that the Holiness Movement's or Simpson's notion of holiness as an "experience" stands in flat contradiction to Hodge, Smeaton, and Kuyper, let alone to the broader liberal movement represented by Schleiermacher. Yet in America this approach flourished in the case of Charles Finney and some Wesleyan Methodists, and became a key emphasis for classical Pentecostalism. Simpson accepted the value of tongues, but not primarily as a missionary gift. Acts depicts the Church as God intended it to be throughout history. Here is another evidence of his anticipation of the Pentecostal tradition not only in its early years, but also in the "latter rain" experiences of the midtwentieth century. He strongly opposed all "cessationist" beliefs, appealing to Joel 2 and 1 Cor. 12:8-10 and 12:28-30. He urged the value of tongues before Charles Parham and William Seymour around 1905.

17.5. John Henry Newman

John Henry Newman (1801-90) represents the most creative mind in nineteenth-century Roman Catholicism, although during the first part of his life he remained a loyal Anglican. Initially under evangelical influence, he entered Trinity College, Oxford, in 1817, and became a Fellow of Oriel at the University of Oxford in 1822. In 1828 he became Vicar of St. Mary's, Oxford. The beginning of his turning point dates from a tour of southern Europe, including Rome, in 1832-33. When he returned to England, he became strongly associated with the Tractarian Oxford Movement. In 1833 he began to produce *Tracts for the Times* (which led to the name *Tractarian*), in collaboration with John Keble and E. B. Pusey. All of them rejected Liberal theology, but sought to restore High Church ideals and rituals in the Church of England.

The Tractarians stressed apostolic succession and a renewed spirituality based on tradition, especially that of the Church Fathers. A. C. Welch writes: "The spirit of the 'Tractarians' was one of the sharpest protests against the spirit of the age on behalf of the church's ancient traditions and her divinely established authority."[126] He further comments, "The primary enemy of the Tractarians was . . . an age blighted by worldliness."[127] Also in 1833 John Keble preached against "National Apostasy," and Newman saw this as the beginning

---

126. Claude Welch, *Protestant Thought in the Nineteenth Century*, vol. 1: *1799-1870* (New Haven: Yale University Press, 1972), p. 207.

127. Welch, *Protestant Thought in the Nineteenth Century*, vol. 1, p. 208.

of the Oxford Movement. The immediate political cause was government "interference" in the organization and reduction of Irish bishoprics. Newman published the first of ninety Tracts three months after Keble's Sermon.

In contrast to the Quakers, Irving, and that tradition, Newman later insisted: "Dogma has been the fundamental principle of my religion; religion as a mere sentiment is to me a dream and a mockery."[128] This brings us closer to Hodge, Smeaton, and Kuyper than to the Quakers and Irving. Welch comments: "English evangelicalism [in which Newman had been brought up] was plagued by its subjectivism. . . . It was a hypochondriac religion, even idolatrous in worshipping religion rather than God."[129] During the first part of his ministry, before "The Parting of the Ways," Newman saw the antidote only in "the Anglican formularies."[130] He insisted that the Reformers did not destroy the "Catholic" element in the Church of England, which was no less devout and "objective" than they were. He resisted the notion that "Pietism" should claim a monopoly over renewal, devotion, and the gift of the Holy Spirit.

In 1843, however, Newman resigned from his Anglican office and preached the sermon "The Parting of Friends." He believed that if Athanasius and Ambrose were to return today, they would find their home in the Roman Catholic Church. He *accepted* the charge that rationalism *"subtracted"* from the Christian faith, but *rejected* the charge that *Rome added* to the faith. Struggling with his doubts about the irrevocable step of moving to Rome, Newman wrote his famous book *An Essay on the Development of Christian Doctrine* (1845).[131] Bernard Reardon calls this book "one of the most significant books of its century," even though he regards its arguments as unconvincing.[132] Owen Chadwick agrees: "The book does not persuade."[133] Newman attempted to offer "seven tests" for the development, as against corruption, of doctrine, which included preservation, continuity, assimilation, and logical sequence.[134] The *Development of Christian Doctrine* was also in the interests of "reserve": God partly hides himself, because even by revelation humans cannot grasp *all* of his transcendent majesty, glory, and grace, all at once. Origen had explained the gradual communication of truth in this

128. John Henry Newman, *Apologia pro Vita Sua* (Boston: Houghton Mifflin, 1956 [from 1864]), and Oxford: Clarendon, 1967), p. 127.

129. Welch, *Protestant Thought in the Nineteenth Century,* p. 212.

130. Newman, *Apologia,* p. 231.

131. John Henry Newman, *An Essay on the Development of Christian Doctrine* (London: Penguin, 1974).

132. Bernard M. G. Reardon, *From Coleridge to Gore: A Century of Religious Thought in Britain* (London: Longman, 1971), p. 146.

133. Owen Chadwick, *Newman* (Oxford and New York: Oxford University Press, 1983), p. 46; cf. Owen Chadwick, *The Victorian Church,* vol. 1 (London: SCM, 1971), pp. 64-75, 170-71.

134. Newman, *Development of Christian Doctrine,* pp. 122-47.

way. He wrote: "God . . . could only communicate as much as they [humans] were able to bear."[135]

Where doctrinal development is legitimate, a bud grows into a flower, a caterpillar into a butterfly. Newman makes much of the development of basic Christology into the more sophisticated doctrines of the fifth and sixth centuries.[136] William Gladstone responded that by this emphasis Newman "places Christianity on the edge of a precipice." In 1847 Newman was ordained in the Roman Catholic Church, and in 1850 he wrote *Lectures on Anglican Difficulties.* He was attacked both by Charles Kingsley from a more liberal tradition, and by E. B. Pusey from a conservative Tractarian position. Meanwhile in 1852 he wrote his brilliant *The Idea of a University,* in which he spoke of the university as training a mind, and of the cultivation of independent judgment. It could today constitute an excellent manifesto for any university Faculty of Arts or Liberal Arts College. Study is to be coherent and critical, not necessarily "useful" for information, wealth, or business. It must include religion. Eventually in 1864 Newman wrote his other famous book, *Apologia pro Vita Sua.* To have written this in three months was broadly considered amazing. He described the history of his conversion to Rome in sensitive, highly personal terms. In 1877 he republished his earlier *Lectures on the Prophetical Office.*

Specifically, Newman especially emphasized the Holy Spirit's "indwelling." In his sermons he declared: "He pervades us . . . as a light pervades a building, or as a sweet perfume the folds of some honourable robe; so that, in Scripture language, we are said to be in him and he in us."[137] However, *Newman distanced himself from "enthusiasts," as well as from the "dryness" of Liberalism.* We must avoid giving to "the gifts of the Spirit" that "rash, irreverent, and self-exalting interpretation, which is one of the chief errors of this time." Such gifts do not have to be "a sort of religious ecstasy, . . . impassioned thoughts, a soft and languid tone of feeling."[138] No doubt Hodge and Kuyper would agree; Irving would disagree. Like the Church Fathers, to whom he looks, Newman insists that *all that the Holy Spirit does, God the Father and God the Son share in as well:* "God is one with every believer as in a consecrated Temple."[139]

Newman argued that the Holy Spirit worked *in and through human actions.* These actions may be overlooked if we speak all the time of the Spirit. This may remind us of Jeremy Taylor. But he certainly rejected as inadequate

---

135. Robin C. Selby, *The Principle of Reserve in the Writings of John Henry Cardinal Newman* (Oxford: Oxford University Press, 1975), p. 7 and throughout.

136. Newman, *Development of Christian Doctrine,* pp. 240-334.

137. Cited in Ian Ker, *The Achievement of John Henry Newman* (London: Collins, and Notre Dame: University of Notre Dame Press, 1990), p. 85; from John Henry Newman, *Parochial and Plain Sermons,* vol. 2 (London: Rivingtons, 1868), p. 222.

138. Newman, *Parochial and Plain Sermons,* vol. 2, pp. 267-68; cited by Ker.

139. Newman, *Parochial and Plain Sermons,* vol. 2, p. 35; cited by Ker.

evangelical preaching which spoke only of "accepting Jesus," without reference to the Father and the Holy Spirit. He also refers to the Spirit in matters of doctrine. He cites Rom. 5:5, "God's love has been poured into our hearts through the Holy Spirit," and sees the Spirit as the author of renewal, and as appropriating or applying justification to the believer. It is through the Holy Spirit that Christ is our justification and sanctification. We should not forget Newman's implicit appeal or presupposition concerning the Holy Spirit in his *dethronement of reason* in *An Essay in Aid of a Grammar of Ascent* (1870). Here Newman does not disparage reasoning as such, but assent, or the view that acceptance of a proposition also depends on will. The will may be open to accept a "whole" even if it does not fully understand individual parts. Rather than replying only on inference, it grasps the *"illative sense,"* for example, of doctrine. This entails judgment. There is here an implicit reference to the light of the Spirit.

The five approaches outlined above represent the diverse legacy bequeathed by nineteenth-century thought. This survey has not been comprehensive, but serves to clarify some main issues that emerge from the nineteenth century. These provide a starting point for the twentieth century. Newman is not typical of the Roman Catholic Church of the time, but many associate him today with the more progressive outlook of Vatican II, and with English Catholicism, in contrast to that of southern Europe. After Schleiermacher, Hegel, and Kierkegaard, he may perhaps be the fourth most creative thinker of the nineteenth century. Hodge, Smeaton, and Kuyper were not included for their creativity, but for their faithfulness to the Reformed and arguably biblical tradition. Yet they also stand in tension with Irving and Simpson. Hodge, Smeaton, Kuyper, and Newman would not have approved of the rise of the Pentecostal and Renewal Movements, but Irving, Irwin, and Simpson largely anticipated at least Pentecostals. Unlike previous centuries, the nineteenth century saw a broad general consensus begin to fragment into varied schools of thought, or a parting of the ways.

18

The Earlier Part of the Twentieth Century

The earlier part of the twentieth century (1900-1959) saw Henry Barclay Swete's thorough, classic, and still standard two-volume work on the Holy Spirit in 1909 and 1912. Later in 1929 and onward came the great theological works of Karl Barth. Smaller works by J. E. Fison and Lindsay Dewar appeared in 1950 and 1959. Finally, the rise of Pentecostal phenomena began before the turn of the century in other parts of the world. But classical Pentecostalism began with Charles Parham and William Seymour in America in 1901 and 1905, to be followed by the Four Square Gospel, the Assemblies of God, and various branches of Pentecostal churches, until an initial or interim plateau in 1920s and 1930s. All this brings us to the end of the 1950s, when the Charismatic Movement began to dawn. Later, Jürgen Moltmann, Ives Congar, Wolfhart Pannenberg, and many other writers produced significant work on the Holy Spirit, which we consider in subsequent chapters.

18.1. Henry Barclay Swete

Henry Swete (1835-1917) became Professor of King's College, London, and then Regius Professor of Divinity at the University of Cambridge from 1890 to 1915. He produced a 400-page volume, *The Holy Spirit in the New Testament,* in 1909, reprinted in 1919 and 1921, and *The Holy Spirit in the Ancient Church,* another 420 pages, in 1912.[1] He also worked on the text of the Septuagint, produced commentaries on Mark (1898) and Revelation (1906), and did the groundwork of a Greek lexicon of the Church Fathers, in due course published as G. W. H. Lampe (ed.), *A Patristic Greek Lexicon* (1961-68), the standard tool for its sub-

---

1. Both published by Macmillan of London.

ject. He collaborated with F. J. A. Hort (1828-92) and B. F. Westcott (1825-1901) at Cambridge.

In his Introduction to *The Holy Spirit in the New Testament* Swete states that this work is an "appeal to the New Testament, not a formal contribution to New Testament theology."[2] His part 1 then sets out the work of the Holy Spirit in the history of the New Testament (pp. 9-110) in seven chapters. Part 2 has seven chapters on the teaching of the New Testament (pp. 111-279), which looks further at the Four Gospels, Paul, and the rest of the New Testament writings. Part 3 is called "A Summary of N.T. Doctrine" (pp. 281-360). This has seven chapters on the Spirit of God, the Spirit of Christ, the Spirit and the Church, and similar topics. Finally, Swete includes no fewer than nineteen additional notes (pp. 361-400) on such special topics as Prophecy, Tongues, Rapture and Ecstasy, and Jewish Apocalyptic.

It cannot be said, as some Pentecostals claim concerning James D. G. Dunn, that Swete allows Paul to overshadow Luke-Acts. He stresses that in Luke John the Baptist "will be filled with the Holy Spirit" before his birth (Luke 1:15, 41, 67). As with some allusions in the Old Testament, Elizabeth is also "filled" with the Spirit. Swete emphatically believes in the conception of Jesus by the Holy Spirit (Luke 1:35).[3] "Physical effects" are often due to the Holy Spirit. Matthew sees this as the fulfillment of prophecy (Matt. 1:20-21). For Jesus the first decisive experience of the Spirit is at his baptism, which all four Gospels attest (Mark 1:9-11; Matt. 3:13-17; Luke 3:21-22; John 1:32-33). Spiritual baptism belongs to the New Age, and heaven is torn asunder. The dove constitutes a further visible sign.[4] The ministry of Jesus begins with Messianic temptations, which were "driven" (Mark 1:12-15) or "led" (Matt. 4:1-11) by the Holy Spirit. This reveals the self-identity of Jesus. He returns from the desert "with power" and authority to perform exorcisms and miracles.[5]

Swete next considers the Pentecostal outpourings in Acts 2:1-47. He notes that the Holy Spirit falls when the apostles are engaged in common prayer, and is given to "all" believers.[6] They can now speak boldly (Greek, *parrēsia*). The Palestinian Church then offers examples of believers "filled with the Spirit" (Acts 4:8). These include the apostles (4:31); Stephen and the Seven (6:3); and Paul (9:17). "Great fear" came upon those who witnessed the fate of Ananias and Sapphira. Philip experiences "the one case" of rapture.[7] Luke recounts the "prophecies" of Agabus and of others (Acts 11:28; 21:4). In "the founding of the

---

2. Henry B. Swete, *The Holy Spirit in the New Testament* (London: Macmillan, 1909, rpt. 1921), p. viii.

3. Swete, *The Holy Spirit in the New Testament*, pp. 13-14 and 24-25 respectively.

4. Swete, *The Holy Spirit in the New Testament*, pp. 45-48 and 365-66.

5. Swete, *The Holy Spirit in the New Testament*, pp. 57-59.

6. Swete, *The Holy Spirit in the New Testament*, pp. 70-72.

7. Swete, *The Holy Spirit in the New Testament*, pp. 93 and 380.

Gentile church" Barnabas is "full of the Holy Spirit" as well as a man of goodness and faith, and Paul and Barnabas are commissioned to evangelize and to
preach with the laying on of hands. They were directed by the Spirit (16:6-7).
The Holy Spirit also fell upon believers and Apollos at Ephesus (19:1-6).

In his part 2, Swete turns to review New Testament teaching. Jesus is
anointed by the Holy Spirit, as prophesied by Isaiah (Luke 4:18). The saying
about "blasphemy against the Holy Spirit" is very serious because it renders
"the source of holiness" as being "as of hell," and calls good, evil.[8] On exorcisms, Jesus "accommodates himself to prevalent belief."[9] The Father will give
the Spirit "to those who ask" (Matt. 7:8). The Holy Spirit will come to our aid
in time of need. Swete takes seriously baptism in the threefold name (Matt.
28:19), which occurs in second-century MSS. Jesus thereby, he claims, asserts
"the Divine Trinity."[10] John's teaching may reflect this (John 14:16, 26). Swete
highlights the new birth from above (John 3:3-5) and the symbolism of water
in the case of the Woman of Samaria (4:10).[11] The Spirit is life; the flesh profits
nothing (6:63). He connects the "flowing," living water with the Feast of Tabernacles (7:37).

Swete gives a separate chapter to the Paraclete Sayings in the Farewell Discourses. Later, in 1927, Hans Windisch would argue that the Paraclete Sayings
could be excised from the Gospel without losing the continuity of the Discourse.[12] These five passages are John 14:16-17; 14:25-26; 15:26-27; 16:7-11; and
16:12-15. However, in a more recent study, after examining this approach of
Windisch, George Johnson concluded, "We cannot discover any decisive reason
for rejecting the traditional position."[13] Swete stresses the Spirit's relation to
Christ. He is "another Paraclete" (*allos parakletos*, 14:16-17). The Paraclete will
be a permanent gift, who will be with you *(par' hymon)* forever (14:16)! Jesus
Christ even says, "*I* will come" (14:18-19) and that the Spirit will teach "all things
that I have said." The Holy Spirit "is to proclaim His [Jesus Christ's] oneness
with the Spirit. . . . The Son came to represent, to interpret, to glorify the Father;
and . . . the Spirit was sent to reveal the Son."[14] Again, in John 15:26-27, "the
Spirit of truth who comes from the Father . . . will testify on my behalf." In 16:9
the Spirit-Paraclete brings judgment "because they do not believe in me," while
"righteousness" relates to Christ's vindication; and judgment, again, because

---

8. Swete, *The Holy Spirit in the New Testament*, p. 117.

9. Swete, *The Holy Spirit in the New Testament*, p. 119.

10. Swete, *The Holy Spirit in the New Testament*, p. 125.

11. Swete, *The Holy Spirit in the New Testament*, p. 137.

12. Hans Windisch, "Die fünf johannische Parakletesprüche," trans. J. W. Cox, in *The Spirit-
Paraclete in the Fourth Gospel* (Philadelphia: Fortress, 1968).

13. George Johnson, *The Spirit-Paraclete in the Gospel of John* (Cambridge: Cambridge University Press, 1970), p. 75.

14. Swete, *The Holy Spirit in the New Testament*, p. 153.

the Kingdom of God in Christ condemns "the ruler of this world" (16:10-11). It is remarkable, we might comment, that many New Testament scholars are overly cautious about the Trinitarian implications of this.[15]

Swete's chapter 4 of part 2 turns to Paul, with a multitude of biblical and Pauline references. The earliest epistle declares, "not in word only but also in power and the Holy Spirit" (1 Thess. 1:5; cf. 2:1-13). This finds corroboration in 1 Cor. 2:1-5. A second theme is that of *"progressive holiness"* (*en hagiasmō*, 1 Thess. 4:7; 5:23; my italics).[16] A third concerns prophecy (1 Thess. 5:19), which is to be valued but also tested, while a fourth is the completion and culmination of the Holy Spirit's work at the Return of Christ, or Parousia. These, as we shall see, resonate with Pentecostal themes, except that Swete stresses "progressive" sanctification, *not* the *event* of Holiness Movements or of "perfectionism." The eschatological emphasis on what is yet to come confirms this.

1 Corinthians speaks at length of the revelation by the Holy Spirit (1 Cor. 2:10, esp. 2:10-16). In this epistle "spiritual" *(pneumatikos)* almost always means "relating to, or given by, the Holy Spirit," which includes ethical action and a Christ-like mind and character. The Spirit brings new life (1 Cor. 6:11; p. 182). Above all, the Spirit witnesses to Christ as Lord (1 Cor. 12:3), and gives gifts to the Church for that purpose. Prophecy "scarcely had its due," largely because the Corinthians saw "tongues" as more attractive, spectacular, and ostentatious. But prophecy is "under the prophet's control" and can be *fallible*.[17] Love is the most crucial of the effects of the Holy Spirit. It is more decisive than tongues. Many Pentecostal splits and divisions would shortly follow Swete's words. Do these splits show more interest in power and personality, like some in Corinth, than in unity and love, especially when "doctrine" is often minimized as too "intellectual"? In 2 Cor. 1:22 the Spirit is the "first installment" *(arrabōn)* of his future presence and gifts. The Holy Spirit gives life (2 Cor. 3:6-11). The Spirit changes believers into *the likeness of Christ* "from one degree of glory to another" (2 Cor. 3:18). Again, this surely indicates "progressive" sanctification. The gift of the Spirit is a proof of genuine ministry (2 Cor. 6:4-10).[18]

Swete now considers Romans and Galatians. The Galatians did not receive the Spirit by "works"; the reverse was the case: the Spirit was given to direct the new life (Gal. 3:1-5). This is confirmed by the argument of 3:6–5:26.[19] This theology contrasts with most rabbinic views, and, according to Luther, with those of the Radical Reformers. Later, some would argue that it also contrasts with the tradition of the Holiness Movement. There is a fine line between praying

---

15. Arthur W. Wainwright, *The Trinity in the New Testament* (London: SPCK, 1962), pp. 199-268, provides a notable exception.

16. Swete, *The Holy Spirit in the New Testament*, p. 172.

17. Swete, *The Holy Spirit in the New Testament*, p. 189.

18. Swete, *The Holy Spirit in the New Testament*, pp. 196-97.

19. Swete, *The Holy Spirit in the New Testament*, pp. 202-10.

for (more of) the Spirit, and seeking to "do" things to expedite the prayers. In Gal. 5:16, 25, Paul sums this up as primarily "living" by the Spirit, in order that believers may *then* "walk" by the Spirit.

Romans speaks of the Spirit as the Agent of Christ's resurrection (Rom. 1:4; 8:9-11). Paul strongly emphasizes that the gift of the Spirit is poured out by God's love (Rom. 5:5). The Spirit gives believers a new mind-set, attitude, or disposition (Rom. 8:2-13). He is the Spirit of God's Son (Rom. 8:14-17). Hence he prays within believers with inexpressible sighs, which long, with creation, for the future (Rom. 8:26-30).[20] Finally, Rom. 12:11; 15:13, 30 apply the Spirit's presence to the everyday life of the Christian.

Chapters 7 and 8 of Swete's work on the New Testament include Philippians, Colossians, and Ephesians, and then Hebrews and the rest of the New Testament. Little distinctive material emerges in Philippians or Colossians, but Ephesians, which Swete seems to accept as Pauline, "abounds in references to the Holy Spirit."[21] Christians are "marked with the seal of the promised Spirit" (Eph. 1:13). The Spirit is "the pledge *(arrabōn)* of our inheritance . . . as God's own people . . ." (1:14). Christians must not "grieve" the Holy Spirit (Eph. 4:30), by whom they were "marked with a seal for the day of redemption." The verb is highly personal, and the noun marks an interim time until the last day. Eph. 1:17 speaks of "a spirit of wisdom and revelation," although this may not denote the Holy Spirit. Eph. 2:18 speaks of access to the Father for both Christian Jews and Gentiles "in one Spirit."

In the light of the multiple divisions among Pentecostals between 1905 and 1920, it is significant that Swete comments: "The Apostle enumerates seven unities which ought to triumph over all the elements of discord that tend to keep believers apart. . . . one body and one hope, . . . one Lord, one faith, one baptism, one God and Father of all" (Eph. 4:3-6).[22] This passage begins by urging humility, gentleness, and patience (v. 2), "making every effort to maintain the unity of the Spirit" (v. 3). Eph. 4:7-16 concludes with ministries like those listed in 1 Cor. 12:4-30 and in Rom. 12:4-8, and makes a plea for the renewal of the mind in Eph. 4:23.

We need not labor the details in Swete by exploring Hebrews and other books at length. We refer the reader to Part I of the present book. But it is worth noting the nineteen additional notes that Swete discusses, including prophecy, tongues, ecstasy and rapture, sanctification, and Jewish apocalyptic. Part 3 of Swete's book is called "a summary of New Testament doctrine," but repeats data which have been considered, under such doctrinal themes as the Spirit and God, the Spirit of Christ, the Spirit and the Church, and the Spirit and the

---

20. Swete, *The Holy Spirit in the New Testament*, pp. 218-21.
21. Swete, *The Holy Spirit in the New Testament*, p. 231.
22. Swete, *The Holy Spirit in the New Testament*, p. 236.

Word.[23] The most distinctive is the first theme listed. *The Spirit is the "Holy Spirit" because holiness derives from none but God, and the Spirit is God's presence and gift.* Swete also argues that in this respect we cannot doubt the Personhood of the Spirit.[24]

In his subsequent work *The Holy Spirit in the Ancient Church,* Swete again restricts himself to sheer description as a historian of doctrine rather than as a systematic theologian. Since the work is limited to the Church Fathers, it virtually constitutes a book of quotations on the Holy Trinity. Perhaps his greatest contribution was to avoid generalizing about epochs and trends, by looking with care at individual figures and situations. Before Nicea and in the pre-Arian age, he says, "The nature of the Spirit . . . continues to be unexplored with a few partial exceptions."[25] After Nicea complex issues in Christology involved a thirty-year additional delay. He does, however, consider Montanism and Tertullian in detail, as well as other pre-Nicene Fathers.

Predictably enough, Cyril of Jerusalem, Athanasius of Alexandria, Basil of Caesarea, and Gregory of Nazianzus receive most attention in the East; and Hilary of Poitiers, Ambrose of Milan, and Augustine of Hippo are most prominent in the West. These seven Fathers are of special significance for the development of the doctrine of the Spirit. All stress repeatedly that the Spirit is "not a creature nor foreign to the divine nature, but belongs to it and is indivisible from the essence of the Son and the Father" *(ou ktisma oude xenon all' idion kai adiaireton tēs ousias tou huiou kai tou patros).*[26]

Swete provides a useful account of the dialogue between Athanasius and the Tropici in which he depends heavily on 1 Cor. 12:4-6 and other passages, especially in 1 Corinthians. But following the Fathers, he necessarily lays more emphasis on the Person of the Holy Spirit as divine than on his work of salvation, which emerges from the later Middle Ages and the Reformation onward. He has provided an excellent, balanced account of the Patristic era, on which we have partly drawn in the present work. In his historical survey, his approach remains generally descriptive, and this main part may contain less revealing comments than his earlier book on the New Testament. But his part 3 (some fifty pages) departs from the merely descriptive, and his last chapters on the Godhead of the Spirit, the Spirit's relation to the Father and to the Son, creation, inspiration, the incarnation, the Paraclete, and sanctification remain more distinctive. This is the case especially in the use of John 16:14-15 and 1 Cor. 12:4-6.[27] Yet much of this material offers little more than a summary of part 2.

---

23. Swete, *The Holy Spirit in the New Testament,* pp. 283-360.

24. Swete, *The Holy Spirit in the New Testament,* respectively pp. 286-88 and 290-92.

25. Henry B. Swete, *The Holy Spirit in the Ancient Church: A Study of Christian Teaching in the Age of the Fathers* (London: Macmillan, 1912), p. 5.

26. Swete, *The Holy Spirit in the Ancient Church,* p. 173.

27. Swete, *The Holy Spirit in the Ancient Church,* pp. 359-409.

18.2. Karl Barth

Karl Barth (1896-1968) was born at Basle (Basel), Switzerland, where he later became a professor (1935) after holding posts in Germany. He studied in Bern and Berlin, where in early years he was influenced by Adolf von Harnack and Wilhelm Herrmann. He was ordained in 1909 and became pastor of Safenwil from 1911 to 1921. In very early years he was impressed by Schleiermacher's emphasis on the immediacy of relation to Christ. He recalls that he "soaked Herrmann in through all my poses," for Herrmann was "not ashamed of the Gospel."

The ten years as pastor at Safenwil contributed, however, to a radical change. He recalls: "In the end I failed as pastor at Safenwil." He began to correspond with Edward Thurneysen, pastor of a neighboring parish. The first shock for Barth was the utter failure of the Liberal theology of Harnack, Jülicher, and Herrmann. The second shock was the invasion of Belgium at the beginning of the First World War (1914), when ninety-three German intellectuals signed a manifesto of support for the Kaiser Wilhelm II, among whom Barth found "almost all of my German teachers." A whole world of exegesis and dogmatics was "shaken to the foundations" by the two events. Barth wrote, "We must begin all over again."

By 1917 Barth had done much of his new thinking. In February 1917 he wrote "The Strange New World within the Bible," which appears in *The Word of God and the Word of Man* (German, 1928). In the Bible, he urged, "A new world projects itself into our old, ordinary world."[28] A central issue is the sovereignty of God. Barth wrote: "It is not right human thoughts about God which form the content of the Bible, but the *right divine thoughts about men*. The Bible tells us not how we should talk with God, but *what he says to us*, . . . how he has . . . found the way to us."[29] Toward the end of this address or essay he asks, "Who is God?" and replies: "The heavenly Father, . . . the Son, . . . the Spirit in his believers" (my italics).[30]

In 1919 Barth wrote the first edition of his *Commentary on Romans* (2nd ed. 1922; Eng. trans. 1933).[31] In the two first editions Barth saw divine grace as the relativizing of all human pretensions and the promise of new creation. He portrayed Judaism as a system of self-affirmation. By 1922, in the second edition, he had appropriated, and drawn on, much of the thought of Søren Kierkegaard, who stressed the transcendence of God as "other." The "hiddenness" of the sovereign God confronts humankind with the dialectic of the "no" on law, sin, and death, and the "yes" of grace, the Holy Spirit, Christ, and new creation. This re-

---

28. Karl Barth, *The Word of God and the Word of Man* (London: Hodder & Stoughton, 1928), p. 37.

29. Barth, *The Word of God and the Word of Man*, p. 43.

30. Barth, *The Word of God and the Word of Man*, pp. 48-49.

31. Karl Barth, *The Epistle to the Romans* (Oxford: Oxford University Press, 1933; 6th ed. 1968).

flects the theme of *Either/Or* in Kierkegaard. God is not the God of human "religion," "religious works," or "religious consciousness." This is because these are "not an achievement of our spirit, but the action of the Holy Spirit . . . because the love of God has been shed abroad in our hearts through the Holy Spirit (Rom. 5:5). . . . The Holy Spirit is the operation of God in faith, the creative and redemptive power of the Kingdom of Heaven. . . . The Spirit of God . . . is the eternal 'Yes!' "[32] Paul stresses "the Wholly-Other-ness of God."[33]

Barth's commentary produced a shock wave throughout Europe. Harnack and Jülicher disowned it as not reflecting critical exegesis. Rudolf Bultmann was initially sympathetic toward its dialectical theology. At all events, it brought Barth to the center of the stage, and from 1921 to 1925 he became Professor of Theology at Göttingen; from 1925 to 1930, Professor of Theology at Münster; and from 1930, Professor of Theology at Bonn, until his move back to Switzerland in the light of Hitler's regime. A key year for his theology of the Holy Spirit seems to have been 1929, when he lectured on *The Holy Spirit and the Christian Life.*[34] We shall return to this work shortly. In 1930 he published his *Anselm: Fides Quaerens Intellectum,* which in 1958 he called a "vital key" to his later work, *Church Dogmatics.*[35] In 1932 he wrote the first edition of the first volume of his *Church Dogmatics,* which grew steadily over the years to fourteen volumes in English.[36] In May 1934 he headed the Barmen Declaration of the Confessing Church, which proclaimed sole and primary allegiance to Christ and Scripture, in direct opposition to the demand for primary loyalty made by Adolf Hitler. This led to the loss of his Chair at Bonn, and to his appointment to a Chair at Basel in Switzerland. He remained there until his retirement in 1962, and death in 1968.

The two main sources for Barth's theology of the Holy Spirit were his lecture or book *The Holy Spirit and the Christian Life* and more fundamentally, in a number of places, his magisterial *Church Dogmatics.* 1929 is the date of his lecture on the Spirit; but it was first published in German in 1938. A further subsidiary source is his early *The Resurrection of the Dead.* This is a brief running commentary on the whole of 1 Corinthians, including chapters 12–14.[37] In the book on the Holy Spirit, Barth underlines the Spirit's work as Creator. Humankind depends on the Holy Spirit for their representing God, as his image.[38]

---

32. Barth, *Romans,* p. 157.

33. Barth, *Romans,* p. 386.

34. Karl Barth, *The Holy Spirit and the Christian Life: The Theological Basis of Ethics* (Louisville: Westminster/John Knox, 1993); cf. also Karl Barth, *The Holy Spirit and the Christian Life,* trans. and annot. Michael Raburn (available on the Internet, 2002) as a translation with commentary.

35. Karl Barth, *Anselm: Fides Quaerens Intellectum* (London: SCM, 1960), Preface.

36. Karl Barth, *Church Dogmatics,* 14 vols. (Edinburgh: T&T Clark, 1957-75).

37. Karl Barth, *The Resurrection of the Dead* (London: Hodder & Stoughton, 1933), pp. 73-106.

38. Barth, *The Holy Spirit* (1993 ed.).

Next, the Spirit prepares us to receive grace. Third, he is the Spirit of promise, who makes the believer "a new creature: God's child."[39] Barth calls these three themes "guiding principles."

Under "The Holy Spirit as Creator," Barth characteristically separates the work of *the Spirit of God* from the *human spirit's* attempt at "religion" or "the highest good."[40] Barth states that the uncreated Spirit can be revealed to created spirits. The Spirit is seen, as in Augustine, as God's love, as inconceivable, undeserved. Barth argues that our participation in the event of revelation is the fundamental significance of the Holy Spirit for the Christian life. The Spirit is not detached from everyday life. Barth writes: we are "equipped by God for God." Through the Spirit we experience "the fabulous wonder of the love of God." Moreover, the Holy Spirit continually makes us *listen to* the Word of the Creator. This revelation is not merely a collection of "already-made desires, . . . turning these urges into a command of God."[41] This is *not simply a matter of feelings, urges, and senses.* God's revelation must become for us the voice of the *living* God, as God says the same things to us that God said through the mouths of the prophets and apostles once for all.

Christians may be "fanatical [enthusiastic] or faithful, devoted," but if this swerves toward the left or right, to "the Papal vogue or . . . the Anabaptists, . . . it evades what God really said." The Holy Spirit meets us "in the scriptural proclamation of the revelation of God," which without the Spirit we cannot hear. "Only in the miracle of the Holy Spirit are they not hidden from us."[42]

Barth now discusses the Holy Spirit as "One Who Atones," or "Reconciler" (German, *Versöhner*). Humans *can* show hostility to the Spirit and to grace. Nevertheless "the love of God has been poured out within out hearts through the Holy Spirit, who was given to us" (Rom. 5:5). Augustine stressed this. On the other hand, we cannot think of *all* sin as *removed,* any more than "we can heal a dead man." We can as little *think* of it as removed "as we can in fact *remove* it ourselves" (Barth's italics).[43] This strongly implies a *progressive, not instantaneous view of sanctification.* Barth appeals to the Reformers. He adds that the Holy Spirit therefore has, "above all, a *disciplinary* office." We must accord with the cross of Christ. We must abandon works righteousness and approach God boldly. We must trust in the Word, and in the death of Christ: "Its joy struggles against the completely radical and hopeless misery which is clearly found within each of us and finds its overt expression in temptation. No one other than the Holy Spirit will give real faith."[44]

39. Barth, *The Holy Spirit,* p. 2.
40. Barth, *The Holy Spirit,* p. 3.
41. Barth, *The Holy Spirit,* p. 9.
42. Barth, *The Holy Spirit,* p. 17.
43. Barth, *The Holy Spirit,* p. 24.
44. Barth, *The Holy Spirit,* p. 35.

Like Luther, Barth elaborates struggle in terms of temptation. Temptation may bring sorrow and "incessant threat hanging over us," but we have his sovereign assistance as Comforter. This is the antithesis to those who "brag so easily and smilingly as some arrogant fanatics (German, *Schwärmergeister*) brag about the Holy Spirit."[45] This becomes a reality in sanctification. The remainder of Barth's essay or lecture follows the consequences of sanctification for ethics. These flow not from a set of external commands, but by showing in life the fruit of the Holy Spirit.

In his study of 1 Corinthians, *The Resurrection of the Dead,* Barth stresses the unity of the thought of this epistle, underlining the value of love over against the pride and splits at Corinth. 1 Corinthians 13 indicates "a great passing away of all those things that are not love."[46] Indeed, Barth has some suspicion about the *phenomenon* of spiritual gifts, which find parallels in pagan religions. He writes: "What we are really concerned with is not *phenomena* in themselves, but with their *whence?* and *whither?* To what do they point?"[47] Clearly Barth is concerned about whether every claim about gifts genuinely originates in the Spirit, and is used for the work which the Spirit promotes. The gifts, Barth urges, are for the common good. In the future the Holy Spirit will be active in bringing about the resurrection of the dead.[48]

In the first volume of *Church Dogmatics* Barth considers the Word of God and the possibility of theology. Can we even speak of God, and can we speak of God as the Holy Spirit? Barth insists that theology is not *about* God, but *from* God, with the inference that it is not *about* the Holy Spirit, but *from* the Holy Spirit. The Word of God addresses us. Barth writes: "The Holy Spirit . . . cannot be separated from the word. . . . His power is . . . the power that lives in and by the Word."[49] Through the Spirit the Word claims and judges us. The Holy Spirit in preaching or in theology thus always says "a final word."[50] God is active through the Spirit, because his revelation is a speech-act.[51] The Holy Spirit is the subjective element in the event of revelation, that is, the one who facilitates appropriation. In harmony with the Western Church Barth understands the Spirit "as the Spirit of both the Father and the Son."[52] Barth explicitly turns to the Holy Spirit in section 12: "The Spirit guarantees man what he cannot guar-

---

45. Barth, *The Holy Spirit,* p. 37.

46. Barth, *The Resurrection of the Dead,* p. 76.

47. Barth, *The Resurrection of the Dead,* p. 80.

48. Barth, *The Resurrection of the Dead,* pp. 191-223; cf. Anthony C. Thiselton, "Luther and Barth in 1 Corinthians 15," in *The Bible, the Reformation and the Church: Essays in Honour of James Atkinson,* ed. W. P. Stephens (Sheffield: Sheffield Academic, 1995), pp. 258-89.

49. Karl Barth, *Church Dogmatics* (henceforth abbreviated *C.D.*) I: 1, sect. 5; Eng. vol. 1, p. 150.

50. Barth, *C.D.* I: 1, sect. 5; vol. 1, p. 182.

51. Barth, *C.D.* I: 1, sect. 5:4; vol. 1, p. 162.

52. Barth, *C.D.* I: 1, sect. 12:2; vol. 1, p. 479.

antee himself."[53] The Holy Spirit "is the Yes to God's Word."[54] Rather than seeing him as "a third person," Barth adopts Augustine's view that "He is the common element, or better the fellowship, the act of communion, of the Father and the Son."[55] Nevertheless, he fully believes in the Holy Spirit as "the Giver of Life" and in "the deity of the Holy Spirit."[56] The work of the Holy Spirit is undivided: *"opera trinitatis ad extra sunt indivisa."*[57]

In the second English volume of *Church Dogmatics* (I: 2, sect. 16) Barth considers further "The Outpouring of the Holy Spirit." Again he calls the Spirit "the subjective reality of revelation."[58] He writes: "The work of the Spirit is that our blind eyes are opened, and . . . in thankful self-surrender we recognize and acknowledge that it is so."[59] "In the Holy Spirit we are free for God."[60] Barth comments, "Christ is revealed in the Bible by the work of the Holy Spirit."[61] Much of this volume concerns time and the Word of God. The Spirit recollects time, and also works moment by moment.

Although volumes 3 and 4 (II: 1 and II: 2) concern the doctrine of God, Barth does not discuss the Holy Spirit other than in passing. Certainly he reiterates that redemption comes from the Father, the Son, and the Holy Spirit.[62] At the beginning of II: 1, Barth insists: "Knowledge of God occurs . . . by the Holy Spirit."[63] The English volumes 5–9, which constitute *C.D.* III: 1–4, concern creation and covenant. In creation "what is true of the Father and the Son is also true of the Holy Spirit. . . . He is the communion of self-impartation realized . . . from all eternity."[64] "It is God the Holy Spirit who makes the existence of the creature as such possible."[65] The aim of this creation is ongoing history, sustained by the Holy Spirit.

In his volumes on Reconciliation (Eng. vols. 9–13; *C.D.* IV: 1–4), Barth discusses the Holy Spirit and the gathering of the Christian community. In IV: 2 he turns to the Spirit and sanctification, and in IV: 3 to the Spirit, the Christian community, and the Christian hope. He declares: "The Holy Spirit is the awakening power in which Jesus Christ has formed and continually renewed his body, i.e., his own earthly-historical form of existence, the one holy, catholic

53. Barth, *C.D.* I: 1, sect. 12:1; vol. 1, p. 453.
54. Barth, *C.D.* I: 1, sect. 12:1; vol. 1, p. 453.
55. Barth, *C.D.* I: 1, sect. 12:2; vol. 1, pp. 469-70.
56. Barth, *C.D.* I: 1, sect. 12:2; vol. 1, p. 471.
57. Barth, *C.D.* I: 1, sect. 11:2; vol. 1, p. 442.
58. Barth, *C.D.* I: 2, sect. 16:1; vol. 2, p. 203.
59. Barth, *C.D.* I: 2, sect. 16:1; vol. 2, p. 239.
60. Barth, *C.D.* I: 2, sect. 16:2; vol. 2, p. 243.
61. Barth, *C.D.* I: 2, sect. 19:2; vol. 2, p. 513.
62. Barth, *C.D.* II: 2, sect. 33:1; vol. 4, p. 105.
63. Barth, *C.D.* II: 1, sect. 25:1; vol. 3, p. 3.
64. Barth, *C.D.* III: 1, sect. 41:1; vol. 5, p. 56.
65. Barth, *C.D.* III: 1, sect. 41:1; vol. 5, p. 56.

and apostolic Church."[66] He quotes Augustine again: "The Holy Spirit has called me by the Gospel, enlightened me with his gifts, sanctified and maintained me in a right faith, as He calls and gathers and enlightens the whole of Christendom, keeping it to Jesus Christ in the true and only faith."[67]

In section 66, Barth expounds the difference between justification and sanctification. They are "two different aspects of the one event of salvation."[68] It is tempting to wonder whether this conflation of terms could suggest what causes problems for "Holiness" movements, but elsewhere Barth regards sanctification as a *process of struggle*. In one sense, all Christians are saints and sanctified. But in another sense holiness involves struggle, temptation, conflict, and maturity over time. Barth robustly declares: "Justification is not sanctification and does not merge into it."[69] In sanctification, "God fashions a people of holy men [people]."[70] In this sense, the Holy Spirit steadily builds up the community.[71] This self-giving of God above all promotes love among Christians "to correspond with the love in which God has drawn him (the Christian) to himself and raised him up."[72]

Finally, in *C.D.* IV: 3, ii, Barth sees the Holy Spirit as sending the community to preach Christ, and as nurturing Christian hope. The Church has "not yet reached its goal, even in the mighty operation of His Holy Spirit."[73] The Spirit belongs to the New Age, but also to the period of "Not Yet."[74] God has not yet become manifest in "universal, exclusive, and ultimate glory."[75] Hence: "God Himself is the Holy Spirit who awakens the Christian to life in hope."[76] There is relatively little by writers of the 1950s and 1960s that has not been anticipated by Barth.

18.3. The Emergence and Rise of the Pentecostal Movements

There are at least four reasons why any "mainstream" scholar would feel trepidation in writing about Pentecostalism. The first is that the warmest, most sympathetic approach is often interpreted as insincere. Reviews of books in *The Journal*

---

66. Barth, *C.D.* IV: 2, sect. 62; vol. 9, p. 643.
67. Barth, *C.D.* IV: 2, sect. 62; vol. 9, p. 645.
68. Barth, *C.D.* IV: 2, sect. 66; vol. 10, p. 503.
69. Barth, *C.D.* IV: 2, sect. 66; vol. 10, p. 503.
70. Barth, *C.D.* IV: 2, sect. 66; vol. 10, p. 511.
71. Barth, *C.D.* IV: 2, sect. 67; vol. 10, pp. 614-726.
72. Barth, *C.D.* IV: 2, sect. 68; vol. 10, p. 727; cf. pp. 727-840.
73. Barth, *C.D.* IV: 3, ii, sect. 73; vol. 12, p. 903.
74. Barth, *C.D.* IV: 3, ii, sect. 73; vol. 12, p. 903.
75. Barth, *C.D.* IV: 3, ii, sect. 73; vol. 12, p. 915.
76. Barth, *C.D.* IV: 3, ii, sect. 73; vol. 12, p. 941.

of Pentecostal Theology have sometimes been dismissed, even if they seek rapport and genuinely admire the commitment and devotion of the movement, as nowadays merely making a "fashionable" comment before some criticism. Until I read a huge amount of Pentecostal literature, I had imagined that my genuine admiration for their warm devotion would permit a dialogue that was both constructive and critical. But I am dismayed by those reviews and articles which say of a writer, "He is not really one of us." Hence, it is implied, what else can we expect?

Yet against this, I am encouraged by two factors. First, many Pentecostals with whom I have spoken express sorrow at such a response, and assert that most Pentecostals would disown such an approach. Second, some of the tenets of the Movement have received some qualification or addition *from within,* by Pentecostals themselves. Gordon Fee, Frank Macchia, and Veli-Matti Kärkkäinen represent three of many examples. Hence even a daring potential "correction," or at least qualification, would be likely to find some support from Pentecostals themselves. Many Pentecostals do, as I do, distinguish genuine experience of God from original misconceptions about terminology in classical Pentecostalism. But we must not be simplistic. Much of the remainder of Part III considers the very varied themes and strata that coexist both among devout Pentecostals and in the Renewal Movement. Although this is not the only reason for giving these movements considerable space in this book, the sheer size and growth of the Pentecostal churches on a global scale suggest that we urgently now need to aim at constructive mutual dialogue. Hence I have gained access not only to numerous Pentecostal writings, but also to Pentecostal Web sites across the world. These range from a narrow dogmatism to sensitive and moving self-criticism.

I have not yet mentioned a third reason for extreme care or even hesitation. *Some* Pentecostal writers, but not all, show what can only be described as at best a latent "persecution" complex or paranoia, or at worst an inverted snobbery about dialogue with so-called recognized scholars. Some scholars are accepted. Gordon Fee, for example, is an excellent New Testament scholar who is also Pentecostal. He has incurred rebuke from fellow Pentecostals by raising questions about the use of the term "baptism in the Spirit" in relation to Scripture.[77] Clark Pinnock is sufficiently sensitive to Pentecostal voices to gain a hearing. James Dunn may be controversial, but he has taken Pentecostal views with sufficient seriousness to merit a huge hearing. In this book we have considered in detail the Pentecostal writers Gordon Fee and Roger Stronstad and the Renewal writer Max Turner, and more broadly Frank Macchia, Veli-Matti Kärkkäinen, and others. *Most* Pentecostals do *not set mind* or brain *against feelings and worship,* recognizing that, for Paul among others, both were important. But I was discouraged by reading the introductory comments of James K. A. Smith,

---

77. See Eldridge, "Pentecostalism, Experimental Presuppositions, and Hermeneutics," at the 20th annual meeting of the Society of Pentecostal Studies (Dallas, Nov. 8-10, 1990).

Thinking in Tongues (2010). He speaks of encountering "A strange brew of academic alarm and snobbery" which degenerated into "awkward pleasantries," as if all biblical or theological scholars shared the Enlightenment or rationalist assumptions which he clearly met on that one occasion.[78] Clearly Pentecostals are of very different kinds and attitudes.

There is one more reason for extreme care and hesitation. Any historian of theology or religion might assume that understanding is best served by looking at early manifestations of the Movement in America under the leadership of Charles F. Parham in 1901 and William Seymour in 1905-6. Yet Pentecostal literature often dismisses this approach as "Eurocentric" (which is curious for America), and cites largely anecdotal accounts of Pentecostal revivals earlier than this in other parts of the world. Again, the reasons for this can easily be understood, and we may readily accept the occurrence of such revivals. *But it does nothing to devalue the global origins and effects of the movement* that began with Parham and Seymour. Indeed, one of my Korean doctoral graduates, Dr. Yongnan Jeon Ahn, who is currently Dean of the Pentecostal Seminary in Daejon, Korea, chose to begin her study of Pentecostal hermeneutics by examining the work of Parham and Seymour.[79] Yet Paulson Pulikottil writes: "Pentecostal histories that are Eurocentric in nature describe Pentecostal history beginning with the Topeka revival [under Parham], and gaining momentum at the Azusa Street Mission [under Seymour] and spreading all over the world."[80] We shall consider Asian and other origins shortly.

We may acknowledge the point that some trace Pentecostal origins to the Holiness Movement, where sanctification is perhaps first seen as "event" rather than "process," including D. L. Moody and Charles Finney. More convincing is the finding of a pre-history in Edward Irwin, while some trace it to Montanism, Tertullian, and even the Syrian church. We shall follow most writers, including many Pentecostals, by beginning with Parham and Seymour, whether or not this movement also began in Calcutta.[81]

(1) *Charles Fox Parham* (1873-1929). Parham has in part become obscured by Seymour among some writers because of Parham's overt racist tone. How-

---

78. James K. A. Smith, *Thinking in Tongues: Pentecostal Contribution to Christian Philosophy* (Grand Rapids: Eerdmans, 2010), p. xii.

79. Yongnan Jeon Ahn, "A Formulation of Pentecostal Hermeneutics and Its Possible Implication for the Interpretation of Speaking in Tongues and Prophecy in 1 Corinthians 12–14" (Ph.D. diss., University of Nottingham, May 2002), pp. 4–29.

80. Paulson Pulikottil, "East and West Meet in God's Own Country: Encounter of Western Pentecostalism with Native Pentecostalism in Kerala," *Cyber Journal for Pentecostal-Charismatic Research, Kerala, India*.

81. Donald W. Dayton, *Theological Roots of Pentecostalism* (Grand Rapids: Baker Academic, 1987), pp. 20-24; Walter J. Hollenweger, *The Pentecostals* (Peabody, MA: Hendrickson, 1972), pp. 21-24; Gary B. McGee (ed.), *Initial Evidence: Historical and Biblical Perspectives on the Pentecostal Doctrine and Spirit Baptism* (Eugene, OR: Wipf & Stock, 2007), pp. xiii-xx and 72-95.

ever, he was pastor of a Methodist church in Kansas, and he founded a Bible school in that state at Topeka. Here he began to teach the "fivefold" or "full" gospel of justification (or conversion), sanctification, Spirit baptism, divine healing, and the imminence of the end time, or the Return of Christ, in a premillennial mode. These five strands became official Pentecostal theology, although the "fivefold" gospel developed into a "full" fourfold gospel: salvation, baptism in the Spirit, healing, and the Return of Christ. Replacing "five" by "four," Donald Dayton comments, "These four themes are well-nigh universal within the movement."[82]

It has been suggested that Parham's concern about healing arose not only from biblical narratives of healing but also from his poor health as a child. He was troubled by rheumatic fever from the age of nine. In 1890 he entered Southwest Kansas College, and struggled with his studies. In 1893 he was ordained in the Methodist Church, but left in 1895 for an independent ministry. His two main activities were the founding of a Healing Home and the editing of a Holiness journal, the *Apostolic Faith*. Through his friend in the Holiness Movement, Frank Sandford (1862-1948), he heard reports of *speaking in tongues,* which he assumed were foreign languages, or instances of *"xenolalia."* He also assumed that this constituted the "latter rain" of the Spirit, in accordance with Joel 2:23 (KJV/AV), ushering in a premillennial Return of Christ. In June 1901 this experience passed to one of his students in Topeka. This then spread to half of his student body.

Like many New Testament scholars today, Parham saw what we might well call "the eschatological character of the Holy Spirit," but for him it was inseparably connected with premillennialism and the term "baptism of the Holy Spirit." In accordance with Joel 2:23 (not 2:28, quoted by Peter in Acts 2:16-21), Parham saw the "early rain" as the fulfillment of the pouring out of the Holy Spirit at Pentecost, and "the latter rain" as a new pouring out of the Spirit immediately before the Return of Christ. Healings and miraculous phenomena would come after a period of "dryness" (especially that of the eighteenth and nineteenth centuries), and presage the End times. The premillennialist view looks to the Return of Christ before the ushering in of an earthly or physical millennium, or thousand-year reign of Christ. The distinctive contribution of Parham was to insist that, in his words, speaking in tongues "is an inseparable part of the Baptism of the Holy Spirit."[83] Apparently such phenomena as floods of joy, shouting, or trances were not "true" signs of the Spirit, while speaking in tongues remained the key evidence. The basis was a simple "Restorationist" reproduction of the Acts narrative in the twentieth century. The encounter of Peter and Cornelius (Acts 10:46) was said to confirm this.

---

82. Dayton, *Theological Roots*, p. 22.

83. Charles F. Parham, *A Voice Crying in the Wilderness* (Baxter Springs: Apostolic Faith Bible College, 1902), p. 35.

Speaking in tongues is thus, *first, a sign of the new Pentecost,* or baptism in the Holy Spirit. *Second, it signifies the end of the age* and the imminent Return of Christ and the millennium. *Third, it plays a role in evangelism* and mission. Parham called this cluster of themes *"the Apostolic Faith movement"* since it reflected, he believed, the age of the apostles. In 1903 he fused these themes with his lifelong emphasis on healing, and in Kansas revival followed, with several thousand converts. Parham then took his "full" gospel to Texas, where it appears that there was further growth in Houston. One such convert was *William Seymour,* who carried this approach to Los Angeles. Parham's movement reached its peak in 1906, with nearly ten thousand followers. Parham attempted to retain their cohesion, but they fell apart into rival factions. As in ancient Corinth, it seemed that "the unity of the Spirit" was exchanged for claims to leadership and power. John Alexander Dowie and Wilbur Glenn Voliva appeared to lead power-hungry splits. In 1907 Parham was accused (or perhaps framed) on a serious charge of immorality. Although the charge was dropped, Parham had lost his credibility and leadership.

(2) *William Joseph Seymour* (1870-1922). Seymour is remembered as pastor of the Apostolic Faith Mission, Azusa Street, Los Angeles, during the Azusa Street Revival of 1906-9. Little is known of his early life, except that his parents were African-American slaves, and that he spent his earlier years in Louisiana and Indianapolis seeking a variety of employments. It is possible that his conversion was in an Episcopal Methodist setting, but he left this church apparently because it did not hold "premillennial" views, nor endorse "prophecies" or "special revelation." Seymour journeyed to Houston in 1902-3, and in 1905 he studied under Charles Parham in his Bible school (as a black person, from outside the window of the lecture room), where he learned of "baptism in the Holy Spirit" from Parham. In 1906 a black community in Los Angeles invited him to become pastor of their small Holiness mission.

After a difficult beginning, Seymour preached regularly at the Azusa Street Mission, and the three years from 1906 to 1909 became the scene of revival. It is said that he used the "call and response" preaching familiar in many black churches. Apparently he drew extensively on such favorite Pentecostal texts as "the Spirit of the Lord is upon me" (Luke 4:18-19); "These signs shall accompany those who believe: . . . they will cast out demons, they will speak in new tongues, they will pick up snakes . . ." (Mark 16:17-18); and "All of them were filled with the Holy Spirit and began to speak in other languages" (Acts 2:4). Seymour wrote that this kind of gathering made all nationalities feel free. He regarded "speaking in tongues" as an ecumenical and international sign of freedom and unity.[84] *Tongues* were seen as a *crossing of boundaries.*

Perhaps unexpectedly, when he visited Seymour's church in October 1906,

---

84. D. T. Irwin, "Drawing All Together in One Bond of Love," *JPT* 6 (1995): 27, esp. n. 5.

Charles Parham reacted with disgust at "animalisms, . . . trances, . . . shaking, jabbering, chattering, . . . meaningless sounds and noises," none of which he perceived as evidence of Spirit baptism.[85] Even Seymour himself disowned some of the phenomena, preferring to emphasize *the fruit of love*. But many journalists and reporters ridiculed his preaching as "a jumble of Scriptures and shouting," which predicted "hellfire and a lake of burning brimstone," and literalist hermeneutics.[86]

Once again the much trumpeted "Holy Spirit of unity" did not prevent Parham from seeking to take over Seymour's church and its revival; but Seymour's followers resisted him. Parham founded a rival community five blocks' distance from Seymour. According to Roebeck, Seymour was gracious and self-effacing, and encouraged critical responses from within his congregation. At the same time Parham disapproved of any mingling between blacks and whites, while Seymour positively encouraged interracial cooperation, and increasingly underlined the need for evidence of Spirit baptism. Speaking in tongues, however, remained his main criterion. Apparently there were up to 50,000 readers of the *Apostolic Faith* newspaper.

In spite of Seymour's call for unity, splits continued. He married in 1908, but this became an occasion for the editor of his paper, Florence Crawford, to take the mailing list of the paper away and move to Portland. Seymour tried to heal the breach, but without success. From 1907 to 1919 he traveled to Alabama, Illinois, and other states. But even this led to conflict with William Durham, who again set up a rival church. Eventually Seymour's congregation dwindled, and he perceived himself forsaken "by the people he had been called to serve."[87] He died of a heart attack in 1922.

(3) *Indigenous Origins in Other Parts of the Globe.* One modern account of the global origins of Pentecostalism can be found in Allan H. Anderson and Walter Hollenweger (eds.), *Pentecostalism after a Century: Global Perspectives on a Movement in Transition.*[88] While this book also considers recent developments, most chapters contain a section on origins. "The Black Roots of Pentecostalism" considers not only Seymour, but also "the Pentecostal or Pentecostal-like 'non-white indigenous churches' in the Third World, usually called 'African independent churches' in Africa."[89] In Africa, Hollenweger argues, "liturgy or oral theology takes *narrative form;* the whole community engages in maximum par-

---

85. C. M. Robeck, "Seymour, William Joseph," in *International Dictionary of Pentecostal and Charismatic Movements (NIDPCM)*, ed. Stanley M. Burgess (Grand Rapids: Zondervan, 2002-3), pp. 1055-56; cf. pp. 1053-58.

86. Robeck, "Seymour," in Burgess, *NIDPCM*, p. 1055.

87. Robeck, "Seymour," in *NIDPCM*, p. 1057.

88. Allan H. Anderson and Walter J. Hollenweger, *Pentecostals after a Century: Global Perspectives on a Movement in Transition*, JPTSS 15 (Sheffield: Sheffield Academic, 1999).

89. Anderson and Hollenweger, *Pentecostals after a Century*, p. 34.

ticipation; and dreams and visions feature widely."[90] These were known in Africa since before the first decade of the twentieth century.

Lee Hong Jung discusses "*Minjung* and Pentecostal movements in Korea."[91] *Minjung* denotes political oppression, coupled with social and cultural alienation. Before 1907 it was imposed by Japanese occupation and by falling victim to power struggles between Japan, Russia, and China. The Great Revival of 1907 at Pyongyang involved the "enthusiasm of the Pentecostal revival movement" with massive revival meetings.[92] On the negative side, however, stood nationalistic tendencies, hatred of the Japanese, and the threat of syncretism. But the Korean Church grew "like wildfire."[93] In 2007 I was privileged to take part in the century celebrations of this revival in Seoul.

Juan Sepúlveda contributes a chapter, "Indigenous Pentecostalism and the Chilean Experience."[94] He writes: "Chilean Pentecostalism is . . . the result of an independent development, contemporary to that of Los Angeles."[95] In 1905 and 1906 two tragedies in the shape of a smallpox epidemic and a devastating earthquake hit Valparaiso. A first contact with "Pentecostal doctrine" occurred in 1907, at first in connection with Minnie Abrams from Mukti, India. A Pentecostal Conference was held in February 1910.

This is not the only account of such worldwide beginnings. Mark Cartledge also recounts the Pyongyang revival in Korea from 1903, which reached a climax in 1907.[96] He also tells about Pentecostal origins outside America in the Welsh Revival of 1904-5 and in Monkwearmouth, Sunderland, in 1908-14. Vinson Synan also cites the Welsh Revival of 1904, and Joseph Smale's involvement in it.[97] Synan also discusses beginnings in India, arguing: "An outbreak of tongues appeared in 1908 that had all the characteristics of the Azusa meeting," adding controversially: "Under the direction of Pandita Ramabai the inmates of a girls' orphanage spoke and prayed in English, Greek, Hebrew and Sanskrit in the years 1905-08."[98] But even most Pentecostals would now doubt whether "tongues" denote *known* foreign languages. Synan traces

---

90. W. J. Hollenweger, "The Black Roots of Pentecostalism," in *After a Century*, ed. Anderson and Hollenweger, pp. 38-39; cf. pp. 33-44.

91. Lee Hong Jung, in *After a Century*, ed. Anderson and Hollenweger, pp. 138-60.

92. Jung, in *After a Century*, ed. Anderson and Hollenweger, pp. 141-43.

93. R. E. Shearer, *Wildfire: Church Growth in Korea* (Grand Rapids: Eerdmans, 1966).

94. Juan Sepúlveda, "Indigenous Pentecostalism and the Chilean Experience," in *Pentecostals after a Century*, ed. Anderson and Hollenweger, pp. 111-35.

95. Sepúlveda, "Indigenous Pentecostalism," in *Pentecostals after a Century*, ed. Anderson and Hollenweger, p. 113.

96. Mark J. Cartledge, *Testimony to the Spirit: Rescripting Ordinary Pentecostal Theology* (Farnham and Burlington, VT: Ashgate, 2010), pp. 2-3.

97. Vinson Synan, *The Holiness-Pentecostal Tradition: Charismatic Movements in the Twentieth Century* (Grand Rapids: Eerdmans, 1971 and 1997), pp. 86-87.

98. Synan, *The Holiness-Pentecostal Tradition*, p. 105.

many world outreaches (including Norway, Denmark, and Germany) to the indirect influence of the Azusa Street phenomenon.

18.4. A Second Phase of Pentecostalism: Consolidation and Division: Garr, Ewart, Bell, and the Assemblies of God

(1) *Alfred G. Garr* (1874-1944) was one of the early leaders who received baptism in the Holy Spirit in 1906 in the Azusa Street revival. Originally a Baptist, he entered Asbury College, Wilmore, Kentucky, and experienced a sense of God's call to missionary work in India. His particular significance for Pentecostalism was his subsequent conviction that, although Parham was broadly right about the "initial experience" of tongues, he was wrong in seeing tongues as a missionary gift, to help in understanding existing languages. He traveled to Calcutta, where a Pentecostal revival was in process. Garr had at first believed that God had given the gift of competence in the Bengali language in his Spirit baptism, just as his wife Lillian thought that she had received the gift of Tibetan and Mandarin Chinese. But both discovered that not only had "tongues" preceded them, but also that their utterance had nothing to do with Bengali or with Tibetan or Mandarin Chinese. Within a few weeks Garr modified Parham's belief about the missionary purpose of tongues. Their function was now perceived to be one of praise, prayer, and perhaps empowerment.

The Calcutta revival spread across parts of India. But in 1907 Garr endorsed the "prophecy" of a Christian woman from Sri Lanka that Colombo, the capital of Ceylon, would be completely destroyed by an earthquake on September 23, followed by the destruction of the island later. As a result, several thousand fled from Colombo, and to Garr's embarrassment the prophecy failed. The Pentecostal movement had suffered a setback. Albert Norton and others, however, carried on. The Pentecostal movement had learned, first, that there could be more than one view about the purpose of tongues; second, "prophecies" invited caution.

(2) *Frank J. Ewart* (1876-1947) presented a further challenge from within the Pentecostal movement.[99] Ewart received "the baptism of the Spirit" in 1908, which caused his dismissal from his Baptist church in Canada. In 1911 he became assistant pastor to William H. Durham in Los Angeles, succeeding him as pastor in 1912. In 1913 he met Robert Edward McAlister (1880-1953), another Canadian Pentecostal pastor, and heard him preach on water baptism in the name of Christ. His reflection on these two relationships led him to challenge or modify the Parham-Seymour debate and tradition in a third direction. He anticipated the "Oneness" movement, that is, the oneness of God, rather than a

---

99. See Walter J. Hollenweger, *The Pentecostals* (Peabody, MA: Hendrickson, 1972), pp. 31-32.

Trinitarian belief, as well as an insistence on baptism in the Name of Christ only, and meditation on the name of Christ. In one sense this was a move away from traditional Trinitarian theology; in another direction it avoided too much preoccupation with the Holy Spirit at the expense of the centrality of Christ. But the "Oneness" movement persisted within the Assemblies of God, becoming known as "the new issue" or "Jesus only." It looked to Durham's teaching on the finished work of Christ, and drove a further split or division into the Pentecostal movement.

(3) *Eudorus N. Bell* (1866-1923) *and the Assemblies of God.* The founding of the Assemblies of God came about in 1913, largely through the work of their first Chairman, Eudorus Bell, and his colleagues, Howard Goss, Mark Pinson, and others. Bell was a former Baptist pastor from Florida who attended Southern Baptist Theological Seminary and the University of Chicago. In 1908 he received the Pentecostal "baptism in the Holy Spirit." In December 1913 he published a "call" to share in a Council of Pentecostal churches at Hot Springs, Arizona, which brought about the *Assemblies of God.* From 1917 to 1919 he edited *The Pentecostal Evangel,* and he was reappointed Chairman of the Assemblies of God in 1920. Yet even now *division and split* lurked in the Assemblies of God: Bell became associated with the "Oneness" movement and became rebaptized, although he later returned to the Trinitarians. Perhaps this move to "Oneness" was to overcompensate for an overemphasis on the Holy Spirit. He also opposed women pastors.

(4) *Aimee Semple McPherson* (1890-1944) *and the Four Square Gospel.* Aimee Semple McPherson was ordained in the Assemblies of God in 1919 as an "evangelist," although she resigned three years later. In 1909 she had been ordained in a Pentecostal community by William Durham. She and her husband became "faith" missionaries in China, until the death of her husband, Robert Semple, during the year of their arrival. In 1921 she settled in Los Angeles and began conducting a series of world mission tours. Her books include *The Second Coming of Christ* (1921). Most important, she began to teach "the Foursquare Gospel," and from 1924 preached numerous radio sermons.

In 1923 Aimee Semple McPherson founded "the Lighthouse for International Foursquare Evangelism" Bible College. She preached Christ as (1) Savior (John 3:16), (2) Baptizer in the Spirit (Acts 2:4), (3) Healer (James 5:14-15), and (4) coming King (1 Thess. 4:16-17).[100] She had an enormous impact on perhaps several million people, some of whom suffered in the Depression. After 1926, much of her ministry seemed to end in controversial and ambiguous circumstances. Such had been the fate of several leaders since Parham. She suffered the further problem of a nervous breakdown in 1930, and the title of her 1936 book,

---

100. Aimee Semple McPherson, *The Four Square Gospel,* ed. Raymond Cox (Los Angeles: Foursquare Publications, 1969), p. 9.

Give Me My Own God, might be noted by admirers and skeptics for the very opposite reasons. In her early years of searching for God, she had heard a few sentences of a sermon which suddenly burst into a "tongues" phenomenon. She had interpreted this as a divine sign of self-witness for unbelievers, and called on this experience.

(5) *Ivan Quay Spencer* (1888-1970) founded the Elim Fellowship of Churches in 1933.[101] He originally attended an Episcopal Methodist Church, but received "baptism in the Holy Spirit" in 1912. In 1915 he became minister of the Elim Tabernacle Church. In 1919 he joined the Assemblies of God in New York, and founded the Elim Bible Institute in 1924. It is difficult to distinguish clearly between "Pentecostal" and "Elim," except that the latter may be broader and perhaps more tolerant of other beliefs and practices than most Pentecostal groups. Nevertheless, it was a member of the Pentecostal Fellowship of North America. On the other hand, the Elim Fellowship, according to Warner, was also criticized for fanatical prophecies and a notion of "selective rapture" of believers. In 1948 Spencer introduced a so-called "New Order of the Latter Rain," a revival movement intended to restore unity, but in fact this became the cause of *disruption and disunity.*

The Elim Fellowship in America should not be confused with *"Elim Pentecostal Church"* of Ireland, which was founded by *George Jeffreys* (1876-1943), a Welsh Pentecostal evangelist, in 1915. In England the Elim Pentecostal Alliance was formed in 1919, and by 1920 it included fifteen assemblies. During the 1920s both Elim communities and Assemblies of God sprang up in Britain. Percy Stanley Brewster (1908-80), for example, was converted under the ministry of George Jeffreys, was a youth leader in East Ham, London, and led successful crusades in Birmingham and in Wales.

18.5. Some Standard Pentecostal Themes and Terminology

In spite of almost endless "splits," some themes and terms remain central to virtually all Pentecostals.

(1) *Restorationists.* This stands at the heart of classical Pentecostalism. It denotes the attempt to restore the biblical conditions of the first century as these are presented in biblical narratives. The precise practices of the apostles in Acts would include exact replication of speaking in tongues in Acts 2, and the first-century practice of baptism, the miraculous, and church order. 1 Corinthians 12–14 would constitute a similar source, but in Acts the issue is to treat narrative as intended replication, not for a purpose related only to its time and place. The corollary of this is that the Patristic and medieval Church represents a decline,

---

101. E. E. Warner, "Elim Fellowship," in *NIDPCM,* p. 598.

not a positive and creative tradition. The Radical Reformers were largely Restorationist, but most would argue that the classical Reformers began this process only selectively.

(2) *Premillennialism and the rapture.* These terms have become familiar in America, but less so in Britain and Europe. Henry Drummond (1786-1860) and Edward Irving (1792-1834) applied many events prophesied in Revelation to the present. John Nelson Darby (1800-1882) then suggested the *premillennialist* view that the *Return of Christ would initiate a thousand-year earthly kingdom,* that is, that Christ would come *before* an earthly millennium. Indeed, Darby believed that Christ would come twice: in his first Return the faithful would be "caught up" or "snatched" in a *Rapture* (with an appeal to 1 Thess. 4:17), which would save them from a period of tribulation; Christ would then return again (on the basis of an appeal to 1 Cor. 15:24). This view became popularized with the use of the *Scofield Reference Bible* (1927). Premillennialism stands at the heart of classical Pentecostalism, but not all "premillennialists" are also Pentecostals. The premillennial view has had considerable influence on American politics and attitudes to world events since 1917, the date of the Balfour Declaration, which led to the founding of the Jewish state in 1948.

We have to imagine that the prophecies of Revelation and some other books applied partly to the first century; *then they remained inapplicable for some eighteen centuries;* then applied to *the twentieth century and thereafter.* John F. Walvoord of Dallas Theological Seminary advocated this view, and it was popularized in Hal Lindsey's *The Late Great Planet Earth* and by Tim LaHaye's *Left Behind* series.[102] A minority of Pentecostals express doubts about this view.

(3) *Baptism in the Holy Spirit.* This is central to Pentecostalism and often to some phases of the Renewal Movement. It constitutes a distinct Christian experience, mostly understood in the light of Acts 2:1-4, and the promise in Mark 1:8. In Acts 2:4, "All of them were filled with the Holy Spirit." There are further references in Acts 11:16 and 10:44-46. Two counterarguments are often used. Most Christians agree that the Holy Spirit brings sanctification. The debate is whether this can be understood as *a single event* with consequences (the Pentecostal view) or as a process over many years often entailing *struggle* (Luther, Hodge, Kuyper). Part of the problem is the double sense of the word "holy." In one sense all Christians are holy, not least because they belong to God. But in a second sense Christians become holy as they share in the process of sanctification. Hence some Pentecostals, for example, Gordon Fee, show reserve about the "event" nature of the term "baptism in the Spirit." Indeed, some prefer to speak of being filled with the Spirit, although this raises problems of a realized eschatology.

---

102. See Anthony C. Thiselton, *1 and 2 Thessalonians through the Centuries,* Blackwell Bible Commentaries (Oxford: Wiley-Blackwell, 2011), pp. 115-45, esp. pp. 143-45.

The second problem about this term is the relation between the meaning of the term in the biblical writings (notably in 1 Cor. 12:13) and its Pentecostal interpretation. This set of questions has most famously been raised by James D. G. Dunn, to which many have offered "replies."[103] Some, including the present writer, affirm the reality of *the experience* to which Pentecostals draw attention, but question whether they use the right biblical *term* for it. It ought not to exclude process, subsequent struggle, and temptation. Even some in the Pentecostal-charismatic tradition, while not abandoning the term "baptism in the Holy Spirit," admit that "renewal in the Holy Spirit" may cause less misunderstanding. Nevertheless, in spite of problems, Frank Macchia has recently described baptism in the Spirit as a virtual identity marker and "organizing principle" of Pentecostals.[104] However, he recognizes that it is "still in the making."[105]

(4) *Speaking in Tongues.* Without question Acts 2 and 1 Corinthians 12–14 establish this as a phenomenon of the first century. (a) Charles Parham saw *"xenolalia"* as *known* foreign languages, and viewed them as an authentic sign of the Spirit, foreshadowing unprecedented missionary activity and the End times. There are fragmentary examples of "tongues" before Parham: certainly among the "heretical" Cathars of the eleventh century, perhaps Hildegard of Bingen, the eighteenth-century French Camisards, and arguably in the nineteenth century the Mormons. Controversially, some argue for a much more widespread early phenomenon.[106] Many or most classical Pentecostals view speaking in tongues as *"initial evidence."*[107] (b) As we saw, Alfred Garr no longer saw "tongues" as foreign languages, but as expressions of joy, delight, and worship, much as the twentieth-century New Testament scholar Ernst Käsemann considers them cries of freedom.[108]

(c) The eschatological connection with speaking in tongues can be seen as the reign of Christ in the heart. 1 Cor. 14:21 and other passages invite continued debate. Several articles still discuss this in the *Journal of Pentecostal Theology.* *The Fundamental Truths of the Assemblies of God* declares: "The baptism . . . in the Holy Ghost is witnessed by the initial physical sign of speaking with other

---

103. James D. G. Dunn, *Baptism in the Holy Spirit* (London: SCM, 1970), is discussed in parts 1 and 3; see also William P. Atkinson, *Baptism in the Spirit: Luke-Acts and the Dunn Debate* (Eugene, OR: Pickwick, 2011).

104. Frank D. Macchia, *Baptized in the Spirit* (Grand Rapids: Zondervan, 2006), pp. 17 and 21.

105. Macchia, *Baptized in the Spirit*, p. 19.

106. Ronald Kydd, *Charismatic Gifts in the Early Church* (Peabody, MA: Hendrickson, 1984); Kilian McDonnell and George T. Montague, *Christian Initiation and Baptism in the Spirit: Evidence from the First Eight Centuries* (Collegeville, MN: Liturgical Press/Glazier, 1991).

107. G. B. McGee (ed.), *Initial Evidence;* and Burgess, *NIDPCM*, pp. 784-91.

108. Ernst Käsemann, "The Cry for Liberty in the Worship of the Church," in Käsemann, *Perspectives on Paul* (London: SCM, 1971), pp. 122-37.

tongues."[109] (d) Recently Frank D. Macchia from inside the movement, and Gerd Theissen from outside it, have perhaps rightly associated "tongues" with "sighs too deep for words" in Rom. 8:26.[110] The debate continues. Meanwhile we discuss Theissen, Macchia, Kärkkäinen, and others further, below. As we comment in Chapter 24, huge advances have been made in our understanding of this phenomenon since the days of Parham and Seymour.

18.6. J. E. Fison, N. Q. Hamilton, and Oscar Cullmann

(1) *Joseph E. Fison* (1906-72) was educated at Queen's College, Oxford, took a first-class degree in theology, and was awarded a postgraduate B.D. After service in the war, he held Canonries at Rochester and Truro, and became Bishop of Salisbury from 1963 to his death in 1972. He wrote *The Blessing of the Holy Spirit* in 1950.[111] Although this small work of 226 pages cannot compare with those of Swete or Barth, it contains many memorable aphorisms and distinctive insights.

Fison's first point would cohere with Pentecostalism. He writes, "The Holy Spirit is the key to the Christian doctrine of the End."[112] Such a comment has become standard among New Testament scholars since at least the work of Oscar Cullmann. Fison compares Gregory Dix's "Become What You Are" with the Keswick Convention's "Possessing Your Possessions."[113] Also like the Pentecostals, he declares, "We have lost the supernatural, and the touchstone of the supernatural is the Holy Spirit."[114] He bewails the absence of creative thought about the Spirit. Like Tillich, he sees confusion between the Spirit and penultimate symbols of the Spirit's action as *idolatry*. Yet appeal to the supernatural should not lead to complacent overconfidence, to what Fison calls "utterly un-Christian and bumptious cocksureness."[115] Replacing the Holy Spirit by tangible objects, even tongues-speaking, fails to do justice to "the incurable self-effacement of the Holy Spirit Himself, and His determination always and only to point to the Lord Jesus Christ."[116] He explains: "As Holy, He is different from

---

109. *Fundamental Truths*, paragraph 8; quoted by Keith Warrington, *Pentecostal Theology: A Theology of Encounter* (London and New York: T&T Clark, 2008), p. 120.

110. Frank D. Macchia, "Groans Too Deep for Words: Towards a Theology of Tongues as Initial Evidence," *Asian Journal of Pentecostal Studies* 1 (1998): 149-73.

111. Joseph E. Fison, *Blessing of the Holy Spirit* (London and New York: Longmans, Green, 1950).

112. Fison, *Blessing of the Holy Spirit*, p. 4.

113. Fison, *Blessing of the Holy Spirit*, p. 8.

114. Fison, *Blessing of the Holy Spirit*, p. 10.

115. Fison, *Blessing of the Holy Spirit*, p. 15.

116. Fison, *Blessing of the Holy Spirit*, p. 22.

all the varying media of His self-manifestation, whether church, sacrament, reason, intuition, Bible, or 'experience.'"[117] He effaces himself in the *kenōsis* of the Spirit.

The Spirit effaces himself through the cross of Christ. Fison declares: "Without a true doctrine of the Holy Spirit, Christianity always goes hard or soft, for either mysticism or morality is lost."[118] He comments, "There is an inevitable tendency to objectify God in the safe world of It, the world which man can handle and manipulate."[119] He quotes from A. G. Hogg, *Redemption from This World*: "There is a kingdom which none enter but children, in which the children play with infinite forces, where the child's little finger becomes stronger than the giant world, a wise kingdom where the world exists only by sufferance, . . . in which the world lies like a foolish, wilful dream in the solid truth of the day."[120] He draws on Old Testament passages about the holy and living God, in contrast to secondhand dependence on what is past (Exod. 3:5; 19:6; 1 Sam. 6:20; Isa. 6:5; 11:9; 23:18; 57:15). A chapter follows on the Spirit in the Old Testament.[121]

Like C. K. Barrett, and unlike James Dunn, Fison insists on "the Silence of the Synoptics" about the Holy Spirit. He acknowledges the role of the Holy Spirit in the birth and baptism of Jesus Christ, but argues: "It is the negative silence of the Synoptics which is the precondition of all the positive riches of the Pentecostal, Pauline and Johannine revelations that ensue."[122] He explains, "Before He could speak of spirit, Jesus had to reinterpret its meaning."[123] Jesus lived in communion with his Father, and lived out his Messianic vocation, which would lead to the cross.

When he turns to Pentecost and to Paul, Fison asserts that everything depends on the eschatological tension between the "now" in Christ and the "not yet" of the promised future. He writes, "Pentecost belongs both to the present age in the manner and form of its manifestation of the Spirit and also to the age to come in the essential context of its revelation of the Spirit: . . . in truth 'the ends of the ages' did overlap (1 Cor. 10:11)."[124] On Paul, Fison declares: "St. Paul's great contribution is to give priority to the ethical without in the least abating one iota of the supernatural and eschatological character of His activity."[125] Many Pentecostals would endorse his verdict: "It is the sense of present

---

117. Fison, *Blessing of the Holy Spirit*, p. 22.

118. Fison, *Blessing of the Holy Spirit*, p. 31.

119. Fison, *Blessing of the Holy Spirit*, p. 38.

120. A. G. Hogg, *Redemption from This World* (Edinburgh: T&T Clark, 1924), pp. 25-26; and Fison, *Blessing of the Holy Spirit*, p. 45.

121. Fison, *Blessing of the Holy Spirit*, pp. 59-80.

122. Fison, *Blessing of the Holy Spirit*, p. 90.

123. Fison, *Blessing of the Holy Spirit*, p. 98.

124. Fison, *Blessing of the Holy Spirit*, pp. 115-16.

125. Fison, *Blessing of the Holy Spirit*, p. 121.

eternity 'in the spirit' that causes the inevitable foreshortening of the temporal future by faith."[126] The Holy Spirit is the "firstfruits" of the future (Rom. 8:23), or the "first installment" of the future harvest (2 Cor. 5:5). The vocational crucifixion with Christ "leaves our personalities utterly open and defenceless."[127] Again, we are to "become what we are . . . by real identification with Christ in His death (Gal. 2:20)."[128]

Fison gives a straightforward account of the Paraclete Sayings in John's Gospel: "The Holy Spirit . . . alone, in P. T. Forsyth's oft-quoted phrase, can 'make Jesus Christ our contemporary.'"[129] Fison then returns to his earlier theme of the peril of idolatry. In his view, this may seek to replace the living Spirit by the Bible, the ministry, the sacraments, or even the Church. He includes here revivalist meetings, such as those of Elim Foursquare Gospellers, which he regards "fanatical."[130] In a subsequent chapter he attacks those who know nothing of "the reciprocal relationships of real life," and especially the preacher who lives "in the world of his own little clique; surrounded by yes-men and yes-women and the sickening entourage of a generally dwindling crowd of admirers and flatterers."[131] Such people, he insists, have shut themselves off from genuine and created openness to the Holy Spirit, because in effect they choose not to hear any voice but their own. By contrast, "God on the cross gave all, . . . and God on the cross received all."[132]

Fison's last chapter concerns holy baptism, which he calls "the sacrament of the Spirit."[133] This constitutes not only transformation by death and resurrection, but also a matter of receiving God's gift. In a controversial statement Fison asserts: *"it is not by seeking the Spirit that we shall find him — that would be to revert to the worked-up psychological and spiritual ecstasies, common to both true and false prophets of all ages"* (my italics).[134] He adds: "The narrow way to the secret of the Spirit is quite different, and is found only by those who face the cross."[135] Baptism is thus "not merely . . . a temporary rite of a moment, but also a permanent principle of a life-time."[136]

From 1900 to 1959 few writers can readily be compared with Swete in their thoroughness, or with Barth in their creativity, or even with Fison for memora-

126. Fison, *Blessing of the Holy Spirit,* p. 122.
127. Fison, *Blessing of the Holy Spirit,* p. 127.
128. Fison, *Blessing of the Holy Spirit,* p. 133.
129. Fison, *Blessing of the Holy Spirit,* p. 141.
130. Fison, *Blessing of the Holy Spirit,* pp. 149, 148-60 and 161-77.
131. Fison, *Blessing of the Holy Spirit,* p. 180.
132. Fison, *Blessing of the Holy Spirit,* p. 197.
133. Fison, *Blessing of the Holy Spirit,* p. 204.
134. Fison, *Blessing of the Holy Spirit,* p. 213.
135. Fison, *Blessing of the Holy Spirit,* p. 213.
136. Fison, *Blessing of the Holy Spirit,* p. 215.

ble aphorisms and insights. A few other books, however, deserve mention for their work on special aspects of the subject. Lionel S. Thornton, *The Common Life in the Body of Christ* (1942; 3rd ed. 1950) comes from the Anglo-Catholic wing of the Church of England; he stresses the *communal or corporate* aspect of the gift of the Holy Spirit. All Christians are "partakers of the Spirit"; the *koinōnia* of the Holy Spirit (2 Cor. 13:13; Phil. 2:1) strictly denotes *not* in the first place "fellowship," still less "companionship," but "participation in or sharing in."[137] Thornton argues that the term denotes "having something in common" or being "a joint shareholder" in something. Hence he traces successively how the apostles had "all things in common," and the apostolic Church had a joint share or common share in Christ, in the Holy Spirit, in God's love, in Christ's victory, in Christ's Sonship, and in the new birth. He writes: "The Holy Spirit [is] its creative author and fountain-source."[138] Rom. 5:5 ("The love of God has been poured out in our hearts through the Holy Spirit") "refers us back to the Day of Pentecost."[139]

Thornton asserts: "Only the Spirit has access to the 'things of God,'" which are freely given to us (1 Cor. 2:2-16).[140] The Holy Spirit also makes us aware of a sonship derived from Christ's status as Son (Gal. 4:1-4).[141] The gift of the Spirit comes through Christ. "Himself anointed with the Holy Spirit, he [Jesus Christ] has poured out the Spirit upon his community."[142] Thornton refuses to think sequentially or chronologically about "stages" of conversion and sanctification. He declares: "When Christ rose, the Church rose from the dead."[143] If someone has to "date" their experience, the center of gravity is around the year A.D. 33.

(2) *N. Q. Hamilton.* Another notable book from the period 1900-1959 is that of Neill Q. Hamilton, *The Holy Spirit and Eschatology in Paul* (1957). It runs to only 94 pages. But in view of the fact that both "mainline" New Testament scholars and Pentecostals stress the link between the Holy Spirit and the last days, Hamilton's short exposition is relevant. He first examines the relation between the Spirit and Christ: "No one can say 'Jesus is Lord' except by the Holy Spirit."[144] Like Dunn, he stresses Rom. 8:9, "Anyone who does not have the Spirit of Christ does not belong to him."[145] He is "the Spirit of His Son" (Gal.

---

137. Lionel S. Thornton, *The Common Life in the Body of Christ* (London: Dacre Press, 1950), pp. 67, 71 and 66-95.

138. Thornton, *Common Life in the Body of Christ*, p. 69.

139. Thornton, *Common Life in the Body of Christ*, p. 104; cf. p. 103.

140. Thornton, *Common Life in the Body of Christ*, p. 109.

141. Thornton, *Common Life in the Body of Christ*, pp. 112-121 and 156-87.

142. Thornton, *Common Life in the Body of Christ*, p. 145.

143. Thornton, *Common Life in the Body of Christ*, p. 282.

144. Neill Q. Hamilton, *The Holy Spirit and Eschatology in Paul*, Scottish Journal of Theology Occasional Paper 6 (Edinburgh: Oliver & Boyd, 1957), p. 8; see pp. 3-16.

145. Hamilton, *The Holy Spirit and Eschatology*, p. 10.

4:6). But "The new relationship of the Spirit to the Lord occurred . . . on the basis of the resurrection *(ex anastaseōs nekrōn)*."[146]

In his second chapter, "The Holy Spirit and Time," Hamilton expounds such terms as "firstfruits" *(aparchē),* "first" *(archē),* "firstborn" *(prōtotokos,* 1 Cor. 15:20, 23; Col. 1:18); and "earnest" *(arrabōn).*[147] Here "more to come" strikes the keynote. But in his next chapter Hamilton discusses "The Spirit and the Eschatological Tension of the Christian Life." This is perhaps his most distinctive contribution. "More to come" also implies that *the present is not the time of total fulfillment.* For example: "Sonship has a not-yet-fulfilled future aspect."[148] *We still long, yearn, and struggle.* He would agree with most Pentecostals that "Confidence in the present is only possible in the light of the future."[149] Pentecostals might also endorse a groaning after, or sighing for, "an eschatological fulfillment still outstanding."[150] But would most "Holiness" movements explicitly accept that while all Christians have become "holy" in Christ, a final culmination of "sanctification" lies ahead, and stress this?

The remaining three chapters are perhaps less creative. They are a fairly routine descriptive exposition of the work of Albert Schweitzer, Charles H. Dodd, and Rudolf Bultmann. Their function is to show the inadequacy of "realized" eschatology in Dodd; of time-conditioned categories in Schweitzer; and of reinterpreted eschatology in Bultmann. These three chapters do add point to the others, but such assessments can be found in many other places. Hamilton concludes by suggesting that it would be a "strain" to try to construct "a cosmos timetable."[151]

(3) *Oscar Cullmann* (1902-99). Hamilton's theme of "now" and "not yet" was already well known before he wrote. Indeed, it had become an established tenet of New Testament scholarship. Much of the earlier credit for this must go to Oscar Cullmann. Cullmann was born in Strasbourg, and became Professor of New Testament in 1930. In 1938 he moved to Basel, Switzerland. His special interests focused on eschatology (especially in *Christ and Time*) and Christology *(The Christology of the New Testament).*[152] Over against C. H. Dodd's "Realized Eschatology" and Albert Schweitzer's future and imminent eschatology, he saw "salvation history" *(Heilsgeschichte),* in which the Christ-event formed a decisive victory (like the D-Day landings in the Second World War) but also pointed toward a final victory yet in the future (like V-Day at the end of the war).[153] He

---

146. Hamilton, *The Holy Spirit and Eschatology,* p. 13.

147. Hamilton, *The Holy Spirit and Eschatology,* pp. 17-19; see also pp. 20-25.

148. Hamilton, *The Holy Spirit and Eschatology,* p. 32.

149. Hamilton, *The Holy Spirit and Eschatology,* p. 33.

150. Hamilton, *The Holy Spirit and Eschatology,* p. 36.

151. Hamilton, *The Holy Spirit and Eschatology,* p. 88.

152. Oscar Cullmann, *The Christology of the New Testament* (London: SCM, 1959 and 1963).

153. Oscar Cullmann, *Christ and Time: A Primitive Conception of Time and History* (London: SCM, 1951), pp. 73-93.

also wrote *Salvation in History, The Immortality of the Soul or the Resurrection of the Body, Baptism in the New Testament,* and *The Johannine Circle.*[154]

In *Christ and Time* Cullmann wrote: "Upon the basis of the Holy Spirit . . . man is that which he will become only in the future. . . . he is already holy, although that becomes a reality only in the future."[155] He declares, "Thus *the Holy Spirit is nothing else than the anticipation of the end in the present*" (my italics).[156] His comment about "being made holy" *now,* but its becoming a "reality" only in the future, may serve to clarify the problem which bedevils the Holiness Movement, namely, how "sanctification" can be seen as an "event" rather than as a process. In Barth, Luther, and Käsemann, and others, this leaves room for struggle and temptation.

154. Oscar Cullmann, *Salvation in History* (London: SCM, 1967).
155. Cullmann, *Christ and Time,* p. 75.
156. Cullmann, *Christ and Time,* p. 72.

19

The Later Twentieth Century to 1985

19.1. Geoffrey Lampe

Geoffrey Lampe (1912-80) was an Anglican theologian, and was Ely Professor of Divinity in the University of Cambridge (1970-78). He was educated at Exeter College, Oxford, gained the Military Cross in the Second World War, and worked mainly in Patristic theology, finally producing his *Patristic Greek Lexicon* (1961). He published *The Seal of the Spirit* in 1951 and *God as Spirit* in 1977.[1]

Lampe's *The Seal of the Spirit* is not simply a study of the doctrine of the Holy Spirit as such. He freely states in his Introduction that his primary purpose is to address "a considerable cleavage of theological opinion about the meaning of the sacrament of Baptism," especially "the relationship between Baptism and Confirmation."[2] This question was an open one in 1951, and has raised its head today in the light of the Renewal Movement. To Anglicans at the Reformed or "Low Church" end of the spectrum, the issue seemed clear. As Lampe argued, it was largely the Tractarians, the Oxford Movement, or "High Church" Anglicans, of the nineteenth century who urged the importance of confirmation as a sign and ceremony of the gift of the Holy Spirit, in contrast to water baptism as a sign of forgiveness of sins and incorporation into the Church. This issue became popularly known as the "Mason-Dix line." It sought a revival of the Anglo-Catholic approach.

In 1890 and 1891 A. J. Mason published his argument in the book *The Rela-*

---

1. Geoffrey W. H. Lampe, *The Seal of the Spirit: A Study in the Doctrine of Baptism and Confirmation in the New Testament and the Fathers* (London and New York: Longmans, 1951); Lampe, *God as Spirit: The Bampton Lectures, 1976* (Oxford: Clarendon, 1977); and "The Holy Spirit in the Writings of Luke," in *Studies in the Gospels: In Memory of R. H. Lightfoot*, ed. Denis E. Nineham (Oxford: Blackwell, 1962), pp. 159-200.

2. Lampe, *The Seal of the Spirit*, p. vii.

tion of Confirmation to Baptism, with a fuller edition of the 1890 book in 1891. Ten years earlier F. W. Puller had contributed a similar argument. A. T. Wirgman replied to these works in 1897, with a mass of Patristic evidence. But this seemed to suggest that "the Fathers had no consistent doctrine on this matter."[3] In 1936 Gregory Dix produced a counterreply, in which baptism seemed to constitute "no more than a prelude to Confirmation."[4] Dix made much of the *Apostolic Tradition* of Hippolytus of Rome, arguing that confirmation could be administered *before* baptism, and in 1946 entered the debate again in *The Theology of Confirmation in Relation to Baptism.*[5] Dix went as far as to say: "The teaching of the New Testament [is] that Baptism in the Spirit is *not* Baptism in water, but something else, which follows closely upon it."[6] Needless to say, this teaching is seized upon by many or some in the Renewal Movement, especially in Episcopal circles. One such example is that of Robert M. Price.[7] Price uses the Mason-Dix arguments against Lampe and Dunn, calling Dunn's argument (1970) even more implausible than Lampe's. He concludes that Episcopalian charismatic renewal becomes very helpful.

Lampe points out that the change in Western terminology from *consignatio* to confirmation reflects a profound shift. A document that requires "sealing" is not valid, he argues, until the seal has been affixed. On the other hand, the "confirmation" of a document may theoretically add to its authority, but in practice the document was already authoritative. The ancient single rite was split into two: baptism and confirmation. Dix, in common with Lionel Thornton, accords too much to confirmation. Thornton argues that the indwelling of the Holy Spirit awaits the completion of the two rites. "Christian Baptism would be reduced to the level of the baptism of John. . . . Confirmation would become . . . the great sacrament."[8]

Lampe now discusses the concept of *sealing* in the New Testament, although perhaps two-thirds of the book concerns the situation in the Church Fathers. He first considers three examples of sealing in Pauline literature: 2 Cor. 1:22; Eph. 1:13; and Eph. 4:30 (mainly *arrabōn*). Here A. Seeberg, A. J. Mason, and Gregory Dix claim that this sealing relates to confirmation, although many today would see this as a historical anachronism. Even J. B. Lightfoot saw these as connected with baptism. But the term denotes "to set a mark of ownership upon," and concerns "faith-response to the grace of God in

---

3. Lampe, *The Seal of the Spirit,* p. ix.

4. Lampe, *The Seal of the Spirit,* p. x.

5. Gregory Dix, *The Theology of Confirmation in Relation to Baptism* (London: Davis, 1946 and 1953).

6. Dix, *The Theology of Confirmation,* p. 22.

7. Robert M. Price, "Confirmation and Charisma," *St. Luke's Journal of Theology* 33, no. 4 (June 1990).

8. Lampe, *Seal of the Spirit,* p. xiii.

Christ."[9] In Rom. 4:11, Paul speaks of his converts as a seal *(sphragis)* "of my apostleship," that is, that which guarantees its reality. In 2 Cor. 1:21-22 Paul uses "seal" to remind his converts that they share in Christ's death and resurrection. "Seal" denotes a stamp made on wax with the stone of a signet ring, and primarily means "a mark of ownership, and also a safeguard . . . against interference."[10] The eschatological content occurs not only in Paul, but in the *Psalms of Solomon* and *4 Ezra*, as "a token by which God recognises and acknowledges his people."[11]

There is "no indication that the rite itself [John's baptism] needed any explanation"; it constituted a "purging" in preparation for the judgment of Mal. 3:3.[12] In a comment similar to that of C. K. Barrett, Lampe asserts: "It . . . allowed the penitent to be numbered among the elect community in the approaching judgment."[13] It is "a cleansing in preparation for judgment."[14]

The baptism of Jesus, to which all four Gospels witness, sums up the Messianic work of Jesus. The "resting" of the Spirit is of a different quality from the temporary and partial Spirit possession of a prophet. Lampe continues: "Like the Church's Baptism, the Baptism of Jesus is proleptically effective. The role of the Servant which He undertakes at His Baptism is fulfilled, not in Jordan, but at Calvary."[15] As far as the Church's reception of the Spirit was concerned, however, "the Spirit was not yet, because Jesus was not yet glorified" (John 7:39).[16] Lampe concludes this chapter: "The Baptism of His followers is also proleptic, signifying . . . in a single moment all the consequences of their faith-union with Christ."[17]

On Luke-Acts, Lampe maintains: "The chief interest of Luke is the advent of the Gospel to the Gentile world"; this "must be borne in mind."[18] The Pentecostal climax in Acts 2 marks the original starting point of the Church's baptism. For it *constitutes an extension of Christ's anointing as a Servant of God.* The subapostolic age brought "a lamentable retrogression . . . from the position which he [in this case, Paul] had reached."[19] In Paul, "As many of us as were baptized into Christ Jesus were baptized into his death. . . . buried with him by baptism into his death" (Rom. 6:3-4).[20] It is a "visible act of trusting response to

9. Lampe, *Seal of the Spirit*, p. 5.
10. Lampe, *Seal of the Spirit*, p. 8.
11. Lampe, *Seal of the Spirit*, p. 15.
12. Lampe, *Seal of the Spirit*, pp. 19 and 21.
13. Lampe, *Seal of the Spirit*, p. 22.
14. Lampe, *Seal of the Spirit*, p. 27.
15. Lampe, *Seal of the Spirit*, p. 38.
16. Lampe, *Seal of the Spirit*, p. 41.
17. Lampe, *Seal of the Spirit*, p. 45.
18. Lampe, *Seal of the Spirit*, p. 48.
19. Lampe, *Seal of the Spirit*, p. 53.
20. Lampe, *Seal of the Spirit*, p. 55.

the prevenient grace of God in Christ, . . . a re-presentation of Christ's own Baptism."[21]

Does Paul or indeed the New Testament suggest that the Holy Spirit comes to believers either in "confirmation" or through some second postbaptismal experience? Lampe briefly considers Philip in Acts 8:39, who is "snatched" by the Spirit; but this is a unique episode in the Church's missionary outreach. In the case of Lydia and the Philippian jailer, baptism appears as the focus. In Acts 10:44 (Cornelius and his friends) "this episode is in no way typical; it is a major turning-point in Luke's narrative. . . . Possibly the Spirit is regarded by Luke as normally, but not universally, imparted through Baptism."[22]

Lampe attends to three passages in which, he admits, the Spirit appears to be mediated through the laying on of hands. The first concerns the visit of Peter and John to Samaria in Acts 8:4-19. Many authors assumed that no one except apostles could mediate the Spirit. But if so, Lampe retorts, why does Paul never allude to this? It is not even listed as a charisma. There is no indication that the apostles laid hands on the three thousand at Pentecost, nor on Philip's Ethiopian eunuch. The word "baptism" "stand[s] for the entire initiatory rite."[23] Lampe also appeals to the Johannine literature as seeing no second rite subsequent to baptism. Many critics of Lampe in the Renewal Movement claim that Lampe undervalues Luke and overvalues Paul. But Lampe insists: "What Luke regards as the distinctive mode of the Spirit's activity in the missionary enterprise [is] the Spirit of power . . . with signs and wonders."[24]

Lampe also pays special attention to Acts 19:1-7, the disciples at Ephesus. This is "another decisive moment in the missionary history. Next to Antioch, in fact in succession to Antioch, Ephesus is the centre of the Gentile mission, the headquarters where Paul makes his longest stay."[25] Lampe concludes that the apostolic laying on of hands was not a regular ceremony, universally employed. It is in no way equivalent to "confirmation."[26] Indeed, he argues that the Syrian practice of associating charismation with the bestowal of the Spirit apparently took its rise in Gnostic circles.

In the remainder of his book, Lampe examines the second-century and Patristic sources. A gulf between the second century and the New Testament rapidly appears, not least in Clement of Alexandria's affinity with Gnosticism, and even in the Ignatian epistles.[27] The Order of Solomon may not be used for orthodox thought. The assumption that confirmation, rather than baptism, "ad-

---

21. Lampe, *Seal of the Spirit*, p. 57.
22. Lampe, *Seal of the Spirit*, p. 66.
23. Lampe, *Seal of the Spirit*, p. 68.
24. Lampe, *Seal of the Spirit*, p. 74.
25. Lampe, *Seal of the Spirit*, p. 76.
26. Lampe, *Seal of the Spirit*, pp. 78-84.
27. Lampe, *Seal of the Spirit*, pp. 101-5.

mits a man into the Church" is "unwarrantable."[28] There is no suggestion, Lampe argues, that the laying on of the bishop's hand is symbolic of the gift of the Spirit. Lampe also examines *The Apostolic Tradition* of Hippolytus. Where it differs from the New Testament, he questions the authenticity of the text.

Finally, Lampe traces the disintegration of the New Testament doctrine of baptism into a multitude of minor liturgical offices. He continues his critique of Mason and Dix through Origen, Cyprian, and others. He also considers the sacramental receiving of the Holy Spirit in relation to Patristic theories of sealing. On the first of these points, he suggests: "We are dealing with a period of theological confusion, when the New Testament teaching on Baptism and the indwelling of the Spirit is rarely fully understood (owing in large measure to a failure to maintain in its completeness the New Testament doctrine of justification)."[29] "Sealing" used to be a symbol of the refashioning of the believer after Christ's image, "the essential status and character of the Christian," but it gradually became "a ceremony of sealing with . . . the gift of the Spirit's indwelling presence, . . . bestowed sacramentally."[30]

Some scholars may suggest that Lampe has gone too far. But in broad terms he has rightly settled the debate in England, and those least satisfied with his position are either a minority of the weakened Anglo-Catholics, fighting a rearguard action in England, or (ironically) Anglo-Catholic charismatics in America, who seek a "second" event in which the Spirit is received *after* what Dunn terms *conversion-initiation*.

In "The Holy Spirit in the Writings of Luke" (1967) Lampe looks at the broader subject of the Spirit more specifically in Luke-Acts, which is so central for Pentecostals and the Renewal Movement. Indeed, much of his essay anticipates the arguments of Roger Stronstad (1984 and 1999) and Robert P. Menzies (1991 and 1994). The Holy Spirit provides the "connecting thread" between Luke and Acts.[31] Lampe writes: "A most striking feature of the opening chapters of St. Luke's work is the outburst of the *prophetic* Spirit which forms the setting for the Forerunner's birth and mission."[32]

In the Old Testament, Lampe argues, the Spirit characteristically inspires the prophets. Moses, Joshua, and others receive the Spirit to prophesy, and *in the Old Testament*, according to Luke, the Spirit is mainly an impersonal force. He argues: "The Spirit of prophecy has been poured out by the exalted Christ."[33] Lampe sees a close association with Jesus, but comments, "Jesus thus

---

28. Lampe, *Seal of the Spirit*, p. 135.

29. Lampe, *Seal of the Spirit*, p. 205.

30. Lampe, *Seal of the Spirit*, p. 269.

31. Lampe, "The Holy Spirit in the Writings of St. Luke," in *Studies in the Gospels*, ed. Denis Nineham, p. 159; cf. pp. 159-200.

32. Lampe, "The Holy Spirit in St. Luke," in *Studies in the Gospels*, p. 165 (my italics).

33. Lampe, "The Holy Spirit in St. Luke," in *Studies in the Gospels*, p. 163.

stands at the climax of the prophetic tradition."[34] The notion that Jesus is the antitype of Elijah thus becomes important. If Stronstad had been more cautious, he might have been more convincing. Lampe concedes, for example: "St. Luke nowhere presses the comparison of Jesus with Moses very far," except in the one case of Stephen.[35] Lampe concludes: "St. Luke's conception of the Spirit is differentiated from that of St. Paul . . . by his predominant interest in it as the power of gospel preaching, the Spirit of prophecy, 'tongues' and 'signs.'"[36]

In *God as Spirit* Lampe brings together several themes. He begins with the two quasi-creedal formulations that the Holy Spirit inspires: "Jesus is Lord" (1 Cor. 12:3) and "Jesus is alive today."[37] In Jesus we experience "God's indwelling presence." Second, in the Old Testament "Word," "Wisdom," "Spirit," and "Angel" provide metaphorical bridges to a transcendent deity.[38] He considers "Spirit" in Philo, the Stoics, and Plato. He takes up the Spirit's relationship with Christ. Like many Pentecostals, he alludes to God's pouring "rain on a thirsty land, showers on the dry ground" (Isa. 44:3-5).[39] This matches Joel's "universal outpouring" (Joel 2:28). He repeats the point of his earlier essay: "To Luke, the Spirit means primarily the Spirit of prophecy. . . . The Spirit is the driving force and inspiration of the mission of Jesus himself, and of its continuation by the apostles' missionaries to the end of the earth."[40] The Spirit guides at "decisive turning points" in the mission of the Church. He acknowledges a tension in Luke between the universality of the gift of the Spirit to *all* Christians and the gift to "a distinct class of prophets within this community."[41] By contrast, in John "the presence of the Spirit is the sign and assurance that Christ himself dwells in us and that we dwell in him" (1 John 3:24; 4:13).[42]

Lampe skillfully rejects the Stoic notion of an immanent Spirit who "pervaded the universe."[43] To be sure, the Spirit animates everything that lives, but this does not provide a bridge between the world and the transcendent God. *Pan-en-theism is not pantheism.* Christian apologists have frequently made this point. Classical orthodoxy always rejected reductionist or psychologizing views of the Spirit. Lampe rejects even Augustine's "artificial distinctions" between Persons of the Trinity based on psychological analogies.[44] Much of the remain-

---

34. Lampe, "The Holy Spirit in St. Luke," in *Studies in the Gospels*, p. 173.
35. Lampe, "The Holy Spirit in St. Luke," in *Studies in the Gospels*, pp. 175-76.
36. Lampe, "The Holy Spirit in St. Luke," in *Studies in the Gospels*, p. 193.
37. Lampe, *God as Spirit*, p. 1, cf. pp. 1-33.
38. Lampe, *God as Spirit*, p. 37.
39. Lampe, *God as Spirit*, p. 63.
40. Lampe, *God as Spirit*, p. 65.
41. Lampe, *God as Spirit*, p. 67.
42. Lampe, *God as Spirit*, p. 91.
43. Lampe, *God as Spirit*, p. 133.
44. Lampe, *God as Spirit*, p. 141.

der of the volume concerns the preexistence of Christ, the Coming of Christ, and the Spirit, the World, and the Church. Like Thornton, he emphasizes the corporate nature of the Spirit's gift. Further, "We experience the presence of God in our relations with other human beings."[45] This brings us to the final points made by Lampe. The Spirit produces love, above all things, and he is creative: "To speak of God's creativity implies his essential otherness in relation to the world."[46] The Holy Spirit is creative, holy, transcendent, and love.

19.2. Lindsay Dewar and Eduard Schweizer

(1) *Lindsay Dewar* contributed a study with some distinctive insights in *The Holy Spirit and Modern Thought*. The first eighty or so pages concern the biblical teaching. He notes: "The common New Testament use of the phrase 'the Spirit' indicates that He is so familiar and central in Christian experience that it is sufficient thus to describe him."[47] The saying about blasphemy against the Holy Spirit "must refer to sin against the light, . . . falsification of conscience, . . . calling good evil and evil good."[48] In the Fourth Gospel the work of the Spirit is to bear witness to Christ.[49] Dewar declares, "Nowhere does St. Luke explicitly state that the Holy Spirit is given by water-baptism," while controversially he claims that the gift of the Spirit to the Gentiles is seen as a kind of "confirmation."[50] The gift of the Spirit to the Samaritans (Acts 8:12-21) comes "through the laying on of the Apostle's hands," while the gift of the Spirit to Cornelius and his friends is "plainly unique — a Gentile Pentecost."[51]

Three specific instances of "speaking in tongues" occur in Acts: Acts 2, Acts 10:46, and Acts 19:6. In each case those involved were "on the tiptoe of expectation. . . . [They are an] unmistakable outward sign of His [Christ's] coming."[52] The traditional signs of wind and fire support this interpretation: "the barrier of the cross, so to say, had been broken down."[53] Dewar accords more than twenty pages to Paul, which are in general helpful but fairly routine. On the personality of the Holy Spirit, however, he adds: "[There is] no possible doubt that he [Paul] thought of him as fully personal — a 'he' and not an 'it.'"[54] The

---

45. Lampe, *God as Spirit*, p. 177.

46. Lampe, *God as Spirit*, p. 207.

47. Lindsay Dewar, *The Holy Spirit and Modern Thought* (London: Mowbray, 1959), p. 17.

48. Dewar, *The Holy Spirit and Modern Thought*, p. 19.

49. Dewar, *The Holy Spirit and Modern Thought*, pp. 36 and 37.

50. Dewar, *The Holy Spirit and Modern Thought*, pp. 52-53.

51. Dewar, *The Holy Spirit and Modern Thought*, p. 54.

52. Dewar, *The Holy Spirit and Modern Thought*, p. 57.

53. Dewar, *The Holy Spirit and Modern Thought*, p. 59.

54. Dewar, *The Holy Spirit and Modern Thought*, p. 71.

eighth chapter of Romans alone would provide sufficient evidence of this. "Helps" (8:26, *synantilambanetai*), he argues, is a strongly personal word. Like Thornton, he calls attention to the common *koinōnia* of the Spirit (Acts 2:42; 1 Cor. 12:18; Gal. 3:28), and to his formation of the Body of Christ (Eph. 4:11-13). Dewar concludes this biblical part: "The Holy Spirit is fully personal and divine, being in an equality with the Father and the Son. . . . He speaks through the prophets. . . . He is at work at two levels — the material and the supernatural. . . . The Holy Spirit will progressively lead believers into all the truth. . . . The Spirit-bearing Body is a sacrificial Body because the root of sacrifice is *agapē*, which comes from the Spirit alone."[55]

The next part of Dewar's volume concerns the history of the doctrine of the Holy Spirit from the Apostolic Fathers to George Fox (1624-91). There is little from Clement of Rome to Augustine to add to our Part II. He jumps to Luther and Calvin, and this outline would merely repeat material already considered. However, he adds material from Richard Hooker (1552-1600), which we omitted. *He admits that Hooker nowhere discusses the Spirit* in his work on natural laws, or indeed in his second book.[56] In the third book Hooker appears *to identify the Spirit with reason.* When he concludes: "There is little, if any, of this teaching [on the Spirit] to be found in Hooker's great work," this accounts for our omission of a special section on Hooker.[57]

Dewar's last part, some fifty pages, concerns "The Psychological Interpretation" of the doctrine of the Spirit. He considers such speculative phenomena as extrasensory perception and psychokinesis, gathered together as *Psi* phenomena. He acknowledges: "It must be frankly admitted that the majority of professional psychologists have not accepted the findings of those who claim to have scientifically established the existence of *psi* phenomena."[58] Much of this part of the book remains speculative. One or two useful points emerge, however. He argues that whereas Freud thought of the unconscious as a closed system, "Jung on the other hand regards the unconscious as being more like an ever-springing fountain of clear water."[59] As we shall later see from Theissen's work, the Holy Spirit works in "the depths" of the human heart, where there are too often self-deception and self-love.

Dewar allows for the revelatory character of some dreams. However, while this may indeed rarely occur, we must acknowledge Thomas Hobbes's dictum that "God spoke to me in a dream" is no different in logic from "I dreamed that God spoke to me." It remains true, nevertheless, that the Holy Spirit works in areas of "pent-up aggression, . . . guilt-ridden sexuality, . . . wretched inferior-

---

55. Dewar, *The Holy Spirit and Modern Thought*, pp. 81-82.
56. Dewar, *The Holy Spirit and Modern Thought*, pp. 148-49.
57. Dewar, *The Holy Spirit and Modern Thought*, p. 151.
58. Dewar, *The Holy Spirit and Modern Thought*, p. 162.
59. Dewar, *The Holy Spirit and Modern Thought*, p. 166.

ity."[60] These are not necessarily conscious states. But conscious life also embodies what Freud calls "narcissism," or self-love, and theologians call that sin. Here the Spirit's outpouring of love and grace takes us forward, to do for us what we cannot do for ourselves. Hence we may speak of being "born again" or "born from above" by the Holy Spirit. From the Holy Spirit come "all holy desires," but we do not need to accept "every thought and desire which comes spontaneously into the mind as coming from him."[61] John wrote, "Believe not every spirit" (1 John 4:1-3).

(2) *Eduard Schweizer* (1913-2006) was a Swiss New Testament scholar who in 1979 became Professor of New Testament at the University of Zurich. He wrote on church order, the Lord's Supper, and what is probably the longest article in the *Theological Dictionary of the New Testament* on the Spirit. This article includes small sections written by Hermann Kleinknecht and Friedrich Baumgärtel, but it was published in English as a book of 119 pages.[62]

In summary, Schweizer finds relatively few references to the Spirit in Matthew and Mark. He writes, "It is no doubt a historical fact that *Jesus Himself seldom referred to the Spirit* (my italics)."[63] This is in startling contrast to James Dunn, as we shall see below. Indeed, Matthew and Mark view the Holy Spirit "in the same way as in the O.T."[64] By contrast, Luke and Acts contain some 37 references. In his Gospel he sees Jesus as "not a pneumatic, but the Lord of the *pneuma.*" He stresses the role of the Holy Spirit in the conception and birth of Jesus more strongly than Matthew. In Acts he underlines visible phenomena at Pentecost (esp. Acts 2:3-6; 4:31), and urges that because Luke is a Hellenist he can portray power *only* in the form of *substance.*[65] Moreover, he appears to restrict the activity of the Spirit in Acts mainly to inspire *speech,* although he allows for "healings," but in the name of Jesus.

Schweizer concludes: "Luke thus shares with Judaism the view that the Spirit is essentially the Spirit of *prophecy.*"[66] He devotes almost a dozen pages in Kittel's *Dictionary* to the Spirit in Luke-Acts, pointing out that *pneuma* occurs three times as often as in Mark. Jesus is explicitly "full of the Holy Spirit" (*plērēs pneumatos hagiou,* Luke 4:1). But he cannot see the decisive manifestation of the Spirit in the exorcisms of Jesus. One of Schweizer's most distinctive claims is that "the power of God [is] manifested in the inspired *utterance* of the witness

---

60. Dewar, *The Holy Spirit and Modern Thought,* p. 171.

61. Dewar, *The Holy Spirit and Modern Thought,* p. 193.

62. Eduard Schweizer, "*Pneuma, pneumatikos,*" in *TDNT,* ed. Gerhard Kittel and Gerhard Friedrich, vol. 6 (Grand Rapids: Eerdmans, 1968), pp. 332-455; and *Spirit of God,* Bible Key Words (London: Black, 1960; German, 1959-60).

63. Schweizer, "*Pneuma,*" in *TDNT,* vol. 6, p. 403.

64. Schweizer, "*Pneuma,*" in *TDNT,* vol. 6, p. 404.

65. Schweizer, "*Pneuma,*" in *TDNT,* vol. 6, p. 407.

66. Schweizer, "*Pneuma,*" in *TDNT,* vol. 6, p. 409.

of Jesus. Luke adopts the typically Jewish idea that the Spirit is the Spirit of *prophecy*."[67] Roger Stronstad and R. P. Menzies will take up and develop this argument in the 1990s, whereas Max Turner will also give it qualified support, with a more guarded proviso that this does not exclude Luke's association of the Holy Spirit with *salvation*. Schweizer several times repeats this theme, and Menzies probably owes more to Schweizer and to Lampe than may appear in his work.

Other features are less open to controversy. For example, Schweizer stresses the *eschatological* character of the gift of the Spirit, but also sees the Spirit as a feature of the Age of the Church. Stephen Wilson has shown decisively that both of these two emphases are far from incompatible in Luke.[68] Luke's community needed eschatology, but it also needed his emphasis on the New Age of the Church.

It is generally agreed, however, as Schweizer urges, that Luke has an interest in physical phenomena and visible manifestations of the Spirit, perhaps because of his Hellenistic background. Thus the physical "rapture" or "snatching away" of Philip in Acts 8:39 stands apart as unique, although it may recall 1 Kings 18:12; 2 Kings 2:16; and Ezek. 3:14; 8:3. In Acts "each of the baptized possesses the Spirit, and does so in a way which is visible and perceptible." As a rule, Schweizer asserts, "baptism in the name of Jesus confers the Spirit," but because of "the freedom of the Spirit," this is not invariable.[69]

Paul has basically been shaped by the Old Testament. Thus the Spirit naturally becomes a sign of something still to come. Again, however, Schweizer claims that Paul thinks of power "in terms of substance," which is more controversial today. But more convincingly he sees the cross and resurrection as a turning point. The Spirit is the Spirit of Christ (Rom. 1:3-4), and Christ, he claims, is "identified with the *pneuma* in 2 Cor. 3:17," although in Part I we rejected the word "identified" here, offering the different explanation of an exegetical "is."[70] In 1 Cor. 15:45 Christ is the life-giving Spirit, "the creative act of the Risen Lord." Yet in 1 Cor. 6:14 Schweizer stresses that the Spirit raises Christians, just as he raised Christ: the resurrection of Jesus and the resurrection of the dead are "the two creative acts of God."[71] The Spirit is also "a sign of what is to come." Schweizer appeals to such terms as *arrabōn* and *aparchē* (firstfruits) in Rom. 8:23 and 2 Cor. 1:22 and 5:5.

Schweizer rightly sees the term *pneumatikos,* "spiritual," as a "master concept." In 1 Cor. 2:4-5 this is what pertains to God, not humankind. The criterion

---

67. Schweizer, *"Pneuma,"* in *TDNT,* vol. 6, p. 407.

68. Stephen G. Wilson, *The Gentiles and the Gentile Mission in Luke-Acts,* SNTSMS 23 (Cambridge: Cambridge University Press, 1973), pp. 59-87.

69. Schweizer, *"Pneuma,"* in *TDNT,* vol. 6, pp. 410 and 413.

70. Schweizer, *"Pneuma,"* in *TDNT,* vol. 6, pp. 415, 416, and 418.

71. Schweizer, *"Pneuma,"* in *TDNT,* vol. 6, p. 421.

of "being spiritual" is the recognition and *confession of Christ as Lord* (1 Cor. 12:2-3). He concludes: "Above all, and unlike Luke, he [Paul] deduces that *the manifestations of the Spirit do not have to be extraordinary. . . .* He reckons among such manifestations *antilēmpseis* [probably administrators] and *kybernēseis* [which I translated *strategists,* or perhaps *guides*] or *diakonia* [*service, ministry*] . . . Rom. 12:7-8; 1 Cor. 12:28" (my italics).[72] Paul values those gifts of the Spirit that *build,* such as *love* (1 Cor. 8:1). In 1 Cor. 2:2, Paul has nothing to preach but Christ crucified. The Spirit is received by faith, involves "openness to God and one's neighbor," and, above all, loyalty to Christ. The Holy Spirit is not the human spirit, which usually denotes a human quality or disposition. *Pneumatikos,* "spiritual," Schweizer re-emphasizes, relates to knowledge and experience of the Holy Spirit.[73]

On John, Schweizer urges, "In John there is no thought of the sporadic coming of the Spirit, the extraordinary nature of his manifestations, ecstatic phenomena or miraculous acts."[74] But even in John the Spirit is the turning point of the old and new ages. He is life-giving power. In the Paraclete passages Jesus himself comes in the Paraclete (John 14:18).

Schweizer then considers the rest of the New Testament. Hebrews, for example, is strongly influenced by Judaism. 1 Peter retains the traditional *prophetic Spirit.* In Revelation "the *pneuma* can lead a man into wonderful regions which the natural man does not perceive" (Rev. 17:3; 21:10). The Spirit of God is represented in his fullness and completeness. Thus within the New Testament there is no either/or between an ecstatic strand and an institutional strand, which emerges too readily in the post-Apostolic writings. Schweizer has in many respects covered the ground traveled by H. B. Swete, except to add a number of insights, but also some temporary baggage from the biblical criticism of the 1950s. For example, few today, since especially Martin Hengel, would replicate Schweizer's sharp division between Judaism and Hellenism. Probably a number would question his overly restrictive re-construction of authentic sayings of Jesus. But the influence of this long article in Kittel's encyclopedia is difficult to overestimate, and he writes as a leading and well-informed New Testament specialist.

19.3. John V. Taylor

John V. Taylor (1914-2001) was educated at Trinity College, Cambridge, was ordained in 1938, and served in two parishes. He then became a missionary-

---

72. Schweizer, *"Pneuma,"* in *TDNT,* vol. 6, p. 424.
73. Schweizer, *"Pneuma,"* in *TDNT,* vol. 6, pp. 430-31 and 433-37.
74. Schweizer, *"Pneuma,"* in *TDNT,* vol. 6, p. 438.

teacher in Bishop Tucker College, Mukono, Uganda. On his return to England, he was appointed General Secretary of the Church Missionary Society in 1963, and served as Bishop of Winchester, the fifth most important bishopric in England, from 1974 to 1985. His two most influential and well-known books were *The Go-Between God,* on the Holy Spirit and mission (1972), and *The Christ-like God* (1992).[75] He chaired the Church of England Doctrine Commission (1978-85). *The Go-Between God* had a wide impact at the time, especially because of its practical nature.

Taylor begins his book on the Spirit with the practical observation that the Holy Spirit was "the chief actor" in the historic mission of the Church. The Spirit *excludes the notion of "It all depends on me"* (my italics).[76] The Spirit is transcendent, yet *operates in everyday life: the Beyond in the midst.* Many of the detailed descriptions of the Spirit use this imagery. They point to his otherness and Personhood. He draws on Martin Buber's *I and Thou* to stress *mutual giving* and *genuine listening* within a personal relationship: "The Holy Spirit is that power which opens eyes that are closed, hearts that are unaware, and minds that shrink from too much reality."[77] In mission, this includes awareness of other people.

As Pannenberg would later urge, the Spirit is no less at work in history, nature, and human living, and is the *Creator Spirit.* God's creativity through the Spirit is also his creative, persuasive love, which may involve "self-oblation."[78] He makes us aware of some "other," and of "some greater whole."[79] Taylor declares, "We must learn to meet the supernatural, if at all, not in discontinuous 'vertical' interactions, but in a universal, 'horizontal' pervasion."[80] The Holy Spirit is *not just an upsurge of the unconscious,* although the Spirit often uses our unconscious for his work. We must discern what is truly the work of the Holy Spirit; this is not necessarily so in "the fever of activity."[81] The eighth- and seventh-century prophets had "a certain revulsion from the more irrational and potentially amoral manifestations of spiritual power."[82] To be confronted by the Holy Spirit as both Creator and Restorer . . . means that thereafter we look upon the present with the pain of judgment and upon the future with the certainty of consummation."[83]

Like Joseph Fison, Taylor inquires about the comparative silence of Jesus

75. John V. Taylor, *The Go-Between God: The Holy Spirit and the Christian Mission* (London: SCM, 1972).

76. Taylor, *Go-Between God,* p. 3.

77. Taylor, *Go-Between God,* p. 19.

78. Taylor, *Go-Between God,* p. 34.

79. Taylor, *Go-Between God,* p. 39.

80. Taylor, *Go-Between God,* p. 45.

81. Taylor, *Go-Between God,* p. 55.

82. Taylor, *Go-Between God,* p. 68.

83. Taylor, *Go-Between God,* p. 75.

concerning the Holy Spirit. In contrast to James Dunn, and like C. K. Barrett, he comments: "We might argue that he scarcely, if ever, thought of his communion with God in terms of the Holy Spirit."[84] But the language of Jesus was bound up with apocalyptic. We do see in Jesus the Creator Spirit when "the *Kairos*-time has come." Taylor asserts, as Dunn will do, that much depends on the *authority* of Jesus, and on his bringing freedom and the new creation. What is significant is the extent to which the Christian Church lost sight of the role of the Holy Spirit as *agent of Christ's resurrection,* as so clearly set forth in the epistles.[85] He also calls the Holy Spirit "a kind of extension of the incarnation."[86] This is far more accurate than the claim that the Church is an extension of the incarnation. He also expounds the "incomparable and inescapable" relationship with Christ, effected by the Spirit.[87]

When we come to part 2, "Style of Life," Taylor names his chapters "Growing, Exploring, Meeting, Playing, and Loving." At the beginning of this part he commends thinking of "the Church being given to the Spirit, [rather] than of the Spirit being given to the Church."[88] The Pentecostal experience was to fuse individual believers *into a fellowship,* with *"awareness of the other."* The gospel is not only about forgiveness, but also about *enabling.* The Spirit enables goodness: "*being* evil is so much worse than *doing* evil" (my italics).[89] The chapter on "Meeting" encourages dialogue with the other, even with those of other faiths.

Taylor declares: "The *charismata,* or grace-gifts, of the Holy Spirit are not themselves of the essence of the Spirit-filled life. They are marked by a certain transience, it is inherent in their nature to 'pass away.'"[90] He adds: "There can be no question of seeking something *extra* beyond the basic gift of the salvation that is offered to us all. . . . To speak of a 'second blessing' is a misnomer."[91] All of the Spirit's gifts, he says, are wonderful; but they are intended for specific tasks. For example, healing may *sometimes* be a special gift, but "marvels" are always ambiguous. The laying on of hands is "an act through which the Holy Spirit within a community expresses his love."[92] He adds: "Speaking with tongues reappears only occasionally in the subsequent history of the church."[93] He cites Eusebius's distaste at the "frenzy" of the Montanists; the scarcity of reference to tongues in the Middle Ages; and the gap of 1,300 years before Hugue-

---

84. Taylor, *Go-Between God,* p. 87.
85. Taylor, *Go-Between God,* p. 102.
86. Taylor, *Go-Between God,* p. 111.
87. Taylor, *Go-Between God,* p. 123.
88. Taylor, *Go-Between God,* p. 133.
89. Taylor, *Go-Between God,* p. 167.
90. Taylor, *Go-Between God,* p. 201.
91. Taylor, *Go-Between God,* p. 202.
92. Taylor, *Go-Between God,* p. 207.
93. Taylor, *Go-Between God,* p. 219.

not peasants: "neither Zinzendorf nor Wesley refers to it. . . . It is not until 1830 that we come upon the next occurrence, [which] . . . inspired Edward Irving to lay stress on this gift."[94] This experience may be a therapeutic one of unconscious tensions released, but it is also "a passionate expression of self-concern," as well as a quest for wholeness.[95]

Taylor concludes by seeing the Spirit as "the very breath of the prayer of Jesus," especially in his cry "*Abba,* Father."[96] Jesus talks to his Father naturally, and a new way of praying is born. The experience of praying in the Spirit with the mind also is nearer to Jesus' experience of the Spirit than "special" gifts for special tasks or occasions. This kind of prayer is an expression of loving. Love of God embraces love of other human beings, and in the experience of love, all is brought before God as Father. "Prayer must advance beyond the cultivation of our own states of feeling and their use as flimsy bridges to bring us to God. . . . [Prayer and the Spirit are] *the embrace of God, his kiss of life*" (my italics).[97]

Although he was not always a parish pastor, none can doubt John Taylor's deep pastoral concern.[98] He became an expert on African affairs. Most readers agree that there are visionary insights in his work, and his book on the Holy Spirit is widely regarded as a classic. He writes from the heart, and, like Fison, produced many pithy and memorable sayings. Parts of this book may suffer criticism; but very much is also inspiring and provokes thought.

19.4. James D. G. Dunn

James Dunn (b. 1939) was for many years Lightfoot Professor of Divinity at the University of Durham. He was educated at the University of Glasgow, and holds the Ph.D. and D.D. from the University of Cambridge. He taught at the University of Nottingham before becoming a professor at Durham. In 1970 he wrote *Baptism in the Holy Spirit,* which many Pentecostal and Renewal adherents regard as a "landmark" for the recognition of issues relating to the Renewal Movement for the mainline churches.[99] He also wrote *Jesus and the Spirit,* while teaching at Nottingham.[100] At Durham he wrote *Christology in the Making;* a

---

94. Taylor, *Go-Between God,* p. 219. He does refer to Thomas Walsh, one of Wesley's preachers, speaking "a language I knew not of."

95. Taylor, *Go-Between God,* p. 220.

96. Taylor, *Go-Between God,* p. 226.

97. Taylor, *Go-Between God,* p. 235 and p. 243.

98. On Taylor's life and career, see David Wood, *Bishop John V. Taylor: Poet, Priest, and Prophet* (London: Church House Publishing, 2002).

99. James D. G. Dunn, *Baptism in the Holy Spirit: A Re-examination of the New Testament Teaching on the Gift of the Spirit in Relation to Pentecostalism Today* (London: SCM, 1970).

100. James D. G. Dunn, *Jesus and the Spirit* (London: SCM, 1975).

two-volume *Commentary on Romans; Jesus, Paul, and the Law; Unity and Diversity in the New Testament;* commentaries on Galatians and on Colossians; *The Theology of Paul the Apostle; The New Perspective on Paul;* and *Jesus Remembered,* as well as many other books and research articles. On our subject he also wrote "Towards the Spirit of Christ" in a volume edited by Michael Welker (2006), and contributed "replies" to the *Journal of Pentecostal Theology.*[101] He is a Fellow of the British Academy.

In his *Baptism in the Holy Spirit* Dunn goes straight to the heart of the question which he addresses by tracing the roots of Pentecostalism to the Holiness Movement and to certain themes among some Puritans and Methodists. Salvation, they claim, is experienced in two stages: first in the experience of becoming a Christian; second, in a later distinct event of a second experience of the Holy Spirit. He also cites some possible evidence of this scheme in John Wesley's *A Plain Account of Christian Perfection.* He even cites, as others do, the Keswick Convention in England, though I stayed for the whole Convention in 1957 and found nothing whatever at that time there about "the second blessing." Indeed, most participants viewed it as a heresy. However, Dunn more credibly refers to Wesley's follower, John Fletcher. He then traces it to the Azusa Street revival, the Topeka Bible College, and the birth of classical Pentecostalism. He rightly asks whether the New Testament and Pentecostals mean the same thing by "baptism in the Holy Spirit."

Dunn asserts, "The Pentecostal doctrine is built chiefly on Acts."[102] Articles in *The Journal of Pentecostal Theology* confirm Dunn's assessment. Probably the most polemical is that by Janet Meyer Everts on Paul (she places Dunn in the "Anglican tradition," although he is Methodist); Roger Stronstad writes on Luke-Acts; and Max Turner gives a more appreciative assessment from the "Renewal Movement" perspective.[103] In *Baptism in the Holy Spirit* Dunn devotes roughly thirty pages to the first three Gospels, sixty pages to Acts, seventy pages to Paul, thirty pages to John, and twenty to the rest of the New Testament. Dunn has not skimped on New Testament themes and exegesis. His purpose in this book is "clarity of thought."[104]

Dunn begins the substance of the argument by considering John the Baptist

---

101. James D. G. Dunn, "Towards the Spirit of Christ: The Emergence of the Distinctive Features of Christian Pneumatology," in *The Work of the Spirit: Pneumatology and Pentecostalism,* ed. Michael Welker (Grand Rapids: Eerdmans, 2006), pp. 3-26.

102. Dunn, *Baptism in the Holy Spirit,* p. 5.

103. Janet Meyer Everts, "The Pauline Letters in J. D. G. Dunn's Baptism in the Spirit," *JPT* 19, no. 1 (2010): 12-18; Roger Stronstad, "Forty Years On: An Appreciation and Assessment of Baptism in the Spirit," *JPT* 19 (2010): 3-11, mainly on Luke-Acts; and Max Turner, "James Dunn's *Baptism in the Holy Spirit,*" *JPT* 19 (2010): 25-31. Dunn offers a response in this number of *JPT* 19, no. 1 (2010), and also writes in *Religious Studies Review* 36 (2010): 147-67.

104. Dunn, *Baptism in the Holy Spirit,* p. 7.

and his words "I baptize you in [or 'with'] water, but he [Jesus] will baptize you in [or 'with,' single dative] the Holy Spirit" (Mark 1:8): "Spirit-and-fire baptism is not offered as an alternative to John's water-baptism. . . . Spirit-and-fire together describe the one purgative act of messianic judgment."[105] He amplifies his case by looking at Mal. 3:2-3; 4:1; Isa. 4:4; 30:28, and John's role as an Elijah. John's baptism *expresses* repentance, and *results* in forgiveness. It is essentially preparative.

The baptism of Jesus remains of crucial importance for all. But its significance lies in the part it plays in salvation history. When the Spirit falls upon Jesus, this is "unique anointing."[106] Dunn opposes both a "Catholic" interpretation of events in terms of a baptism followed by "confirmation" and a Pentecostal interpretation of them as baptism followed by a second blessing: "we are dealing here not with two ritual actions, but only one — baptism."[107]

Part 2 begins with Pentecost. As appears throughout these latter chapters, Dunn's huge difference from most Pentecostals is the interpretation of "bare historical narratives": do they point beyond themselves? Dunn claims, "Pentecostals and Catholics alike have again missed the principal significance of the story" as "a watershed in salvation history."[108] "The descent of the Spirit upon Jesus was Jesus' *own* entry with the new age."[109] As we shall shortly note, Stronstad and Turner preferred a different hermeneutics of Luke-Acts. Dunn insists, "Pentecost inaugurates the age of the Church. For Luke, Pentecost constitutes the disciples as the new covenant people of God."[110]

Necessarily, when addressing his subject, Dunn discusses the famous controversial events which follow Pentecost: "the riddle of Samaria" in Acts 8:5-8; the conversion of Paul in Acts 9, 22, and 26; the conversion of Cornelius in Acts 11:15-17; and the "disciples" at Ephesus in Acts 19:1-7. These all constitute foundational passages for a Pentecostal doctrine of baptism in the Holy Spirit. We have already discussed these in Part I, and also in Swete, Dewar, Lampe, and others. Dunn points out that in Acts 11:15 "the Holy Spirit fell on them as on us *at the beginning*," followed by 11:17, "*when we believed* in the Lord Jesus Christ" (his italics).[111] Acts 8 is parallel. Dunn comments, "There is complete silence about any confirmatory coming of the Spirit."[112] The passage underlines that the Samaritans were fully accepted: "In New Testament times the possession of the Spirit was *the* hallmark of the Christian" (his italics).[113] The

105. Dunn, *Baptism in the Holy Spirit,* p. 11.
106. Dunn, *Baptism in the Holy Spirit,* p. 26.
107. Dunn, *Baptism in the Holy Spirit,* p. 37.
108. Dunn, *Baptism in the Holy Spirit,* p. 40.
109. Dunn, *Baptism in the Holy Spirit,* p. 41.
110. Dunn, *Baptism in the Holy Spirit,* p. 49.
111. Dunn, *Baptism in the Holy Spirit,* p. 52.
112. Dunn, *Baptism in the Holy Spirit,* p. 59.
113. Dunn, *Baptism in the Holy Spirit,* p. 66.

key background is the religious and social animosity between Jerusalem and Samaria.

The conversion of Paul is a favorite passage of Pentecostals, because "Paul was converted, . . . and *three days later* he was baptized in the Spirit" (his italics).[114] Such non-Pentecostal scholars as Johannes Weiss and John Knox also emphasize such a sequence. Dunn insists, however, that the "three-day experience was a unity. . . . Paul seems to make no distinction between what commissioning he received outside Damascus, and the commissioning he received through Ananias."[115] Next, Cornelius responded as far as he could, but "he only entered into this Christian experience when he received the Spirit."[116] We again address a single experience.

Acts 19:1-7 represents another "foundational" text for Pentecostals. But the "disciples" did not belong to a Christian group *(hoi mathētai)* at Ephesus. Apollos "knew only the baptism of John and needed fuller instructions about 'the way of God' (Acts 18:25-6)."[117] The two events are parallel, so both had to undergo the complete initiation. Dunn concludes: "One of Luke's purposes in recording these unusual instances is to show that the one thing which makes a man a Christian is the gift of the Spirit."[118] Thus he concludes part 2 on Acts, and we cannot claim, as some Pentecostals do, that his exegesis is shallow or skimpy merely because in later years he concentrates increasingly on Paul, and becomes increasingly a world-renowned Pauline specialist.

On Paul (part 3) Dunn considers the early work in Thessalonians and Galatians, the transition to the middle period in 1 and 2 Corinthians, the central work in Romans, and then the later Pauline apostles. In fact, before he begins, he singles out Rom. 8:9 as expressing the heart of the matter: "Rom. 8:9 rules out the possibility both of a *non*-Christian possessing the Spirit, and of a Christian *not* possessing the Spirit: only the reception and consequent possession of the Spirit makes a man a Christian" (his italics).[119]

We need not explore all the Pauline passages once again. Rom. 8:9-10 is so clear: "The Spirit of God dwells in you. Anyone who does *not* have the Spirit of Christ does *not* belong to him" (NRSV). We select a sample. 1 Thess. 1:5-9 and 2:13 speak of the Word preached, the response of faith, and reception of the Holy Spirit. Gal. 3:26-27 introduces the word *baptizō* and shows that "to be baptized in Christ is the same thing as putting on Christ."[120] At first glance Gal. 4:6-7 may seem to suggest a Pentecostal interpretation: "Because you are sons, God has sent

---

114. Dunn, *Baptism in the Holy Spirit*, p. 73.
115. Dunn, *Baptism in the Holy Spirit*, pp. 74 and 75.
116. Dunn, *Baptism in the Holy Spirit*, p. 82.
117. Dunn, *Baptism in the Holy Spirit*, pp. 86 and 88.
118. Dunn, *Baptism in the Holy Spirit*, p. 93.
119. Dunn, *Baptism in the Holy Spirit*, p. 95.
120. Dunn, *Baptism in the Holy Spirit*, p. 112.

the Spirit of his Son into your hearts." But any sane exegesis shows that the text between the two clauses "is logical, not chronological."[121] It does *not* imply "two stages" of experience. "There is no talk of a subsequent coming of the Spirit."[122]

In the Corinthian epistles, 1 Cor. 6:11 speaks of "spiritual cleansing." Dunn rightly rejects any sacramentalist talk of a "baptismal aorist" fashionable in the earlier half of the twentieth century. He avoids presuppositions, which is why he frequently uses "conversion-initiation," to avoid pre-judging the relation between the two.[123] Similarly, 1 Cor. 6:14-20 speaks of becoming a Christian. The only place where Paul speaks of "baptism in the Spirit" is 1 Cor. 12:13. But Dunn observes: "Once the initiatory and incorporative significance of the metaphor is grasped, the Pentecostal arguments fall to the ground. For Paul, to become a Christian and to become a member of the Body of Christ [i.e., in baptism] is synonymous."[124] In my commentary on the Greek text of 1 Corinthians, I discuss the verse and add a note on 12:13 on Pentecostal traditions.[125] I refer to Sarah Parham's *Life of Charles F. Parham,* Joseph Seymour, N. Bloch-Hoell, Roger Stronstad, K. L. Archer, Frank Macchia, and others, as well as to Dunn. Dunn discusses 2 Cor. 1:21-22 and 2 Cor. 3:3-8.

Dunn turns to a number of passages in Romans and in the later Pauline epistles. He notes that Holiness preachers often mistakenly treated Romans 7 as a record of autobiographical struggle and dispute in contrast to "victory" in Romans 8, and is at one with all New Testament specialists in showing that *this is not the case.*[126] We have already considered Rom. 8:9 as "the most embarrassing verse in the New Testament to the crude Pentecostal view."[127] He repeats: "The thing which determines whether a man is a Christian is not his profession of faith in Christ, but the presence of the Spirit."[128] The later references simply confirm this point: Col. 1:13; 2:11-13; 2:20–3:14; and Eph. 1:13-14; 2:4-6; 4:1-6 and 20, and 5:25-29.

The Pentecostal argument from John is "that the disciples were regenerate before Pentecost, and had received the Spirit before Pentecost."[129] Dunn argues that the weakness here is to assume that the narratives in Luke-Acts and John are historical and chronological reports: "a flat plain of homogeneous historicity."[130] John's aim, however, is to show the continuity between Jesus and the

---

121. Dunn, *Baptism in the Holy Spirit,* p. 114.
122. Dunn, *Baptism in the Holy Spirit,* p. 115.
123. Dunn, *Baptism in the Holy Spirit,* pp. 6-7.
124. Dunn, *Baptism in the Holy Spirit,* p. 129.
125. Anthony C. Thiselton, *The First Epistle to the Corinthians: A Commentary on the Greek Text,* NIGTC (Grand Rapids: Eerdmans, 2000), pp. 997-1001.
126. Dunn, *Baptism in the Holy Spirit,* pp. 147-48.
127. Dunn, *Baptism in the Holy Spirit,* p. 148.
128. Dunn, *Baptism in the Holy Spirit,* p. 149.
129. Dunn, *Baptism in the Holy Spirit,* p. 173.
130. Dunn, *Baptism in the Holy Spirit,* p. 173.

Spirit-Paraclete. John points only to one uniting event of the Spirit's coming, linking together the glorification of Jesus and his uplifting. Chronology remains important, but "the gift of the Spirit is the immediate result of the Son of Man's being lifted up," as Edmund Hoskyns, R. H. Lightfoot, and Raymond Brown all maintain.

Dunn concludes that there "is much to be praised" in the Pentecostal attempt to restore a New Testament emphasis, but it has "led to two unfortunate aspects." The first is the "separation of Spirit-baptism from the event of conversion-initiation" as if to make the reception of the Spirit a second, subsequent experience. Dunn comments, "This is quite contrary to New Testament teaching."[131] The second mistake, he urges, is to separate faith from water baptism: "so that a man is a Christian before his water baptism, and the latter is little more than a confession of a past commitment. This may well accord with present Baptism practice, but it is not the New Testament pattern."[132]

Five years later Dunn published *Jesus and the Spirit*. He concedes in his Introduction that "Wider reading has thrown up some . . . often striking parallels to the 'charismatic' phenomena reported in the New Testament."[133] We shall endeavor only to take account of those themes and assessments which clearly go beyond *Baptism in the Holy Spirit*.

Part 1 concerns the religious experience of Jesus. The prayer life of Jesus provides an important point of departure. All strata of the first three Gospels stress the importance of prayer for Jesus. "Q" has the saying about "ask, seek, and knock" (Matt. 7:7-11//Luke 11:9-13). In Matt. 21:13 the temple is valued as a house of prayer. The account of Gethsemane in Mark 14:32-42 is strong testimony to Jesus' dependence on *prayer*, which could include boundless terror and suffering.[134] For Christians, Jesus' use of *Abba*, "dear Father" (Mark 14:36), is distinctive, and may be repeated by Christians, who derive their sonship from Christ's Sonship (Rom. 8:15; Gal. 4:6).[135] Joachim Jeremias is right to view "Abba" as a family word, even if, Dunn comments, "Jeremias has pressed his argument too far. . . . Nevertheless much of value remains."[136] Adolf von Harnack was right to single out the Fatherhood of God as a distinctive theme in the teaching of Jesus. It does not simply arise from the post-Easter Church. But, further, it tells us much about the consciousness of Jesus. We may note, however, that Dunn views this as an implicit reference to the Spirit, whereas John Taylor and Joseph Fison spoke of Jesus' specific avoidance of language about his dependence on the Holy Spirit.

---

131. Dunn, *Baptism in the Holy Spirit*, p. 226.
132. Dunn, *Baptism in the Holy Spirit*, p. 227.
133. Dunn, *Jesus and the Spirit*, p. 5.
134. Dunn, *Jesus and the Spirit*, pp. 17-21.
135. Dunn, *Jesus and the Spirit*, pp. 21-26.
136. Dunn, *Jesus and the Spirit*, p. 23.

In his third chapter Dunn is more explicit about Jesus' experience of the Spirit. Jesus was conscious of "God's Spirit upon and working through him. . . . Jesus speaks about his work as an exorcist, and . . . the prophecy of Isa. 61:1ff. being fulfilled in and through him."[137] There are a number of passages which record Jesus' healing of "mentally deranged and/or 'demon-possessed' people."[138] These belong to the base-rock of historical probability, which even David Strauss accepted. Dunn lists passages about the Beelzebub charge (Mark 3:22-26; Matt. 12:24-26//Luke 11:15-18); the Spirit or "finger" of God (Matt. 12:27-28//Luke 11:19-20); and the "strong man" saying (Mark 3:27). Dunn comments: "It was an *awareness* of *otherly* power working through him, together with the *conviction* that power was *God's* power" (his italics).[139]

Dunn expounds further the significance of Isa. 61:1 for Jesus. This also belongs to authentic Jesus tradition: "It is clear that Luke himself was influenced by Isa. 61:1 . . . in his presentation of Jesus' ministry."[140] Hence the Sonship of Jesus, the Spirit, and his experience of God are brought together: "Jesus believed himself to be empowered by the Spirit and thought of himself as God's son."[141] This was underlined by his baptism.

In view of the prevalence of the Renewal Movement, chapter 4 may appear to be more controversial than perhaps it was intended to be. It bears the title: "Was Jesus a Charismatic?" But the definition may allay fears: "As soon as we recognize Jesus as a man inspired, it becomes appropriate to describe him as a *charismatic* figure. . . . 'Charismatic' . . . could describe anything from the ecstatic frenzy of the early prophets (e.g., 1 Sam. 19:20-24; Hos. 9:7) to the majestic utterances of Second Isaiah."[142] Dunn cites the ministry of Jesus as miracle-worker, exercising *dynameis,* "power," in Mark 6:2, 5, 14 and Acts 2:22. It is more open to question whether, in view of its modern usage, "the power of a charismatic personality . . . may underlie some . . . of the so-called 'nature miracles.'"[143] Nevertheless the discussion of the *authority* of Jesus remains relevant (Luke 10:19). Clearly "Jesus had the reputation of a prophet."[144] Yet "there is no evidence of ecstatic behavior."[145] The "already–not yet tension" may lessen the difference between James Dunn on one side and Barrett and Fison on the other, which otherwise may seem startling.[146]

---

137. Dunn, *Jesus and the Spirit,* p. 43.
138. Dunn, *Jesus and the Spirit,* p. 44.
139. Dunn, *Jesus and the Spirit,* p. 47.
140. Dunn, *Jesus and the Spirit,* p. 54; cf. p. 55.
141. Dunn, *Jesus and the Spirit,* p. 63.
142. Dunn, *Jesus and the Spirit,* p. 68.
143. Dunn, *Jesus and the Spirit,* p. 73.
144. Dunn, *Jesus and the Spirit,* p. 82.
145. Dunn, *Jesus and the Spirit,* p. 85.
146. Dunn, *Jesus and the Spirit,* p. 89; cf. C. K. Barrett, *The Holy Spirit and the Gospel Tradition*

Part 2 of *Jesus and the Spirit* moves to the earliest Christian communities. Some of this material, but not all, overlaps with that in *Baptism in the Holy Spirit*. On the issue of continuity and discontinuity, Dunn observes, "The Spirit can be described by Luke and Paul as the Spirit of Jesus (Acts 16:7; Phil. 1:19)."[147] Paul's experience of the appearance of the risen Christ was not merely an experience of the Spirit. Paul experienced the risen Jesus as one who sent him forth with the message of the new age. Paul sees Jerusalem as the center of Christianity, as Galatians 1 and 2 confirm. Pentecost involved "a communal vision." Glossolalia was clearly here an ecstatic phenomenon (Acts 2:4–13:9; 2:33). It entailed the "abandoning of conscious control of the speech organs to the subconscious."[148] Further, "Many present thought they recognized words of praise to God in other languages."[149] Many questions remain unresolved, but the event launched the mission of the Church.

The key effect, Dunn concludes, was to lead the early Christians to place their hope *not in themselves, but in the exalted Jesus.* He agrees, however, with many that Luke stands in contrast to Paul, John, and the rest of the New Testament. Controversially he suggests: "His attitude seems to be: the more eye-catching the miracle, the greater the propaganda value. All this is in notable contrast to . . . elsewhere in the New Testament."[150] If the suggestion is right, Luke's Hellenism would explain much of this contrast. Dunn likewise notes Luke's interest in prophecy, although this is not peculiar to Luke. In all this the Spirit is the principal source of authority. But in Acts the emphasis falls also on the community and its worship. Dunn concludes, *"Luke is a valuable but undiscriminating guide when it comes to asking questions about the religious experience of the earliest Christian communities"* (his italics).[151]

I have already anticipated much of part 3 when we considered the Pauline Churches in Part I of this book. We noted that Paul preferred the term *charisma* to *pneumatika* to emphasize that all gifts were free gifts of *grace.*[152] We also argued that to describe celibacy as a *charisma* (1 Cor. 7:7) implied that not all *charismata* were spontaneous.[153] We also considered the gifts of grace in 1 Cor. 12:8-10, sometimes citing Dunn's comments. No *charisma* can be used according to human will.[154] As we noted, these gifts are to build *(oikodomeō)* the

---

(London: SPCK, 1958), pp. 46-99, 113-121, and 140-62; Joseph E. Fison, *The Blessing of the Holy Spirit* (London and New York: Longmans, Green, 1950), pp. 81-102.

147. Dunn, *Jesus and the Spirit*, p. 95.
148. Dunn, *Jesus and the Spirit*, p. 148.
149. Dunn, *Jesus and the Spirit*, p. 152.
150. Dunn, *Jesus and the Spirit*, p. 167.
151. Dunn, *Jesus and the Spirit*, p. 195.
152. Dunn, *Jesus and the Spirit*, pp. 201-12.
153. Dunn, *Jesus and the Spirit*, p. 206.
154. Dunn, *Jesus and the Spirit*, p. 221.

Church "for the common good" (1 Cor. 12:7). Certainly *charisma* is not to be confused with human talent. Like Lionel Thornton, but without Thornton's sacramentalism, Dunn turns finally in part 3 to the Body of Christ and to the Spirit of Jesus. He comments: "The body of Christ only comes to realization in any place through the manifestations of grace [i.e., the gifts of the Spirit]."[155]

Secondly, however, the Church must reflect dying and being raised with Christ. Hence, in *contrast* to many in the Renewal Movement, Dunn also writes: "*For Paul, the religious experience of the believer is characterized by paradox and conflict, the conflict of Spirit and flesh.* It is a religion of *Anfechtung* — of faith always assailed by question and doubt, life is always assailed by death. . . . It is a life of tension . . . (Rom. 8:22-23; 2 Cor. 5:4) — the tension of belonging to two opposed worlds at the same time . . . *a life-long tension:* the cry of frustration in Rom. 7:24 is the life-long cry of the Christian" (Rom. 7:25b; 8:10; Dunn's italics).[156] Much of this volume acknowledges the truth of some themes in the Renewal Movement and in Pentecostalism. But it rejects others as not corresponding with the New Testament. In particular, the last comment would well harmonize also with Luther and the mainline Reformers, rather than with notions of "the second blessing" or even with elements distinctive of the Holiness Movement. Dunn adds: "The distinctive essence of Christian experience lies in the relation between Jesus and the Spirit."[157] Further, for the earliest Christians God was a "living reality," who gave vibrant life to the Church.

19.5. The Earlier Phase of the Renewal or "Charismatic" Movement

(1) *Its rise.* Documentation remains scattered, and, as in Pentecostalism before 1985, much was anecdotal. However, since around 1990 a wealth of more scholarly literature has sprung up. For this early stage, we depend especially on Stanley Burgess (ed.), *The New International Dictionary of Pentecostal and Charismatic Movements,* and on the article "Charismatic Movement" by P. D. Hocken.[158] Although many charismatic exponents use the term "charismatic," we have tried to follow Ives Congar in usually speaking of the Renewal Movement.

It is well recorded that in 1959 Dennis Bennett, Rector of St. Mark's, Van Nuys, California, and Frank Macguire, together with John and Joan Baker, claimed to have received "baptism in the Holy Spirit." By spring 1960, seventy members of St. Mark's had a similar experience. In April 1960 Bennett pro-

---

155. Dunn, *Jesus and the Spirit*, p. 297.

156. Dunn, *Jesus and the Spirit*, p. 338.

157. Dunn, *Jesus and the Spirit*, p. 358.

158. Peter D. Hocken, "Charismatic Movement," in *The New International Dictionary of Pentecostal and Charismatic Movements (NIDPCM)*, ed. Stanley Burgess (Grand Rapids: Zondervan, 2nd ed. 2003), pp. 477-519. Numerous other books are helpful.

claimed this publicly. Nevertheless hostility was expressed from within St. Mark's, and Bennett moved to St. Luke's, Seattle, which in due course became a center of the Movement. I know that, as is claimed, he visited seminaries all over the world, for in the early 1960s I heard him speak at a seminary in Bristol, England, although he did not greatly impress me. In the very early 1960s the Renewal ministry of the long-standing Pentecostal, David du Plessis, also emerged. Some traced the earlier roots of this to Oral Roberts and to his "healing" evangelism in the Holiness Movement of the 1940s and 1950s, but this is where the Renewal Movement and Pentecostalism became intertwined. Strictly, "Renewal" is understood to take place within the "mainline" churches or traditions. In the early 1960s, Jean Stone was a further voice in the spread of the Movement.

In England and the British Isles, many discussed the controversial claims of Michael Harper, a Church of England curate, who founded the Fountain Trust. Many were also influenced by the remarkable book of David Wilkerson in America, *The Cross and the Switchblade* (1963). From 1963, John Collins, Vicar of St. Mark's, Gillingham, Kent, began to promote the Movement. David Watson became known for his work at York; and John Perry, for his work at St. Andrew's, Chorleywood. But in the main, John Stott and most Evangelical and Anglican leaders had strong reservations about the view of sanctification which the Renewal Movement promoted, and found its terminology and aspects of its doctrine surprisingly "unbiblical." In the early years, it became associated with specific figures and parish churches, and with a series of conferences. By 1970, when it entered the Catholic Church, some "high Church" Anglicans, such as John Gunstone, became leading Renewal figures.

In Germany the first major gatherings seemed to begin around 1965, with conferences near Frankfurt. In France it is claimed that Renewal had begun earlier in the Reformed Church. In Holland, David du Plessis led an influential meeting in 1965 in Utrecht. In Belgium influential support came from the Catholic Primate, Cardinal Léon-Joseph Suenens, since at least 1972. Poland remains a strongly Catholic country, and the first Renewal groups probably emerged in about 1975 and 1976 in Warsaw, with the encouragement of the former Pope, then Archbishop of Krakow. In Scandinavia the origins were mainly in the early 1970s, with strong Pentecostal influence. Italy saw its origins in 1970-71, and Spain in 1973-74.

There were said to be stirrings in Brazil in the middle and late 1950s in Baptist circles. By the mid-1960s, Methodists, Presbyterians, and Congregationalists became involved. In Argentina "baptism in the Holy Spirit" emerged among the Open Brethren in 1967. In Chile an Anglican missionary carried the Renewal Movement forward after visiting England in the mid-1960s.

The origins on the African continent are more difficult to trace, not least because often both Christians and non-Christians see life in terms of a struggle against evil spirits, and in many countries there are as many "independent" churches as mainline denominations. North India can look back on a century of Pentecostal missionaries, especially in Calcutta, but the Renewal Movement appears to have emerged first in Mumbai (Bombay), then in Pune (Poona) and Delhi, mainly within the Catholic Church. Matthew Naiekomparambil claimed "baptism in the Spirit" in the early 1970s, and became a leader in the Renewal Movement. In China, the death of Mao Tse-tung provided a measure of freedom, which has allowed the House Church Movement to seek Renewal, but the relation to "mainline" churches remained ambiguous.

The upshot of all this is the conclusion that the Renewal Movement, which began on a small scale in 1959-60, has blossomed into a vast, worldwide global Movement. Rather than nurturing a mutually critical and suspicious relationship with the traditional denominations, both sides have recognized an urgent need for mutual respect and mutual listening. *The problem, however, is how this can be promoted in a way that allows for mutual understanding and respect, together with honest mutual criticism and mutual correction.* This has become one of the most urgent tasks that confronts the credibility and unity of the Church in the world. We echo much of what Yves Congar has said, namely, that while we respect the yearning for fresh springs of the Holy Spirit in a "dry land," we cannot and should not expect that all will become "charismatic." For it is often accompanied by a baggage of "unbiblical" terminology, a populist subculture, and an unthought-through theology of sanctification which cannot simply be swept under the carpet. To admire the commitment and devotion which often follow "baptism in the Spirit" is not merely an idle and formal compliment. Sincerity, on both sides, must be respected. Fortunately "corrections" are voiced *within* major denominations about the *need for renewal and zeal,* and are voiced *within* the Renewal Movement regarding *terminology, subculture, and occasionally theology.* Mutual correction does not involve visible defensiveness if it is truly led by the Holy Spirit. The Renewal Movement was marked in its earlier years, from 1960 to around 1980 or 1985, with a brittleness which it has largely left behind, although the "Third Wave" of the Movement, as we shall see, has tended to reopen old mutual suspicions.

(2) *Consolidation and early assessments on both sides.* Before we discuss this later trend, however, we may follow the Renewal Movement beyond its rise to its *consolidation and development.* The development of the Renewal Movement within the Catholic Church in America owed much to events at Duquesne University, Pittsburgh, and at the University of Notre Dame, Indiana, in 1967. Those involved were influenced by debates which followed the decrees of Vatican II in 1963-65. They saw the outpouring of the Holy Spirit as God's answer to Pope John's prayer for a new Pentecost.

Within the Catholic Renewal Movement, several prominent leaders played a decisive part. Stephen B. Clark (b. 1940) and Ralph Martin (b. 1942) worked together from 1967 onward especially through the Cursillo Movement (the Spanish for "a little course"). Both were prominent leaders. Clark was educated at Yale, Freiburg, and Notre Dame, published *Baptized in the Spirit* (1969), *Spiritual Gifts* (1970), and *Growing in Faith* (1972), and conducted seminars on "Life in the Spirit." He also published *Building Christian Communities* (1972) and in 1982 established the Sword of the Spirit community. Ralph Martin remained a lay leader, and worked with the Sword of the Spirit community through the 1980s. He moved to Brussels to work more closely with Cardinal Suenens. Within the Renewal Movement he is generally regarded as a teacher and a prophet. Clearly conferences, courses, and communities became as important as books.

Among Protestants, Lawrence ("Larry") D. Christenson (b. 1928) became an important Renewal leader among American Lutherans, after graduating from Luther Theological Seminary in St. Paul, Minnesota. In 1974 he organized Lutheran Charismatic Renewal Services and wrote *The Renewal Mind*. Dennis Bennett (1917-91) remained an influential Renewal leader in the Episcopal Church of the United States of America. For twelve years he nurtured Renewal at St. Luke's, Seattle, and was involved in founding what became Episcopal Renewal Ministries. With his second wife, Rita, he published *The Holy Spirit and You* (1971), which became a best-seller, a book on healing (1984), and *How to Pray for Release of the Spirit* (1985).[159] Michael G. Harper (b. 1931) became a leader in Britain, where in 1962 he had been curate (assistant minister) to John Stott at All Souls, Langham Place, London. In 1964 he became General Secretary of the Fountain Trust, in 1966 editing its journal, *Renewal*. He traveled to America and New Zealand in 1965-67, but in 1995 he resigned Anglican orders to join the Greek Orthodox Church.

Meanwhile, opposition grew also. In America the Southern Baptist Convention opposed the Charismatic Renewal Movement, and in England many Protestants experienced either theological resistance or confusion, especially during the 1960s and 1970s. Many became puzzled that although in theory the Renewal Movement still gave a prominent place to the Bible as the Word of God, in practice it seemed as if "promptings of the Spirit" were given a higher authority. Many local churches became split over whether "prophecies" constituted a genuine Word of God, or whether they were a way of giving a special status to the private welling up of subjective convictions, often sincerely held. Many recognized that "prophecy" could in the worst case become a tool for power and control, unless very carefully tested by Scripture and other means.

In 1978 the General Synod of the Church of England expressed the wish "to conserve the new life it [Renewal] has brought to many parishes"; nevertheless

---

159. Dennis and Rita Bennett, *The Holy Spirit and You: A Study Guide to the Spirit-Filled Life* (Eastbourne: Kingsway, 1971).

it asked for a Report to explore "the reasons for this upsurge, to pinpoint the particular distinctive features of spirituality and ethos which the movement presents, and indicate the points of tension which exist with traditional Anglicanism."[160] It also asked for guidance on "how the riches of the movement may be conserved for the good of the Church." From knowing the contributors, I should guess that three or four members would stand with the resolution, while two or three had "Renewal" credentials. Michael Harper was consulted.

The Committee found it difficult at first to define charismatic renewal.[161] "Pentecostal" was considered but rejected because it was associated with a specific denomination.[162] It was a pity that it began so soon with "order and decorum," which is an issue about its culture.[163] On the other hand, "groaning and crying aloud" was the form in which most Anglicans encountered it.[164] Michael Harper's report on the origins of the Renewal Movement accords with our account above. What is most relevant is the comment: "A particular focus of debate about 'baptism in the Spirit' occurred on the staff of the 'Mecca' of evangelism, All Souls, Langham Place. . . . The Rector, John Stott, and some other members of staff . . . were unconvinced, and were concerned that the teaching of the baptism in the Spirit was not thoroughly conformable to Scripture, and would be highly divisive to practice. . . . This . . . marks a milestone in England."[165]

The Report well sums up the key problem, together with the fact that "charismatics had inevitably to adopt a high profile" during the earlier days. James D. G. Dunn's book *Baptism in the Holy Spirit* (1970) and Walter Hollenweger's *The Pentecostals* (1972) addressed some of the issues. Furthermore, more than one tradition within the Church became involved in Renewal. Distinctive music gave the Movement force and distinctiveness, drawn from such sources as *Living Waters* (1974) and *Fresh Sounds* (1976), but at the cost of expressions of a division of musical taste. An attempt at mutual understanding was published in the Evangelical Council's "Gospel and Spirit" (1976).[166] By 1980, the Report states, "The second and third generations of believers in charismatic parishes may often welcome their spiritual inheritance without feeling the same necessity to exhibit 'tongues' and 'prophecy' on all possible occasions."[167] These were too often simply "recognition-symbols."

160. General Synod Report (Chaired by Colin Craston), *The Charismatic Movement in the Church of England* (London: Church Information Office, 1981).

161. Synod Report, *Charismatic Movement*, p. 1.

162. Synod Report, *Charismatic Movement*, p. 2.

163. Synod Report, *Charismatic Movement*, p. 4.

164. Synod Report, *Charismatic Movement*, pp. 6-7.

165. Synod Report, *Charismatic Movement*, p. 7.

166. Report, "Gospel and Spirit," *The Churchman*, April 1977; cf. James I. Packer, "Theological Reflections on the Charismatic Movement," *The Churchman* 94 (1980).

167. Synod Report, *The Charismatic Movement*, p. 11.

The Report then explores a number of specific case studies of parishes. The upshot may be to distinguish between the theological, practical, and subcultural. (a) *Theologically,* many welcome the genuine emphasis on Renewal, but have reservations about: (i) the *self-advertising prominence* of the Holy Spirit, who is to testify above all not to himself, but to Christ; (ii) "Is Christian initiation," the Report asks, "a one-stage or a two-stage affair?"[168] Pentecostalism is usually firm on this; but the Report suggests that in the approach toward 1980 "the renewal movement perhaps moved." However, the underlying issue is whether with the "Holiness" tradition (hardly known in England) sanctification and consecration constitute an *event,* or a *process,* often accompanied by *struggle and temptation.* (iii) The stubborn point remains: is "baptism in the Spirit" used *in the New Testament* for the very genuine experience of "fullness of the Spirit" or openness to the Spirit, as often described by Renewal practitioners? The balance between Bible and Spirit does not quite come under this list of *theological* points, since Renewal exponents claim to be fully "biblical." It does, however, become a practical issue.

(b) *Practical Issues* largely revolve around "prophecy." Until the nineteenth century, such writers as Aquinas and Calvin assumed that "prophecy" included *preaching,* as well as perhaps more *occasional* "special" revelation. The practical problem is that "prophecy" is so often not *anti*-biblical, but *extra*-biblical, with little to test it but the consensus of a community. Hence we cannot too easily blame those who suggest that in *practice* (not in theory) the authority of prophecy sometimes appears to be more primary than that of the Bible. The debate, however, remains an open one, with advocates on both sides.

(c) *Cultural or subcultural.* We shall note that, in spite of his strong sympathies for Renewal, Cardinal Congar has suggested that the Renewal Movement cannot expect its gifts to be for *all,* since many *are deeply uncomfortable* with the visible *manifestations* of such phenomena as hand waving, popular music and bands, or entirely "free" prayer, rather than drawing on historic liturgy. The notion of "recognition symbols" raises its head when one compares the types of hymns or songs often used. Lord Coggan, previous Archbishop of Canterbury, called them "ditties," and lamented their omission of strong theological themes about God in favor of too many subjective themes about "me."

It is a pity that such reservations intrude, for the devotion and outreach or evangelism of the Renewal Movement are usually to be welcomed by churches. However, the Movement has also become divisive. This constitutes a contradiction in terms if it is really prompted (in all its phenomena) by the Holy Spirit of unity and continuity. We shall consider its further fruition in the twenty-first century, when this Movement broadened further. Often in this latest phase Pentecostals seem more ready to engage in serious self-criticism and growth than

---

168. Synod Report, *The Charismatic Movement,* p. 20.

the Renewal Movement, with its "Third Wave" and its effects. Meanwhile, there are some encouraging signs of mutual dialogue and mutual criticism, notably in such works as those which we shall note by Donald Carson in America, and by Tom Smail in Britain.

20

Three Pentecostal or Renewal New Testament Scholars:
Fee, Stronstad, and Turner

Since the Pentecostal and Renewal movements have become so strong in numbers, influence, and global expansion, we need to select those representatives of greatest scholarly reputation and integrity. Clearly Gordon Fee in North America and Max Turner in England rank high in scholarly reputation. For a third, we considered including either Roger Stronstad or R. P. Menzies. But we could include only one of them, for reasons of length and space, and Turner wrote, "Roger Stronstad's . . . work marked the entrance of Pentecostal writers to Lukan scholarship."[1] At the time of writing not many Renewal or Pentecostal writers are established New Testament specialists, and if we had broadened the net such writers as Russell Spittler and Frank Macchia might have been included. However, Stronstad is the most polemical of our three scholars, while Fee and Turner have wider concerns and present a good case for Renewal.

20.1. Gordon Fee

Gordon Fee (b. 1934) was born in Ashland, Oregon, and was educated at Seattle Pacific University and the University of Southern California. He taught at Gordon-Conwell Theological Seminary and at Regent College, Vancouver. He wrote a major commentary on 1 Corinthians and more recently *God's Empowering Presence*.[2] He is explicitly a Pentecostal, the son of an Assemblies of God minister, but also questions the Assemblies of God's Article 7, concerning

---

1. Max Turner, *Power from on High: The Spirit in Israel's Restoration and Witness in Luke-Acts*, JPTSS 9 (Sheffield: Sheffield Academic, 1996), p. 62.

2. Gordon Fee, *God's Empowering Presence: The Holy Spirit in the Letters of Paul* (Peabody, MA: Hendrickson, and Carlisle: Paternoster, 1994); and Fee, *The First Epistle to the Corinthians*, NICNT (Grand Rapids: Eerdmans, 1987).

baptism in the Holy Spirit. If a group of Pentecostals are asked to name their most impressive scholars, most will include Fee among their top one or two. He is neither defensive nor insular. In a recent interview he expressed a special debt to the New Testament theology of N. T. Wright, former Bishop of Durham.

In his Introduction Fee states that he wishes to emphasize the Holy Spirit as a Person and as "the personal presence of God himself."[3] Whether we see "a human face in the Spirit" is not quite as easy to assert or to defend as the principle that God is seen in the *human* face of *Christ.* As Eberhard Jüngel observes, "God defined himself as love on the cross of Jesus"; God becomes thinkable, conceivable, and credible *in Jesus Christ.*[4] Fee would not deny this, but whether God is to be revealed equally concretely through "seeing" the Person of the Spirit seems at first sight more controversial, since above all the Spirit witnesses *to Christ.* He effaces himself in the manner identified by Fison, Taylor, and Congar.

This, however, is one of my very few points of questioning Fee's work. Indeed, he rightly states, "Person, Presence and Power . . . are what the Holy Spirit is to the Apostle Paul."[5] Another query, however, might concern his exposition of 1 Thess. 5:19-20. Fee sees "quench not the Spirit" as referring to "charismatic manifestations."[6] But he does not discuss whether this alludes to a wider frame of reference, as many of the Church Fathers suggest. Athanasius, for example, sees the meaning as a warning that ingratitude, impurity, or lack of holiness may impede the Spirit's presence and work (*Letters,* 4:4; *NPNF,* vol. 4, p. 514). John Chrysostom understands 1 Thess. 5:19-20 as referring to suppressing the Holy Spirit's illumination (*Homily on 1 Thessalonians,* 11; *NPNF,* vol. 13, p. 370). This is also Augustine's view (*On the Psalms,* 77:4; *NPNF,* ser. 1, vol. 8, p. 361). Thomas Aquinas understands "prophecy," as we have noted, as "divine doctrine," and prophets as *"preachers."*[7] John Calvin sees "prophetic teaching" as "the interpretation of Scripture properly applied to the people present."[8] These writers may not be right about *all* prophecy or action of the Spirit; but neither is this *always* spontaneous and "charismatic." This verse may have in mind any who are weary of hearing the Word of God, in more than one form.

Fee gives a very good account of 1 Corinthians, as we might expect, including its "Christocentric" character and its strong emphasis on grace.[9] Genuine

---

3. Fee, *God's Empowering Presence,* pp. 5-6.

4. Eberhard Jüngel, *God as the Mystery of the World* (Edinburgh: T&T Clark, 1983), pp. 220-21; cf. pp. 203, 224, 229, and 105-396.

5. Fee, *God's Empowering Presence,* p. 8.

6. Fee, *God's Empowering Presence,* p. 59.

7. Thomas Aquinas, *Commentary on 1 Thessalonians and Philippians* (Albany: Magi Books, 1969), p. 52.

8. John Calvin, *1 and 2 Thessalonians* (Wheaton, IL: Crossway Commentary, 1999), p. 60.

9. Fee, *God's Empowering Presence,* pp. 85-86.

power is from the Spirit, not of human cleverness.[10] He might have stressed the transcendence of the Holy Spirit in the Greek *to pneuma to ek tou theou* in 2:12.[11] But 2:10-16 is well expounded. Fee misses an opportunity to discuss *charismata* as *settled habits and dispositions* in 7:7, with Paul's comment about the Christian's attitude to *celibacy* as a *charisma*.[12] But he rightly stresses the Trinitarian nature of 12:4-6.[13] He is excellent on the *charismata* of 1 Cor. 12:8-10, where *logos sophias . . . logos gnōseōs* is best translated not as "word of wisdom" or "word of knowledge," but as "the message of (Christ crucified as God's) true wisdom" and the "message of knowledge" in the sense of interpreting the meaning of Scripture.[14]

Surprisingly, Fee thinks that "gifts of healing" need "little comment."[15] But the plural has rightly suggested to many commentators either a generic "*different kinds* of healings" (at least from the time of T. C. Edwards), or at least "natural and supernatural healings." Prophecy "consisted of spontaneous, Spirit-inspired messages." But this may *include* both spontaneous and prepared revelations, since the Holy Spirit may convey *both* sudden and unmediated perceptions of a revelation, *and, equally, work through the mind* to provide inferences from a revelation or expansions of it.[16] However, Fee is undoubtedly correct in asserting: "There is no Pauline evidence for the phenomenon known in contemporary circles as 'personal prophecy' whereby someone prophesies over another as to very personal matters in their lives."[17] He is also constructive on the gift of discerning between prophecies.

Fee's translation "different kinds of tongues" is helpful. He acknowledges that the literature on this subject "is immense," and cites a small selection of both Pentecostal and traditional literature. He does not specify one type, other than seeing tongues as "visible and extraordinary manifestations of the Spirit."[18] This caution is probably wise. In my commentary I cite numerous theories, including a basic six.[19] Fee rules out "ecstasy" on the basis of 1 Cor. 14:27-28, as well as speaking "a known earthly language." His comment on "interpreting of tongues" is also wise, both in excluding "translation" and in asserting "that it may be given *either to the tongues-speaker or another*."[20] *There is*

10. Fee, *God's Empowering Presence*, pp. 91-92.

11. Fee, *God's Empowering Presence*, p. 103.

12. Fee, *God's Empowering Presence*, p. 138.

13. Fee, *God's Empowering Presence*, pp. 162-64.

14. Fee, *God's Empowering Presence*, pp. 166-68.

15. Fee, *God's Empowering Presence*, p. 168.

16. Anthony C. Thiselton, *The First Epistle to the Corinthians: A Commentary on the Greek Text*, NIGTC (Grand Rapids: Eerdmans, 2000), pp. 956-65 and 1128-68.

17. Fee, *God's Empowering Presence*, p. 170.

18. Fee, *God's Empowering Presence*, p. 172.

19. Thiselton, *First Epistle to the Corinthians*, pp. 970-89; cf. pp. 1094-1130.

20. Fee, *God's Empowering Presence*, p. 173.

no Greek word for someone (tis) *in 1 Cor. 14:3,* which suggests *the probability of the former.*

On 1 Cor. 12:13 Fee is less uncomfortable with the *traditional "mainstream"* (non-Pentecostal) interpretation of "baptized in one Spirit" than are most Pentecostals. Like Dunn, he also argues: "One is hard pressed in Paul's letters to find an equation between baptism and the reception of the Spirit."[21] He refers here to Rudolf Schnackenburg as well as to Dunn. In 1 Corinthians 12–14 the *charismata* have value for the whole Church "as one awaits the consummation."[22] In 14:13 he rightly says that "one who speaks in tongues [is] to pray for the gift of interpretation."[23]

2 Cor. 3:8 and 17 receive helpful comments, especially on the background of 3:17 in Exodus. The section on Gal. 3:1-5 also receives entirely useful comments about Paul's converts' initial reception of the Spirit "predicated on faith" and the gospel of Christ.[24] Fee also handles Rom. 8:1-11 with care and insight. He carefully disentangles a complex syntax to conclude that the righteousness of Christ is the basis for the Spirit's indwelling the believers.[25] On Rom. 8:12-15 Fee echoes Fison's maxim: "By the Spirit's help they are to *'become what they are'*" (my italics).[26] On Rom. 8:26-27 he asks whether "inexpressible sighs" might refer, at least in part, to *tongues* (as Frank Macchia understands it), noting many parallels; but he also singles out the Spirit's praying as the main point of the verses.[27] Finally, Fee includes a careful exposition of relevant passages in the Captivity Epistles, including that in Eph. 1:13-14 (which is related to 2 Cor. 1:21-22), where the Spirit is again the pledge of God's ownership and of our future inheritance.[28]

Clearly apart from minor points over which any two New Testament specialists may well disagree, this 800-page work shows careful exegesis and an approach which differs little from that of well-informed Pauline scholars, allowing also for its welcome attention, where relevant, to the Holy Spirit. This coheres with a recent article on Gordon Fee by Julian Lukins in *Charisma*.[29] Lukins calls Fee "the first Bible scholar of the modern Pentecostal movement." He recounts Fee as saying, however: "I don't think of myself as a Pentecostal scholar; I think of myself as a scholar who happens to be a lifelong Pentecostal."

---

21. Fee, *God's Empowering Presence,* p. 179; cf. Rudolf Schnackenburg, *Baptism in the Thought of Paul* (Oxford: Blackwell, 1964), p. 83; and J. D. G. Dunn, *Baptism in the Holy Spirit* (London: SCM, 1970), pp. 199-202.

22. Fee, *God's Empowering Presence,* p. 199.

23. Fee, *God's Empowering Presence,* p. 223.

24. Fee, *God's Empowering Presence,* p. 381; cf. pp. 381-89.

25. Fee, *God's Empowering Presence,* pp. 544-48.

26. Fee, *God's Empowering Presence,* p. 559.

27. Fee, *God's Empowering Presence,* pp. 578-86.

28. Fee, *God's Empowering Presence,* pp. 668-72.

29. Julian Lukins, "A Professor with Spirit," *Charisma,* September 1, 2010, pp. 1-3.

He acknowledges that he has sometimes faced "an uphill battle in Pentecostal circles," where many are "wary of theological endeavors." Fee concludes: "Having a Ph.D. has not stopped me from being Spirit-filled." He has strong reservations about whether Paul used "baptism in the Spirit" in the way in which it is usually used in Pentecostal and Charismatic circles. But, as we have seen, he is more than happy to use the term "Spirit-filled," with which many Christians would wholly agree.

20.2. Roger Stronstad

In 1984 *Stronstad* wrote *The Charismatic Theology of Saint Luke,* and in 1999 *The Prophethood of All Believers.*[30] He began with the polemical statement: "It still remains a commonplace to read Luke through Pauline glasses. James D. G. Dunn was guilty of this in his 1970 benchmark study *Baptism in the Holy Spirit.* . . . In spite of significant criticism . . . some two decades later he still insists 'that the pneumatology [Pentecostals love that ugly word!] of Luke is essentially one with the pneumatology of Paul.'"[31] This reminds us that most Pentecostals find in Luke-Acts what many claim is virtually a canon within the canon, in contrast to the Reformers' allegedly giving privilege to Paul. This renders our discussion of Stronstad and Turner more challenging than our dialogue with Gordon Fee on Paul.

The central thesis of Stronstad's book (first developed from a thesis at Regent College, Vancouver) is that the Holy Spirit in Acts is most closely associated with "vocation," *not with salvation.* He admits: "I have consistently interpreted the problematic, ambiguous texts vocationally rather than soteriologically. . . . The gift of the Spirit of prophecy . . . which was received by Cornelius is identical to the vocational gift of the Spirit which was poured out on the disciples on the day of Pentecost."[32] Chapter 1 on interpreting and applying Luke-Acts is a key part of the argument. Much of Luke-Acts is *narrative* (*diēgēsis,* Luke 1:1, or *logos,* Acts 1:1). Often report becomes "historical narrative." Its center, or its "paradigm," Stronstad believes, is "selective history" in which what Luke *omits* is as important as what he includes. Its context in the Greco-Roman world is an interpretative key, as are its "multiplex purpose" and the Spirit's driving ahead God's plan of salvation history.[33]

---

30. Roger Stronstad, *The Charismatic Theology of Saint Luke* (Peabody, MA: Hendrickson, 1984); and Stronstad, *The Prophethood of All Believers: A Study in Luke's Charismatic Theology,* JPTSS 16 (Sheffield: Sheffield Academic Press, 1999).

31. Stronstad, *The Prophethood of All Believers,* p. 10; James D. G. Dunn, "Baptism in the Holy Spirit: A Response to Pentecostal Scholarship in Luke-Acts," *JPT* 3 (1993): 3-27.

32. Stronstad, *Prophethood of All Believers,* p. 11.

33. Stronstad, *Prophethood of All Believers,* pp. 18-27.

Few New Testament specialists would so far disagree. Whether the center-piece is also the anointing by the Spirit of Jesus, Stephen, Philip, Peter, and Paul would meet with varying responses. The *anointing of Jesus* in Luke is uncontroversial, although the emphasis in J. E. Fison, C. K. Barrett, and in Ives Congar on Messianic *kenōsis* is missing.[34] Paul also received the designation "prophet" in the work of K. O. Sandnes.[35] But it is when Stronstad discusses "applying the paradigm" that we begin to suspect a circular argument. When he selects "evangelical" opponents (mainly John Stott and the Pentecostal Gordon Fee), his major question now becomes: "Granted that most of Luke-Acts is *narrative*, and it provides the major source for Pentecostalists, how are we to interpret and *apply* biblical narrative to the present?" (my italics). He attacks (quite brutally) Stott and Fee for arguing that narrative yields reports, not didactic material.[36] Admittedly he is correct to call this theological history or theological narrative, as I. Howard Marshall has well argued.[37] However, he calls the approach of even Fee "Hermeneutics of Denial," in contrast to his own "Hermeneutics of Affirmation."

This rumbustiously polemical style may be appreciated in some parts of North America, but will not win over British readers. Why does he not engage with the great narrative theorists, who could offer something of what he seeks? My Pentecostal doctoral graduate Yongnan (Sarah) Jeon Ahn from Korea also discusses "Pentecostal Experience as a 'Pentecostal' Experience" in her doctoral dissertation; but in considering Acts, she dialogues with Martin Dibelius, Hans Conzelmann, and Ernst Haenchen, and their theories of an "idealized" church in Acts; and with Joseph Fitzmyer, Luke T. Johnson, and above all Paul Ricoeur (as well as R. T. Menzies and Max Turner) on narrative in Acts.[38] Where is such dialogue or engagement in Stronstad? He does not allude to some earlier in-depth discussion. I have also carefully discussed the implications of narrative genre in my *New Horizons in Hermeneutics*.[39]

Stronstad is entirely correct about examples of "fillings" of the Holy Spirit in Luke. He gives at least nine good examples from Luke-Acts.[40] He modifies his earlier first impression by a more careful discussion of "applying the histori-

---

34. C. K. Barrett, *The Holy Spirit and the Gospel Tradition* (London: SPCK, 1958), pp. 158-59; J. E. Fison, *The Blessing of the Holy* Spirit (London and New York: Longmans, Green, 1950), pp. 92-102, and throughout; on Congar, see below, Chapter 21.

35. K. O. Sandnes, *Paul — One of the Prophets? A Contribution to the Apostle's Self-Understanding*, WUNT 2.43 (Tübingen: Mohr, 1991).

36. Stronstad, *Prophethood of All Believers*, pp. 28-30.

37. I. Howard Marshall, "The Present State of Lukan Studies," *Themelios* 14 (1989): 52-57; and Marshall, *Luke: Historian and Theologian* (Exeter: Paternoster, 1970).

38. Yongnan Jeon Ahn, "A Formulation of Pentecostal Hermeneutics" (Ph.D. diss., University of Nottingham, 2002), pp. 139-70 and 231-33.

39. Anthony C. Thiselton, *New Horizons in Hermeneutics* (London: HarperCollins; rpt. Carlisle: Paternoster, and Grand Rapids: Zondervan, 1992), pp. 351-73, 479-507, 566-75, and 604-11.

40. Stronstad, *Prophethood of All Believers*, pp. 25-28.

cally particular."[41] At first this looks promising, as when he excludes application of time-span lapses or chronological gaps, and the laying on of hands. But when he comes to something crucial, he exempts it from the discussion of criteria and norms. He states, "Speaking in tongues . . . is not a practice like church government, or even *celebrating the Lord's Supper. . . . It is a gift from God, and not a human rite [as if the Lord's Supper were not!]. Therefore it is inappropriate to include it in a discussion about applying practices within the early Church to a contemporary Christian practice*" (my italics).[42] In other words, speaking in tongues is not only exempt from hermeneutics; worse, speaking in tongues is more "of God" than the ordained sacraments of the Lord's Supper and water baptism.

Much in the remaining chapters 2–7 is good and acceptable. It is true that Luke sees Jesus as the eschatological prophet.[43] But Stronstad seems consistently to underplay complementary views, for example, "This is My Son," as if this were an either/or.[44] This is a case where more argument and less assertion on the part of the writer would have given his work more weight. The saddest part is the author's apparent lack of awareness that he cannot read *everything* in Scripture on the basis of an arbitrarily *selected paradigm*. Even if he thinks that others do this with a different "paradigm," two wrongs do not make a "right." Some might imagine that this is a case of "Pentecostal hermeneutics." But I have orally discussed hermeneutics with so many Pentecostals that I am not convinced that they always involve such arbitrariness. His work on Stephen, Barnabas, Agabus, Peter, and Paul may be useful; but overstatement is seldom the object of reflection.[45] This work reminds me once more of the comment in the *Journal of Pentecostal Theology* about a major scholar: "He is not one of us."

20.3. Max Turner

Max Turner is Emeritus Professor of New Testament at the London School of Theology (originally the London Bible College) since his retirement from teaching in 2011. We should note that Turner is not a Pentecostal, but is a major writer explicitly in the Renewal Movement. He has published two books which deserve our attention, not least for their wide reading and generosity of spirit. The first of the two books on the Holy Spirit, *The Holy Spirit and Spiritual Gifts Then and Now* arose from an invitation by the Theological School to provide a half-module on this subject. Chapters 2, 4, and 5 depend heavily on Turner's ar-

41. Stronstad, *Prophethood of All Believers*, pp. 30-32.
42. Stronstad, *Prophethood of All Believers*, pp. 33-34.
43. Stronstad, *Prophethood of All Believers*, pp. 35-39.
44. Stronstad, *Prophethood of All Believers*, pp. 41-44.
45. Stronstad, *Prophethood of All Believers*, pp. 85-101.

ticle in *The Dictionary of Jesus and the Gospels*.[46] Chapters 12–20 are a revision of an article first published in 1985.[47] But in addition to its didactic value, it also draws on a mass of meticulous research from the mid-1980s to 1995. On the other hand, *Power from on High* is fundamentally a research volume of 500 pages on the Holy Spirit in Luke-Acts. Its first chapter engages with Hermann Gunkel (1888), H. Leisegang (1919 and 1921), Friedrich Büchsel (1926), and Hans von Baer (1926), and it interacts with more recent major writers in the rest of the book. The book draws on very wide reading, as can be seen from the impressive bibliography and index.

In *The Holy Spirit and Spiritual Gifts* Turner considers the Old Testament and Intertestamental Judaism, concluding that the Spirit is "largely understood as 'the Spirit of prophecy' enabling revelation, wisdom and inspired speech."[48] This largely accords with Lampe's approach, while Eduard Schweizer and Robert Menzies polarize the debate to exclude soteriology. Turner argues that even in Judaism the Spirit gives *life* to the community, as well as "empowerment." Thus even "wind" or "breath" sometimes denotes "vitality."[49] Although he questions whether in the Old Testament and in Judaism the Spirit is a "personal" being, the Spirit is so closely related to God that the verse "They rebelled and grieved his holy Spirit" (Isa. 63:10) might naturally refer to God himself. Indeed, to Jewish Wisdom and in Philo this might mean "God's own 'mind' or 'will' at work" (Isa. 30:1-2; 40:12-14; Wis. 7–9; Philo, *On the Creation of the World* 135, 144; *On the Special Laws* 4:123; *That the Worse Attacks the Better*, 80–81, 83–84; *On Noah's Work as Planter* 18; *Allegorical Interpretation* 1:142).[50] Exceptions might include Num. 11:17, 29, where Moses' endowment is shared with the seventy elders.

Naturally enough, the Old Testament writers looked forward to an eschatological gift of the Spirit to *all* Israel (Joel 2:28; cf. Isa. 32:15; 44:3; Ezek. 39:29). "Spirit of prophecy" remains the prominent theme. In the period of Judaism this becomes pronounced (*Jubilees* 31:12; Philo, *On Flight and Finding* 186), and is related to revelation and guidance.[51] Turner includes a number of rabbinical and targumic sources, for example, *Tosefta Pesaḥim* 2:15. Further "From Philo's perspective charismatic wisdom is similar to charismatic revelation," which explains why the "Spirit of Prophecy" gives "wisdom."[52] The unaided human

---

46. Joel Green, Scot McKnight, and I. Howard Marshall (eds.), *Dictionary of Jesus and the Gospels* (Leicester: Inter-Varsity Press and Downers Grove, IL: InterVarsity Press, 1992), pp. 341-51.

47. Max Turner, "Spiritual Gifts Then and Now," *Vox Evangelica* 15 (1985): 7-64.

48. Max Turner, *The Holy Spirit and Spiritual Gifts Then and Now* (Carlisle: Paternoster, 1996), p. xii.

49. Turner, *Holy Spirit*, p. 2.

50. Turner, *Holy Spirit*, p. 3.

51. Turner, *Holy Spirit*, p. 6.

52. Turner, *Holy Spirit*, p. 9.

mind cannot perceive this alone (cf. *4 Ezra* 14:22; Sir. 39:6). Classic Old Testament allusions include the example of Balaam (Num. 23–24) and Saul (1 Sam. 10 and 19:20, 23). Against the popular impression, Turner insists that after the last canonical books the Spirit of prophecy was not "withdrawn, but 'rare.'"[53] He offers a critique of Schweizer, Menzies, and Stronstad *for their overly exclusive either-or on the polarization between the Spirit of prophecy and the Spirit of salvation,* as we also have suggested.[54] Turner asserts: "Judaism did attribute miracles of power to 'the Spirit of Prophecy.'"[55] His accumulation of evidence from Jewish writings is impressive. This includes Qumran.

At the beginning of Luke's Gospel evidence for the Spirit of prophecy is not difficult to find. Elizabeth, Zechariah, Mary, and John the Baptist fall into this category. Davidic hopes are partly drawn from Isa. 11:1-4, and allusions to the Son of God are fulfillments of Ps. 2:7 and 2 Sam. 7:11-14. Turner is right to argue that the Messianic temptations, which follow his baptism, test his vocation. Turner rightly emphasizes that the temptations are *vocational.* He might have spelled out more clearly, however, their specifically *Messianic* nature. He concedes that the Spirit gives him "messianic empowering"; but they are specifically *Messianic temptations.* Will the Messiah take the easier way of trying to do God's will by popularity, by use of the miraculous, or by "evil that good may come"?[56] His use of the Exodus theme and the Strong Man Bound seems right.

Turner has some excellent comments on the Holy Spirit's being "*the driving force within Lucan salvation history,*" and the Spirit's legitimizing the mission in Acts.[57] He begins to draw a contrast between the role of the Spirit in Luke's Gospel as "the Spirit of prophecy" and his role in Acts as "empowering for witness."[58] He admits, with other writers, that Acts shows more interest in the Church and community than in the renewal of the individual. But in the onward movement of salvation history and the outreach of the Church, the Spirit may equip specific individuals for specific tasks. Along with James Dunn, he attacks the ideas of "confirmation" argued by Dix and Thornton. He concludes, "Acts 2:38, 39 paradigmatically associate the gift of the Spirit with conversional faith and baptism; . . . the only passage which postpones the gift of the Spirit to a point discernibly later than Christian baptism is Acts 8:12-17, and 8:16 implies this was exceptional."[59] He adds that Acts 19:1-6 is often *regarded as*

---

53. Turner, *Holy Spirit,* pp. 12-13 and 193-95.

54. R. P. Menzies, *The Development of Early Christian Pneumatology with Special References to Luke-Acts* (Sheffield: Sheffield Academic Press, 1991); and Menzies, *Empowered for Witness* (Sheffield: Sheffield Academic Press, 1994).

55. Turner, *Holy Spirit,* p. 14.

56. Turner, *Holy Spirit,* pp. 29 and 35.

57. Turner, *Holy Spirit,* p. 37 (his italics).

58. Turner, *Holy Spirit,* p. 38.

59. Turner, *Holy Spirit,* p. 45.

a counterexample, but concludes that it is probably not. He generously considers the arguments of Stronstad and Menzies to the contrary.

Like John V. Taylor and J. E. Fison, Turner stresses that "the Spirit has a role in the everyday life of the Christian."[60] But this does exclude "exceptional and powerfully charismatic *intensifications* of ordinary Christian virtues" (his italics).[61] In the Gospel of John Turner recognized the role of *revelation,* and that John nowhere attributes liberating acts of exorcism or healing to the Spirit. He carefully examines John 4:10, 13-14; and 6:32-58, 60-63. He comments, "The supreme revelation of God's wisdom" holds the key; as in 1 Corinthians 1–2 the "offense" is that "Jesus will ascend through the cross."[62] The background of John 3:3 (born from above, *anōthen*) alludes to Ezek. 36:25-27, where the nation's "cleansing" by water is also inspired "by God's indwelling Spirit. . . . 'I will *create* in them a holy spirit' (cf. Ezek. 36:26; Ps. 51:12)."[63] Both the cross and revelation are central in John. The Discourse on the Paraclete (John 14–16) confirms this. Turner writes: "The coming Spirit does not merely *replace* Jesus' presence, but also mediates the presence of the Father and of the glorified Son to the disciple (John 14:16-26)."[64]

On Paul, Turner criticizes F. W. Horn's theory of a three-stage development of teaching about the Spirit. He notes the problem of chronology, where Horn places Galatians in a "middle" stage, but an early dating from Galatians (with the so-called South Galatian theory) "cannot be dismissed so easily"; while if 1 Thessalonians is a "friendship" letter, too much attention cannot be given to 1 Thess. 5:19-21 as Paul's "view" of the Holy Spirit.[65] Again, Menzies is said to pit the "prophecy" aspect against the "salvation" aspect unduly. Turner gives a good account of major Pauline themes: the Spirit and the new covenant (2 Cor. 3); new creation (2 Cor. 3–5); the Spirit of Christ (Rom. 5:12-21; 1 Cor. 15:20-22, 45-49); and the Spirit and the resurrection (1 Cor. 15:42-49). N. T. Wright and I have discussed at length *sōma pneumatikon* (spiritual body), and vigorously argued, as Turner does, that this means a vehicle of being "corresponding to the new creation of the Spirit."[66]

Turner's part 1 concludes with a valuable argument on the "implicitly Trinitarian" nature of New Testament thought about the Spirit. The Spirit is "the

---

60. Turner, *Holy Spirit,* p. 49.

61. Turner, *Holy Spirit,* p. 49.

62. Turner, *Holy Spirit,* p. 65.

63. Turner, *Holy Spirit,* p. 69.

64. Turner, *Holy Spirit,* p. 80.

65. Turner, *Holy Spirit,* pp. 108-9; F. W. Horn, "Holy Spirit," in *The Anchor Bible Dictionary,* ed. D. N. Freedman, 6 vols. (New York: Doubleday, 1992), vol. 3, pp. 265-78; and F. W. Horn, *Das Angeld des Geistes: Studien zur paulinischen Pneumatologie* (Göttingen: Vandenhoeck & Ruprecht, 1992).

66. Turner, *Holy Spirit,* p. 124; Thiselton, *The First Epistle to the Corinthians,* pp. 1271-81; N. T. Wright, *The Resurrection of the Son of God* (London: SPCK, 2003), pp. 347-56.

expansion of God's *own* personality."[67] *Very many writers have too easily slipped into a largely "binitarian" view of the Trinity and the Holy Spirit,* as Arthur Wainwright and some others would rightly agree.[68]

Part 2 of Turner's *The Holy Spirit and Spiritual Gifts Then and Now* considers specifically the "gifts" of the Holy Spirit in relation to the present. It constitutes almost half of the book. He considers primarily but not exclusively the nine gifts of 1 Cor. 12:8-10, together with various meanings of "charismatic gifts." His first subject is prophecy. Like most writers, he sees prophecy as "the application of revealed truth rather than the argumentation of it."[69] Such a definition would include much (but not all) preaching. I should want to find room for a more substantial overlap than Turner, but the difference is one of degree rather than of kind. Turner argues that the Septuagint draws a sharper distinction than the later *koinē* Greek. Yet if prophecy denotes "God's mouthpiece to the people," this was one of the principles suggested to many about the character of good preaching.[70] Turner does allow for both phenomena. He writes, "Alongside the non-invasive type of prophecy . . . there appears to have been a compulsive, charismatic sort of prophecy."[71] The only problem with the word "invasive" is whether it could possibly imply a dualism between what charismatics call "supernatural working" and "natural processes." The Holy Spirit was just as active in inspiring Paul's reasoning and argumentation as some "prophecy" in Acts, just as he is in directing sermon preparation as much as, or sometimes more than, "spontaneous" delivery.

Ultimately Turner recognizes this. He agrees that the relation between *prophētēs* and phenomena in the churches is complex. He agrees with Wayne Grudem, David Aune, and Christopher Forbes that probably "Paul did not anticipate 'ecstatic' . . . types of prophecy (not even behind 1 Cor. 12:3)."[72] His strongest argument is that Paul placed "prophets" above teachers and second only to apostles in 1 Cor. 12:28-29; but this still may have included *applied* preaching.

I am not entirely convinced that Turner fully answers Thomas W. Gillespie, who, with Ulrich Müller and David Hill, allows room for prophecy as pastorally applied preaching. But perhaps both Gillespie and Turner in the end argue for inclusive understanding. Gillespie concludes: "The task of the prophets, as Paul understands it, is to explicate through divine revelation, and the implications,

---

67. Turner, *Holy Spirit*, p. 171; cf. pp. 169-83.

68. Turner, *Holy Spirit*, p. 169; cf. p. 170, and Arthur W. Wainwright, *The Trinity in the New Testament* (London: SPCK, 1962), pp. 199-234.

69. Turner, *Holy Spirit*, p 185; quoted from J. I. Packer, *Keep in Step with the Spirit* (Leicester: Inter-Varsity Press, 1984), p. 215.

70. Turner, *Holy Spirit*, p. 191.

71. Turner, *Holy Spirit*, p. 192.

72. Turner, *Holy Spirit*, p. 203.

theological and behavioral, of the apostolic kerygma (1 Cor. 15:3b-8)."[73] He also emphasizes its reflective nature. David Hill adds, "The proclamation of the prophet is *pastoral preaching* which by its very nature offers guidance and instruction to the community."[74] In his volume *New Testament Prophecy* Hill defines a Christian prophet as one *"who functions within the Church, occasionally or regularly, as a divinely called and divinely inspired speaker who receives intelligible and authoritative messages which he is impelled to deliver publicly in oral or written form."*[75] I have supported these views in my commentary on 1 Corinthians, and understand 1 Cor. 14:25 to allude to the preaching of the gospel, which involves the hearer in perceiving judgment as well as grace.[76]

There is not a vast difference between Turner and Gillespie. All of us agree that prophecy is for edification and exhortation and comfort.[77] *Controversy* concerns (a) whether *applied biblical and gospel exposition* and *proclamation* are *primary* or *secondary* to *specific revelations about people* or *groups;* and, secondly, (b) whether the Spirit may provide revelation and prophecy *primarily through reflection and sustained discourse as well as sometimes a more "free," intuitive and spontaneous burst of a shorter utterance,* or whether *"spontaneous," staccato "words" or messages are primary, as well as a longer, more reflective discourse on occasion.* Both recognize that the two overlap, but on which is Paul's primary emphasis? I am convinced that in 1 Corinthians 14 prophecy primarily denotes preaching the gospel, not private disclosures about, or private messages to, an individual. If the latter occurred, we should need much convincing that it was genuine.

With regard to Christian tradition in 1 Thess. 5:20, "Do not despise the words of prophets," we have already seen that many of the Church Fathers suggest a broad interpretation. (1) Tertullian sees this primarily as an exhortation to purity.[78] (2) Athanasius views it similarly as a warning against unholy deeds.[79] (3) Ambrosiaster says that prophecy *could* mean biblical exposition.[80] (4) Augustine sees prophecy as explanatory exposition, which is like a lantern.[81]

---

73. Thomas W. Gillespie, *The First Theologians: A Study in Early Christian Prophecy* (Grand Rapids: Eerdmans, 1994), p. 262.

74. David Hill, "Christian Prophets as Teachers or Instructors in the Church," in *Prophetic Vocation in the New Testament and Today,* ed. Johannes Panagopoulos, NovTSup 45 (Leiden: Brill, 1977), p. 114 (his italics); cf. pp. 108-30.

75. David Hill, *New Testament Prophecy* (London: Marshall, Morgan & Scott, 1979), pp. 8-9 (his italics).

76. Thiselton, *The First Epistle to the Corinthians,* pp. 1127-30; see also 956-65 and 1128-68.

77. Gillespie, *The First Theologians,* p. 141; Turner, *Holy Spirit,* pp. 205, 210, and 217.

78. Tertullian, *Against Marcion,* 5:15; *ANF,* vol. 3, p. 462.

79. Athanasius, *Letters,* 4:4; *NPNF,* ser. 2, vol. 4, p. 514.

80. Ambrosiastri qui dicitur, *Commentarius in Epistolas Paulinas* (Vindobonae: Hoelder-Pichler-Tempsky, 1969), vol. 3, p. 232.

81. Augustine, *On the Psalms,* on Ps. 77:4; *NPNF,* ser. 1, vol. 8, p. 361.

(5) Thomas Aquinas asserts: "Prophesying . . . may be understood as divine doctrine. . . . Those who explain divine doctrine are called prophets. . . . Do not despise . . . preachers."[82] (6) John Calvin rejects "foretelling the future." He writes, "'Prophecies' mean the art of interpreting Scripture; a prophet is the interpreter of the will of God."[83] (7) Matthew Henry says: "By prophesying, here understand the preaching of the word, interpreting and applying the Scripture; we must not despise preaching. . . . We must search the Scriptures."[84] (8) John Wesley, whom many claim to be an inspiration for Pentecostalism, writes: "'Prophesyings,' that is, preaching, for the Apostle is not speaking of extraordinary gifts."[85] To be fair, three writers or sources may think otherwise. John Cassian (fifth century) is ambiguous about "things heavenly," which does not tell us much.[86] Matthew Poole speaks of "extraordinary gifts in primitive times."[87] J. B. Lightfoot refers to "unchastened enthusiasm in the first flush of their devotion to the Gospel."[88]

I find Turner's comments on these gifts "today" on the whole helpful and informative. As someone well versed in linguistics, he is especially informative on "Tongues Speech Today."[89] Curiously, the one chapter about which I have most reservation is that on prophecy. I need not repeat what I have already said. But I must add a new point. Whereas the other gifts tend to enrich the church, this gift *may* become an exercise in power, control, and easy deception, guiding a local church or community into arbitrary paths. I think that Deut. 18:20 should be placed as a banner in such churches: "If any prophet . . . who presumes to speak in my name a word that I have not commanded the prophet to speak — that prophet shall die." Turner is simply *inadequate on the constant danger of mistaken prophecy and the urgent need for testing* in this chapter. Yet he does refer to such episodes as that of those who took it upon themselves to prophesy that David Watson would not die of cancer, when the reverse occurred. Something like Walter Moberly, *Prophecy and Discernment* (2006), is required.[90]

In other respects, Turner is informative when he describes aspects of the phenomena of prophecy today. He begins with a dissertation by Mark J. Cart-

82. Thomas Aquinas, *Commentary on St. Paul's First Letter to the Thessalonians and the Letter to the Philippians* (Albany: Magi Books, 1969), p. 52.

83. Calvin, *1 and 2 Thessalonians*, p. 60.

84. Matthew Henry, *Concise Commentary* (CD ROM, Bible Truth Forum) on 1 Thess. 5:20.

85. John Wesley, *Notes on the New Testament* (CD ROM, Bible Truth Forum) on 1 Thess. 5:20.

86. John Cassian, *The Second Conference of Abbot Isaac*, 12; *NPNF*, ser. 2, vol. 11, p. 409.

87. Matthew Poole, *Commentary on the Holy Bible* (London: Banner of Truth, 1963), p. 751.

88. Joseph B. Lightfoot, *Notes on the Epistles of St. Paul* (London: Macmillan, 1895), p. 82.

89. Turner, *Holy Spirit*, pp. 303-14.

90. R. W. L. Moberly, *Prophecy and Discernment* (Cambridge: Cambridge University Press, 2006), esp. pp. 169-254.

ledge, who has now published several books on tongues and charismatic phe-nomena, and discusses the *oracular nature of prophecy*. This, of course, has a flip side, because, as Wolfhart Pannenberg as well as Günther Bornkamm point out, Paul deliberately *avoided an oracular mode of discourse* and used *rea-soning and argument*, although it took him very much more trouble. No less worrying, however, is the use of "pictures, . . . dreams or visions, . . . a 'word,' . . . 'impulses.'"[91] As a writer on linguistics, he would surely know Ludwig Wittgenstein's later philosophy of language. A major theme in the later Wittgenstein concerns *the limits and ambiguity of ostensive definition:* "A pic-ture of the object comes before the child's mind when it hears the word," but it can be *variously interpreted:* "Uttering a word is like striking a note on the key-board of the imagination."[92] Such exclamations as "Water!" or "Away" can de-note a host of possibilities in terms of content and use. "Water" may mean: "Don't walk here; it is marshy and wet." Or it may just mean: "Would you like a glass of water?" Or: "If you come here, your thirst can be quenched and you can be refreshed."[93]

In early years I considered the example "Poison!" It may mean: "Don't drink this; it is harmful"; or "I have been poisoned, avenge me"; or it can mean "You have put sugar in my tea." Wittgenstein observes: "An ostensive definition can be variously interpreted in *every* case" (his italics).[94] We see an object: Wittgenstein urges, "Point to a piece of paper. — And now point to its shape — now to its colour — now to its number (that sounds queer) — How did you do it?"[95] He concludes, "Naming is so far not a move in a language-game — any more than putting a piece in its place on the board is a move in chess. . . . *Noth-ing* has so far been done when a thing has been named."[96] Yet "prophets" seem prepared to move congregations to major activities on the strength of a picture or word which may point, at whim, in any of several directions. "Pictures" fare no better. What matters is how a picture is *applied,* and this requires interpreta-tion and cognitive reflection. Elsewhere Wittgenstein speculates a picture of a boxer. Depending on how we interpret the picture, it may mean "Don't fight like this," or "Fight like this."

We have already noted that Hobbes's maxim that "God spoke to me in a dream" *can* simply mean "I dreamed that God spoke to me." Logically they are equivalent. In his *Zettel* Wittgenstein explores the perplexity caused by dreams for the conscious and unconscious. He considers "'True' and 'false' in a dream":

---

91. Turner, *Holy Spirit,* pp. 316-17.

92. Ludwig Wittgenstein, *Philosophical Investigations* (Oxford: Blackwell, 2nd ed. 1958), sect. 6.

93. Anthony C. Thiselton, *Language, Liturgy, and Meaning* (Nottingham: Grove Books, 1975 and 1986), pp. 10-16.

94. Wittgenstein, *Philosophical Investigations,* sect. 28.

95. Wittgenstein, *Philosophical Investigations,* sect. 33.

96. Wittgenstein, *Philosophical Investigations,* sect. 49.

"I dream that it is raining, and that I say 'It is raining' — on the other hand: I dream that I say 'I am dreaming.' Has the verb 'to dream' a present tense? How does a person learn to use this?"[97] Or, to return to pictures, "There is good reason to say that we altered our visual impression through our attitude."[98] We are *not* suggesting for one moment that pictures, dreams, and visions *cannot* be revelatory. But the interpretation and assessment of them are highly complex, and simple "pictures" are highly ambiguous. No one need deny that there are historical precedents in Hildegard of Bingen and other medieval mystics. But the contexts and circumstances of their interpretation are not entirely clear, they were usually tested against the tradition of the Church, and some might even have misled some sincere inquirers.

Paul Ricoeur confirms that symbols are "double meaning" expressions. Dreams are still more complex, multi-layered experiences. Dreams, he argues, are "*disguised, substitutive and fictive* expressions of human wishes or desires."[99] On top of this, what has to be interpreted is *not the dream-as-remembered or recounted* ("the dream-content"), but its underlying text. In the dream as actually dreamt, events may become *displaced, condensed, or "scrambled."*[100] *None* of this suggests that God *cannot* or *never* speaks in dreams. God did use dreams in the Old Testament in the case of Joseph and Pharaoh (Gen. 41:1-8, 15-24), and in the New Testament a dream or vision was experienced by Peter (Acts 12:6-17). The point is that someone who claims to have heard the voice of God through a picture, dream, or vision has to be enormously careful that this is the case. It is notable that this often appears to involve women, from Hildegard to the present day. We may only hope that mistakes are not made, and the "revelations" not too hastily claimed. Wittgenstein and Ricoeur show the massive potential for error; yet who would deny that the Holy Spirit may work through the subconscious, or "secrets of the heart"?

Max Turner appears to reach safer ground with the other gifts. For example, Turner shows that tongues-speech in Acts could not be "initial evidence" of receiving the Spirit (as argued by R. Menzies) for several reasons, but especially because "tongues" marked "occasions of powerful or significant irruptions of the Spirit," such as Pentecost itself, the inclusion of Gentiles at Caesarea, the inclusion of Samaritans in Acts 8:18, and the occasion at Ephesus (Acts 19:11).[101] He argues that *xenolalia*, actual foreign languages, provide a better explanation for *heterais glōssais lalein* (to speak in other tongues or languages) than the notion that the first disciples, eager to convert the world, "merely prattled

97. Ludwig Wittgenstein, *Zettel* (Oxford: Blackwell, 1967), sects. 398 and 399.

98. Wittgenstein, *Zettel*, sect. 205.

99. Paul Ricoeur, *Freud and Philosophy: An Essay on Interpretation* (New Haven and London: Yale University Press, 1970), p. 5 (my italics).

100. Ricoeur, *Freud and Philosophy*, p. 93 (my italics).

101. Turner, *Holy Spirit*, p. 225.

incomprehensively" or had an ecstatic experience.[102] In any case, the "hearing" of the tongues, many suggest, could be a miracle of hearing.

I have discussed twelve possibilities in my commentary on First Corinthians, and wish that Turner had considered the views of Krister Stendahl (who received simply a footnote on p. 221) and Gerd Theissen's brilliant study *Psychological Aspects of Pauline Theology*, which does not appear to be mentioned.[103] However, Turner asserts: "There is no contradiction between tongues viewed as an aid in devotion and what is said in 1 Cor. 14:22 ["tongues are a sign not for believers but for unbelievers"] . . . and Acts 2:1-13, unless one arbitrarily asserts tongues may only have one function."[104] This is a key comment and, like the first one, allows me to give *general support to Turner, even if we dissent over details*. He argues that tongues-speech is "definitely non-ecstatic."[105] In terms of its use today, "Psychologically 'tongues-speech' is not the product of what is usually meant by 'ecstasy.'"[106] Further: "Some claims to have recognized *xenolalia* have been made this century, but most of them are ill-documented . . . and the languages prove to have been 'recognized' by people who are not competent speakers of the tongue in question."[107] Of the many tape recordings of "tongues" submitted to specialists in linguistics, "few if any" have the structure or grammar of a natural language.[108] Mostly, tongues are "orientated towards the Lord."[109]

Turner even makes more than a gesture toward the Holy Spirit's interaction "with people at the subconscious level," which for me is the key to the whole phenomenon.[110] On the "interpretation of tongues," Turner concedes that 1 Cor. 14:13 may invite the tongues-speaker himself ("someone," Greek *tis*, does not appear in the Greek) to pray for the Spirit to teach him to put it into articulate speech. Turner argues that it may also refer to "someone else." Personally, I think this less likely, but not impossible. Both "gifts" may well be from the Spirit: one the gift of "release"; the other, the gift of articulation for the Church.

On "healing," Turner has many insights. He concedes, against his own inclinations, "In the euphoria and excitement of revival, miracles have been testified to in abundance, but rarely verified."[111] In contrast to John Wimber, Turner

---

102. Turner, *Holy Spirit*, pp. 222-23.

103. Gerd Theissen, *Psychological Aspects of Pauline Theology* (Edinburgh: T&T Clark, 1987), esp. pp. 74-114 and 292-341.

104. Turner, *Holy Spirit*, p. 233.

105. Turner, *Holy Spirit*, p. 238.

106. Turner, *Holy Spirit*, p. 305.

107. Turner, *Holy Spirit*, p. 307.

108. Turner, *Holy Spirit*, p. 308.

109. Turner, *Holy Spirit*, p. 309.

110. Turner, *Holy Spirit*, p. 310.

111. Turner, *Holy Spirit*, p. 333.

sees "both healing and the lack of it as in different ways 'normal' in this age."[112] God's will is also one of wrath and judgment on . . . our sinful humanity."[113] Believers "should be able to combine a truly Christocentric and lively expectation of God's saving interventions with an equally cruciform acceptance of weakness."[114] It is cruel to accuse sufferers or those whose relatives and friends have *not* witnessed miraculous healing of showing inadequate faith and prayer. I recall declaring in the Church of England General Synod that its Healing Report was good but seriously inadequate because it failed to address situations of apparent "non-healing," only to receive a public reply from the Chairman of the Report Group: "We are not the Doctrine Commission; it would be beyond us!" I endorse Turner's insistence that this forms a vital part of the issue, on both theological and pastoral grounds.

These are the most distinctive elements of *The Holy Spirit and Spiritual Gifts Then and Now*. It is a book full of wise judgments and generosity, even if we may disagree over many important details. This may be in part because his meticulous scholarship on Luke-Acts is supported by research recounted and argued in his careful book *Power from on High: The Spirit in Israel's Restoration and Witness in Luke-Acts* (also 1996), to which we now turn. Some of it covers ground already examined in *The Holy Spirit*, so our discussion of it will be short. We have already mentioned that the first chapter of this book examines the views of Hermann Gunkel, H. Leisegang, F. Büchsel, and H. van Baer. Turner then examines the work of Geoffrey Lampe, the "personality" or personhood of the Holy Spirit in Luke-Acts, and Luke's language of Spirit endowment as "metaphor for different aspects of the activity of the Spirit . . . perhaps best explained as a metaphorical way of referring to the inception of a specific new activity."[115]

Turner next considers the work of James D. G. Dunn. Dunn insists that "power for service" is not the primary purpose of the anointing of Jesus, but only a corollary to it. Dunn sees Pentecost as a continuing fulfillment of God's covenant promise. Paul elucidates these themes in 2 Cor. 3:3, 6-8. "Receiving the Spirit" is virtually equivalent to "the matrix of the Christian life."[116] Turner argues that this is because Dunn sees Ezekiel 36 behind Paul's thought, whereas he suggests that it is more plausibly Isa. 61:1-2 (Luke 4:18-21), which speaks of "empowering."

On the other hand, Turner is at one with Dunn in rejecting the arguments of N. Adler in favor of references to "confirmation." If confirmation is viewed

---

112. Turner, *Holy Spirit*, p. 344.
113. Turner, *Holy Spirit*, p. 345.
114. Turner, *Holy Spirit*, p. 345.
115. Turner, *Power from on High*, p. 47.
116. Turner, *Power from on High*, p. 51.

as extending "the baptismal graces of justification, Sonship and faith, no viable criteria can be offered for distinguishing between a baptismal level and a confirmation level."[117] This not only seems correct, but also reflects the Reformed tradition within Anglicanism.

Turner continues the theme that Lampe and Dunn find a safer and a more secure ground in Paul than in Luke-Acts. Luke insists on seeing the Spirit as "missionary-empowering."[118] However, he also criticizes Eduard Schweizer, Roger Stronstad, and R. P. Menzies for *too exclusive an emphasis* on "the Spirit of Prophecy." How can the Holy Spirit be a universal gift if only some are "prophets" while he is primarily the Spirit of prophecy?[119] In this context he discusses the work of G. Haya-Prats.

Turner's part 2 concerns the Spirit of prophecy in Judaism as the background to Luke. He argues: "For the Judeans of Luke's day, the Spirit was largely, if not exclusively, the 'Spirit of prophecy.'"[120] The Spirit gives inspired speech and revelation. Few could deny this. Nor does Turner have any difficulty in insisting on the importance of the Targums for our understanding of Judaism. Indeed, his use of Targumic evidence is impressive. He gives many examples from *Targum Pseudo-Jonathan* on passages in Genesis, some from *Targum Onqelos*, and one from *Targum Neofiti*.[121] He argues that these suggest "charismatic revelation" and "charismatic wisdom." The evidence from the multiplication of references cannot be doubted.

The next four chapters are more distinctive, arguing for the Spirit's work of miracle and even ethical influence and restoration in the Septuagint, Targums, and rabbinic writings. This includes Messianic references in *1 Enoch, Psalms of Solomon*, Qumran, and other sources.[122] Ethical influence features in the argument. John Levison endorses some of Turner's conclusions in an earlier article on the "invasive" character of the Spirit in Judaism.[123] The research on Judaism seems impeccable. How much of this influences Luke the "Hellenist," however, remains yet to be seen. Much of the argument seems to be directed primarily against the claims of Menzies. The most interesting arguments concern alterations by the Targums or the Septuagint to the Hebrew text of the Old Testament. For example, *Targums Neofiti* and *Pseudo-Jonathan* change Gen. 6:3, "My

---

117. Turner, *Power from on High*, p. 34.
118. Turner, *Power from on High*, p. 57.
119. Turner, *Power from on High*, pp. 61 and 73.
120. Turner, *Power from on High*, p. 82.
121. Turner, *Power from on High*, pp. 93-99.
122. Turner, *Power from on High*, pp. 105-18.
123. John R. Levison, *The Spirit in First-Century Judaism* (Boston and Leiden: Brill, 2002), p. 253; cf. Max Turner, "The Spirit of Prophecy and the Power of Authoritative Preaching in Luke-Acts: A Question of Origins," *NTS* 38 (1992): 85.

spirit will not abide (or contend) with man forever, for they are flesh," so that *Pseudo-Jonathan* has, "Did I not put my holy spirit in them that they may perform good deeds?"[124]

On the coming of the Messiah, Turner covers much of customary ground about the prophetic Spirit in Zechariah, Mary, and Elizabeth in Luke 1–2. The relation of John the Baptist to Jesus reflects Mal. 3:1, and leads to a "charismatic revelation."[125] To be "full of" the Spirit occurs twenty-seven times in Luke-Acts, but only five times in Paul.[126] Turner comments on empowering the Messianic Son and the anointing of Jesus by the Spirit.[127] He sees Pentecost as the enthronement of Jesus as Messiah of Israel and the Spirit as his executive power for Israel's restoration.

Several further chapters take us through Acts. As we might expect, Turner underlines the "charismatic" experience of the Church in Acts: revelatory visions and dreams, perception and discernment, the Samaritan episode (which "provides a clear break with the norm"), the rapture of Philip, and Paul's reception of the Spirit.[128] We have discussed much of this material already. But he adds a special note on the Cornelius episode, in which he argues that James Dunn's arguments "fall just short of proof at each stage."[129] Cornelius received "the Spirit of prophecy" as a witness to the inclusion of the Gentiles. But in Acts 10:2, following his introduction to the Roman centurion in 10:1, Luke describes him as a "God-fearer, with all his household . . . who prayed constantly to God," that is, *as all but a pious Jew*" (Turner's italics).[130] The episode relates to the cleansing and restoration of Israel, but also to the Gentiles' place in this Messianic cleansing.[131] On the Ephesian Twelve (Acts 19:1-7), Turner takes more traditional paths, following not Ernst Käsemann's view of their being "anomalous semi-Christians," but the explanation by Donald A. Carson and others that they are Christians who somehow missed out on Pentecost.[132]

In his concluding chapter Turner stresses again that "The 'Spirit of prophecy,' anticipated in Judaism, prototypically afforded revelation, wisdom and invasive prophetic and doxological speech."[133] Nevertheless (against Stronstad and Menzies) "salvation and its benefits are made present in the ministry only

---

124. Turner, *Power from on High*, p. 123.

125. Turner, *Power from on High*, pp. 151 and 153.

126. Turner, *Power from on High*, pp. 165-69.

127. Turner, *Power from on High*, pp. 188-266.

128. Turner, *Power from on High*, p. 360; cf. pp. 348-78.

129. Turner, *Power from on High*, p. 381; cf. pp. 378-87.

130. Turner, *Power from on High*, p. 386.

131. Turner, *Power from on High*, p. 387.

132. Turner, *Power from on High*, p. 390; cf. pp. 388-400.

133. Turner, *Power from on High*, p. 431.

through Jesus-empowered-by-the-Spirit."[134] We cannot justify the claim that the reception of the Spirit is not necessarily *soteriological* or constitutes a *supplementary* gift. The Spirit plays an important role in leading up to conversion. In conclusion Turner sees his work as "a challenge to non-Pentecostal/non-charismatic sectors of the Church."[135] But it might equally constitute a *challenge to a formalized, overly sacramentalist Church.* The Spirit is seen as "the transcendence of God over, to, and through, the Church, . . . the *self-manifesting presence of God*" (his italics).[136] But many, including the present writer, have believed and *even explicitly taught this* since before they ever heard of "the Charismatic Movement" in the mid-1960s.

What are we to make of the two books? *The Holy Spirit and Spiritual Gifts* offers a good blend of New Testament scholarship and practical observations. I have indicated broad general agreement, but with a number of specific reservations. The book is a useful advance in friendly and ecumenical dialogue on crucially important issues. *Power from on High* gives meticulous attention to Intertestamental Judaism and to Luke. It challenges the attempt to view Luke through Pauline spectacles. In the conclusion it is forthright in giving through Luke-Acts "a challenge to classical Pentecostalism"; first, in terms of a Pentecostal theology of sequence; second, in terms of "evidential tongues"; third, in terms of the notion of "Initial Evidence"; fourth, in terms of a broader recognition of the Pentecostal gift.[137]

The arguments must generate sympathy that a search for Renewal may seem so often to look for within the horizon of Acts. But Krister Stendahl warns us about a correspondingly youth-like experience in many Christians. He writes: "It seems to me that few human beings can live healthily with high-voltage religious experience over a long period of time. . . . I am very concerned about what happens to charismatics after five or ten or twenty years. From my observations, it seems that they need us; they need to know that their home is the larger church in which their status as children of God does not depend on the intensity of their experiences. . . . The lesson can be learned only in a church where we rejoice with the charismatics in the gifts given to them, . . . where such gifts can grow in faith without feeling threatened, if their experiences change during a long and honest life."[138]

As we shall see in the next chapter, Yves Congar has expressed a similar dual concern in his consideration of the Renewal Movement. He has welcomed it, but gives reasons why *every* Christian should *not* become a charismatic. After

134. Turner, *Power from on High*, p. 435.
135. Turner, *Power from on High*, p. 439.
136. Turner, *Power from on High*, p. 439.
137. Turner, *Power from on High*, pp. 445-53.
138. Krister Stendahl, *Paul among Jews and Gentiles* (Philadelphia: Fortress, 1976, and London: SCM, 1977), p. 123; from the section "Glossolalia — The New Testament Evidence," pp. 97-125.

all, while Turner is right to shed the spotlight on Luke-Acts, Luke is but one voice within the canon. We are still left with the problem of how to relate what are largely *narratives* to our own times. Whether Luke looked for replication of the early years that he recounts as a blueprint for all time remains an open question for further debate.

21

Five Major Theologians: Congar, Moltmann,
Pannenberg, Lossky, and Zizioulas

These eminent theologians can hardly be mentioned in the same breath as the other twentieth-century writers whom we have considered. Georges-Yves Congar (1904-95) stands alongside Karl Rahner, Hans Urs von Balthasar, and Hans Küng as one of the four major Roman Catholic theologians of our times. He has explicitly written on the Holy Spirit and the Renewal Movement, and his thoughts are judicious and very helpful. Jürgen Moltmann (b. 1926) scarcely needs any introduction, as he (with Pannenberg) is perhaps the most widely read, creative, and inspiring Protestant theologian of our age. Wolfhart Pannenberg (b. 1928) is majestic, profound, and meticulously learned, and draws on biblical, historical, and philosophical theology to offer enormously impressive writings. John Zizioulas and Vladimir Lossky represent respectively Greek and Russian traditions within Eastern Orthodoxy, and are creative and impressive on our subject. All five have produced a multitude of writings, and in my personal judgment are beyond compare.

21.1. Georges-Yves Congar

Congar trained for the priesthood in Paris, and entered the Dominican Order in 1925. He attended courses in Thomism, studying under the philosophical Neo-Thomist Jacques Maritain (1882-1973), and came under the influence of Réynold Garrigou-Lagrange (1877-1964). His particular areas of interest came to be those of historical theology, ecclesiology, and ecumenism. His thesis was on Johann A. Möhler. Like Balthasar, he became attracted to Karl Barth's emphasis on the sovereignty of God, grace, and his polemic against Liberalism. In 1937 he visited England, where A. Michael Ramsey (1904-88) introduced him to the Anglican tradition. During the Second World War he became a prisoner in

Colditz, where he met many Protestants. His first book in 1937 was *Divided Christendom* (Eng. 1939). After a period during which he was out of favor with the Vatican, Pope John XXIII appointed him consultant to the preparatory Commission of the Second Vatican Council. He was made a Cardinal in 1994.

After the war, Congar wrote on the *Reform of the Church* (1950), *Lay People in the Church* (1952), and later a study of Catholic-Orthodox relations in *After Nine Hundred Years* (1954; Eng. 1959). He wrote *Tradition and Traditions* (1960-63; Eng. 1966) while Vatican II was in session. His full-scale magisterial work on the doctrine of the Holy Spirit, *I Believe in the Holy Spirit,* appeared in 1979-80 (Eng. 1983).[1] He was born the same year as Karl Rahner (1904-84), and one year before Hans Urs von Balthasar (1905-88).

Congar's *I Believe in the Holy Spirit* has appeared in three volumes.[2] Studies of Congar's theology of the Holy Spirit have been published by Elizabeth Teresa Groppe and by Aidan Nichols.[3] The first of Congar's three volumes explores biblical and historical material. The Spirit is known, he argues, by his *effects*, so it is necessary to look at those historical and contemporary figures who claim to have experienced the Holy Spirit. Like Joseph Fison, however, he also emphasizes the *kenōsis,* or self-emptying, of the Holy Spirit. Fison spoke of this as the Spirit's "self-effacing" reticence, but Congar goes even further. *The Spirit empties himself of his own personality* in order to become what Augustine saw as the personal bond of love between God the Father and God the Son. Congar sees the Spirit as especially the bond between God and human beings. He refuses to accept that we should pit revelation and experience against each other; they are complementary. Thus the third distinctive characteristic of this volume is that Congar sees the effects of the Spirit *both* in high points of mystical experience *and* in the *ordinary, everyday living* of Christians, as Taylor does.

Congar sees the intermittent endowment by the Spirit in the Old Testament as bringing forward God's purpose in history, whether this be through the prophets and Messianic preparation or in cosmic wisdom. The New Testament witness to the Holy Spirit begins with the public ministry of Jesus, including his conception, birth, and especially his baptism: "The Spirit enters the history of mankind as a messianic gift and . . . as an eschatological gift."[4] Congar cites Thomas Aquinas as seeing the form of the dove as a *visible* mission. The Pauline material stresses the effects of the Spirit in the everyday life of the Christian, as Käsemann also notes with reference to the lordship of Christ. But

---

1. Aidan Nichols, *Yves Congar* (New York: Geoffrey Chapman, and Oxford: Morehouse-Barlow, 1989), provides a short account of life and theology.

2. Yves Congar, *I Believe in the Holy Spirit: Lord and Giver of Life* (New York: Seabury, and London: Chapman, 1983).

3. Elizabeth Teresa Groppe, *Yves Congar's Theology of the Holy Spirit* (New York: Oxford University Press, 2004), and Nichols, *Congar,* pp. 141-72.

4. Congar, *I Believe in the Holy Spirit,* vol. 1, pp. 15-16; also cited by Nichols.

Congar's distinctive emphasis concerns the Church, and the Spirit's activity in forming it and indwelling it. *The Church is the sphere of the Spirit.* Luke's special contribution underlines the continuity between Christ and the Church.

Patristic exegesis usually sees the universality of Pentecost as the reversal of Babel and the ability to hear the gospel in a variety of languages. This is reflected in events in Jerusalem (Acts 2; 4:25-31), in Samaria (Acts 8:14-17), in Caesarea (Acts 10:44-48), and in Ephesus (Acts 19:6). The "tongues" constitute a sign of giving praise to God for the outreach of the gospel and the expansion of the Church. Luke sees the effects of the Spirit primarily in corporate and historical time. Paul also views the effects of the Spirit in personal terms, such as "the fruits of the Spirit" (Gal. 5:22).

The Johannine discourses on the Paraclete also, as in Luke, underline the continuity between Christ, the Spirit, and the Church: "I will come to you" (14:3, 18); "The Holy Spirit, whom the Father will send in my name, will teach you everything" (14:26); "The Spirit of truth . . . will guide you into all truth" (John 16:13). After the departure of Jesus, he continues to do the work of Jesus.

The development of tradition through the Fathers does not set up an opposition between the "institutional" and the "charismatic." The Holy Spirit worked *both* through successive bishops and the institutional Church *and* in spontaneous ways through the people of God. Congar traces, like many others, the development of the doctrine of the Spirit through Athanasius and the Cappadocian Fathers, especially Basil, with his teaching on the threefold *Gloria.* He affirms the formulation of the Council of Constantinople (381) and of Augustine, especially in *The Trinity.* As the Eastern Church stresses, the Spirit proceeds "in the first place" *(principaliter)* from the Father (John 15:26), but also through Christ as the Western Church urges. He will discuss this further in his volume 3.

Volume 2 contains some of Congar's most distinctive and creative work. He first argues: "the Church is made by the Spirit."[5] He speaks of the "two missions" which lead to "the Co-instituting of the Church." The Greek words *pempein* and *apostellein* are used virtually synonymously: God "sends" his Son, and God "sends" the Spirit of his Son to commission the apostles for the outreach and mission of the Church.[6] Congar reminds us that, as we have noted, Irenaeus saw the Son and the Spirit as the two "hands" of God. This does not mean that "the institutional" and "charismatic" oppose each other: "they are complementary."[7] The Spirit thus "makes the Church one."[8] *The unity of the Spirit* is not merely an abstract ideal, but central to his work of forming the

---

5. Congar, *I Believe in the Holy Spirit,* vol. 2, p. 5.
6. Congar, *I Believe in the Holy Spirit,* vol. 2, pp. 7-12.
7. Congar, *I Believe in the Holy Spirit,* vol. 2, p. 11.
8. Congar, *I Believe in the Holy Spirit,* vol. 2, p. 15.

Church. He works in the everyday life of Christians. The Holy Spirit is also "earnest money" of the future, looking to the perfect unity of the Church. Its "catholicity" also implies the bringing together of diversity. This involves "the part played by the Spirit in the understanding of Scripture" and "the unity of the whole of Scripture."[9] Interestingly he also comments: "Does he [the Spirit] still speak through the prophets? Who would dare to say that he does not?"[10] Yet because the Spirit is also transcendent and mysterious, he borrows Hans Urs von Balthasar's phrase concerning the Holy Spirit as the "Unknown One beyond the Word."[11] He makes the Easter event of Jesus Christ present today.

The Holy Spirit also preserves the Church as "apostolic." In parallel with "Restorationist" ideas in Pentecostalism, Congar defines "apostolic" as "conformity with the origins of Christianity."[12] He again refers to the "two missions" of the apostles and the Paraclete (sending by the Son, John 15:16, 20; 17:18; and sending by the Holy Spirit, John 14:16, 26 and 15:26). The Spirit gives the transcendent principle of *faithfulness*, as in "Guard the truth that has been entrusted to you by the Holy Spirit" (2 Tim. 1:14). He endorses Wolfhart Pannenberg's exposition of apostolicity as "dynamic catholicity," not merely as a witness.[13] As we might expect, Congar includes a chapter on the holiness of the Church, referring to the Holy Spirit as forming the people of God into a holy temple (1 Cor. 3:17), and as a holy Bride of Christ (2 Cor. 11:2; Eph. 5:25-27, 29-31). The Church, the Bride of Christ, whom God calls to be "gentle and loving" (Matt. 11:29), "has often been proud and hard in history."[14]

Congar considers the whole third article of the Creed as if it were one piece altogether: "I believe in the Holy Spirit, the Lord and Giver of life. . . . I believe in one Catholic and Apostolic Church. . . ." This is the formulation of the "Nicene Creed." But similar clauses under the third article come together in the later "Apostles'" Creed: "I believe in the Holy Spirit; the holy Catholic Church; the communion of Saints; . . . the Resurrection of the Body. . . ." Congar therefore now considers "the Communion of Saints." He discusses the earliest explanations, which regard the phrase as referring to the saints: "the community of the blessed, anticipated in the Catholic Church."[15] He cites Rahner's comment: it is possible for us "to believe beyond this world, and to love as far as God's world, even with and into (Rahner's phrase) his heart."[16] Congar also considers the bond of love and the work of the Spirit in Augustine's tradition.

---

9. Congar, *I Believe in the Holy Spirit*, vol. 2, p. 28.
10. Congar, *I Believe in the Holy Spirit*, vol. 2, p. 30.
11. Congar, *I Believe in the Holy Spirit*, vol. 2, p. 33.
12. Congar, *I Believe in the Holy Spirit*, vol. 2, p. 39.
13. Congar, *I Believe in the Holy Spirit*, vol. 2, p. 50.
14. Congar, *I Believe in the Holy Spirit*, vol. 2, p. 57.
15. Congar, *I Believe in the Holy Spirit*, vol. 2, p. 59.
16. Congar, *I Believe in the Holy Spirit*, vol. 2, p. 60.

Part 2 of the second volume concerns the Spirit and personal lives. Congar declares: "The Spirit is the principle of love, and realizes our lives as children of God in the form of a Gift."[17] Again he considers the Pauline theme of the Spirit as an earnest of the future, and the whole New Testament theme of the gift of the Spirit in the Messianic era. He then examines Gal. 4:6: "God has sent the Spirit of his Son into our hearts." Like Moltmann, he speaks of the Spirit's indwelling, his glory, and the Jewish or Aramaic *shekinah* of God.[18] He also underlines the fact that "every action performed by God is common to all three Persons of the Trinity. . . . Even the *incarnation is common to the three Persons*" (my italics).[19] This is parallel to Moltmann and Pannenberg in their New Testament *narrative* approach to the Trinity. Like Moltmann, Congar speaks of the Spirit of life and the Holy Spirit's part in initiating prayer.[20] He concludes this part with a section on the Spirit and freedom and the gifts and fruit of the Spirit.[21]

There follows a *judicious discussion of Renewal* in the Spirit. Congar prefers the term *Renewal Movement* to the term "Charismatic Movement." He traces the movement, which "spread like wildfire in the traditional churches," since 1956 among Protestant churches and since 1967 in the Catholic Church.[22] He sees the Renewal Movement largely (but not exclusively) as "trying to compensate for a depressed and humiliating way of life" on the part of "believers who are seeking spiritual independence."[23] Whatever our personal assessment, we must recognize that "amazing changes . . . are taking place in the world. . . . This is a world-wide movement."[24] In place of such a term as the Pentecostal "Restorationist," Congar prefers to speak of "re-sourcement, . . . a simple return to the source of the Christian faith."[25] This reflects a Trinitarian perspective. Again, he stresses that we should *not oppose institution and "charism."* The Renewal Movement, he observes, does not despise the sacraments.

Congar rightly insists, "All experience has to be checked, tested and proved authentic."[26] He cites Cardinal Suenens as defending the authenticity of many experiences. The movement seeks to go beyond "excessively organized and cerebral religion"; he then discusses "hand-clapping, raised hands, cries and sounds, very rhythmical singing, dancing, and the laying on of hands."[27] Con-

---

17. Congar, *I Believe in the Holy Spirit*, vol. 2, p. 67.
18. Congar, *I Believe in the Holy Spirit*, vol. 2, p. 79.
19. Congar, *I Believe in the Holy Spirit*, vol. 2, p. 85.
20. Congar, *I Believe in the Holy Spirit*, vol. 2, pp. 100-118.
21. Congar, *I Believe in the Holy Spirit*, vol. 2, pp. 119-41.
22. Congar, *I Believe in the Holy Spirit*, vol. 2, p. 149; cf. pp. 149-201.
23. Congar, *I Believe in the Holy Spirit*, vol. 2, p. 149.
24. Congar, *I Believe in the Holy Spirit*, vol. 2, p. 149.
25. Congar, *I Believe in the Holy Spirit*, vol. 2, p. 150.
26. Congar, *I Believe in the Holy Spirit*, vol. 2, p. 154.
27. Congar, *I Believe in the Holy Spirit*, vol. 2, p. 154.

gar suggests that these *can* be inspired by the Holy Spirit; but these *also can* occur in pagan cults (1 Cor. 12:2). In the light of this, he insists, *"I do not believe that the Renewal, in the form in which it appears now, can be extended to the whole of the Church"* (my italics).[28] This is because "the style of . . . meetings is *not acceptable to everyone*," and "the Spirit's gifts are given 'for the common good,' for the good of all believers. . . . the flock in love will always *avoid imposing charismatic manifestations* as a *law* in his community" (my italics).[29] It appears, for example, that the church at Rome did not lead that kind of life. The Movement must not claim that the *whole* Church will become "charismatic."

We have noted that Congar expresses reservation about the term "charismatic" although he happily speaks of the Renewal Movement. This is partly because the terms "charisma" and "charismatic" are understood in three distinct ways. The narrowest sense of the term is associated with speaking in tongues, "prophecy," and miracles or healing. Then a distinct risk emerges of restricting *grace* and *gift* only to "the level of extraordinary and even exceptional manifestations."[30] *Renewal, in Congar's judgment,* avoids the pitfall. On the other hand, he does not follow Chrysostom in seeing such gifts as being only for the beginning of the Church. Congar discusses whether "tongues" denote unknown foreign languages, or an outburst of joy and praise. He does not follow Frank Macchia in seeing tongues in terms of Rom. 8:26, the sighs of the Holy Spirit. Although he expresses some reticence about the question, he asserts: "It is not a question of speaking a foreign language," or of "translation."[31] Paul declares, ". . . to another, various kinds of tongues" (1 Cor. 12:10). "Healing" may sometimes occur, but within the corporate or "brotherly" context of prayer in the community.

On the other hand, Congar traces the phrase "baptism in the Spirit" to the Holiness Movement and the two stages of rebirth or conversion and sanctification. The Assemblies of God, he reminds us, distinguish three aspects: conversion, baptism of the Spirit, and sanctification. 1 Cor. 12:13 speaks of "being plunged in the Spirit"; but "this constitutes the process of becoming a Christian."[32] He adds, "Catholic Renewal . . . interprets the term 'baptism in the Spirit' perhaps a little too facilely. . . . At other times — fortunately — the term . . . is avoided and other expressions are used instead: 'pouring out or outpouring of the Spirit' or 'renewal in the Holy Spirit.'"[33]

All this is meticulously scholarly, with enormous, detailed footnotes and documentation, yet he also recognizes, albeit with caution, the claims of the Re-

28. Congar, *I Believe in the Holy Spirit*, vol. 2, p. 156.
29. Congar, *I Believe in the Holy Spirit*, vol. 2, pp. 156-57.
30. Congar, *I Believe in the Holy Spirit*, vol. 2, p. 163.
31. Congar, *I Believe in the Holy Spirit*, vol. 2, p. 177.
32. Congar, *I Believe in the Holy Spirit*, vol. 2, p. 190; cf. pp. 189-201.
33. Congar, *I Believe in the Holy Spirit*, vol. 2, p. 198.

newal experience. I am broadly in agreement with his careful assessment of the Renewal Movement.

In his third volume, Congar considers the ecumenical dimension of the Eastern Church and the Western Church, and of orthodox and Catholics. On the West's *filioque* clause, he sees the Eastern Church as unduly influenced by Photius of Constantinople, whose work we noted above. Photius did not confine himself to scriptural arguments and Patristic texts. Broadly, the West is more analytical and the East more reliant on symbols.[34] In fact, the Orthodox and Catholic formulations complement each other. "The Holy Spirit proceeds from the Father" describes the *ultimate* Source, but "and the Son" denotes "through the Son" as mediate channel. Both forms are equivalent and complementary. An increasing number of theologians now recognize this. These three volumes constitute a major and judicious exposition of the Person and work of the Holy Spirit.

21.2. Jürgen Moltmann

Jürgen Moltmann (b. 1926) is without doubt one of the three or four most widely read and influential of twentieth-century- and early-twenty-first-century theologians. He was for many years Professor of Theology at Tübingen, and has written over a dozen major, influential volumes, as well as numerous shorter books and many research papers. Yet his books are easily readable and designed to reach a wide public, as well as serving the Church. His volume *The Spirit of Life* (German, 1991; English, 1992) is of most immediate concern to our subject.[35]

(1) *Context and guidelines for the book,* The Spirit of Life. Moltmann's other volumes on Systematic Theology provide a context for his argument in *The Spirit of Life*. In *The Trinity and the Kingdom of God* he shows the Trinitarian communion of the Holy Spirit with the Father and the Son.[36] In this volume he rightly approaches the Trinity in terms of *the concrete narrative of the New Testament, not of abstract metaphysics or analogues*. He writes: "The New Testament talks about God by proclaiming in narrative the relationships of the Father, the Son and the Spirit; which are relationships of fellowship and are open to the world."[37] Thus from the first the *narrative* of the conception, birth, and baptism of Jesus entails the activity of the Holy Spirit and the "sending" of the Father. In the climax to the ministry of Jesus, "The Father raises the Son

---

34. Congar, *I Believe in the Holy Spirit,* vol. 3, p. 8.

35. Jürgen Moltmann, *The Spirit of Life: A Universal Affirmation* (London: SCM, 1992).

36. Jürgen Moltmann, *The Trinity and the Kingdom of God: The Doctrine of God* (London: SCM, 1981).

37. Moltmann, *Trinity and the Kingdom,* p. 64.

through the Spirit."[38] We ask not only: "How do I experience God? . . . [but] also how does God experience me?"[39] This sees God in action as Holy Spirit, as does "A God who cannot suffer cannot love either."[40]

In *God in Creation* Moltmann "looked at the Spirit as the power and life of the whole creation."[41] He first stresses "the difference between God and the world: God is not to be understood in worldly terms."[42] But he nevertheless manifests himself in "making, preserving, maintaining, and perfecting" the world, as well as more especially "indwelling, sym-pathizing, participating, accompanying, enduring, delighting and glorifying" it, which are "relationships of mutuality . . . of living between God the Spirit and all his created beings."[43] He invokes the rabbinic notion of *Shekinah* and the Christian doctrine of the Trinity to amplify this. With respect to the latter he expounds *perichōresis* or "mutual interpenetration."[44] As in his later work on the Holy Spirit, he emphasizes "creation out of nothing," the giving of life, even if this involves "a self-limitation by God" in "making room" for the new.[45]

In *The Way of Jesus Christ* Moltmann has explored the complementary relation between the Holy Spirit and Christ. His "Spirit Christology" is not an alternative to "Logos" Christology but "a necessary complement."[46] He writes: "Jesus' history as the Christ does not begin with Jesus himself. It begins with . . . the Holy Spirit."[47] Thus his birth is "from the Holy Spirit."[48] In the baptism of Jesus we see both "the *kenōsis* of the divine Spirit" and "Jesus' endowment with the Spirit."[49] In both respects the Holy Spirit works *through Jesus*.

Moltmann begins *The Spirit of Life* with a brief consideration of approaches to the Spirit today. Twenty years ago we could speak of a "forgetfulness of the Spirit," or of the Spirit as "the Cinderella of Western Theology." A survey of the present book will show how all this has changed since the 1980s. This forgetfulness "gave way to a positive obsession with the Spirit"; yet no new paradigm in pneumatology had appeared.[50] He states, however, a basic principle: "Word and

---

38. Moltmann, *Trinity and the Kingdom*, p. 88.

39. Moltmann, *Trinity and the Kingdom*, p. 3.

40. Moltmann, *Trinity and the Kingdom*, p. 38.

41. Moltmann, *Trinity and the Kingdom*, p. 17.

42. Jürgen Moltmann, *God in Creation: An Ecological Doctrine of Creation* (London: SCM, 1985), p. 13.

43. Moltmann, *God in Creation*, p. 14.

44. Moltmann, *God in Creation*, p. 15.

45. Moltmann, *God in Creation*, pp. 86-88.

46. Moltmann, *God in Creation*, p. 17.

47. Jürgen Moltmann, *The Way of Jesus Christ: Christology in Messianic Dimensions* (London: SCM, 1990), p. 73.

48. Moltmann, *Way of Jesus Christ*, p. 76.

49. Moltmann, *Way of Jesus Christ*, p. 91.

50. Moltmann, *Spirit of Life*, p. 1.

Spirit [exist] in a mutual relationship, not as a one-way street."[51] "Revelation" does not pose a false alternative to experience of the Spirit; yet we must not lose "the qualitative difference between God and humans."[52] But Moltmann rejects the absolute contrast between a God as "Other" and his immanent working, which Hendrikus Berkhof and Alisdair Heron also see as a major problem. I have tried to parallel this call for a complementary perspective by describing the Holy Spirit as "the Beyond Who Is Within."

Moltmann sets out what is virtually a programmatic agenda: we must avoid undue individualism; we must continue to wrestle with the *filioque* clause; we must reemphasize the Holy Spirit as the agent of resurrection; and we must not lose sight of the personhood of the Holy Spirit. He declares, "The Holy Spirit has a wholly unique personhood."[53] He is always also a "being-in-relationship."[54]

(2) *An appeal to experience. The Spirit of Life* has three main points. The first concerns "Experience." Experiences that are genuinely decisive or formative for us are akin to "limit situations" such as death and deep love. Moltmann recounts his early experience of the death of a friend during the bombing of Hamburg in the Second World War, and it provokes the question: "Where is God?" and "Why am I not dead too?"[55] The primary experience is passive rather than active, namely, experiences which *happen* to us and *befall* us. Such experiences change us.

In this sense, a theology which listens to experience stands in utter contrast to the modern obsession for methodological detached objectivism of the kind which many draw from Descartes and perhaps the scientific method. We need to abandon "the narrow subject-object pattern."[56] This does not mean being subject-centered. It means being open to the Spirit as a "Thou" as the fountain of life: to experience God in everything presupposes that the transcendent is immanent in things. The infinite is in the finite, the eternal in the temporal.[57] Hans-Georg Gadamer has shown us the fallacy of treating a text as only a passive object; especially in the case of the Bible, the text becomes active, addressing us as "objects," while we listen.[58]

---

51. Moltmann, *Spirit of Life*, p. 3.
52. Moltmann, *Spirit of Life*, p. 5.
53. Moltmann, *Spirit of Life*, p. 12.
54. Moltmann, *Spirit of Life*, p. 14.
55. Moltmann, *Spirit of Life*, p. 21; expounded more fully in Jürgen Moltmann, *A Broad Place* (London: SCM, 2007), pp. 16-18.
56. Moltmann, *Spirit of Life*, p. 33.
57. Moltmann, *Spirit of Life*, p. 35.
58. Hans-Georg Gadamer, *Truth and Method* (London: Sheed & Ward, 2nd Eng. ed. 1989), pp. 3-34, 101-29, and 265-306; cf. Anthony C. Thiselton, *Hermeneutics* (Grand Rapids: Eerdmans, 2009), pp. 206-15.

Moltmann turns next to historical experience, to "an experience of God which happens to people in the medium of history through historical events."[59] This is the point of Part II of the present book. Thus Moltmann considers uses and experiences of *rûach* in the Old Testament. The Hebrews often experience this as "the creative power of God."[60] Often this "came upon" chosen individuals, as, for example, in the book of Judges, the Spirit came upon Gideon (Judg. 6:34) and Samson (Judg. 13:25; 14:6, 19), or as he empowered Saul. Notably, "the king's endowment with the Spirit is ritualised in Israel," which provides "a messianic perspective."[61] But "inward experience" occurs in such passages as Ps. 51:10-11, "Cast me not away from thy presence, and take not thy Holy Spirit from me."

When Christians talk about the Holy Spirit, Moltmann writes, they always mean "God himself." To make this vivid he takes up the word *Shekinah* from Rabbinic Judaism. The word had originally denoted "tabernacle" or "dwelling," and comes to mean "God himself," and yet "distinct from God," or "God's self-distinction" in Hegel's thought. This is seen in God's co-suffering with Israel: "In all their affliction he was afflicted" (Isa. 63:8-9).[62] This completely coheres with the suffering of the Holy Spirit-with-Christ: "The Spirit of the LORD shall rest upon him, the Spirit of wisdom and understanding . . ." (Isa. 11:2; cf. the Spirit of judgment in Isa. 4:4). Prior to the Messianic anointing, the rebirth of Israel by the Spirit becomes a corporate hope (in Isaiah and Ezekiel 37). After that, the hope narrows again to rest on Jesus, as he proceeds to his cross and resurrection, carrying the hopes of the true Israel. Jesus is filled with the Spirit.[63]

The Church then shares this anointing of Jesus by the Spirit. Jesus prays "Abba, dear Father," and the Church echoes it. Jesus receives the Spirit "without measure" (John 3:34). In the Messianic temptations the Messianic kingship of Jesus is "put on trial," and Jesus is strengthened and upheld by the Spirit in the journey to the cross. There Christ "through the eternal Spirit offered himself without blemish to God" (Heb. 9:14). The Church takes up this attitude of trust, obedience, and Sonship in Rom. 8:15 and Gal. 4:6 where the Spirit impels the cry, "Abba, dear Father."[64] Moltmann writes, "The other side of Jesus' death is also presented as his experience of the Spirit" through the resurrection and his living presence.[65] This is also "Trinitarian communion," for "God was in Christ, reconciling the world to himself" (2 Cor. 5:19). Christology and eschatology are brought together.

59. Moltmann, *Spirit of Life*, p. 39.
60. Moltmann, *Spirit of Life*, p. 42.
61. Moltmann, *Spirit of Life*, p. 45.
62. Moltmann, *Spirit of Life*, pp. 48-49.
63. Moltmann, *Spirit of Life*, p. 60.
64. Moltmann, *Spirit of Life*, p. 63.
65. Moltmann, *Spirit of Life*, p. 65.

Moltmann adds a distinctive chapter on the Trinitarian mutuality of Christ's saving event. He expresses concern about the *filioque* clause in the Creed.[66] The Father breathes out his Word in the eternal Spirit.

The gift of the Spirit is also "the reason for the eschatological longing for the completion of salvation, the redemption of the body, and the new creation of all things."[67] "The creation waits with eager longing for the revealing of the children of God; . . . creation itself will be set free from its bondage to decay. . . . We ourselves who have the firstfruits of the Spirit, groan inwardly while we wait for the adoption, for the redemption of our bodies" (Rom. 8:19-23; 2 Cor. 1:22; 5:5; Eph. 1:14; cf. Heb. 6:5). The more deeply we experience this, and in fellowship with one another, the more certain and assured the hope for the Spirit's universal coming will be.

Part 2 of this book is the longest, embracing the Spirit of life, liberation for life, rebirth to life, the sanctification of life, the charismatic powers of life, and other themes. Christ accomplished salvation; the Holy Spirit "confers" it. Moltmann traces the theme of the vitality of the life which the Spirit confers partly through the work of Dietrich Bonhoeffer, showing how different it is from Friedrich Nietzsche's diagnosis of Christian faith as weakness and mediocrity. He observes: "We shall interpret vitality as love of life."[68]

In this sense, the contrast between the Spirit and flesh denotes strength versus frailty; trust versus self-sufficiency; the eternal versus the transitory; to be "sold under sin" (Rom. 7:14; 8:6) and deliverance. Sin, injustice, and death are confronted by the salvation longed for in apocalyptic. In Gnosticism people ceased to hope for any "redemption of the body": "In this Gnostic form, the Christian hope no longer gazes forward to a future when everything will be created anew. It looks upwards to the soul's escape from the body."[69] Without the Holy Spirit, people become centered in themselves.[70] Self-destruction follows. Mysticism can masquerade as a supposedly Christian way of becoming "turned in on oneself," in contrast to personal sociality. The life of the Spirit is "the full and unreserved 'yes' to life, and the full and unreserved love for the living, . . . 'the well of life.'"[71] How pathetic this makes Nietzsche's portrayal of Christianity look!

Moltmann explores this further in his next chapter on liberation. He notes the aims of Liberation Theology, and its vision of changing the world. For the Christian, he argues, freedom is not found "in the autonomous right of disposal of oneself and one's property," but in "the hitherto unexplored creative

---

66. Moltmann, *Spirit of Life*, pp. 71-73.
67. Moltmann, *Spirit of Life*, p. 73; cf. pp. 74-77.
68. Moltmann, *Spirit of Life*, p. 86.
69. Moltmann, *Spirit of Life*, p. 90.
70. Moltmann, *Spirit of Life*, p. 91.
71. Moltmann, *Spirit of Life*, p. 97.

powers of God," which are thrown open through the Spirit and which are "life-giving through love."[72] He adds that this freedom shows itself in sociality, or mutual love. Only through such love does human freedom enter a free world.[73] Justification also brings freedom. Guilt weighs heavily on those who have done wrong. It destroys their self-esteem and results in self-justification or self-destruction. However, God bears the pain of his love. He atones by transferring human guilt into divine suffering, through "carrying human sin."[74] "For our sake he made him to be sin who knew no sin" (2 Cor. 5:21; cf. Gal. 3:13). God's Spirit works not only in the renewal of people, but also "destabilizes" human systems of injustice.

Moltmann discusses the Nicodemus discourse in John 3:3-5 on rebirth to life and New Testament language about *palingenesia* (Tit. 3:5). The Reformers and Pietists tended to miss the *cosmic* character of new birth with its *apocalyptic* background. Taking up a quotation from Luther, Moltmann comments: "To go forward in God's ways means continually beginning afresh. . . . Not to go forward . . . means going backward."[75] Luther also saw sanctification and justification as closely related. Moltmann recounts a memorable and informative conversation between Wesley and Zinzendorf.[76] This is highly significant for those who see in Wesley the roots not only of the Holiness Movement, but also of Pentecostalism and the Renewal Movement. Clearly Zinzendorf thinks that Wesley has departed from his religion, which puzzles and perplexes Wesley. Zinzendorf accuses Wesley of denying that Christians remain "miserable sinners" *(miseros peccatores),* and even "glor[ying] over them." Wesley responds that the end of our faith, even in this life, is "Christian Perfection" *(Christiana perfectione).* Zinzendorf retorts: "I acknowledge no inherent perfection in this life. This is the error of errors. . . . I trample on it: I devote it to utter destruction. Whoever follows inherent perfection denies Christ." Further, "we are perfect in Christ; in ourselves we are never perfect." Wesley dismissed this as merely "striving about words."

Zinzendorf puts his finger on the problem when he accuses Wesley of confusing two distinct senses of "sanctification": one comes with being-in-Christ; the other depends on a long process of the Holy Spirit's work. Of course both agree, "We are renewed day by day," but what does this mean? Moltmann insists that all these terms depend upon time and context.[77] He acknowledges, however, that "Methodist testimony" to sanctification can be therapeutic.

Nevertheless with the erosion of values today we need to *search for* what ac-

72. Moltmann, *Spirit of Life,* p. 115.

73. Moltmann, *Spirit of Life,* p. 118.

74. Moltmann, *Spirit of Life,* pp. 133 and 134.

75. Moltmann, *Spirit of Life,* p. 155 (from Luther).

76. Moltmann, *Spirit of Life,* pp. 167-71.

77. Moltmann, *Spirit of Life,* p. 171.

cords with life. We need to recall our own vulnerability and frailty.[78] In one sense of the Word, "'sanctification' is . . . used for a divine act through which God chooses something for himself. . . . In this way he sanctifies his chosen people Israel, making them his people. . . . What God loves is holy."[79] But we must "sanctify what God has already sanctified."[80] Thus Luther insisted that a Christian is *semper iustus, semper peccator*. The reformed Church is *reformata reformanda*, reformed but in need of reformation. *The Holy Spirit completes his work only after this life on earth has been ended.*

When he moves on to consider "charismatic powers of life," Moltmann distinguishes between the Pauline and Lucan doctrine of the *charismata*. Yet both, however, place call and endowment together. We may speak of "special *charismata*," but "the *whole* of life and *every* life in faith is charismatic, for the Spirit is 'poured out upon all flesh.'"[81] *Kerygmatic charismata* include the gifts of apostles, prophets, teachers, evangelists, speaking with tongues and other ways of expressing faith. *Diaconal* or charitable *charismata* include deacons, people who care for the sick, those who give faithfully for charity, and widows.[82] Moltmann would not call special gifts "*supernatural* over against the '*natural*' charismata"; for believers put their natural gifts at the service of the congregation. Speaking with tongues may spring spontaneously from a situation where body language, such as throwing oneself on the ground, or raising one's hands, may respond to an intense revelation.[83] Prophetic speech is also a special *charisma*.

Healings may also occur today, although "the body of Christ needs weak and handicapped members as well as strong ones, and God gives the weak and handicapped members the most 'honor and glory' (1 Cor. 12:24)."[84] For the body of Christ is the body of one "exalted and humiliated, the risen and the crucified Christ."[85]

The last chapter of the long part 2 considers mystical experiences: "What they describe is in fact the love affair between human beings and God."[86] It often concerns the liberation of a passion for God. In ancient tradition, Fathers of the Church comprehended things with their eyes. Today we need more balance between the active life and the contemplative life. However, "Christian meditation is not transcendental meditation."[87] Its "innermost heart" is meditation on

78. Moltmann, *Spirit of Life*, p. 173.
79. Moltmann, *Spirit of Life*, p. 174.
80. Moltmann, *Spirit of Life*, p. 175.
81. Moltmann, *Spirit of Life*, p. 182 (his italics).
82. Moltmann, *Spirit of Life*, p. 183.
83. Moltmann, *Spirit of Life*, p. 185.
84. Moltmann, *Spirit of Life*, p. 193.
85. Moltmann, *Spirit of Life*, p. 193.
86. Moltmann, *Spirit of Life*, p. 199.
87. Moltmann, *Spirit of Life*, p. 203.

the passion of Christ. We may well become aware of "Christ for us" in institutionalized religion, but for Paul and others "Christ within us" is no less important.[88] Moltmann concludes that mysticism and discipleship go together and are vitally important for the Church.[89]

Moltmann is right to distinguish Christocentric and Theocentric mysticism *from counterfeit examples*. But some would argue that historically even Christian mysticism can sometimes be beguiling. It might well have been helpful if Moltmann had included a strong critique of the excesses of some mysticism. Visions and dreams could be caused *either* by sustained piety *or* by eating moldy and decaying foods; these phenomena may be self-induced, even by Christians. Luther, Emil Brunner, and Reinhold Niebuhr express reservations, as well as approval. *They are particularly critical of a "ladder of experience or piety" which penetrates to the inner presence of God*, as if to query justification by grace through faith. Moreover, "passivity" *can dull critical self-awareness* over against genuine experience of God. Few would convincingly challenge many of Moltmann's positive claims. However, the warnings from Luther, Brunner, and Niebuhr against self-deception, the undermining of grace, and the possible erosion of personhood in much mysticism are vital. They do more than complement the picture.

Part 3 of the volume contains only two chapters: on the fellowship of the Spirit, and on the Personhood of the Spirit. Moltmann defines fellowship as "opening ourselves for one another, giving one another a share in ourselves."[90] The primary biblical reference is 2 Cor. 13:13, "The fellowship of the Holy Spirit be with you all." Hence the Spirit "gives himself." The concept of *koinōnia* as fellowship is strongly "Trinitarian," in that the Spirit "enters into a relationship of reciprocity and mutuality," not unilaterally, as he is with the Father and the Son which is thus a Trinitarian relationship.[91] This includes "the love that binds," between the Spirit and his people, and between people within this fellowship.[92] Moltmann explicitly rejects a Unitarian concept of community or fellowship.

Fellowship becomes a process. (We may think of Thornton's allusion to "grafting": being grafted into Christ makes us one with him; the grafting grows ever more deeply and inextricably one.)[93] Moltmann also argues for the community in *time as well as place* "between the generations."[94] In a family or local community, parents and grandparents have special gifts for their children;

88. Moltmann, *Spirit of Life*, p. 204.
89. Moltmann, *Spirit of Life*, p. 209.
90. Moltmann, *Spirit of Life*, p. 217.
91. Moltmann, *Spirit of Life*, p. 218.
92. Moltmann, *Spirit of Life*, p. 220.
93. Lionel S. Thornton, *The Common Life in the Body of Christ* (London: Dacre, 3rd ed. 1950), pp. 144-45.
94. Moltmann, *Spirit of Life*, p. 237; cf. pp. 236-39.

more widely there is coherence with, and respect for, past tradition, in parallel with concerns with the worldwide Church. "Sociality" may be expressed in practical terms as we "find God's love *in* human love, and human love *in* God's love."[95] Friendship and affection in freedom are other manifestations of this: "We only become free when someone likes us and affirms us with affection."[96] Usually like-minded attracts like-minded, but the Holy Spirit Who Is Beyond, still draws us into his fellowship: "Love makes life worth living — it is the source of new life."[97] Often this is enhanced by physical expressions, whether this be an embrace, a handshake, "the holy kiss," or a liturgical laying on of hands.[98]

Moltmann's final chapter concerns the unique Personhood of the Holy Spirit. He claims that he is not a "person" in exactly the same sense as God the Father and God the Son, but uniquely personal.[99] To express this uniqueness he draws on metaphors which are applicable to the Spirit, and on relations in the Spirit's origin to the Holy Trinity.

The metaphors are of four kinds: personal ones such as "Lord"; "formative" ones such as "energy"; movement language such as "fire" and "love"; and mystical ones such as "light" and "water." I argued in Part I of the present book, and shall repeat in the Conclusion, that the personal metaphors are in no way compromised by what Bultmann called "dynamistic" ones. Such language as "filled" or "poured out" is what Ian Ramsey calls "qualifiers," which reshape the "personal models." Where Moltmann speaks of "unique" personhood, I spoke and will speak of the "suprapersonal" nature of the Holy Spirit.

The personal status of *Lord* comes every Sunday in the Nicene-Constantinopolitan Creed: "the Spirit, the Lord and Giver of life."[100] 2 Cor. 3:17 states, "The Lord is the Spirit," whether or not this alludes to the passage in Exodus under discussion. The Spirit as life-giver comes especially in 1 Cor. 15:45: "the life-giving Spirit." The *Paraclete* is also a personal word, whether we interpret it as *Comforter, Advocate,* or even once as *Prosecuting Counsel.*

Moltmann's "formative" metaphors should *not* be thought to "depersonalize" the Spirit. He is perhaps overly generous in suggesting that person and power blur into each other. Rather, such language as *energy* or *space* decisively qualifies the personal. Indeed, Moltmann points out that this language does *not* denote the Spirit *as agent,* but his *effects.*[101] The notion of energy as vital power goes back to the use of the Hebrew *rûach.* The Spirit can be an "energizing

95. Moltmann, *Spirit of Life,* p. 248 (his italics).
96. Moltmann, *Spirit of Life,* p. 256.
97. Moltmann, *Spirit of Life,* p. 259.
98. Moltmann, *Spirit of Life,* pp. 263-67.
99. Moltmann, *Spirit of Life,* pp. 268-69.
100. Moltmann, *Spirit of Life,* p. 270.
101. Moltmann, *Spirit of Life,* pp. 274-78.

stimulus" who "awakens unguessed of vitality." The joy that he gives may be infectious. Jer. 17:13 speaks of "the fountain of living water," as does John 4:14; cf. 7:38. He may give "multifarious configurations of life."

Movement metaphors are familiar: fire, tempest, and love, or "the rushing of a mighty wind" (Acts 2:2-4). Fire often accompanies visions of God's presence and glory, from Moses' sight of the burning bush (Exod. 3:2) to the pillar of fire by night which assured Israel of God's presence (Num. 9:15). Fire cleanses, burns, heats, and shines. "Our God is a consuming fire" (Deut. 4:24) suggests, Moltmann declares, that "he is a passionate God."[102] A characteristic promise is: "He will baptize you with the Holy Spirit and with fire (Matt. 3:11; Luke 3:16), namely, the fire of purification. Light, water, and fertility are described as mystical metaphors: "Where light, water, and warmth come together, the meadows become green and trees blossom and bear fruit."[103] Thus we also speak of the "well of life" for the thirsty.

Again, the Personhood of the Holy Spirit is Trinitarian "because his subjectivity is constituted by his inter-subjectivity."[104] Moltmann believes that the traditional way of thinking about the Holy Spirit is too "monarchical," as if God the Father always takes first place in our thoughts; the Son, second; and the Spirit, third.[105] It may be difficult, however, to hold together Moltmann's insistence on a co-equal reciprocity and mutuality in all circumstances, when, especially in Romans, 1 Corinthians, and 1 Thessalonians, God as Father seems at times to be portrayed as having some form of primacy. Critics might suggest that Moltmann interprets the relations within the Trinity in terms of a prior concern for equality in a social, almost "democratic" sense. Yet what he says needs to be heard as a corrective to an unduly metaphysical and monarchical approach to the Trinity. It is perhaps enough to bear in mind that this century is almost obsessive about "democracy" and "equality," at least in the West, in contrast to earlier generations.

Moltmann recognizes this. He asserts that the historical concept of the Trinity is connected to the monarchical concept, reversing it to the order of the times of the Father, the Son, and the Holy Spirit.[106] This much is surely right. It is not true to associate creation with the Father, redemption with the Son, and the era of the Church with the Holy Spirit. As the Church Fathers stress, all three Persons of the Trinity are involved in *every creative, redemptive, and sanctifying act.* The term "economic" Trinity could mislead us in this sense. It is also true that in what Moltmann calls "the Eucharistic Concept of the Trinity," God the Father, the Son, and the Holy Spirit all undergo a *kenōsis* or self-emptying. It is not only

102. Moltmann, *Spirit of Life*, p. 279; cf. pp. 278-81.
103. Moltmann, *Spirit of Life*, p. 283; cf. pp. 281-85.
104. Moltmann, *Spirit of Life*, p. 289.
105. Moltmann, *Spirit of Life*, pp. 290-95.
106. Moltmann, *Spirit of Life*, p. 295.

in the incarnation and the cross that this occurs. The Father, Son, and Holy Spirit give themselves in creation, in the cross, and in the life of God's people. All co-work to bring about the new creation. Moltmann writes that the eucharistic concept of the Trinity reverses the monarchical concept. The order Father → Son → Spirit in the eucharistic concept becomes Spirit → Son → Father in the monarchical one.[107] Nevertheless Moltmann recognizes that both directions of thought have a complementary place. In the end, Moltmann concedes: "Both patterns are economic concepts of the Trinity — indeed, they really sum up the two sides of salvation history, which comes 'from God' and leads 'to God.'"[108]

Only in doxology can these complementary approaches become united into one. As in the threefold *Gloria* of the Creed ("who with the Father and Son together is worshipped and glorified"), in co-equal *perichoretic* relationship, the Holy Spirit is no longer simply the third Person of the Trinity.[109] The three models of monarchical, historical, and Eucharistic Trinity are thereby brought together in doxology. As a postscript Moltmann considers again the *filioque* clause of the Creed. If all three Persons of the Trinity are involved in all God's deeds, the procession from the Father and the Son is presupposed. In this sense "the *filioque* addition contributes nothing new"; while *with* this addition the Holy Spirit takes third place in the primordial relationship of the Trinity.[110]

A simpler, shorter, and more user-friendly version of this volume is published as *The Source of Life*.[111] Five of the eleven chapters were first delivered as oral lectures in 1990, 1995, and 1996. Chapter 11, however, "What Are We Doing When We Pray?" is entirely fresh. "To come to God only with entreaties is hardly the expression of a true love for God."[112] Hence he begins with a cry to God which includes complaint, silence, wishes, craving, groaning, thinking, praising, and rejoicing. God is more than a heavenly helper. If God is *Abba*, our dear Father, children address their parents trustfully about what is on their mind. Even friends share their sorrows and joys, and are bonded to each other in affection. In relation to God, this is "prayer in the Holy Spirit."

A section on bodily posture follows. There is biblical precedent for kneeling (Ps. 95:6; Phil. 2:10). But early Christian figures depicted in catacombs in Rome and Naples "are standing upright, heads raised and eyes open. Their arms are stretched above their heads, their hands open, palms upwards."[113] It suggests expectation. The upright stance shows that God is no longer feared.

---

107. Moltmann, *Spirit of Life*, p. 300.

108. Moltmann, *Spirit of Life*, p. 300.

109. Moltmann, *Spirit of Life*, p. 304.

110. Moltmann, *Spirit of Life*, p. 306.

111. Jürgen Moltmann, *The Source of Life: The Holy Spirit and the Theology of Life* (London: SCM, 1997).

112. Moltmann, *The Source of Life*, p. 125.

113. Moltmann, *The Source of Life*, p. 128.

Each one may correspond to a specific situation, but standing seems to have many advantages.

Moltmann then considers the world as "full of praise." "All the trees of the wood sing for joy" (Ps. 96:12). "All creatures are aflame with the present glory of the Lord."[114] Only our modern era can see the natural world as dumb. Prayer may be specific and as unreserved as possible: "we begin to love God for his own sake. . . . we forget ourselves."[115] We pray in the name of Jesus, and support others in specific intercessions.[116] All this becomes possible through the Person and work of the Holy Spirit, through Christ, according to the loving will of God our Father.

In the exposition of Jürgen Moltmann, the Person and work of the Holy Spirit have become the most practical of subjects. As the subtitle of the major volume indicates, this study is broad and universal in its scope. It adheres closely to the New Testament, but also draws on experience and history. It is closely related to *The Trinity and the Kingdom of God, God in Creation,* and *The Way of Jesus Christ.* It considers the role of experience and what this amounts to, transcending merely individual experience. It looks at new creation and sanctification and considers "gifts of the Spirit." Like Congar's books from the Catholic side, it engages with the Renewal Movement. It would be unreasonable to expect agreement with, or endorsement of, every paragraph. But the three contributions considered in this chapter have been selected not only because of the stature of each writer, but also because, in my own view, they also invite a very large measure of agreement.

21.3. Wolfhart Pannenberg

Wolfhart Pannenberg (b. 1928) became Professor of Systematic Theology first at Mainz and then at Munich. He holds numerous doctorates, and is deservedly one of the very few overseas Fellows of the British Academy. His most wide-ranging and influential work is his three-volume *Systematic Theology* (German, 1988-93; English, 1991-98).[117] His three volumes of *Basic Questions in Theology* appeared in English in 1970, 1971, and 1973 (German, 1967 and 1972).[118] His *Theology and the Philosophy of Science* was translated into English in 1976; his *Reality and Faith* in 1977, and *Jesus — God and Man* in 1968.[119] He

---

114. Moltmann, *The Source of Life,* p. 134.

115. Moltmann, *The Source of Life,* p. 140.

116. Moltmann, *The Source of Life,* pp. 140-44.

117. Wolfhart Pannenberg, *Systematic Theology,* 3 vols. (Grand Rapids: Eerdmans, and Edinburgh: T&T Clark, 1991-98).

118. Wolfhart Pannenberg, *Basic Questions in Theology,* 3 vols. (London: SCM, 1970-73).

119. Wolfhart Pannenberg, *Jesus — God and Man* (London: SCM, and Philadelphia: Westminster, 1968; German 1964).

has written numerous other volumes, too many to list. He first came to significant notice in 1961 for his work with colleagues known as "the Pannenberg Circle," *Revelation as History.* Since that time the twin themes of the resurrection and history in its broadest sense have marked his work. Some have written of him as the first great alternative to Barth and Bultmann. Pannenberg's own account of his early studies can be found in the volume edited by Carl Braaten and Philip Clayton.[120]

Pannenberg studied at the Universities of Berlin, Göttingen, Basel, and Heidelberg. His first teaching posts were at Heidelberg and then with Moltmann at Wuppertal, until he became a professor at Mainz. At Heidelberg Hans von Campenhausen introduced him to Augustine's interpretation of history in *City of God,* and Gerhard von Rad influenced his views on prophecy, promise, and fulfillment in history. This was amplified by the work of Walter Zimmerli and Oscar Cullmann. But the decisive step for Pannenberg was his own strong and positive view of the resurrection of Jesus Christ as the central point of the meaning of history, and its promise, meaning, and fulfillment. This constitutes the most distinctive claim of Christian faith. It also involves rational processes, and (against Bultmann) is not the mere product of the Church's faith. Pannenberg comments, "History is the most comprehensive horizon of Christian theology. All theological questions and answers are meaningful only within the framework of the history which God has with humanity and . . . his whole creation."[121]

Historical-critical procedures and methods are marred by "anthropocentricity."[122] These methods are "inspired within an anthropocentric worldview" and often concern the "ghetto of redemptive history."[123] "Agreement with normal, ordinary, repeatedly attested modes of occurrences and conditions as we know them" would exclude apocalyptic hope of new creation, the resurrection, and much of the work of the Holy Spirit.[124] In the light of the resurrection and the coming of the Holy Spirit "What formerly seemed insignificant may perhaps appear later as of fundamental importance. . . . The first steps have barely been taken towards a decisive breakthrough to the primacy of the future," which then reveals history as a whole.[125]

In this sense, Pannenberg approaches the theology of the Holy Spirit in two distinctive ways. In *Jesus — God and Man* he sees "God's presence in Jesus, . . .

120. Carl E. Braaten and Philip Clayton, *The Theology of Wolfhart Pannenberg* (Minneapolis: Fortress, 1988), pp. 11-18.

121. Pannenberg, "Redemptive Event and History," in *Basic Questions,* vol. 1, p. 15; cf. pp. 15-80.

122. Pannenberg, *Basic Questions,* vol. 1, p. 39.

123. Pannenberg, *Basic Questions,* vol. 1, pp. 40 and 41.

124. Pannenberg, *Basic Questions,* vol. 1, p. 44.

125. Pannenberg, "Eschatology and the Experience of Meaning," in *Basic Questions,* vol. 3, pp. 201 and 207.

characterized by the concept of the Spirit."[126] But it is scarcely surprising that for most of their narrative the writers of the Gospels see Jesus from the *previous* side of the resurrection: "the pre-Easter Jesus, the eschatological prophet."[127] The context is largely that of *traditions from the past.* But this is not adequate for Paul. Because of *the resurrection and the Holy Spirit,* he was able to speak about the sending of the preexistent Son of God into the flesh," according to the Spirit (Rom 1:3-4).[128] From this vantage point we can arrive at a full Christology of the incarnation and resurrection and a doctrine of the Holy Spirit.[129]

The second distinctive way of speaking about the Holy Spirit emerges in the third volume of Pannenberg's *Systematic Theology.* Pannenberg sees the whole of the *event of creation* as a *Trinitarian event,* involving the Father, the Son, and the Holy Spirit. He comments: "God's Spirit is not only active in human redemption as he teaches us to know the eternal Son of the Father in Jesus of Nazareth, and moves our hearts to praise God. . . . The Spirit is at work already in creation as God's mighty breath, the origin of all movement and life."[130] We must not restrict the work of the Holy Spirit to *"supernatural"* gifts; he is "none other than the Creator of all life in the whole range of natural occurrences, and also in the new creation of the resurrection of the dead."[131] Paul speaks of his "indwelling" believers, but we must perceive his creative work "everywhere" and finally in his "triumph over death."[132]

After such a beginning, and within the framework, Pannenberg then addresses the work of the *Holy Spirit in sanctification.* The medieval period and the Reformation brought together a theology of the Spirit and grace. But one of the achievements of New Testament scholars in the twentieth century remains the re-discovery of the close link between the *Holy Spirit and eschatology.* Otto Weber and Karl Barth also spoke of the "awakening power" of the Spirit. One common element between the Spirit as Creator and the Spirit as Sanctifier is his "fashioning" or "transfiguring power."[133] Thereby God's creatures may share in his glory. In this process, however, the Holy Spirit above all is the Spirit of Christ. Hence Christ as Lord "imparts" the Spirit to the disciples of Jesus (John 20:22). The Father and the Son "work together in sending the Spirit."[134] Jesus is also seen as recipient of the Spirit. Pannenberg is also one of the relatively few to note (as N. T. Wright and I have done) that *sōma*

---

126. Pannenberg, *Jesus — God and Man,* p. 116.
127. Pannenberg, *Jesus — God and Man,* p. 117.
128. Pannenberg, *Jesus — God and Man,* p. 119.
129. Pannenberg, *Jesus — God and Man,* pp. 121-23.
130. Pannenberg, *Systematic Theology,* vol. 3, p. 1.
131. Pannenberg, *Systematic Theology,* vol. 3, p. 2.
132. Pannenberg, *Systematic Theology,* vol. 3, p. 2.
133. Pannenberg, *Systematic Theology,* vol. 3, p. 4.
134. Pannenberg, *Systematic Theology,* vol. 3, p. 5.

pneumatikon, spiritual "body," denotes that which is given and *characterized by the Holy Spirit* (1 Cor. 15:44).[135]

The pre-Easter life of Jesus is seen to be filled with the Holy Spirit, in the light of the Easter event. This especially colors John's Christology and theology of the Spirit. When the Spirit is at work in believers, he "is not just . . . an invisible and incomprehensible field of force," but the *Spirit of Christ.*[136] He imparts *himself* in a creative, dynamic way. Pannenberg urges: "Only to the degree that the Son is manifested in creaturely life does the work of the Spirit in creation take on the form of gift."[137] He now makes the profound point that whereas gifts and endowments to individuals, or even the nation in the Old Testament, end, at the latest, at the moment of death (Eccl. 12:7), for Christian believers the *Spirit effects the resurrection and beyond* (Rom. 8:11).[138] The Holy Spirit constitutes an eschatological endowment. The Spirit is "a lasting possession of believers," and makes possible "participation in the eternal life of God."[139]

Pannenberg then considers the outpouring of the Holy Spirit at Pentecost in Acts 2. He views the experience of "tongues" as a collective experience of ecstatic speech (Acts 2:4, 12-15). But he acknowledges that it is hard to be precise. He comments, "Luke leaves room for the spontaneity of the experience of the Spirit as the source of the community's proclamation of Christ."[140] At all events, it is about *universal missionary proclamation.* Some speak of Pentecost as the "foundation" of the Church; but for Paul *only Christ is the foundation* (1 Cor. 3:1). The Spirit's close link with Christ appears in John, and in Rom. 8:14-16 as well as elsewhere in Paul: "The Spirit and the Son mutually indwell one another as Trinitarian persons."[141] The Spirit's manifestations, Pannenberg urges, show individuality and plurality, but differences between gifts should not occasion division in the Church (1 Cor. 12:11). Like so many other contemporary thinkers, he opposes and regrets a false opposition between the Word and the Spirit. However, the Spirit's listening to Christ can act "as a brake on the unregulated enthusiasm that, with an appeal to the dynamic of the Spirit, breaks free from the Church's tradition and institutional order."[142] Such "breaking free" is not to be counted as a sign of spiritual vitality.

---

135. Pannenberg, *Systematic Theology,* vol. 3, p. 6; Anthony C. Thiselton, *Life after Death: A New Approach to the Last Things* (Grand Rapids: Eerdmans, and London: SPCK, 2012), pp. 122-28; Thiselton, *The First Epistle to the Corinthians: A Commentary on the Greek Text,* NIGTC (Grand Rapids: Eerdmans, 2000), pp. 1276-89; N. T. Wright, *The Resurrection of the Son of God* (London: SPCK, 2003), pp. 353-55.

136. Pannenberg, *Systematic Theology,* vol. 3, p. 7.

137. Pannenberg, *Systematic Theology,* vol. 3, p. 9.

138. Pannenberg, *Systematic Theology,* vol. 3, p. 10.

139. Pannenberg, *Systematic Theology,* vol. 3, p. 12.

140. Pannenberg, *Systematic Theology,* vol. 3, p. 14.

141. Pannenberg, *Systematic Theology,* vol. 3, p. 17.

142. Pannenberg, *Systematic Theology,* vol. 3, p. 20.

After an appendix on the Church, Pannenberg also writes on the relations between the Holy Spirit, the Church, and the Kingdom. *Kingdom and Church are not identical. God's reign* as sovereign *King* requires justice and total obedience from his subjects. Thus the *Church cannot be "a full expression" of the Kingdom of God.* It is "an anticipatory sign of God's coming rule."[143] A sign points beyond itself. Hence, like Moltmann, Pannenberg never sees the Church as existing for itself, but as responding to the Spirit in building itself up and in bringing in the Kingdom. Historically Augustine implied this in his dealings with the Donatists. There can be no "pure" Church on this side of the grave. Rudolf Schnackenburg, Pannenberg notes, has stressed this distinction between the Kingdom and the Church. As Karl Rahner urged, the Church may be thought of as a visible sign, or sacrament, *of that to which it points,* namely, *"final salvation."*[144] Hence the nature of the Church is "a pilgrimage toward a future that is still ahead. . . . The church, then, is not identical with the Kingdom of God. It is a sign of the Kingdom's future of salvation."[145] Vatican II defined the Church in this way, as "a sacrament of salvation."

The Holy Spirit, therefore, does not abolish the institutional, but *relativizes it.* There is nothing permanent about the institution, but it can facilitate faithfulness and *continuity.* The *Spirit points beyond this,* and empowers the pilgrim church to move forward on its way. Yet the Holy Spirit's work is cosmic in scope. Pannenberg paints grand, majestic pictures of the Spirit, the world, and history, from *creation, through the present, onward to the eschaton.*

21.4. Vladimir N. Lossky and John D. Zizioulas

The mistaken popular image that there was little development in Eastern Orthodox theology after the era of the Church Fathers is wide of the mark. The intellectual vigor of the Russian Orthodox Church arguably reached a climax in Vladimir Nikolaevich Lossky (1903-58), who was exiled from Russia in 1922. His biographer, Olivier Clément, calls him the theologian of the Person and work of the Holy Spirit, in order to identify his two major concerns. John D. Zizioulas (b. 1931), Metropolitan of Pergamon, is described by many, including Kärkkäinen, as "the most significant Eastern Orthodox theologian of our day."[146] He shares some of Lossky's themes. Zizioulas stresses the mutuality of Christology and the doctrine of the Holy Spirit in the New Testament and in the Eastern Fathers. In effect, there is no "Christ" without the Holy Spirit. This theme is em-

---

143. Pannenberg, *Systematic Theology,* vol. 3, p. 32.
144. Pannenberg, *Systematic Theology,* vol. 3, p. 35.
145. Pannenberg, *Systematic Theology,* vol. 3, pp. 36-37.
146. Veli-Matti Kärkkäinen, *Pneumatology* (Grand Rapids: Baker Academic, 2002), p. 106.

bedded in the later twentieth-century expression of the Greek Orthodox tradition. Nikos A. Nissiotis, for example, sees "Pneumatology [as] the heart of the Christian religion, touching all aspects of our faith in Christ."[147]

(1) *Vladimir Lossky.* Lossky was educated in St. Petersburg, but was forced to leave Russia in 1922. After further training in Prague, he arrived in Paris in 1924 and studied more extensively at the Sorbonne. He soon began work on the medieval mystic Meister Eckhart, who remained a lifelong interest. His first degree had been in the field of medieval history. His most important book is probably *The Mystical Theology of the Eastern Church,* in which he expounds "Deification," or more accurately *theōsis,* as a central concept.[148] Alongside his work on the mysticism of Eckhart, Lossky wrote an early work on the theology of negation in Pseudo-Dionysius. Negative theology implied, for Lossky, that God cannot be grasped by human analytical concepts, descriptions, or formulas. A cardinal theme is the difference between objective *"nature,"* or "natural" individuality, and *personal being.* Personal being is known, in Rowan Williams's helpful words, "in *ekstasis* and *kenōsis,* self-transcending and self-forgetting, the overcoming of the boundaries of mutual exclusion that define individuals over against each other."[149] God is the supreme paradigm of personal being, of a life wholly lived in *ekstasis* and *kenōsis.* At the same time Lossky also drew on the medieval thought of Gregory Palamas (1296-1359). Gregory drew a careful distinction between God's "essence," which lies beyond human knowledge, and God's "energies," through which he can be known and in which human beings can participate. Lossky spoke explicitly of "the Palamite synthesis."[150]

The Holy Spirit reproduces the image of God through the Christian Church. The Spirit enables us to be the kind of "personal being" that, like God, does not divide oneself off from anyone else or from the world, but takes the "risk" of entering into a mutual relationship with "a free and independent other": "divine freedom is accomplished through creating this supreme risk: another freedom."[151] But creation is a work of the whole Trinity. The Father is "Maker of heaven and earth"; the Son is he "by whom all things were made"; and the Spirit is "the Giver of Life."[152] On the same page he quotes Athanasius: "The Father created all things by the Son in the Holy Spirit." He also quotes Ba-

147. S. Paul Schilling, *Contemporary Continental Theologians* (London: SCM, 1966), p. 231.

148. Vladimir N. Lossky, *The Mystical Theology of the Eastern Church* (New York: St. Vladimir's Seminary Press, 1988). The French appeared in 1944, and the English in 1957.

149. Rowan Williams, "Eastern Orthodox Theology," in *The Modern Theologians,* ed. David Ford (Oxford: Blackwell, 3rd ed. 2005), p. 579; cf. pp. 572-88.

150. Vladimir N. Lossky, *The Vision of God* (New York: St. Vladimir's Seminary Press, 1983), p. 153.

151. Vladimir N. Lossky, *Orthodox Theology* (New York: St. Vladimir's Seminary Press, 2001), p. 54.

152. Lossky, *Mystical Theology,* p. 100.

sil: the Father is the "primordial cause" of creation; the Son is the "operating cause"; the Holy Spirit is "the perfecting cause."[153]

A "person," then, can be unified with God by the Holy Spirit, by way of *theōsis* or transfiguration, in the process of "becoming." Unless there are mutuality, relationality, and movement, a person remains a "thing," or part of nature, to be *objectified* as an "it." Lossky appeals to the concept in Irenaeus of the Son and the Spirit as the two "hands of God," so that the sanctified Christian community forms a whole "within the hand of God."[154] This becomes the "ecclesiastical" new creation. Anticipating Zizioulas, he sees an authentic person, led by the Spirit, not as an isolated individual who erects defensive barriers around the self, but as a person in the interconnected give-and-take of communion *(koinōnia)*. Through the Holy Spirit this becomes a community of love. Lossky develops further his contrast between nature and person in his book *In the Image and Likeness of God*.[155] Through the Spirit humans are to become like their Creator, in the process of divinization, deification, or *theōsis*.

(2) *John D. Zizioulas.* Zizioulas represents the Greek Orthodox Church rather than the Russian, but shares many of Lossky's concerns. His main arguments are encapsulated in the title of his book *Being as Communion*.[156] Born in 1931, he took a D.Theol. degree at the University of Athens in 1965, was a professor at the University of Glasgow from 1973 to 1987, and became Metropolitan of Pergamon in 1986. He has written a number of books, including *Eucharist, Bishop, and Church* (2001) and *Communion and Otherness* (2006). The Church, he argues, is founded on a twofold economy: that of Christ, and that of the Holy Spirit. From one point of view, he writes, "the Spirit is given by Christ, particularly the risen and ascended Christ ('there was no Spirit yet, for Christ had not yet been glorified [John 7:39]')." The other point of view suggests "that there is, so to say, *no Christ until the Spirit is at work,* not only as a *forerunner* announcing his coming, but also as the one who *constitutes his very identity as Christ,* either at his baptism (Mark) or at his very biological conception (Matthew and Luke). Both of these views could coexist happily in one and the same biblical writing" (first italics his; second, mine).[157]

The centrality of both Christ and the Spirit, as well as that of the Holy Trinity, cannot be doubted. Zizioulas's second theme, that of communion or relationality, almost replicates the view of Lossky, except that in the case of Zizioulas the Church becomes more dominant. He writes: "Ecclesial being is

153. Lossky, *Mystical Theology*, pp. 100-101; Basil, *On the Holy Spirit*, 16:38.

154. Lossky, *Mystical Theology*, p. 106.

155. Vladimir N. Lossky, *In the Image and Likeness of God* (New York: St. Vladimir's Seminary Press, 1974).

156. John D. Zizioulas, *Being as Communion: Studies in Personhood and the Church* (New York: St. Vladimir's Seminary Press, 1997).

157. Zizioulas, *Being as Communion*, pp. 127-28 (his italics).

bound to the very being of God. . . . It is a way of *relationship* with the world, with other people, and with God, an event of *communion*. . . . It cannot be realized as the achievement of an *individual,* but only as an ecclesial *fact*" (his italics).[158] The Church must be an image of the way in which God exists.

Zizioulas writes, "God is a relational being: without the concept of communion it would not be possible to speak of the being of God. . . . 'God' has no ontological content, no true being, apart from communion."[159] He adds: "Nothing exists as an 'individual,' conceivable in itself. . . . Communion does not come from a 'hypostasis.'"[160] He believes that a proper synthesis "between Christology and Pneumatology" is "the basis of . . . ecclesiology."[161] On the subject of the Holy Spirit, Zizioulas strikingly declares: "The Holy Spirit is not one who *aids us* in bridging the distance between Christ and ourselves, but he is the person of the Trinity who actually *realizes in history that which we call Christ,* this absolutely relational entity, our Saviour. In this case, Christology *is essentially conditioned by Pneumatology*" (my italics).[162]

Zizioulas argues that Vatican II did not allow Pneumatology to play a sufficiently important role. When it did refer to the Spirit, the Spirit "was brought into ecclesiology *after* the edifice of the Church was constructed with Christological material alone."[163] To Zizioulas the reason was all too plain. Christ *instituted* the Church as an institution, or, in Lossky's language, as an *objective* or objectified entity. But Zizioulas and Lossky see the Spirit as giving life to the Church in *its charismatic* aspect. However, Zizioulas concedes: "The problem *how* to relate the institutional with the charismatic, the Christological with the Pneumatological aspects of ecclesiology, still awaits treatment by Orthodox theology."[164] But there is a key principle: "The unity between Christology and Pneumatology remains unbreakable."[165]

Finally, the doctrine of the Holy Spirit ensures "the importance of the *local* church in ecclesiology."[166] This does not deny or reduce the Church's catholicity. This is *not* Congregationalism. The Eucharist, Zizioulas argues, demonstrates "the *simultaneity* of both local and universal."[167] It is *not* "a confederation of local churches."[168] He concludes: "Pneumatology must be made constitutive of

---

158. Zizioulas, *Being as Communion*, p. 15.
159. Zizioulas, *Being as Communion*, p. 17.
160. Zizioulas, *Being as Communion*, p. 18.
161. Zizioulas, *Being as Communion*, p. 107.
162. Zizioulas, *Being as Communion*, pp. 110-11.
163. Zizioulas, *Being as Communion*, p. 123.
164. Zizioulas, *Being as Communion*, p. 125.
165. Zizioulas, *Being as Communion*, p. 129.
166. Zizioulas, *Being as Communion*, p. 132.
167. Zizioulas, *Being as Communion*, p. 133.
168. Zizioulas, *Being as Communion*, p. 136.

Christology and ecclesiology, i.e., the condition of the very being of Christ and the Church."[169]

So far we have omitted one very important part of the concerns of Zizioulas. He is deeply concerned to show that all his comments derive from the Fathers of the Eastern Church, and ultimately from Scripture. The work which he and Lossky present has often been called "hermeneutical," in the sense of offering a careful re-presentation of the work of the Eastern Fathers for today. Both frequently cite Athanasius, Basil, and the other Cappadocian Fathers in support of their claims. Basil, for example, is "rather unhappy with the notion of substance as an ontological category and tends to replace it — significantly enough for our subject here — with that of *koinōnia*."[170] With Ignatius and Irenaeus (who had roots in both East and West) we find the beginnings of "the identification of being with life."[171] The work of both theologians largely facilitates our appreciation of Eastern Orthodoxy, both Russian and Greek. Zizioulas concludes that the Holy Spirit does not "add" to the essence of the Church; the Spirit "is the very essence of the Church."[172]

In this chapter we have considered Congar, Moltmann, Pannenberg, Lossky, and Zizioulas. All these thinkers are creative and to be taken with the utmost seriousness. In strictly personal terms, I find these five thinkers among the most satisfying writers on this subject. All write with judiciousness and sensitivity, yet each represents a different strand of tradition within theology and the Church.

---

169. Zizioulas, *Being as Communion*, p. 139.
170. Zizioulas, *Being as Communion*, p. 134.
171. Zizioulas, *Being as Communion*, p. 93.
172. Zizioulas, *Being as Communion*, p. 132.

22

Other Writers from the End of the Century: 1986-2000

22.1. The Blossoming of the Renewal Movement and Its "Third Wave"

During the 1980s, Peter Hocken declared: "The majority of denominations adopted positions of cautious openness, neither welcoming C.R. [Charismatic Renewal] with enthusiasm, not rejecting it as inauthentic."[1] Generally they accepted the validity of Pentecostal experience and its "gifts of the Spirit." But they rejected the Pentecostal theology of a "baptism in the Spirit" subsequent to faith-initiation or conversion, and the "initial evidence" of this "baptism" in glossolalia. Meanwhile the Renewal Movement, like Pentecostalism, became an increasingly international Movement. It also crossed the boundaries of traditional denominations, even sometimes or often leaving traditions for "house churches."

During the 1980s "house churches" often used the term "Restoration" in the Pentecostal sense of an alleged return to Apostolic Church theology and practices by seeking especially to replicate the early years recounted in Acts. The ministry of the laity was emphasized, together with the warmth and friendship of more intimate groups. Indeed, on the Internet many ascribe their involvement with either Pentecostalism or the Renewal Movement as primarily due to the warm social ethos which they found there. In the 1990s they more often became known as "new churches." In the Church of England "Fresh Expressions" came later to be introduced as a way of encouraging this kind of growth, but strictly within constraints approved by the bishop of the relevant diocese, or his deputy.

Another main phenomenon occurred in the increasing attention to *intellectual competence,* mainly in Pentecostalism and more slowly in the Renewal

---

1. Peter Hocken, "Charismatic Movement," in *NIDPCM,* p. 483.

Movement. A number of *seminaries* were founded, for example, Glynn Hall among Assemblies of God in America, and Mattersey Hall, for a time under David Petts, near Sheffield in England. Some explicitly Pentecostal and Renewal students attended and still attend Fuller Theological Seminary, Pasadena, and Gordon-Conwell Theological Seminary in South Hamilton, MA.[2] John Wimber lectures at Fuller on "The Miraculous and Church Growth," which is both popular and controversial. Even more significant has become *The Journal of Pentecostal Theology,* with a wide range of articles, and the *Journal's JPT* Supplements, which are sometimes or often of a high scholarly quality. Gordon Fee, Roger Stronstad, and Max Turner, as we saw throughout Chapter 20, have published scholarly New Testament contributions, Fee on Paul, and Stronstad and Turner on Luke-Acts. From within the Roman Catholic tradition, Kilian McDonnell (b. 1921) has collected numerous documents in his *Presence, Power, and Praise* (3 vols., 1980); and published *Christian Initiation and Baptism in the Holy Spirit* (1991) and *Towards a New Pentecost* (1993).

Pentecostals sometimes offer self-criticisms which seem to find little parallel in the Renewal Movement. Perhaps this is because officially, at least, the Renewal Movement seems to affirm the tenets of the particular major denomination within which they function. By contrast, Pentecostals usually see themselves as a distinctive tradition or denomination. The Internet teems with examples, some on Facebook. One comes from Paul Alexander.[3] He pleads with Assemblies of God to reconsider their stance toward (1) racism: this demands "repentance"; (2) war and military service: Assemblies of God have changed their stance from earlier years, and need fresh theological consideration; (3) Israel/Palestine: we need to become "less dispensational and less one-sidedly Zionist"; and (4) gender: too many fail to support women as senior pastors. Alexander concludes by urging: "Seek Jesus" more seriously; and "Journey forward in confession and truth-telling regarding our racist past."

To be sure, a few are bold enough to express concerns about "Charismatic Reformation," and below we consider Tom Smail's perceptive comments. J. Lee Grady, contributing editor of *Charisma* and author of *The Holy Spirit Is Not for Sale,* lists fifteen criticisms of the Charismatic Movement. He argues that "The so-called 'Spirit-filled' Church of today struggles with many of the same things the Catholic Church [and Luther] faced in the 1500s."[4] He continues: "We don't have popes — we have super-apostles. We don't support an untouchable priesthood — we throw our money at celebrity evangelists who own fleets of private jets." In place of negative criticism, he pleads for a reform

---

2. Cecil M. Robeck, "Seminaries and Graduate Schools," in *NIDPCM,* pp. 1045-50.

3. Paul Alexander, "Four Suggestions for Assemblies of God," *Internet,* March 27, 2010, pp. 1-3.

4. J. Lee Grady, "It's (Past) Time for a Charismatic Reformation," *Internet,* October 26, 2011, pp. 1-2.

"of our theology"; a return to the Bible; "we charismatics must stop blaming everything on demons"; "gentleness is a fruit of the Holy Spirit"; "we must stop giving platforms to ministers who make outlandish claims of supernatural financial returns"; the need for "independent" evangelists to be accountable; and nine other "reforms."

Peter Hocken suggests that after 1980 the era of big conferences ended, and some even spoke of a "decline" in the Movement.[5] It had become less of a novelty to the traditional churches, and rather than speaking of "decline," many would see this era as a blossoming after a rather defensive and more aggressive phase. Some were happy to speak of "being open to the Spirit," or "being filled" or simply "renewed" by the Spirit," rather than being "baptized in the Spirit," and to regard tongues no longer as "initial evidence" of this experience, but rather as *one gift among others.* The Movement also became more varied, and in 1983 Peter Wagner began to use the term "Third Wave." Some described this as "neo-charismatic."

The "Third Wave," however, did not represent any dilution of a charismatic emphasis. It stressed healings, casting out demons, and receiving and announcing "prophecies"; but "baptism in the Spirit" was now thought to occur at regeneration or conversion (1 Cor. 12:13) rather than as a "second blessing."[6] After conversion the hope was for *multiple renewal* or more than one filling with the Holy Spirit. Speaking in tongues was not considered as an "initial evidence" of filling by the Spirit. Most of all, this "Third Wave" sought *to avoid divisiveness* and to shun any thought that the "Spirit-filled" were a first-class spiritual elite in comparison with other Christians.

Some movements, however, might be perceived as traveling in a different direction. In the 1990s some traditional Christians expressed consternation at the so-called "Toronto Blessing." This was associated with the Vineyard Movement and often with "The Third Wave." John Wimber had founded the Vineyard Christian Fellowship in 1987. Manifestations of revival occurred at the Toronto Airport Vineyard Network in 1994, and these were apparently carried back to England, especially to Holy Trinity, Brompton, in central London. The pastor of Vineyard, John Arnott, preferred to use the term "The Father's Blessing" to "Toronto Blessing." It gave rise to nightly renewal meetings, each attended by two to four thousand people. Stories were told of people "slain in the Spirit," or "resting in the Spirit," apparently so overcome by the Holy Spirit as to seem to become inanimate. "Holy Laughter" was a manifestation which had appeared in earlier years.[7] There were apparently numerous unusual physical ex-

---

5. Hocken, "Charismatic Movement," in *NIDPCM*, pp. 485-86.

6. C. Peter Wagner, "Third Wave," in *NIDPCM*, p. 1141.

7. Joe Maxwell, "Laughter Draws Toronto Charismatic Crowds," *Christianity Today* 38, no. 12 (1994).

pressions of "release" brought about by the Spirit. But in 1995 the Airport Church was disaffiliated from the Vineyard Movement. Holy Trinity, Brompton, is now said to be far from extreme.

Since Peter Wagner is associated with the "Third Wave" of the Renewal Movement, we may refer to his description of its content and distinctiveness. He writes, "The desire of those in the third wave is to experience the power of the Holy Spirit in healing the sick, casting out demons, receiving prophecies and participating in other charismatic type manifestations without disturbing the current philosophy of ministry governing their congregations."[8] Wagner then expounds five distinctive themes.

Three distinctive themes include: (1) "belief that the baptism of the Holy Spirit occurs *at conversion* (1 Cor. 12:13) rather than [as] a second work of grace"; (2) "expectations of *multiple fillings* of the Holy Spirit subsequent to new birth"; and (3) "a *low-key* acceptance of tongues as one of many New Testament gifts . . . *not* considered the *initial physical validation* of a certain spiritual experience . . . but a gift used by some for . . . prayer language."[9] These three characteristics clearly distinguish the "Third Wave" from classical Pentecostalism, and would be broadly accepted, although with considerable caution, by many "mainline" churches, denominations, or traditions, but probably not by all.

Wagner adds fourth and fifth distinctive elements, which seem sufficiently *broad and general* also to win general assent and approval: "ministry under the power and *anointing of the Holy Spirit*" (my italics), and references to the *worshiping community rather than to a faith-healer*. The fifth principle arises explicitly from the aim of *"avoidance of divisiveness."* Unity has been fundamental to the work of the Holy Spirit since Acts, Paul, John, Ephesians, and Clement of Rome. But what exactly does the fourth theme involve? Many traditional churches would not endorse the generalized expectancy of healing the sick, casting out demons, and receiving and announcing prophecies as outlined above.

It is possible that there is a divergence between theology and practice here. Mark Bonnington comments, "John Wimber's Vineyard movement and their so-called 'third wave' teaching are consciously attempting a synthesis of charismatic ideas with traditional evangelical ones. Spirit 'baptism' is played down in favour of other metaphors ('filling') in line with the fact that the 'initial' experience of the Spirit is subordinated to repeated Spirit-filling. Nevertheless the experiences or 'sensible' nature of Spirit-filling remains central."[10] As well as

---

8. C. Peter Wagner, "Third Wave," in *NIDPCM*, p. 1141.

9. Wagner, "Third Wave," in *NIDPCM*, p. 1141 (my italics).

10. Mark Bonnington, *Patterns in Charismatic Spirituality* (Cambridge: Grove Books, 2007), p. 7.

making secondary the notion of "baptism in the Spirit" as a "second blessing," the Third Wave remains thoroughly *Trinitarian*.

What of the early Pentecostal vision of the "Foursquare" Gospel of Christ as Savior, Baptizer in the Spirit, Healer, and Coming King? The first and the fourth are held firmly by "mainline" churches, even if Pentecostals are right to emphasize the fourth more clearly than many established churches tend to do in practice. We have seen that the second is largely modified into an extended and multiple *process,* but still requires a quasi-physical "experience." The most sensitive remains the third, where the very large Report on Healing by the Church of England Synod leads to a different degree of expectancy and centrality from what characterizes most established churches. This brings with it a corresponding pastoral shift.

We may return to Mark Cartledge's account of Third Wave worship. He describes "the classic Vineyard model" as involving not only "songs" and a sermon. Additional to this, there is a strong expectation of supposedly replicated "words of knowledge," "public invocation of tongues," and other "charismatic" phenomena.[11] The problem here is that "the word of knowledge" has little correspondence with our exegetical work in Part I, and with the account of tongues-speech in Luke-Acts and in Paul. These do not seem to follow "invocation." Worse, Harvey Cox recounts that in his writings "Wagner himself asserts that 'Satan delegates high-ranking members of the hierarchy of evil spirits to control nations, regions, cities, tribes, peoples, groups, neighborhoods and other significant networks of human beings throughout the world.'"[12] Hence exorcisms and casting out demons became a regular feature of the Third Wave meetings. Cox's appeal to C. S. Lewis that we should neither magnify the influence of demons nor discount them altogether is probably right.[13] But, as Yves Congar wisely points out, these practices are not the standard practices of any "mainline" denomination, and take us much nearer to Pentecostal theology, with its frequent *dualism of the natural and supernatural.* Further, Mark Cartledge in another work endorses the verdict of Vinson Synan with respect to the Third Wave: "While rejecting the hardline Pentecostal opinion, most theologians were willing to admit that tongues were the 'usual,' 'normal' or most common 'consequence' of receiving the 'baptism.'"[14]

11. Mark J. Cartledge (ed.), *Speaking in Tongues: Multi-Disciplinary Perspectives* (Milton Keynes: Paternoster, 2006), pp. 209-10.

12. Harvey Cox, *Fire from Heaven: The Rise of Pentecostal Spirituality and the Reshaping of Religion in the Twenty-First Century* (Cambridge, MA: Da Capo, 1995), p. 284.

13. Cox, *Fire from Heaven,* p. 285.

14. Mark Cartledge, *Charismatic Glossolalia: An Empirical-Theological Study* (Aldershot, Hants, and Burlington, VT: Ashgate, 2002), p. 75; and Vinson Synan, "The Role of Tongues as Initial Evidence," in *Spirit and Renewal,* ed. Mark W. Wilson, JPTSS 5 (Sheffield: Sheffield Academic Press, 1994), p. 74; cf. pp. 67-82.

Cartledge does put forward at least two good reasons why tongues today should not be discounted or discouraged. First, he argues that the *"otherness"* or transcendence of God should not reduce our horizons to those of *rationalism.* They serve to prevent "the 'otherness' of divine revelation . . . from being domesticated and merely striving for my own interests."[15] Second, we should ensure that any speaking in tongues is *not triumphalist,* but accords with "the cross of Christ, . . . which is the true test of Christian identity and also contemporary relevance."[16] For this second reason Frank Macchia urges that intimacy with God should be understood Christologically and be transforming. Expressing it in more widespread terms, Gordon Fee rightly sets tongues within the "now" and "not yet" of eschatology.[17] Rom. 8:26-27 is a standard text which makes this point explicit.

However, the "Third Wave," as described by Cartledge and others, does not appear to reflect this balance. We have already observed that an over-expectancy of "healing" emphasizes the "now" of eschatology, and avoids the "not yet." Hence, Bonnington observes, "This worship is often identified as exuberant — physically and emotionally expressive of its own particular style of music."[18] Many, he comments, "see charismatic worship as *'Radio 2'* worship. . . . it does not suit the taste of Radio 3 purists with their high-culture commitment to classical style (choirs, robes, and liturgical precision), nor the more intellectual approach of Radio 4."[19] To understand Bonnington's excellent analogy, readers outside Britain will need to know that the B.B.C. Radio 3 mainly broadcasts classical music, and is therefore sometimes accused of being "elitist"; Radio 4 usually broadcasts informative talks; while Radio 2 is largely a channel for pop music. As someone who has no idea even how to find Radio 2 by button or tuning dial, and listens only to Radio 3 or 4, this correct description sums up an immense stumbling block for me and many others!

As we have already seen in Parts I and II, the practice of giving and expecting "words of knowledge," "words of wisdom," and "prophecies" in this "charismatic" way narrows each category from that suggested by careful contextual biblical interpretation to an overly specific understanding of these gifts. It also differs in historical practice from that suggested by Ambrose, Aquinas, Calvin, and many others, although there are exceptions, as Kidd and Burgess point out. Each of the nine or so gifts from 1 Cor. 12:8-10 is interpreted in a particular way, which accords with popular expectation. Indeed, for many the practice of the

---

15. Cartledge, *Charismatic Glossolalia,* p. 200.

16. Cartledge, *Charismatic Glossolalia,* p. 200.

17. Gordon Fee, "Toward a Pauline Theology of Glossolalia," in *Pentecostalism in Context: Essays in Honour of William W. Menzies,* ed. Robert P. Menzies and Wonsuk Ma, JPTSS 11 (Sheffield: Sheffield Academic Press, 1997), pp. 24-37.

18. Bonnington, *Patterns in Charismatic Spirituality,* p. 16.

19. Bonnington, *Patterns in Charismatic Spirituality,* pp. 16-17.

Roman Catholic tradition may seem to guarantee a more "biblical" and histori-cal balance between spontaneous *and* ordered and "institutional" than this "Third Wave" as it is practiced in the style of John Wimber's or Peter Wagner's "Vineyard" or "New Wine" meetings.

On the positive side, its *Trinitarian framework* and its broader *multiple* in-terpretation of "baptism in the Holy Spirit" place this tradition more firmly in the tradition of the established churches. But it is hard to determine the bound-aries between a style of worship that carries over subcultural baggage and ele-ments of worship designed specifically for outreach to the unchurched and to a younger generation. We have noted already that there seems to be much less self-criticism in the Renewal Movement than in Pentecostal circles, especially about biblical exegesis of "the gifts of the Spirit." This, we may hope, is the next stage to come.

Meanwhile, an excellent "middle way" is advocated by Donald A. Carson in his closing pages of *Showing the Spirit*.[20] As far as tongues-speech is concerned, on one side he acknowledges that this "is usually recognized as learned behav-ior"; but on the other side it "often conveys a mild sense of well-being, personal integration, and power. It is not dangerous in itself, but can be psychologically damaging in some of the *uses* to which it is put" (his italics).[21] On office and gift, he rightly argues that there *need not be tension*. He suggests: "The ideal breaks down when the office is held by those who have not been endowed with the requisite grace-gift, or when the church fails to discharge its responsibilities to test and hold accountable those who serve as leaders."[22]

Carson then provides a moving account of how his church was formerly split between "a few pro-charismatics" and those who opposed it. This is a fre-quently experienced situation, which an increasing number of clergy and pas-tors now face. A series of meetings addressing the concerns of each side helped the situation. On one side, biblical exegesis and a widespread recognition that tongues could promote pride would address those who wished for Renewal; on the other side, resentment at being "relegated to second class status" began to promote mutual understanding. One exponent of Renewal conceded that he used to speak in tongues, but now apparently did not need it because he had matured as a Christian. Carson concludes that the church agreed "that we would not *foster* tongues-speaking in public meetings but we would not oppose [it] if [it] occurred, provided [it] fell within Pauline stipulations. Those who felt they had the gift were encouraged to use it in private, rather than in a public assembly, where [some] would have been more than a little uncomfortable."[23]

---

20. Donald A. Carson, *Showing the Spirit* (Grand Rapids: Baker, 1987), pp. 183-88.
21. Carson, *Showing the Spirit*, p. 184.
22. Carson, *Showing the Spirit*, p. 185.
23. Carson, *Showing the Spirit*, p. 187.

He adds: "In short, the church must hunger for personal and corporate submission to the Lordship of Christ."[24]

Some of the most constructive thinkers are those who used to have a high profile in the Charismatic Movement, but have since that time demonstrated a broader concern. Tom A. Smail (b. 1928) provides a case in point. In 1975 he was Director of the Fountain Trust, a charismatic network in Britain associated with Michael Harper. But in 1980 Smail wrote *The Forgotten Father;* in 1998, *Once and for All: A Confession of the Cross;* and in 2006, *Like Father, Like Son: The Trinity Imagined in Our Humanity.* In *The Giving Gift* (1994) he proposed a revision of the *filioque* clause in the Nicene Creed. The titles and subtitles of Smail's books show precisely the creative, *broadened, and self-critical stage* of writing for which we have hoped. *Like Father, Like Son* not only claims a Trinitarian framework; it also argues for the need for Christians to live out participation in the mutual relations between the Father, the Son, and the Holy Spirit.

The clearest and most helpful book of the kind for which I have been searching is one written by Tom Smail, Andrew Walker, and Nigel Wright. It bears the long title *The Love of Power or the Power of Love: A Careful Assessment of the Problems within the Charismatic and Word-of-Faith Movements* (1994).[25] The three writers describe themselves as all having been deeply involved in the Renewal Movement, and are writing for those who are "basically sympathetic to . . . renewal." But they long for a "more reflective phase in which people are not simply content to worship with swaying bodies and closed eyes. . . . The movement is becoming confident enough to be self-critical, and mature enough to exercise the gift of discernment, which is one of the most necessary but most neglected gifts of the Spirit."[26]

In the first part, Smail expresses concern lest the movement forget that "The way to Pentecost is Calvary" (as J. E. Fison stressed).[27] Smail writes: "We are indeed rejuvenated and empowered at Pentecost, but we are judged, corrected and matured at the cross."[28] He also declares: "The Spirit is meant to engage our thoughts as well as our emotions."[29] He also recalls why he reacted ambiguously to Dennis Bennett in 1965. This strikes a chord with me: I felt totally ill-at-ease listening to Dennis Bennett in Bristol in 1965. Smail pleads for more serious appropriation of Luther's *theologia crucis.*

---

24. Carson, *Showing the Spirit,* p. 188.

25. Thomas Smail, Andrew Walker, and Nigel Wright, *The Love of Power or the Power of Love: A Careful Assessment of the Problems within the Charismatic and Word-of-Faith Movements* (Minneapolis: Bethany House, 1994).

26. Smail et al., *Love of Power or Power of Love,* p. 8; cf. pp. 13-36.

27. Smail et al., *Love of Power,* p. 19.

28. Smail et al., *Love of Power,* p. 19.

29. Smail et al., *Love of Power,* p. 16.

Nigel Wright then considers John Wimber's style of worship, and "signs and wonders" in his "Vineyard Ministries" in California, as well as the associated "Third Wave" of Peter Wagner. He describes the phenomenon of "trembling, falling, trances, weeping, unrestrained laughter, and the release of anguish and pain in a startling and sometimes frightening manner."[30] He concedes that worship is also "at the same time restrained"; that "spiritual anointing" tends to replace "baptism in the Spirit; and the Restorationist use of the Bible is largely abandoned." Yet he expresses concern about a "laid-back, non-dogmatic, pragmatism."[31] Even more seriously, he exposes what has been a major criticism throughout this book. He attacks "a *heightened dualism* [which] resolves the whole of reality into God and Satan, good and evil, and *eclipses the realm of the natural*" (my italics).[32] He is also deeply concerned that "the rhetoric about miraculous healing far exceeds reality."[33] He does not deny that miracles may occur, but deplores exaggerated anecdotal reports. God heals when and where *he* pleases, and *only* then and there.

Andrew Walker addresses the vexed question of demons. Too much emphasis on this can encourage paranoia, a mental state in which we mistrust and suspect others.[34] In Scripture "devil" does not appear in the Old Testament, but in the New Testament almost entirely in the context of the ministry of Jesus.[35] But in terms of this conflict, "that battle has been fought and won once and for all by Christ."[36]

The book contains ten useful essays in all, and we cannot consider all of them. The fourth essay in which the three writers join suggests that the Word of Faith Movement does not correspond with the Greek Fathers' notion of "deification." The "Word of Faith" Movement is associated with Kenneth Hagin (b. 1917) and Kenneth Copeland (b. 1937), who taught not only "gifts of healing" but also that God's desire to "bless" included wealth and prosperity. Many speak of a "wealth" gospel in parts of America. Our three writers condemn the movement outright as being incompatible with the core of the gospel. It can generate positively anti-Christian attitudes.

In the fifth essay Smail expresses concern lest *charismatic worship* sometimes "bypasses the rational faculties." He states, "All is not well with it; . . . the high praise of God had *degenerated into endless repetitive chorus singing that*

---

30. Nigel Wright, "The Theology of Signs and Wonders," in Smail et al., *Love of Power*, p. 38, cf. pp. 37-52.

31. Wright, "Signs," in Smail et al., *Love of Power*, p. 39.

32. Wright, "Signs," in Smail et al., *Love of Power*, p. 41.

33. Wright, "Signs," in Smail et al., *Love of Power*, p. 43.

34. Andrew Walker, "Demonology and the Charismatic Movement," in Smail et al., *Love of Power*, pp. 55-64; cf. pp. 53-72.

35. Walker, "Demonology," in Smail et al., *Love of Power*, pp. 64-72.

36. Walker, "Demonology," in Smail et al., *Love of Power*, p. 72.

was in danger of *becoming a bore and burden rather than a release and a joy*" (my italics).[37] He comments, "In the midst of the noisy and exuberant striving for the spiritual mountaintops, there was little room for silent listening and patient waiting upon God."[38] Worship must relate not only to moments of joy, but also to "dull days, when we are empty and unresponsive . . . and can only hold out empty hands for the bread and wine. . . ."[39]

Finally, in the sixth essay Nigel Wright writes on "The Rise of the Prophetic."[40] He compares many of the trivial and idiosyncratic "prophecies" of the Renewal Movement with the genuinely prophetic ministries of Martyn Lloyd-Jones and Martin Luther King. In the seventh essay Andrew Walker reinforces what has been said about *dualism and rhetorical exaggeration about miracles* in earlier essays.

No one can doubt the serious commitment of these three writers to the Renewal Movement. They represent a reflective and self-critical mellowing, of which the Renewal Movement stands in much need. They perhaps promise a new era of ecumenical and reconciling hope, and, as we move into the twenty-first century, an era of greater mutual dialogue and understanding.

22.2. Gerd Theissen

Gerd Theissen (b. 1943) received his doctorate in Theology and Habilitation from the University of Bonn, and in 1978 became a professor at the University of Copenhagen. He has been a professor at Heidelberg since 1980. A series of essays in the 1970s appeared in England as *The Social Setting of Pauline Christianity* (1982), and his *Psychological Aspects of Pauline Theology* appeared in German in 1983 and in English in 1987. The latter partly drew on the experiences of his wife, who is a psychotherapist, and Theissen has written up to twenty books. His main work is both in New Testament and in theology. On the subject of the Holy Spirit, his work on the operation of the Spirit in the subconscious is valuable. He is also well versed in 1 Corinthians.

Theissen's *Psychological Aspects of Pauline Theology* begins with issues about learning theory, the structuring of a life-world, and psychic processes. Then his part 2 on "The Secrets of the Heart" considers Rom. 2:16; 1 Cor. 4:1-5; 14:20-25; and 2 Cor. 3:4–4:6. He rightly follows Bultmann, as I have here, in asserting: "Paul is familiar with the idea of unconscious impulses within human

---

37. Tom Smail, "In Spirit and in Truth: Reflections on Charismatic Worship," in Smail et al., *Love of Power*, pp. 96 and 97; cf. pp. 95-103.

38. Smail, "Reflections," in Smail et al., *Love of Power*, p. 97.

39. Smail, "Reflections," in Smail et al., *Love of Power*, p. 98.

40. Nigel Wright, "The Rise of the Prophetic," in Smail et al., *Love of Power*, pp. 105-11.

beings. . . . God . . . probes even inner motives and thoughts."[41] 1 Cor. 4:1-5 pre-supposes the concept of the "unconscious." Paul asserts: "I do not even judge myself. . . . I am not thereby acquitted. It is the Lord who judges me. Therefore do not pronounce judgment before . . . the Lord comes." As in 2 Cor. 5:10, he speaks of "hidden intentions of the heart" *(tas boulas tōn kardiōn).*[42] Presumably this must have been unconscious. Paul, in psychological terms, becomes "reconciled" with his unconscious. He does not repress it.[43]

Rom. 2:16 speaks similarly of "the secrets of human beings." Here "secrets refer to inner processes" human knowledge of which is strictly limited, but "God's omniscience is presupposed."[44] In 1 Cor. 14:20-25 Paul again speaks of the secrets of the heart, but in the context of prophecy as a gift of the Holy Spirit disclosing such secrets: "Prophecy . . . discloses the secrets of the hearts of unbelievers and outsiders."[45] Theissen also argues, "Prophecy . . . accomplishes what the Corinthians expect from speaking in tongues."[46] This prompts him to examine the Spirit's working in the "human heart." He writes: "God's omniscience extends above all to the human *heart*" (his italics).[47] Paul declares: "He who searches the hearts of men knows what is in the mind of the Spirit, because He intercedes for the saints, according to the will of God" (Rom. 8:27).[48] 2 Cor. 4:6 also speaks of "light shining in our hearts, . . . an inner process."[49] In psychological terms, the Holy Spirit overcomes "cognitive dissonance."[50]

We may note Theissen's work on Romans 7 and 9. He follows W. G. Kümmel and most modern commentators in describing the "I" of Rom. 7:7-25 as a "rhetorical fictive 'I,' as a rhetorical means of illustrating a general train of thought. This 'I' does not include the person of Paul."[51] The "wretched man" cannot fulfill the Law (Rom. 7:24): it is impossible to assess Romans 7 as a statement of Paul about himself. Theissen sees these chapters in terms of the contrast of the "flesh" and the Holy Spirit. In Romans 8 he depicts overcoming the flesh by the Spirit. In Rom. 7:7-13 he traces the origin of sin, with clear allusions to the story of the Fall. He devotes about a hundred pages to these two chapters.

41. Gerd Theissen, *Psychological Aspects of Pauline Theology* (Edinburgh: T&T Clark, 1987; rpt. 1999), p. 57.
42. Theissen, *Aspects,* p. 61.
43. Theissen, *Aspects,* pp. 63 and 66.
44. Theissen, *Aspects,* p. 74.
45. Theissen, *Aspects,* p. 75.
46. Theissen, *Aspects,* p. 77.
47. Theissen, *Aspects,* p. 87.
48. Theissen, *Aspects,* p. 111.
49. Theissen, *Aspects,* p. 123.
50. Theissen, *Aspects,* pp. 153-58,
51. Theissen, *Aspects,* p. 177.

Theissen turns next to 1 Corinthians 12–14. In 1 Cor. 12:2 he compares Paul's allusion to pagan states of ecstasy as "led astray."[52] On pagan frenzy he comments: "Unconscious impulses develop in the ecstatic state and overcome deeply rooted moral inhibitions."[53] He does *not* suggest that the Corinthians borrowed from such cults as that of Dionysus, even if there may be certain parallels. For example, an outsider would involuntarily have had to ascribe to the Christians a ritual *mania*. And Paul is well aware of this: "This . . . ritualization of an irrational dynamic of drives . . . [is] socially learned and based on pre-established roles of conduct . . . positively or negatively influenced by social reinforcers."[54] He argues: *"Glossolalia is socially learned behaviour."*[55]

Theissen is *not about to deny that tongues-speech,* or selected examples of it, may be given *by the Holy Spirit.* But there is a warning signal here. I have regularly read through comments on the Internet on "Pentecostal Theology Worldwide" and noted that frequently the answer to the question "What drew you to Pentecostalism?" was answered in terms of the *intense social fellowship* that was found there. People seldom learn to receive tongues-speech in isolation, but in a community which has certain "learned behavior." Hence Theissen warns us about an artificial social expectancy of tongues-speech, which may obscure the genuine gift. He compares "Dionysian ecstasy" with other forms of inspiration such as those of Plato, Socrates, Philo, and Montanism.[56]

Theissen maintains: "Paul's chief goal is to reduce through argumentation the social reinforcement of *glossolalia*."[57] He therefore does two things: first, he places prophecy above glossolalia; second, he urges "the privatization" of glossolalia. . . . In the private realm all social reinforcements are lacking."[58] Tongues-speech cannot "build" the community. Within the community Paul argues for intelligible speech (1 Cor. 14:6, 19). Tongues-speech, claims Theissen, "is — or can be — a symbol of belonging to a group."[59] For the Corinthians this could mean all too easily that "only speakers in tongues were considered pneumatics (1 Cor. 14:37)."[60] When he asks, "Do all speak with tongues?" (1 Cor. 12:30), *Paul assumes that there are genuine Christians at Corinth who do not speak with tongues.*

Theissen also appeals to J. P. Kildahl for the view that tongues-speech depends not only on a social bond within groups, but also on "charismatic leaders"

---

52. Theissen, *Aspects*, p. 276.
53. Theissen, *Aspects*, p. 277.
54. Theissen, *Aspects*, p. 281.
55. Theissen, *Aspects*, p. 292 (my italics).
56. Theissen, *Aspects*, pp. 277-91.
57. Theissen, *Aspects*, p. 293.
58. Theissen, *Aspects*, p. 293.
59. Theissen, *Aspects*, p. 294.
60. Theissen, *Aspects*, p. 295.

(as well as "a like-minded group").[61] If we accept these arguments, they would explain much about the theme of "initial evidence" and a fairly tight, even defensive, boundary around a tongues-speaking group. Some may admittedly doubt the force of these arguments. The allusion to the role of "charismatic leaders," however, may less controversially explain the frequent splintering of Pentecostal groups in the early days of Pentecostalism, and provide an explanation for the divisions into subgroups within the church at Corinth. Theissen observes, "Paul criticizes a Corinthian dependence-syndrome with clear words: 'Each one of you says, "I belong to Paul" or "I belong to Apollos" or "I belong to Cephas . . ." (1 Cor. 1:12). Paul proposes a counter-thesis: "All are yours" (1 Cor. 3:22).'"[62]

Theissen refuses to speculate about a correspondence between social classes and tongues-speakers, except to pass the general comment that a "higher evaluation of *Glossolalia* would then be [involve] a higher evaluation of the groups . . . active in speaking in tongues."[63] Dale Martin makes the same point.[64] But he recognizes the value of the gift for the individual (1 Cor. 14:4). Although he compares tongues-speech with a foreign language (1 Cor. 14:10-11), Paul insists that even the tongues-speaker, let alone others, cannot understand it. In any case, 14:10-11 is only an analogy. He concludes: *"Glossolalia is language of the unconscious — language capable of consciousness. . . . Glossolalia makes unconscious depth dimensions of life accessible"* (my italics).[65] It may even bring to the surface what has been repressed.

On the negative side, Theissen concedes that these "babbling monologues" *may be egocentric.* In my larger commentary on the Greek text, I noted Philipp Vielhauer's argument that in 1 Cor. 14:4 to build up *(oikodomeō)* oneself implies "self-sufficiency or self-affirmation."[66] But on Rom. 8:26, Theissen *considers* the possibility, also argued by Frank Macchia, a Pentecostal scholar, that "inexpressible sighs" could be a manifestation of tongues. He concedes, however, that Rom. 8:26 may well constitute *silent* yearning, whereas tongues are audible. Moreover, the "sighs" in context appear as a *collective* prayer, whereas tongues are individual. The former is an expression of suffering with creation, whereas the latter are "ecstatic rapture."[67] In the end, therefore, *he rejects the identifica-*

---

61. Theissen, *Aspects*, p. 297; cf. John P. Kildahl, *The Psychology of Speaking in Tongues* (New York: Harper & Row, 1972), p. 44.

62. Theissen, *Aspects*, p. 299.

63. Theissen, *Aspects*, p. 301.

64. Dale B. Martin, *The Corinthian Body* (New Haven: Yale University Press, 1995), pp. 87-103.

65. Theissen, *Aspects*, p. 306.

66. Philipp Vielhauer, *Oikodomeō: Das Bild vom Bau in der christlicher Literatur vom Neuen Testament bis Clemens Alexandrinus* (Karlsruhe: Harrassowitz, 1940), pp. 91-98; Anthony C. Thiselton, *The First Epistle to the Corinthians: A Commentary on the Greek Text*, NIGTC (Grand Rapids: Eerdmans, 2000), p. 1095.

67. Theissen, *Aspects*, p. 317.

tion. Tongues-speech may either be liberating or destructive, whereas the "sighing" is *always* positive.[68]

Where there is genuine experience of the Holy Spirit, or "pneumatic experience," this must be integrated, Theissen urges, with an "interpretation of reality as a whole."[69] This is also implied by 1 Cor. 2:6-16, where Paul contrasts the wisdom and revelation of the *Holy Spirit* and the "foolishness" of the cross with purely *human wisdom.* Paul draws here on Jewish Wisdom traditions. Theissen writes: "It is only through conferral of the divine Spirit that an expansion of consciousness beyond the limits of the *psyche* can occur."[70] The *Spirit who comes from God* (1 Cor. 2:12) becomes *"a formative influence from without"* (my italics).[71] Yet even among Christians there can be resistance, symbolized by the powers, or *archontes.* In general, "both simple believers and 'advanced' pneumatics are grasped by the symbol of the cross. . . . Only the latter penetrate the unconscious connexion in which the preaching of the cross functions. . . . They emancipate themselves consciously from the compulsive standards of this world. Their consciousness has opened itself into unknown depths. . . . They have grown beyond human consciousness."[72] For all Christians Paul presupposes the existence of a new world, and envisages transformed and transforming behavior.

Theissen has called his book *Psychological Aspects of Pauline Theology* because he wants to show how well psychology can be used to illuminate Pauline *theology.* In my view, he succeeds. But in another context he might have called his book *Paul's Theology of the Holy Spirit.* Many relevant questions are asked and answered.

22.3. The Church of England Doctrine Commission Report "We Believe in the Holy Spirit" (1991)

We include the Church of England Doctrine Commission's Report of 1991 because it sought to combine academic rigor with pastoral relevance, and it has some distinctive themes. It was chaired first by John Baker, then Bishop of Salisbury (who retired from the Chairmanship because of ill health), and subsequently by Alec Graham, the Bishop of Newcastle. The Commission included ten members with university posts, and two whose work was primarily pastoral. I served as Acting-Chairman for the period between the two bishops.

Our Introduction concedes that the doctrine of the Holy Spirit has become

68. Theissen, *Aspects,* pp. 319-20.
69. Theissen, *Aspects,* p. 337.
70. Theissen, *Aspects,* p. 364.
71. Theissen, *Aspects,* p. 368.
72. Theissen, *Aspects,* p. 385.

a vast and untidy subject, made more difficult by "the self-effacing character of the Holy Spirit," whose work is chiefly to bear witness to Christ (John 15:26).[73] It affirms the Personhood of the Holy Spirit as God within the Trinity, and within a Christocentric faith. It explains that "we have avoided using the term 'Spirit' in a broad and generalized way," not because it is illegitimate to speak of "spirituality" in this sense, but because the New Testament and Christian tradition speak of the Spirit in relation to Christ, or in a Trinitarian way.[74] Finally, the Report recognizes gifts of the Spirit for particular individuals, but insists that God does not thereby "suspend our human ways of knowing and give[s] us a kind of other-worldly infallibility."[75]

The chapter on "Praying 'in the Spirit'" and Charismatic Experience takes as its point of departure the chapter "God as Trinity: An Approach through Prayer" in the previous Report, *We Believe in God* (1987). There it was argued that Christians "are graciously caught up in a *divine conversation*" (my italics), in which the *Holy Spirit* intercedes for us and prays within us (Rom. 8:16, 26) *to God the Father through Jesus Christ.*[76] The Holy Spirit inspires prayer. In "charismatic experience" the private use of tongues appeared to emerge in interviews as a kind of "'love language' *to* God" (1 Cor. 14:2): "it is in the private use of tongues that the most interesting material emerged in discussion with the Anglicans."[77] In interviews many seemed to be unhappy with psychological language about "releasing the unconscious" or "exposing one's inner life," but most agreed on its immediacy or directedness and the danger of "short-circuiting normal checks and defences."[78] Interviewers also agreed about the possibility of mood swings, depression, and guilt if certain prayers (e.g., for healing) were not "answered." The presence of the Spirit, as Bernard of Clairvaux observed, was the desire for even greater grace.

A chapter called "Is This That?" addresses the problem of assuming that experience today exactly matches, or could match, that of the New Testament churches. Several notes of caution are struck. "The present Christian experience of the reader may impose a pattern of understanding upon the New Testament text."[79] This may apply equally to Renewal groups and to others. Renewal groups tend to value highly the narrative of Acts or Luke-Acts, as well as summaries of "gifts" in 1 Cor. 12:8-10 and 1 Pet. 4:8ff. But we must be careful "lest we

---

73. Church of England Doctrine Commission, *We Believe in the Holy Spirit* (London: Church House Publishing, 1991), p. 3.

74. *We Believe in the Holy Spirit*, p. 11.

75. *We Believe in the Holy Spirit*, p. 15.

76. Church of England Doctrine Commission, *We Believe in God* (London: Church House Publishing, 1987), p. 108.

77. *We Believe in the Holy Spirit*, p. 25.

78. *We Believe in the Holy Spirit*, p. 27.

79. *We Believe in the Holy Spirit*, p. 39.

convert into a universal doctrine . . . three or four special occasions in the Acts of the Apostles."[80]

The phrase "baptism in the Spirit" has "a certain first-blush plausibility: a baptism is a once-for-all event; it has a God-given objectivity: the term can be used metaphorically (as by Jesus about his death). . . . However, we need to exercise caution. . . . This experience, which is often called *baptism in the Spirit,* should be both welcomed and also tested. It is . . . not universal; true commitment, discipleship and experience of the Spirit can and do exist *without such a crisis.* Hence it should not be erected into an essential requirement of the faith, and to call such an experience the baptism in the Spirit can convey the wrong message, as though it were a norm for every Christian. We need . . . some descriptive term . . . more in accord with scriptural usage."[81]

The chapter closes with a brief reflection on the California evangelist John Wimber, his Vineyard churches, "power evangelism," and "signs and wonders." However, in mainline churches "The Kingdom of God" is distinct from the Church (as Pannenberg insists). In Wimber, on the other hand, the Kingdom is to be found *within* the Church, not beyond it. Further, not all "Renewal" or "Charismatic" Christians follow John Wimber, and the phenomena which accompany his work "are open to . . . more than one theological explanation."[82] Even his exegesis of "word of knowledge" (1 Cor. 12:8) offers differing interpretations. After more than twenty-five years (to 1991) the Renewal Movement has learned some self-criticism and sensitivity; yet Wimber reflects the bolder claims of the earlier phase of the Renewal Movement. Specifically on baptism in the Holy Spirit, the Report refers favorably to the work of James D. G. Dunn, considered above. On healing, "We do not find evidence in the scriptures to support the view that the Church has been given by the Lord the *certainty* that . . . cure . . . will *always* accompany the deeper healing offered."[83]

The chapter concludes: "*Openness to change, vitality, warmth and surprise all need to be balanced by continuity, regularity, stability and rationality*" (my italics).[84] The ebullience characteristic of *some* charismatics may be *inappropriate* in many lives for different reasons. "*Continuous euphoria*" *cannot be a model for all Christians.* Nor can what many call "hotline" guidance from God in all, or at least nearly all, situations be such a model. In relation to such phenomena, "a friendly critique" is required.

The classic criticism of this, the Commission argues in the next chapter, comes in 1 Corinthians, where Paul examined the purpose of the gifts, especially for the building up of the community. These "gifts of the Spirit" are espe-

---

80. *We Believe in the Holy Spirit,* p. 45.
81. *We Believe in the Holy Spirit,* pp. 44-45.
82. *We Believe in the Holy Spirit,* p. 46.
83. *We Believe in the Holy Spirit,* p. 52 (my italics).
84. *We Believe in the Holy Spirit,* p. 55.

cially centered in the glorification of Christ, and come from the Spirit of Jesus, who is *love*. The greatest gift is love, or, in different terms, "Christlikeness" or even "Godlikeness." Jesus is Spirit-filled: "We encounter God the Spirit in the 'overflow' towards us of the life of Father and Son."[85] According to the Orthodox theologian Paul Evdokimov, "we could speak of the Spirit proceeding from the Father and the Son if we also spoke of the Son coming forth from the Father *and the Spirit*."[86] This is one of several attempts to reconcile Eastern and Western traditions.

In a chapter on sacraments and structures, it is said that both remind us that "the process of our salvation is not complete," just as we stretch out our hands "in needful expectancy at Holy Communion."[87] Both gifts come from the Holy Spirit. Those "on the margins" may thereby miss some of the Spirit's gifts.

A chapter on the Spirit and power acknowledges the superhuman resources of the Holy Spirit, but adds, "On the other hand there is weakness, failure, shame, in dereliction in the passion narratives in all four Gospels," from which Christians who share in the cross are not exempt.[88] "In the early chapters of 1 Corinthians Paul is *re-evaluating the nature of power;* in so doing he is laying the foundation for his treatment of the corporate life of the Church in chapters 12 to 14."[89] In the New Testament, "signs and wonders" do take place, but *"seeking"* a sign is *not* "an imperative of the gospel."[90] Jesus renounced the use of popularity and brute "power," for example, in the Messianic temptations.

The Spirit is the Spirit of truth. Hence he "exposes falsehoods, dissolves the self-deception of illusion, and witnesses to the truth of God."[91] We must distinguish the Spirit *from subjective feelings, or convictions of certainty.* The Spirit of God brought *order* to the chaos of a featureless waste in creation, and his creative work provides "the thinkableness of the universe."[92] "He exposes that which needs attention, so that life can then be grounded in reality rather than in illusion."[93] Truth transcends flat description, as when a mapmaker displays a three-dimensional reality in two dimensions. So Christ definitively discloses the heart of God. In Eberhard Jüngel's words, cited above, Christ also makes God "thinkable and conceivable." The Spirit "anticipates disclosures which in principle belong to the last judgment" (John 16:7ff.).[94] When we consider the

85. *We Believe in the Holy Spirit,* p. 67.
86. *We Believe in the Holy Spirit,* p. 67; cf. pp. 68-72.
87. *We Believe in the Holy Spirit,* p. 81.
88. *We Believe in the Holy Spirit,* p. 95.
89. *We Believe in the Holy Spirit,* p. 97.
90. *We Believe in the Holy Spirit,* p. 104 (my italics).
91. *We Believe in the Holy Spirit,* p. 112.
92. *We Believe in the Holy Spirit,* p. 114.
93. *We Believe in the Holy Spirit,* p. 116.
94. *We Believe in the Holy Spirit,* p. 128.

canon of Scripture, "*This* is where we hear the witness of the Spirit" (the Report's italics).[95]

Like Pannenberg, the Commission considers the Spirit and creation. The Report discusses cosmic history, including the Big Bang theory of cosmologists, the hand of God in continuous creation, the apparent predictability of a Newtonian world, and the apparent abolition of precise determinism in quantum theory and the so-called Butterfly Effect. The Holy Spirit did not first come onto the scene at Pentecost. "Creation is a painful thing in which the Spirit shares."[96] We wait for what we do not yet see, while the Spirit works "within the physical process" with patience.[97] The sciences and the arts both explore the Spirit's creativity. Albert Einstein expressed wonder and submission to the way things are, and his celebrated remark "God does not play dice" was specifically a response to Heisenberg's uncertainty principle.

The final chapter considers the Holy Spirit and the future, and, again, "the Holy Spirit as the one beyond and yet within."[98] It was noted that biblical language uses *temporal formulations* more frequently than perhaps spatial ones (Heb. 11:1). "The yearnings and longings, as well as the joys and promises, which the Spirit of God places in the human heart do not stand in sharp discontinuity with the promised future."[99] The Spirit gives "the glorious body" for which Christians wait at the resurrection. "The event of the resurrection is a corporate event as one which involves us as individuals."[100] Meanwhile the yearnings of the Holy Spirit, *as a divine discontent within,* find expression in deeds of love, and long for the future which God alone can bring.[101]

22.4. Friedrich W. Horn and Christopher Forbes

(1) *Friedrich W. Horn* published *Das Angeld des Geistes* (The Deposit of the Spirit) in 1992 as his Habilitation, which was submitted in 1989. He also produced an extensive article on the Holy Spirit in *The Anchor Bible Dictionary* (some twenty pages, or fifty columns) in 1992.[102] He is Professor of New Testament Studies at the Gutenberg University of Mainz, and has previously written

95. *We Believe in the Holy Spirit*, p. 132.
96. *We Believe in the Holy Spirit*, p. 144.
97. *We Believe in the Holy Spirit*, p. 146.
98. *We Believe in the Holy Spirit*, p. 171.
99. *We Believe in the Holy Spirit*, p. 177.
100. *We Believe in the Holy Spirit*, p. 182.
101. *We Believe in the Holy Spirit*, p. 186.

102. Friedrich W. Horn, *Das Angeld der Geistes: Studien zur paulinischen Pneumatologie* (Göttingen: Vandenhoeck & Ruprecht, 1992); and "Holy Spirit," in *The Anchor Bible Dictionary*, ed. David N. Freedman (New York and London: Doubleday, 1992), vol. 3, pp. 260-80.

on Luke-Acts. He subsequently published books on the interpretation of the New Testament (1995) and on the relation between the indicative and imperative (2009).

Horn describes the allusion to the Spirit of God in the Old Testament as almost incidental, but sees development in Judaism, especially in the New Testament. The specific combination of "Holy" and "Spirit" does not occur in Greek literature. Indeed, the only explicit occurrences in the Old Testament are limited to these: Isa. 63:10-11 and Ps. 51:11. In Intertestamental Judaism we can refer to *Jubilees* 1:21; *4 Ezra* 14:22; *Ascension of Isaiah* 5:14; and *Testament of Levi* 18:11. In secular Greek *pneuma* is derived from *pneō*, meaning "blow" or "breathe," but then has metaphysical extensions, often as invisible spirit or prophetic spirit (Plato, *Definitions* 40). It could refer to inspiration in the oracle of Apollo at Delphi, and to a part of the body in Stoicism.

Modern study of *pneuma*, Horn maintains, began with F. C. Baur and Hermann Gunkel. Baur (1831, 1845) expounded the term in the New Testament as relating to self-consciousness, in the context of an *idealist philosophy inherited from Hegel*. Hermann Gunkel (1888 and 1909), by contrast, approached the subject in terms of *experience*.[103] Gunkel writes, "We must first of all distinguish the experience of the pneumatic himself from the interpretation given it by him or his observers."[104] He chooses to look at *"popular* views held in the community" (of Paul's converts). The community is not concerned with doctrine, but with experience. These include glossolalia and prophecy.[105] Wilhelm Bousset (1901) then called for a greater comparison with Hellenistic and Jewish *parallels*. Horn cites these as illustrating the diversity of approaches and the need for more rigorous conceptual examination.

Horn rightly gives a special place to the Easter experience. The resurrection of Christ opens the possibility of speech about the Holy Spirit (Rom. 1:4; 8:11; 2 Cor. 13:4; Gal. 6:8).[106] But his main thesis begins early in the book. He examines the Pauline letters in chronological sequence, beginning with 1 Thessalonians.[107] He looks especially at 1 Thess. 4:1-10; 5:19 and 23 and assertions about the Holy Spirit in the context of Paul's theology in 1 Thessalonians. He believes that 1 Thessalonians is removed in time from later letters of Paul. He finds similar terms to those addressed to Jews, the contrast between word and power, and expressions of confident hope for the future. The bereaved should "not grieve, as others do." The theme of *sanctification* by the Spirit emerges in 1 Thess. 4:3-7.[108] In 1 Thess. 5:19 Paul states that prophets must be esteemed because their

103. Hermann Gunkel, *The Influence of the Holy Spirit* (Minneapolis: Fortress, 2008).
104. Gunkel, *The Influence of the Holy Spirit*, p. 5.
105. Gunkel, *The Influence of the Holy Spirit*, pp. 30-38.
106. Horn, *Das Angeld des Geistes*, pp. 105-6.
107. Horn, *Das Angeld des Geistes*, pp. 121-60.
108. Horn, *Das Angeld des Geistes*, pp. 126-27.

work is that of the Spirit.[109] Paul gives this exhortation because "prophets" might otherwise be regarded as of low esteem in a Hellenistic community. But the contrasts Spirit/flesh and Spirit/law come mainly in his *later* letters.

Next, Horn considers the dispute with "Pneumatic Enthusiasm in Corinth."[110] The Corinthians saw *pneuma* as a "substance" that led to salvation. Horn cites 1 Cor. 2:13; 3:1; 12:1; and 14:37, although I doubt whether these verses positively support the argument. He is on surer ground in citing "the strong" and enthusiastic over-confidence: "All things are lawful" (6:12), "all of us possess knowledge" (8:1), and even "there is no resurrection of the dead" (15:12). But most of his section concerns baptism and glossolalia. Baptism, according to Horn, works "a substantive transformation."[111] For the Corinthians, it is a sacramental incorporation into the pneumatic *kyrios* (1 Cor. 6:11). In contrast to this, 1 Thessalonians does not consider baptism. On tongues-speech, the gifts of the individual manifest endowment by the Holy Spirit.[112] Hence Paul writes with irony: "Already you are filled! Already you have become rich!" (1 Cor. 4:8). The contrast, however, between Spirit and flesh begins to take on a distinctive meaning for Paul (1 Cor. 3:1-3).[113]

The next passages to be considered are 2 Corinthians 10–13 and 2 Corinthians 1–9. In the latter the Spirit is associated with the Lord, and the contrast between letter and Spirit emerges. Then Galatians and Romans are considered.[114] Finally, Horn examines all that relates to the Holy Spirit as "earnest," "pledge," "down payment," or "deposit" *(Angeld).*[115] Throughout he has engaged with parallels from Judaism. But the heart of his argument is to distinguish sharply between three stages in the development of Pauline thought: (1) 1 Thessalonians; (2) 1 Corinthians; (3) Galatians, Romans, and Philippians. In all three phases the notion of the Holy Spirit as a *pledge or deposit* is prominent. But only after the dispute with pneumatic enthusiasm does Paul clarify the relationship between the Holy Spirit and Christ, and then with eschatology and the Church.[116]

The criticisms invited by Horn's book may be predicted. Did Paul compromise with either the Corinthians' view of baptism or with their overrealized eschatology and "enthusiasm"? This seems highly doubtful. Were 2 Corinthians, Galatians, Romans, and Philippians dominated by Paul's dispute with Jewish-

109. Horn, *Das Angeld des Geistes,* pp. 127-30.
110. Horn, *Das Angeld des Geistes,* pp. 160-274.
111. Horn, *Das Angeld des Geistes,* pp. 205-6.
112. Horn, *Das Angeld des Geistes,* pp. 206-74.
113. Horn, *Das Angeld des Geistes,* pp. 274-86; cf. pp. 287-313.
114. Horn, *Das Angeld des Geistes,* pp. 346-84.
115. Horn, *Das Angeld des Geistes,* pp. 385ff.
116. This emerges most clearly and briefly in Horn, "The Holy Spirit," in *Anchor Bible Dictionary,* vol. 3, pp. 275-76.

Christian "nomism"? This seems too close to F. C. Baur, who argued that every "authentic" Pauline epistle reflected a Judaizing controversy, and thus ended up ascribing authenticity only to the four major epistles. On top of this is the problem of chronology. Horn places Galatians too late, if we accept the "South Galatians theory" of Paul's travel, with its implications for an early date. Indeed, several of these criticisms have been made by Max Turner.[117] We remain unconvinced by Horn's reconstructive and theological theory.

(2) *Christopher Forbes* wrote three years later in 1995, about prophecy and glossolalia, comparing their treatment by Paul and the New Testament churches with supposedly parallel phenomena in Greco-Roman religion. He argues that claims to find parallels *cannot* be supported. His 1995 book bears the title *Prophecy and Inspired Speech in Early Christianity and Its Hellenistic Environment*.[118] At the time of writing he is Senior Lecturer in the Department of Ancient History at Macquarie University, Sydney, Australia. He laments that many claim to find parallels within the world of Hellenistic popular religion with inspired speech in the churches of the New Testament without adequate direct firsthand evidence. He concludes: "The consensus is based on only the flimsiest evidence."[119] The two sets of phenomena are radically different.

Forbes engages in an impressive survey of literature on tongues-speech, including Stendahl, Meeks, Dautzenberg, Horsley, Gundry, and a variety of writers, assessing the relation of their work to Bacchic frenzy in Euripides, to the Delphic Apollo, and to Cassandra in Aeschylus. He refers to David Aune's argument that 1 Cor. 12:2 probably extended to experiences of possession or trance.[120] After the survey, Forbes examines tongues-speech in the New Testament, looking at R. A. Harrisville, C. G. Williams, and others. In Acts 10:46 the members of the household of Cornelius speak in tongues and praise God; they do not address humans (1 Cor. 14:2). The modern term "ecstatic" does not correspond exactly with the Greek *ekstasis*. He approves of Aune's broader term "altered states of consciousness."[121] He adds: "It is not possible to argue any simple opposition between, say, 'ecstatic' glossolalia and 'non-ecstatic' prophecy."[122] After looking at various options, he concludes: "Paul, like Luke, understands glossolalia as the miraculous ability to speak unlearned human and (possibly) divine or angelic languages."[123] I remain less convinced of this than

---

117. Max Turner, *The Holy Spirit and Spiritual Gifts Then and Now* (Carlisle: Paternoster, 1986), pp. 107-9.

118. Christopher Forbes, *Prophecy and Inspired Speech in Early Christianity and Its Hellenistic Environment*, WUNT 2.75 (Tübingen: Mohr, 1995).

119. Forbes, *Prophecy*, p. 5.

120. Forbes, *Prophecy*, pp. 12-43.

121. Forbes, *Prophecy*, p. 55.

122. Forbes, *Prophecy*, p. 56.

123. Forbes, *Prophecy*, p. 64.

he is, although he has presented a fair discussion, with the exception that he shows no awareness of Gerd Theissen's *Psychological Aspects of Pauline Theology.*

In his next chapter Forbes looks at tongues-speech among the Church Fathers, acknowledging John Chrysostom's "negative evidence."[124] He also recognizes differences of conclusions about supposed early evidence.[125] At all events, he argues that "tongues will cease" (1 Cor. 13:8-12) does not refer to the close of the biblical canon, but to an eschatological future.[126] On the function of tongues, he sets out three views: they are a *form of praise* or inspired prayer (1 Cor. 14:15); they may function as a *"sign"* to draw attention to something else; or they may be *"revelatory,"* especially if or when they are interpreted (which would perhaps corroborate my view that it is the tongues-speaker who should interpret the tongues).[127]

Forbes now returns to review Hellenistic inspiration with reference to the Delphic and Delian Apollo, and with reference to Plato. "Prophecy" *(mantikē)* is superior to augury *(oiōnistikē)*, just as inspired madness *(mania)* from the gods is superior to sanity *(sōphrosynē)*, which is merely human (Plato, *Phaedrus* 244 A–D).[128] We must distinguish "incoherent babbling" from the well-known obscurity of Pythian oracular utterances. But probably the only "inspired" or "charismatic" speech known to the ordinary public was the form known at Delphi and popularized by wandering soothsayers.[129] Certainly in Delphic practice "there were no unknown languages."[130] Forbes also considers the cults of Dionysus and Cybele, examining Euripides' *Bacchae.* The main "frenzy" is that of the rites of Bacchus or Dionysus. But King Pentheus is also driven to his death by a kind of frenzy. The demands of Dionysus also included dancing. Forbes writes: "Characteristic of the cults of Dionysus and Cybele are outbreaks of shouting, the music of symbol, drums and flutes, and frenzied dancing."[131] Forbes concludes that *the criticisms* of supposed parallels with the New Testament by T. W. Manson and Robert H. Gundry "are thoroughly justified."[132]

It is important to note that examples of "frenzy" do take place in pagan religions. As Barth observed, far more important than the *phenomena* of religion

---

124. Forbes, *Prophecy,* p. 83.

125. Forbes, *Prophecy,* pp. 75-79.

126. Forbes, *Prophecy,* pp. 85-91.

127. Forbes, *Prophecy,* pp. 93-99; cf. Anthony C. Thiselton, "The Interpretation of Tongues: A New Suggestion in the Light of Greek Usage in Philo and Josephus," *JTS* 30 (1979): 15-36; and Thiselton, *The First Epistle to the Corinthians,* pp. 1107-11 and 970-88.

128. Forbes, *Prophecy,* p. 105.

129. Forbes, *Prophecy,* p. 117.

130. Forbes, *Prophecy,* p. 123.

131. Forbes, *Prophecy,* p. 135.

132. Forbes, *Prophecy,* p. 147. Cf. Robert H. Gundry, "'Ecstatic Utterances' (NEB)?" *JTS* 17 (1966): 299-307.

are their *source* and *purpose*. Forbes has carried out a thorough and informative piece of work. He concludes that "no convincing parallels have been found within the traditions of Greco-Roman religion" and the New Testament.[133] His work as an ancient historian is excellent. On his narrower view of "prophecy," however, I should have reservations, and broadly follow Hill and Gillespie. I am uncertain about his view of tongues-speech, but he has made an excellent contribution.

133. Forbes, *Prophecy*, p. 316.

23

The Twenty-First Century

The writers whom we note and discuss in this chapter largely belong, in terms of their publication, to the twenty-first century. There are two exceptions. Michael Welker wrote his main work on the Spirit in 1994, and another on this subject in 2006. Furthermore, he displays a favorable attitude to postmodern themes, which places him among some of the most recent expositors of the doctrine of the Holy Spirit. Our second writer, Harvey Cox, published in 1995, and it may be more difficult to justify placing him in this chapter. But he addresses many of the issues that still persist among Pentecostals even today. Others have all published in the twenty-first century.

23.1. Michael Welker

Michael Welker (b. 1947) received his first Ph.D. for work under Jürgen Moltmann at Tübingen in 1973, and his second Ph.D. in 1978 in philosophy. He wrote his 1980 habilitation on A. N. Whitehead and Process Philosophy at Heidelberg. From 1983 to 1987 he was Professor of Systematic Theology at Tübingen, then from 1987 to 1991 Professor of Reformed Theology at Münster, and finally since 1991 Professor of Dogmatics at Heidelberg. He has also lectured widely in America, China, and elsewhere. In 1994 (German, 1992) he published *God the Spirit* and edited *The Work of the Spirit: Pneumatology and Pentecostalism,* to which such scholars as James Dunn, Veli-Matti Kärkkäinen, Frank Macchia, and John Polkinghorne have contributed. He has written some nine other books.[1]

---

1. Michael Welker, *God the Spirit* (Minneapolis: Fortress, 1994); and Michael Welker (ed.), *The Work of the Spirit: Pneumatology and Pentecostalism* (Grand Rapids: Eerdmans, 2006).

Welker's main book, *God the Spirit,* is not easy reading, partly because he sets up a constant dialectic of proposing a view, and then radically qualifying it. Further, behind his theological thought lie two philosophical presuppositions. First he engages positively with *process thought,* associated especially with Alfred N. Whitehead (1861-1947). This sees the importance of change, or becoming, often in terms of emergence. One positive aspect of his work is to focus on action and effect rather than "things," which coheres with a theology of the Holy Spirit. But "connections" and "interconnections" between change, process, and temporality raise complex issues, and the book clearly recognizes complexity. More questionable, however, are the *pluralism and postmodernism* that pervade the book. In certain respects the postmodern is *healthy in opposing the standardization of knowledge,* especially within a scientific paradigm, but its attention to diffusion and *fragmentation has an unhealthy side,* which Christians too readily think is beneficial to Christian faith. Postmodernity and pluralism constitute complex phenomena, and I have tried to offer in four studies a balance sheet of encouragement and warnings, which on the whole remains less positive than Welker's.[2] Curiously, there seems to be a dearth of reviews on this book and subject, especially in American and British journals.

Welker has given us a glimpse of his primary concerns in an article, "The Holy Spirit" (1989).[3] His first *dialectic or nonsystematic "paradox"* is to situate the experiences of the Holy Spirit in "the poles of, on the one hand, the experience of God's proximity, and on the other, the consciousness of God's distance."[4] Renewal or "Charismatic" followers emphasize the first. They now include vast numbers. Welker gives a brief sketch of the beginnings of Pentecostalism at Topeka, Kansas, and its spread to Latin America and Africa, and the "second charismatic awakening" from 1960 onward. He also cites "Neo-Pentecostalism, as a third branch, with an emphasis on "baptism in the Spirit" and on speaking in tongues. Finally, he distinguishes a "Third Wave" of the Charismatic Renewal Movement from 1980 onward.[5] All these stress what Gordon Fee calls the "power and presence" of God. From outside the Movements, however, we must ask about "the Spirit of *truth,*" in contrast to "the retreat into subjective feelings," and resist the assumption that pragmatic *success* is a criterion of truth, which it is not.[6]

Welker endorses *pluriformity* in a *postmodern* age, and compares liberation

---

2. Anthony C. Thiselton, *Interpreting God and the Postmodern Self* (Edinburgh: T&T Clark, 1995); Thiselton, "Postmodernity, Postmodernism," in *A Concise Encyclopaedia of the Philosophy of Religions* (Oxford: Oneworld, 2002), pp. 233-35; Thiselton, *The Living Paul* (London: SPCK, 2009), pp. 148-62; and Thiselton, *Hermeneutics* (Grand Rapids: Eerdmans, 2009), pp. 327-48.

3. Michael Welker, "The Holy Spirit," *Theology Today* 46 (1989): 5-20.

4. Welker, *God the Spirit,* p. 7.

5. Welker, *God the Spirit,* pp. 8-11.

6. Welker, *God the Spirit,* pp. 14-15.

and feminist theologies. He writes: "Powerful and invigorating forms of plural-ism are there just as much to be distinguished from disintegrative and debilitat-ing forms."[7] He adds: "The gifts of the Spirit take as their starting-points typical differences that are bound together by the Spirit: old and young, rich and poor. . . ."[8] He concludes this section: "Realistic, honest, self-critical, penitent renewal, not idealistic and moral skimming over the surface, is what accords with the action of the Spirit, . . . sensitive to difference."[9] Structural patterns of life are involved. He then defines "the postmodern" as follows: "Theorems or intellectual positions are called 'postmodern' if they abandon the assumption of the 'unity of reality' and of the 'unity of experiences.'"[10] This almost pro-vides its key to his theology of the Spirit. He rejects "old European metaphysics" and "social moralism."[11] Somehow "metaphysical *totalization*" carries with it the illusion that God's power is at our disposal.[12]

Further dialectic emerges in the recognition of the *universality* implied by the work of the Holy Spirit and the Spirit's work within *specific conflicts*. This is amplified in terms of dialectic between moralism and what goes beyond moral-ism. There is a sense in which Anglo-Americans will welcome this attention to the particular case, in contrast to the frequent generalizations from some French and German writers.

Welker next spends a long time with creative readings of biblical passages, often going beyond traditional interpretations. Sometimes, he acknowledges, meanings seem ambiguous. For example, he rightly examines the gift of the Spirit of God to empower individuals for God's task in the book of Judges. But, surprisingly, he asserts: "God's Spirit is anything but a spirit of war."[13] Although these people were warriors, such leaders as Jephthah, Samson, and even Gideon and Saul were not "supernatural heroes," but all too human and sinful: "Gideon remains a doubting, sceptical, person" (Judg. 6:13ff., 36ff.); "this charismatic even ends up erecting an idol in his city (Judg. 8:27)."[14] Jephthah's daughter is sacrificed for Jephthah's feisty enthusiasm. Samson "throws a drinking party" (Judg. 14:10ff.) and is caught up in "dismaying, brutal stories . . . involved in ruffians' squabbles."[15]

Nevertheless the effect of each of these charismatic leaders was to deliver Israel "from fear, paralysis, and mere complaint," under the oppression of the

---

7. Welker, *God the Spirit*, p. 23.
8. Welker, *God the Spirit*, p. 23.
9. Welker, *God the Spirit*, p. 25.
10. Welker, *God the Spirit*, p. 37.
11. Welker, *God the Spirit*, pp. 41 and 44.
12. Welker, *God the Spirit*, p. 47.
13. Welker, *God the Spirit*, p. 52.
14. Welker, *God the Spirit*, p. 59.
15. Welker, *God the Spirit*, p. 66.

Philistines to a situation of collective restoration. Israel's sin led to the loss of its coherence. The point of the Judges accounts is "restoring the community of God's people, . . . raising up of the 'crushed and oppressed,' and the renewal of the forces of life."[16] Welker adds: "*A differentiated public and differentiated public-opinion correspond to the changing identity of Samson, the one on whom the Spirit comes.* On the one hand public opinion says, 'Keep clear of the Philistines. . . . They are sly and dangerous.' . . . On the other hand public opinion also says, 'Don't worry about the Philistines! If the Spirit of God is with us, we are their betters'" (Welker's italics).[17] The Spirit delivers Israel from overpowering enemies. Welker applies the same contrast to Saul and to Moses. He concludes: "God's Spirit simultaneously empowers people *and* disempowers them" (his italics).[18] These passages do *not* address "*even a homogeneous public*" (his italics).[19]

The Messianic texts announce God's chosen bringer of salvation, on whom the Spirit "remains." This makes way for the universal spread of justice (Isa. 11:1-5, 9-10; 42:1-4, 6-8). "Mercy" is not a charitable act, but "an act of establishing righteousness" (cf. Isa. 61:3, 8, 11).[20] The readiness to remove wrongs implies forgiveness and structural transformation. In practice this means removing hatred of minorities, exploitation, the disparaging of Jesus or Black people, and a host of similar things. Yet the Spirit and the Bearer of the Spirit "extend beyond morality."[21] When the Spirit is poured out "from heaven," heaven "is understood as a domain that is not accessible to human measurement, . . . a domain of reality that is relatively inaccessible to us."[22] That statement reminds us of Fison on the Spirit. The Spirit acts upon a variety of structures, some of which are foreign to one another, promoting life and reciprocal interconnections among different races, young and old, men and women (Joel 2:28-32). "When the Spirit of God is poured out, the different persons and groups of people will open God's presence with each other and for each other."[23]

In the Person of Christ the Spirit is universalized, yet also made concrete. Jesus overcomes "powerlessness" in others, just as the judges did. We can see this in his exorcisms: "It is characteristic of the suffering caused by *demons* that woe and powerlessness are given a long-term status."[24] We may compare Mark 1:23-24; 5:2-14; Matt. 8:29; Luke 4:33-34; 8:28, 31. Nevertheless Welker declares,

16. Welker, *God the Spirit*, p. 65.
17. Welker, *God the Spirit*, p. 73.
18. Welker, *God the Spirit*, p. 83.
19. Welker, *God the Spirit*, p. 91.
20. Welker, *God the Spirit*, p. 117.
21. Welker, *God the Spirit*, p. 123.
22. Welker, *God the Spirit*, pp. 137 and 139.
23. Welker, *God the Spirit*, p. 151.
24. Welker, *God the Spirit*, p. 199.

"It is striking that in Jesus' pre-Easter activity, the demons' powers are not removed with one blow, but are 'driven out' in a multitude of individual, concrete acts of liberation, . . . not by means of an 'organized' liberation action."[25] This also epitomizes Welker's concrete and diversified approach to the experience of the Spirit. On the "Messianic secret," or commands to silence, Welker adopts the same approach, once again, as J. E. Fison: "Jesus does not want to act in such a way that his messianic identity is made known only in the light of healings he has performed."[26] It is only in the light of suffering and the cross that resurrection is possible.

Welker's 1989 article "The Holy Spirit" at first seems to say little that does not appear in more detailed form in this book. However, at this point, where the article remains parallel with the book, some of its terminology seems clearer and more explicit. Welker speaks of the Spirit working in "poly-concreteness." Where J. E. Fison speaks of the "self-effacement" of the Spirit, Welker speaks of the Spirit's "selflessness" in pointing away from himself to Jesus (John 14:26; 15:26; 16:13-14).[27]

In his book Welker turns to Acts, especially to Acts 2:1-16. This portrays "an experience of power which enables persons of different background, education, interests, and expectations . . . to understand, . . . to have shared experiences of commonality . . . constituted by unexpected, universal, but not homogeneous clarity."[28] There is a shared understanding of God's deeds of power in which God *"effects a world-encompassing, multilingual, polyindividual testimony to Godself"* (his italics).[29] He calls "baptism in the Spirit" "the fullness of the Spirit's action."[30] Life is life in God's presence. In this context Paul lists gifts of the Spirit in 1 Cor. 12:8-10.[31] These gifts encourage hope. Once again Welker stresses the diversity of those who receive these gifts: people with specific backgrounds, specific countries, and specific cultures. He writes, "The action of the Spirit touches me in the unique and unrepeatable concretization of this 'here and now.'"[32] But as "self-giving and self-bestowing," the Spirit brings forth reciprocity and love. It is a matter of "free self-withdrawal for the benefit of others," which gives space to others.[33]

The two most controversial and divisive workings of the Spirit, Welker

---

25. Welker, *God the Spirit*, p. 202.

26. Welker, *God the Spirit*, p. 207.

27. Welker, "The Holy Spirit," *Theology Today* 46 (1989): 18; and *God the Spirit*, pp. 222-23 and 283-302.

28. Welker, *God the Spirit*, p. 234.

29. Welker, *God the Spirit*, p. 235.

30. Welker, *God the Spirit*, p. 237.

31. Welker, *God the Spirit*, pp. 241-43.

32. Welker, *God the Spirit*, p. 247.

33. Welker, *God the Spirit*, p. 249.

claims, are *speaking in tongues* and *the inspiration of Scripture*. First, he examines Mark 16:17 (Mark's longer and disputed text); Acts 10:46; 1 Cor. 12:10, 28, 30; 13:8; and 14:2-25. He sees tongues-speech as "a prayer directed to God that in praise and thanksgiving serves to build up those who are praying in tongues — but only those who are praying in tongues."[34] He affirms that tongues-speech *is* a gift of the Spirit, but in a universal generalization claims that "it is undisputed" that the descent of the Spirit is *necessarily* bound up with tongues, and that tongues are also not the highest or most important gift (1 Cor. 14:19). Most, but not all, Pentecostals would now agree with both claims. Tongues become divisive if too much emphasis is placed on "the numinous" and corresponding "experiences."[35] It is also a "protest phenomenon" — against placing too little emphasis on the Spirit, and too much on formalism and abstraction. This links with "polyconcrete" postmodernism in contrast to abstract modernism.

The problem of the inspiration of Scripture is that many take this to mean "an event in which God implemented the precise wording of the text in the authors . . . *throughout*. . . . Each individual word is of equal significance" (Welker's italics).[36] This inspiration is to preserve the community of faith from disintegration, but is also to give a voice to "a plurality of testimonies . . . present in the biblical traditions" (his italics).[37] The text reflects God's presence, Welker asserts, in a variegated manner.

The last chapter addresses the Personhood of the Spirit. Welker warns us that so often spirit counts as the essence of the human person, and is confused with the Spirit of God. This point is fundamental. He accuses Nicholas Berdyaev and Walter Kasper of this, and even Yves Congar, though the last is a surprise, and perhaps because Welker sees this as not his main emphasis. Second, Welker rejects the notion of spirit in Aristotle as remaining too much an *abstract principle*. Even Hegel noted this. Similarly, a theology of the Spirit must recognize "the specific selflessness of the Spirit of God."[38] This is seen in the Spirit's pointing to Christ and in his effective engagement with the world and with others. Too much Western theology, Welker claims, is based on Aristotle's notion of Being and actuality. He appeals to Eberhard Jüngel. A center of action of such does not become a person without some *reciprocal relationship or relationality* such as we see in the Holy Trinity. Welker writes: "Self-relation indeed 'is' only *in* its en-acted constant activation and renewal."[39] He rejects "essential abstractedness." His perspective is active and dynamic. We go back, it seems, to the early Hebrew view of the living God, and to the wind, which can

---

34. Welker, *God the Spirit*, p. 265.
35. Welker, *God the Spirit*, p. 268.
36. Welker, *God the Spirit*, p. 272.
37. Welker, *God the Spirit*, p. 275.
38. Welker, *God the Spirit*, p. 295.
39. Welker, *God the Spirit*, p. 299.

be seen only in its effects. He might well have added Paul Ricoeur for support, especially in *Oneself as Another.*

Welker concludes, "Through human beings and in their midst, God *inscribes* Godself in this world by the Spirit; through human beings Christ addresses the world (cf. 2 Cor. 3:3)" (his italics).[40] He adds: "The mystery of self-giving, of free self-withdrawal for the benefit of the world, is revealed to these persons defined by the Spirit."[41] We recall that this was a distinctive feature of Jürgen Moltmann's argument in *The Spirit of Life,* who was formerly Welker's supervisor of research. Forgiveness of sins provides the foundation for the renewal and restoration which the Spirit offers to the world.[42] The final goal of all this is resurrection by the Spirit, intimacy with God, and participation in God's glory.[43]

What reviews there are of this complex book rightly call it "sensitive" and "pastoral." They consider the philosophical backgrounds from which Welker succeeds in drawing the best from postmodernism. But Welker does not warn us about the negative effects of postmodernism on Christianity. As we have observed, there is much of benefit in postmodernism. But some aspects of this movement or network can be poisonous, and it is a pity that Welker gives no warning about what is harmful, as well as rightly selecting some more helpful points. This is all the more the case since in Pentecostal literature a naive affinity with the postmodern has become increasingly fashionable, often buried beneath the impression of great sophistication! Welker's book is theologically and pastorally perceptive. It almost deserves to be placed beside Moltmann's, Congar's, and Pannenberg's works. They, too, have Hegel in the background, but they give less emphasis to the dubious themes of process philosophy and other questionable philosophical movements.

In his essay of 2006, Welker largely repeats what he has said in *God the Spirit.* He speaks again of "the multi-contextual and polyphonic presence of the Spirit," and of the need to move beyond the concept of "person" in Aristotle.[44] The pouring out of the Spirit, he repeats, brings about a pluralistic striving for God's righteousness and truth. (Pannenberg and Moltmann, like Barth, would probably have replaced "striving" with "grace.") God works through frail and finite creatures. In accord with process thought, the Church works in "emergent" ways, reconfiguring clusters of relations and countering evil forces. God's

---

40. Welker, *God the Spirit,* p. 309.

41. Welker, *God the Spirit,* p. 310.

42. Welker, *God the Spirit,* pp. 315-25.

43. Welker, *God the Spirit,* pp. 325-41; cf. Anthony C. Thiselton, "The Beatific Vision," in Thiselton, *Life after Death: A New Approach to the Last Things* (Grand Rapids: Eerdmans, and London: SPCK, 2012), pp. 185-215.

44. Welker, "The Spirit in Philosophical, Theological, and Interdisciplinary Perspectives," in *The Work of the Spirit: Pneumatology and Pentecostalism,* ed. Welker (Grand Rapids: Eerdmans, 2006), p. 228; cf. pp. 221-32.

Kingdom comes not like a storm, but as an "emergent reality."[45] In ecumenical and interdisciplinary work we should both be alert for "resonances" and distinguish between spirits. "Baptism in the Spirit" remains a positive "symbol in the framework of the polycontextual and polyphonic dwelling of the Spirit"; it mediates between "initiation events of faith and the insistence that the 'Spirit of truth' is characterized by its connection to Jesus Christ and a Wisdom that operates in astounding, though not necessarily spectacular ways."[46]

23.2. Harvey Cox and Amos Yong

(1) *Harvey Cox* (b. 1929) wrote *Fire from Heaven* in 1995. He was Research Professor of Divinity at Harvard Divinity School, from which he retired in 2009. He was ordained as a Baptist minister in 1957, and is best known for his book *The Secular City*, published in 1965, which sold over a million copies. Many will also know his book *The Seduction of the Spirit* (1985), and at least a dozen other books. In 1995 he produced *Fire from Heaven*, which traces the rise and partial development of Pentecostal spirituality, including interviews with many Pentecostals worldwide.[47]

There is no need to rehearse again the origins of the Pentecostal Movement, which we discussed in Chapter 18. Cox discusses millennialism in America, the Azusa Street Revival, the prophecy of "latter rain," and the work of Charles F. Parham in Topeka, Kansas.[48] He notes the Black African roots of Pentecostalism with William Seymour, and Parham's conservative stance on race. He recounts William H. Durham's attack on Seymour, in which he argued that sanctification was not "a *second* work of grace," and Seymour's response that tongues was only *one* of the gifts of the Spirit.[49] He then speaks of the Welsh revival, and of similar phenomena in India. All this gives birth to "a narrative theology whose central expression is the testimony."[50] He briefly discusses the cessationist view of Benjamin B. Warfield, and the comment by the devout G. Campbell Morgan that Pentecostalism was "the last vomit of Satan."[51]

Very relevantly, Cox now traces the *disputes* which broke out: between Parham, Durham, and Seymour. These concerned whether *sanctification* em-

---

45. Welker, "The Spirit," in *The Work of the Spirit*, p. 229.
46. Welker, "The Spirit" in *The Work of the Spirit*, p. 231.
47. Harvey Cox, *Fire from Heaven: The Rise of Pentecostal Spirituality and the Reshaping of Religion in the Twenty-First Century* (Cambridge, MA: Da Capo, 1995).
48. Cox, *Fire from Heaven*, pp. 19-55.
49. Cox, *Fire from Heaven*, pp. 62-64.
50. Cox, *Fire from Heaven*, p. 71.
51. Cox, *Fire from Heaven*, p. 75; cf. G. Campbell Morgan, *The Spirit of God* (London: Hodder & Stoughton, 3rd ed. 1902).

braced two stages or three. Indeed, "The most amazing thing about the runaway divisiveness in the young Pentecostal movement is that while the spats and squabbles continued, so did its spread. The more Pentecostals fought, the more they multiplied. . . . The pattern of division and proliferation continued apace."[52] I cannot help wondering, since they claimed no system of doctrine, how many of these "divisions" were grouped around strong personalities who gave rise to power struggles, just as these occurred at Corinth. Strangely, "the unity of the Spirit" did not seem to matter.

Cox next considers "the recovery of primal speech," which he sees as glossolalia or "ecstatic utterance." This goes hand in hand with "primal piety," which includes trance, vision, healing, dress, and dance; and with "primal hope" with its millennial eschatology.[53] He gives a vivid description of "speaking in tongues" in various assemblies. He sees this as relating to "pressing needs, demanding urges, and tumultuous emotions."[54] Historically he alludes to the Montanists, to Wesley, and to Jacob Boehme.

On "signs and wonders" Cox alludes to African spirituality and to Asia and other parts of the world. He sees a broad searching for the miraculous, from Lourdes to other groups and sites. In history he alludes to Joachim of Fiore. He concludes controversially: "'Pentecostalism' is not a church or . . . religion, but a *mood* . . . millennial sensibility" (his italics).[55] Predictably he then discusses "prophecy" with special reference to Aimee Semple McPherson. He comments that she made *use of popular culture.* He argues that "women have become the principal carriers of the fastest-growing religious movement in the world."[56] Music now appears on the discussion agenda. Here the African roots make themselves felt, with reference to tambourines and jazz improvisations.[57]

Part 3 of the book now moves to manifestations of Pentecostalism in Latin America, Europe, Asia, Black Africa, and America. Emilio Willems considers its spread in Latin America. Cox looks in particular at Brazil, where he finds more Pentecostal pastors than Catholic priests.[58] It is claimed that in Europe, from 1985 to 1990, Baptists, Methodists, Presbyterians, and Anglicans all lost members to Pentecostal churches.[59] He notes "the recent success of Pentecostals in China, Russia and Ukraine."[60] In Asia, he discusses the new generation in Korea, where "Hyun Kyung Chung is one of an emerging group of theolo-

52. Cox, *Fire from Heaven*, pp. 77-78.
53. Cox, *Fire from Heaven*, pp. 81-83.
54. Cox, *Fire from Heaven*, p. 88; cf. pp. 81-97.
55. Cox, *Fire from Heaven*, p. 116.
56. Cox, *Fire from Heaven*, p. 137.
57. Cox, *Fire from Heaven*, pp. 142-52.
58. Cox, *Fire from Heaven*, pp. 175-77.
59. Cox, *Fire from Heaven*, p. 187. No authoritative source is quoted.
60. Cox, *Fire from Heaven*, p. 179.

gians from the fast-growth area of Christianity."[61] Chung is not explicitly Pentecostal, but Pentecostalism in Korea seems to transcend its boundaries, even absorbing characteristics of shamanism.[62] Cox reports that three of the largest ten churches in the world are in Seoul. Shouting, singing, and other physical phenomena accompany the worship. According to one report, nearly 80 percent of all Korean Christians "have experienced 'the baptism of the Holy Spirit.'"[63]

Black Africa, however, represents the special "home" of Pentecostals.[64] Cox attended assemblies in their thousands in Zimbabwe, and visited many African independent churches. These include Full Gospel, Assemblies of God, and "Apostolic" churches. Even before Pentecostal missionaries arrived, "protest-based denominations [were] . . . already present."[65] But in South Africa Pentecostalism did not succeed in exorcising "the demon of race." Finally, Cox returns to America. He recounts a broad variety of experiences, including the estate of Jimmy Swaggart, where he found "weeping, scolding, dancing, singing along with his choir. . . . Swaggart was something of a shaman, . . . putting himself into an ecstatic state of consciousness, with hundreds of millions of people watching [i.e., on television]."[66] Yet Swaggart ended up with "his tearful confession of his various rendezvous with prostitutes, and his defrocking by the Assemblies of God."[67]

Cox's survey is itself primarily a *phenomenological* survey of *worldwide* Pentecostalism in 1995, as he sees it. He begins with his autobiography, moving from the portrayal of our era as "post-religious" in *The Secular City* (1965) to a confirmation that traditional churches usually or often do not engage with the spirit of our age, to the different "solution" that, far from being "post-religious," our age in the 1990s seeks a more primal religion and primal language than the traditional churches can provide. His assessment of Pentecostalism is therefore largely or partly positive, noting that it meets a genuine need, in contrast to the "dryness" and "rationalism" of formal religion. But he readily notices fallibilities, eccentricities, and power plays, with which probably most Pentecostals would agree. I can fully understand why for many Pentecostals Cox's book seems to hover between very cautious approval in its recognition of *worldwide numbers and relevance* to our age, and ambiguity or even skepticism for its *pragmatic and phenomenological* stance, as over against a genuine theological one.

61. Cox, *Fire from Heaven*, p. 215.
62. Cox, *Fire from Heaven*, p. 219.
63. Cox, *Fire from Heaven*, p. 233.
64. Cox, *Fire from Heaven*, pp. 243-62.
65. Cox, *Fire from Heaven*, p. 249.
66. Cox, *Fire from Heaven*, p. 277.
67. Cox, *Fire from Heaven*, p. 278.

(2) *Amos Yong* tells us that his upbringing took place in the context of Pentecostalism but that he then moved toward "Evangelicalism." At the end of a pilgrimage, he turned to Eastern Orthodoxy, where he belongs. But he insists that he consciously retains these three strands of spiritual life: Pentecostal, Evangelical, and Eastern Orthodox. All this can be found in his preface to *Spirit–Word–Community* (2002), which is largely devoted to arguing for a triadic or threefold method of *biblical hermeneutics*.[68] However, he also tells us that Frank Macchia and Stanley Grenz encouraged the publication of these themes as a book. Since the later 1990s, "Pentecostal Hermeneutics" has become a subject of serious concern. In the 1980s and in earlier history, this was not the case. Indeed, even in 1998 Veli-Matti Kärkkäinen wrote in "Pentecostal Hermeneutics in the Making" that Pentecostal thought was far from developed in this area.[69] Gordon Fee spoke in 1991 of a disregard of scientific exegesis and a carefully thought-out hermeneutics.[70] Amos Yong attempts to take the discussion about hermeneutics further, particularly in this book, published in 2002

Virtually all writers agree that there is no single "Pentecostal hermeneutic." Most authors would agree with many mainstream Christian interpreters that "canonical hermeneutics focuses on interpreting the scripture as Christian texts gathered together by the Church for the Church."[71] Yong cites Francis Watson and Charles Scalise, but he might well have cited Telford Work (2002), Jens Zimmermann (2004), Daniel Trier (2008), Mark Bowald (2008), Richard Briggs (2011), Joel Green (2012), and many others, all of whom aim to reestablish a *theological* hermeneutics. Yong writes: "My focus, then, is intentionally on theological hermeneutics."[72] His starting point is "pneumatological," but he is anxious to avoid the subjectivism that threatens to accompany a purely "Spirit-centered" hermeneutic or "charismatic exegesis." He is aware of Hans Robert Jauss's Reception Theory as well as Kevin Vanhoozer's work on hermeneutics and deconstruction.[73] Jauss's work is of major importance in reminding us of "Reception" and "Tradition."

Yong's positive solution is to offer a threefold hermeneutic, which, following Vanhoozer, he compares with a "Trinitarian" proposal. Like Welker, he is perhaps too readily seduced by postmodernism to welcome *pluralism and frag-*

---

68. Amos Yong, *Spirit–Word–Community: Theological Hermeneutics in Trinitarian Perspective* (Aldershot, Hants, and Burlington, VT: Ashgate, 2002), pp. ix-xi.

69. Veli-Matti Kärkkäinen, "Pentecostal Hermeneutics in the Making: On the Way from Fundamentalism to Postmodernism," *Journal of the European Pentecostal Theological Association* 18 (1998): 76-115.

70. Gordon D. Fee, *Gospel and Spirit* (Peabody, MA: Hendrickson, 1991), pp. 85-86.

71. Yong, *Spirit–Word–Community*, p. 3.

72. Yong, *Spirit–Word–Community*, p. 5.

73. Yong, *Spirit–Word–Community*, p. 10.

mentation as over against "any totalizing metanarrative."[74] Here he follows Paul Feyerabend in his thesis *Against Method,* concerning which many will have serious critical reservations, although he is correct to oppose the modernist notion of a "single general method" for all texts in all situations: "*Sola spiritus* inspires an 'enthusiastic' or radically individualistic Christianity."[75] I agree with *this.* But in practice *he is utterly far from the first to argue for a triadic balance between the author* (the Spirit of God and his agent), the *word* (Christ and the text), and the *response of the wider community* (Reader-Response theory). In 1992, in *New Horizons in Hermeneutics,* I tried to argue that this was needed for *some or many* situations. Indeed, I set out *ten models* of different hermeneutical methods for ten *kinds* of texts and situations.[76] Although Yong lists *New Horizons* in his bibliography, along with two of my smaller works, several of my more serious volumes have appeared between 2002 and 2011. Nevertheless, in terms of the work of the Holy Spirit, Yong, like Macchia and perhaps Vanhoozer, shows us that this must always be within the framework of the Holy Trinity and Church tradition, as well as with an eye to the context and genre of the text.[77]

23.3. Jim Purves

Purves is a Baptist minister in Edinburgh, and completed a doctoral study of the Holy Spirit and the Charismatic Movement at the University of Aberdeen. In 2004 he published *The Triune God and the Charismatic Movement.*[78] He explains that since 1975 he has been "both a Charismatic and a student of Reformed truths."[79] He engages with what he perceives to be "a great gap" between Christian dogma and "the experience I had entered." In this respect he understandably draws on the work of Tom Smail and James Dunn, who respectively value the Charismatic Movement and "experience," but who do not view the Movement without some criticism.[80] He also draws on the earlier work of Edward Irving.

Purves rightly regards 1975 as the "heyday" of the Charismatic Movement,

---

74. Yong, *Spirit–Word–Community,* p. 311.

75. Yong, *Spirit–Word–Community,* p. 312.

76. Anthony C. Thiselton, *New Horizons in Hermeneutics: The Theory and Practice of Transforming Biblical Reading* (Grand Rapids: Zondervan, and London: HarperCollins, 1992), pp. 558-619.

77. See especially Yong, *Spirit–Word–Community,* pp. 245-73.

78. Jim Purves, *The Triune God and the Charismatic Movement: A Critical Appraisal of Trinitarian Theology and Charismatic Experience from a Scottish Perspective,* Paternoster Theological Monographs (Carlisle: Paternoster, 2004).

79. Purves, *The Triune God,* p. xvii.

80. Purves, *The Triune God,* pp. 176-207.

when Dennis and Rita Bennett were still influential, and Michael Harper was promoting Renewal within the whole Church. In those days, many in established churches regarded the Movement as owing much to Pentecostals, and many within the Movement sought "baptism in the Spirit," accompanied by glossolalia. In Scotland David Black affected the Movement, and became the first Director of Scottish Church Renewal in 1974. But in the late 1970s tensions came about within the historic churches. Black asked: "Do we create suspicion . . . because we attach too much significance to the gifts of the Spirit?"[81] Yet where there was greater acceptance, it may have led to a lack of critical reflection on the part of Charismatics. They nevertheless were aware of "experiencing God . . . construed in terms of experiencing the Holy Spirit."[82]

Purves seeks to arrive at a new understanding of the Holy Trinity, partly through his study of the Ante-Nicene Fathers. He examines Post-Nicene developments, including those of Pseudo-Dionysius and John Calvin. Calvin, like the Charismatic Movement, saw the work of the Holy Spirit as "suprarational."[83] He also viewed the Spirit as "Epistemic Agent" within a Trinitarian framework and a Christocentric gospel.[84] Purves then considers the opposing models of the Trinity in Edward Irving and T. F. Torrance.[85] If Torrance's approach is correct, he writes, the beliefs of advocates of Renewal in Scotland "would be untenable."[86]

The seventh chapter concerns Tom Smail and James Dunn. Purves examines Smail's books *Reflected Glory, The Giving Gift,* and *The Forgotten Father. Reflected Glory* advocates the need for a Christocentric focus. But all three books stress the importance of the Church and the need to reformulate the Trinitarian framework of Renewal. *The Forgotten Father* "reflected something of Smail's disillusionment with the development of the Charismatic Movement."[87] (This would be even clearer in Smail's more recent book, *The Love of Power or the Power of Love.*) Smail stressed the prevenient grace of the sovereign God more than most Charismatics, and the relation between God the Father and the Son. Dunn begins with "experience" rather than dogma, but questions, as we have seen, whether baptism in the Holy Spirit is genuinely based on New Testament evidence. Purves concludes: "The Charismatic Movement in Scotland makes no ready connection between a rediscovered Pneumatology and the Trinitarian models offered to them."[88]

---

81. Purves, *The Triune God,* p. 11.
82. Purves, *The Triune God,* p. 25.
83. Purves, *The Triune God,* p. 91.
84. Purves, *The Triune God,* pp. 101-8.
85. Purves, *The Triune God,* pp. 132-75.
86. Purves, *The Triune God,* p. 174.
87. Purves, *The Triune God,* p. 182.
88. Purves, *The Triune God,* p. 203.

Purves leaves us with the following dilemma: "The Charismatic Movement's emphasis on supra-rational experience carries separate connotations from those associated with the Spirit's work in the sacraments. A tendency in the Charismatic Movement towards the ecstatic and phenomenal contrasts with a more subtle and implicit understanding of the Spirit's suprarational work in those areas of Scottish sacramental theology we have looked into."[89] A way ahead seems to be found in a closer relationship between the Holy Spirit and Jesus Christ, and perhaps also in the notion of communion advocated by Zizioulas. Purves concludes that Irving, Smail, and Dunn may help us in our search.

23.4. Frank D. Macchia

Frank Macchia (b. 1952) remains one of the most forward-looking, open, and ecumenically concerned Pentecostal leaders, perhaps alongside Veli-Matti Kärkkäinen. He took a Master's degree at Wheaton College, a Master of Divinity degree from Union Theological Seminary, and a Doctorate in Theology from the University of Basel (1989). Since 1999 he has been Professor of Theology at Vanguard University in California. He is Senior Editor of *Pneuma, The Journal for Pentecostal Studies*, and in 2006 published *Baptized in the Spirit*.[90] He has published several other books, including *Spiritual and Local Liberation* and *Justified in the Spirit*. Harvey Cox describes *Baptized in the Spirit* as a comprehensive and balanced re-casting of Christian theology that assigns an appropriate role to the Holy Spirit.

In his chapter "Framing the Issue" Macchia recognizes the different perspectives of Luke-Acts and Paul, and with reservations endorses the work on Luke-Acts of Robert Menzies and Roger Stronstad (see Chapter 20, where these are discussed). But his reservations *reflect those of Max Turner:* Menzies' notion of prophetic speech is too narrow, as is Stronstad's notion of charismatic gifting. He rightly suggests, in accordance with New Testament scholarship and Church tradition, "a broader *eschatological* framework as a *Trinitarian* act" and recovering early Pentecostals' vision of eschatological "latter-day rain." He strikingly adds: "An *eschatological* interpretation of Spirit-baptism can help us to mend the rift between Spirit-baptism as a *soteriological* and as a *charismatic* category" (my italics).[91] To this he also adds a renewed and corrected emphasis on the Kingdom of God as "the reign of divine love" (Rom. 5:5). In due course

89. Purves, *The Triune God*, p. 210.

90. Frank D. Macchia, *Baptized in the Spirit: A Global Pentecostal Theology* (Grand Rapids: Zondervan, 2006).

91. Macchia, *Baptized in the Spirit*, p. 17.

he will dialogue with Pannenberg, who, we noted, views "Kingdom of God" as a "pure" church. The aim of this corrected vision is to explore "how Spirit-baptism might function as an organizing principle of a Pentecostal theology."[92]

Macchia appeals to Veli-Matti Kärkkäinen to confirm the view that Spirit-baptism remains "at the forefront of the theological agenda in modern theology."[93] This is surely right. Many, the present writer included, wish to affirm much in the Renewal Movement, but certainly *not* that the New Testament uses the term "baptism in the Spirit" for the kind of genuine experience which has the *wrong name* in Pentecostalism. It is encouraging, however, that Macchia and Kärkkäinen call this a "doctrine still in the making." Macchia begins to provide a new context by appealing to the *transformation of creation and new creation, and a central focus in Jesus Christ* (Heb. 1:1-3).

There can be no doubt about the diversity of Pentecostalism. Macchia paints a delightful picture of the stereotypical Pentecostal, who understands Spirit-baptism as empowerment for ministry, as distinct from regeneration or initiation into Christ, and then linked with extraordinary gifts, especially healings and tongues-speech. However, he argues that this stereotype is far from universal: "Oneness Pentecostals" are *Christocentric;* "Chilean and German Pentecostals . . . regard Spirit-Baptism as *regeneration*" (my italics).[94] Macchia agrees with Simon Chan that Pentecostals have reached no agreement about their distinctive features.[95] Yet all seem to agree with the Korean Koo Dong Yon that baptism in the Spirit is somehow *central,* even if some *disagree about its meaning.* Hence, Macchia argues, baptism in the Spirit may serve as a *lens through which* to view different ecclesiologies. Steven Land, he notes, in *Pentecostal Spirituality* takes issue with F. Dale Bruner's description of Pentecostal theology as "*pneuma-* to *baptisto*-centric," as "missing the point altogether."[96] Yet Macchia regrets that "the baptism in the Spirit" has virtually disappeared from Pentecostal authors since Harold Hunter and Howard Ervin some twenty years ago (1980 and 1984). He made the very same comment orally at a conference on "Recent Developments in Pentecostal Theology," jointly sponsored by the Templeton Foundation and U.S.C. College, and posted on "Pentecostalism Worldwide" on the Internet.

Macchia deplores the diversity that has led to Pentecostal theology's be-

---

92. Macchia, *Baptized in the Spirit,* p. 17.

93. Macchia, *Baptized in the Spirit,* p. 19.

94. Macchia, *Baptized in the Spirit,* p. 20.

95. Simon Chan, *Pentecostal Ecclesiology: An Essay on the Development of Doctrine* (Blandford Forum: Deo, 2011).

96. Macchia, *Baptized in the Spirit,* p. 24; Steven J. Land, *Pentecostal Spirituality: A Passion for the Kingdom* (Sheffield: Sheffield Academic Press, 1993), pp. 62-63. Cf. Frederick Dale Bruner, *A Theology of the Holy Spirit: The Pentecostal Experience and the New Testament Witness* (Grand Rapids: Eerdmans, 1970), pp. 56-117

coming "a disconnected cafeteria of ideas."[97] *Part of the problem has been "our Holiness legacy."*[98] This is a mixed blessing, because the Holiness Movement emerged out of a "Revivalist" context, in which "its hallmark was a crisis experience following regeneration."[99] Macchia declares, *"The problem is that the revivalist influence of the Holiness Movement caused it to transform John Wesley's more process-orientated understanding of sanctification into a high-voltage crisis experience"* (my italics).[100] *This represents a key admission.* It can lead into a "higher life" or *elitist* mentality (as, we may comment, at Corinth). Nevertheless, why, he asks, abandon a "fruitful metaphor" just because of "technical problems"?[101] I am doubtful that this is merely a "technical problem," but I thoroughly endorse the argument about Pentecostalism's roots in Wesley and the Holiness Movement.

The exegetical problems are not the only ones for an apparent decline of interest in baptism in the Spirit. Because Pentecostalism has become global, different regions offer different agenda. With some it is speaking in tongues, for example; with others it is healing; with yet others, as Donald Dayton argues, it is eschatology and "the latter rain." Some strive for such abstractions as "purity" or "power." Yet all seek a "life-transforming" response to the reign of God.[102] Macchia appeals to Wolfhart Pannenberg for the warning that particular moments of renewal can eclipse *continuity* in the Christian life. With Pannenberg he also stresses the distinctive goal of looking for, and bringing in, the Kingdom of God. With Steven Land and Jürgen Moltmann, he looks for "a Trinitarian understanding of the eschatological realization of the Kingdom of God in history, so as to keep the continuity of Christ and the Spirit in one's understanding of the . . . way of salvation."[103] Indeed, the Protestant theme "Kingdom of God" coheres with the Catholic theme, "union with God," and with the Eastern Orthodox theme, "Participation in God."[104]

Macchia reproaches Walter Hollenweger for conveying the impression that Pentecostals see doctrine as of secondary importance, and argues that his Birmingham colleague or successor Allan Anderson leaves the same negative impression. He sees the *cross*, for example, as one of the organizing *doctrinal principles* of Pentecostalism, and commends Geoffrey Wainwright's bringing together of doctrine and worship. However, he commends Hollenweger and Emil Brunner for their emphasis on continuity of life and doctrine. In the end,

---

97. Macchia, *Baptized in the Spirit*, p. 27.
98. Macchia, *Baptized in the Spirit*, p. 28.
99. Macchia, *Baptized in the Spirit*, p. 28.
100. Macchia, *Baptized in the Spirit*, p. 30.
101. Macchia, *Baptized in the Spirit*, p. 32.
102. Macchia, *Baptized in the Spirit*, p. 41.
103. Macchia, *Baptized in the Spirit*, p. 44.
104. Macchia, *Baptized in the Spirit*, p. 45.

Macchia insists, with Stronstad and Menzies, that the Lukan concept of "baptism in the Spirit" is charismatic and for empowerment, but leaves room for a much *broader definition* of what it means.[105]

Part of the further progress is to recognize that baptism is not only related to the Church but also to bringing in the *Kingdom of God,* or awaiting it. This preserves the aspect of eschatology and new creation. Another is to recognize the *Trinitarian* framework, on which Macchia has already written. A third advance, which Turner pleads for, is the concern with *soteriology* and regeneration. Here Macchia appeals to both Karl Barth and Karl Rahner. He writes: "The key question involved in Spirit baptism thus becomes how the story . . . played out in the death and resurrection in Jesus comes to involve us."[106] He is happier with James Dunn's interpretation than some of his colleagues seem to be. *Empowerment by the Spirit,* however, remains at the heart of the experience (Acts 1:8).[107] Macchia concludes that "Implied is that all Christians are charismatic."[108] This is undoubtedly true if it means that "all are recipients of grace"; but it raises questions if it means that "all are given grace for particular tasks" (1 Cor. 12:28-31).

Macchia is still willing to speak of a "Christological focal point," even the "Full" or fourfold gospel.[109] He acknowledges that within Pentecostalism some have seen baptism in the Spirit as an outpouring of divine love (Rom. 5:5; and E. W. Bell). Frank Ewart even spoke of Calvary as unlocking the flow of God's love. He further admits that "early Pentecostals separated sanctification from Spirit baptism" by defining it narrowly as a cleansing and separation from sin. *Transformation is the key theme* (2 Cor. 3:18). Eschatology and the Trinitarian perspective are the currently neglected aspects. Macchia cites Moltmann's language about advent, and the discontinuity of new from old.[110] "Fire" in Acts 1:8; 2:3 are probably signs of God's presence.[111] He is clearly right that the goal of history is "that God may be all in all" (1 Cor. 15:28). Metaphorically, "baptism in the Spirit reflects a fullness of spiritual experience," as well as the Spirit's incorporating the Christian in Christ. He rejects "the elitist assumptions of Pentecostal revivalism."[112] The goal is that Christ might "fill all things" (Eph. 4:10).

Much of Macchia's thought about the Trinity is rightly assisted by drawing on Moltmann and Pannenberg. He traces their Trinitarian narrative in the New Testament to its *cosmic* perspective, as well as their insight into God's chosen

---

105. Macchia, *Baptized in the Spirit,* pp. 57-60.
106. Macchia, *Baptized in the Spirit,* p. 66.
107. Macchia, *Baptized in the Spirit,* p. 75.
108. Macchia, *Baptized in the Spirit,* p. 77.
109. Macchia, *Baptized in the Spirit,* p. 80.
110. Macchia, *Baptized in the Spirit,* p. 95.
111. Macchia, *Baptized in the Spirit,* p. 101.
112. Macchia, *Baptized in the Spirit,* p. 113.

"vulnerability to be affected by the world."[113] However, Macchia concludes: *"Spirit baptism is a powerful experience received with, or at a moment distinct from, Christian initiation"* (my italics).[114] The alternative or addition "received with" marks a huge concession.

Macchia's two remaining chapters concern ecclesiology and the fruit of *love*. The key word for his long chapter on ecclesiology is *koinōnia*: "*koinōnia* grants Spirit baptism in relational dynamic . . . and involves the diversely-interactive charismatic structure of the Church in the church's living witness to the kingdom."[115] He cites 1 Cor. 12:13 in the context of bringing *diversity together in solidarity*. Communal life involves sharing (Eph. 5:19). But for many it may seem a leap to insist on any *antihierarchical "egalitarian" system*, which does indeed *anticipate the kingdom*, but *leaves aside the joining of struggle and fallibility until we reach the kingdom*. Again, Macchia is right about the unity of Pentecost in Acts 2:5; but the narrative of Acts depicts a developing structure, as in the appointment of the Seven in Acts 6.[116] Yet he expounds the traditional "marks" of the Church as one, holy, catholic, and apostolic.[117] In many ways, this recalls Moltmann on the Church.

In his final chapter Macchia asserts that without divine love at its Spirit-baptism it would be "little more than raw energy without substance or direction, feeding little more than an emotional release. . . . Love is God's supreme gift, for it transcends all emotion, conceptuality, action, only to inspire all three. . . . There is nothing beyond love."[118]

Macchia has genuinely grounded "baptism in the Spirit" in a Christocentric, Trinitarian, and eschatological foundation. A very high percentage of his work will be appreciated by all Christians, especially its dialogue with serious theologians. It is open, and provokes thought. Critics, however, may wonder whether Macchia makes baptism in the Spirit so inclusive, so potentially ready to include everything, that it risks becoming nothing in particular: so blurred at the edges that it becomes acceptable to all. Yet he also seems to pin Pentecostal identity on the use of this term. The remaining question which some will ask is: Why retain *this* phrase for an experience so profound and central? Why does not Scripture, especially Paul and John, make more of it? Even granted the "occasional" character of so much New Testament teaching, for example, on the resurrection or the Lord's Supper, why do some many allusions to Spirit-*baptism* appear to carry less weight than Macchia places on them? Granted that so much of what he says is generous and right, does he neverthe-

113. Macchia, *Baptized in the Spirit*, p. 125.
114. Macchia, *Baptized in the Spirit*, p. 153.
115. Macchia, *Baptized in the Spirit*, p. 165.
116. Macchia, *Baptized in the Spirit*, p. 218.
117. Macchia, *Baptized in the Spirit*, pp. 204-41.
118. Macchia, *Baptized in the Spirit*, p. 259.

less have the right term to describe the experience which all New Testament writers, including Luke, would have recognized as actually describing the experience? This does not undervalue the generosity or perceptiveness of his work. Rather, it may question the legacy to which he wants to give credibility and currency.

23.5. Eugene Rogers and Veli-Matti Kärkkäinen

(1) *Eugene F. Rogers.* Rogers was educated at Princeton, Tübingen, Rome, and Yale, and has taught at Yale Divinity School and Princeton University. He has written on Aquinas and Barth, and on sexuality and the body. In 2005 he published his book *After the Spirit.*[119] He endorses the testimony of the Church Fathers that "the acts of the Trinity toward the world are indivisible."[120] But this could also lead to an unintended problem. If the mission of the Holy Spirit is indistinguishable from that of Christ, might the Spirit then become an obscure, even shadowy, figure virtually overshadowed by the visible and public ministry of Jesus Christ, and by the Father's "sending" of the Son? Rogers constructively seeks to restore a needed emphasis on the Holy Spirit by exploring a *narrative theology of the Trinity* within which the Spirit works in a Trinitarian framework. The fruitfulness of the *biblical narrative approach to the Trinity* has been amply demonstrated by Moltmann and by Pannenberg. It saves us from the endless distraction of metaphysical and analogical approaches.

The events of the annunciation, baptism, transfiguration, resurrection, and ascension of Jesus *all demonstrate "intra-Trinitarian relations."* To this group of events in the life and ministry of Jesus Rogers gives the overall title "the Spirit rests on the Body of the Son." He makes a centerpiece or paradigm of the baptism of Jesus.[121] He writes, "The baptism of Jesus is primarily to be understood as an intra-Trinitarian event. . . . It is an event in which the Spirit bears witness to the love between the Father and the Son." He continues: "In the baptismal interaction, the Father expresses his love ('this is my son, my Beloved'); the Spirit hovers over the waters of Jordan as she hovered over the waters of creation. . . . Jesus receives the love and witness in a way that other human beings can participate in."[122]

The resurrection of Jesus is no less "intra-Trinitarian" than the other events. Rom. 8:11 and less directly Rom. 1:4 demonstrate this. Rogers sees the same pattern in the annunciation, commenting, "What the Trinity does . . . has

---

119. Eugene F. Rogers, *After the Spirit: A Constructive Pneumatology from Resources outside the Modern West* (Grand Rapids: Eerdmans, 2005, and London: SCM, 2006).

120. Rogers, *After the Spirit*, p. 7.

121. Rogers, *After the Spirit*, pp. 135-71.

122. Rogers, *After the Spirit*, pp. 136-37; cf. p. 145.

its character from what the Trinity does in its own life."[123] Rogers concludes by noting the Spirit's role in prayer.

(2) *Veli-Matti Kärkkäinen* holds the Doctor of Theology degree from the University of Helsinki, Finland, and joined the faculty of Fuller Theological Seminary in 2000, where he became a full professor in 2003. He also holds a teaching position at the University of Helsinki. He has published nearly a dozen books in English, including *The Trinity: Global Perspectives* (2007); *One with God: Salvation as Deification and Justification* (2004); *Pneumatology: The Holy Spirit in Ecumenical, International, and Contextual Perspective* (2002); and most recently *Holy Spirit and Salvation: The Sources of Christian Theology* (2010).[124] Kärkkäinen has lectured in many countries, and is well known as a progressive and creative Pentecostal speaker and writer. He deserves more space than we can give to him here.

In *Pneumatology* Kärkkäinen distinguishes between different Pentecostal traditions and positions. In his part 1 he summarizes these positions, and in historical terms shows how various developments responded to "the challenge that drove the church toward a fuller understanding."[125] He considers Montanism, the Eastern Fathers, Augustine, Hildegard of Bingen, the "Left Wing" Radical Reformers, and others. Later in the book he compares Eastern Orthodox, Roman Catholic, Lutheran, and Pentecostal views. These include the perspectives of John Zizioulas, Karl Rahner, Wolfhart Pannenberg, Jürgen Moltmann, and Michael Welker.

In October 2006 Kärkkäinen took part in a Colloquium or Consultation sponsored by the Templeton Foundation and U.S.C. College, which included "Recent Developments in Pentecostal Theology," to which he and Frank Macchia contributed. He began his presentations by explaining that: (a) Pentecostals do not build on tradition; (b) Pentecostals have produced relatively little writing or literature; (c) they are *more Christocentric* than is popularly believed by others; (d) they consist of a wide *diversity of theologies and practices;* and (e) in general they have failed adequately to engage with wider social and ecumenical issues. He notes that *more than 40 percent of Pentecostals do not speak in tongues,* and emphasizes this. He saw ways forward as achieved by placing more emphasis on *eschatology and mission,* which is part of their raison d'être. He commended the new work of Amos Yong, and some Hispanic Pentecostals' concern for the poor.

Most of *Holy Spirit and Salvation* is devoted to historical and geographical surveys. We have tried to include any important insight in our Part II, above, in

---

123. Rogers, *After the Spirit,* p. 117.

124. Veli-Matti Kärkkäinen, in *Holy Spirit and Salvation: The Sources of Christian Theology* (Louisville: Westminster/John Knox, 2010); and Kärkkäinen, *Pneumatology: The Holy Spirit in Ecumenical, International and Contextual Perspective* (Grand Rapids: Baker Academic, 2002).

125. Kärkkäinen, *Pneumatology,* p. 38.

our historical section, and also in Chapter 18. Kärkkäinen begins with pre-Nicene writings; he then includes the post-Nicene Fathers, the medieval Church, and the Reformation and Post-Reformation writers up to the nineteenth century. Part 2 then discusses twentieth-century theologies of the Holy Spirit in Eastern Orthodox thought, Roman Catholic writers, and Protestant traditions, including Evangelical and Pentecostal theologies. The Orthodox tradition includes "Deification" and Vladimir Lossky, in whose writings "The Spirit leads us, through the Son, to the Father, where we discover the unity of the three. . . . The Son is sent by the Father and is incarnate by the Holy Spirit. . . . The Holy Spirit does not have the character of a work which is subordinate."[126] Hence Lossky opposes the Western "proceeds from the Father *and the Son (filioque)."*

Under this Orthodox heading, Kärkkäinen also discusses John Zizioulas's *Being as Communion* (1985) as "a landmark theological work."[127] Zizioulas calls for a proper synthesis between Christology and Pneumatology, while Kallistos (Timothy) Ware stresses the "secret hidden quality" about the Spirit.[128] Kärkkäinen also considers Sergius Bulgakov.

Kärkkäinen looks at Vatican II, Hans Urs von Balthasar, Yves Congar, Karl Rahner, and Kilian McDonnell in the Roman Catholic tradition; and Karl Barth, Hendrikus Berkhof, Jürgen Moltmann, Wolfhart Pannenberg, and Michael Welker in the Protestant tradition.[129] His selection from "Evangelical Theologies" includes Stanley Grenz, Donald Bloesch, and Clark Pinnock; and from Pentecostal and Charismatic testimonies Steven J. Land, Allan Anderson, Harvey Cox, and Kilian McDonnell.[130] Finally, he looks at Women's Pneumatologies (e.g., Rosemary Ruether, 2005); African Pneumatologies (e.g., John Mbiti, 1975), and Pneumatologies from Asia and Latin America. As he says in various publications, "Pentecostalism and independent charismatic movements are the most rapidly growing Christian force in Latin America."[131] We have moved a long way from the classical Pentecostalism of the early years of the twentieth century.

23.6. Finny Philip and Arie Zwiep

(1) *Finny Philip* was educated at Serampore University, and took a Ph.D. from the University of Durham in 2003. He has now returned to a college associated

---

126. Kärkkäinen, *Holy Spirit and Salvation*, pp. 278 and 279.
127. Kärkkäinen, *Holy Spirit and Salvation*, p. 282.
128. Kärkkäinen, *Holy Spirit and Salvation*, p. 285.
129. Kärkkäinen, *Holy Spirit and Salvation*, pp 307-37.
130. Kärkkäinen, *Holy Spirit and Salvation*, pp. 363-81.
131. Kärkkäinen, *Holy Spirit and Salvation*, p. 455.

with Serampore as Academic Dean. Born in 1966, he published *The Origins of Pauline Pneumatology* in 2005.[132]

Like many who write on the Holy Spirit, he begins with a review of scholarship. This includes Otto Pfleiderer, Hermann Gunkel, Eduard Schweizer, Roger Menzies, and Gordon Fee. He describes Gunkel's emphasis on ordinary people's experience against a Jewish background as "remarkable."[133] He recounts Schweizer's achievement in the same kind of language, although Geoffrey Lampe might be credited with a broadly similar approach. Menzies, however, uses a more "rigid" concept of prophecy.[134] Horn is a "significant milestone" in that he distinguishes two themes in Judaism which emerge in the New Testament.[135] Horn's extensive discussion of the eschatological content of the Holy Spirit in 1 Thessalonians is congenial to his own thesis. The Spirit is the *arrabōn* or guarantee of what is to come, which is in effect the title of Horn's book. For Fee, too, eschatology is important: "The Spirit had played a leading role in Paul's expectation of the end-times."[136] Ezek. 36:26-27 constitutes a key point in Pauline thought. In fulfillment of Old Testament prophecy *all of God's people now prophesy.* Fee also stresses God's personal presence through the Spirit.

Although Philip claims that there is a "lacuna" in previous scholarship, his thesis seems to be close to Horn's. On the other hand, Philip places more stress on Paul's mission to the *Gentiles:* "The Spirit is freely given to the Gentiles; . . . the Spirit was the key to his own preaching of the gospel to the Gentiles."[137] Hence in his part 1 Philip examines the conceptual background for the *eschatological bestowal of the Spirit,* looking especially at Ezek. 36:26-27 (as Fee does); Ezek. 37:1-14; Isa. 32:9-20 and 44:1-5; and Joel 3:1-2.[138] In his third chapter Philip considers postcanonical Judaism, including *Jubilees, 4 Ezra,* and Qumran; and in the fourth chapter Wisdom and Philo.[139] The remainder of the study discusses how Paul drew on themes which are found in the Old Testament and Judaism. He calls his part 2 "Paul's Convictional Background," and his part 3, "Paul and the Holy Spirit."[140]

Philip concludes that Paul's conversion experience and his conviction that God had poured out his Spirit on the Gentiles, confirmed by the experience at

---

132. Finny Philip, *The Origins of Pauline Pneumatology: The Eschatological Bestowal of the Spirit,* WUNT 2.194 (Tübingen: Mohr, 2005).

133. Philip, *Origins,* p. 8.

134. Philip, *Origins,* p. 15.

135. Philip, *Origins,* pp. 16-17.

136. Philip, *Origins,* p. 22.

137. Philip, *Origins,* p. 26.

138. Philip, *Origins,* pp. 34-76.

139. Philip, *Origins,* pp. 77-119.

140. Philip, *Origins,* pp. 125-62 and 164-225 respectively.

Antioch, constitute the driving motivations of Paul's theology of the Holy Spirit. In his conversion experience Paul encountered the Holy Spirit, seeing "the glory of God in the face of Jesus Christ" (2 Cor. 3:1–4:6). It would be difficult to say that Philip's conclusions are startling. Some anticipation comes in a different form from N. Q. Hamilton and Friedrich Horn. This, however, does not underrate the distinctive work, including Philip's use of sources. It is a useful marker to signpost where interest lay in 2005.

(2) *Arie W. Zwiep* (b. 1964) published *Christ, the Spirit and the Community of God* in 2010.[141] He studied at Louvain, Belgium, and at the University of Durham, England, under James D. G. Dunn. He has been Assistant Professor at the Free University of Amsterdam since 2004, and has written *The Ascension of Isaiah in Lukan Christology* (1997). The volume on the Holy Spirit collects eight essays, some of which have appeared in journals, on mainly the early chapters of Acts. The first four deal with the text of the ascension narratives, resurrection and heavenly exaltation, and the death of Judas Iscariot in the context of anti-Semitic trends.

The fifth essay concerns Luke's view of "baptism in the Holy Spirit." Zwiep argues that Luke sees it as an eschatological, corporate, and barrier-breaking event, which holds future promise and present experience together in tension. It is based on a paper given at Amsterdam in 2006 at a Pentecostal/Charismatic conference held to celebrate the one hundredth anniversary of the Azusa Street Revival, and was given particularly in response to Robert P. Menzies' work on Luke-Acts. Like Max Turner, he sees Menzies (like Stronstad) as making the entrance of Pentecostalism into serious New Testament scholarship.[142] Zwiep values dialogue rather than "socio-pragmatic hermeneutics, that is, reading the Bible to find confirmation of what one already believes."[143] These hermeneutical issues are even more important than exegetical ones.

Zwiep first marks out common ground between Pentecostals and Evangelicals. These include a common recognition that (a) Luke writes as *both* a theologian *and* a historian; (b) Luke must not be read through a Pauline lens; (c) "cessationism," especially as a dispensationalist view, "is rapidly in the retreat in evangelical circles"; (d) first-century Judaism provides the most plausible context for understanding Luke-Acts; and (e) there is growing consensus about the power-mission aspect of Luke's concept of the Spirit, especially in the wake of work by Eduard Schweizer.[144] The common ground, Zwiep argues, is much larger than it was thirty years ago.

Unexpectedly perhaps, Zwiep argues that *both* James Dunn's "conversion-

---

141. Arie W. Zwiep, *Christ, the Spirit and the Community of God: Essays on the Acts of the Apostles*, WUNT 2.293 (Tübingen: Mohr, 2010).

142. Zwiep, *Christ, the Spirit and the Community*, p. 100.

143. Zwiep, *Christ, the Spirit and the Community*, p. 101.

144. Zwiep, *Christ, the Spirit and the Community*, p. 104; cf. pp. 101-5.

initiation" thesis *and* the Pentecostal "second blessing" thesis are akin to Luke's perspective.[145] What may spoil the debate is an alleged "systematization fallacy." This stands in contrast to Hans-Georg Gadamer's emphasis on the concrete and particular, and helps us forward. Luke's allusion to the promise of the last days is based on Joel 2:28-32, Ezekiel 36–37, and Isa. 32:15 and 44:3-5. John the Baptist's words in Luke 3:16-17, "He will baptize you with the Holy Spirit and fire," likewise look to such passages, including the Day of Judgment. Mark and "Q" also imply *eschatological judgment.* In Luke it is linked with Acts 1:5. "The crucial question, however, is *how* the relation between the two baptisms is to be defined" (his italics).[146] Did Luke envisage the fiery baptism promised by John the Baptist to be *fulfilled at Pentecost?* Or did he see Pentecost as a *partial* fulfillment in *anticipation* of judgment at the eschaton? Zwiep argues: "Pentecost is not the definitive and final fulfillment of the eschatological promises and expectations, but an *anticipation . . .* of eschatological promises" (his italics).[147] After all, the symbolism in Peter's speech, "the sun . . . turned to darkness, and the moon to blood" (Acts 2:19-20), is apocalyptic and eschatological. At this stage the Holy Spirit is the first installment *(arrabōn)* of more to come (2 Cor. 1:22; Eph. 1:14).

Can we seriously imagine that Luke envisages a succession of *individual* experiences, such as those which Pentecostal theology would imply? Zwiep quotes Menzies as claiming that this "baptism" is to be experienced *"by every individual believer."* . . . "power *for every believer"* (Zwiep's italics).[148] Zwiep calls for a deeper theological and pastoral understanding, and claims some support from parallels from Qumran. He argues, "This 'already–not yet' tension looks very much like what we find in the New Testament."[149] Pentecost is also a "Barrier-Breaking Event": "In Acts 2:17-18 the classic walls of division are explicitly broken down."[150]

Zwiep surely is right. His argument is convincing, although perhaps he has missed one trick. Charles F. D. Moule and Alan Richardson, as well as Oscar Cullmann, see baptism itself as an anticipation of the Last Judgment. C. F. D. Moule describes baptism as "also a pleading guilty, an acceptance of the sentence" (i.e., at the Last Judgment).[151] Alan Richardson asserts: baptism accepts

---

145. Zwiep, *Christ, the Spirit and the Community,* p. 105.

146. Zwiep, *Christ, the Spirit and the Community,* p. 108.

147. Zwiep, *Christ, the Spirit and the Community,* pp. 108-9.

148. Zwiep, *Christ, the Spirit and the Community,* p. 111; Robert P. Menzies, *Spirit and Power: Foundations of Pentecostal Experience* (Grand Rapids: Zondervan, 2000), p. 101.

149. Zwiep, *Christ, the Spirit and the Community,* p. 116.

150. Zwiep, *Christ, the Spirit and the Community,* p. 117.

151. Charles F. D. Moule, "The Judgement Theme in the Sacraments," in *The Background to the New Testament and Its Eschatology: In Honour of C. H. Dodd,* ed. David Daube and W. D. Davies (Cambridge: Cambridge University Press, 1956), p. 465; cf. pp. 464-81.

the verdict "guilty," and so it brings us past the great assize and the Final Judgment.[152] Further, Tom Holland convincingly argues that baptism is a *corporate*, rather than an individual-oriented, sacrament.[153] *His judicious emphasis on the "now" and "not yet" of eschatology, and on the corporate or communal aspect of baptism of any kind, provides, in my view, a decisive rejection of the classical Pentecostal view of an individualist and "single event" character of "baptism in the Spirit."*

This is one of the most relevant essays to our discussions. But Zwiep's sixth essay on the Church is also relevant to some degree.[154] First, he argues that the Church is a "charismatic" community, in which miracles, prophecy, and other experiences occur. Acts does not pay as much attention to organization as do the Pastoral Epistles. Thus: "Acts cannot and should not play a role in the debate about *ecclesiology*. . . . There is a strong sense of *uniqueness (Einmaligkeit)* in his portrayal of the earliest Christian communities."[155] Indeed, Zwiep concludes: "The New Testament does not provide us with a uniform and authoritative 'model' of being church. Church structures and organizational principles vary from place to place. . . . Acts does not give a detailed blueprint for successful church building. . . . Luke did not write a handbook on church planting."[156] We know that it bridged social and ethnic barriers, but *the form of the Church varied* in order to serve Christ and the gospel, under the direction of the Holy Spirit. To end, in effect, with Zwiep thus provides a fitting climax to this study.

152. Alan Richardson, *Introduction to the Theology of the New Testament* (London: SCM, 1958), p. 341.

153. Tom Holland, *Contours of Pauline Theology: A Radical New Survey of Influences on Paul's Biblical Writings* (Fearn, Ross-shire: Mentor, 2004), pp. 141-56.

154. Zwiep, *Christ, the Spirit and the Community*, pp. 120-38.

155. Zwiep, *Christ, the Spirit and the Community*, p. 124 (first italics mine; second, Zwiep's).

156. Zwiep, *Christ, the Spirit and the Community*, p. 137.

24

Summary, Conclusions, Mutual Dialogue,
and Personal Reflections

This chapter differs from the others in that I have discarded the use of footnotes altogether, on two grounds. First, it may make for easier reading. It is my aim simply to reflect on what I have written in Chapters 1 to 23, with some evaluative comments. Second, no claim is put forward in this last chapter for which we have not given ample documentation in the twenty-three previous chapters. I begin by listing seven fundamental themes on this subject, as they have emerged from our biblical, historical, and contemporary studies. Toward the end of each of the seven principles or themes, I have added a practical consequence. This may be only one of a variety of possible "applications."

I have simply suggested "a" practical principle in each case to show that this study constitutes more than simply an exercise in theoretical doctrine, or an abstract study in biblical, historical, and contemporary theology. However, it is *not less than* this. I have included, where possible, the Pentecostal and Renewal Movements, not least because of their immense impact on this subject over the last hundred or so years, as well their sheer numbers and influence today. But the tendency of both movements until very recently indeed has been to devalue sheer biblical and doctrinal scholarship, as if this were somehow an alternative to "experience"; even sometimes to substitute *"feeling"* for *"thought."* We need a fresh review of biblical teaching and historical doctrine, and this last undocumented chapter seeks to build on this, including some personal reflections. Some may be controversial.

After noting these seven fundamental themes, I shall attempt a mutual dialogue with Pentecostals and advocates of the Renewal Movement in the hope of our drawing more closely together, and even learning on both sides from the other. Finally, I shall look further at some implications of this study for hermeneutics and biblical interpretation.

24.1. Seven Fundamental Themes

(1) *The Personhood of the Holy Spirit.* It has become a constant theme of every chapter that the Holy Spirit is a "Person." But at the outset we acknowledge that the Spirit is *not a Person in exactly the same sense* as we call human beings *persons.* We appeal to what Ian Ramsey has said concerning all language about God. We may use a near but approximate *model,* such as Person, provided that we sufficiently *qualify* the word in such a way as to cancel off any unwanted meanings. God, he suggests, may be the *cause,* but only in the sense of the *first* cause; God is not part of the causal chain of nature or contingent events. God is *Father,* but only if God is *heavenly* Father, or Father of Jesus.

Rudolf Bultmann has claimed that Paul does not understand the Holy Spirit as fully personal because he also uses such images as *filling* or *pouring out.* He calls these "dynamistic" metaphors or images, and concludes on this basis that Paul did not consider the Holy Spirit personal. But this argument shows only that the *model "person"* must be *qualified* by such *dynamistic metaphors as* *"filling"* or *"pouring."* The Spirit is no *less* a person because of this; this suggests *not* that the Holy Spirit is *subpersonal* but that the Spirit is *suprapersonal.* The Holy Spirit is *more* than a person, but *not less* than a person.

Three points may be made, the first in support of this, and the other two to consider some inferences from it. First, both in the Bible and throughout the centuries, writers have argued that to experience the Holy Spirit is to experience *God.* We noted, for example, Gordon Fee's description of the Spirit as "God's Empowering Presence." This must mean that the Holy Spirit participates in *God's personhood.* This has been emphasized by the Church Fathers in both the East and the West, by the Church of the Middle Ages, by the major Reformers, and by post-Reformation writers. Ambrose, we saw, stresses the *inseparability* of all three Persons of the Trinity in sanctification, and that "they share together in every stage of salvation." Basil the Great insisted on the cooperation and co-equality of the Persons of the Trinity in their activities, and in the Church's worship through the threefold *Gloria.* In the Middle Ages, Anselm argued, "The Spirit possesses in every respect the attributes [or character] of the Father and the Son." Calvin urged that we recognize *God through* the Holy Spirit. This includes the concept of Personhood with respect to the Father and the Spirit no less than it remains unquestioned in the case of the Son. This has been carefully argued in our Part I, on biblical teaching. In Part III, we saw that the work of Moltmann, Zizioulas, and others clarified this point.

Second, in the light of this and of everything that has been said above, it remains astonishing that so many refer to the Holy Spirit as *"it."* This can have only the effect of *demeaning the Holy Spirit,* and of implying a reversal of the great debate in which Hilary, Ambrose, Athanasius, and Basil answered the objections of their opponents. They urged unanimously that the Holy Spirit is *not a created being, or a "thing."* In particular, Athanasius led the attack on any notion that the Spirit is a creature or part of *creation,* that is, an *"it."* In the biblical accounts, the Holy Spirit often does what only a Person can do. The *Spirit prays, is grieved,* bears active witness or "cries in our hearts," speaks through prophets, and much more. In Martin Buber's language, the Holy Spirit relates to us as *I and Thou, not* as *I and it.* Hilary, Athanasius, and Basil contributed to this point.

Third, we come to what may perhaps constitute a more controversial and sensitive issue, but offer it on grounds of commonsense semantics and linguistics. This concerns the unfortunate confusion between *grammatical* and *personal* or identity-gender. James Barr and others in linguistics rightly insist that we should *not confuse conventional grammatical gender* with a gender of *personal identity. Rûach,* the Hebrew word for "spirit," is *grammatically* feminine. But the Greek word for "spirit," *pneuma,* is *grammatically* neuter; while John uses the masculine *paraklētos* and *ekeinos.* Barr points out that assigning grammatical gender has nothing to do with the legendary eroticism of the French on the ground that French assigns a *grammatical* gender to a host of words for objects! Nor does grammatical convention suggest anything about *personal* gender in Greek, Latin, Hebrew, French, or Turkish. In Greek the word for "child" *(teknon)* is grammatically neuter. But it would be absurd to infer from this anything about Greek attitudes toward children as mere objects. When we call the Holy Spirit personal, we do not need to ascribe personal gender. Gender concerns the *human creation;* God is *beyond* gender, as the Holy Spirit is also. This does not prevent the analogical application of *fatherly or motherly qualities* to God or to the Spirit. These are modes of describing divine action *analogically,* and they have precedents in the Old and New Testaments. Nor does it prevent gender being ascribed to Jesus when he chooses to become one with humankind. Incidentally, the translator of the Greek-speaking John Zizioulas uses the masculine pronoun in his work.

A Practical Consequence: The Holy Spirit is no less personal than God. We should never give in to the widespread popular trend of calling the Spirit "it." As a Person, the Spirit *addresses* us, and we may offer worship to the Holy Spirit, usually, but not always, in the form of the threefold *Gloria,* as urged especially by Basil the Great. If the Spirit were not a Person, what would it suggest about the Holy Trinity? It would be a serious mistake to think of the Holy Spirit simply as no more than a "force" or a "power."

(2) *The transcendence, distinctiveness, and "otherness" of the Holy Spirit.* In the Old Testament, clearly the Holy Spirit comes from "Beyond," as well as often operating "within" human beings. I have urged that the Spirit can rightly be called "the Beyond who is within." This phrase seeks to retain a balance between the transcendence and the immanence of much of the Spirit's work. The word "within," however, must be understood both in a *corporate* and in an *individual* sense: as both within the universe, the world, and the Church and within

the individual believer. A major theme of the Old Testament is that of human beings receiving the capacity to perform superhuman tasks. The gift of the Spirit to the judges provides one example. Virtually all the judges had some human weakness. But the Spirit enabled them to deliver Israel beyond their natural strength from their oppressors. The Spirit guarded Israel's cattle from marauders, and in Ezekiel the Spirit of God gave life to dry bones.

In the New Testament, too, the Holy Spirit is transcendent. Paul, as we have seen, carefully distinguishes the Spirit of God from the spirit of the world, and defines the Holy Spirit as *to pneuma to ek tou theou* (literally, "the Spirit, the out-from-God One"; i.e., "the Spirit who comes forth from God"; 1 Cor. 2:12). The Paraclete in John does not even speak on his own initiative, but his work is to witness to *Christ* (John 15:26-27; 16:12-15; cf. 1 Cor. 2:15-16).

This has strong implications for the widespread use of the adjective "spiritual" in a very broad and indeterminate way. "Spiritual" in this case refers primarily to the anthropological use of "spirit" as a merely human capacity or as *pertaining to the nonmaterial or religious aspirations of human beings.* This applies at least as conspicuously and no less misleadingly to the noun "spirituality." It is crystal clear, and impossible to deny, that when Paul uses the Greek word *pneumatikos,* "spiritual," he is alluding specifically to the agency, work, and effects of *the Holy Spirit,* for whom the lordship of *Jesus Christ* has become the supreme criterion (1 Cor. 12:3). When in 1 Corinthians he uses *pneumatikos* ("spiritual person"), Paul is referring to those whose life and thought are characterized by the Holy Spirit. When he uses *pneumatika* ("spiritual things"), Paul is referring to spiritual truths which the Holy Spirit reveals and imparts. He is not using either term in some quasi-Gnostic or anthropological sense, to mean "appertaining to the human spirit." This would imply a view of humankind which Paul does not hold. It is true that many Greeks, and some of the Corinthian Christians themselves, held this view of spirit. But to attribute this view *to Paul* and *to most of the biblical writers* would be a serious mistake. Just as we have noted the widespread popular error of referring to the Holy Spirit as "it," so we note the widespread popular error of using "spirit," "spiritual," and "spirituality" in a way which is wholly unbiblical, and does not reflect Paul's own use of the vocabulary. Our point does not reduce the immanence of the Spirit's work.

Such misuse has seduced us in many ways. For example, Paul speaks of the magnificent promise of God that the Holy Spirit will bestow upon us a *spiritual body* at the resurrection of the dead. This holds forth God's promise of a *mode of existence wholly* under *the control of the Holy Spirit,* animated by the Spirit's ever-fresh, *ever-new presence.* The Holy Spirit will lead us to fresh revelations and wonders, not the static "perfection" envisaged by Plato and probably Aquinas. The Pauline and biblical vision can be destroyed by thinking of *spiritual body* merely as some kind of purely human nonmaterial existence, as if *spirit* were a component of human nature. It would lose the dynamic, onward-moving power and presence of God as Holy Spirit. It would have reduced a dynamic picture of an existence determined by *God* through his Spirit into the purely *abstract, nonbodily notion* of an ideal Form. Such an abstraction could be absorbed into the All of many Eastern religions. This even threatens to diminish God's love for, and preservation of, the individual as well as the Church. It transposes the glorious promise of resurrection into that of a unit of created existence deprived of all that is important in life, simply to exist only perhaps as a shadow or "soul." To conceive of "the body" animated by the Holy Spirit places us in an entirely different universe of discourse. In this context the Holy Spirit brings to completion the *holiness, newness, well-being, and ongoing life* of which in this life we received only the *pledge* or guarantee *(arrabōn)* of more to come.

We are not suggesting that the word "spirituality" can *never on any occasion* be used in its broader sense. We simply propose that if the term *has* to be used in this way, it is made abundantly clear that this is *not the primary* biblical or indeed Christian usage. We must retain what is distinctive about the work of the Holy Spirit. This includes such qualities as witness to Christ, a Christ-like mind and character, holiness, "otherness" or "beyond-ness," and love. This does not undermine the point made by Zizioulas that Christ and the Spirit are complementary, or even that there would be no "Christ" without the Holy Spirit.

A Practical Consequence: From the time of Paul and the Church Fathers, especially Augustine, it has been urged that the Spirit of God should never be confused with "spirit" in the broader or anthropological sense. If we do confuse the two, this entire reorientation of language about the Holy Spirit becomes open to serious risk of distortion. We can ensure the glory, wonder, and "otherness" of the work of the Spirit if we stress the Holy Spirit's transcendence and "otherness" *beyond the merely human,* as well as the Spirit's work within the Church and world. Of the many effects, the work of the Holy Spirit in the resurrection of the dead would constitute a major example.

(3) *The Holy Spirit and the Holy Trinity.* One of the outstanding points of progress in our thinking about the Holy Trinity and the Holy Spirit within it has been a shift away from abstraction and metaphysical analogies and pictures to a *narrative exposition* of the Trinity *in the New Testament.* At first this seemed *specifically to come from Jürgen Moltmann and Wolfhart Pannenberg,* but others, for example, *Eugene F. Rogers,* have now decisively adopted it. This constitutes a *breakthrough* in formulating the role of the Holy Spirit within a Trinitarian framework, which almost every historical theologian of the Spirit has attempted to do. It provides a straightforward introduction to why such a complex phenomenon is necessary for Christians. This approach can readily be used in sermons, and can do much to explain the roots of the doctrine in biblical terms.

The baptism of Jesus provides a prime example, as Rogers shows. At his baptism Jesus was anointed for his Messianic work by the Holy Spirit (Mark 1:10), and then the Holy Spirit drove him (as in Mark 1:12) or led him (Matt. 4:1; Luke 4:1) into the wilderness for the testing and confirmation of this Messianic task. But this is not the whole of the account. It is equally the case that God the Father expresses his approval through the heavenly voice, which declared: "You are my Son, the Beloved [Greek, *ho agapētos*], with you I am well pleased" (Greek, *en soi eudokēsa;* Mark 1:11). The baptismal narrative recounts: "As he was coming up out of the water, he saw the heavens torn apart and the Spirit descending like a dove [Greek, *hōs peristeran*] on him" (Mark 1:10). All four Gospels testify to this narrative (Matt. 3:13–4:11; Luke 3:21-22; 4:1-13; John 1:32-34). The baptism of Jesus was a Trinitarian event in that all Persons of the Holy Trinity shared in a cooperative work.

The conception and Virgin Birth of Jesus equally take place within a Trinitarian framework. The originator of "sending" the Son into a human life remains God the Father, who "sent his Son into the world" (John 3:16). The mediate and efficient cause involved the agency and activity of the Holy Spirit. Simply on the basis of parallels with divine births in Greek religions, we are not entitled to dismiss Luke's account (Luke 1:35-38). In the creation of the world we have seen that the vast majority of scholars, including those as diverse in their specialist fields as C. K. Barrett and Wolfhart Pannenberg, insist that the Spirit "hovers creatively" over the waters of chaos (Gen. 1:2). They implicitly reject the NRSV translation: "a wind from God swept over the face of the waters." They see the creative Spirit *(rûach)* of God hovering or brooding as One about to bring order out of chaos. This coheres with Isa. 63:11-14, where the dynamic, creative Spirit or Agent of God brought Israel up from the sea. Indeed, since the Spirit of God stands guard over Israel in the wilderness, so the Spirit empowers and keeps Jesus in his recapitulation of Israel's journey. Hence the allusion to a visible dove in Luke's narrative depends not on Greek parallels, but on Luke's concern to show the parallel between creation and new creation. With retrospective insight, we attribute both acts of creation to Trinitarian cooperation.

Narrative has come to be recognized as an increasingly important biblical genre for given purposes. This does not mean that we subscribe to an often uncritical obsession with "story" today. As I argued in *New Horizons in Hermeneutics* and elsewhere, narrative is especially valuable if we take it seriously enough to bring to bear the additional resources of Gerard Génette and Paul Ricoeur in literary theory. In expounding the mystery of the Holy Trinity, biblical narrative has proved itself to be an invaluable didactic and explanatory source. As Gregory of Nazianzus rightly insisted, "three" has *nothing* to do with *numerical* values. Gregory's comment ought to make us pause before using distracting models like shamrocks or clover. The role of the Holy Spirit emerges most clearly from understanding the Spirit's part in major biblical narratives, not by playing with numerical analogies.

Perhaps few today are taught the Catechism from the Book of Common Prayer (1662). It begins with some introductory questions and answers, then rehearses the Apostles' Creed and asks the candidates what they have learned from the creed. The catechumen answers: "I learn to believe in God the Father, who hath made me, . . . in God the Son, who hath redeemed me, . . . in God the Holy Ghost, who sanctifies me." It is *not wrong* to differentiate between respective operations characteristic of each Person of the Trinity. But from an early date the Church Fathers, East and West, have firmly stressed that all three Persons of the Holy Trinity share jointly in the work of creation, redemption, sanctification, and resurrection. In this respect, the Prayer Book Catechism, while not at all "wrong," is to be regretted, as giving rise to a widespread movement of thought.

A Practical Consequence: It will help us to avoid mistakes in seeking to understand the Person and work of the Holy Spirit if we understand this within a Trinitarian frame. If we begin with a proper exposition of the New Testament narrative of Jesus, the Holy Trinity will no longer seem to be a theoretical doctrine inherited from the contingent events surrounding fourth- and fifth-century councils. This approach will be seen as an imperative of the New Testament, to which the Church Fathers appealed. This affects our two-way intercourse with God. In worship, as Tom Smail and others have urged, we address the threefold *God* through the mediation of the *Son* in the power of the *Spirit.* In prayer the Spirit inspires us and gives us the longing and the words; we normally address prayer to the Father; and it is always "through Jesus Christ our Lord." All Persons of the Holy Trinity uphold and prolong our life; all Persons of the Trinity created us and brought us into existence because the whole Godhead loves us. All are involved in giving us the Scriptures, and maintaining the Church in continuity. This gives further reason for Basil's insistence on our use of the threefold *Gloria.*

In another direction Eugene Rogers has shown how the Christian's *baptism,* like Christ's, remains a *work of the whole Holy Trinity,* Father, Son, and Spirit. The Holy Spirit binds us to Christ in the love of the Father. As Cullmann and others have shown, baptism *anchors us* in the events of the cross and resurrection. We are buried and raised with Christ (Rom. 6:2-11), and bound to Christ and raised from death by the Holy Spirit (Rom. 8:11). This is a communal event as well as an individual one.

(4) *The Holy Spirit is shared out as a common possession of the whole people of God.* In the Old Testament the Spirit of God is often given to chosen individuals to perform designated tasks. The classic source for this idea is the book of Judges. When Israel sinned, God gave them into the hand of their enemies. When Israel cried to the Lord in distress, "the Spirit of the LORD came upon Jephthah" (Judg. 11:29), or "the Spirit of the LORD rushed upon him [Samson]" (14:6), and in the latter case "he tore a lion apart barehanded, as one might tear

apart a kid" (14:6b). But although these individuals become *individual* "judges" or "saviors," the gift is *only for the sake of the whole of corporate Israel, or for all of God's people.*

As Filson pointed out, this scheme of individual endowment for corporate benefit is carried forward to the New Testament. Paul clearly states, "To each is given the manifestation of the Spirit *for the common good*" (1 Cor. 12:7). He then proceeds to enumerate nine particular grace-gifts (12:8-10) which are "activated by one and the same Spirit, who allots to each one individually just as the Spirit chooses" (12:11), for the benefit of the whole community of the Church. Paul immediately proceeds to expound "the one body" with many limbs (12:12-27). But this is *exactly the context* in which he states, "*In one Spirit, we [plural] were all baptized into one body*" (12:13). Zwiep, as we saw, emphasized the *communal and eschatological* context of this passage. He is probably not alone in this, but his exposition gives the verse special point in discussing initiation and the work of the Holy Spirit. We shall consider and discuss the mistakenly individualist interpretation of 12:13 when we attempt mutual dialogue with Pentecostals on the "baptism in the Spirit."

The ramifications of this insight about community are numerous. Lionel Thornton, we noted, was probably one of the first to insist that Paul's prayer that the "grace of our Lord Jesus Christ, the love of God, and the communion *(koinōnia)* of the Holy Spirit be with all of you" (2 Cor. 13:13; or in some versions of v. 14) referred to a *"joint share"* or *"participation"* in the Holy Spirit. He argues from the use of the cognate Greek noun to denote *shareholders* or *participants.* The word certainly does not mean, as I have heard it paraphrased in a church, "the companionship" of the Holy Spirit. To be a *participant,* whatever our particular gifts, will promote the Spirit's gift of *mutuality,* and will prevent any kind of elitism or arrogance. The Holy Spirit is not "mine," but graciously "ours."

This invites respect and care for all fellow believers as those who also make up the holy temple of God, which is consecrated as holy by the corporate indwelling of the Holy Spirit (1 Cor. 3:16-17; 6:19). It is argued that 6:19 speaks of an *individual* temple, while 3:16-17 speaks of the one holy temple *made up of the community.* If that is true, other Christians deserve respect, if not reverence, as temples of the Spirit. To commit an offense against a fellow believer has therefore been described as *sacrilege.* But does Paul *necessarily* refer to the individual in 6:19? Paul uses *the plural* in both passages: Greek, *naos theou este kai to pneuma tou theou oikei en hymin* (3:16); *to sōma hymōn naos tou en hymin hagiou pneumatos estin* (6:19). On the other hand, since body is likely to denote "physical body" in this context, and not the Church, the latter passage may well be interpreted in individual terms. This does not invalidate the argument that the Holy Spirit is never the exclusive possession of one person, in contrast to another.

A Practical Consequence: We noted John Taylor's down-to-earth comment that the presence and power of the Holy Spirit *excluded* our ever thinking: *"It all depends on me."* Even if we fail in some task, the Holy Spirit indwells and activates the whole Church of which at best we are only a tiny fragment. But if this encourages us, it also humbles us. The Holy Spirit is *never* simply *"mine";* as if the Spirit were anyone's exclusive possession or monopoly. This may offer one reason why "gifts of the Spirit" are apportioned out, "each one of them, as he chose" (1 Cor. 12:18). *No single individual can possess all the gifts of the Spirit.* Hence the exclusion of "It all depends on me" is balanced by the exclusion of "I am more favored than you." Gifts for individuals never undermine, or *should* never undermine, any gift given for the good of *all.* This also rules out any envy. As Paul states in the next chapter, "Love is not envious or boastful or arrogant . . . it is not irritable or resentful" (13:4-5). There is no reason for envy if the Spirit selects someone to carry responsibility for others. That person will be duly accountable.

(5) *The Holy Spirit is "holy" because the Spirit is an extension of God.* Throughout the pages of the New Testament and throughout the centuries of history, Christians have wrestled with the task of how to do justice to the Holy Spirit's conveying the very presence of God, and yet not reducing the Spirit *only* to a mode or extension of God's Being. This constituted the ancient heresy of Modalism or Sabellianism, which the Church has sought to avoid ever since the time of Hippolytus.

It is difficult to be certain to what degree late Old Testament and Jewish writers conceived of the *Wisdom, Word,* and *Presence* (Hebrew, *pānîm;* literally, "face") of God as *"extensions"* of God. To what degree and at what time did the Hebrews or Jews conceive of a *semi-independent hypostasis* which *represented* God? Angels are not of the same order, for they are creatures, *created* beings, of God. In many texts, to see God is to experience his gracious *face* or *presence* (Job 33:25-26; Ps. 17:15). To seek God's face becomes a standard expression (1 Chron. 21:30; Ps. 24:6). But *to seek the Holy Spirit cannot be other than to seek God himself.* In Ps. 139:7 "Spirit" and "presence" form what is commonly called "synonymous parallelism" in Hebrew poetry: "Where can I go from your Spirit? Or where can I flee from your presence?" In Ps. 51:11, "Do not cast me away from your presence" is parallel with "Do not take your Holy Spirit from me." At the level of words they constitute *synonyms,* in which each could replace the other.

We also noted that only God is "Holy" in an absolute sense. Hence the term "Holy Spirit" derives from the attribution of "holy" to *God alone.* In a secondary sense, it leads to the distinctive work of the Holy Spirit in *sanctification:* both the sanctification of individuals, and the sanctification of the whole people of God. The person in whom the Holy Spirit dwells becomes "holy." This applies individually and *corporately* (1 Cor. 3:16-17 and 6:19-20). But the biblical writers, as is common knowledge, use "holy" in two senses. First, anything that belongs to God is holy. Second, holiness is also a goal, reached after long growth and often struggle. The first describes the sense in which all Christians are holy. The second is usually called sanctification. Confusion between these two meanings may account in part for the notion in most Holiness Movements that "becoming holy" constitutes an event, not a process. "Perfectionism" not only denies the sinfulness of Christians; it also robs a future eschatological hope of its reality. We doubt whether Wesley should be credited or blamed for this doctrine as much as some claim. It was perhaps different in the case of Fletcher and some of Wesley's followers.

The work of the Holy Spirit especially concerns sanctification. The Church Fathers concentrated on ensuring that the Holy Spirit was regarded as uncreated, proceeding from God. This tradition lasted into the earlier Middle Ages. But theologians in the later Middle Ages, the Reformation, the Post-Reformation era, and into modern times emphasized this distinctive activity of the Holy Spirit, while at the same time recognizing that the whole Trinity co-operated in every stage of creation, redemption, sanctification, and resurrection into eternity.

A Practical Consequence: The Holy Spirit is not a *substitute* for God. The Spirit conveys God's presence, power, and love. 1 Thessalonians and Romans focus on *God,* just as in the Gospels Jesus Christ proclaimed not himself but the coming reign of *God.* It seems that some Corinthians invited Paul's rebuke for speaking constantly of their more easily approachable "Lord," Christ, while pushing "God" into more remote and shadowy margins of their lives. This is why the so-called "subordination" passages occur in 1 Corinthians. Paul tells them that "God is the head of Christ" (1 Cor. 11:3); that "all things come from God" (11:12); that at the end time Jesus Christ will "hand over the kingdom to God the Father" (15:24), and "the Son himself will also be subjected to the one who put all things in subjection under him, so that God may be all in all" (15:28). In spite of the "pneumatics" at Corinth, there seems to have been no parallel problem about special worship of the Spirit. But that is not to say that a minority of Pentecostals or advocates of the Renewal Movement could not fall into this mistake. This is by no means to criticize the correct emphasis of Hilary, Athanasius, Basil, Moltmann, and many others, on the co-equality of the Persons of the Trinity. But Paul and the writer of Revelation (Rev. 4:8-11 and 5:1-10) seem to hold this together with pastoral advice not to neglect the ultimate nature and ultimate source of Being as God the Father. If we use the term "*Holy* Spirit," it is appropriate also to use the term "*Holy* Trinity."

(6) *The Holy Spirit is identified or recognized by the Spirit's effects, but what is claimed as the Spirit's effects is not always of the Spirit.* The meaning of *rûach* and *pneuma* as "wind" reminds us of a truth of which a number of Old Testament writers have reminded us. We cannot "see" the wind as such, but we can certainly *see its effects* in fallen trees, waving cornfields, higher or lower temper-

atures, and icy blasts. Philosophers who discuss the existence of God often talk of "inference from activity," or more precisely "inference from the effects of activity." We cannot see God, but we can see the effects of his working. We cannot "see" the Holy Spirit, but we can see the Spirit's *effects*. We did not have to wait for Rudolf Bultmann to use a *functional rather than metaphysical* approach to the Person of the Holy Spirit. As we noted, Bonaventura emphasized "the vestiges, footprints, or traces" of God (*Journey of the Mind*, 1:2), and so did many of the Fathers and medieval writers.

Yet this talk and direction of inferences can sometimes be hazardous. Fallen trees, for example, may have fallen for many reasons besides the wind. As we noted, when he wrote about the phenomena which Paul discussed in 1 Corinthians 12–14, Karl Barth reminded us that the key to understanding the phenomena was not what came to view in itself, but, *in Barth's language, the whence (from whom or from what did this come?) and the whither (for what purpose did it exist, and to what did it lead?)*. In other words, did *every* piece of the phenomena genuinely come *from* the Holy Spirit? And did it lead *to* the building up of the Church and *to* the glorifying of Christ?

It is a truism that some phenomena that purport to come from the Holy Spirit turn out to be nothing of the kind. The Church, with much heartache, has discovered how easily purely human forces can mimic and replicate what at first passes for the work of the Spirit. For countless generations, since the earlier period of the Old Testament, through the First Epistle of John, the *Didache*, Montanism, and the medieval church, until today, the sensitive subject of *"false prophecy"* has been prominently on the agenda. Recently Walter Moberly, as we noted, has written a helpful book on this subject. History has witnessed to many *self-proclaimed prophets*. It is not always the answer to seek to test prophecy with reference to the tradition of the Church, or what Irenaeus called "the rule of faith." For this might result in the endless repetition of the Church's tradition, in which "office" or the "institutional" triumphed over everything that was more novel, creative, or "charismatic." We are reminded of Hodge's curious boast that Princeton, his seminary, had thankfully never produced an original idea.

Yet we cannot vacate the field to deception and human whim. Many have sincerely seen as "prophecy" what their contemporaries or successors have seen as the projection of deep-seated desires, or even the desire for "celebrity" status, or simply a sincere mistake. The one "effect" which is clearly stipulated in the Bible is the *confession of Jesus as Lord* (1 Cor. 12:3). This passage features in virtually every historical writer on the Holy Spirit. The shift to Christological criteria is faithful to Paul, 1 John, and Church tradition. The problem then arises that in the modern era, Christology has sometimes suffered blurred edges. Irenaeus would have appealed to publicly mediated "apostolic tradition" or the rule of faith. But no criterion is watertight, and perhaps this is why *"discernment of spirits"* is a spiritual gift. Some argue that this "gift" has become the most important and most essential of all. There is still a division of opinion about Montanism. John Wesley famously changed his mind about it.

One of the unresolved puzzles, to which we shall return, is that the early Pentecostal claim to have rediscovered the ministry of the Holy Spirit (during the twenty years from 1905 to 1925) was beset by so much division, or what Harvey Cox has called "squabbles," based often on struggles for power. Does this manifest the "unity of the Spirit" (Eph. 4:3); or "one new humanity" (2:15); or "the measure of the full stature of Christ" (4:13)? Yet a perfect unity without quarreling would be the "pure" Church, which was consistently rejected by Augustine and the "mainline" Fathers in the Donatist controversy. It is a regression to the narrower perspective of the Puritans. What it does demonstrate, however, is not the suppression of all prophecies, but the habit of extreme care and the most rigorous testing. Christology, ethical lifestyle, and the continuity of the Church must somehow become involved.

The latter part of Deuteronomy contains the many blessings and curses attributed to Moses before he relinquished his leadership. I almost wish that Deuteronomy 18 could be placed on display in every Pentecostal Assembly and every Renewal Movement meeting. Moses acknowledges that God will raise up prophets (Deut. 18:15-19). But then he concludes this chapter: "Any prophet . . . who presumes to speak in my name a word that I have not commanded the prophet to speak — that prophet shall die. . . . It is a word that the LORD has not spoken. The prophet has spoken presumptuously; do not be frightened by it" (18:20, 22).

A Practical Consequence: Many writers have spoken of the *kenōsis,* self-emptying, reticence, or "self-effacement" of the Holy Spirit, just as Jesus Christ experienced *kenōsis* in the incarnation (Phil. 2:5-11). Part of this concerns the Spirit's mystery and invisibility apart from the phenomena or effects which she produces. It becomes all too possible on this basis to misidentify what is truly a work of the Holy Spirit, even in oneself or in one's community. This makes "discernment of spirits" (1 Cor. 12:10) one of the most important of the gifts of the Spirit. This becomes acute in mysticism. Mysticism can promote delightful, intimate experiences of God through the Spirit. This in turn, however, can generate either "revelations" by the Holy Spirit, or hallucinations which have been unconsciously self-generated. Hildegard, Catherine of Siena, and perhaps Julian of Norwich and Teresa of Avila confront us with the kind of problems for which Walter Hilton was eager to find criteria and restraints. We have seen Wittgenstein's warnings about the multiple possibilities of understanding and interpreting the "meaning" of a "picture," or Ricoeur's warning about the complexity of interpreting dreams.

We take to heart opposite warnings of Congar and Moltmann that it would be overly daring to deny the validity of *all* "private" prophecy. But the consequences of a mistake in identifying "phenomena" with the Holy Spirit can be disastrous. The other related problem is to see the Holy Spirit's work of sanctification as an *upward ladder* of all-too-human disciplines of religious aspirations from humans to God. As Luther and Calvin insisted, sovereign grace moves in the *opposite direction: from God to humans,* mediated through Christ and the Spirit. To conceive of the Christian life as a "journey" has the advantage of encouraging us to see *sanctification as a process,* and to find a balance between "now" and "not yet" eschatology. But it risks inverting the direction of God's sovereign grace. At least generally the medieval mystics were sufficiently aware of the tradition of the Church to avoid offering any "revelation" in flat contradiction to it. The wisdom of George Ridding, the first Bishop of Southwell (now Southwell and Nottingham), in the Litany which he composed for those about to be ordained, can come to our rescue: "Alike from stubborn rejection of new revelations and from hasty assurance that we are wiser than our fathers, save us and help us, we humbly beseech Thee, O Lord" (*A Litany of Remembrance,* p. 7).

(7) *The Holy Spirit co-shares in the glorification of the Father and the Son.* The threefold *Gloria* has become a feature of most liturgical worship since at least the time of Basil, but less of informal worship. The *Gloria* cuts both ways: it provides a salutary reminder both to those who neglect the Holy Spirit, and to those who *constantly* speak almost obsessively of the Holy Spirit more than of God or Christ.

Some might suggest that the Church Fathers since Hilary and Athanasius spent too much energy and time in constantly reaffirming the deity of the Holy Spirit and in insisting that the Spirit was not a "creature." But the practical thrust of this was to stress the contrast between two orders of being. The divine order consisted of God the Father, God the Son, and God the Holy Spirit, who alone are worthy of worship and glorification. The created order consists of human beings, angels, saints, even Mary, and all creatures. To adore them transforms glorification and worship into idolatry. This may seem controversial, but too many Protestants seem to have forgotten why they ever expressed anxiety about the saints and Mary in the first place. The reply will be that in Catholic, Orthodox, and Anglo-Catholic traditions veneration is not worship. But we have only to visit parts of Southern Europe to see that this distinction is not often popularly understood by the masses. Both in the case of Catholicism and the Renewal Movement leaders may offer theological explanations for certain practices which simply sail over the heads of the masses.

It is here that the second of the Ten Commandments becomes especially relevant. God's image is intended to be borne by humans and God's people. As those who worshiped in pagan temples in the ancient world well knew, images in their temples were not "copies" of the deity but *"representations"* of the deity. God appointed human beings to *represent* him to the world. This was their vocation. The people of God must not make statues or images of God because these are *false substitutes for the representation of God* that is the duty of humans. The original task of humanity to be God's representative to the rest of creation is formulated in Gen. 1:26: "Let us make humankind in our image, according to our likeness"; cf. Gen. 9:6; Ps. 8:4-8; 1 Cor. 11:7; Heb. 2:6-8. One aspect of this is what Thomas Aquinas and others called "dominion." To represent God's sovereign *kingship* invites "ruling" as kings. But in God's purposes, this did not mean only, if at all, "power *over*," which may seem to involve force. It included "power for," which *involves care and stewardship, at least as much as sovereignty and control.* The Epistle to the Hebrews is adamant that where humans *failed* in this, Christ and his kingdom succeeds (Heb. 2:6-8; Col. 1:13-17). To worship any *created* being remains idolatry. Nowadays constructs of God made *only by humans* may be *conceptual.* But the principle remains. Maintaining the distinction drawn by the Church Fathers and the Bible thereby gives honor and worship to the Holy Spirit.

A Practical Consequence: This final point concerns both worship and the Holy Trinity, and may therefore seem to go over previous ground. But this seventh principle seeks to enhance the positive by comparing the negative. Each Christian subtradition carries with it its own dangers. What we wish to revere is important, whether, according to our tradition, this is a particular text of the Bible; the sermon; the two or seven sacraments; traditional saints and Mary; the Spirit-filled community; our spiritual leaders; our historic roots; or anything that Paul Tillich called the "penultimate," rather than God as Holy Trinity. To look to these with any attitude akin to worship may turn out to be a way of unconsciously dishonoring the Holy Spirit, who may well *use* some or all of these to work his ministry among us.

We do not suggest that these seven principles provide an exhaustive account of the Holy Spirit's Person and work. We might well have included, for example, the relation of the Holy Spirit to futurity or to inspiration. But in the light of the biblical writings, the history of the Church, and modern literature, they offer at least *seven firm starting points* on which we find for the most part general agreement.

24.2. The Need for Mutual Dialogue on Six Issues with Pentecostals and the Renewal Movement, and a Postscript from Church History

Until very recently the lack of dialogue has been acute. In practice, the tone of *some* reviews and discussions has been surprising. In the *Journal of Pentecostal Theology,* for example, writers have on occasion suggested that although a particular book may be helpful, the writer's conclusions eventually leave much to be desired because he or she is "not one of us." I have never seen a comparable attitude in Catholic-Protestant or Orthodox-Catholic discussion, which I should have assumed involved deeper historical differences. I hasten to add that this Pentecostal comment is far from typical, but it shows the seriousness of such misunderstanding. In the case of the Renewal Movement the situation is often the reverse. It is often nurtured within the "mainline" traditions, but displays such a loose fit to established patterns of worship that traditional Christians often find themselves alienated, often to the surprise of those involved in Renewal. Sometimes such phenomena as exuberant and repetitive songs, expectation of healing, prophecies, and perhaps even tongues, antagonize some of the faithful. This applies especially to what Mark Bonnington, we noted, called with great honesty a "Radio 2" ethos.

Yet on the other side "the faithful" often engage in a *routine* of worship, Scripture, and sacraments that needs new life and more flexible horizons. Worship can be dry, formal, and repetitive, in a different sense. It is sometimes reduced to what William Law called "saying prayers," in contrast to "praying." Its worst and saddest description is "being religious," as if it were simply a human performance or activity. Rather than using the term "baptism in the Spirit," established traditions sometimes resort to such phrases as "committed Christians" or "believers who are open to the Spirit" to mark this crucial difference. When Pentecostals and participants in the Renewal Movement attend traditional formal worship, they feel like the writer of Psalm 63: "You are my God, . . . my soul thirsts for you; my flesh faints for you, as in a dry and weary land where there is no water" (Ps. 63:1). At their best, Pentecostalism and the Renewal Movement have gifts that can be shared with the *whole* Church, *if only they are shared sensitively*. Recently there have been excellent signs of hope from both sides. From the side of Pentecostalism Gordon Fee, Frank Macchia, and Veli-Matti Kärkkäinen have creatively engaged with biblical, historical, and theological thought in the "mainline" churches.

From the side of the Renewal Movement, Max Turner, Tom Smail, Andrew Walker, and Nigel Wright have produced excellent work. On the border, perhaps facing both ways, Ives Congar, Jürgen Moltmann, Donald Carson, and others have shown deep, sympathetic understanding of Renewal experience, even if voicing needed reservations about given aspects. Indeed, Tom Smail and his co-writers seem to represent a very rare self-criticism from within the Renewal Movement. On the other hand, the Pentecostal worldwide web ranges from some with dogmatic certainty to very healthy self-criticism. Gordon Fee has risked the ire of fellow Pentecostals by his critique of "baptism in the Spirit" as a poor fit to informed New Testament exegesis. All these writers have been discussed in detail in Part III of this book. The descriptive work done by Harvey Cox, Mark Cartledge, Jim Purves, and Mark Bonnington has been invaluable in clarifying issues and themes.

The following represent issues in which there is probably widespread agreement in principle, but where practical implications in life and worship have to be explored further.

(1) *The Trinitarian framework of every experience of the Holy Spirit.* No orthodox Christian, no Pentecostal, and no exponent of Renewal would normally wish to challenge this. It represents common ground among the three traditions. But in practice there are divergences of emphasis in worship, prayer, and other areas. The biblical pattern suggested in Paul's letters is that of prayer addressed *to* God the Father, *through* Christ the Mediator, initiated *by* the Holy Spirit. It does not imply that other modes of prayer are wrong. But it offers a norm for usual praying. A fixation on one Person of the Holy Trinity, not least a fixation on the Holy Spirit as the main addressee in prayer, does not follow the *normal* Christian pattern. Tom Smail has written at length on this. At all events we have seen throughout the book that *all* Persons of the Trinity are involved in every aspect of creation and redemption.

Jürgen Moltmann has shown in his work on the Trinity how God the Father does more than "send" his Son to die on the cross. The Father and the Holy Spirit are deeply involved at every step of the incarnation, passion, and resurrection of Christ, as a narrative exposition of Trinitarian theology shows. Even the final Coming of the Kingdom of God, to which Pentecostals rightly look forward, is not only a glorious appearing of Christ but a climactic fulfillment of the purposes of God the Father, and it ushers in a genuine "fullness" of the Holy Spirit in resurrection life. As Cullmann has urged, this side of the future goal, "Christians still sin, and Christians still die." The Kingdom, as the titles of Moltmann's books suggest, is entirely Trinitarian.

Our prayer and devotion, then, should reflect this. This diminishes none of the Persons of the Trinity. It simply enhances the glory of the wholeness of the one God, seen in terms of three Persons.

(2) *The unity of the Holy Spirit nurtures the unity of the Church.* It is understandable if Pentecostals, those in the Renewal Movement, and traditional Christians should all think that they have to "give up" something precious and important if they are asked to be sensitive to the attitudes and experiences of other Christians. Yet how can anyone claim that the Holy Spirit is within them or within their church if this were to lead to defensiveness or even polemic? I still find the early history of Pentecostalism with its many splits and power struggles quite incomprehensible, especially since this seems often to be regarded almost with pride or complacency as inevitable. If some think the Holy Spirit is leading them in opposite directions, does it imply that the Holy Spirit's leading is virtually self-contradictory? Or is this an example of human fallibility, laying claim to the Spirit?

Martin Luther found it intolerable that some of the Radical Reformers claimed that the Holy Spirit had urged them *to kill* nobles who owned property. Supposedly the Holy Spirit initiated the Peasants' Revolt. The most outrageous acts have been performed by self-proclaimed "prophets" in the name of the Holy Spirit. If the Spirit is genuinely the Holy Spirit of unity (Acts 2:44-47; 1 Cor. 12:7; Eph. 4:3-6), how can the Spirit cause such disunity? Yet the history of the late-nineteenth- and early-twentieth-century churches portrays endless squabbling, power plays, and fragmentation of the churches allegedly under the guidance of the Holy Spirit. Do fragmentation and "independent" church work really represent a response to the Holy Spirit of unity? Or does "independent" denote "I am free of accountability" to all but like-minded admirers, and free from any "external" discipline? The virtues of sensitivity to others and sharing with "the other" in solidarity are akin to Paul's theme that the fruit of the Spirit is love.

Ancient Corinth is as relevant here as ever. As we have noted, L. L. Welborn and others have rightly seen the "splits" at first-century Corinth in terms of power struggles between dominant and forceful personalities, who were each admired by their own circle of followers. In 1 Cor. 1:10 Paul appeals to them "to be united," and not to be seduced into loyalty to what to them were "big" figures. He exclaims, "Has Christ been divided? Was Paul crucified for you?" (1:13). "The message about the cross" (1:18) concerns not only redemption and salvation, but the end of self-centeredness and of the world's notion of "power," which is quite different from that of God in Christ, which Paul preached through the Holy Spirit. Church history from the nineteenth and early twentieth centuries is littered with divisions in the name of the Holy Spirit of unity. Many in these two movements have pleaded for a more Christ-centered and cross-centered approach. Hence this is not an "external" caveat, but gives added voice to what many have said within the Movements.

(3) *The Holy Spirit and the appeal to "present experience" and "new things."* Pentecostalism and the Renewal Movement rightly do not allow Christian faith to become formalized and routinized into the performance of "religious acts." Christianity must be of the heart, and not, they argue, of the intellect and will. These two movements exercise a prophetic ministry to prevent the rest of the Church falling into mere "religiosity," religious performance, and routine. One of the most important observations of William Law concerned the crucial difference between *"saying prayers"* and *"praying."*

However, just as the Holy Spirit unites Christians throughout the world, of which the tongues in Acts 2 constituted a sign, so the Spirit also ensures *continuity of faith throughout the ages. It is extraordinary that some in the Renewal Movement constantly look for something "new" as if to imply that the Holy Spirit has not genuinely been at work in the godly Christians of the past.* Do we expect the Holy Spirit to *contradict* what the Spirit has already done? Here traditionalists and charismatics can learn something from each other. To become *mired in the past without willingness to change can on occasion* be a traditionalist failure. Conversely, always to look *for what is new and "exciting" can on occasion* become the Renewal Movement's mistake of *denigrating the past and despising tradition* handed down from godly predecessors. It may undervalue insights from the past in the name of the pragmatic fashion of the moment. As we saw, George Ridding, again, wisely writes: "Alike from stubborn rejection of new revelations and from hasty assurance that we are wiser than our fathers, save us and help us, we humbly beseech Thee, O Lord" (*A Litany of Remembrance*, p. 7).

Some argue that Pentecostals and the Renewal Movement strike a chord of resonance with the modern world by stressing *"feeling."* "Experience" is very often translated by media interviewers as "How do you *feel* about this or that?" Often Pentecostals and Renewal advocates also regard "feeling" as the key to resisting the intellectualization of experience. It also appeals, it is claimed, to society and the world. But is this a genuinely *Christian* insight to facilitate outreach? Might it not be *surrender to the seductions of the world?* It is inescapable that the mass media, including television, radio, and the papers, have largely replaced "What do you think about this?" by the subjective "How do you feel about this?" It is more than a change in linguistic idiom. *Thinking requires careful reflection and argument; feeling is subjective and either predictable or groundless.* A well-known "Marriage Enrichment" course has as one of its key slogans: "Feelings are never right or wrong." They don't have to be defended or regarded as potentially blameworthy. Therefore they provide a "safe" method of communication between couples. It is just as inescapable that certain kinds of hymns, songs, and worship deliberately nurture (if not manipulate) *emotion.*

There is much misunderstanding about "feeling." Love, Wittgenstein pointed out, is not a feeling. We recall his example, which we have noted above. It makes sense to say of a genuine feeling or sensation: "Oh! I am in terrible pain! . . . Oh, it's all right, it has gone off now." But we cannot convincingly say of love: "Oh! I love you so deeply. . . . Oh, it's gone off now." This is because love, unlike pain, is a sustained disposition or attitude, which shows itself in actions. God can hardly command us to have a feeling, any more, Wittgenstein suggests, than to give the order: "Laugh at this joke!" As Pannenberg argues, faithfulness can be demonstrated only over a time span because it is not a fleeting feeling.

This brings us back to Renewal music and songs. These have shifted away from recounting God's great acts of the past in the Bible and history, which nourished the eighteenth-century hymn writers. We may recall Philip Doddridge (1702-51), who wrote, "O God of Bethel"; Charles Wesley (1707-88), who wrote, "Hail the Day That Sees Him Rise"; Thomas Olivers (1725-99), who wrote, "The God of Abraham Praise"; Augustus Toplady (1740-78), who wrote, "Rock of Ages"; William Cowper (1731-1800), who wrote "God Moves in a Mysterious Way"; Isaac Watts, John Newton, and others. By contrast, many "Renewal" songs appear to focus on the present fleeting moment. In some cases they can be almost wholly subjective and individualistic. Does that matter? Worship is primarily addressed to God, and celebrates what God has done and is doing. The great hymns of the eighteenth century rightly allow for some heart-searching, but seldom as a focus which distracts us from God. This is far from true of *all* Renewal music, but some might suggest too high a proportion. Moreover, to stress the heart and personal emotion does not constitute an alternative to intellect and will, but complements them.

Yet the Holy Spirit has been given to testify, to teach, and lead into all truth (John 15:26; 16:8-13). Teaching and training nurture *permanent dispositions* and explain the *basis* of the emotions that we may feel. As Krister Stendahl has reminded us, emotions may come and go. The Spirit works in emotions *and* intellect *and* will; but to focus on emotions alone is far from adequate. This is perhaps the greatest of the problems unmasked by Mark Bonnington's excellent analogy of "Radio 2" worship. The Renewal Movement's hymns and songs may perhaps perform a service to the whole Church in promoting self-involvement and social bonding. But many often perform a grave disservice to the Church by becoming intellectually without content, repetitive, and even trivial. Some of them are centered not on the deeds of God, but on the subjective awareness of the individual. They may even unwittingly encourage a narrow self-centeredness. The encouraging feature is the slow but steady realization among Protestant and Renewal advocates themselves that this problem needs to be addressed. Tom Smail's *The Love of Power or the Power of Love* is worth its weight in gold in this respect. We have quoted in Chapter 22 Smail's words: "The high praise of God had degenerated into endless repetitive chorus singing that was in danger of becoming a bore and burden, rather than a release and a joy." He is equally adamant about the need to complement emotions with intellectual content, teaching, and concern. On a theology of the Holy Trinity, we have noted some of Purves's reservations about the Charismatic Movement, although, like Smail, this is his roots.

The Bible constantly enjoins us to have trained and taught minds. In Pentecostalism, with the era of Gordon Fee, Frank Macchia, Veli-Matti Kärkkäinen, and others, we are beginning to rise above the notion of attacking thinkers and academics, as if human beings could never use their heads, hearts, and wills together. Those of us who long for deeper sanctification by the Holy Spirit pray that the Spirit will be at work in every part, including our unconscious desires.

(4) *The Holy Spirit gives a gift of healing, but not with a divided dualism of "natural" and supernatural.* With the exception of "cessationists" like Hodge, who believe that the "gifts of the Spirit" were exclusively for the apostolic age before the formation of the canon of Scripture, most Christians believe that *the sovereign God can heal and does heal.* An acid test is how many of *us* pray to God for healing, health, and survival if or when we are beset with health problems. My own life gives the lie to Rudolf Bultmann's simplistic claim that no one could use medicine and radio and electronic devices and at the same time pray fervently to God for health and healing. I do both every day. Most churches re-

ceive regular requests to pray for the sick. Normally this denotes *more than* fortitude under suffering, or the offering of a placebo. It is a feature of classical Pentecostalism that the "full" gospel, as exemplified by Aimee Semple McPherson, whom we discussed above, sees Jesus as Savior, Baptizer in the Spirit, Divine Healer, and Coming King. The "full gospel" movement expanded this into five: justification, sanctification, healing, the premillennial return of Christ, and baptism in the Holy Spirit, as evidenced by tongues.

The emphasis on eschatology or "the Coming King" accords with the conclusion of many New Testament scholars that the miracles of Jesus, especially exorcisms and healing miracles, constitute anticipatory signs of the *inbreaking of the Kingdom of God in the Person of Jesus.* The Pentecostal idea of associating healing with the inbreaking of the Kingdom of God seems entirely right. Jesus performed healings on a number of occasions. Mark 1:34 states: "He cured many who were sick with various diseases and cast out many demons" (with parallels in Matt. 4:23-24 and Luke 4:40; Greek, *therapeuō*). Mark 3:22-27 relates this to the Kingdom. In Mark 3:14-15 Jesus gave the Twelve authority to heal. We may compare Mark 6:13; Matt. 8:7, 16; 9:35; 10:1, 8; 12:22; Luke 9:6; 13:14; and so on. Acts 14:9 and 1 Cor. 12:9, 28 take up the theme of healing for the apostolic Church.

The problem that arises is the *timing* of eschatological fulfillment. It is generally agreed that the Kingdom of God is *both present and future.* Many New Testament studies or theological textbooks leave this as a flat statement without spelling out its significance. But in fact it explains the ambiguity of expectancy and prayer in relation to healings. Sometimes God allows, as it were, the opening of Christmas presents before Christmas, and heals *as if* the End were already here. But clearly *The End Is Not Yet,* as the title of one of Ulrich Simon's books expresses it. It might be argued that healing campaigns attempt in some cases to force God's hand about the timing of the End. God heals only where and when he pleases or chooses. Even the book on healing by Kimberly Ervin Alexander is packed with descriptions of healings, but includes not much more than two pages on the acknowledged tension between the "already" and the "not yet." It seems a distraction from this important eschatological question to browbeat us with the question: Is it the will of God to heal? Of course it is; but when and where? If expectancy is raised to a high pitch, there must be a degree of *depression and misplaced self-recrimination* from those for whom it is claimed that their Christian *faith and trust* was somehow deficient. If healing were a uniform and universal phenomenon, in cases of disappointment this would make the problem of suffering and evil much more acute.

There is another very serious problem, with which a number of Pentecostals agree. Writers and preachers tend to speak of "supernatural" healings. But, as Walter Hollenweger, Tom Smail, and others firmly stress, we do not wish to promote a "dualist" or two-level picture of the world. God is sovereign over his own creation. Purves significantly prefers to speak of the "suprarational." The Holy Spirit may choose to use "natural" or everyday medication, or to use some surprising method which is not fully understood. It is noteworthy that the eminent Pentecostal Donald Gee apparently believed that "gifts of healing" could include natural processes, as did Pietists such as Bengel. John Wimber was right to associate healing with the Kingdom of God. But whether, away from the context of the incarnation and ministry of Jesus, he was right to raise such a level of daily expectation may be doubted. This became one of those phenomena which made many "ordinary" Christians become distinctly uncomfortable, and could lead to *exaggeration and disappointment.* Not only do a number of Pentecostals make this point, but Tom Smail, Andrew Walker, and Nigel Wright also lament *the "heightened dualism," the frequent exaggerated claims, and the "paranoid" preoccupation with demonic forces* which too often arises within the Renewal Movement, to which they are still loyal. They write as critics of Wimber and the Renewal Movement *from within the Movement.* Furthermore, in our examination of understandings of the Spirit's gifts over the centuries, we saw that the Latin terms used by Ambrose were broader in scope than popular writers often understand them today.

(5) *The Holy Spirit and "prophecy" and tongues.* Since the "rediscovery" of speaking in tongues by Parham, Seymour, and others at the beginning of the twentieth century, there has arisen a huge volume of research in biblical studies, linguistics, psychology, religious experience, and other areas into prophecy and tongues-speech. Yet for many, nothing at all might have happened over the last one hundred years. Mark Cartledge is one among others who have adopted a many-sided, or multi-disciplinary, approach. Moreover, claims to speak as a *prophet* have more serious effects in the Church than the debate about *tongues.* A number of Pentecostals, including Veli-Matti Kärkkäinen, admit that often too much has been made of tongues, and are openly embarrassed that some still regard tongues as "initial evidence" of baptism in the Spirit. Such forward-looking movements as Pentecostalism and the Renewal Movement, which seek precisely not to be locked in a dead past, might well wish to draw upon biblical and historical insights and experiences which were perhaps not open to Parham and Seymour and their immediate successors at that time.

Claims to *prophecy* have been a source of difficulty over many centuries, as we have seen. They rank alongside irresponsible claims to encourage people to do things in the name of the Bible, when the biblical text does not really say what is claimed for it. That is why biblical writers are adamant about the need to "test" prophecy against the criterion of the lordship of Christ and related phenomena. In Part II on the Holy Spirit through the centuries, we have repeatedly noted many warnings about claiming to speak on behalf of the Holy Spirit when the words spring from self-deception. John Owen and Jonathan Edwards, for example, express this warning with eloquence and vigor.

I have usually placed "prophecy" in inverted commas. This is *not* because I do not believe in prophets or prophetic inspiration. But I am convinced that this term has a much *broader range of meaning than most people allow.* I do not believe that David Hill, Ulrich Müller, and Thomas Gillespie have *excluded* "charismatic" prophecy. They did not intend to do this. But I believe that they are right to view it *normally* as *applied preaching,* especially as *biblical,* or *gospel,* applied preaching. We have seen in this study that Philipp Vielhauer and K. O. Sandnes consider *Paul himself a "prophet," even though he almost always uses reflective and persuasive argumentation rather than simply asserting: "Thus says the Lord." Augustine, John Calvin, Matthew Henry, John Wesley, and James Denney believed that the term denoted the public preaching of the biblical message,* as we have noted in Parts I and II. Indeed, I have so often promoted this argument that it is unnecessary to repeat it further.

Nevertheless it is worth making a final comment on the underlying theological issue. The most serious theological issue is whether God is believed to work through processes of *training, reflection, and thought,* or simply by intuition and feeling that may be "spontaneous." The coming of a "thought" into a mind made empty is not necessarily "revelation," although it *might* be *on rare occasions.* It is a matter of extreme concern that major decisions and strategies in a local church *may* be guided by random thoughts *believed* to be "prophetic" on little evidence other than claims by those who make it. John Locke famously made the statement that sheer intensity of conviction does not guarantee the truth of what is claimed. I still recall some fifty years ago being confronted on the Piccadilly Circus underground (subway) by a lady with intense staring eyes, who began: "I have a message for you." At the time I was wearing a clerical collar, so I was perhaps fair game. But the "message" was so bizarre and irrelevant to my circumstances that it did not even require much elaborate "testing"!

In this connection I do have concerns, as I have indicated, about the *"pictures"* often shared as "prophetic" in some Renewal circles. I do not dismiss the pictures which Hildegard, Catherine of Siena, and similar mystics of the Middle Ages claim to have seen. In most cases, however, they held a high view of the tradition of the Church, including the Bible and Church Fathers. On the other hand, a devout Roman Catholic medieval specialist suggested that I should not discount the quite likely notion that their frequent diet of moldy bread may well have given rise to hallucinatory phenomena. The use of "pictures" becomes problematic when we are interpreting *not* God's great deeds of redemption, but allegedly *"domestic" needs* for guidance. The greatest care must be taken to ensure that even these are sincere, authentic, and not colored by subjective interpretations. It is worse if these arise from manipulation. The "interpretation" of a picture, of course, takes us at once into the cognitive realm. I cannot overemphasize my concern about the influence of "pictures," in the light of Wittgenstein's astute observations that "A picture can be variously interpreted," and, indeed, "A picture held us captive." Might a picture mean: "*Don't* do this!" We must respect the biblical call for "testing" and "discernment" with the utmost seriousness.

In very recent years the question of tongues-speech has become a far less urgent matter for "mainline" churches than prophecy. Mistakes in claims to "prophecy" can set churches off in the wrong direction and become unwitting (or conscious) vehicles of power play, as in ancient Corinth. But classical Pentecostalism seems less eager than it used to be to make tongues "initial evidence" of baptism in the Spirit. Many Pentecostals, like Kärkkäinen, say honestly that they do not speak in tongues. Most admit that even if it is a gift of the Holy Spirit, it may also be "learned behavior" to which issues of social bonding and the practices and expectations of the group may apply. No Pentecostal would belittle tongues, but many see *confession of Christ and the cross,* and the *Spirit's fruit of love,* as more obvious "evidence" of the Spirit. This is not too far away from some of Seymour's early concerns.

The Renewal Movement has not in general seen tongues as "initial evidence" of a "second blessing" by the Holy Spirit, whatever we call the event. Because the Movement is widely diffused, of the six possible views of tongues, including the two or three main views, none seems to be universal. Most advocates of Renewal recognize that in Paul, at least, there is specific instruction about its "private" use, and that it is addressed to God, not to human beings (1 Cor. 14:2, 4, 6-12). Therefore the work by specialists in linguistics such as Samarin or Goodman does not unduly seem to trouble them, when they suggest that "tongues-speech" is not a structured "language." Further, unless they hold an old-fashioned "dualist" view of reality as natural and supernatural, they would usually not be alarmed by Krister Stendahl's comments about "high-voltage religion." Nor would they necessarily resist Gerd Theissen's theological notion of the Spirit's work in the unconscious. At its lowest, this gift may allow for release from tension or neurosis, and encourage *integration of the personality.* At its highest, it may signal *intimate expressions of longings, prayer, or praise to God* (Rom. 8:26-27). Given the Pauline safeguards, this need not disrupt a traditional worshiping community.

Acts 2 and related passages in Acts present a more difficult problem. But most Renewal advocates do not wish to drive a wedge between Luke and Paul, even if Luke may seem to be more problematic. In spite of Turner's work on Luke, and his lament about reading the New Testament through the lenses of Paul, many in the Renewal Movement are happy to remain in the clearer and safer ground of Paul, whom they usually see as Luke's companion in missionary travel.

(6) *"Baptism in the Spirit."* A difference emerges here between most Pentecostals and most exponents of the Renewal Movement. Since the "Third Wave," the majority in the Renewal Movement have come to sit loose to the term "bap-

tism in the Spirit," although they usually insist on some alternative term which
has greater biblical precedent. In the *Dictionary of Pentecostal and Charismatic
Movements,* however, J. R. Williams insists that "Baptism in (or with) the Holy
Spirit occupies a place of critical importance" for both Pentecostals and "Charismatic Churches." Indeed, M. P. Hamilton claims that to be "charismatic" implies experiencing baptism in the Spirit. Admittedly this *Dictionary* was published in 2002 and 2003, and some reconsideration may have occurred by 2012,
ten years later. Sometimes those in the Renewal Movement claim to be "Spirit-
filled" Christians. They can appeal to the example of Stephen and the Seven for
this term (Acts 6:5). On the other hand, this term tends to suggest an *eschatological fulfillment* or climax, so the search for a suitable biblical term continues.
Some speak of being "open" to the Holy Spirit, but others reject the term as too
broad, since many outside the Movement lay claim to be open to the Spirit.
However, they tend to look for an "event" term rather than a "process" term, although many would remain hesitant about the theology of sanctification which
this implies.

The situation becomes different among Pentecostals. Some indeed have begun to question the biblical propriety of the term. Scholarly New Testament
specialists such as Gordon Fee have openly challenged the traditional Pentecostal use of "baptism in the Spirit." Yet more broadly the same biblical texts feature in appeals for the biblical grounds of the term: Acts 2:1-5; 2:38-39; 10:44-45;
11:16; Mark 1:4, 8; and 1 Cor. 12:13. The terms "filling" and "fire" are closely associated with it. Many of the texts on closer inspection simply refer to receiving
the Holy Spirit. We have explored these references in Part I in our work on the
Acts of the Apostles. The notion of a "second Pentecost," in our view, refers to
decisive "boundary-crossing" in the successive stages of the expansion of the
gospel.

Frank Macchia is very progressive and creative on other subjects. But he regards this one as the *crucial identity-marker of Pentecostals.* For many in "mainline" churches, it remains extraordinary to interpret 1 Cor. 12:13, "in the one
Spirit we were all baptized into one body," as relating to baptism in the Spirit,
because the context concerns not *holiness* but *unity,* and because the verse is addressed to *all* Christians. It is not much easier to interpret Mark 1:8 in this way.
This concerns the different ministries of John the Baptist and Jesus. Acts 1:4-5,
"you will be baptized with the Holy Spirit," is again addressed to *all* Christians,
as they enter the New Age of world history *together.* The main concerns of committed traditional Christians are, first, that this experience may in principle be
multiple, renewable, and repeatable; and second, that it can be applied in principle to *any* Christian or to *all* committed Christians. It should never become
the monopoly of an "elite." If it does, we are back with the elite "spiritual people" at Corinth, whom Paul rebukes.

If there is no chance of persuading Pentecostals to change their terminology, we must stress that this may remain a *respected experience*, but it will continue to cause perplexity as long as it is anchored to *biblical passages which do not seem to speak of this experience at all*. Many will respect the *experience* but regret the *terminology*. It would be tragic if this were due to the historical accident of becoming intertwined with the *Holiness Movement*. In the case of the Holiness Movement, many will applaud their aims but regret their doctrines. It will at once be seen that at the root of this lies a parting of the ways on the basis of biblical interpretation, or hermeneutics. This will constitute the final topic of this book.

A Postscript: Seven Issues from Church History. Almost every good and positive movement prompted by the Holy Spirit in the history of the Church has given rise to exaggerations or distortions. I hesitantly suggest the following selective list of seven qualities. The insights do not necessarily degenerate, but such phenomena as perhaps Montanism, and more clearly the "Radical Reformers," suggest that a brief and selective checklist may be helpful for ongoing dialogue:

(a) The experience of new creation, newness of life, praise, and joy may degenerate into a loss of the Christian need for waiting, pilgrimage, struggle, and self-discipline. (b) The revelation of a genuinely Trinitarian life in the Holy Spirit may degenerate into a Spirit-centered life, with little focus on Christ. (c) The experience of personal intimacy with God may degenerate into individualism and lack of social concern. (d) Daily renewal and a focus on promise and new things of the future may degenerate into a disparagement of history, tradition, the past, and continuity. (e) The revelation of prophecies (in the popular sense) may degenerate into an interpretation of all the gifts of the Spirit as a "spontaneous" experience, rather than seeing most of these gifts in terms of settled habits. (f) An appreciation of God's sovereign power to heal may degenerate into a expectancy that God will always do so, as if the End had already arrived. (g) The yielding of one's heart and feelings to God may degenerate into failing to see that the whole person also entails intellect and judgment.

24.3. Five Issues in Hermeneutics and Two in New Testament Exegesis

(1) *The status of Luke-Acts in relation to "pre-understanding" as an influence on exegesis.* It is an irony that some Pentecostals find themselves fellow travelers with biblical critics in sometimes appearing to relish a sharp *contrast between Luke and Paul.* It is often claimed that traditionalists see the Holy Spirit *through the lenses of Paul,* while Pentecostals view the Spirit *through the lenses of Luke.* This nowadays does not seem to trouble Pentecostals, nor those in the Renewal Movement, usually because they claim that hermeneutical inquiry reveals that everyone *reads the Bible on the basis of "presuppositions," "pre-understanding," or*

some preliminary understanding. The implication seems to be that one pre-understanding is as good as another. It seems to be forgotten that while *Paul writes explicitly to instruct, to build, or to correct the churches,* Luke's aim is either clearly expressed in his preface, or is, at the very least, *still controversial.*

We must first address the widespread misunderstanding about "pre-understanding." We have already made this point, but, after all, this is a summary, and hugely important. It is correct that Schleiermacher, Heidegger, Bultmann, Gadamer, Lonergan, and many others have underlined that understanding cannot be achieved by approaching the biblical text as if one were an "empty head." To repress every piece of prior knowledge does not make for true *objectivity,* except in the entirely negative sense of *objectivism* or *positivism.* But each of these exponents of hermeneutics insists that *the text itself speaks back to correct and to refine our initial pre-understanding.* This is why "presupposition" is an unfortunate word, giving the suggestion of a *fixed and immovable* starting point. Even if our pre-understanding is partly theological, it still remains *open to challenge and revision* in the light of the biblical text itself.

This is one reason why *any* preliminary understanding, in contrast to another, will not be good enough to unlock the meaning of the text. An *antitheistic* pre-understanding, for example, would quickly receive correction from a biblical text. "Secular" biblical critics seem to be amazingly absent-minded on this point. To indulge one of my favorite concerns or themes, for instance, how can anyone read Paul's claim to be a "prophet," alongside his long use of *argument and diatribe,* and *not* see Pauline texts as challenging the narrowing down of "prophecy" to *only the spontaneous and charismatic?* Even if we reject this example as a hobbyhorse which I have done to death, what could undermine the general principle? Pre-understandings are *not permanent* "lenses," but *temporary footholds* from which *to begin.* We move on from them to engage in a long (if necessary) process of dialogue with the biblical text.

There is a second issue which causes concern. Pentecostals and most in the Renewal Movement do not usually subscribe to any but the gentlest of biblical criticism. Yet many seem ready to make common cause with critics about a radical difference of approach between Luke and Paul. No one could deny differences of perspective. Most sane writers no longer wish to defend the Bible as a monochrome landscape. But are we claiming that the difference between Luke and Paul gives adequate grounds for a fundamentally different understanding of the Holy Spirit, and fundamentally different Church practices?

It does not trouble many New Testament critics to see the notion "Luke" (as the author of Acts) and Paul as travelling companions for many miles *on the basis of a purely literary or rhetorical device.* But would most Pentecostals or Renewal advocates not envisage that Paul and Luke conversed together for many miles and many days? Unless we believe that "Luke" did not write Acts, can we really imagine that this "Luke," the traveling companion of Paul, declined to dis-

cuss the Spirit with him on the ground that, as a Hellenist, his approach would
be different? Again, Luke and Paul of course retain their own perspectives, but to
overpress a radically sharp contrast between them seems implausible. We should
have to begin all over again the lengthy discussion about the authorship and date
of Acts. Some place these in the second century. Philipp Vielhauer regards Luke
as nearer to the apologists than to Paul. Ulrich Wilckens accepts that there are serious differences, but attributes these to different situations.

Yet, as is well known, there are numerous counterexamples to the alleged
extreme lateness of Luke. Long ago, Marcel Simon demonstrated the early and
distinctive theology of Israel's history in Stephen's speech in Acts 7. J. A. T. Robinson argued for the very early Christology of Acts 3:19-21. C. F. D. Moule recognized Christological affinities between Luke and Paul, including their common
use of *Kyrios, Lord.* When he considers Acts yet once more in his *New Testament
Theology* (2004), I. Howard Marshall admits that the relation between the Gospel of Luke and Acts is "complex," but that nevertheless Luke's Gospel and Acts
imply each other. Furthermore, we need not simply appeal to the possible identification with Luke of the "man of Macedonia," who beckons Paul to Greece
and Europe, in Acts 16:9. This event, perhaps involving Luke, is followed at once
by an inexplicable change from "they" to "we," which many have likened to
Luke's diary. What is more, we need not depend on the Acts narratives for the
suggestion that Luke traveled with Paul; it is also clear from Col. 4:14; 2 Tim.
4:11; and Phlm. 24. It seems, however, that *The New International Dictionary of
Pentecostal and Charismatic Movements,* edited by Burgess, does not consider it
appropriate to include articles on Luke and Acts. A reader would never imagine
that the whole of both Movements virtually depends on given evaluations of
Luke-Acts. Admittedly it is *not* a *biblical* dictionary, but such an article would
be far more fundamental to these Movements than many of the very minor figures on which the contributors spend time and space.

Admittedly since the time of the Deists, many have argued that Luke
painted a much more harmonious picture of the earliest Church than we might
expect. Since that time, there have always been those who described Luke's reconstruction as "idealized," and not corresponding to reality. But if the aim expressed in the preface is valid, Luke would not wish to paint more negative pictures than was fair and necessary to a Roman inquirer. Selectivity does not
imply deception, guesswork, or error. Later F. C. Baur was not comparing Acts
with Paul, but specifically with a Paul reduced to a controversialist with Christian "nomists," as in Romans and Galatians. In Britain the line of defenders of
the early date of Acts progressed from J. B. Lightfoot and William Ramsay
through F. F. Bruce, I. Howard Marshall, and Bruce Winter; while outside Britain, the line came from Theodore von Zahn and Adolf von Harnack to Luke T.
Johnson and others. This is not the place to argue this point; only to show that
such a conclusion should not be regarded as without argument or simply *fool-*

ish. But, as we have seen, only Stronstad and Menzies from the Pentecostal side seem still to speak of *preliminary understanding* as *permanent "glasses"* rather than as temporary starting points which need revision, refinement, and correction in the light of dialogue with the biblical text, its genre, and its purpose.

(2) *The "zeal" or "fire" of earlier New Testament books, including "the major epistles," in comparison with its later writings.* The following point is controversial and of the nature of a "thought experiment." Even James Dunn sets in *contrast* the warm passion of Paul in the early and major epistles with the cooler, more formal concern with the doctrine of the Church and church order in Ephesians, the Pastoral Epistles, and later New Testament writings. He makes no bones about understanding this contrast, as very many do, *as a disappointing degeneration from zealous concern for the gospel and the Holy Spirit* into secondary matters of church order. He even suggests a possible hint of puzzlement about how the lateness of John, alongside its warmth and concern, seems at first sight to undermine such a neat *chronological* scheme. But in canonical and hermeneutical terms, there might be an alternative explanation for this alleged turn from the "charismatic" to the institutional. At least there is room for a "thought experiment" about it. Might we suppose that this is *not* due to a cooling off of the fires of zeal, but to a *complementary* conviction that the "charismatics" had begun to lead to abuse. Perhaps, as 1 John testifies, self-proclaimed prophets arose who risked *maverick innovations.* Might later writers, or even Paul after a sustained period of enforced house arrest in Rome, wish to begin to focus increasingly on matters of the *Church* (as in Ephesians) or on the tested validity of *ministerial appointments* (as in the Pastoral Epistles)?

A number of reputable scholars, who include J. N. D. Kelly, Bo Reicke, Gordon Fee, Bruce Metzger, and Joachim Jeremias, view the Pastoral Epistles as genuinely Pauline, partly on the basis of a secretary being responsible for style and vocabulary. Many more view the author of Ephesians, 1 and 2 Timothy, and Titus as either Paul or at least a devoted disciple of Paul. The first century, in any case, utilized secretaries more often than we might imagine, as specialists on this subject have shown. This would account for radical differences of style and vocabulary.

If we can speculate, we do not know what befell Paul for many years. He may have remained under guard or protective custody, receiving many visitors who carried reports of the churches to him. In the quietness of careful reflection, is it so surprising that Paul's thoughts might turn increasingly to the churches? Might it even come about that, as he develops in his mind the theme of the Church as one and universal or worldwide, he offers this as a theme in Ephesians, for which we have evidence that this might have become a circular letter to several Pauline communities? Could it be that his converts had learned too well about the liberty of the Holy Spirit, and needed now the sober reflection prompted by his pastoral letters to Timothy and Titus? It is not irrational to suggest that errors began to grow in the light of self-proclaimed prophecy. Paul did not wish to *attack* prophecy as such, especially in the light of his earlier comment in 1 Thess. 5:19. But he may have wanted to introduce some safeguards, which become explicit in the qualifications required for bishops (or overseers), presbyters (or elders), and deacons.

The hermeneutical point is that *absence* of *references to the Holy Spirit* can tell us nearly as much as discourses like those in 1 Corinthians 2 and 12–14 that are *full* of references to the Spirit. This is where our attitude to the *canon as a whole* enters the picture.

(3) *The purpose of the Acts of the Apostles.* The purpose of Acts should not be confused with the first point about pre-understanding. This also becomes an important *hermeneutical* issue. Was Acts genuinely intended as a *blueprint* for church organization in the future or for all time, as Restorationists claim? Or was it Luke's attempt to portray the Christian faith as an unstoppable expansion of the one community of faith, overseen by God in accordance with his purpose at that time? Beverly Gaventa, among others, has convincingly argued for this view. The author of Acts, like other ancient historians, selects his material, even perhaps forgoing some episodes or events in order to present the initial history of the expansion of the early Church. How can we know what Luke might have said when unpredicted situations emerged in later history? In other words, the Restorationist assumption that Luke intended to offer a blueprint for all time is regrettably *extrinsic* to the biblical writings. It does *not come from the Bible,* but from *assumptions about* the Bible.

This does not mean that this assumption is "wrong." It simply means that we cannot call this a clearly *biblical* assumption, but must pray and weigh up *other arguments* in favor of, or against, its validity. This is where Luke and Paul do not stand on an equal footing. Paul often states that he is writing in response to specific questions about church life. To suggest that we simply *"prefer"* some reading or book changes the issue from one of *evidence and argument* to mere subjective *desire.* We discussed above a canonical approach to the Bible as a whole, in which we saw that Deuteronomy and sometimes Proverbs, with their optimism that God always seems to prosper the obedient and godly, is well balanced by Ecclesiastes and Job, with their realistic and more pessimistic provisos that God does not always choose to will human affairs in that way. In other words, Ecclesiastes and Job offer counterexamples, which suggest that we should avoid treating Deuteronomy as a simple blueprint for all life for all time.

This does not undermine the relevance of the Bible to individual and communal daily life. It suggests that reflection on the relevance of biblical texts must be historical. It must take account of two moving and expanding horizons. I have called these the horizon of the text and the horizon of the reader. In the first of my series of books on hermeneutics, published in 1980, I suggested that this constituted a first principle of hermeneutics. The book was called *The*

Two Horizons. Twelve years later I sought to correlate the *kind* of biblical text, for example, didactic, symbolic, narrative, hymnic, legal, historical, prophetic, existential, self-involving, poetic, Reader-Response, and others, with specific life-situations to which they respectively especially apply. If traditionalists, Pentecostals, and those in the Renewal Movement could undertake more exploration of this kind, we might come closer together "under Scripture."

(4) *The gifts of the Spirit and the two horizons.* It is inevitable that we ask some questions about "gifts of the Holy Spirit" which Paul or Luke or other biblical writers would not have asked in quite that way. One of the clearest examples would be to wonder how Paul might have reacted to being asked whether the gift of healing was "supernatural." It would not be entirely true to suggest that such language had no currency in the days of Paul, Augustine, or Aquinas. But Deism and the Enlightenment have drastically changed the resonance and cash value of the term to modern readers or inquirers. We have written several times concerning "miracles" in this book that Walter Hollenweger, Nigel Wright, and many others have warned us against imposing on Paul and on Luke a "dualist" view of the universe that they would not have recognized as "Christian." To them, God has acted as Sovereign over the whole of creation, whatever his chosen mode of action. Here we need to look both at the biblical texts and at the given historical situation of ourselves as readers. Many scholars now call this our "historicity," or the way in which our era, gender, and education have conditioned us.

A kindred problem to which I have given much attention concerns the alleged "spontaneity" of many gifts of the Holy Spirit. Because of our historicity, many imagine that intuition or spontaneity provides the most reliable guarantee or indication that these gifts come genuinely from without. We have not fabricated them as counterfeit human constructs. But this assumption owes more to our own perceptions and historical conditioning than to the biblical text. If we patiently examine the text with openness to the Spirit, we shall see that many of the gifts of the Spirit *cannot be construed as "spontaneous" or intuitive gifts, but as trained dispositions.* We have argued above that "an utterance of wisdom" in 1 Cor. 12:8 is related to the wisdom of God expressed in the *gospel,* in line with the Wisdom literature of the Old Testament. To receive such wisdom from the Spirit would be a *habit,* but *nonetheless a gift of the Spirit, just* because it relates to a sustained and learned disposition. We saw that *Bezalel's craftsmanship* was *both* a gift from the Spirit *and* a trained skill. *Apostleship and teaching* can no less constitute a *sustained* gift than that of *administration.* We observed that many Pentecostals are happy with the idea that speaking in tongues is usually *a learned behavior.*

In our Part II, we noted that many of the Latin terms given to gifts of the Holy Spirit, especially by Ambrose, suggested more training or habits for such gifts as administration or teaching than many often assume today. Some could even argue that this accords with horizons of expectation in Ambrose. But at least it reinforces the point about the importance of taking account of "two horizons." Some Pentecostals and advocates of the Renewal Movement (only some) tend to give *the present* experience of the *twentieth-* or *twenty-first-*century reader priority over either the *biblical text* or the majority reception of texts over the centuries. This seems as disrespectful to the text and to history as *radical versions of Reader-Response theory* in literary criticism today. We may cite the kind of Reader-Response theory advocated by Stanley Fish or David Bleich, rather than the more judicious kind advocated by Wolfgang Iser. Here literary poems are one thing; the text of Scripture is another. For all the talk of "hermeneutics" in recent Pentecostal literature, I have seen little or nothing on Reader-Response theory and the need to reach a careful balance in considering the two horizons of the text and the reader.

(5) *The power of the Holy Spirit as the personal presence of God.* I am not sure whether these fifth through seventh points count as genuinely *hermeneutical* points, or simply as exegetical or *theological* ones. So I shall consider these more briefly. "Power" is used constantly in some circles as if it denoted sheer force, or as if it offered a parallel to "power" in such industrial contexts as steam power or electric power. But the biblical writings, of course, pre-date any notion of industrial power. In the Bible "power" does not denote some independent force but *"effective"* agency, and "the *effective presence and activity of God."* Whatever in the range of varied tasks is carried out in the strength of the Holy Spirit becomes an *effective* task. There are two perils here. One is to assimilate the concept to modern industrial and mechanical society; the other is to conceive of a "spiritual" version of brute force, in contrast to personal love. Many will find such terminology as "power evangelism" and "power healing," titles of two of John Wimber's books (1986) and (1987), as at least problematic, and at most insensitive, to the associations which we have outlined. It seems also to undermine the self-effacing character of the Holy Spirit, as expounded by J. E. Fison and many others.

Karl Barth, we noted, avoided this problem by rendering the word "power" as *"effectiveness"* or "effective *action."* Paul tells the church in Corinth, "The message about the cross is foolishness to those who are perishing, but to us who are being saved it is the power of God" (1 Cor. 1:18). In my larger commentary on 1 Corinthians, I expounded this as "operative, effective, and actualized." The Greek terms *dynamis* and *dynatos* refer to competence to perform a given function. Because, as Fee and others rightly insist, the Holy Spirit cannot be separated from God, the power of the Spirit denotes the omni-competency of God. Again, we can repeat John Taylor's comment: it rules out any notion of "It's all up to me." Above all, the Holy Spirit should not be depersonalized; nor should love become subsumed under brute force.

(6) *The Holy Spirit's anointing of Jesus Christ.* This sixth issue concerns pri-

marily theology and exegesis rather than hermeneutics as such. The principle
commands universal assent, and therefore again can be set out briefly. It is well
supported over the centuries, including strong support from Gregory the Great.
We may infer from the Spirit's anointing of Christ that *all* the gifts of the Spirit
are derived from the Christian's being in Christ; conversely, it is due to the Holy
Spirit that Christians are "in Christ" (1 Cor. 12:3). Believers are sons of God because sonship is *derived* from Jesus Christ. Christ is "the only begotten Son"
(John 3:16) from the Father; Christians are "adopted" by God because they are
"clothed with Christ" (Gal. 3:27). Down the centuries writers have rightly seen
the importance of the Spirit's anointing of Christ, as Christ experienced this in
the paradigmatic event of his baptism, which is recounted in all four Gospels as
of special importance (Mark 1:9-11; Matt. 3:13-17; Luke 3:21-22; John 1:32-33).
The Holy Spirit leads him through his Messianic temptations. Zizioulas, we
saw, speaks of two complementary economies. The complementary point is
that without the Holy Spirit, in his words, "there is no "Christ."

In Acts 1:8 the purpose of the coming of the Holy Spirit is to be "my
[Christ's] witnesses in Jerusalem, in all Judea and Samaria, and to the ends of
the earth." In John, the Spirit "will not speak on his own [initiative]" (John
16:13; *aph' heautou*), "He will glorify me" (16:14). In Paul the criterion of receiving the Holy Spirit is the confession "Jesus is Lord" (1 Cor. 12:3), and to be "spiritual" is to "have the mind of Christ" (1 Cor. 2:15-16). But Paul never suggests
that Christ and the Spirit are identical: "The Lord is the Spirit" (*ho kyrios to
pneuma estin*, 2 Cor. 3:17), we noted, is an *exegetical "is,"* referring back to Exodus. The upshot of all this is that the criterion for "being spiritual" is *being like
Christ.* Most Pentecostals are eager to assert this, although it remains a topic of
discussion on several Pentecostal websites on the Internet.

(7) *The Holy Spirit and inspiration.* To speak of the inspiration of Scripture
may seem to constitute a prosaic conclusion, since it has been constantly asserted in Judaism, the Church Fathers, the Church of the Middle Ages, the Reformation, and beyond. The rise of biblical criticism does not negate this. It
simply stresses that the Holy Spirit can speak through a variety of genres, a variety of writers, and a variety of situations. Graf Henning von Reventlow and
others have diagnosed the problem of denial of inspiration of the Bible to Deist
writers. They have also explained the *reasonableness* of this belief in theism.
Nicholas Wolterstorff, the Yale philosopher, has also demonstrated the reasonableness of belief in the use of *varied* mouthpieces as *agents* of the Holy Spirit.
Whether an utterance or a letter is authentic, he argues, depends on the identity
of the writer. But in everyday life, we frequently encounter deputized discourse.
Secretaries provide an example. The secretary may even choose the phraseol-
ogy, the vocabulary, and the style of the letter. But its authoritative currency depends entirely on whether it is written on behalf of an authoritative figure.
Variations of style and vocabulary do not make "deputized discourse" an un-

reasonable belief. This provides one reason among others to heed the advice of Tom Wright in referring inspiration and authority not directly to the Bible as such, but to *God* and to God the Holy Spirit *through* the Bible.

The Holy Spirit's inspiration of the Bible does not exclude the study and use of biblical criticism. This can assist us to appreciate the variety of different voices through which the Spirit speaks. Mikhail Bakhtin and Fyodor Dostoevski have helped us to see how *polyphonic discourse* can be used harmoniously to convey a reality or situation which is far too profound and complex to be communicated through monophonic discourse. Similarly, the Jewish scholar Robert Alter has shown that, for example, the two accounts of the anointing and rise to power of David are not drawn from "contradictory" sources, but deliberately convey a stereoscopic view of David's situation: one from the point of view of divine sovereignty and election; the other in terms of "the hurly-burly of human life."

This does not, in the end, represent a tame and prosaic ending to our study. It reminds us that the Holy Spirit persists with us through ordinary everyday situations. It is not only a so-called "perfect church" that experiences the Holy Spirit. Those who need the Holy Spirit most are those whom we might not expect. But "God's love has been poured into our hearts through the Holy Spirit that has been given to us" (Rom. 5:5).

Parallel to the Spirit's descending ministry of inspiration is his ascending ministry of initiating and inspiring prayer. Just as "descending" blessing from God to human beings depends on the Holy Spirit's presence to create, to sanctify, and to give hope, so also does the principle, sometimes neglected, that the "ascending" ministry of the Spirit from human beings to God is just as essential in the form of worship, prayer, and thanksgiving. Descending blessings may not only include above all Scripture, but also preaching, the sacraments, and many other gifts. Prayer may include adoration and contemplation. At all events, the Holy Spirit enables *two-way communion with God.* Christians down the centuries echo the threefold *Gloria* through the two-way inspiration of the Holy Spirit: "Glory be to the Father, to the Son and to the Holy Spirit, as it forever shall be." Interpreting the Bible still leaves us wrestling with history. The threefold *Gloria* takes us out of our history-bound situation, to proclaim what is outside history, as that which "forever shall be."

Bibliography

Ahn, Yongnan Jeon, "A Formulation of Pentecostal Hermeneutics and Its Possible Implication for the Interpretation of Speaking in Tongues and Prophecy in 1 Corinthians 12–14" (Ph.D. diss., University of Nottingham, May 2002).

Alexander, Kimberly Ervin, *Pentecostal Healing: Models in Theology and Practice*, JPTSS (Blandford Forum: Deo Publishing, 2006).

Ambrosiastri qui dicitur, *Commentarius in Epistolas Paulinas* (Vindobonae: Hoelder-Pichler-Tempsky, 1969), vol. 3, p. 232.

Anderson, Allan H., and Walter J. Hollenweger, *Pentecostals after a Century: Global Perspectives on a Movement in Transition*, JPTSS 15 (Sheffield: Sheffield Academic, 1999).

Aquinas, Thomas, *Commentary on St. Paul's First Letter to the Thessalonians and the Letter to the Philippians* (Albany, NY: Magi, 1969).

————, *Summa Theologiae*, 60 vols., Latin and English (London: Eyre & Spottiswoode, and New York: McGraw-Hill, Blackfriars ed. 1963).

Archer, Kenneth J., "Pentecostal Hermeneutics: Retrospect and Prospect," *JPT* 8 (1996): 63-81.

Arnold, John H., and Katherine J. Lewis, *Companion to the Book of Margery Kempe* (Cambridge: Brewer, 2004).

Artz, Frederick B., *The Mind of the Middle Ages* (New York: Alfred Knopf, 3rd ed. 1958).

Atherton, Mark (ed.), *Hildegard of Bingen: Selected Writings* (London: Penguin, 2001).

Atkinson, James, *Luther: Early Theological Works*, LCC 16 (London: SCM, 1962).

————, *Martin Luther and the Birth of Protestantism* (London: Penguin, 1968).

Atkinson, William P., *Baptism in the Spirit: Luke-Acts and the Dunn Debate* (Eugene, OR: Pickwick, 2011).

Aune, David E., *Prophecy in Early Christianity and the Ancient Mediterranean World* (Grand Rapids: Eerdmans, 1983).

————, *Revelation*, 3 vols. (Dallas: Word, 1997-98).

Barr, James, *The Semantics of Biblical Language* (Oxford: Oxford University Press, 1961).

Barrett, C. K., *The Holy Spirit and the Gospel Tradition* (London: SPCK, 1958).

————, "The Holy Spirit in the Fourth Gospel," *JTS* 1 (1950): 1-15.

Barth, Karl, *Anselm: Fides Quaerens Intellectum* (London: SCM, 1960).

————, *Church Dogmatics*, 14 vols. (Edinburgh: T&T Clark, 1957-75).

————, *The Epistle to the Romans* (Oxford: Oxford University Press, 1933; 6th ed. 1968).

————, *The Holy Spirit and the Christian Life*, trans. and annot. Michael Raburn (available on the Internet, 2002) with commentary.

————, *The Holy Spirit and the Christian Life: The Theological Basis of Ethics* (Louisville: Westminster and John Knox, 1993).

————, *The Resurrection of the Dead* (London: Hodder & Stoughton, 1933).

————, *The Theology of Schleiermacher: Lectures at Göttingen, 1923-24* (Grand Rapids: Eerdmans, 1982).

————, *The Word of God and the Word of Man* (London: Hodder & Stoughton, 1928).

Bauckham, Richard, *Jesus and the Eyewitnesses: The Gospels as Eyewitness Testimony* (Grand Rapids: Eerdmans, 2006).

————, *Testimony of the Beloved Disciple* (Grand Rapids: Baker Academic, 2007).

Baumgärtel, Friedrich, "*Pneuma*," in *Theological Dictionary of the New Testament (TDNT)*, ed. Gerhard Kittel and Gerhard Friedrich, vol. 6 (Grand Rapids: Eerdmans, 1968), pp. 359-67. [See also Schweizer.]

Beare, F. W., *The First Epistle of Peter* (Oxford: Blackwell, 1961).

Beasley-Murray, George R., *John*, Word Biblical Commentary, vol. 36 (Nashville: Nelson, 2nd ed. 1999).

Bede, *In Epistolas VII Catholicas*, ed. D. Hurst (Turnhout: Brepols, 1983).

————, *In Marci Evangelium Expositio*, ed. D. Hurst, CCSL 120 (Turnhout: Brepols, 1960).

————, *On the Nature of Things* and *On Times*, trans. with an intro. by Calvin B. Kendall and Faith Wallis (Liverpool: Liverpool University Press, 2010).

Behm, Johannes, "*Paraklētos*," in *TDNT*, vol. 5, pp. 800-814.

Beker, J. Christiaan, *Paul the Apostle: The Triumph of God in Life and Thought* (Edinburgh: T&T Clark, 1980).

Bengel, J. A., *Gnomon Novi Testamenti* (Stuttgart: Steinkopf, and London: Dulau, 1866).

Bennett, Dennis and Rita, *The Holy Spirit and You* (Eastbourne: Kingsway, 1974).

————, *The Holy Spirit and You: A Study Guide to the Spirit-Filled Life* (Eastbourne: Kingsway, 1971).

Best, Ernest, *The First and Second Epistles to the Thessalonians* (London: Black, 1972).

————, *1 Peter*, New Century Bible Commentary (London: Oliphants, 1971).

Bittlinger, Arnold, *Gifts and Graces: A Commentary on 1 Corinthians 12–14* (London: Hodder & Stoughton, 1967).

Bonnington, Mark, *Patterns in Charismatic Spirituality* (Cambridge: Grove, 2007).

Bornkamm, Günther, *Early Christian Experience* (London: SCM, 1969).

————, "Faith and Reason in Paul," in G. Bornkamm, *Early Christian Experience* (London: SCM, 1969), pp. 29-46.

————, *Paul* (London: Hodder & Stoughton, 1972).

Botte, Bernard, *La Tradition Apostolique*, Sources Chrétiennes (Paris: Editions du Cerf, 1984).

Botterweck, G. J., and H. Ringgren (eds.), *Theological Dictionary of the Old Testament (TDOT)* (Grand Rapids: Eerdmans, 1980).

Bowald, Mark A., *Rendering the Word in Theological Hermeneutics* (Grand Rapids: Baker Academic, 2007).

Braaten, Carl E., and Philip Clayton, *The Theology of Wolfhart Pannenberg* (Minneapolis: Fortress, 1988).

Brent, Allen, *Hippolytus and the Roman Church in the Third Century* (Leiden: Brill, 1995).

Bridges, Cheryl, and Frank Macchia, "Glossolalia," in *The Encyclopedia of Christianity*, vol. 2 (Grand Rapids and Cambridge: Eerdmans, 2001), pp. 413-16.

Bromiley, Geoffrey W. (ed.), *Zwingli and Bullinger*, LCC 24 (London: SCM, 1955).

Brooke, George J., *The Dead Sea Scrolls and the New Testament* (London: SPCK, 2005).

Brown, Francis, with S. R. Driver and C. A. Briggs (eds.), *The New Hebrew and English Lexicon* (Lafayette, IN: Associated Publishers, 1980).

Brown, Raymond E., *The Gospel according to John*, 2 vols., Anchor Bible (New York: Doubleday, 1966 and 1971).

Bruce, F. F., *The Book of Acts*, NICNT (Grand Rapids: Eerdmans, and London: Marshall, Morgan & Scott, 1965).

————, "Commentaries on Acts," *Epworth Review* 8 (1981): 82-87.

————, *The Epistle to the Hebrews*, NICNT (Grand Rapids: Eerdmans, 1964).

Bruner, F. Dale, *A Theology of the Holy Spirit: The Pentecostal Experience and the New Testament Witness* (Grand Rapids: Eerdmans, 1970).

Bucer, Martin, *The Common Places of Martin Bucer*, ed. David F. Wright (Abingdon, Eng: Sutton Courtenay, 1972).

Bultmann, Rudolf, *A Commentary on the Johannine Epistles*, Hermeneia (Philadelphia: Fortress, 1973).

————, *The Holy Spirit: Eastern Christian Traditions* (Peabody, MA: Hendrickson, 1989).

————, *The Holy Spirit: Mediaeval Roman Catholic and Reformation Traditions* (Peabody, MA: Hendrickson, 1997).

————, "Is Exegesis without Presuppositions Possible?" in Bultmann, *Existence and Faith: Shorter Writings of Rudolf Bultmann* (London: Collins, Fontana ed., 1964), pp. 342-51; German, *Glauben und Verstehen* (Tübingen: Mohr, 1965-85), vol. 3, pp. 142-50.

————, *The New International Dictionary of Pentecostal and Charismatic Movements*, *NIDPCM* (Grand Rapids: Zondervan, rev. ed. 2003).

————, "*Pisteuō; faith*," in *TDNT*, ed. Gerhard Kittel and Gerhard Friedrich, vol. 6 (1968), pp. 217-22.

————, *Theology of the New Testament*, 2 vols. (London: SCM, 1952 and 1955).

Burgess, Stanley M., *The Holy Spirit: Ancient Christian Traditions* (Peabody, MA: Hendrickson, 1984).

Burns, J. Patout, and Gerald M. Fagin, *The Holy Spirit: Message of the Fathers of the Church* (Wilmington, DE: Glazier, 1984).

Caird, George B., *The Language and Imagery of the Bible* (London: Duckworth, 1980).

————, *The Revelation of St John the Divine* (London: Black, 1966).

Calvin, John, *Commentary on the Psalms of David*, 3 vols. (Oxford and London: Thomas Tegg, 1840).

————, *The Epistles of Paul to the Galatians, Ephesians, Philippians and Colossians* (Edinburgh: Oliver and Boyd, 1965).

————, *1 and 2 Thessalonians* (Wheaton, IL, and Nottingham: Crossway, 1999).

————, *The First Epistle of Paul to the Corinthians* (Edinburgh: St. Andrew's, 1960).

————, *Institutes of the Christian Religion*, trans. Henry Beveridge, 2 vols. (London: James Clarke, 1957).

————, *The Second Epistle of Paul to the Corinthians; The Epistles of Paul to Timothy, Titus and Philemon* (Edinburgh: St. Andrew's, 1964).

Carpenter, J. Estlin, *The Johannine Writings: A Study of the Apocalypse and the Fourth Gospel* (London: Constable, 1927).

Carrington, Philip, *The Primitive Christian Catechism: A Study in the Epistles* (Cambridge: Cambridge University Press, 1940).

Carson, Donald A., *The Gospel according to John*, The Pillar New Testament Commentary (Grand Rapids: Eerdmans, 1991).

————, *Showing the Spirit* (Grand Rapids: Baker, 1987).

Cartledge, David, *The Apostolic Revolution: The Restoration of Apostles and Prophets in the Assemblies of God in Australia* (Chester Hill, N.S.W.: Paraclete Institute, 2000).

Cartledge, Mark J., *Charismatic Glossolalia: An Empirical-Theological Study* (Aldershot, Hants, and Burlington, VT: Ashgate, 2002).

————, "The Practice of Tongues," in *Speaking in Tongues: Multi-Disciplinary Perspectives*, ed. Mark J. Cartledge (Milton Keynes: Paternoster, 2006), pp. 206-34.

————, *Testimony to the Spirit: Rescripting Ordinary Pentecostal Theology* (Farnham and Burlington VT: Ashgate, 2010).

Chadwick, Henry, "Literarische Berichte und Anzeigen: Hermann Dörries, *De Spiritu Sancto*," *Zeitschrift für Kirchengeschichte* 69 (1958): 335-37.

Chadwick, Owen, *Newman* (Oxford and New York: Oxford University Press, 1983).

————, *The Reformation* (London: Penguin, 1964 and 1972).

————, *The Victorian Church*, vol. 1 (London: SCM, 1971).

Chan, Simon, *Pentecostal Ecclesiology: An Essay on the Development of Doctrine* (Dorset, Blandford Forum: Deo, 2011).

Chung, Paul S., *The Spirit of God Transforming Life: The Reformation and the Holy Spirit* (New York: Palgrave/Macmillan, 2009).

Church of England Doctrine Commission, *We Believe in God* (London: Church House Publishing, 1987).

————, *We Believe in the Holy Spirit* (London: Church House Publishing, 1991).

Church of England Synod Report, *A Time to Heal: A Contribution to the Ministry of Healing: A Report for the House of Bishops* (London: Church House Publishing, 2000).

Collins, John N., *Deacons and the Church* (Leicester: Gracewing, and Harrisville: Morehouse, 2002).

Collins, R. F., *First Corinthians*, Sacra Pagina (Collegeville, MN: Glazier/Liturgical Press, 1999).

Congar, Yves, *I Believe in the Holy Spirit: Lord and Giver of Life,* 3 vols. (New York: Seabury, and London: Chapman, 1983 and 1997).

Conway, Colleen M., "Gospel of John," in *The New Interpreter's Dictionary of the Bible,* 5 vols. (Nashville: Abingdon, 2008), vol. 3, pp. 356-70.

Conzelmann, Hans, *Acts of the Apostles,* Hermeneia (Minneapolis: Fortress, 1987).

————, *1 Corinthians: A Commentary,* Hermeneia (Philadelphia: Fortress, 1975).

————, "*Phōs,*" in *TDNT,* vol. 9, pp. 310-58.

————, *The Theology of Luke* (London: Faber, and New York: Harper & Row, 1961).

Cothenet, E., "Les Prophètes Chrétiens comme Exégètes Charismatiques de l'Écriture," in *Prophetic Vocation in the New Testament and Today,* ed. J. Panagopoulos, NovTSup 45 (Leiden: Brill, 1977), pp. 77-107.

Cox, Harvey, *Fire from Heaven: The Rise of Pentecostal Spirituality and the Reshaping of Religion in the Twenty-First Century* (Cambridge, MA: Da Capo, 1995).

Crafton, J. A., *The Agency of the Apostle,* JSNTSS 51 (Sheffield: Sheffield Academic, 1991).

Cranfield, Charles E. B., *A Critical and Exegetical Commentary on the Epistle to the Romans,* 2 vols., ICC (Edinburgh: T&T Clark, 1975 and 1979).

————, *1 & 2 Peter and Jude* (London: SCM, 1960).

————, *The Gospel according to Saint Mark* (Cambridge: Cambridge University Press, 1963).

Cullmann, Oscar, *Christ and Time: A Primitive Conception of Time and History* (London: SCM, 1951).

————, *The Christology of the New Testament* (London: SCM, 1959 and 1963).

————, *Salvation in History* (London: SCM, 1967).

Dallimore, Arnold A., *Forerunner of the Charismatic Movement* (Chicago: Moody, 1983).

Danker, Frederick W., in W. Bauer, F. W. Danker, W. F. Arndt, and F. W. Gingrich, *Greek-English Lexicon of the New Testament* (BDAG) (Chicago: University of Chicago Press, 3rd ed. 2000).

Dautzenberg, G., "Zum religionsgeschichtlichen Hintergrund der *diakriseis pneumatōn* (1 Kor. 12:10)," *Biblische Zeitschrift* 15 (1971): 93-104.

Davey, J. Ernest, *The Jesus of St. John* (London: Lutterworth, 1958).

Davids, Peter H., *The Epistle of James: A Commentary on the Greek Text,* NIGTC (Grand Rapids: Eerdmans, and Carlisle: Paternoster, 1982).

Davies, Brian, *The Thought of Thomas Aquinas* (Oxford: Clarendon, 1992).

Davies, J. G., "Pentecost and *Glossolalia,*" *JTS* 3 (1952): 228-31.

————, "The Primary Meaning of *Parakletos,*" *JTS* 4 (1953): 35-38.

Davies, W. D., *Paul and Rabbinic Judaism* (London: SPCK, 2nd ed. 1955).

Davis, Henry, *St. Gregory the Great: Pastoral Care* (New York: Newman, 1950).

Dayton, Donald W., *Theological Roots of Pentecostalism* (Grand Rapids: Baker Academic, 1987).

Dewar, Lindsay, *The Holy Spirit and Modern Thought* (London: Mowbray, 1959).

Dix, Gregory, *The Theology of Confirmation in Relation to Baptism* (London: Davis, 1946 and 1953).

————, *The Treatise on the Apostolic Tradition of St. Hippolytus of Rome, Bishop and Martyr* (London: Alban, 1992).

Dodd, C. H., *The Historical Tradition in the Fourth Gospel* (Cambridge: Cambridge University Press, 1963).

————, *The Interpretation of the Fourth Gospel* (Cambridge: Cambridge University Press, 1953).

Dörries, Hermann, *De Spiritu Sancto: Der Beitrag der Basilius von Plotin* (Berlin: de Gruyter, 1964).

Dunn, James D. G., *Baptism in the Holy Spirit: A Re-examination of the New Testament Teaching on the Gift of the Spirit in Relation to Pentecostalism Today* (London: SCM, 1970).

————, "Baptism in the Holy Spirit: A Response to Pentecostal Scholarship in Luke-Acts," *JPT* 3 (1993): 3-27.

————, *Jesus and the Spirit: A Study of the Religious and Charismatic Experience of Jesus and the First Christians as Reflected in the New Testament* (London: SCM, 1975).

————"A Response," *JPT* 19, no. 1 (2010); and *Religious Studies Review* 36 (2010): 147-67.

————, *The Theology of Paul the Apostle* (Edinburgh: T&T Clark, 1998).

————, "Towards the Spirit of Christ: The Emergence of the Distinctive Features of Christian Pneumatology," in *The Work of the Spirit: Pneumatology and Pentecostalism,* ed. Michael Welker (Grand Rapids: Eerdmans, 2006), pp. 3-26.

Edwards, Jonathan, *Basic Writings,* ed. Ola Winslow (New York: New American Library, 1966).

————, *Select Works of Jonathan Edwards,* vol. 2: *Sermons* (London: Banner of Truth Trust, 1959).

————, *The Sermons of Jonathan Edwards,* ed. Wilson H. Kinnach (New Haven: Yale University Press, 1999).

————, "A Treatise concerning Religious Affections," in *Select Works of Jonathan Edwards,* vol. 3 (London: Banner of Truth, 1959).

————, *Works of Jonathan Edwards,* vol. 2: *Religious Affections,* ed. John Smith (New Haven: Yale University Press, 2009).

Eichrodt, Walter, *Theology of the Old Testament,* 2 vols. (London: SCM, 1964).

Eldridge, "Pentecostalism, Experimental Presuppositions, and Hermeneutics," at the 20th Annual Meeting of the *Society of Pentecostal Studies* (Dallas, November 8-10, 1990).

Ellis, E. Earle, "The Role of the Christian Prophet in Acts," in E. E. Ellis, *Prophecy and Hermeneutic in Early Christianity* (Grand Rapids: Eerdmans, 1978), pp. 23-62 and 129-45.

Engels, Donald, *Roman Corinth* (Chicago: University of Chicago Press, 1990).

Erb, Peter C. (ed.), *Pietists: Selected Writings* (London: SPCK, 1983).

Eriksson, Anders, *Traditions as Rhetorical Proof: Pauline Argumentation in 1 Corinthians* (Stockholm: Almqvist & Wiksell, 1998).

Ervin, Howard, *Conversion-Initiation and Baptism in the Holy Spirit: A Critique of James D. G. Dunn, "Baptism in the Holy Spirit"* (Peabody, MA: Hendrickson, 1987).

————, "Hermeneutics: A Pentecostal Option," in *Essays on Apostolic Themes: Studies in Honor of Howard M. Ervin,* ed. Paul Elbert (Peabody, MA: Hendrickson, 1985), pp. 11-25.

Everts, Janet Meyer, "The Pauline Letters in J. D. G. Dunn's Baptism in the Spirit," *JPT* 19, no. 1 (2010): 12-18.

Fairweather, Eugene R. (ed.), *A Scholastic Miscellany: Anselm to Ockham* (London: SCM and Philadelphia: Westminster, 1956).

Faller, Otto, *Sancti Ambrosii Opera, pars nona* (Vindobonae: Hoelder-Pichler-Tempsky, 1964).

Fee, Gordon, *The First Epistle to the Corinthians* (Grand Rapids: Eerdmans, 1987).

————, *God's Empowering Presence: The Holy Spirit in the Letters of Paul* (Milton Keynes: Paternoster, 1995, and Peabody: Hendrickson, 1994).

————, *Gospel and Spirit: Issues in New Testament Hermeneutics* (Peabody, MA: Hendrickson, 1991).

————, *Paul, the Spirit, and the People of God* (Peabody, MA: Hendrickson, 1996).

————, "Toward a Pauline Theology of Glossolalia," in *Pentecostalism in Context: Essays in Honour of William W. Menzies,* ed. Robert P. Menzies and Wonsuk Ma, JPTSS 11 (Sheffield: Sheffield Academic, 1997), pp. 24-37.

Filson, Floyd V., *The New Testament against the Environment* (London: SCM, 1950).

————, *Who Was the Beloved Disciple?* (London: Marshall, Morgan & Scott, 1977).

Fish, Stanley, *Is There a Text in This Class? The Authority of Interpretive Communities* (Cambridge, MA: Harvard University Press, 1980).

Fison, J. E., *The Blessing of the Holy Spirit* (London and New York: Longmans, Green, 1950).

Fitzmyer, Joseph A., *The Acts of the Apostles,* Anchor Bible (New Haven: Yale University Press, 1998).

————, *Romans,* Anchor Bible (New York: Doubleday, 1992).

Forbes, Christopher, *Prophecy and Inspired Speech in Early Christianity and Its Hellenistic Environment,* WUNT 2.75 (Tübingen: Mohr, 1995).

Foster, Richard J., and James B. Smith (eds.), *Devotional Classics: Selected Readings* (San Francisco: Harper, rev. ed. 1990).

Fox, George, *The Journal of George Fox* (Leeds: Pickard, 6th ed. 1836).

————, *The Journal of George Fox* (New York: Cosimo Books, 2007).

France, R. T., *The Gospel of Mark: A Commentary on the Greek Text,* NIGTC (Grand Rapids: Eerdmans, 2002).

Franks, R. S., *The Work of Christ* (London: Nelson, 1962).

Fuchs, Ernst, *Christus und der Geist bei Paulus* (Leipzig: Hinrichs, 1932).

Furnish, Victor P., *2 Corinthians,* Anchor Bible (New York and London: Doubleday, 1984).

Gadamer, Hans-Georg, *Truth and Method* (London: Sheed & Ward, 2nd Eng. ed. 1989).

Gardner-Smith, P., *St. John and the Synoptic Gospels* (Cambridge: Cambridge University Press, 1938).

Gaventa, Beverly Roberts, *The Acts of the Apostles,* Abingdon New Testament Commentaries (Nashville: Abingdon, 2003).

Gee, Donald, *Concerning Spiritual Gifts* (Stockport: Assemblies of God, 1928, 3rd ed. 1937).

————, *Spiritual Gifts in the Work of the Ministry Today* (Springfield, MO: Gospel Publications, 1963).

General Synod Report (Chaired by Colin Craston), *The Charismatic Movement in the Church of England* (London: Church Information Office, 1981).

Gerrish, B. A., *A Prince of the Church: Schleiermacher and the Beginning of Modern Theology* (London: SCM, 1984).

Gillespie, Thomas W., *The First Theologians: A Study in Early Christian Prophecy* (Grand Rapids: Eerdmans, 1994).

Godet, F., *Commentary on St. Paul's First Epistle to the Corinthians,* 2 vols. (Edinburgh: T&T Clark, 1886).

Goodman, Felicitas, *Speaking in Tongues: A Cross-Cultural Study of Glossolalia* (Chicago: University of Chicago Press, 1972).

Grady, J. Lee, *The Holy Spirit Is Not for Sale* (Grand Rapids: Baker/Chosen, 2010).

Green, Joel B., *The Gospel of Luke,* NICNT (Grand Rapids: Eerdmans, 1997).

————, *Practicing Theological Interpretation* (Grand Rapids: Baker Academic, 2011).

Green, Joel, and Scot McKnight (eds.), *Dictionary of Jesus and the Gospels* (Leicester, Eng., and Downers Grove, IL: InterVarsity Press, 1992).

Greer, Rowan A. (ed.), *Origen: An Exhortation to Martyrdom, Prayer, and Selected Works,* Classics of Western Spirituality (London: SPCK, 1979; also Paulist Press, Mahwah, NJ).

Gregory the Great, *Forty Gospel Homilies* (Kalamazoo, MI: Cistercian Publications, 1990).

Griffith Thomas, W. H., *The Holy Spirit of God* (London and New York: Longmans, Green, 1913).

Groppe, Elizabeth Teresa, *Yves Congar's Theology of the Holy Spirit* (New York: Oxford University Press, 2004).

Grudem, Wayne A., *The Gift of Prophecy in 1 Corinthians* (Washington, DC: University Press of America, 1982).

Grundmann, Walter, and Marinus de Jonge, "*Chriō, Christos, Chrisma,*" in *TDNT,* vol. 9, pp. 493-580.

Gundry, Robert H., "Ecstatic Utterances (N.E.B.)?" *JTS* 17 (1966): 299-307.

Gunkel, Hermann, *The Influence of the Holy Spirit* (Minneapolis: Fortress, 2008).

Gunstone, John, *Live by the Spirit* (London: Hodder & Stoughton, 1984).

Gutjahr, Paul C., *Charles Hodge: Guardian of American Orthodoxy* (Oxford and New York: Oxford University Press, 2011).

Gwatkin, Henry M., *Early Church History to A.D. 313,* 2 vols. (London: Macmillan, 1912).

Haenchen, Ernst, *The Acts of the Apostles: A Commentary* (Oxford: Blackwell, 1971).

Hagner, Donald A., *Hebrews* (Peabody, MA: Hendrickson, 1990/1995).

Hamilton, Neill Q., *The Holy Spirit and Eschatology in Paul,* Scottish Journal of Theology Occasional Paper 6 (Edinburgh: Oliver & Boyd, 1957).

Hanson, Anthony T., *Jesus Christ in the Old Testament* (London: SPCK, 1965).

Harnack, Adolf von, *History of Dogma,* vol. 2 (New York: Russell & Russell, rpt. 1938).

Harrington, D. J., "Charisma and Ministry: The Case of the Apostle Paul," *Chicago Studies* 24 (1985): 245-57.

Harris, Ralph W., *Spoken by the Spirit: Documental Accounts of "Other Tongues" from Arabic to Zulu* (Springfield, MO: Gospel Publishing House, 1973).

Hatch, Edwin, and Henry A. Redpath, *A Concordance to the Septuagint*, 2 vols. (Athens: Beneficial Books, 1977).

Hauschild, W.-D., *Basilius von Caesarea: Briefe* (Stuttgart: Hiersemann, 1973).

Haykin, Michael A. G., *The Spirit of God: The Exegesis of 1 and 2 Corinthians in the Pneumatomachian Controversy of the Fourth Century*, Supplement to *Vigiliae Christianae* 27 (Leiden and New York: Brill, 1994).

Hegel, Georg W. F., *Lectures on the Philosophy of Religion*, 3 vols. (London: Kegan Paul, Trench & Trübner, 1895).

——, *The Phenomenology of Mind*, Harper Torchbooks (New York: Harper & Row, 1967).

Heidegger, Martin, *Being and Time* (Oxford: Blackwell, 1962).

Heine, Ronald E., *The Montanist Oracles and Testimonia* (Macon, GA: Mercer University Press, 1989).

—— (ed.), *Origen: Commentary on the Gospel according to John, Books 1-10* (Washington, DC: Catholic University of America Press, 1989).

Hendry, George S., *The Holy Spirit in Christian Theology* (London: SCM, 1966).

Hengel, Martin, *Acts and the History of Earliest Christianity* (London: SCM, 1979).

Henry, Matthew, *Concise Commentary* (CD ROM from Bible Truth Forum).

Heron, Alasdair, *The Holy Spirit* (London: Marshall, Morgan & Scott, 1983).

Hester, James D., *Paul's Concept of Inheritance: A Contribution to Paul's Understanding of Heilsgeschichte* (Edinburgh: Oliver & Boyd, 1968).

Hilborn, David, "Glossolalia as Communication," in *Speaking in Tongues*, ed. Mark Cartledge (Milton Keynes: Paternoster, 2006), pp. 111-46.

Hill, David, "Christian Prophets as Teachers or Instructors in the Church," in *Prophetic Vocation in the New Testament and Today*, ed. J. Panagopoulos (Leiden: Brill, 1977), pp. 108-30.

——, *New Testament Prophecy* (London: Marshall, 1979).

Hocken, Peter D., "Charismatic Movement," in *New International Dictionary of Pentecostal and Charismatic Movements (NIDPCM)*, ed. Stanley Burgess (Grand Rapids: Zondervan, 2nd ed. 2003), pp. 477-519.

Hodge, Charles, *The First Epistle to the Corinthians* (London: Banner of Truth, 1958).

——, *Systematic Theology*, 3 vols. (Grand Rapids: Eerdmans, 1946).

Hodgson, Peter C., "Georg Wilhelm Friedrich Hegel," in *Nineteenth-Century Religious Thought in the West*, vol. 1, ed. Ninian Smart, John Clayton, Patrick Sherry, and Steven Katz (Cambridge: Cambridge University Press, 1985).

Hogg, A. G. *Redemption from This World* (Edinburgh: T&T Clark, 1924).

Holder, Arthur C., "Bede and the New Testament," in *The Cambridge Companion to Bede*, ed. Scott De Gregorio (Cambridge: Cambridge University Press, 2010).

Holland, Tom, *Contours of Pauline Theology: A Radical New Survey of Influences on Paul's Biblical Writings* (Fearn, Ross-shire: Mentor, 2004), pp. 141-56.

Hollenweger, Walter J., "The Black Roots of Pentecostalism," in *Pentecostals after a Century: Global Perspectives on a Movement in Transition*, ed. Allan H. Anderson and Walter J. Hollenweger, JPTSS 15 (Sheffield: Sheffield Academic, 1999), pp. 33-44.

——, "Critical Issues for Pentecostals," in *Pentecostals after a Century: Global Perspec-*

tives on a Movement in Transition, ed. Allan H. Anderson and Walter J. Hollenweger, JPTSS 15 (Sheffield: Sheffield Academic, 1999), pp. 176-96.

————, *Der 1 Korintherbrief, eine Arbeitshilfe zur Bibelwoche* (Kingmünster: Volksmissionarisches Amt der Pfälizischen Landeskirche, 1964).

————, *The Pentecostals* (Peabody, MA: Hendrickson, 1972).

Horn, Friedrich, *Das Angeld der Geistes: Studien zur paulinischen Pneumatologie* (Göttingen: Vandenhoeck & Ruprecht, 1992).

————, "Holy Spirit," in *The Anchor Bible Dictionary,* ed. David N. Freedman (New York and London: Doubleday, 1992), vol. 3, pp. 260-80.

Hoyle, R. Birch, *The Holy Spirit in St. Paul* (London: Hodder & Stoughton, 1927).

Hudson, Neil, "Strange Words and Their Impact on Early Pentecostals," in *Speaking in Tongues,* ed. Mark Cartledge (Milton Keynes: Paternoster, 2006), pp. 52-80.

Hull, J. H. E., *The Holy Spirit in the Acts of the Apostles* (London: Lutterworth Press, 1967).

Hurtado, L. W. *Lord Jesus Christ: Devotion to Jesus in Earliest Christianity* (Grand Rapids: Eerdmans, 2005).

Hussey, M. Edmund, "The Theology of the Holy Spirit in the Writings of St. Gregory of Nazianzus," *Diakonia* 14 (1979): 224-33.

Irving, Edward, *Collected Writings,* ed. G. Carlyle (London and New York: Straham, 1866), vol. 1: *Catholic Apostolic Church;* vol. 2: *Orations of God.*

Irwin, D. T., "Drawing All Together in One Bond of Love," *JPT* 6 (1995).

Jantzen, Grace, *Julian of Norwich: Mystic and Theologian* (London: SPCK, 2000).

Jeremias, Joachim, *New Testament Theology,* vol. 1: *The Proclamation of Jesus* (London: SCM, 1971).

Johnson, George, *The Spirit-Paraclete in the Gospel of John* (Cambridge: Cambridge University Press, 1970).

Johnson, Luke T., *The Gospel of Luke,* Sacra Pagina 3 (Collegeville, MN: Glazier/Liturgical Press, 1991).

Jones, John D., *Pseudo-Dionysius the Areopagite: The Divine Names and Mystical Theology* (Milwaukee: Marquette University Press, 1980).

Julian of Norwich, *Revelations of Divine Love* (London: Penguin, 1998).

Jüngel, Eberhard, *God as the Mystery of the World* (Edinburgh: T&T Clark, 1983).

Kärkkäinen, Veli-Matti, *Holy Spirit and Salvation: The Sources of Christian Theology* (Louisville: Westminster/John Knox, 2010).

————, "Pentecostal Hermeneutics in the Making: On the Way from Fundamentalism to Postmodernism," *Journal of the European Pentecostal Theological Association* 18 (1998): 76-115.

————, *Pneumatology: The Holy Spirit in Ecumenical, International, and Contextual Perspective* (Grand Rapids: Baker Academic, 2002).

Käsemann, Ernst, "The Cry for Liberty in the Worship of the Church," in Käsemann, *Perspectives on Paul* (London: SCM, 1971), pp. 122-37.

————, *New Testament Questions of Today* (London: SCM, 1969).

Keddie, John W., *George Smeaton: Learned Theologian and Biblical Scholar* (Darlington: Evangelical Press, 2011).

Keener, Craig S., *Miracles: The Credibility of the New Testament Accounts,* 2 vols. (Grand Rapids: Baker Academic, 2011).

Kelly, J. N. D., *The Epistles of Peter and Jude* (London: Black, 1969).

Kepler, Thomas S. (ed.), *An Anthology of Devotional Literature* (Nappanee, IN: Jordan, 2001).

Ker, Ian, *The Achievement of John Henry Newman* (London: Collins, and Notre Dame: University of Notre Dame Press, 1990).

Kierkegaard, Søren, *Philosophical Fragments* (Princeton: Princeton University Press, 1985).

Kildahl, John P., *The Psychology of Speaking in Tongues* (New York: Harper & Row, 1972).

Klemm, David E., *Hermeneutical Inquiry,* 2 vols. (Atlanta: Scholars Press, 1986).

Knowles, David, *The Evolution of Mediaeval Thought* (London: Longmans, 1962).

Knox, Ronald A., *Enthusiasm: A Chapter in the History of Religion* (Oxford: Clarendon, 1950).

Kuhn, Thomas S., *The Essential Tension* (Chicago: University of Chicago Press, 1977).

————, *The Structure of Scientific Revolutions* (Chicago: University of Chicago Press, 1st ed. 1962; 2nd ed. 1970).

Kümmel, Werner G., *Introduction to the New Testament* (London: SCM, 1966).

Kuyper, Abraham, *The Work of the Holy Spirit* (New York and London: Funk & Wagnalls, 1900).

Kydd, Ronald, *Charismatic Gifts in the Early Church* (Peabody, MA: Hendrickson, 1984).

Kysar, Robert, *The Fourth Evangelist and His Gospel* (Minneapolis: Augsburg, 1975).

Lake, Kirsopp, *The Apostolic Fathers,* 2 vols., Greek and English, LCC (London: Heinemann, and Cambridge, MA: Harvard University Press, 1965).

————, "The Gift of the Spirit on the Day of Pentecost," in *The Beginnings of Christianity,* ed. F. J. Foakes-Jackson and Kirsopp Lake, vols. 1-5 (London: Macmillan, 1920-33), vol. 5 (1933), pp. 111-20.

Lampe, Geoffrey W. H., *God as Spirit: The Bampton Lectures, 1976* (Oxford: Clarendon, 1977).

————, "The Holy Spirit in the Writings of St. Luke," in *Studies in the Gospels: Essays in Memory of R. H. Lightfoot,* ed. D. E. Nineham (Oxford: Blackwell, 1967), pp. 159-200.

————, *The Seal of the Spirit: A Study of the Doctrine of Baptism and Confirmation in the New Testament and the Fathers* (New York and London: Longmans, Green, 1951).

———— (ed.), *A Patristic Greek Lexicon* (Oxford: Clarendon, 1961).

Land, Steven J., *Pentecostal Spirituality: A Passion for the Kingdom* (Sheffield: Sheffield Academic, 1993).

Lane, William, *The Gospel of Mark,* NICNT (Grand Rapids: Eerdmans, and London: Marshall, Morgan and Scott, 1974).

————, *Hebrews,* 2 vols., Word Biblical Commentary 47A (Dallas: Word, 1991).

Law, William, *A Serious Call to a Devout and Holy Life* (London and Toronto: Dent, and New York: Dutton, 1906).

Leaney, A. R. C., *The Rule of Qumran and Its Meaning* (London: SCM, 1966).

Lee, Edwin K., *The Religious Thought of St. John* (London: SPCK, 1950).

Léon-DuFour, Xavier, "Towards Symbolic Understanding of the Fourth Gospel," *NTS* 27 (1981): 439-56.

Levison, John R., *The Spirit in First-Century Judaism* (Boston and Leiden: Brill, 2002).

Lightfoot, Joseph B., *Notes on the Epistles of St Paul* (London: Macmillan, 1895).

Lindars, Barnabas, *The Gospel of John*, New Century Bible Commentary (London: Oliphants, 1972).

Lossky, Vladimir N., *In the Image and Likeness of God* (New York: St. Vladimir's Seminary Press, and London and Oxford: Mowbray, 1974).

———, *The Mystical Theology of the Eastern Church* (New York: St. Vladimir's Seminary Press, 1988).

———, *Orthodox Theology* (New York: St. Vladimir's Seminary Press, 2001).

———, *The Vision of God* (New York: St. Vladimir's Seminary Press, 1983).

Loyd, Philip, *The Holy Spirit in Acts* (London: Mowbray, 1957).

Lukins, Julian, "A Professor with Spirit," *Charisma*, September 1, 2010, pp. 1-3.

Luscombe, David, *The School of Peter Abelard: The Influence of Abelard's Thought in the Early Scholastic Period* (Cambridge: Cambridge University Press, 2008).

Luther, Martin, *Against the Heavenly Prophets*, in *Luther's Works* (St. Louis: Concordia, 1958).

———, *The Large Catechism* (Philadelphia: Fortress, 1959).

———, *Luther's Works* (St. Louis: Concordia, 1959).

———, *Paul's Epistle to the Galatians* (London: James Clarke, 1953).

———, "Preface to the New Testament," in *Works of Martin Luther*, vol. 6 (Philadelphia: Fortress, 1943).

Luz, Ulrich, *Matthew 1–7: A Commentary* (Edinburgh: T&T Clark, 1990).

———, *Matthew 8–20: A Commentary* (Minneapolis: Fortress, 2001).

Lyotard, Jean-François, *The Differend* (Manchester: Manchester University Press, 1990).

———, *The Postmodern Condition* (Manchester: Manchester University Press, and Minneapolis: University of Minnesota Press, 1984).

Macchia, Frank D., "Babel and the Tongues of Pentecost: Reversal or Fulfilment? — A Theological Perspective," in *Speaking in Tongues*, ed. Mark J. Cartledge (Milton Keynes: Paternoster, 2006), pp. 34-51.

———, *Baptized in the Spirit: A Global Pentecostal Theology* (Grand Rapids: Zondervan, 2006).

———, "Groans Too Deep for Words: Towards a Theology of Tongues as Initial Experience," *Asian Journal of Pentecostal Studies* 1 (1998): 149-73.

———, "Sighs Too Deep for Words: Toward a Theology of Glossolalia," *JPT* 1 (1992): 47-73.

Macquarrie, J., *Studies in Christian Existentialism* (London: SCM, 1966).

Marshall, I. Howard, *The Epistles of John*, NICNT (Grand Rapids: Eerdmans, 1978).

———, *The Gospel of Luke*, NIGTC (Grand Rapids: Eerdmans, 1978).

———, *Luke: Historian and Theologian* (Exeter: Paternoster, 1970 and 1989).

———, *New Testament Theology* (Downers Grove, IL: InterVarsity Press, 2004).

———, "The Present State of Lukan Studies," *Themelios* 14 (1989): 52-57.

Martin, Dale B., *The Corinthian Body* (New Haven: Yale University Press, 1995).

Martin, David, and Peter Mullen, *Strange Gifts? A Guide to Charismatic Renewal* (Oxford: Blackwell, 1984).

Martin, P. J., *James and the Q Sayings of Jesus* (Sheffield: Sheffield Academic, 1991).

Mason, Arthur J., *The Five Theological Orations of Gregory of Nazianzus*, Greek text (Cambridge: Cambridge University Press, 1899).

Maxwell, Joe, "Laughter Draws Toronto Charismatic Crowds," *Christianity Today* 38 (1994): 12.

McDonnell, Kilian, and George T. Montague, *Christian Initiation and Baptism in the Holy Spirit: Evidence from the First Eight Centuries* (Collegeville, MN: The Liturgical Press, 1991).

McDonnell, Kilian (ed.), *Presence, Power and Praise: Documents on the Charismatic Renewal*, 3 vols. (Collegeville, MN: The Liturgical Press, 1980).

McGee, Gary B. (ed.), *Initial Evidence: Historical and Biblical Perspectives on the Pentecostal Doctrine of Spirit Baptism* (Eugene, OR: Wipf & Stock, 1991 and 2007).

McLynn, N. B., *Ambrose of Milan: Church and Court in a Christian Capital* (Berkeley: University of California Press, 1994).

McPherson, Aimee Semple, *The Four Square Gospel*, ed. Raymond Cox (Los Angeles: Foursquare Publications, 1969).

Menzies, Robert P., *Development of Early Christian Pneumatology with Special Reference to Luke-Acts* (Sheffield: JSOT Press, 1992).

————, *Empowered for Witness: The Spirit in Luke-Acts* (Sheffield: JSOT Press, 1994).

————, "The Essence of Pentecostalism," *Paraclete* 26 (1992).

————, "Evidential Tongues: An Essay on Theological Method," *Asian Journal of Pentecostal Studies* 1 (1999): 111-23.

Merklein, Helmut, "Der Theologe als Prophet: Zur Funktion prophetischen Redens im theologischen Diskurs des Paulus," *NTS* 38 (1992): 402-29.

Meyer, H. A. W., *Critical and Exegetical Handbook to the Epistles to the Corinthians*, 2 vols. (Edinburgh: T&T Clark, 1892).

Migne, Jacques-Paul (ed.), *PG*, up to 161 vols. (Paris: Garnier, 1857-66).

———— (ed.), *PL*, up to 73 vols. (Paris, Garnier, 1844-55).

Moberly, R. W. L., *Prophecy and Discernment*, Cambridge Studies in Christian Doctrine (Cambridge: Cambridge University Press, 2006).

Moltmann, Jürgen, *A Broad Place* (London: SCM, 2007).

————, *The Crucified God* (London: SCM, 1974).

————, *God in Creation: An Ecological Doctrine of Creation* (London: SCM, 1985).

————, *The Source of Life: The Holy Spirit and the Theology of Life* (London: SCM, 1997).

————, *The Spirit of Life: A Universal Affirmation* (London: SCM, 1992).

————, *The Trinity and the Kingdom of God: The Doctrine of God* (London: SCM, 1981).

————, *The Way of Jesus Christ: Christology in Messianic Dimensions* (London: SCM, 1990).

Montague, George T., *The Holy Spirit: The Growth of a Biblical Tradition* (Eugene, OR: Wipf & Stock, 1976).

Montefiore, Hugh, *A Commentary on the Epistle to the Hebrews* (London: Black, 1964).

Morgan, G. Campbell, *The Spirit of God* (London: Hodder & Stoughton, 3rd ed. 1902).

Moule, Charles F. D., "The Judgement Theme in the Sacraments," in *The Background to the New Testament and Its Eschatology: In Honour of C. H. Dodd,* ed. David Daube and W. D. Davies (Cambridge: Cambridge University Press, 1956), pp. 464-81.

Moulton, W. F., and A. S. Geden, *A Concordance of the Greek Testament* (Edinburgh: T&T Clark, 1899).

Mounce, Robert H., *The Book of Revelation* (Grand Rapids: Eerdmans, and London: Marshall, Morgan and Scott, 1977).

Mounce, William D., *Pastoral Epistles,* Word Biblical Commentary 46 (Nashville: Nelson, 2000).

Mountain, W. J. (ed.), *S. Aurelii Augustini, De Trinitate,* 2 vols., CCSL 50 and 50A (Turnholt: Editores Pontificii, 1968).

Müller, Ulrich B., *Prophetie und Predigt im Neuen Testament* (Gütersloh: Mohn, 1975).

Müntzer, Thomas, *Collected Works* (Edinburgh: T&T Clark, 1988).

Mussner, Franz, *The Historical Jesus in the Gospel of St. John,* Quaestiones Disputatae 19 (London: Burns & Oates, 1967).

Neufeld, Vernon H., *The Earliest Christian Confessions* (Leiden: Brill, and Grand Rapids: Eerdmans, 1963).

Newman, John Henry, *Apologia pro Vita Sua* (Boston: Houghton Mifflin, 1956 [from 1864], and Oxford: Clarendon, 1967).

————, *An Essay on the Development of Christian Doctrine* (London: Penguin, 1974).

————, *Parochial and Plain Sermons,* vol. 2 (London: Rivingtons, 1868).

Nichols, Aidan, *Yves Congar* (New York: Geoffrey Chapman, and Oxford: Morehouse-Barlow, 1989).

Nolland, John, *The Gospel of Matthew: A Commentary on the Greek Text,* NIGTC (Grand Rapids: Eerdmans, 2005).

Nunn, H. P. V., *The Son of Zebedee and the Fourth Gospel* (London: SPCK, 1932).

O'Meara, John J. (ed.), *Origen: Prayer and Exhortation to Martyrdom,* Ancient Christian Writers (New York: Paulist Press, 1954, rpt. 1979).

Orr, James, *Revelation and Inspiration* (London: Duckworth, 1909).

Owen, John, *The Holy Spirit* (Grand Rapids: Kregel, 1954).

————, *The John Owen Collection: A Discourse concerning the Holy Spirit* (Rio, WI: Ages Software, 2004).

Packer, James I., *Keep in Step with the Spirit* (Leicester: InterVarsity Press, 1984).

————, "Theological Reflections on the Charismatic Movement," *The Churchman* 94 (1980).

Pannenberg, Wolfhart, *Basic Questions in Theology,* 3 vols. (London: SCM, 1970-73).

————, *Jesus — God and Man* (London: SCM, and Philadelphia: Westminster, 1968; German 1964).

————, *Systematic Theology,* 3 vols. (Grand Rapids: Eerdmans, and Edinburgh: T&T Clark, 1991, 1994, and 1998).

Parham, Charles F., *A Voice Crying in the Wilderness* (Baxter Springs, KS: Apostolic Faith Bible College, 1902).

Pelikan, Jaroslav, *The Christian Tradition,* vol. 3: *The Growth of Mediaeval Theology (600-1300)* (Chicago: University of Chicago Press, 1978).

Perrin, Norman, *The Kingdom of God in the Teaching of Jesus* (London: SCM, 1963).

Perves, Jim, *The Triune God and the Charismatic Movement: A Critical Appraisal of Trinitarian Theology and Charismatic Experience from a Scottish Perspective* (Carlisle: Paternoster, 2004).

Petry, Ray C. (ed.), *Late Mediaeval Mysticism*, LCC (London: SCM, and Philadelphia: Westminster, 1957).

Philip, Finny, *The Origins of Pauline Pneumatology: The Eschatological Bestowal of the Spirit*, WUNT 2.194 (Tübingen: Mohr, 2005).

Pogoloff, Stephen M., *Logos and Sophia: The Rhetorical Situation of 1 Corinthians* (Atlanta: Scholars Press, 1995).

Poole, Matthew, *Commentary on the Holy Bible* (London: Banner of Truth, 1963).

Powell, Cyril H., *The Biblical Concept of Power* (London: Epworth, 1963).

Powers, Janet Evert, "Missionary Tongues?" *JPT* 17 (2000): 39-55.

Prenter, Regin, *Spiritus Creator: Luther's Concept of the Holy Spirit* (Philadelphia: Muhlenberg, 1953).

Price, Robert M., "Confirmation and Charisma," *St. Luke's Journal of Theology* 33, no. 3 (June 1990).

Pulikottil, Paulson, "East and West Meet in God's Own Country: Encounter of Western Pentecostalism with Native Pentecostalism in Kerala," *Cyber Journal for Pentecostal-Charismatic Research, Kerala, India*.

Rad, Gerhard von, *Wisdom in Israel* (London: SCM, 1972).

Ramsey, B., *Ambrose* (London: Routledge, 1997).

Ramsey, Ian T., *Religious Language: An Empirical Placing of Theological Phrases* (London: SCM, 1957).

Reardon, Bernard M. G., *From Coleridge to Gore: A Century of Religious Thought in Britain* (London: Longman, 1971).

Rengstorff, Karl L., *"Apostolos,"* in *TDNT*, vol. 1, pp. 407-47.

Report, "Gospel and Spirit," in *The Churchman*, no. 1 (1978).

Richard, Earl J., *First and Second Thessalonians*, Sacra Pagina (Collegeville, MN: Glazier, 1995).

Richardson, Alan, *Introduction to the Theology of the New Testament* (London: SCM, 1958).

Richardson, Neil, *Paul's Language about God*, JSNTSS (Sheffield: Sheffield Academic, 1994).

Ricoeur, Paul, *Freud and Philosophy: An Essay on Interpretation* (New Haven and London: Yale University Press, 1970).

————, *Oneself as Another* (Chicago: University of Chicago Press, 1992).

————, *Time and Narrative*, 3 vols. (Chicago: University of Chicago Press, 1984, 1985, and 1988).

Robeck, Cecil M., "The Gift of Prophecy in Acts and Paul," *Studia Biblica et Theologica* 5 (1975): 15-38, and 39-54.

————, "Seminaries and Graduate Schools," in *NIDPCM*, ed. Stanley Burgess, pp. 1045-50.

————, "Seymour, William Joseph," in *NIDPCM*, ed. Stanley Burgess, pp. 1053-58.

Roberts, Alexander, and James Donaldson (eds.), *ANF*, 10 vols. (Edinburgh: T&T Clark, and Grand Rapids: Eerdmans, rpt. 1993).

Robertson, A., and A. Plummer, *The First Epistle to the Corinthians,* ICC (Edinburgh: T&T Clark, 2nd ed. 1914).

Robinson, John A. T., *The Body: A Study in Pauline Theology* (London: SCM, 1952).

————, *The Human Face of God* (London: SCM, 1973).

Rogers, Eugene F., *After the Spirit: A Constructive Pneumatology from Resources outside the Modern West* (Grand Rapids: Eerdmans, 2005, and London: SCM, 2006).

Rupp, E. Gordon, and Benjamin Drewery (eds.), *Master Luther — Documents of Modern History* (London: Arnold, 1970).

Ruthven, Jon, *On the Cessation of the Charismata: The Protestant Polemic on Postbiblical Miracles* (Sheffield: Sheffield Academic, 1993).

Samarin, William J., *Tongues of Men and Angels: The Religious Language of Pentecostalism* (New York: Macmillan, 1972).

Sanders, J. N., and B. A. Mastin, *The Gospel according to St John* (London: Black, 1968).

Sandnes, K. O., *Paul — One of the Prophets? A Contribution to the Apostle's Self-Understanding,* WUNT 2.43 (Tübingen: Mohr, 1991).

Scaer, David, "The Concept of *Anfechtung* in Luther's Thought," *Concordia Theological Quarterly* 47 (1983): 15-30.

Schaff, Philip (ed.), *NPNF,* ser. 1, 14 vols. (Edinburgh: T&T Clark, and Grand Rapids: Eerdmans, rpt. 1993).

Schaff, Philip, and Henry Wace (eds.), *NPNF,* ser. 2, 14 vols. (Edinburgh: T&T Clark, and Grand Rapids: Eerdmans, rpt. 1991).

Schatzmann, Siegfried, *A Pauline Theology of Charismata* (Peabody, MA: Hendrickson, 1987).

Schilling, S. Paul, *Contemporary Continental Theologians* (London: SCM, 1966).

Schlechter, S., *Some Aspects of Rabbinic Theology* (London: Black, 1909).

Schleiermacher, Friedrich D. E., *The Christian Faith* (Edinburgh: T&T Clark, 1989; from 2nd ed. 1830).

————, *Hermeneutics: The Handwritten Manuscripts,* ed. Heinz Kimmerle (Missoula: Scholars Press, 1977).

————, *On Religion: Speeches to Its Cultured Despisers* (London: Kegan Paul, Trench & Trübner, 1893).

Schnackenburg, Rudolf, *Baptism in the Thought of Paul* (Oxford: Blackwell, 1964).

Schrage, W., *Der erste Brief an die Korinther,* 4 vols., EKKNT 7/1-4 (Neukirchen: Neukirchener, 1992-2001).

Schweitzer, Albert, *The Mysticism of Paul the Apostle* (London: Black, 1931).

Schweizer, Eduard, "*Pneuma, Pneumatikos,*" in *TDNT,* ed. Gerhard Kittel and Gerhard Friedrich, vol. 6 (Grand Rapids: Eerdmans, 1968), pp. 332-455.

————, *Spirit of God,* Bible Key Words (London: Black, 1960; German, 1959-60).

Scott, Ernest F., *The Spirit in the New Testament* (London: Hodder & Stoughton, 1924).

Selby, Robin C., *The Principle of Reserve in the Writings of John Henry Cardinal Newman* (Oxford: Oxford University Press, 1975).

Sepúlveda, Juan, "Indigenous Pentecostalism and the Chilean Experience," in *Pentecostals after a Century,* ed. Allan H. Anderson and Walter J. Hollenweger (Sheffield: Sheffield Academic Press, 1999), pp. 111-35.

Shapland, C. R. B., *The Letters of Saint Athanasius concerning the Holy Spirit* (London: Epworth, 1951).

Shearer, R. E., *Wildfire: Church Growth in Korea* (Grand Rapids: Eerdmans, 1966).

Sjöberg, Erik, "*Rûach* in Palestinian Judaism," in *TDNT,* vol. 6, pp. 375-89.

Smail, Tom, *The Forgotten Father* (London: Hodder & Stoughton, 1980).

———, "In Spirit and in Truth: Reflections on Charismatic Worship," in Smail et al., *Love of Power,* pp. 95-103.

Smail, Thomas, Andrew Walker, and Nigel Wright, *The Love of Power or the Power of Love: A Careful Assessment of the Problems within the Charismatic and Word-of-Faith Movements* (Minneapolis: Bethany House, 1994).

Smalley, Beryl, *The Study of the Bible in the Middle Ages* (Notre Dame, IN: University of Notre Dame Press, 5th ed. 1964).

Smalley, Stephen S., *1, 2, and 3 John* (Waco, TX: Word, 1984).

Smeaton, George, *The Doctrine of the Holy Spirit* (London: Banner of Truth, rpt. 1958, from the 1882 ed.).

Smith, James K. A., *Thinking in Tongues: Pentecostal Contributions to a Christian Philosophy* (Grand Rapids: Eerdmans, 2010).

Snaith, Norman, and Vincent Taylor (eds.), *The Doctrine of the Holy Spirit,* Headingly Lectures (London: Epworth, 1937).

Southern, R. W., *Saint Anselm: A Portrait in Landscape* (Cambridge: Cambridge University Press, 1990).

Spawn, Kevin L., and Archie T. Wright, *Spirit and Scripture: Exploring a Pneumatic Hermeneutic* (London: T&T Clark International/Continuum, 2012).

Speiser, E. A., *Genesis,* Anchor Bible (New York: Doubleday, 1964).

Spener, Philipp Jakob, *Pia Desideria,* conveniently at hand in *Pietists: Selected Writings,* ed. Peter C. Erb (London: SPCK, 1983), pp. 31-49.

Staley, Lynn (ed.), *The Book of Margery Kempe,* bk. 1 (Kalamazoo, MI: Medieval Institute, 1996).

Stanley, C. D., *Paul and the Language of Scripture,* SNTSMS 69 (Cambridge: Cambridge University Press, 1992), pp. 197-205.

Stanton, G. N., *Jesus of Nazareth in New Testament Preaching,* SNTSMS 27 (Cambridge: Cambridge University Press, 1974).

Stelten, Leo F., *Dictionary of Ecclesiastical Latin* (Peabody, MA: Hendrickson, 1995).

Stendahl, Krister, "Glossolalia — the New Testament Evidence," in his *Paul among Jews and Gentiles* (London: SCM, 1977), pp. 109-24.

———, *Paul among Jews and Gentiles* (London: SCM, 1977, and Philadelphia: Fortress, 1976).

Stephens, W. Peter, *The Holy Spirit in the Theology of Martin Bucer* (Cambridge: Cambridge University Press, 1970).

Stewart, Roy A., *Rabbinic Theology* (Edinburgh: Oliver & Boyd, 1961).

Strachan, Charles G., *The Pentecostal Theology of Edward Irving* (London: Darton, Longman & Todd, 1973, and Peabody, MA: Hendrickson, 1988).

Stronstad, Roger, *The Charismatic Theology of Saint Luke* (Peabody, MA: Hendrickson, 1984).

————, "Forty Years On: An Appreciation and Assessment of Baptism in the Spirit," *JPT* 19 (2010): 3-11.

————, "Pentecostal Experience and Hermeneutics," *Enrichment Journal* (formerly a paper at the 20th Annual Meeting of The Society of Pentecostal Studies, Dallas, November 1990).

————, *The Prophethood of All Believers: A Study in Luke's Charismatic Theology*, JPTSS 16 (Sheffield: Sheffield Academic, 1999).

Suurmond, Jean-Jacques, "A Fresh Look at Spirit-Baptism and the Charisms," *The Expository Times* 109 (1998): 103-6.

Swete, Henry B., *The Holy Spirit in the Ancient Church: A Study of Christian Teaching in the Age of the Fathers* (London: Macmillan, 1912).

————, *The Holy Spirit in the New Testament* (London: Macmillan, 1909, rpt. 1921).

Synan, Vinson, *The Holiness-Pentecostal Tradition: Charismatic Movements in the Twentieth Century* (Grand Rapids: Eerdmans, 1971 and 1997).

————, "The Role of Tongues as Initial Evidence," in *Spirit and Renewal*, ed. Mark W. Wilson, JPTSS 5 (Sheffield: Sheffield Academic, 1994), pp. 67-82.

Taylor, Jeremy, *Selected Writings*, ed. C. H. Sisson (Manchester: Carcanet, 1990).

Taylor, John V., *The Go-Between God: The Holy Spirit and the Christian Mission* (London: SCM, 1972).

Taylor, Vincent, *The Person of Christ in New Testament Teaching* (London: Macmillan, 1958).

Thayer, Joseph H. (from Grimm-Thayer), *Greek-English Lexicon of the New Testament* (Edinburgh: T&T Clark, 4th ed. 1901).

Theissen, Gerd, *Psychological Aspects of Pauline Theology* (Edinburgh: T&T Clark, 1987).

Thielicke, Helmut, *The Evangelical Faith*, 3 vols. (Grand Rapids: Eerdmans, 1974-82).

Thiselton, Anthony C., *1 and 2 Thessalonians: Through the Centuries*, Blackwell's Bible Commentaries (Oxford: Wiley-Blackwell, 2011).

————, *1 Corinthians: A Shorter Exegetical and Pastoral Commentary* (Grand Rapids: Eerdmans, 2006).

————, *The First Epistle to the Corinthians: A Commentary on the Greek Text*, NIGTC (Grand Rapids: Eerdmans, 2000).

————, *Hermeneutics: An Introduction* (Grand Rapids: Eerdmans, 2009).

————, *The Hermeneutics of Doctrine* (Grand Rapids and Cambridge: Eerdmans, 2007).

————, "The Holy Spirit in the Latin Fathers with Special Reference to Their Use of 1 Corinthians 12 and This Chapter in Modern Scholarship," *Communio Viatorum* 53 (2011): 7-24.

————, "The Interpretation of Tongues: A New Suggestion in the Light of Greek Usage in Philo and Josephus," *JTS* 30 (1979): 15-36.

————, *Interpreting God and the Postmodern Self* (Edinburgh: T&T Clark, 1995).

————, *Language, Liturgy, and Meaning* (Nottingham: Grove, 1975 and 1986).

————, *Life after Death: A New Approach to the Last Things* (Grand Rapids: Eerdmans, and London: SPCK, 2012).

————, *The Living Paul* (London: SPCK, 2009).

————, "Luther and Barth on 1 Corinthians 15," in *The Bible, the Reformation and the*

Church: Essays in Honour of James Atkinson, ed. W. P. Stephens (Sheffield: Sheffield Academic, 1995), pp. 258-89.

————, *New Horizons in Hermeneutics: The Theory and Practice of Transforming Biblical Reading* (Grand Rapids: Zondervan, and London: HarperCollins, 1992).

————, "Postmodernity, Postmodernism," in *A Concise Encyclopaedia of the Philosophy of Religions* (Oxford: Oneworld, 2002), pp. 233-35.

————, "The Supposed Power of Words in the Biblical Writings," *JTS* 25 (1974): 282-99; also rpt. in *Thiselton on Hermeneutics: Collected Works with New Essays* (Grand Rapids: Eerdmans, and Aldershot: Ashgate, 2006), pp. 53-68.

————, *The Two Horizons: New Testament Hermeneutics and Philosophical Description* (Grand Rapids: Eerdmans, and Exeter: Paternoster, 1980).

————, "Wisdom in the New Testament," *Theology* 115 (2011): 260-68.

————, "Wisdom in the Old Testament and Judaism," *Theology* 114 (2011): 163-72.

Thornton, Lionel S., *The Common Life in the Body of Christ* (London: Dacre, 3rd ed. 1950).

Trevett, Christine, *Montanism: Gender, Authority and the New People Prophecy* (Cambridge: Cambridge University Press, 1996).

Trier, Daniel J., *Introducing Theological Interpretation of Scripture: Recovering a Christian Practice* (Grand Rapids: Baker Academic, 2008).

Turner, Max, "Early Christian Experience and Theology of Tongues — A New Testament Perspective," in *Speaking in Tongues: Multi-Disciplinary Perspectives,* ed. Mark J. Cartledge (Milton Keynes: Paternoster, 2006), pp. 1-33.

————, *The Holy Spirit and Spiritual Gifts Then and Now* (Carlisle: Paternoster, 1996).

————, "James Dunn's *Baptism in the Holy Spirit,*" *JPT* 19 (2010): 25-31.

————, *Power from on High: The Spirit in Israel's Restoration and Witness in Luke-Acts,* JPTSS 9 (Sheffield: Sheffield Academic, 1996).

————, "Spiritual Gifts, Then and Now," *Vox Evangelica* 15 (1985): 7-64.

Twomey, D. Vincent, and Janet E. Rutherford (eds.), *The Holy Spirit in the Fathers of the Church: The Proceedings of the Seventh International Patristic Conference, 2008* (Dublin: Four Courts Press, 2010).

Van Dusen, Henry P., *Spirit, Son and Father* (New York: Scribner, 1958).

Van Gemeren, W. (ed.), *New International Dictionary of Old Testament Theology and Exegesis,* 5 vols. (Carlisle: Paternoster, 1997).

Vanhoye, A., *Homilie für haltbedürftige Christen* (Regensburg: Pustet, 1981).

Vawter, Bruce, *On Genesis: A New Reading* (New York: Doubleday, 1977).

Vermès, Géza, *The Complete Dead Sea Scrolls in English* (London: Allen Lane, 1997).

Vielhauer, Philipp, *Oikodomē: Das Bild vom Bau in der christlichen Literatur vom Neuen Testament bis Clemens Alexandrinus* (Karlsruhe: Harrassowitz, 1940).

Vriezen, T. C., *An Outline of Old Testament Theology* (Oxford: Blackwell, 1962).

Wagner, C. Peter, "Third Wave," in *NIDPCM,* pp. 1141-42.

Wainwright, Arthur W., *The Trinity in the New Testament* (London: SPCK, 1962).

Walker, Andrew, "Demonology and the Charismatic Movement," in Tom Smail et al., *Love of Power* (Minneapolis: Bethany House, 1994), pp. 53-72.

Warfield, Benjamin B., *Counterfeit Miracles* (London: Banner of Truth, 1996).

Warrington, Keith, *Pentecostal Theology: A Theology of Encounter* (London and New York: T&T Clark, 2008).

Watkin-Jones, Howard, *The Holy Spirit in the Mediaeval Church: A Study of Christian Teaching concerning the Holy Spirit and His Place in the Trinity* (London: Epworth, 1922).

Watson, Francis, *Text, Church and World: Biblical Interpretation in Theological Perspective* (Edinburgh: T&T Clark, 1994).

Welborn, L. L., "Discord in Corinth," in L. L. Welborn, *Politics and Rhetoric in the Corinthian Epistles* (Macon, GA: Mercer University Press, 1997), pp. 1-42.

————, *Paul, the Fool of Christ: A Study of 1 Corinthians 1–4* (London and New York: T&T Clark International, 2005).

Welch, Claude, *Protestant Thought in the Nineteenth Century,* vol. 1: *1799-1870* (New Haven: Yale University Press, 1972).

Welker, Michael, *God the Spirit* (Minneapolis: Fortress, 1994).

————, "The Spirit in Philosophical, Theological, and Interdisciplinary Perspectives," in *The Work of the Spirit: Pneumatology and Pentecostalism,* ed. Michael Welker (Grand Rapids: Eerdmans, 2006), pp. 221-32.

———— (ed.), *The Work of the Spirit: Pneumatology and Pentecostalism* (Grand Rapids: Eerdmans, 2006).

Wenham, Gordon, *Genesis 1–15,* Word Biblical Commentary (Nashville: Nelson, 1987).

Wesley, John, *Journal* (London: Isbister, 1902).

————, *Notes on the New Testament* (CD ROM, Bible Truth Forum).

————, "On the Holy Spirit: Sermon 141," edited by George Lyons (Nampa, ID: Northwest Nazarene College, from Christian Classics Ethereal Library, 1999).

————, Sermon 55, "On the Trinity," ed. David R. Leonard (Nampa, ID: Northwest Nazarene College, from Christian Classics Ethereal Library, 2011).

Westcott, B. F., *The Epistles of St. John: Greek Text with Notes* (Abingdon, Berkshire: Marcham Manor, and Grand Rapids: Eerdmans, 1966).

————, *The Epistle to the Hebrews: The Greek Text* (London and New York: Macmillan, 3rd ed. 1903).

Whiteley, D. E. H., *The Theology of St. Paul* (Oxford: Blackwell, 1964; 2nd ed. 1971).

Williams, Cyril G., *Tongues of the Spirit* (Cardiff: University of Wales Press, 1981).

Williams, D. H., *Ambrose of Milan and the End of the Nicene-Arian Conflicts* (Oxford: Oxford University Press, 1995).

Williams, George H. (ed.), *Spiritual and Anabaptist Writers,* LCC 25 (London: SCM, 1957), p. 47.

Williams, Ronald R., *The Acts of the Apostles,* Torch Commentary (London: SCM, 1953).

Williams, Rowan, "Eastern Orthodox Theology," in *The Modern Theologians* (Oxford: Blackwell, 3rd ed. 2005), pp. 572-88.

Wilson, Mark W. (ed.), *Spirit and Renewal,* JPTSS 5 (Sheffield: Sheffield Academic, 1994).

Wilson, Stephen G., *The Gentiles and the Gentile Mission in Luke-Acts* (Cambridge: Cambridge University Press, 1973).

Windisch, Hans, "Die fünf johannische Parakletesprüche," trans. J. W. Cox, *The Spirit-Paraclete in the Fourth Gospel* (Philadelphia: Fortress, 1968).

————, *Johannes und die Synoptiker* (Leipzig: Hinrichs, 1926).

Winstanley, Edward W., The *Spirit in the New Testament* (Cambridge: Cambridge University Press, 1910).

Winter, Bruce W., "The Public Honouring of Christian Benefactors," *JSNT* 34 (1988): 87-103.

————, "Religious Curses and Christian Vindictiveness, 1 Cor. 12–14," in Bruce Winter, *After Paul Left Corinth* (Grand Rapids: Eerdmans, 2001), pp. 164-83.

Wire, Antoinette C., *The Corinthian Women Prophets: A Reconstruction* (Minneapolis: Fortress, 1990).

Witherington, Ben, III, *Jesus the Sage: The Pilgrimage of Wisdom* (Minneapolis: Fortress, 2000).

Wittgenstein, Ludwig, *Philosophical Investigations* (Oxford: Blackwell, 2nd ed. 1958).

————, *Zettel* (Oxford: Blackwell, 1967).

Work, Telford, *Living and Active: Scripture in the Economy of Salvation* (Grand Rapids: Eerdmans, 2002).

Wright, N. T., *The Resurrection of the Son of God* (London: SPCK, 2003).

Wright, Nigel, "The Theology of Signs and Wonders," in Tom Smail et al., *Love of Power* (Minneapolis: Bethany House, 1994), pp. 37-52.

Yong, Amos, *Spirit–Word–Community: Theological Hermeneutics in Trinitarian Perspective* (Aldershot, Hants, and Burlington, VT: Ashgate, 2002).

Zimmermann, Jens, *Recovering Theological Hermeneutics* (Grand Rapids: Baker Academic, 2004).

Zinn, Groves A. (ed.), *Richard of St. Victor: The Twelve Patriarchs. The Mystical Book, Book Three of the Trinity,* Classics of Western Spirituality (London: SPCK, 1979).

Zizioulas, John D., *Being as Communion: Studies in Personhood and the Church* (New York: St. Vladimir's Seminary Press, 1997).

Zwiep, Arie W., *Christ, the Spirit and the Community of God: Essays on the Acts of the Apostles,* WUNT 2.293 (Tübingen: Mohr, 2010).

Zwingli, Huldrych, *The Defence of the Reformed Faith* (Allison Park, PA: Pickwick Publications, 1984).

Index of Modern Authors

Pre-modern authors prior to 1800 are listed with subjects; **boldface** page numbers indicate main references.

Index of Subjects

Pre-modern writers before 1800 are included in this subject index, not with modern authors; **boldface** page numbers indicate main references.

Abba, Father, 40-41, 70, 79, 175, 267, 403, 410

abbot: at the Abbey of St. Victor, 237; Bernard of Clairvaux as, 233; Rupert of Deutz as, 231

Abelard, Peter, 222, **232-33**

Absolute, the, 299

activity (vs. essence), 217

Acts: fivefold structure of, 49; purpose of, **496-97**

administration, 9, **91-92**, 107, 110, 222; spontaneous administrator, **92**

adoration, of God, 500

Advocate, 141, 189, 304, 408

Africa, African independent churches, 95, 332

African-American slaves, 331

Agabus, 67

Against the Celestial Prophets (Luther), 260

Agent of creation, 194

agents of God, 3, 8-11

Albert the Great, 243

Alcuin of York, **227-28**

Alexandria, 182

alienation, homesickness, 119

all Christians, 70, 277, 302, 305, 314, 459

all the gifts of the Holy Spirit, 476

all three persons of the Trinity, 298

ambiguity: of expectation, 487; of language, **75-77**, 153; of ostensive definition, **386**

Ambrose, **196-201**, 202

America, 283, 293, 312, 316, 337, 421, 428, 450

Anabaptists, 263

analogy, human, 204

Anathema Iēsous, **80-81**

Anfechtung, 268. *See also* struggle

angels, 4, 13, 35, 212, 310; angelic speech, 119

Anglican, 261, 313, 394

animalisms, trances, shaking, 332

Annunciation, 128, 461

anointing, 5, 8-10, 13, 34-35, 42, 47, 130, **136**, **145-46**, 171, 174-75, 197, 200, 212, 216, 303, 378

Anselm, **230-31**

anticipating the end in the present, 344

anti-hierarchical approach: of Carlstadt and Müntzer, 262, of Macchia, 460

Antioch, 66

apocalyptic, 20, 13, **25-26**, 54, 119, 150, 159, 179, 259, 278, 312, **404**, **422**

apophatic theology, 225

apostasy, 154

529

Index of Scripture and Other Ancient Sources